WITHDRAWN

Geographical Inquiry
and American
Historical Problems

Geographical Inquiry and American Historical Problems

CARVILLE EARLE

STANFORD UNIVERSITY PRESS

Stanford, California

1992

Stanford University Press
Stanford, California

© 1992 by the Board of Trustees of the Leland Stanford Junior University

Printed in the United States of America

CIP data are at the end of the book

For my parents and parents-in-law, in gratitude

Carville R. Earle and Doris R. Earle

Lewis R. Curlett, Jr. and Vera H. Curlett

Acknowledgments

The central ideas in this book—the virtues of a geographical perspective upon important problems in American history, of comparative inquiry across American regions and periods, of skepticism toward received historiographic and cliometric wisdom—trace their origins to my youth and to the remarkably creative place where I was raised and, in the main, educated. I have here to acknowledge the seminality of that place in my thinking and writing on the American past. Baltimore's secret, I suspect, has to do with a certain obliqueness of perspective that the city imparts to anyone who has lived there for a sustained period. And could it have been otherwise in a city of such mixed provenience, a city that is part northern and part southern, part Menckenian iconoclasm and part Hopkins intellectualism?

Growing up in the northernmost southern city and the southernmost northern city in the 1950s held certain curious intellectual advantages, not the least of which was the daily encounter with conflicting regional cultures. My sympathies, however, ran counter to the aims of Baltimore's regional partisans. In these encounters, I preferred detachment rather than engagement, dispassion rather than commitment. At an early age (and without much reflection) I learned that the protean clash of regions and history is a subject better suited to analysis and comparison than to rhetoric and contention. The simple fact of the matter is that I had too many friends on either side to enlist in their partisanal campaigns.

In making sense of these regional cleavages, I naturally turned toward history and eventually toward the comparative history of American regions, that is to geographical history. Much to my astonishment, I discovered that my hometown was arguably the fount of modern historical scholarship in the United States. Intrigued by this coincidence, I read a great deal about the ambitious program initiated by the historian Herbert Baxter Adams of Johns Hopkins University and of his declaration of history as past politics—the meaning of which I have slowly come to understand. And then I read Frederick Jackson Turner—a Hopkins graduate student in history during the late 1880s and early 1890s. Turner's early writings on the American frontier and, more particularly, his skillful blending of history and geography, offered a beacon of illumination upon the regional and sectional tensions that I had experienced (and failed to explain).

And then there was the brooding presence of H. L. Mencken. It is hard to imagine anyone coming of age in Baltimore during the 1950s without absorbing in the process a healthy dose of Mencken's skepticism and iconoclasm. It was not really necessary to read Mencken (which I didn't) for his thoughts and his style were all around you, in the vapors so to speak. Indeed, the everyday conversations of thinking Baltimoreans (of whom there was a goodly number) were regularly punctuated with Menckenia and seasoned with his perversely witty and irreverent style. Even now, far from the influences of Mencken's thought, I find it difficult to refrain from a style of argumentation and a point of view acquired osmotically during my youth in the Monumental City.

My experiences in Baltimore failed me, however, when I began to pursue my curiosity about regional and sectional division into the American past. As a city dweller, I was desperately ill-equipped for this journey into the foggy realms of rural history and agrarian systems. Fortunately for me, I stumbled on the outset across two well-thumbed volumes written by Lewis Cecil Gray, the dean of southern agrarian history. With Gray's magnificent volumes as a guide, I gained entree to the rural worlds of American history, worlds that at once had shaped the evolution of American regions and the sectional tensions that ensued. Yet I doubt that even a scholar as sensitive to agrarian systems as Lewis Gray discerned all of the tendrils that ran from these rural worlds into the higher spheres of regional economy, society, and polity, from prosaic agrarian systems into the central problems in American history—to slavery and freedom, industrialization and urbanization, socialism and trade unionism, stasis and change. It is this deceptive power of rural life that constitutes the interpretive subtext in the essays that follow. Insofar as that subtext provides a compelling reinterpretation of the American past, the credit redounds to that impeccable scholar who guided me from Baltimore far back into the rural worlds of the American past.

Although my origins on the edge of north and south are indelibly imprinted upon these essays, I would like to think that they transcend provincialism, that their themes and interpretations have an appeal for a larger and more cosmopolitan audience of historians, geographers, and social science historians. Indeed, several of the essays in this volume previously have attempted to address these audiences in scholarly journals or as chapters in books. I thank the editors of these publications and my coauthors on four of these essays—Ronald Hoffman of the University of Maryland College Park for chapters three and five and Sari Bennett of the University of Maryland Baltimore County for chapters nine and eleven—for permission to reprint them here. The response to their initial publication has been gratifying and I trust that reprinting will foster in a new generation of students a keener appreciation for American geographical history. All of the essays, old and new, have been rewritten for consistency of style as well as in acknowledgment of new evidence that has come to light. In a few cases, I have amplified somewhat the original arguments and interpretations or revised them so as to eliminate ambiguity.

Essays written over fifteen years invariably benefit from the kind and constructive criticism of scholars and friends. I gained many insights from my coauthors, Ron Hoffman and Sari Bennett. Many others have tried to refine my thinking and sharpen my arguments, among whom I count Shannon Brown, Lois Carr, Daniel Doeppers, Stanley Engerman, William Hutchinson, James Knox, Allan Kulikoff, Russell Menard, the late Franklin Mendels, James Mohr, Peter Temin, and Lorena Walsh. I owe a special thanks to Leonard Hochberg for the germ of an idea that evolved into this book and to Sir H. J. Habakkuk for his generous note of support at a moment when the disciples of his seminal work on American and British industrialization voiced unveiled skepticism over my contrary thesis of cheap labor as the foundation of American industrialization. My appreciation also extends to Daniel S. Allen, Lary Dilsaver, Elizabeth Hines, Darrell Kruger, Sheila McGlynn, and Gregory Veeck who read the manuscript in part or in full and offered constructive comment. And in the end, I have benefited from wise advice generously offered by Norris Pope and Peter J. Kahn of Stanford University Press. The errors that remain, of course, are my own.

As the son of a secretary, I know a good one when I see one. Fortunately for me, I have been blessed by association with three wonderful manuscript typists and equally wonderful people. To Fran Meo in Baltimore, Peggy Christian in Ohio, and Maudrie Eldridge in "Lusiana," my sincerest thanks. My gratitude also extends to Mary Lee Eggart, Clifford Duplechin, and James Kennedy for the mystical transformation of my crude manuscript maps and graphs into works of art.

And lastly, for their unusual tolerance and forbearance during the course of what came to be known as "the book," my thanks and my love to Mary Lou, Rick, Jim, Randy, and Elizabeth—Baltimoreans all.

Several of my essays have already appeared in slightly different form in journals and books over the years. I am obliged to the editors and publishers for permission to reprint them here.

Chapter 1 appeared as "Environment, Disease, and Mortality in

Early Virginia," in *The Chesapeake in the Seventeenth Century: Essays on Anglo-American Society,* edited by Thad Tate and David Ammerman. © 1979 by The University of North Carolina Press. Reprinted by permission of the UNC Press and the Institute of Early American History and Culture; and the *Journal of Historical Geography* 5 (1979), pp. 365–90.

Chapter 2 appeared as "The First English Towns of North America," in *Geographical Review* 66 (1977), pp. 34–50, and is reprinted by permission of the American Geographical Society.

Chapter 3 appeared as "Staple Crops and Urban Development in the Eighteenth-Century South," in *Perspectives in American History* 10 (1976), pp. 5–78 (with Ronald Hoffman).

Chapter 5 appeared as "The Foundation of the Modern Economy: Agriculture and the Costs of Labor in the United States and England, 1800–1860," in *American Historical Review* 85 (1980), pp. 1055–94 (with Ronald Hoffman).

Chapter 6 appeared as "A Staple Interpretation of Slavery and Free Labor," in *Geographical Review* 67 (1978), pp. 51–65, and is reprinted by permission of the American Geographical Society.

Chapter 7 appeared as "The Myth of the Southern Soil Miner: Macrohistory, Agricultural Innovation, and Environmental Change," in *The Ends of the Earth: Perspectives on Modern Environmental History,* edited by Donald Worster (Cambridge: Cambridge University Press, 1988), and is reprinted with permission of the publisher.

Chapter 9 appeared as "The Geography of Strikes in the United States: 1881–1894," in *The Journal of Interdisciplinary History* 13 (1982), pp. 63–84 (with Sari Bennett). © 1983 by the Massachusetts Institute of Technology and the editors of *The Journal of Interdisciplinary History.*

Chapter 11 appeared as "Socialism in America: A Geographical Interpretation of Its Failure," in *Political Geography Quarterly* 2, no. 1 (1983), pp. 31–55 (with Sari Bennett).

In addition to these essays, two figures are adapted here from published sources. Fig. 12.5 is from "The Diffusion of the Use of Tractors Again" by Richard Morrill, in *Geographical Analysis* 17 (1985), and is reprinted by permission. © 1985 by the Ohio State University Press. All rights reserved.

Fig. 12.7 is from *The Dynamics of Agricultural Change* by David Grigg, p. 161, and is reprinted by permission of the publishers, St. Martin's Press, Inc., and Hutchinson Educational. © 1982. All rights reserved.

C. E.

Contents

Geographical Inquiry and American Historical Problems

Introduction

The Practice of Geographical History

The surest way toward an appreciation of the art and science of geographical inquiry is through deed rather than word, through concrete and poignant illustration rather than methodological prescription. This series of essays in American geographical history, accordingly, is less a didactic primer than a gentle introduction to a discipline at work in history, less a systematic survey than a series of apt historical problems viewed through the lenses of locational and ecological inquiry, less a theory of history than a set of parables from times past.

The twelve essays in this volume reexamine a handful of perennial problems in American history from a geographical point of view. I have chosen historiographic problems which interest me and which lend themselves to ecological and locational reinterpretation. The essays encompass the first three centuries of American history, beginning with the nightmarish world of disease and death that was early Virginia and ending with the melancholy demise of socialism earlier in this century. The principal themes concern processes that defined the American experience—colonization, regional development and sectionalism, slavery and freedom, urbanization, industrialization, working-class politics, and the long-run periodization of the American past—and the geographical factors that shaped them. The essays are arranged in a chronology of three roughly equal parts: the colonial period between 1607 and 1776; the early national and antebellum periods between the 1780s and 1860; and the postbellum period and the age of reform between 1865 and 1920. Flanking these parts is a concluding chapter which offers at once a synthesis of the various historiographic case studies and an interpretation of the rhythms of American macrohistory and geography's role therein.

These essays in American geographical history are dedicated to the several muses that have inspired them—to history, geography, and the precocious offspring of their union, social science history. To history they offer a fresh angle of vision on the past, a varied series of locational and ecological reinterpretations of familiar historical problems, and a reasonably comprehensive synthesis of American macrohistory; to geography, a subversion of our complacency toward a geographical interpretation of human affairs, our eagerness to deny geography's significance for history and social change (there are exceptions of course—one thinks immediately of the contributions of historical geography and the *Annales* school and its legatees—but in the main, western scholarship has been ageographical, if not anti-geographical; it has steadfastly obscured, denied, or just plain ignored the "geographical factor" in the study of history and social change); and to social science history, one more in a series of promising signs of a revitalization of geographical inquiry in the analysis of social change—of, among other things, an impending rapprochement between geography and history, a reconsideration of the geographical factors in the history of society, and a growing dissatisfaction with the timeless and spaceless models of consensus history and functionalist social theory. The problems and issues taken up here are important, the time spans long, the space extensive, and the methods of inquiry varied. It may be appropriate therefore on the outset of these essays to say at least a few words about geographical history in the large—about the constraints, opportunities, and achievements of this distinctive interpretive point of view.

The Constraints upon Geographical History

That geography's dual themes of space and man-environment relations have not been especially well received by the Western intellectual community is hardly a novel point, and scholars sufficiently detached from that community have made it previously. In speaking of space, the noted French philosopher-historian Michel Foucault remarked that the West regards space as dead, inert, and undialectical while time is seen as alive, vibrant, and dialectical.[1] And with respect

1. Michel Foucault, *Power/Knowledge: Selected Interviews and Other Writings, 1972–1977* (New York: Pantheon Books, 1980), pp. 63–77.

to geography's man-environment theme, the polymath C.P. Snow implicitly underlined the difficulties of such inquiry when conducted within an intellectual tradition which draws a sharp separation between the study of nature and the study of mankind.[2] It is in this unpromising habitat that geographical inquiry has taken place and at times flourished—a habitat which treats space as dead and the relations of nature and culture as an awkward structural bridge.

Geographers are at once pleased and provoked by these philosophical exposés of Western thought: pleased by their provision of a philosophical justification for the discipline; provoked by the icy detachment of the philosophers' prose when juxtaposed against the sense of quiet desperation which gripped geography during the 1930s and 1940s. And rightly so, for American geography could have used a philosophical champion in these difficult times of economic retrenchment, when the discipline struggled valiantly to preserve its distinctive locational and ecological points of view within the academy.

Whatever its other benevolences, the era of the New Deal was not kind to the discipline of geography. Geographers found themselves boxed in by Western thought. The hard times, the intellectual milieu of functionalism and consensus, and geography's position at the bottom of the Western intellectual hierarchy conspired against the discipline. Geographers were driven almost inescapably toward two tactical decisions which simultaneously redefined and foreshortened their field of inquiry. First, they conceded the impracticality of reversing the powerful anti-geographical currents in Western thought. That is to say that geographical inquiries on the problems of history and social change were largely abandoned. And second, they adopted instead a far more constrained version of geographical inquiry, one in which interpretation was restricted almost exclusively to the dependent variables of place and landscape. These decisions, while they may have insured geography's viability, came at the expense of its vitality. Henceforth, geographers set aside the problems of history and social change, that is, of geographical history; locational and ecological modes of inquiry were cultivated in relative obscurity; methods of analysis were quietly refined; and theories, albeit modest ones, adduced. Only on rare occasions did geographers ven-

2. Charles Percy Snow, *The Two Cultures and the Scientific Revolution* (Cambridge: Cambridge University Press, 1959).

ture out into the stormy world of historical and social interpretation, and when they did, the reactions were usually swift and almost always unpleasant.

Thus it was that geographical history found itself caught in a double bind. Geographers for their part had abandoned history, and historians (not to mention Western scholars more generally) had abandoned geography. For those who persisted in doing geographical history, these were joyless and unrewarding times indeed.

But times change. One senses that the world which produced these blunderous misadventures has changed for the better; that geographical forays into social and historical interpretation are not only welcome but imperative in a global system. It is time, one suspects also judging from the favorable reception accorded the geographical inclinations of *inter alia* Wallerstein, Tilly, Skinner, and Worster, for geographers to set aside their disciplined humility and forbearance in favor of a more ambitious and provocative geographical history of social change. In doing so, geographers join with these scholars in the larger project of reconfiguring Marxian and Weberian analyses for a locationally and ecologically interdependent world in the past, present, and future.[3]

On the eve of such a felicitous conjuncture in Western thought, it would be pointless to lament geography's marginal status in the past and, worse yet, to rail against it. But having said that, I am not prepared to wipe the slate clean—at least not before pointing out the paradoxical creativity that has flowed from geography's marginalization and with some demonstration of the ways in which those

3. See for example the works of Immanuel Wallerstein, *The Modern World-System: Capitalist Agriculture and the Origins of the European World-Economy in the Sixteenth Century* (New York: Academic Press, 1974); *idem, The Modern World-System II: Mercantilism and the Consolidation of the Euorpean World-Economy, 1600–1750* (New York: Academic Press, 1980); *idem, The Modern World-System III: The Second Era of Great Expansion of the Capitalist World-Economy, 1730–1840s* (San Diego, California: Academic Press, 1989). Edward Shorter and Charles Tilly, *Strikes in France, 1830–1968* (Cambridge: Cambridge University Press, 1974); Charles Tilly, *The Contentious French* (Cambridge: Harvard University Press, 1986). G. William Skinner, ed., *The City in Late Imperial China* (Stanford: Stanford University Press, 1977). Donald Worster, *Dust Bowl: The Southern Plains in the 1930s* (New York: Oxford University Press, 1979); *idem, Nature's Economy: A History of Ecological Ideas* (New York: Cambridge University Press, 1977); *idem, Rivers of Empire: Water, Aridity, and the Growth of the American West* (New York: Pantheon, 1985). Alfred W. Crosby, *The Columbian Exchange: Biological and Cultural Consequences of 1492* (Westport, Conn.: Greenwood Press, 1972); *idem, Ecological Imperialism: The Biological Expansion of Europe, 900-1900* (New York: Cambridge University Press, 1986). Eugene D. Genovese and Leonard Hochberg, *Geographic Perspectives in History* (Oxford, England: Basil Blackwell, 1989).

uniquely geographical methods and themes may aid us in the understanding of human affairs. In my case that means historical human
affairs, since by training and temperament, I have been drawn to
the historiographical issues and controversies of American history,
or more precisely to Anglo-American history between the times
of Queen Elizabeth and those of Woodrow Wilson. After nearly a
decade and a half of research and writing on this domain, I am persuaded that geography offers an interesting angle of vision on historical problems, and particularly on those problems stalled in historiographic traffic. I am further persuaded by the offhand remark of
an historian who, as we wrestled with a problem, stared at me in
amazement and said: "You think differently." I took that as a compli-
ment not so much on my own meditations on the past as on the field
of inquiry which had prepared me to think in this peculiar fashion—a fashion fundamentally transverse to the channels of Western
thought. And lastly, I am persuaded by a slight extension of Philip
Abrams's interrogatory for social interpretation—try asking questions about human affairs and see if you can do without historical—
and, I would add, geographical—answers. Time, space, and ecology
invariably constitute the scaffolding upon which these interpretations
are framed.[4]

Opportunities: Locational, Ecological, and Macrohistorical Inquiry

What is it about geography that makes us think differently about
human affairs, past and present? This is not a question requiring
an arcane treatise, indeed quite the opposite since the way we think
is rather easily described—though less easily acquired. Geography's
mission is the comprehension of changes on the earth's surface,
and toward that end, human geographers ponder the interactive
effects of nature and culture within specific locations and times.
That easy definition of the field, however, belies the dense connective logic peculiar to geography. Indeed the essence of the field is
its methodo*logic*, which entails connecting human actions (e.g., historical events) with their immediate environs (ecological inquiry)
and connecting these with the specific coordinates of place and re-

4. Philip Abrams, *Historical Sociology* (Ithaca, N.Y.: Cornell University Press, 1982),
esp. p. 1.

gion (locational inquiry).[5] If one concedes—and can we do otherwise?—that every human action from the revolutionary to the prosaic is embedded in its context, that is, in place- and time-specific ecologies, then it follows that any reasonable theory of social change must begin with geographical history or, if you prefer, historical geography.

Geographers have made much ado about the labeling of this point of departure for social theory. Frankly, I think that the distinctions made between geographical history and historical geography have been overdrawn and excessively canonical. The main point is that the way in which we do human geography, the way in which we view locational and ecological relationships, may vary in subtle but important ways. The perspective of historical geography, in the first instance, focuses upon those relationships which have shaped the evolution of place and landscape; geographical history, in contrast, focuses upon those relationships which have shaped human affairs in the past. The former curls back into geography; the latter into history and historical interpretation. Both perspectives, of course, are useful and both are necessary for a full understanding of society and history. But regardless of the perspective deployed, all geographical inquiry—whether of event or of place—invariably begins with location.

Locating these relationships on maps—the first task in *locational inquiry*—is not always as easy as it sounds, especially in a societal context that regards space as dead and inert. But once the mapping is completed, the locational patterns arising from the map shed almost magically new light on old problems. The power of spatial method is not trivial. As one scholar has counseled, many of our current historiographical and social-scientific controversies might be resolved through a proper specification of events in time and space.[6] The principal reason for this explanatory power, of course, is that spatial method directly addresses one of the fundamental axioms of West-

5. The spirit of geographical inquiry is perhaps best conveyed in Carl Sauer's "The Quality of Geography," *California Geographer* 11 (1970), pp. 5–9. Also, Gary L. Gaile and Cort Willmott, eds., *Geography in America* (Columbus, Ohio: Merrill Publishing Company, 1989). On historical geography, see Carville Earle et al., "Historical Geography," *ibid.*, pp. 156–91; William Norton, *Historical Analysis in Geography* (London: Longman, 1984).

6. On the need for proper specification in time and space, see the work of G. William Skinner, *The City in Late Imperial China*; *idem*, "Presidential Address: The Structure of Chinese History," *Journal of Asian Studies* 44 (1985), pp. 271–292. Also, John A. Agnew, *Place and Politics: The Geographical Mediation of State and Society* (Boston: Allen & Unwin, 1987).

ern intellectual inquiry, namely that causality requires the dual proofs of temporal precedence and spatial proximity or association. Without them, causal analysis collapses like a house of cards.

The spatial method (or more simply, map method) thus acquires its power by aligning the effect (*explanandum*) in proper locational position so that potential hypotheses on the causal variables (*explanans*) immediately leap to mind. Virtually all of the essays in this volume deploy this simple yet powerful method of locational inquiry, first querying the spatial distribution of historical events at various scales (why was mortality in early Virginia highest in a small zone along the James River? why did cities flourish in early Pennsylvania, Massachusetts, and Carolina and not elsewhere along the Atlantic seaboard? why was Boston the vanguard of the American Revolution? why was slavery southern and freedom northern? and so on) and then pursuing the ecological basis of their causality.

The logic of spatial method is extremely suggestive of powerful explanations of human affairs, but—and this is critical—it is only suggestive. It remains sterile in the absence of connected attributes within space and time.[7] And it is on this point that geography offers a substantive connection. These are the relationships between man and environment—the focal point of *ecological inquiry*. While not every problem of human affairs is illuminated by this nexus, many are, and all the more so in societies that rely on primary production in agriculture, mining, and forestry. This geographical domain is fairly large because it includes not only all of the developing world today, but all of the rest of the world prior to the 1920s. History therefore is a particularly apposite domain for geographical inquiry.

The notions of man-environment relations or the man-land tradition are a kind of shorthand for geographers, but these notions fail miserably in conveying the variety of methods used in exploring the connective tissue between nature and culture. Our methodological styles vary from precisely quantified models to loosely integrated conceptual interpretations. My preferred variant (though not the only one used in the ensuing essays), and one which has had some success in historical reinterpretation, focuses on the point of mediation between nature and culture, i.e., on primary production (agri-

7. Robert D. Sack, "Geography, Geometry, and Explanation," *Annals of the Association of American Geographers* 62 (1972), pp. 61–78. Andrew Sayer, "The Difference that Space Makes," in *Social Relations and Spatial Structures*, ed. by Derek Gregory and John Urry (New York: St. Martin's Press, 1985), pp. 49–66.

culture, forestry, fishing) and its technology—what I will call, in a word, the staple or "ag-tech" approach.

This ecological perspective has four principal intellectual sources: the commodity approach in economic geography (an approach which became unfashionable during geography's rush toward quantification and abstract spatial models in the 1960s); the ecological approach exemplified in the detailed agronomic thinking of the geographer Carl Sauer in his brilliant reconstructions of agricultural origins and dispersals; the provocative linkages of subsistence technology and societal evolution in the work of the anthropologist Julian Steward; and, lastly, the "staple thesis" pioneered by both economic historians and geographers.[8]

Staple inquiry is characterized methodologically by its attention to the ecological details of primary production and their societal ramifications: to the details of environmental constraints; of crop choice; of crop attributes (bulk, weight, perishability, seasonality); and of agrarian technology (both material and organizational). The method's hallmark is in connecting these details of everyday agrarian life with larger structures of regional economy, society, and politics. These connections are extensive in number and substantial in magnitude, and it is the purpose of this book to demonstrate them through a series of articles on important American historical problems. From the prosaic particulars of crop production and often rudimentary technology, our connections take us a great distance from these modest origins to embrace critical human issues far removed from the usual confines of agricultural geography.[9] These tracings in the American case lead to reinterpretations of such fundamental historical issues as the contrasting trajectories of regional development in the north and south; the choice of free labor or slav-

8. The "commodity approach," though discredited by quantitative and theoretical geographers during the 1960s, taught a great deal of the agronomic detail which one requires for understanding the constraints and opportunities facing agrarian societies. A good, albeit dated, introduction is John W. Alexander's *Economic Geography* (Englewood Cliffs, N.J.: Prentice-Hall, Inc., 1963). Carl O. Sauer, *Agricultural Origins and Dispersals* (New York: American Geographical Society, 1952). Julian Steward, *Theory of Culture Change: The Methodology of Multilineal Evolution* (Urbana, Illinois: University of Illinois Press, 1955). On staples, Harold A. Innis, *The Fur Trade in Canada: An Introduction to Canadian Economic History*, revised ed. (Toronto: University of Toronto Press, 1956); and especially, Robert Baldwin, "Patterns of Development in Newly-settled Regions," *The Manchester School of Economic and Social Studies* 24 (1956), pp. 161–79.

9. The theoretical specification of staple linkages appears in Carville Earle, "The Significance of Staples in American History," *Ohio Geographers* 13 (1985), pp. 54–69.

ery; the coming of the Civil War; and the failure of American socialism.

These ecological reinterpretations of American history may at first seem strained, even contrived, for an audience distanced by time and urbanity from our rural origins. It is incumbent upon these essays, accordingly, to turn back time, to nurture in urbane readers an appreciation of the immense complexity of past agrarian systems, not to mention their countless points of intersection with regional society, polity, and economy. What we are seeking in these essays is nothing less than a reacquaintance with the rural worlds of American history, a patient tracing of the manifold agrarian connections between nature and culture in worlds we have lost, a suspension of modernity's disbelief in the extraordinary power of prosaic agrarian systems, and, in the process, an exposition of a new interpretation of the American past.

The intent of these essays is to make space come alive with the vibrance of dense and extensive ecological connections between nature, culture, and location. But these alone are an insufficient interpretation of human affairs, past or present. Lest we invoke fears of a pervasive ecological determinism, it may be wise to sketch the rather stringent interpretive limits of an ecological staple theory, to remind ourselves precisely what staple theory does—and what it does not do.

In an important sense, staple theory is little more than a method for unravelling or unpacking the social effects of a particular crop produced by a fixed level of technology in a particular region. However useful this may be—and I think it very—the theory does not get at first principles. It does not tell us how and why staples were established in the first place (beyond some obvious and usually trivial connections made between nature's endowment and the specific botanic limits of a crop or certain general remarks on comparative advantage). Nor does it tell us how and why staples and their technologies are modified or abandoned in succeeding historical periods. This is to say that staple theory as it stands now is partial, functionalist, and ahistorical over the long run of history. Left out are the dynamics of agrarian innovation, diffusion, and the ensuing reconfiguration of agrarian practice. Left out too are the parameters that guide and channel agrarian innovation and staple change—parameters such as the dynamics of price, as mediated through a capitalist world system susceptible to periodic crises; of natural calamity; of agrarian policy; of agrarian knowledge and epistemology; and, ultimately, of human agency's capacity for distilling these signals and acting upon them in blundering or novel ways.[10]

As it happens, of course, one cannot study American history over an extended period without engaging the dynamics of agrarian innovation. Staple theory is no exception. The profundity of that theory hinges on its attention toward first principles, toward the causes and not merely the consequences of fundamental agrarian innovations. The trick is to connect staple theory's preoccupation with effects—with the societal ramifications of staple production and marketing—to a vibrant and dialectical temporal dimension which accommodates long-run agrarian innovation and change—a connection attempted later in this volume through a macrohistorical interpretation of the American past. This interpretation, however provisionally and heuristically, proposes that American history is periodic in nature with conjunctures of economic, societal, and political rhythms in recurrent periods of a half century (more or less) and, within periods, recurrent phases.

This provisional interpretation of the American past has several virtues. First, the periodic structure derives directly from the historical periodizations defined by traditional American historians. Second, it provides, as it were, a natural history of the American past, a delineation that enables us to isolate analogous historical periods and phases, compare them, and interpret the remarkable variability of historical action which ensues. Perhaps the principal contribution of this macrohistory, however, is the hypothesis that the mechanism driving the rhythms of American history is explicable within a spatial and ecological framework. The half-century cycles, I propose, are propelled by place-specific agrarian technical innovations and their spatial diffusion in response to periodic demographic stagnation, policy impotence, and economic crisis in capitalist systems—the latter of which are dialectically the result of a thoroughly diffused technology introduced and adopted a half century earlier. This integra-

10. On the role of innovation, see Carl O. Sauer with a commentary by Martin Kenzer, "Regional Reality in Economy," ed. by Martin Kenzer, *Association of Pacific Coast Geographers Yearbook* 46 (1984), pp. 35–49. Lakshman S. Yapa, "Innovation Bias, Appropriate Technology, and Basic Goods," *Journal of Asian and African Studies* 17 (1982), pp. 32–44; Derek Gregory, "Suspended Animation: The Stasis of Diffusion Theory," *Social Relations and Spatial Structures*, pp. 296–336.

tive interpretation of time, space, and ecology in American history offers at once a novel view of our past and a cautionary tale for our future.

The Achievements of Geographical History

In writing these essays in American geographical history, I have been sustained by the convictions that history and geography are inextricable, that historical and social interpretations have a geographical imperative. These convictions, though repeatedly tested by the anti-geographical impulses of Western thought, have been continually reaffirmed by good works in geographical history—by scholars in such diverse fields as social science history, the *Annales* school, historical demography, and historical geography, not to mention the work of Giddens and structuration theorists. In these works, I believe, are contained the signs of an impending rapprochement between history and geography within the hospitable and capacious domain of social science history.[11] Yet even as we anticipate a promising future for geographical history, we would do well to understand something of its arduous past, and most particularly of the momentous contributions of scholars such as Bloch and Febvre, Sauer and Darby, Whittlesey and Fox—in my mind, geographical historians all—during the past half century. Curiously enough, the prologue to geographical history's oft-troubled past is to be found in the field's remarkably vibrant present.

Befitting a discipline at the margins of Western thought, geographical history has been conducted on the borderlands of epistemological realms, between history and social science, between narration and generalization, between synthesis and analysis. These

11. In addition to the authorities cited in note 3 above, see Alan Baker, "Reflections on the Relations of Historical Geography and the *Annales* School of History," in *Explorations in Historical Geography: Interpretative Essays*, ed. by Alan Baker and Derek Gregory (Cambridge: Cambridge University Press, 1984), pp. 1–27 and sources cited therein. On structuration theory, see Anthony Giddens, *Central Problems in Social Theory: Action, Structure, and Contradiction in Social Analysis* (Berkeley: University of California Press, 1979); *idem, The Constitution of Society: Outline of the Theory of Structuration* (Cambridge: Polity Press, 1984). Also, Derek Gregory, "Human Agency and Human Geography," *Transactions of the Institute of British Geographers* ns. 6 (1981), pp. 1–18; Allan Pred, *Place, Practice, and Structure: Social and Spatial Transformation in Southern Sweden, 1750–1850* (Totowa, N.J.: Barnes & Noble Books, 1986).

epistemological marchlands, of course, fall within the larger domain of social science history, that curious but fertile mix of historians, economists, sociologists, political scientists—and geographical historians. At the risk of caricaturing the exquisite variety of this youthful field, it may be said that these scholars share certain predispositions toward social inquiry, predispositions that derive, on the one hand, from misgivings over functionalist social theory and consensus historiography, and on the other, from the curiously productive synergy of science and history. Social science historians (geographical historians included) accordingly are inclined to be: (1) *anti-synchronist* in their commitment to temporal interpretations of social systems; (2) *contextualist* in their specification of the temporal and spatial scope conditions of theory and interpretation; (3) *conjunctivist* in their accommodation of the interplay of human agency and social structures; (4) *historicist* in their interpretation of actions as contingent upon the operative norms and values ("rules of the game") in particular times and places; (5) *comparativist* in their analysis of behavioral variability in times and spaces with similar scope conditions; and (6) *iconoclastic* in their insistence on superseding the categories and interpretations of nineteenth-century social theory, that is, of Weberian and Marxian analysis.[12]

These predispositions have always been congenial for students of geographical history and for good reason. Not only was geography there at the creation of social science history in France during the 1930s and 1940s, but in an important sense geography consummated these continental predispositions during those bleak days of depression and war—when, ironically, Anglo-American geography was in full retreat from history and social inquiry. For scholars seeking a constructive means of expressing their dissatisfactions with an ascendent functionalist social science and consensus historiography, geographical history provided a new vantage point for the reinterpretation of continental social change. Geographical history was not only refreshingly novel in perspective but rather more generous in its accommodation of behavioral variations in time and space—variations which depression and war had accentuated in Western Europe and

12. These predispositions are conveniently displayed in Charles Tilly's provocative volume, *Big Structures, Large Processes, Huge Comparisons* (New York: Russell Sage Foundation, 1984); as well as in G. William Skinner's ongoing analyses of Chinese, Japanese, and French regional systems. See also David Hackett Fischer, *Historians' Fallacies: Toward a Logic of Historical Thought* (New York: Harper & Row, 1970), pp. 216–19; and Robert F. Berkhofer, Jr., *A Behavioral Approach to Historical Analysis* (New York: The Free Press, 1969).

which functionalism and consensus rather too readily papered over. Geographical inquiry ever since has figured prominently in this genre, in the writings of such non-geographers as Fernand Braudel and Emmanuel Le Roy Ladurie of the famed *Annales* school, Jan DeVries, G. William Skinner, Charles Tilly, and Immanuel Wallerstein, to name only a few of the more prominent exponents of ecological and spatial interpretation of past societies and social change.[13]

Geography's rapprochement with historical interpretation was not entirely fortuitous, coming as it did amidst the husky creative atmosphere of the 1930s and amongst the French with their distinctively oblique view of human affairs. Only the French, one suspects, had the élan to elevate geography from a marginal mode of inquiry to a position of interpretive preeminence. But they in addition had the luck of intellectual history on their side.

Historians in France, unlike historians elsewhere, had been nurtured for decades on the principles of geographical history. Indeed, the generation of French historians which came of age during the 1930s and 1940s was heir to a bidisciplinary alliance which dated its origins to the days of the "Great War" and the influence of Paul Vidal de la Blache, the master of French regional geography, upon the youthful historians Marc Bloch and Lucien Febvre. Incorporating Vidalian emphases upon region, location, and ecological association, Bloch and Febvre founded a new mode of historical interpretation in the 1930s which henceforth was known (after their journal) simply as the "*Annales* school." Following World War II, a second generation of students led by Braudel, Ladurie, and Goubert assumed the mantle of the *Annales* school and, in turn, transmitted this eclectic though invariably geographical methodology to a generation of so-

13. See Fernand Braudel's three-volume series, *The Structure of Everyday Life: Civilization and Capitalism 15th-18th Century*, volume 1 (New York: Harper & Row, 1981); *The Wheels of Commerce: Civilization and Capitalism 15th-18th Century*, volume 2 (New York: Harper & Row, 1982); and *The Perspective of the World: Civilization and Capitalism 15th-18th Century*, volume 3 (New York: Harper & Row, 1984). E. Le Roy Ladurie, *Times of Feast, Times of Famine: a History of Climate since the Year 1000* (Garden City, N.Y.: Doubleday, 1971); *idem, The Peasants of Languedoc* (Urbana: University of Illinois Press, 1974). Jan De Vries, *Economy of Europe in an Age of Crisis* (Cambridge: Cambridge University Press, 1976); *idem*, "Patterns of Urbanization in Preindustrial Europe, 1500–1800," in *Patterns of European Urbanization since 1500*, ed. by H. Schmal (London: Croom Helm, 1981), pp. 77–109. Skinner, *The City in Late Imperial China; idem*, "Presidential Address: The Structure of Chinese History." Shorter and Tilly, *Strikes in France*; Tilly, *The Contentious French*. Wallerstein, *The Modern World-System; idem, The Modern World-System II; idem, The Modern World-System III*.

cial science historians within and without the Francophone world.[14]

We can never underestimate the role of the *Annales* school in the evolution of a geographically sensitive social science history; yet the impressive achievements of that school might have fallen on barren ground had it not been for a concurrent if modest revival of geographical history in the English-speaking world. The story begins, as many important stories do, in the 1930s when a handful of geographers—Carl Sauer of Berkeley, H. C. Darby of Cambridge, and Derwent Whittlesey of Harvard—resisted their discipline's attempt to eradicate history from the mainstream of Anglo-American geographic thought.

Their efforts in behalf of history and historical interpretation met formidable opposition from geography's mainstream in the American Midwest. Chastened by an earlier dalliance with Darwinian and Spencerian evolutionary theory and an overarching and overstated environmental determinism, geographers such as Richard Hartshorne and Robert Platt were intent upon purging the discipline of any remnant of this painful past—remnants which included nothing less than the relations of nature and culture, history, and social interpretation. And, in the main, they succeeded in effecting a new and safer geography—functionalist, ahistorical, and descriptive; securing its hegemony during the 1930s; and effectively sealing off the profession from discourse and inquiry on the problems of society and history—not to mention environmental change.[15]

14. In the history of the *Annales* school, two dates stand out above all others—1929 and the founding of the *Annales d'Histoire, économique et sociale* by Marc Bloch and Lucien Febvre; and 1947 with the establishment of the Sixième Section of the Ecole Pratique des Hautes Etudes (under the direction of Febvre) as "a focus for cooperation among social scientists with historians playing the leading roles." Baker, "Reflections on the Relations of Historical Geography and the *Annales* School of History," pp. 3–4; Samuel Kinser, "Annaliste Paradigm? The Geohistorical Structuralism of Fernand Braudel," *American Historical Review* 86 (1981), pp. 63–105. Traian Stoianovich, *French Historical Method: the Annales Paradigm* (Ithaca, N.Y.: Cornell University Press, 1976); Peter Burke, ed., *A New Kind of History: From the Writings of Febvre*, trans. K. Folca (New York: Harper and Row, 1973), pp. ix–xvi. It is ironic, given geography's instrumental role in the origins of social science history and the *Annales* school, that a recent survey of the state of social science history uses a sampling design that ignores geography and geographers altogether. See J. Morgan Kousser, "The State of Social Science History," *Historical Methods* 22 (1989), pp. 13–20. And similarly, that Bloch's biographer has so little to say about his associations with Vidal de la Blache and geographical methodologies. Carole Fink, *Marc Bloch: A Life in History* (Cambridge: Cambridge University Press, 1989).

15. The philosophy and the accomplishments of this new geography are presented respectively in Richard Hartshorne, "The Nature of Geography," *Annals of the Association of American Geographers* 29 (1939), pp. 173–658; and Preston E. James and Clarence F.

I belabor this painfully familiar episode in Anglo-American geographical thought—what Sauer called the "great retreat"—merely for the purpose of providing context for the subterranean resistance to geography's purge of history. The resistance, which in time resurfaced and converged with the geographical history of the *Annales* school, came from several quarters—Berkeley (and later Wisconsin), Cambridge, Harvard—and it assumed several forms. But most of all, it was embodied in three men who, in style and substance, could hardly have been more unlike: Carl Sauer at Berkeley, the hard-driving, opinionated field man from Berkeley; Clifford Darby, the scrupulous and reserved Cambridge don; and Derwent Whittlesey, the mysterious, star-crossed geographer at Harvard. Each, in his own fashion, played a decisive role in preserving a place for history in Anglo-American geographical inquiry.

Sauer was characteristically unequivocal in opposing the new geography. Early on, he launched a vigorous and systematic critique of the new geography's mindless retreat from historical and environmental inquiry, a critique which he sustained through methodological essay and counterexample. In Sauer's opinion, all geography was historical geography; anything else was one-dimensional and uninteresting. When not lampooning the new geography, Sauer and his students produced a spectacular array of archival and field inquiries on historical and cultural geography—on the evolution of the cultural landscape, on agricultural origins and dispersals, on European expansion, acculturation, and the progressive destruction of the environment, on changing resource evaluation and use, and so on.[16] Sauer eventually tired of defining what was geography and what was not; he preferred instead to identify interesting ecological questions

Jones, eds., *American Geography: Inventory and Prospect* (Syracuse, N.Y.: Syracuse University Press, 1954). Critical reviews of this phase in geography's history appear in Preston E. James and Geoffrey J. Martin, *All Possible Worlds: a History of Geographical Ideas* (New York: John Wiley, 1981); David Harvey, *Explanation in Geography* (London: Edward Arnold, 1969); and David Slater, "The Poverty of Modern Geographical Enquiry," *Pacific Viewpoint* 16 (1973), pp. 159–76.

16. Carl O. Sauer, "Foreword to Historical Geography," *Annals of the Association of American Geographers* 31 (1941), pp. 1–24; *idem, Agricultural Origins and Dispersals* (New York: American Geographical Society, 1952); *idem, The Early Spanish Main* (Berkeley: University of California Press, 1966). John Leighly, ed., *Land and Life: a Selection from the Writings of Carl Ortwin Sauer* (Berkeley: University of California Press, 1967). The historical and ecological themes in Sauer's scholarship largely defined the contents of the classic anthology by William Thomas, ed., *Man's Role in Changing the Face of the Earth* (Chicago: University of Chicago Press, 1956).

and to pursue them wherever they happened to lead—which for him was invariably into culture history.

Whereas Sauer opposed every aspect of the new geography, Clifford Darby sought reformation of the new geography from within. In a manner better suited perhaps to a prospective Cambridge don, he sidestepped programmatic declarations on history and geography and instead voiced his opinions indirectly through impeccable scholarship on English historical geography from the time of William the Conqueror to the present. With characteristic modesty and indefatigable archival research, Professor Darby preserved a historical perspective in English geography—but at no small cost. His bargain with the new geography was Faustian in proportion and it entailed upon him eventually an act of contrition, performed through the enunciation of a series of *obiter dicta* declaring, among other things, the illegitimacy of geographical history. Driven by the inexorable logic of the internal reformer, Darby insisted that historical geography's domain was confined to inquiry on changes in landscape and region; to do otherwise, to deploy geographical inquiry for the study of human affairs, of society, economy, and polity, constituted trespass on the domain of history. But if Darby was rigidly and indefensibly doctrinaire on this point, his students were not. In their repeated transgressions into geographical history, they pushed the dignified resistance of their mentor toward the brink of rebellion and toward social science history.[17]

But that would get us ahead of our story since there was one last pocket of resistance during the 1930s. One does not think of Harvard as an especially revolutionary place, but it indeed assumed that role in staving off, however momentarily, the new geography and providing a safe house for geographical history. In 1939, a professor of geography at Harvard published a volume which was at once a

17. H. C. Darby, *An Historical Geography of England before A.D. 1800* (Cambridge: Cambridge University Press, 1936); *idem, The Domesday Geography of England*, 7 volumes (Cambridge: Cambridge University Press, 1952–77); *idem, A New Historical Geography of England before 1600* (Cambridge: Cambridge University Press, 1976). Darby's critique of geographical history had a chilling effect; see his "On the Relations of History and Geography," *Transactions and Papers of the Institute of British Geographers* 19 (1953), pp. 1–11; *idem*, "Historical Geography," in *Approaches in History: a Symposium*, ed. by H.P.R. Finberg (London: Routledge and Kegan Paul, 1962), pp. 127–56. The *Annales* school has consistently deplored the artificial separation of history and geography. See the reviews of Marc Bloch, *Annales d'histoire economique et sociale* 1 (1929), pp. 606–11; and Robert Mandrou, "Geographie humaine et histoire sociale," *Annales: économies, sociétés, civilisations* 12 (1957), pp. 619–26.

classic in political geography and a cogent defense of historical methodology. Derwent Whittlesey's *The Earth and the State*, while it had only modest impact in geography, was extraordinarily influential for historians in general and one in particular, the European historian Edward Fox.[18] Fox, who had studied under Whittlesey at Harvard, borrowed from him the notion that the history of nation-states consists largely in the regional contention between an emergent core area and peripheral adversaries. These notions informed Fox's lifework on Western civilization and ultimately his magnificent little volume *History in Geographic Perspective: The Other France*—a volume which, despite its unadorned geographical analyses, provides one of our most provocative statements on the regional dynamics of state formation.[19]

It was in the classroom, however, that this extraordinary teacher may have had his greatest influence. There, Fox insinuated in his lectures Whittlesey's notions on geographical history and transmitted them to an entire generation of historians and social scientists who were trained at Cornell University. It is no accident therefore that geographically inclined scholars such as the anthropologist G. William Skinner, the historians Allan Bogue and Morton Rothstein, and the sociologist Leonard Hochberg all received their education at Cornell; nor perhaps that the similarly inclined Eugene Genovese would marry Fox's daughter.[20]

Fox's training as a European historian *qua* geographical historian had prepared him for an even more critical role in improving the relations between geography and history in the English-speaking world. Following the lead of the *Annales* school which he knew so intimately from his scholarship on France, Fox placed geography in

18. Derwent Whittlesey, *The Earth and the State: a Study of Political Geography* (New York: Henry Holt & Company, 1939). Whittlesey's trials and tribulations at Harvard University are examined in Neil Smith, "'Academic War Over the Field of Geography': The Elimination of Geography at Harvard," *Annals of the Association of American Geographers* 77 (1987), pp. 155–72. Ironically, Smith seems oblivious to Whittlesey's impact, via Fox, on the renaissance of geographic perspective among historians and social science historians. See, for example, *idem*, "Geography Redux? The History and Theory of Geography," *Progress in Human Geography* 14 (1990), pp. 547–59.

19. Edward Fox, *History in Geographic Perspective: the Other France* (New York: W.W. Norton & Company, 1971).

20. Fox infused his geographical perspective upon history into Cornell's curriculum through his teaching and his role as editor of *The Development of Western Civilization Series: Narrative Essays in the History of our Tradition from its Origins in Ancient Israel and Greece to the Present* (Ithaca, N.Y.: Cornell University Press, 1951–.)

the service of historical interpretation. His inversion of Whittlesey's historical geography into geographical history was as refreshing as it was radical for Anglo-American scholars. Henceforth, Fox joined with the *Annales* school in regarding the historical event as the central problem for inquiry, the dependent variable, if you will, of a geographical history. Such a radical reformulation was inconceivable, however, among the students of Sauer and Darby who, unlike the Cornell historian, were restrained by disciplinary allegiances. For these geographers, historical geography entailed the description and interpretation of the evolutionary development of landscape and spatial organization; it was not to be concerned with ecological and locational impacts on society, polity, and economy. Yet even as these scholars discounted (and often discredited) geographical history in their programmatic writings, they were doing it (or encouraging their students to do so) in their substantive work. Geographical history did not die; quite the contrary, it flourished in the subterranean and often guilt-ridden strata of historical geography. The scholarship of Andrew Clark—a student of Sauer—and his students offers a case in point.

Andrew Clark was a geographical historian in spite of himself. Although he frequently declared that his agenda was always centered on the themes of geographical change and changing geographies, in practice Clark just as often ventured across the line into geographical history. During the 1960s and early 1970s, for example, he supervised a series of exceptionally fine dissertations which owed much of their verve and originality to historiographical themes. These included Cole Harris's evaluation of the impact of the seigneurial system in French Canada, James Lemon's examination of the agrarian basis of liberalism in eighteenth-century Pennsylvania, Sam Hilliard's reassessment of the self-sufficiency controversy in the antebellum South, and Robert Mitchell's test of the frontier thesis in the backcountry of colonial Virginia. This was geographical history by any other name. It displayed all of the accoutrements of the historian's craft—tenacious archival research, critical evaluation of primary sources, and, above all, engagement in and resolution of historiographic controversy.[21]

21. Andrew H. Clark, "Historical Geography," in *American Geography: Inventory and Prospect*, pp. 70–105; *idem*, "Geographical Change as a Theme for Economic History," *Journal of Economic History* 20 (1960), pp. 607–16. R. Cole Harris, *The Seigneurial System in Early Canada: a Geographical Interpretation* (Madison: University of Wisconsin Press, 1966);

The generational drift toward geographical history was not limited to North America. At Cambridge during the 1970s and 1980s, Darby's students contradicted their mentor and eagerly embraced a geographical interpretation of history and social change. Scholars such as Alan Baker, Derek Gregory, Mark Billinge, Mark Overton, Richard Smith, and David Harvey, while continuing to profess historical or human geography, engaged in what can only be described as geographical history. In the small, their undeclared version of geographical history had a much harder edge than that of their American counterparts. Whereas American scholars in the Clark tradition engaged historiography and historical reinterpretation, the Cambridge group drew more explicitly upon the philosophies of Marxism and structurationism. Their interpretations revolved around the issues of class and class conflict, the relative roles of structural forces and human agency therein, and the resonances of this contention in contemporary British society. The presentist impulse in this work is unmistakable and sharply at variance with the somewhat softer, pragmatic, and insular historical interpretations of Clark's American disciples.[22]

In the large, these subtly different perspectives on geographical

---

James T. Lemon, *The Best Poor Man's Country: a Geographical Study of Early Southeastern Pennsylvania* (Baltimore: Johns Hopkins University Press, 1972); Sam B. Hilliard, *Hog Meat and Hoecake: a Geographical View of Food Supply in the Old South, 1840–1860* (Carbondale: Southern Illinois University Press, 1972); Robert D. Mitchell, *Commercialism and Frontier: Perspectives on the Early Shenandoah Valley* (Charlottesville: University Press of Virginia, 1977). One indicator of geographical history's achievement is its increasingly frequent inclusion in mainstream historical geography. See, for example, the interpretation of the coming of the American Revolution in Donald Meinig, *The Shaping of America: a Geographical Perspective on 500 Years of History, Volume 1, Atlantic America, 1492–1800* (New Haven: Yale University Press, 1986).

22. The fascination of Darby's students with past (and present) politics marks a significant departure from their mentor. See, for example, Baker, "Reflections on the Relations of Historical Geography and the *Annales* School," pp. 1–27; Alan R.H. Baker, "On Ideology and Historical Geography," in *Period and Place: Research Methods in Historical Geography*, ed. by Alan R.H. Baker and Mark Billinge (Cambridge: Cambridge University Press, 1982), pp. 233–43; Derek Gregory, "The Discourse of the Past: Phenomenology, Structuralism, and Historical Geography," *Journal of Historical Geography* 4 (1978), pp. 161–73; *idem*, "Action and Structure in Historical Geography," in *Period and Place*, pp. 244–50; and David Harvey, *The Urbanization of Capital: Studies in the History and Theory of Capitalist Urbanization* (Baltimore: Johns Hopkins University Press, 1985); *idem*, *Consciousness and the Urban Experience: Studies in the History and Theory of Capitalist Urbanization* (Baltimore: Johns Hopkins University Press, 1985). The predispositions of these scholars are critically assessed in my book review of Baker and Gregory's *Explorations in Historical Geography* in *Annals of the Association of American Geographers* 77 (1987), pp. 480–84.

history have been inextricably bonded. If at times unreflective on precisely what they were doing and how they were doing it, the practitioners of geographical history—from the French *Annales* school to Edward Fox, from Carl Sauer to Andrew Clark, and from Clifford Darby to Alan Baker—were appreciative nonetheless of the similarities in their goals and their modes of inquiry. All that remains is for their legatees to seize what Marc Bloch regarded as history's most creative moment—and confer upon themselves the title of "geographical historians."[23]

Overview

These essays in American geographical history would not have been possible had it not been for the impressive achievements of the geographers, historians, and social scientists cited above. In a very real sense, they initiated the arduous task of reversing the powerful anti-geographical current that runs through Western thought. I trust that these essays in American geographical history, insofar as they demonstrate geography's capacity for illuminating the problems of history, will extend these heroic efforts.

These essays, like the muses which have inspired them, embrace the fullness of the historical experience. Whatever élan they convey is owing, I am sure, to an attempt to understand the integrity of that experience in all its wholeness, that is, in ecological assemblages over space and across time. Doing so entails, however, the engagement of a variety of themes and a range of methods, all of which may prove unsettling to the more disciplined reader. It seems wise, if not imperative, then, to offer a brief sketch of the feral tendencies contained within this volume and its four thematic sections.

The first section, consisting of four chapters on the colonial pe-

23. Marc Bloch, *The Historian's Craft* (New York: Knopf, 1953). Doubtless some geographers will object to geographical history, seeing it as a capitulation to history and a loss of disciplinary autonomy. See, for example, James Vance's review of Donald Meinig's *The Shaping of America* in *Annals of the Association of American Geographers* 77 (1987), pp. 479–80. There Vance declares that historical geographers should follow Professor Meinig in providing "a clear presentation of a methodology differentiated from that of the historian." The irony is that of all of Professor Meinig's major works, it is this one which most effectively blurs the lines between geography and history, which speaks directly to history, which provides a "geographical perspective on 500 years of history," and which most closely heeds Carl Sauer's warning that "when a subject is marked, not by inquisitiveness, but by definition of its boundaries, it is likely to face extinction. This way lies the death of learning. . . ." Sauer, "Foreword to Historical Geography," p. 4.

riod, reinterprets American colonization and regional development. The first essay deals with the murderous ecological milieu of early Virginia, the tragic settlement experience there, and the eventual dissolution of the Virginia Company; the second, with the locational logic behind the English colonization of the Atlantic Seaboard of North America; the third, with the agrarian basis of regional divergence in southern colonial society, economy, and polity; and the fourth, with Boston's role as locational vanguard of the American Revolution.

The colonial period chapters highlight several themes: English misperceptions of the robust American environment and their implications for mortality in early Virginia, as well as the regional destinations of Puritans, Quakers, and Anglicans during the seventeenth century; the variable role of ethnocultural and economic factors in the initial formation of pluralist early American regions; the ecological effects of agrarian staple crops upon the ensuing social and economic development of these same regions; and the gathering of revolutionary dissent in Boston, perhaps the most unusual of all regions in British North America.

The second set of essays unravels the causes of sectional differences in north and south during the early national and antebellum periods. The main point is that sectionalism rested upon divergent agrarian systems and their societal ramifications, ramifications that led in the north to an industrial, urbanized, and free society and in the south to an agrarian, slave society. Employing a staple approach to regional development, these essays reveal that what have often been dismissed as prosaic attributes of crops—their growing season, seasonality, bulk, weight, and perishability, and associated technologies—have in fact touched all facets of regional life, from location (south or north) to labor systems (slave or free), from settlements (plantation or family farm) to social structures (egalitarian or inegalitarian), and from urban wages (dear or cheap) and industrialization and urbanization (modest or large) to the nature of the American working class (unified or divided).

The staple perspective in these essays also invites a reassessment of the nature of agrarian society, south and north. Neither was as static and conservative as prevailing historiography tends to portray them. Agrarian society in the south was different to be sure, but it was not necessarily backward by comparison with the north. As one of these essays makes clear, the southern planter had a penchant for

recurrent, and often wise, agrarian innovations that belies the enduring myth of a feckless, lazy, and backward society. Another of the
essays offers an equally new perspective on the northern farmer—
and perhaps also upon current interpretations of the causes of the
American Civil War. In our haste to explore the slavery debate in its
national and territorial dimensions, we seem to have overlooked the
intraregional tensions arising from the advocacy of slavery by more
than a few farmers in the midwestern corn belt during the 1840s and
1850s. Their strident insistence upon slavery's superiority in corn
production (and staple theory suggests that they were probably right)
touched off a tremor in midwestern geopolitics and resonated fears
of an impending expansion of the peculiar institution north of the
Ohio River and to the nation at large. More generally, agrarians
north and south had more supple responses to conditions surrounding them than our mythology of agrarian conservatism usually allows. Many of them openly entertained innovation and change, even
if it imperiled the course of regional and national affairs.

The third set of essays shifts to the American urban scene, tracing agrarian society's tendrils into the geography of labor and labor
politics between the Civil War and World War I. The first essay
reconstructs the spatial distribution of worker protest during the
Gilded Age and refines Herbert Gutman's hypothesis on industrialization and the declension of labor power; the second essay reports
on the American Federation of Labor and the formative roles of the
general strike of 1886, the ensuing Haymarket riot, and the geographical lessons that they taught; and the last essay reconsiders the
geography of American socialism and traces its failure to a schism in
the wages and material interests of skilled and unskilled workers—all
of which curve back in one fashion or another to agrarian society and
the role of staple commodities in regional wage determination.

The volume concludes with perhaps the grandest problem of all
for a student of American history—the capacity to make sense out
of the past, to tell a story which speaks to our present condition as
well as to our richly documented past. The final essay attempts to
do just that, knotting the strands of earlier chapters into a provisional interpretation of American macrohistorical rhythms and their
agrarian basis. The chapter is centered around three propositions:
(1) that the periods of American history, along with their policy
cycles, long waves, and religious revitalizations, flow with a logistic
rhythm of fifty years more or less; (2) that each period consists of a

six-phase natural history, which begins in economic and social Crisis, progresses through sequential phases of Creativity, Conflict (international war), Diffusion, Dissent, and Decline, and returns a half century or so later to Crisis; and (3) that recurrent, dialectical, and institutionalized processes of agrarian innovation and diffusion, also lasting about a half century more or less, are the driving forces in the periodic rhythms of American macrohistory. These propositions are provisional, heuristic, and more or less problematic in that they offer ample scope for the play of free will, indeterminacy, and unpredictability in some phases (notably Crisis, Creativity, and Dissent) and in some locations in American history.

The several essays in this volume are at once autonomous and interdependent. They are autonomous in the sense that each of these historical problems has its own vast literature, its own set of historiographical controversies, and, in a few cases, its own scholarly journals. The careful reader, I trust, will discern an undercurrent of thematic continuity running through these essays—that *where* something happened in the past deserves, indeed requires, interpretive consideration; that *when* it happened was conditioned by ecological (innovation) and locational (logistic spatial diffusion) considerations; and that *how and why* it happened depended very often upon the kinds of crops or other staples that were tended in that place or region. Geographical history, in other words, offers something of estimable value for scholars who are dedicated to recovering and understanding the American past.

CHAPTER 1

The Ecological Causes of the Virginia Mortality Crisis, 1607-1624

T he English colonization of North America resembled an epic geographical comedy. Captivated by the facile belief that latitude controlled climate and environment, the English transfigured America in their minds into a pristine, temperate Europe.[1] Along the fresh face of the Atlantic Seaboard of North America, they envisaged familiar Old World environments—environments of moderation, of temperate maritime climate consisting of more humid lands to the north in what they would call, after their analogue, New England, and Mediterranean-like lands in the latitudes of Virginia and the Carolinas. Here was a premise for uproarious comedy and, at times, tragedy.

Seldom has such a misguided theory produced so many bizarre consequences. In the latitude of Spain, the English colonists dutifully tended vineyards that yielded insipid wine. In the latitude of France, the settlers tried valiantly to produce silk, but the imported worms, reared on the white mulberry of Europe, refused to feed on the abundant reds of America. And Virginians watched in amusement as Polish potash-makers, especially imported from the dense stands of pine in the European plain, wandered fruitlessly in search of the infrequent and scattered pines in early Virginia.[2] Countless tales of

This essay benefitted immeasurably from the comments of David Ammerman, Daniel Doeppers, James Knox, Allan Kulikoff, and Russell Menard.

1. Gary Dunbar, "Some Curious Analogies in Explorers' Preconceptions of Virginia," *Virginia Journal of Science*, n.s. 3, no. 9 (1958), pp. 323–26; H. Roy Merrens, "The Physical Environment of Early America: Images and Image Makers in Colonial South Carolina," *Geographical Review*, 59 (1969), pp. 530–56; Charles M. Andrews, *The Colonial Period of American History* (4 vols.; New Haven, Conn.: Yale University Press, 1964); and Carville V. Earle, "The First English Towns of North America," *Geographical Review*, 67 (1977), pp. 34–50.

2. In addition to the sources cited above, see Irene W. D. Hecht, "The Virginia Colony, 1607–1640: A Study in Frontier Growth," (Ph.D. diss., University of Washington,

this sort of blundering relieve the story of relentless English expansion during the seventeenth century, yet on occasion the tales cross the line from comedy into tragedy. For in the nightmarish world of early Virginia, these fanciful environmental theories conspired with short-sighted geographical policies to produce levels of disease and mortality unsurpassed in the annals of English colonization.

Faulty environmental models plagued the colony from the very beginning in 1607. Colony officials in England drew analogies between the European and American environments that glossed over decisive differences—to the misfortune of the Virginia settlers. The American mainland was a lustier and more robust land than Europe, with unanticipated seasonal extremes.[3] New World winters were colder and snowier, and summers were hotter. River and stream levels fluctuated greatly, swelling after the winter melt and spring rains and receding markedly during the scorching American summers. The English also discovered that rainstorms were more intense, thunder more violent, lightning more flashing, and all were more frequent. Other environmental details failed to accord with the Englishmen's maritime model of America. American forests, for instance, contained an enormous diversity of species and lacked the large, homogeneous stands of maritime Europe, while American precipitation, which in theory should have declined toward the tropics, in fact increased substantially.

The English were slow learners. Gradually they abandoned their maritime model and their latitudinal analogies for a more realistic assessment of the New World environment, in the process leaving us a bountiful supply of amusing anecdotes. But it was in Virginia that the maritime model stood the first test, and the learning was painful indeed. The Company leaders could not comprehend the enormous environmental changes taking place along the James River estuary between spring and late summer, and hence they obstinately insisted that the colony remain centered at Jamestown, which proved to be a dynamic and deadly location.

Disease has long been suspected as one of the principal causes of

---

1969); Edmund S. Morgan, "The Labor Problem at Jamestown, 1607–18," *American Historical Review*, 76 (1971), pp. 595–611; *idem, American Slavery, American Freedom: The Ordeal of Colonial Virginia* (New York: W. W. Norton & Co., 1975).

3. Carl O. Sauer, "The Settlement of the Humid East," *Climate and Man, Yearbook of Agriculture, 1941* (Washington, D.C.: GPO, 1941), pp. 157–66; Donald W. Meinig, "The American Colonial Era: a Geographical Commentary," *Proceedings, Royal Geographical Society of Australia, South Australian Branch*, 59 (1958), pp. 1–22.

death in early Virginia, with Jamestown as the locus. The association of place, disease, and mortality, although often observed, has seldom been understood. This essay examines the seasonal changes in the estuarine environment and the Virginia Company's failure to respond to those changes, and it sets out a geographical model of disease mortality that accounts for spatial, seasonal, and annual mortality variations in Jamestown and the James River estuary between 1607 and 1624. The model, derived from the first year in Jamestown, suggests the probable causes of disease-related deaths and offers a logical and consistent account of the pathogenic organisms, the sources of infection, the incidence of infection, morbidity and mortality, and the recurrence of epidemics. The plan of the essay entails, first, the derivation of the model based on the first year at Jamestown, second, its application and testing for the years 1608–24, and third, a discussion of the Virginia Company's inability to understand the New World environment and adopt policies that would have led to lower mortality rates, and some speculations on the causes of declining mortality after 1624 in Virginia and the English colonies generally.

The first year in Virginia portended the dreadful mortality that ravaged the colony until 1624. Things went well at first. The expedition of three vessels and 144 persons left England in December 1606, headed south and west to the West Indies, and then north to the Chesapeake Bay, entering it on 26 April 1607. Shortly thereafter, the colonists established Jamestown on the north side of the James River, nearly 50 miles from its mouth (Figure 1.1).[4] The Virginia spring was beneficent, and when Captain Newport departed on 22 June he left 104 healthy colonists. But by late summer the colony took on a more somber attitude. On 6 July, George Percy's journal mentioned the death of one John Asbie by the "bloudie fluxe," and three days later George Floure died of the "swelling." In the space of one month, 21 colonists died, causing Percy to lament that "our men were destroyed with cruell diseases, as swellings, Flixes, Burning Fevers, and by warres, and some departed suddenly, but for the most part they died of meere famine . . . ."[5] Forty-six were dead by the

4. "Observations of Master George Percy, 1607," pp. 5–23 of Lyon Gardiner Tyler, ed., *Narratives of Early Virginia, 1606–1625* (New York: Charles Scribner's Sons, 1907); on the selection of Jamestown, see Earle, "The First English Towns."

5. "Observations of Master George Percy," p. 20. One hundred and five colonists are claimed in "The Proceedings of the English Colony," *Travels and Works of Captain John Smith* I, Edward Arber, ed., Burt Franklin: Research and Source Work Series no. 130, (2 parts; New York: Burt Franklin reissue, originally published 1910), p. 94. Hereafter cited as Arber, ed., *Travels and Works*.

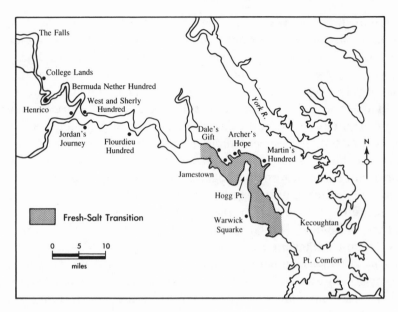

FIGURE 1.1.   The James River, 1607–24.

end of September, and in January, when the first supply arrived in
Virginia, just 35 of 104 colonists were alive.[6]

   The abundance of death demanded an explanation. Let us look
first at Percy's comment that "meere famine" was the chief cause of
death. In support of his view, the colonist's daily ration—just half
a pint of wheat and another of barley mixed in a gruel—yielded
roughly half the caloric intake required for an active man of the
average colonist's stature.[7] But there may have been a political aspect
to his comment: we know that the selection of Jamestown over the
Archer's Hope site had displeased him, and he may have been a sup-
porter of the faction accusing President Wingfield of hoarding the
colony's food and drink for presidential favorites. Whatever Percy's
motives, his emphasis on famine spotlighted attention on President
Wingfield. The president, of course, denied these allegations.[8] His
rebuttal draws indirect support from one of his enemies, Captain

   6. Arber, ed., *Travels and Works*, I, pp. lxxvi, 9, 95. Alexander Brown, *The First Republic in America* (New York: Houghton Mifflin, 1898), p. 55.

   7. Herbert Renardo Cederberg, Jr., "An Economic Analysis of English Settlement
in North America, 1583–1635" (Ph.D. diss., University of California, 1968), p. 144. Arber,
ed., *Travels and Works*, II, pp. 391–92.

   8. "A Discourse of Virginia per: Ed: Ma: Wingfield," Arber, ed., *Travels and Works*,
I, pp. lxxiv–xci.

John Smith. Smith made little of the shortage of provisions, stating matter-of-factly on several occasions that the colony still had so many weeks of supplies remaining. He knew that the colony had a supplementary source of food in the annual sturgeon run. Thousands of these fish entered the James estuary in April and May, and their run to freshwater spawning grounds continued through the summer, when the big fish came in. "From the end of May till the end of June," wrote Smith, "are taken few but young Sturgeons of 2 foot or a yard long. From thence till the midst of September, them of 2 or three yards long and few others. And in 4 or 5 houres with one nette were ordinarily taken 7 or 8: often more."[9] A few years later, John Rolfe related that two men in a few hours axed forty sizable sturgeon.[10] Since the Atlantic sturgeon averages above 100 pounds, the output of two axe-wielding men would have totalled 4,000 pounds, or nearly 40 pounds per colonist per day.[11] A daily intake of two pounds of sturgeon, some sea crabs, and the wheat-barley gruel was more than adequate for the colonists' metabolic needs. Furthermore, two pounds of fish daily would have provided 90 percent of what we now consider the daily thiamine requirement, so that the outbreak of beriberi postulated by the medical historian Blanton seems unlikely.[12]

Thus the food supply during Jamestown's first summer, though unappealing, provided sufficient nourishment to ward off starvation and vitamin-deficiency diseases. Although starvation did not cause death, the possibility was a constant fear of the colonists, and by mid-September they felt it was imminent. Newport had left them supplies for 13 or 14 weeks; even allowing for the extra food resulting from the death of 50 colonists, by September there were only enough supplies for four to eight weeks, the sturgeon run was falling

9. *Ibid.*, I, pp. 8–9, 51.

10. Philip A. Bruce, *Economic History of Virginia in the Seventeenth Century* (2 vols.; New York: Macmillan, 1896), I, p. 112.

11. Edward C. Raney, "Freshwater Fishes," *The James River Basin, Past, Present, and Future*, Virginia Academy of Science, James River Project Committee (Richmond: 1950), p. 154. James Wharton, *The Bounty of the Chesapeake: Fishing in Colonial Virginia*, Jamestown 350th Anniversary Historical Booklets, No. 13 (Williamsburg: Virginia 350th Anniversary Celebration, 1957).

12. H. L. A. Tarr, "Changes in Nutritive Value through Handling and Processing Procedures," *Fish as Food* (4 vols.; New York: Academic Press, 1961–65), II, p. 248; Wyndham B. Blanton, "Epidemics, Real and Imaginary, and other Factors Influencing Seventeenth Century Virginia's Population," *Bulletin of the History of Medicine*, 31 (1957), pp. 454–62.

off, and additional supplies were not expected until October at the earliest.

Although Percy blamed famine for Virginia's troubles, his list of clinical symptoms brings us closer to what I believe to have been the actual causes of death—typhoid, dysentery, and perhaps salt poisoning. Medical historians are generally agreed that Percy's "flixes" or "bloudie Flixes" describe dysentery, while "Burning Fevers" are symptomatic of typhoid fever.[13] The "Swellings," though they may be associated with dysentery, could also have resulted from salt intoxication from the salty river water.[14] These three diseases are also indicated by the incidence and rapidity of death, as chronicled by Percy. Typhoid fever progresses rapidly from infection by the bacterium *Salmonella typhosa*. The first week may be symptomless, as the organisms spread through the bowel wall and into the lymphatic glands. In the second week, the organism enters the bloodstream, causing a rapid rise in body temperature, recognized by colonials as the "burning fever." The illness peaks in the third week, and death may result. Before the use of antibiotics, it is estimated that 15–20 percent of those infected died.[15]

Dysentery, caused by amoebic parasites, produced the "bloudy flux." While several types of amoebic parasites reside in the human intestinal tract, most are harmless commensals or bring on diarrhea

13. Very useful are John Duffy, *Epidemics in Colonial America* (Baton Rouge: Louisiana State University Press, 1953); Wyndham B. Blanton, *Medicine in Virginia in the Seventeenth Century* (Richmond: William Byrd Press, 1930), pp. 3–77; Thomas P. Hughes, *Medicine in Virginia, 1607–1699*, Jamestown 350th Anniversary Historical Booklets (Williamsburg: Virginia 350th Anniversary Celebration, 1957); Richard Harrison Shryock, *Medicine and Society in America, 1660–1860* (New York: New York University Press, 1960), pp. 82–116.

14. Hans G. Keitel, *The Pathophysiology and Treatment of Body Fluid Disturbances* (New York: Appleton-Century-Crofts, 1962), pp. 162–64; John H. Bland, "Clinical Physiology and Four Avenues of Loss and Gain," *Clinical Metabolism of Body Water and Electrolytes* (Philadelphia: W.B. Saunders, 1963), pp. 133–64.

15. The fever lasts 21 days usually, and occasionally up to 33 days. Frederick P. Gay, *Typhoid Fever Considered as a Problem of Scientific Medicine* (New York: Macmillan, 1918), pp. 13–24; Gay shows 15–27 percent mortality for the London Fever Hospital, 1848–70. See also William Budd, *Typhoid Fever: its Nature, Mode of Spreading, and Prevention* (New York: n.p., 1931); Jacques M. May, *The Ecology of Human Disease* (New York: MD Publications, 1958), pp. 171–88. In general, I agree with Jones that typhoid fever killed numerous Virginians in 1607. I disagree with him on the following points: (1) that typhoid, aided by beriberi, was the principal killer; (2) that typhoid was probably introduced by Reverend Robert Hunt; and (3) that the Jamestown environment was essentially passive in the typhoid epidemic. Gordon W. Jones, "The First Epidemic in English America," *Virginia Magazine of History and Biography*, 71 (1963), pp. 3–10.

or mild dysentery. More dangerous is *Entamoeba histolytica*, which may invade the bowel wall, causing ulceration and the bloody stools that gave the disease its seventeenth-century name. More serious complications arise when these parasites bore into a large blood vessel, causing massive hemorrhaging, or when they enter the bloodstream and travel to other organs. Dysentery is often fatal, especially when populations are weakened by other illnesses or malnutrition. Pre-antibiotic mortality rates of 12–25 percent have been recorded.[16] Like typhoid, dysentery can act quickly, though the rates of incubation vary with the individual.[17] Clinical symptoms usually appear within 1–4 weeks, but the range may be from a few days to several months.

An epidemic of typhoid fever and dysentery accords with Percy's description of death and sickness at Jamestown. Percy first noted disease-related deaths on 6 July, and sickness and death continued "for the space of sixe weekes"—a time span in keeping with the progression of both diseases. Furthermore, the mortality rate of 46 percent (50 of the 104 colonists had perished by mid-September) exceeds just slightly the sum of expected pre-antibiotic mortality rates for typhoid (15–20 percent) and dysentery (12–25 percent). Even if some colonists died of both pathogens, so that the separate rates cannot be taken as simply additive, my guess is that the correct estimate of disease mortality probably lies in the 27–45 percent range, and near the upper end. This supposition is based on several considerations. First, the Jamestown population was probably under 30 years of age, and hence included the most susceptible age groups for typhoid (15–25 years) and dysentery (26–30 years).[18] Furthermore, the concentration and confinement of the population facilitated the incidence and spread of these diseases and perhaps increased their virulence.[19]

16. Ernest Carroll Faust, *Amebiasis*, Publication No. 191, A Monograph in American Lectures in Internal Medicine (Springfield, Ill.: Charles C. Thomas, 1954). "Parasitism in Southeastern United States: A Symposium," *Public Health Reports*, 70, no. 10 (1955), pp. 957–75; Blanton, *Medicine in Virginia in the Seventeenth Century*, p. 63; Arthur L. Bloomfield, "A Bibliography of Internal Medicine: Amebic Dysentery," *Journal of Chronic Diseases*, 5 (1957), pp. 235–52; May, *The Ecology of Human Disease*, pp. 189–215.

17. "In controlled experiments with human volunteers Walker and Sellards found that the prepatent period, i.e., from exposure until the amebas appeared in the stools averaged nine days, varying from one to 44 days in the 17 of 20 exposed individuals who became infected." Faust, *Amebiasis*, p. 58.

18. *Ibid.*, p. 28. About 50 percent of all typhoid cases occur in the age group 15–25 years; Gay, *Typhoid Fever*, p. 13.

19. Faust, *Amebiasis*, p. 26. Modern surveys for *Entamoeba histolytica* in the southeastern United States average 11 percent positive in the general population; but among the

The role of typhoid and dysentery may be further clarified by a discussion of the disease agents, their introduction, and the sources of human exposure. Introduction is not problematic, since the colony undoubtedly contained numerous carriers of both diseases. According to modern laboratory diagnostic surveys, *E. histolytica* is carried by 40 percent of the population in the 26–30 age group (with a decreasing incidence away from that peak),[20] and typhoid bacilli are carried by 2–30 percent of the general population.[21] Carriers of both may be symptomless, and the diseases are therefore almost impossible to detect in the absence of laboratory diagnoses. The Jamestown carriers must have passed millions of disease organisms in their feces, and also through their urine in the case of typhoid. The diseases were then transmitted, in all probability, through the ingestion of a contaminated water supply.[22]

But what was the water supply, and why was it contaminated in July and August and not earlier or later? The colonists drank river water. In spring, with river flow at a maximum owing to high precipitation, low evaporation, and high runoff, the water was safe. The fresh running water swirled around Jamestown Island and flushed disease organisms downstream. But dramatic changes occurred as summer set in. River flow lessened, water levels receded some 10–15 feet, and Jamestown Island became a peninsula attached to the mainland.[23] Pools of standing water and stagnant marshes rimming the

concentrated populations of a mental hospital and an orphanage, the positives rose to 40 and 55.5 percent, respectively. Willard H. Wright, "Parasitism in Southeastern United States: Current Status of Parasitic Diseases," *Public Health Reports*, 70, no. 10 (1955), pp. 966–75. Gay, *Typhoid Fever*, pp. 14–15, 43–45.

20. Faust, *Amebiasis*, p. 28.

21. Gay, *Typhoid Fever*, p. 43.

22. As one expert on typhoid fever has observed, "it must be remembered that a single discharge of the bowels of a typhoid patient may contain one billion typhoid bacilli, perhaps more at times, and that 1 percent of one billion is ten million, a number of bacilli large enough to do immense damage." George C. Whipple, *Typhoid Fever: its Causation, Transmission and Prevention* (New York: John Wiley & Sons, 1908), pp. 49–50.

23. The normal regime of Chesapeake estuaries is described here. Discharge, however, will depart from the norm of spring highs and summer lows under atypical meteorological conditions, e.g. prolonged drought or excessive rainfall, variable evapotranspiration, variable snow-melt water. Virginia, Virginia Conservation Commission, Division of Water Resources, *Surface Water Supply of Virginia: James River Basin*, Bulletins nos. 5, 13, 17, and 25 (Charlottesville and Richmond: 1944–61). On Jamestown's transformation from an island to a peninsula attached to the mainland, see C. A. Browne, "Reverend John Clayton and His Early Map of Jamestown, Virginia," *William and Mary Quarterly*, 2nd Series, 19 (1939), pp. 5–6. The recession in river depth is estimated from depths of the main

mainland side of the island created a virulent wetland environment for *S. typhosa* and *E. histolytica.*

Even more deadly was the summer contamination of the river water with salt, sediment, and fecal material. As fresh water flow fell, salt water invaded some 30 miles up the James estuary from a point below Hog Point in the spring to Jamestown by mid-summer. And along the inland-moving fresh-salt boundary, sediments and organic wastes were trapped by the salt plug, particularly on the north side of the James owing to the rightward deflection of the marine incursion by the earth's rotation.[24] Percy put it succinctly: "our drink was cold water taken out of the River, which was at floud very salt, at low tide full of slime and filth, which was the destruction of many of our men . . . ."[25]

At flood tide, the colonists drank water containing salt in concentrations of over five parts per thousand—far above the recommended standard today for constant daily usage of one part per thousand. The colonists suffered from salt poisoning, with its characteristic symptoms of "swellings" (edema), lassitude, and irritability. The "idle, lazy and factious" behavior of the early Virginians was, in part, the result of a steady summer diet of salty water.[26] The ebb tide, though less saline, was very turbid, organically polluted, and deadly. The trapped pathogens of typhoid and dysentery must have

---

channel at Jamestown. Percy gives 6 fathoms (36 feet) in spring; an English pilot, interrogated by the Spanish in 1611, put the depth at 3 1/2 fathoms (21 feet) at the least. The river's annual range is 15 feet. Alexander Brown, *The Genesis of the United States* (2 vols; Boston, 1890), I, p. 519. Samuel H. Yonge, *The Site of Old "James Towne," 1609-1698* . . . (Richmond: Hermitage Press, 1907).

24. An excellent survey of the James is Maynard M. Nichols, "Sediments of the James River Estuary, Virginia," *Geological Society of America, Memoir*, 133 (1972), pp. 169-212.

25. "Observations of Master George Percy" (cited in n. 4), pp. 21-22.

26. Drinking water preferably should contain not more than 0.5 parts per thousand salt content; however, some contemporary municipal water supplies use 2 parts per thousand without public complaint. Thomas R. Camp and Robert L. Meserve, *Water and Its Impurities*, 2nd ed. (Stroudsburg, Penn.: Dowden, Hutchinson & Ross, 1974), p. 2; Keitel, *Pathophysiology and Treatment of Body Fluid Disturbances*, pp. 162-64, 209-10. J.H. Bland, "Clinical Physiology and Four Avenues of Loss and Gain." A composite of early Virginian behavior would include irritability, short tempers, factiousness, and hyperbolic perceptions. The extremity of their situation accounts for some of these behaviors, salt poisoning accounts for them all. On idleness in early Virginia, see Morgan, "The Labor Problem at Jamestown," (cited in n. 2). On apathy induced by the range of early Virginia's problems, see Karen Ordahl Kupperman, "Apathy and Death in Early Jamestown," *Journal of American History* 66 (1979), 7-24.

floated back and forth past Jamestown with every summer tide. The danger from contaminated water passed in September as river flow increased, pushing the salt incursion and its deadly associates downstream toward Hog Point.

The 1607 epidemic of fevers, fluxes, sickness, and death was the first of many such summer epidemics between 1607 and 1624. Supporting the thesis that the repeated epidemics were outbreaks of typhoid and dysentery is the fact that these diseases confer only limited immunity to repeated attacks. Severe dysentery attacks invoke a limited antibody response for two weeks after the infection, but thereafter the survivor is susceptible to reinfection.[27] Typhoid attacks confer somewhat more immunity: recurrence is usually put at 0.75–4.2 percent; however, the recurrence rate rises to between 8 and 15 percent in especially virulent and massive infections, like those we posit in Jamestown.[28] Thus, survivors of dysentery and typhoid epidemics at Jamestown would have been only slightly less susceptible to these diseases than new arrivals. Survivors of a Virginia summer may have become "seasoned" to some new diseases, but they were not immune to future epidemics of typhoid and dysentery or to the effects of salt poisoning. These recurred with the annual summer invasion of salt water up the James and with the resulting contamination of the Jamestown water supply.

This close relationship between environment, disease, and mortality in 1607 Jamestown may be stated more generally for all Chesapeake estuaries. For our purposes, an estuary is an ecological unit wherein fresh water from the land is mixed with encroaching water from the sea, producing several salinity zones: (1) the zone of fresh water, with salinity less than 0.5 parts per thousand; (2) the zone of fresh-salt transition (the oligohaline), with salinities of 0.5–3 parts per thousand; and (3) the zone of salty water, with salinity above 3 parts per thousand (this can be further divided into the mesohaline, polyhaline, and marine).[29] Sediment and fecal material entering

27. Faust, *Amebiasis*, pp. 30–32.
28. Gay, *Typhoid Fever*, p. 148.
29. Chesapeake estuaries are moderately stratified—i.e., turbulence by tidal action mixes underlying salty water and overriding fresh water, thus bringing salt to the surface. The variety of estuaries is discussed in a massive compendium, George H. Lauff, ed., *Estuaries*, Publication no. 83, American Association for the Advancement of Science (Baltimore: Horn-Shafer, 1967). Several articles therein are pertinent: Donald W. Pritchard, "What is an Estuary: Physical Viewpoint," pp. 3–5; *idem*, "Observation of Circulation in Coastal Plain Estuaries," pp. 37–44; M. M. Nichols and R. L. Ellison, "Sedimentary Pat-

an estuary are flushed out of its freshwater portion, temporarily trapped or plugged up by the salt incursion in the oligohaline, and eventually flushed for the most part downstream into the saltier water. Thus, pathogenic river-borne organisms are least in the freshwater zone, maximum in the oligohaline zone, and intermediate in the mesohaline and polyhaline zones near the estuary mouth. Contamination also varies by bank side. Left bank contamination exceeds right bank owing to the deflection of the salt incursion by the earth's rotation.

This geographic distribution of estuarine contamination is, in turn, directly correlated with human exposure, infection, and mortality from the pathogens of typhoid and dysentery.[30] Mortality also varies seasonally with the migrations of the salt incursion. In the oligohaline zone, the probability of infection increases when the salt-fresh boundary passes by; clinical symptoms and mortality lag behind during the prepatent period, with a normal lag of about one week to one month. The location of this deadly boundary zone migrates with river discharge. In the Chesapeake estuaries, low discharge usually occurs in summer, as the salt water invades up-estuary to its landward maximum; on the James, it migrates 30 miles to the vicinity of Jamestown, where mortality rates should peak in July and August. Highest discharge customarily comes in spring and pushes the salty water to its seaward maximum; on the James, the retreat is to Hog Point, where mortality should peak in April and May. Within the salty water, mortality should rise slightly in spring because of the proximity of the salt trap; however, this zone receives tidal flows of

---

terns of Microfauna in a Coastal Plain Estuary," pp. 283–88; and J. L. McHugh, "Estuarine Nekton," pp. 581–620, which contains the salinity classification. Also see Donald W. Pritchard, "Salinity Distribution and Circulation in the Chesapeake Bay Estuaries System," *Journal of Marine Resources*, 11 (1952), pp. 106–23.

30.   The distribution of disease organisms within an estuary depends on their point of entry, the circulation and flushing time of the estuary, and the life expectancy of the disease organisms. Laboratory experiments show that coliform bacteria, an indicator of disease contaminants, die off rapidly to one-tenth their original population in a period of 0.5 to 2–3 days. The extent of downstream contamination increases when river circulation is rapid and the pollutants are flushed downstream before death. Bostwick H. Ketchum, "Distribution of Coliform Bacteria and other Pollutants in Tidal Estuaries," *Sewage and Industrial Wastes*, 27 (1955), pp. 1288–96; Clarence J. Velz, *Applied Stream Sanitation* (New York: Wiley-Interscience, 1970), pp. 339–79; *Wastes Management Concepts for the Coastal Zone: Requirements for Research and Investigation*, Committee on Oceanography and Committee on Ocean Engineering, National Academy of Engineering (Washington, D.C., 1970).

fecal material throughout the summer, thus assuring summer sickness and death. Recurrent epidemics were possible when the population occupied the fresh-salt and salt-water zones.[31]

This geographic model of mortality is of course fairly crude, coarsely subdividing estuaries into three salinity zones and hypothesizing the variable mortality within them. A more refined model might specify the precise concentrations of contaminants as a function of estuarine flushing and transport and the life expectancies of pathogens, as well as the expected levels of infection and mortality. But the hydrologic information for early Virginia does not permit such refinements. Nonetheless, ample records survive to afford several opportunities of testing the basic geographic model of mortality. For the period 1607–24, deaths may be calculated from contemporary statistics of population and immigration, though these must be used with caution, since early Virginians regularly juggled population estimates to suit their purposes. The most probable causes of death are deduced from colonists' descriptions of the timing and symptoms of disease and the plausibility of their explanations of the causes of death. The locations of population and of mortality derive from contemporary accounts. Particularly useful is the geographic census of the living and dead for 1623–24.

The first matter at issue is the relationship between mortality and the location of population in early Virginia. A chronological survey of the period 1607–24 reveals the recurrent deadliness of Jamestown summers. When population was concentrated in the town, mortality rates invariably rose above 30 percent; and when the population dispersed, death rates declined sharply. The first two summers in Virginia were disastrous: by October 1608, of perhaps 244 colonists who had come to Jamestown, 149 were dead.[32] But the third summer offered the first glimmer of hope. The death toll between

31. The expected timing and location of disease morbidity and mortality rest on the assumption of "average" climatic conditions and "normal" estuarine circulation—i.e., peak discharge and salt retreat in spring, and low discharge and salt incursion in late summer. Atypical weather conditions could alter the timing and location of disease incidence. The timing of epidemics is affected also by physiological factors. The increased incidence of typhoid and dysentery in late summer also may have to do with increased human output of pathogens at that time, as counts of coliform bacteria in the Detroit River suggest (see Velz, *Applied Stream Sanitation*, pp. 239–42). The reasons underlying this increased productivity are incompletely understood, but for our purposes it should produce higher mortality on the landward edge of the oligohaline than on the seaward edge.

32. In December 1606, 144 colonists went to Virginia; 104 were left by Newport in June 1607; 38–40 survived in January 1608; 100–120 immigrants arrived between Janu-

FIGURE 1.2. A portrait of Captain John Smith appearing on the map of New England that accompanied Smith's tract entitled *The Generall Historie of Virginia, New England and The Summer Isles* (London: I. D. and I. H. for Michael Sparkes, 1624). Captain Smith, though given to hyperbole and self-promotion, was a gifted geographer and ethnographer. His tactical dispersal of settlers from Jamestown effected a reduction in disease and death that was matched only by Thomas Dale's removal of settlement from Jamestown to Henrico in 1613.

October 1608 and mid-summer 1609 was just 21 of 130 persons, including 11 who died by drowning.[33] Captain John Smith claimed credit for this success, and rightly so.

---

ary and September 1608; and 60 were alive in October 1608. The mortality rate in the text is from Hecht, "The Virginia Colony" (cited in n. 2), p. 68, and Brown, *The First Republic* (cited in n.6), pp. 55, 58–59, 68. Brown's population and immigration figures are usually accurate, and I rely on them frequently. However, his friendliness toward the Sandys administration from 1619 to 1624 and its "democratic" character leads him to minimize the mortality problem then, while he is excessively critical of mortality under Thomas Smythe's administration before 1617 and the Crown's after 1624.

33. Friends of Smith claimed that only 7 or 8 of 200 died. Brown shows 130 alive in October 1608; 11 drowned in mid-January, and not more than 109 survived. Arber, ed., *Travels and Works*, I, pp. 154–57. Brown, *The First Republic*, pp. 70–71. Philip L. Barbour,

Smith, though a vainglorious man, was also a sensitive ethnographer.[34] He carefully recorded the Indians' movements, and in all probability he understood the adaptive value of their seminomadic economy. In the spring, the Indians congregated along the James estuary, subsisting on marine life while they planted their crops of corn, pumpkins, and beans. United and hungry after a long lean winter, the Chesapeake tribes were especially dangerous at this season in their annual cycle. As summer approached, the tribes left the estuarine zone and dispersed into smaller groups, residing usually on a hill with a freshwater spring, yet near enough to the river to gather fish, oysters, and crabs. By dispersing, the Indian bands avoided the unhealthy estuarine zone while exploiting scattered edible plants and animals during this leanest of seasons.[35] But dispersal

---

The Jamestown Voyages under the First Charter, 1606–1609, Hakluyt Society, 2nd Series, 137 (Cambridge: published for the Hakluyt Society at the University Press, 1969), II, p. 411.

34. The full story of Smith's ecological and ethnographic sensitivity and his application of this knowledge remains untold. Arber, ed., *Travels and Works*, I, pp. 61–70; Maurice A. Mook, "Virginia Ethnology from an Early Relation," *William and Mary Quarterly*, 2nd Series, 23 (1943), pp. 101–29. Philip L. Barbour, *The Three Worlds of Captain John Smith* (Boston: Houghton Mifflin, 1964), pp. 243–76. Smith can be eulogized too much. While others died in Jamestown, he explored the healthier reaches of the Chesapeake. In 1608, Smith returned to Jamestown long enough to see the summer sickness, before he was off again. Brown, *The First Republic*, p. 60.

35. For the Indians, the zone of the fresh-salt transition was assuredly unhealthy and perhaps as deadly as for the English. Indian dispersal may have been designed to avoid water-borne disease. Although some scholars maintain that typhoid and dysentery were not present in America before 1492—the evidence is not overwhelming on this score—these diseases could have spread into the Virginia tidewater as a result of sixteenth century European contact. In pre-settlement New England, for instance, very slight European contact with the Indians contributed to a massive epidemic of plague in 1617. Similarly, the Virginia tribes could have been infected by tribes in the vicinity of the Roanoke colony during the 1580s or possibly by the lost colonists who, legend has it, lived among the Indians. One student of Indian disease believes that dysentery was widespread among the North American woodland Indians before the permanent settlement of the English and French. Woodrow Borah, "Hispania Victrix; American Debellata: The Demographic Meaning of Conquest," *Revista de Historia* (São Paulo), in press, as summarized and cited in William M. Denevan, ed., *The Native Population of the Americas in 1492* (Madison: University of Wisconsin Press, 1976), p. 5; Whipple, *Typhoid Fever*, pp. 117–18; Sherburne F. Cook, "The Significance of Disease in the Extinction of the New England Indians," *Human Biology*, 45 (1973), pp. 485–508; Frank D. Ashburn, ed., *The Ranks of Death: A Medical History of America* (New York: Coward-McCann, 1947), pp. 158–59; Alfred W. Crosby, Jr., *The Columbian Exchange: Biological and Cultural Consequences of 1492*, Contributions in American Studies, 2 (Westport, Conn.: Greenwood, 1972). More recently, researchers on the James River have discovered a new water-borne bacterial disease called the "coastal disease," a potentially fatal disease of the lungs. *The Baltimore Sun*, 25 Oct. 1977, p. A8.

to healthier sites had its price: the scattered bands were politically and militarily weak. They sniped at their vulnerable, sick, and weak English enemies, but a summer war of attrition was impossible.

This flux in Indian power eluded most Virginians. Percy fully expected annihilation in the summer of 1607, and he marveled that God had saved them by putting "a terrour in the Savages hearts."[36] Smith saw things more clearly: the dispersed and fragmented Indian bands were almost as vulnerable as the whites. In 1609, he dispersed his men with impunity. Smith also understood Indian generosity in the fall. Then the dispersed Indians reassembled, harvested their crops, and gorged themselves. Their full bellies made them charitable, and they brought "Bread, Corne, Fish and Flesh in great plentie" to the confounded colonists.[37] With the onset of winter, the Indians once again fragmented into small bands and migrated upland into their piedmont hunting grounds, where they stalked deer, bear, and other game animals. Smith's genius was in placing the Indians' puzzling behavior and their subsistence strategies into a coherent ecological whole. He comprehended that the colony's survival depended on emulating the Indians' seminomadism, at least during the deadly summer season.[38]

In late May 1609, President Smith scattered the Jamestown settlers into the surrounding countryside. His scheme infuriated Captain Gabriel Archer, who described more than he understood: "Howbeit when Captaine Argoll [Argall] came in about [July 10, 1609], they were in such distresse, for many were dispersed in the Sauages townes, living vpon their almes for an ounce of Copper a day; and four score lived twenty miles from the fort and fed upon nothing but oysters eight weekes Space . . . ."[39] Smith's scheme of dispersal, though repugnant to Archer, was the wisest to date.

But the scheme encountered other opposition in August with the arrival of 185–270 immigrants. Smith was able to dispatch one-

36. "Observations of Master George Percy," p. 22.

37. *Ibid.*

38. The conclusion that Smith fully appreciated Indian ecology and its seasonal avoidance of unhealthy areas seems, to me at any rate, inescapable. Smith's careful ethnographic descriptions of the Indians preceded his accession to the colony's leadership and his decision to send the colonists out to live in scattered bands among the Indians. The Captain knew that dispersal was an extraordinary measure since it directly contravened the Company's instructions insisting on a clustered settlement on a defensible site, preferably an island. For background see Alden T. Vaughan, *American Genesis: Captain John Smith and the Founding of Virginia* (Boston and Toronto: Little, Brown, 1975).

39. Arber, ed., *Travels and Works*, I, p. xcvi.

third of the colonists to Nansemond on the south side of the river in the salt water and another one-third to the fresh water at the Falls near the head of the James. But the rest stayed in Jamestown, assuredly against Smith's better judgment. Predictably, sickness ravaged 100 Jamestown colonists, and 50 died by October. Yet at Nansemond in the salt and at the Falls in the fresh, few sickened and none died.[40] Indian behavior had given Smith the key to life in the James estuary, but this precious knowledge was soon lost. He was relieved of the presidency in October and returned to England; with him went the schemes of seminomadism and summer dispersal. The colony once again clustered at Jamestown, and death hung heavy over the settlement.

Between Smith's departure and Gates's arrival in May 1610, the colony experienced the infamous "starving time." The accounts of hundreds starving, of cannibalism, and of other inhumanities have proven irresistible. But these accounts are biased, sensationalized, and exaggerated. They have warped the death toll and its causes out of all proportion and have diverted attention from the summer epidemics. In the first place, the death toll in the winter of 1609–10 was much less than is usually assumed. The most common error has been the belief that 490–500 immigrants came to Virginia in October, that just 50–60 survived when Gates arrived in May 1610, and hence that over 400 died.[41] In fact, the Virginia population in October stood at 250 or less; and after Smith departed with 30 unruly youths, 220 colonists remained. At least 15 of these were killed by Indians, and 25–30 others returned to England, leaving 180 in the colony.[42]

40. Staying in Jamestown during August was inconsistent with Smith's strategy, and so I conclude that his opponents were responsible for the return to the town. By summer's end 1609, the population stood at 250. *A Voyage to Virginia in 1609: Two Narratives Strachey's "True Reportory" and Jourdain's "Discovery of the Bermudas,"* Louis B. Wright, ed. (Charlottesville: University Press of Virginia, 1964), p. 83.

41. The starving time is embedded in Virginia's historical lore, embracing everything from AAA guidebooks to Edmund Morgan's sophisticated research. Yet another and less dramatic explanation may be suggested. Proponents of the starving time err in assuming that 490–500 immigrants reached Virginia before the winter of 1609–10. In fact, only 185–270 arrived, and joined about 109 survivors, making a total of 294–379. An estimate of three hundred seems about right, and it fits with Strachey's estimate. Fifty of these died at Jamestown in August 1609. Brown, *The First Republic,* pp. 97, 109, 112–13. One hundred were alive when Gates arrived in May 1610. *A Voyage to Virginia,* pp. 82–83, 115.

42. Brown, *The First Republic,* pp. 97, 109, 112–13. Despite his careful analysis of mortality, Brown is anxious to blame Captain Smith and the Company's administration; and so accepts too readily the thesis of starvation promulgated in "'A Trewe Relaycon':

When Gates arrived in May, he found 40 men in good health, along with President Percy, at Point Comfort near the mouth of the James. And at Jamestown, 60 ragged men dragged out to meet Gates.[43] In other words, 100 survived the winter, 15 were killed by the Indians, and 80 died from other causes.

Was starvation the cause of death? Enemies of the Company and Sir Thomas Smythe's administration placed the blame on starvation resulting from inadequate provisions. Purportedly, "famine compelled us wholly to devoure those Hoggs, Dogges & horses that weare then in the Collony . . ." along with vermin and human flesh.[44] Yet there are serious inconsistencies surrounding the "starving time." Gates reported that 600 hogs were destroyed, which at conservative dressweights of 50 pounds per hog amounted to 30,000 pounds for 200 colonists or less—or about 150 pounds per capita during the seven months.[45] And supplemented by 500 chickens, dogs, 7 horses, rats, snakes, and other vermin, the colonists' diet seems sufficient to have warded off starvation—even without human flesh.[46]

Gates offered a different interpretation. He noted that Powhatan stepped up hostilities, confining the colonists to Jamestown between October and May. Some of the colonists were murdered, others fled, "and most by drinking of the brackish water of James Fort weakened and endangered, famine and sickness by all these means increased."[47] Brackish water, probably contaminated with typhoid and dysentery, is implicated once again, but this time in winter. One source of salty water, of course, was shallow wells, tapping brackish aquifers contaminated by pathogens percolated downward into the groundwater. Another possible source of bad water was the river, contaminated during the severely cold winter of 1609–10. Clima-

---

Virginia from 1609 to 1612," *Tyler's Quarterly Historical and Genealogical Magazine*, 3 (1922), pp. 264–70; "A Brief Declaration of the Plantation of Virginia . . . in 1624," *Colonial Records of Virginia* (Richmond: R.F. Walker, Superintendent of Public Printing, 1874), pp. 70–73; William Smith, *The History and the First Discovery and Settlement of Virginia*, introduction by Darrett B. Rutman (New York: Johnson Reprints, 1969), pp. 108–17.

43. Percy's abandonment of Jamestown for the healthier Point Comfort site was pragmatic, though not the most heroic of gestures. *A Voyage to Virginia*, pp. 62–63.

44. "A Brief Declaration," p. 71.

45. Gates's comments are excerpted in *A Voyage to Virginia*, p. 99; also Strachey's remarks, *ibid.*, pp. 86–87.

46. Gates's hog estimate is confirmed by Smith. *A Voyage to Virginia*, pp. 86–87. Arber, ed., *Travels and Works*, I, p. 167.

47. The tragedy was also blamed on "idleness," perhaps the result of salt intoxication. *A Voyage to Virginia*, pp. 98–99.

tologists have observed that cold temperatures and subsiding air depress rainfall. A cold, dry winter, common in many parts of the mid-latitudes during the late sixteenth and early seventeenth centuries, would have lowered river discharge and delayed the retreat of the estuarine salt incursion, fecal material, and sediment from Jamestown.[48]

We cannot say conclusively that typhoid, dysentery, and salt poisoning were the principal causes of death in that winter; however, we can suggest that the case for massive starvation is far from proven. For instance, the mortality rate of 44.4 percent is much lower than the rate usually suggested by proponents of the "starving time." Starvation appears dubious given the livestock available and consumed in the winter of 1609–10. Moreover, the mortality rate is very similar to expected and observed rates of death from typhoid and dysentery for 1607 and 1608. Finally, winter mortality in early Virginia was rare except in extremely severe winters (e.g., 1607–8 and 1609–10).[49] Cold, dry winters and estuarine hydraulics could have produced a contaminated water supply and epidemic typhoid and dysentery in the so-called "starving time."

With the arrival of Lord de la Warr in June 1610, Jamestown was retained as the colony center. Three hundred and fifty were alive in mid-June, the sickness began one month later, and 150 (43 percent) had died by the end of summer. Fifty more died by April 1611.[50]

48. On seventeenth-century climate, see H. H. Lamb, "The History of our Climate: Wales," in *Climatic Change with Special Reference to Wales and its Agriculture*, James Taylor, ed., Memorandum No. 8 (1965), University College of Wales, Aberystwyth, pp. 1–18; C.E.P. Brooks, *Climate Through the Ages: A Study of the Climatic Factors and their Variations*, 2nd rev. ed. (New York: Dover, 1970), pp. 359–78; the extremely cold winter of 1609–10 is noted in Brown, *The First Republic*, p. 113. Salty water at Jamestown in the winter of 1609–10 would explain the presence of water too cold to wade in for oysters, yet unfrozen because the salt incursion lowered the freezing point. "A Brief Declaration," p. 71. Twentieth-century records of the James River provide evidence of winter discharge falling below late summer levels. However, salinity records are too recent and spotty to confirm a winter salt incursion. Virginia Conservation Commission, *Surface Water Supply*, nos. 5, 13, 17, and 25.

49. Arber, ed., *Travels and Works*, I, pp. 23, 98; Brown estimates that 57 of 110 colonists died between January and April 1608 and that 25 of 83 died between April and October 1608. The winter mortality of 52 percent exceeds slightly the 44 percent rate (80/180) for the cold winter of 1609–10. Brown, *The First Republic*, p. 57. Arber, ed., *Travels and Works*, II, pp. 398, 407, 434.

50. Gates and 200 settlers withdrew from Jamestown in June 1610. The 40 others at Point Comfort probably were not included in this count. The colony thus numbered 200–240. De la Warr arrived with 150 men, putting the colony's population at 350–390. The colonists were heartened when De la Warr announced he had provisions for 400 men

Colony leaders strongly suspected the Jamestown water supply as the cause of death. Gates and Strachey stated as much, and Gates and de la Warr, on their return to England in the fall of 1610, communicated their fears to the Company.[51] Jamestown's days were numbered, or so it seemed.

The establishment of a healthier town site took time, and meanwhile summer death continued. Thomas Dale arrived in Virginia on 22 May 1611 with 300 colonists, bringing the colony strength to 450.[52] By mid-June, Dale had chosen a new town site—the Falls at the head of the James—but building did not commence until September. The colonists spent the summer in Jamestown, and the sickness began in early July. A few days later Dale instituted martial law. But tough discipline did not thwart disease. At least 240 of the colonists became so sick they could not work.[53] A death toll of about one-third of the population, or 160, would be consistent with summer mortality and with later population estimates. At summer's end in 1611, the colony population stood as follows: Dale's 320 survivors, plus 300 immigrants brought by Gates in August, all of whom were evacuated to the healthier Falls site, and 62 brought by Argall in late September. This put the colony total at 682—a figure just slightly below the 700 estimated for early 1612 by a Spanish prisoner at Jamestown.[54]

Construction of Henrico, the new town near the Falls, began in the autumn of 1611 and continued through the winter. But the schedule was interrupted by spring planting in 1612, and full-scale

---

for 1 year. They would have been less cheerful if De la Warr had brought 200–300 immigrants, as is sometimes asserted. *A Voyage to Virginia*, pp. 85, 115. Brown, *The First Republic*, pp. 116, 128, 134–39. Richard L. Morton, *Colonial Virginia* (2 vols; Chapel Hill: University of North Carolina Press, 1960) I, pp. 27–28; Hecht, "The Virginia Colony," p. 330; "'A Trewe Relaycon': Virginia from 1609 to 1612," pp. 269–70.

51. For Strachey's insights, *A Voyage to Virginia*, pp. 82–83. Morton, *Colonial Virginia*, I, pp. 28–29.

52. One hundred and fifty were alive in March 1610; 30 arrived soon after, and Dale brought 300 in May 1611—a total of 450. Brown, *The First Republic*, pp. 138–39, 149. Ralph Hamor, *A True Discourse of the Present State of Virginia*, introduction by A. L. Rowse (Richmond: The Virginia State Library, 1957), p. 26.

53. Brown, *The First Republic*, pp. 149–55; Morton, *Colonial Virginia*, I, pp. 25–31; Brown, *Genesis* (cited in n. 3), I, pp. 506–07; Darrett B. Rutman, "The Virginia Company and its Military Regime," pp. 1–20 of *The Old Dominion: Essays for Thomas Perkins Abernathy* (Charlottesville: The University Press of Virginia, 1964).

54. Brown, *The First Republic*, pp. 156, 172; Arber, *Travels and Works*, II, p. 509; "Letter of Diego de Molina, 1613 May," *Narratives of Early Virginia*, pp. 220, 223–24.

settlement of the new town awaited the end of the harvest. My guess is that the majority of colonists spent the summer at Jamestown and the mortality results suggest as much. The Spanish prisoner Molina reported that 300 to 350 died out of a total population of 700. Molina's report appears accurate since seven hundred colonists seems about right for the spring of 1612. The death rate in 1612–13 was probably 50 percent or more.[55]

With the establishment of Henrico and the general dispersal of population between 1613 and 1616, early Virginia enjoyed its healthiest era. By 1614, Jamestown had dwindled as the colony's center, and the population shifted toward the head of the James River. Rolfe's description of settlement in 1616 revealed that Jamestown contained just 19 percent of the colony population, and that over 32 percent resided in the oligohaline (Dale's Gift and Jamestown) and the salt-water zone (Kecoughtan). The remaining 68 percent occupied fresh-water zones at Henrico, Bermuda Nether Hundred, and West Sherley Hundred.[56] Mortality was rarely mentioned in the contemporary correspondence or accounts of these years, and for good reason: the mortality rate had declined sharply. Between May 1613 and May 1616 only 45 immigrants arrived, yet by the latter date 351 colonists survived.[57] Assuming no natural increase, the Virginia population either held steady or declined at a rate of about 15 deaths per year—an astonishing annual mortality rate of only about 3.8 percent.

The marked improvement following the redistribution of popu-

55.   As late as May 1613, Jamestown contained almost one-half of the colony's population, and Henrico only one-third. The pattern surely changed by the summer of 1613. "Letter of Diego de Molina, 1613," pp. 223–24. Hamor, *A True Discourse*, p. 32. Dale's letter of June 1614 is enlightening. Although his obligation in Virginia was complete, he believed the colony was in "desperate hazard." Abandoning her might reflect on his reputation. Perhaps too, Dale had to endure another summer to see if the healthy year preceding (1613) had resulted from his settlement policies or from dame fortune. *Ibid.*, pp. 51–59.

56.   John Rolfe, *A True Relation of the State of Virginia Lefte by Sir Thomas Dale Knight in May last 1616* (New Haven, Conn.: Yale University Press, 1951), pp. 33–41; Hamor, *A True Discourse*, pp. 26–33; Charles E. Hatch, Jr, *The First Seventeen Years: Virginia, 1607–1624*, Jamestown 350th Anniversary Historical Booklets, no. 6 (Williamsburg: The Virginia 350th Anniversary Celebration, 1957), pp. 32–33.

57.   Brown, *The First Republic*, pp. 220, 224, 229. Hecht, "The Virginia Colony," p. 332. Writing in 1614 about the martial law invoked in 1611, Hamor defended Dale's measures, "for more deserued death in those daies, then do now the least punishment." Healthful conditions had marvelously reformed idle, factious, and apathetic Virginians! Hamor, *A True Discourse*, p. 27.

lation into healthy freshwater environments is consistent with the model proposed here. However, proponents of the "seasoning" thesis have maintained that the reduction in immigration was what reduced death rates. Immigrant mortality was very high, but survivors, who were then seasoned to the Virginia disease environment, were less susceptible (immune) to disease in future years, they claim. Since immigration to Virginia came to a virtual standstill in the summer of 1611, the "seasoning" thesis would posit a sequence of high mortality rates in that summer, the survival of seasoned colonists, and a sharp mortality reduction in the summer of 1612. In fact, as we have shown, mortality remained high in both summers. Death rates only dropped dramatically in 1613, after the Virginians shifted their settlements into the freshwater zone. Environment and location thus were the decisive factors lowering mortality between 1613 and 1616. Immigration and seasoning were largely irrelevant.[58]

The healthy era, 1613–16, was the product of a lengthy and painful process of environmental learning and adjustment. The three years from 1607 to 1610 were spent enduring death and identifying its geographic pattern and its causes. By the spring of 1610, colonial leaders had associated death, water supply, and the Jamestown environment. They persuaded the Company in London by the fall of that year. Implementation of a new settlement distribution consumed the next three years from the winter of 1610–11 to the fall of 1613. During these years, Dale reconnoitered, chose a site, began construction of Henrico, cleared land for crops, and instituted an aggressive Indian campaign. Curiously, Dale's provocative encroachment into Powhatan's territory at the head of the James met little resistance from the chief. Perhaps Powhatan's advanced age and

58. Seasoning was at once a well-recognized process in Virginia and a theory of curative medicine, i.e., treatment of individuals. By exposing the individual to infection in a new disease environment, future susceptibility was reduced. The theory worked fine for self-immunizing or debilitating diseases such as malaria, bacillary dysentery, and paratyphoid. But curative medicine worked miserably on non-immunizing, virulent diseases. Exposure to these diseases brought death year after year. The only effective remedy against them, at least before vaccines and antibiotics, was the preventive medicine of environmental modification or avoidance. Since Virginians were powerless to change the oligohaline, the best course was to avoid that zone. An excellent discussion of the seasoning process and the role of malaria is Darrett B. Rutman and Anita H. Rutman, "Of Agues and Fevers: Malaria in the Early Chesapeake," *William and Mary Quarterly*, 3rd Series, 33 (1976), pp. 31–60; see also Blanton, *Medicine in Virginia* (cited in n. 13), pp. 37–41; Ashburn, *The Ranks of Death* (cited in n. 35), pp. 118–23, 519–60; Duffy, *Epidemics in Colonial America* (cited in n. 13), pp. 214–18; May, *The Ecology of Human Disease* (cited in n. 15), p. 26.

the capture of his daughter Pocahontas tempered his retaliation, or perhaps the chief had his hands full with the hostile Monacans on his western flank, and temporarily conceded Dale the James River head. Whatever Powhatan's motives, the English colony profited from his passivity.[59]

When Dale left Virginia in the spring of 1616, he felt confident that the colony would endure. The mortality problem had been solved by diminishing Jamestown's importance and locating the settlements in healthier zones. With sickness and death on the wane, the healthy colonists produced a surplus of food. Trade relationships altered: where formerly the colonists had begged, stolen, or traded for Indian food, now the Indians came seeking the colony's corn.[60] Healthy conditions continued through the summer of 1616. There were no reports of widespread mortality, and the colony probably contained 335–351 colonists. But with the arrival of a new governor in the spring of 1617, all of Dale's insights were abandoned, to be painfully relearned.

Governor Samuel Argall was not one to learn from his mistakes. This was the same Argall who earlier had condemned Smith's dispersal of colonists in the summer of 1609. As governor in the spring of 1617, Argall was again appalled by the state of the colony and Jamestown where: "he found but five or six houses, the Church down, the Palizado's broken, the Bridge in pieces, the Well of fresh water spoiled; the Store-house they used for the Church, the market-place, and streets, and all other spare places planted with Tobacco: . . . the Colonie dispersed all about, Planting Tobacco."[61] On 9 June Argall wrote to the Company that he "likes James Town better than Bermudas 40 miles aboue it; and will strengthen it."[62] Argall must have succeeded in realigning settlement, for that summer a great mortality ensued. Death struck 105–115 of the 415

59.   Hamor, *A True Discourse*, pp. 54–55; William Strachey, *The Historie of Travell into Virginia Britania*, ed. by Louis B. Wright and Virginia Freund, 2nd Series, no. 103 (Hakluyt Society, 1953), pp. 105–6; Nancy Oestrich Lurie, "Indian Cultural Adjustment to European Civilization," pp. 33–60 of *Seventeenth-Century America*, James Morton Smith, ed. (Chapel Hill: University of North Carolina Press, 1959). Wesley Frank Craven, *White, Red, and Black: the Seventeenth-Century Virginian* (Charlottesville: The University Press of Virginia, 1971), pp. 46–50.

60.   Rolfe, *A True Relation*, p. 36.

61.   Arber, ed., *Travels and Works*, II, pp. 535–36.

62.   Susan Myra Kingsbury, ed., *The Records of the Virginia Company of London* (4 vols; Washington, D.C.: GPO, 1933), III, p. 73.

TABLE 1.1

Population Distribution by Estuarine Zone, 1622–24

Estuarine zone	Massacre deaths, 1622	Living, 1623–24	Dead, 1623–24	Total	Pct. of population
Fresh-water	209	289	57	555	28.5%
Oligohaline	145	603	211	959	49.3%
Salt-water	0	330	101	431	22.2%

SOURCES: "Lists of the Livinge & Dead in Virginia, February 16, 1623 [4]," *Colonial Records of Virginia*, (cited in n. 42), pp. 37–60. Kingsbury, ed., *Records of the Virginia Company*, III, pp. 565–71. The census of 1623–24 alone gives a misleading impression of population distribution between 1618 and 1622. Massacre casualties on 22 Mar. 1622 were heaviest upriver from Jamestown, and hence I have included them as a more accurate representation of population geography under the Sandys administration.

NOTE: Does not include population on the eastern shore or on the recently arrived vessels.

colonists, and suddenly the mortality rate had risen from nil to 25 percent.[63]

The realignment of settlement begun by Argall and continued under the Sandys administration was, I believe, one of the principal causes of death until 1624. The hard-won knowledge of the environment and the adjustments made between 1607 and 1617 were abandoned. Between 1617 and 1623, 36 new settlements dotted the James estuary, and 13 of them occupied the oligohaline and the salt-water zone.[64] More importantly, population shifted into the lower estuary, and Jamestown was reaffirmed as chief city and center of government. The extent of realignment is revealed in two sources: the census of 1623–24, and the listing of deaths from the massacre of March 1622. These help provide a more accurate picture of population distribution from 1618 to 1622 (see Table 1.1), and they show that 71 percent of the Virginia colonists resided in the oligohaline and salt-water zones, whereas only 28 percent occupied the fresh-water zone—almost a direct reversal of the pattern under Dale, when 65 percent lived in the fresh-water zone.

Increased mortality accompanied the shift in population. Several

63. *Ibid.*, p. 92. The mortality rate is based on the following: probably 335 (my estimate) were alive in May 1617, plus 80 brought in by Argall, or a total of 415. In May 1618 the colony contained about 400, of whom 90–100 had arrived between March and May 1618. Subtracting these from the 400 yields 300–310 alive in March 1618. Thus, between May 1617 and March 1618, 105–115 had died. Arber, ed., *Travels and Works*, II, pp. 535–36; Brown, *The First Republic*, pp. 253–56, 260, 277; Hecht, "The Virginia Colony," pp. 333–34; Evarts B. Greene and Virginia D. Harrington, *American Population Before the Federal Census of 1790* (New York: Columbia University Press, 1932), p. 135.

64. Hecht, "The Virginia Colony," pp. 174, 361–63.

thousand colonists died between 1616 and 1624, and disease was an important cause. Comments on summer sickness and death increasingly punctuated colonial correspondence. But disease was not the sole killer. Indian attacks, starvation, and plague also contributed. While the surviving evidence precludes a precise bill of mortality, some estimates of disease-related deaths can be made from the census of 1623–24.

As a benchmark year, 1623–24 is here used for estimating the usual 1616–24 mortality rate from typhoid, dysentery, and salt poisoning. Several bits of evidence suggest these diseases as the principal causes of death in 1623–24: (1) the reports of summer sickness and death in that year; (2) the absence of other reported causes of mortality; and (3) the abundant food supply, making starvation an unlikely cause of death. Moreover, the census listing of colonists killed, presumably by the Indians, permits exclusion of these deaths from our disease estimate.[65] Typhoid and dysentery are also implicated by the spatial pattern of death recorded in the census of 1623–24. Among those settlements reporting deaths during the year, 16.7 percent died in the fresh-water zone; 37.1 percent in the oligohaline; and 23.3 percent in the saltier portion of the James estuary (see Table 1.2). The match between reality and our estuarine model is good, but not perfect. Fresh-water death rates are higher than expected, perhaps reflecting the severe disruptions in this area caused by the massacre of 1622. Another peculiarity is Hog Island in the oligohaline, where only 8.8 percent died. A safer right bank location, the removal of pollutants toward the north bank by a river meander, and the small population probably combined to make Hog Island a healthy micro-environment. Otherwise, the census pattern points toward death by typhoid and dysentery in the oligohaline and the salty lower James.

Having isolated these diseases as probable causes of death, we can estimate their usual contribution to Virginia mortality. The annual disease mortality rate (shown in Table 1.3) is estimated as the sum of the products of the ecological zone death rates (Table 1.2) and the population distribution for 1616–24 (Table 1.1). A disease mortality rate of 28.3 percent per year is indicated; for typhoid, dysentery, and

---

65. Brown, *The First Republic*, pp. 569–70; Edmund S. Morgan, *American Slavery, American Freedom*, pp. 104–5. The year following the massacre of 1622 was very sickly, but the resulting mortality probably antedated the census of 1623–24. Tyler, ed., *Narratives of Early Virginia* (cited in n. 4), p. 438; Morton, *Colonial Virginia*, I, pp. 83–90.

TABLE 1.2

Mortality Rates by Estuarine Zones, 1623–24

Estuarine zone and settlements	Total population	Number dead	Pct. dead
Fresh-water zone	299	50	16.7%
College Land	33	0	0.0
Neck of Land	41	4	9.5
West & Sherlow Hundred	56	10	17.9
Jordan's Journey	50	8	16.0
Flourdieu Hundred	63	18	28.6
West & Sherlow Hundred Island	56	10	17.9
Oligohaline zone	558	207	37.1
James Cittie within the Corporation	272	89	32.7
Plantation over against James River	142	65	45.5
Hog Island	34	3	8.8
Martin's Neck	51	26	51.0
Warwick Squarke	59	24	40.7
Salt-water zone	420	98	23.3
Elizabeth City	420	98	23.3

SOURCE: "Lists of the Livinge & Dead."
NOTE: The table includes only those settlements returning lists of dead. "Killed" colonists are not included.

TABLE 1.3

Estimated Annual Disease Mortality Rates Based on Population Distribution and Estuarine Zone Mortality Rates, 1618–24

Estuarine zone	Pct. of colony population (1)	Annual mortality rate (2)	Pct. of total mortality rate (1 × 2)
Fresh water	28.5%	16.7%	4.8%
Oligohaline	49.3	37.1	18.3
Mesohaline, polyhaline	22.4	23.3	5.2
Estimated annual disease mortality rate for Virginia			28.3%

salt poisoning alone, 23.5 percent, with the oligohaline contributing 18.3 percent and the salt water 5.2 percent. In the fresh water 4.8 percent died, but the causes are not known.

Argall and the Sandys administration, by redistributing Virginians into the most deadly zones, share the responsibility for the deaths of 24–28 percent in any single year. But the gravity of their offense worsened with time. Epidemics struck year after year, killing immigrants and seasoned colonists alike. Disease thus claimed considerably more colonists than 28 percent between 1618 and 1624.

TABLE 1.4

Disease-Related Death Estimates in Virginia, *1618–24*

Time period	Population at		Immigrants	Population at risk	Deaths from disease (using estimate of 28.3% per year)	Deaths from disease as pct. of total deaths
	Beginning	End				
Dec. 1618–Mar. 1620	600	887	814–914	1,414–1,514	402–430 (28.3%)	68.8%
Mar. 1620–Mar. 1621	887	843	1,051	1,095–1,938	550 (28.3%)	50.2%
Mar. 1621–Mar. 1622	843	1,240	1,580	2,463	688 (28.3%)	58.2%
Mar. 1622–Apr. 1623	1,240	1,241	695	1,935	347 (17.9%)[a]	50.0%
Apr. 1623–Feb. 1624	1,241	1,275	405	1,646	371 (22.5%)[b]	100.0%

SOURCES: Population estimates for 1618–22 and 1624 are from Brown, *The First Republic*, pp. 328–29, 375, 381, 415, 462, 464, 466–67, 503–5, 612; Morgan, *American Slavery, American Freedom*, pp. 412–13; Greene and Harrington, *American Population*, pp. 134–36; immigration estimates are from Brown, *The First Republic*; Hecht, "The Virginia Colony," pp. 334–45. The unknown population of April 1623 is estimated by working backwards, i.e., population of February 1624 (1,275) minus immigrants between April 1623 and February 1624 (405) plus deaths during the period (371) equals population as of April 1623 (1,241); "Lists of the Livinge & Dead," pp. 37–60.
[a]Since 347 known deaths occurred in the massacre, the remainder are assigned to disease.
[b]The overall death rate fell below the disease rate, hence all deaths are assigned to disease.

The overall contribution of disease to death is estimated from the several censuses and immigration figures, and the basic data are set out in Table 1.4. Between December 1618 and February 1624, about 5,145 persons resided in or immigrated to Virginia; 24.8 percent survived in 1624, 49.3 percent had died from disease, and 25.9 percent had died from other causes or went back to England. Two of every three deaths resulted from typhoid, dysentery, and salt poisoning. These diseases were the principal killers in some years, and they were significant contributors in all.[66]

Although the Company and colony leaders tried desperately to reduce summer mortality, they failed because they misunderstood its causes. Preventive measures were aimed at the immigrants, for whom guest houses (hospitals) were established and whose arrivals were scheduled for fall after the sickly summer months—all on the false assumption that "seasoned" colonists would survive.[67] But seasoned colonists stood little chance of survival in the oligohaline zone, as revealed in the muster of 1625.

Fifty-seven settlers gave arrival dates before 1616. Twenty-four resided in the freshes, 25 in the salt, and just 9 in the oligohaline. Older settlers, those arriving before 1620 of all giving arrival dates, made up about one-fifth of the population in the oligohaline, one-third in the salt water and two-fifths in the fresh.[68] These spatial and environmental patterns of death went undetected by the Company, but were instrumental in its dissolution. Henceforth, direction of the Virginia colony was assumed by the Crown.

The demise of the Virginia Company in 1624 signaled a new era in Virginia demography. The old constraints focusing the colony on

66. These estimates of annual disease mortality permit an assessment of other causes of death. For example, Morgan has suggested starvation and malnutrition, occasioned by control of Virginia's food and labor supply by a handful of private capitalists. The most likely years for this were 1620–22, when causes other than Indian killings and diseases contributed 40–50 percent of all deaths. Morgan, *American Slavery, American Freedom*, pp. 92–107. Note, however, that immigration was also heaviest in these years—suggesting Craven's point of inadequate provisioning of the immigrants by the Company. Probably both Company and private policies were responsible for the increased death rate; in any case, the critical years seem to have been 1620–22. Wesley Frank Craven, *The Dissolution of the Virginia Company: The Failure of a Colonial Experiment* (Gloucester, Mass.: Peter Smith, 1964), pp. 152–53.

67. The Company believed in the curative medicine of seasoning rather than the preventive medicine of settlement dispersal. Craven, *Dissolution of the Virginia Company*, pp. 145–75; Kingsbury, ed., *Records of the Virginia Company*, III, pp. 275, 301–02.

68. John Camden Hotten, ed., *The Original Lists of Persons of Quality . . . 1600–1700* (New York: Empire State, 1931), pp. 200–265.

TABLE 1.5

*Population Growth, 1625–34, Under Pre-1625 Disease Mortality Rates
and a Fitted Mortality Rate*

Date	Scenario A: The pre-1625 disease mortality rate of 28.3 pct. per year		Scenario B: A fitted mortality rate of 14.2 pct. to account for the actual population in 1625–34	
	Population and immigrants	Survivors	Population and immigrants	Survivors
1625–6	1,210 + 1,000	1,582	1,210 + 1,000	1,896
1626–7	1,582 + 1,000	1,849	1,896 + 1,000	2,485
1627–8	1,849 + 1,000	2,040	2,485 + 1,000	2,990
1628–9	2,040 + 1,000	2,177	2,990 + 1,000	3,423
1629–30	2,177 + 1,000	2,275	3,423 + 1,000	3,794
1630–1	2,275 + 1,000	2,344	3,794 + 1,000	4,113
1631–2	2,344 + 1,000	2,394	4,113 + 1,000	4,387
1632–3	2,394 + 1,000	2,430	4,387 + 1,000	4,622
1633–4	2,430 + 1,000	2,456	4,622 + 1,000	4,824
1634–5	2,456 + 1,000	2,475	4,824 + 1,000	4,997

NOTE: The actual population in 1634 was 4,914. The above calculations assume no natural increase. Some children were born in the colony during the period, but the imbalanced sex ratio favoring males and other evidence suggest that children contributed little to population growth at this time.

Jamestown and the oligohaline were relaxed, and mortality fell. Between 1625 and 1634, Virginia's population grew from 1,210 to 4,914, with an estimated 9,000 immigrants.[69] Although over half of the population died in the nine-year period, this figure obscures the marked improvement in annual mortality. Had the pre-1624 mortality rate of 28.3 percent per year continued, Virginia in 1634 would have numbered 2,456 settlers instead of 4,914. In effect, annual mortality was cut in half (to about 14.2 percent) during the early royal period (see Table 1.5).[70]

69. One thousand immigrants per year is the estimate of Morgan, *American Slavery, American Freedom*, p. 159. Morgan underestimates somewhat the magnitude of declining mortality rates after 1624. A lower death rate is not inconsistent with his literary evidence. Ship captains experienced high mortality (42 percent in 1636) precisely because they plied the oligohaline zone. And 1,800 deaths in 1636, given the population and increased immigration in that year, produces a mortality rate in between the high rate of the period 1618–24 (28.3 percent) and the lower estimated rate after 1624 (14.2 percent).

70. Morgan's 1625–40 estimate of 1,000 immigrants per year has been questioned as too high by Menard. He suggests that immigration varied directly with tobacco prices, and accordingly Virginia immigration peaked at about 2,000 in 1635–36 and generally fell in preceding years (1625–35) substantially below 1,000 per year. If Menard is correct, then annual mortality rates for the period 1625–34 were even lower than the 14.2 percent presented here. Russell R. Menard, "Economy and Society in Early Colonial Maryland" (Ph.D. diss., University of Iowa, 1975), pp. 167–70.

Several factors caused the decline in mortality. By far the most important was the shift in population patterns. By 1634, the deadliest zone along the James, including James City, Warwick, and Warrowerguyoake counties, contained 45 percent of the total population. But population had spread into healthier zones, including the lower York in the salt on the south side of that river, the fresh water at the head of the James, and the lower James and the Eastern Shore.[71] The general dispersal of tobacco plantations within all ecological zones also favored life. Typhoid and dysentery could not become epidemic when settlement was scattered. And as population grew, settlement progressed inland away from the deadliest parts of the James and onto the hills, ridges, and drainage divides where fresh springs provided a safe water supply. Dietary habits probably changed, too, with increased consumption of wine, beer, and cider instead of water, and reduced consumption of oysters and clams during May to August when these bivalves concentrate microorganisms. As the "new healthiness" of the country took hold, Virginians and their visitors usually attributed it to improvement in the climate as a result of forest clearance. More accurately, the spread and dispersal of settlement along with certain dietary adjustments were the keys to life.[72]

Frontier expansion and plantation dispersal continued during the rest of the seventeenth century, with generally beneficial demographic effects. Although travelers commented on the pallid complexions, sickness, and death in the salt-water environments of the lower estuaries, the population there was generally much healthier than in the fresh-salt transition.[73] As the frontier expanded into the

71. "A List of the Number of Men, Women and Children . . . within the Colony of Virginia, Anno Dne, 1634," *Colonial Records of Virginia* (cited in n. 42), p. 91.

72. On dispersal and tobacco, see Morton, *Colonial Virginia*, I, pp. 122–33; Hecht, "The Virginia Colony," pp. 195–207; Craven, *Dissolution of the Virginia Company*, pp. 170–71. In a revealing note, Governor Wyatt in 1623 blamed the colony's ill-fortune on "the intemperate drinking of water." "To plant a colony by water drinkers was an inexcusable errour in those who laid the first foundation and have made it a received custome." Kingsbury, ed., *Records of the Virginia Company*, IV, pp. 10–11, 453; Wharton, *The Bounty of the Chesapeake* (cited in n. 11), p. 46; William Ancisz and C. B. Kelly, "Self-purification of the Soft Clam *Mya arenaria*," *Public Health Reports*, 70 (1955), pp. 605–14.

73. Gilbert Chinard, ed., *A Huguenot Exile in Virginia, or Voyages of a Frenchman Exiled for his Religion with a Description of Virginia & Maryland* (New York: Press of the Pioneers, 1934), pp. 130, 174. Recognition of the fresh-salt transition and its dangers is incipient in Bullock's "flowing of the salt." Clayton thought all salt water bad, because it impregnated the air and thus damaged the human body. William Bullock, *Virginia impartially Examined . . .* (London, 1649), p. 4; Edmund Berkeley and Dorothy Smith Berkeley,

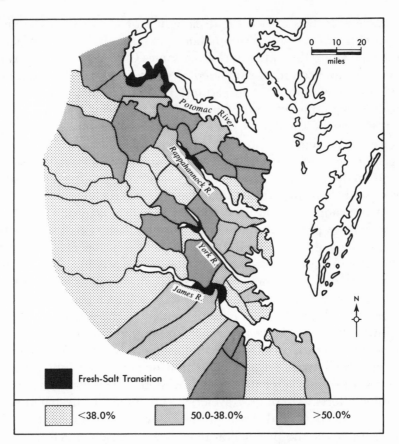

FIGURE 1.3.   The Pattern of Mortality in Virginia Parishes in 1725–26: Proportion of Burials to Births. Source: Public Record Office, C.O. 5/1320, f. 74.

oligohaline zones of the York, Rappahannock, and Potomac rivers, death rates rose above those in either the salt or the fresh-water zones. The spatial pattern of mortality, as reconstructed from a Virginia parish census of births and deaths for 1725–26, tends to confirm the persistence of disproportionate death in the oligohaline (Figures 1.3 and 1.4).[74] Along the four principal Virginia estuaries,

---

eds., *The Reverend John Clayton . . . his Scientific Writings and other Related Papers* (Charlottesville: University Press of Virginia, 1965), p. 54.

74.   The census records births and burials for the year beginning 15 April 1725. I have assumed that census recording procedures were uniform among Virginia parishes, but they undoubtedly were not. More thorough studies of Virginia demography may reveal whether the parishes departing from the estuarine-disease model reflect actual differ-

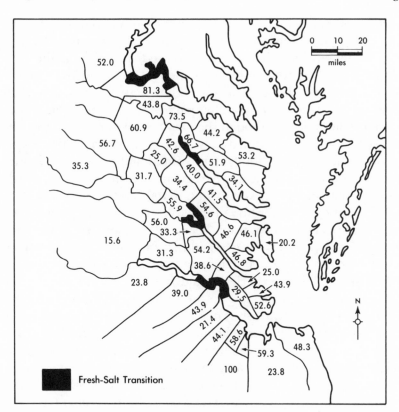

FIGURE 1.4.   The Proportion of Burials to Births in Virginia Parishes, 1725–
26. Source: Public Record Office, C.O. 5/1320, f. 74.

the pattern of mortality hypothesized by the estuarine model for
early Virginia remains recognizable a century later. Progressing
downriver, the proportion of burials to births is generally least in
the fresh-water zones, peaks in the oligohaline, and drops slightly in
the salt-water zones of the lower estuaries. Left-bank (north-side)

ences or recording biases in the census. Parish boundaries are roughly accurate. The four
Henrico County parishes are aggregated on the maps. Charles Francis Coke, *Parish Lines,
Diocese of Virginia*, Virginia State Library Publications, 25 (Richmond: Virginia State Li-
brary, 1967); George Carrington Mason, *Colonial Churches of Tidewater Virginia* (Richmond:
Whittet and Shepperson, 1945). The fresh-salt transition zones are located according to
Nichols, "Sediments of the James River" (cited in n. 24), pp. 171–79. See also H. C. Whaley
and T. C. Hopkins, *Graphical Summary Reports Nos. 1–2: Atlas of the Salinity and Temperature
Distribution of Chesapeake Bay*, Chesapeake Bay Institute, The Johns Hopkins University,
Reference 52–4 and 63–1 (Baltimore: 1952 and 1963); Chinard, *A Huguenot Exile*, p. 174.

mortality is usually higher than the corresponding right-bank (south-side). The maps' subtleties and their several departures from the model—notably the higher than expected mortality in the upper Rappahannock as well as in Nansemond County in the salt-water zone of the lower James, plus the rather higher levels of mortality along the Potomac estuary as compared to the other valleys—warrant more attention. Although the chances for survival in the Chesapeake had improved dramatically after 1624, the mortality maps of a century later strongly imply that typhoid and dysentery continued as important causes of death, particularly in the zone of the fresh-salt transition and, to a lesser extent, in the zone of salt water.[75]

The demographic history of early Virginia is both sad and tragic: sad because so many died; tragic because they died needlessly. Smith, Dale, and others intuitively grasped that the recurring summer sicknesses were spawned by contaminated and salty water in the vicinity of Jamestown. Their experience and their observation of the Indians suggested that dispersing in the summer or shifting settlement permanently into the fresh-water zone were the best ways to save lives. But their insights were abandoned with the arrival of new colonial leaders or a new Company administration. Jamestown was reclaimed, mortality rose, and the painful environmental learning process began again from ground level. Governor Sandys and his administration never learned. The nexus of environment and mortality confounded and eluded them. They mistakenly believed that the "seasoning" process would eventually take hold and that Vir-

75. This geographical pattern of mortality might be explained by other models, such as the Rutmans' malarial endemicity in which malarial "morbidity climbs as endemicity rises, since a greater percentage of infectious bites by *Anopheles* leads to symptomatic malarial attacks. Yet the rate of morbidity will be balanced at some point by the rate of immunities in the population and then will begin to decline until, in a hyperendemic situation, morbidity is largely limited to children, non-immune newcomers to the community, and pregnant women." Translated into spatial terms, endemicity should follow more or less the frontier of settlement—i.e., old settled areas should be hyperendemic, newly settled areas should have low but rising morbidity, and middle-aged areas should have very high morbidity. Accordingly, the James River area, as the oldest settled zone, should show similarly low values on our map, followed by very high values in the middle-aged tier of Gloucester, Middlesex, Lancaster, Westmoreland, and Northumberland counties, and low values elsewhere. I do not detect such a pattern, and thus favor the three-zone estuarine model of enteric diseases. Rutman and Rutman, "Of Agues and Fevers," pp. 37–39, 44–45. Also, Lorena S. Walsh and Russell R. Menard, "Death in the Chesapeake: Two Life Tables for Men in Early Colonial Maryland," *Maryland Historical Magazine*, 69 (1974), pp. 211–27; and Robert V. Wells, *The Population of the British Colonies in America before 1776* (Princeton, N.J.: Princeton University Press, 1975).

ginia's population would grow. But typhoid and dysentery were no respecters of flawed theories of immunity. From a demographic standpoint, the best thing that happened in early Virginia was the dissolution of the Company with its fixation on Jamestown.

Never again would Englishmen in America occupy such a persistently deadly location as early Jamestown. Indeed, across the entire sweep of British expansion, only Calcutta and the West African slave ports match the levels of mortality in early Virginia.[76] North American colonization was, in fact, remarkably healthy after 1624. Epidemics of enteric disease such as those in early Virginia were virtually unknown during the rest of the seventeenth century. In large measure, this was so because the English took greater care in the selection of town sites. Salty ocean or bay water virtually surrounded the towns of Boston and Newport in New England and Charles Town in Carolina. These briny locations minimized disease epidemics because the salt water was, in the first place, undrinkable, and because river and tidal action flushed out the pathogens and lowered their concentrations in the surrounding bays and ocean. Moreover, at each of these town sites, drinking water was supplied by excellent and steady springs, located usually at higher elevations. Equally salubrious was the site of Philadelphia, located in the "freshes" of the Delaware River beyond the reaches of the deadly oligohaline.[77]

These healthier locations were not felicitous accidents; rather they reflected a heightened perception of the more extreme New World environment and of estuarine dynamics and water supply. The settlers of Massachusetts in 1630 exemplify a striking change in their approach to the environment. Whereas Virginians struggled through 17 years of death at Jamestown, the Puritans learned more rapidly. Soon after disease broke out in Charlestown (Massachusetts) in 1630, the majority of Puritans left for other sites, particularly the salt-enshrouded and elevated peninsula of Shawmut, or, as we know

76. Philip D. Curtin, "Epidemiology and the Slave Trade," *Political Science Quarterly*, 83 (1965), pp. 190–216; and Rhoads Murphey, "The City in the Swamp: Aspects of the Early Growth of Calcutta," *Geographical Journal*, 130 (1964), pp. 241–56; and W. E. Morgan, "The Influence of European Contacts on the Landscape of Southern Nigeria," pp. 193–208 of R. Mansell Prothero, ed., *People and Land in Africa South of the Sahara* (New York: Oxford University Press, 1972).

77. Earle, "The First English Towns" (cited in n. 1); Carl Bridenbaugh, *Cities in the Wilderness: Urban Life in America, 1625–1742* (New York: Capricorn Books, 1964); Darrett B. Rutman, *Winthrop's Boston: a Portrait of a Puritan Town, 1630–1649* (Chapel Hill: University of North Carolina Press, 1965).

it today, Boston.[78] The Puritans abandoned the analogue of America as a temperate maritime environment; instead, their locational strategy was guided by practice rather than theory, and thus afforded the best preventive medicine against enteric water-borne diseases in the dynamic American coastal environment. Henceforth, densely populated English settlements avoided the zone of the fresh-salt transition and thus escaped the epidemics of typhoid and dysentery that ravaged Jamestown in the late summer.

We have not heard the last word on mortality in the oligohaline. These predominantly rural zones will, I suspect, achieve a cruel prominence as historical demographers and geographers continue probing the geography of early American mortality. When the map of mortality is finally drafted, the oligohaline will stand out and nowhere more prominently than in the marshes and tidal swamps in the wet rice districts of Carolina and Georgia. Where the ebb and flow of fresh and salt water were integral parts of wet rice culture and where slaves were unable to escape from the lethal environment, the specter of disease and death is sadly predictable.[79]

78. Rutman, *Winthrop's Boston*, pp. 23–40.
79. Duffy, *Epidemics in Colonial America* (cited in n. 13). It has been suggested that slaves in South Carolina were relatively more immune to yellow fever and malaria than were white Europeans, thus giving blacks an advantage in wet rice cultivation; however, slaves would not have been immune to water-borne typhoid or dysentery, which probably were commonplace in the wet rice fields where they worked. Peter H. Wood, *Black Majority: Negroes in Colonial South Carolina from 1670 through the Stono Rebellion* (New York: Alfred A. Knopf, 1974), pp. 63–91; Peter A. Coclanis, *The Shadow of a Dream: Economic Life and Death in the South Carolina Low Country, 1670–1920* (New York: Oxford University Press, 1989). On the use of fresh and salt water flows in the tidal rice fields, see Sam B. Hilliard, "Antebellum Tidewater Rice Culture in South Carolina and Georgia," in James R. Gibson, ed., *European Settlement and Development in North America: Essays on Geographical Change in Honour and Memory of Andrew Hill Clark* (Toronto: University of Toronto Press, 1978), pp. 91–115.

CHAPTER 2

Why the Puritans Settled in New England

The Problematic Nature of English Colonization in North America, 1580–1700

N ew England." "Boston." In the pantheon of American regions and places, these two evoke redolent images of quaint farming villages, revolutionary patriotism, and Yankee ingenuity. But it was not always so. Three-and-a-half centuries ago, "New England" was more nearly an epithet in the English mercantile mind. Etymologically, it stood for an old England writ new, for a redundant region with dour prospects for improving the balance of English economic accounts. Much better, mercantilists believed, to point their energies farther south to the estuaries and sounds of the Chesapeake and North Carolina, where, in the same latitudes as southern Europe, they predicted vast wealth and profit from grapes, wine, silk, and citrus. It was a dream, and a bad one at that—but it was nonetheless the vision that guided the crown's allocation of colonies along the Atlantic Seaboard. That is why dissenters wound up in New England, and royal favorites and friends in the "mediterranean lands" to the south.

This etymological tale speaks volumes about our ignorance of that enormous undertaking known as the English colonization of North America. Standard historical accounts, for example, rarely if ever mention English preconceptions about the North American environment. Nor is there much interest in why the English colonized where they did. The whole matter of English colonization—its directions and destinations—is taken as an unproblematic given. Early American history thus begins with the colonies in place, and no one understands precisely its geography. Why the Puritans settled in New England and Virginians in the Chesapeake seems a matter of profound disinterest. All of which is curious indeed, for in that geography lies the seeds of American pluralism.

Geographers, to their credit, have regarded colonization as a problem worthy of reflection and inquiry. James Vance and Donald Meinig, in particular, have reconsidered these locational issues and suggested provocative new lines of thought. For geographers, it matters a great deal that the Puritans settled in New England—a land perceived as of marginal environmental worth—and that Boston became its regional capital. Yet it is fair to say that geographic interpretations of colonization are themselves guilty of great oversimplification. Our colonization models, with their economistic accent upon staple trades and urban entrepôts, leave out much the most interesting parts of the story. The problem is not with geographical models per se, for these are useful means of simplifying reality in order to elucidate complex processes. But when our colonization models gloss over, or altogether ignore, such key elements as environmental perceptions and evaluations of the American coastline, the politics of royal colonial allocations, the cultural and administrative roles of colonial cities, and the different migration patterns of various groups of colonists, our simplifications run the risk of misconstruing the way that historical geography actually happened—and, perhaps worse, of fabricating a uniformitarian colonization model from a process that was specific to England in the seventeenth century. Our task, as I see it, is one of resolution, of reintroducing a degree of historical complexity into the skeletal geographic models of English colonization.

The Mercantile Model of Colonization and Early American Towns

Although geographers have illuminated the contemporary urban scene, geographical insights dwindle at an accelerating pace as we move back toward the seventeenth century—the dark ages of American urban geography.[1] To insist that geographers redress this imbal-

---

1. Geographical discussions of colonial urban patterns may be found in James T. Lemon, "Urbanization and the Development of Eighteenth-Century Southeastern Pennsylvania and Adjacent Delaware," *William and Mary Quarterly*, 3rd ser., 24 (1967), pp. 501–43; Douglas R. McManis, *Colonial New England: A Historical Geography* (New York: Oxford Uni-

ance is pointless given today's pressing urban problems, and impractical owing to the discipline's traditional bias toward present landscapes and spatial patterns. In such a context, the seventeenth century is remote indeed. Yet neglect of this era places geographers in the curious position of having no satisfactory explanation for the origins and early growth of several important cities in the contemporary urban system. New Amsterdam (New York), Philadelphia, Boston, and Charleston are just a few of the places that were rooted in the first European frontier, and their historical durability is reason enough for inquiry and interpretation.

A large step in that direction is James E. Vance's model of mercantile colonization and the origins of American cities and their urban systems, perhaps the best-known geographical theory of American colonization.[2] Vance maintains, principally on evidence assembled from the colonial period of American history, that initial settlement was regulated primarily by commerce in staple commodities. Economic activity, in other words, guided the location and growth of these early frontier towns. The sufficiency of a mercantile interpretation of colonial settlement for early American history is, however, open to question. After a brief review of Vance's model and the historical evidence for and against it, I will propose a complementary model of frontier settlement that, in its fidelity to the historical context, is more appropriate to English colonization during the seventeenth century. Whereas Vance's colonial model emphasizes the role of the economy and long-distance mercantile trade, the monopolist-migration model I will present accents ethnocultural factors rooted in religion, politics, and demography. Whereas in Vance's model, trade precedes towns, in mine, towns precede trade. The applicability of these two models to other frontiers will be discussed in the conclusion.

Vance's mercantile model offers a comprehensive interpretation of

---

versity Press, 1975); David Ward, *Cities and Immigrants: A Geography of Change in Nineteenth-Century America* (New York: Oxford University Press, 1971); and Joseph A. Ernst and H. Roy Merrens, "'Camden's Turrets Pierce the Skies!': The Urban Process in the Southern Colonies During the Eighteenth Century," *William and Mary Quarterly*, 3rd ser., 30 (1973), pp. 549–74.

   2. James E. Vance, Jr., *The Merchant's World: A Geography of Wholesaling* (Englewood Cliffs, N.J.: Prentice-Hall, 1970). Donald Meinig's imperial model of colonization is essentially identical to the mercantile model, particularly in the early phases of exploration and initial settlement. See his *The Shaping of America: A Geographical Perspective on 500 Years of History: Volume I, Atlantic America, 1492–1800* (New Haven, Conn.: Yale University Press, 1986).

the evolution of settlement on capitalist frontiers. Although the entire model is fascinating and controversial, this essay focuses only on the early stages of colonization—the years leading up to and including the first several decades of settlement. In Vance's model a frontier region prior to settlement contains an infinite number of potential town sites. The mercantile model narrows these down by specifying the probable zones of initial settlement on the basis of presettlement exploration and trade. Early explorers gather information about economic possibilities along the frontier, highlighting promising zones that are then periodically exploited by merchants and traders dealing in fish, furs, skins, or other staples. In the most productive trading zones, profits become sufficiently large to warrant year-round trade. There, merchants and entrepreneurs establish towns—entrepôts— that serve as staple-collecting depots and staging areas for extensions of the staple frontier. The fate of these first mercantile towns thus hinges almost exclusively upon the long-distance trade in staples and overseas demand. Although Vance identifies subsequent stages in the model—an expanding staple frontier, a linear urban system, and central place infilling—these stages go far beyond what is at issue here, namely the origins of the first urban settlements (or points of attachment, in Vance's language), their viability during infancy, and, in certain cases, their enduring initial advantage.

Vance's mercantile interpretation, though undeniably decisive for long-run urban development in colonial America, seems less satisfactory as an explanation of initial English colonization and urban origins in the seventeenth century. His ideal-typical sequence of the transition from periodic staple trading to permanent mercantile towns may apply in the valleys of the Delaware, Hudson, and Connecticut rivers— all areas of Dutch hegemony—but the Dutch proliferation of Indian trading-post towns stands in sharp contrast with the mere handful of towns established under English colonization.[3] The historical evidence is unequivocal. The English customarily erected one or at most a few towns in each colony, and scarcely any of them secured a staple

3. Van Cleaf Bachman, *Peltries or Plantations: The Economic Policies of the Dutch West India Company in New Netherland, 1623–1639* (Baltimore: Johns Hopkins University Press, 1969); Gerald F. DeJong, *The Dutch in America, 1609–1674* (Boston: Twayne Publishers, 1975), pp. 1–27; Adrian C. Leiby, *The Early Dutch and Swedish Settlers of New Jersey*, New Jersey Historical Series, Vol. 10 (Princeton, N.J.: D. Van Nostrand Co., 1964); Albert E. McKinley, "The English and Dutch Towns of New Netherland," *American Historical Review* 6 (1900), pp. 1–18; Clinton A. Weslager, *Dutch Explorers, Traders, and Settlers in the Delaware Valley, 1609–1664* (Philadelphia: University of Pennsylvania Press, 1961).

commodity until a decade or so after settlement. The staple trade, in sum, does not seem to have been their raison d'être.

Historians of the Carolinas, the Jerseys, Maryland, Pennsylvania, and Virginia tell a very different story: colonists there invariably established towns first and only then set about the frustrating business of finding a staple crop.[4] Some confusion may arise about New England because a seasonal fishing industry did indeed foster the growth of Salem—perhaps the only English town to fit Vance's model.[5] Yet in nearby Boston, neither the fishing trade nor any other presettlement staples contributed substantially to the town's location or its ensuing development. The Puritans were much less interested in commercial possibilities than in creating a self-sufficient, interdependent urban theocracy focused on Boston—a millennial "city upon a hill." The absence of a staple trade notwithstanding, Boston grew into a sizable town of 1,200 in its first decade (1630–40); and a half-century later Boston's achievement was reenacted (albeit more spectacularly) in Philadelphia and Charles Town.[6] The English frontier experience thus constitutes a serious dilemma for Vance's staple trading model. If trade did not determine initial settlement locations or the astounding urban growth that on occasion ensued, what did?

I address these questions by reexamining the early history of English colonization on the Atlantic Seaboard of seventeenth-century North America. At issue are the determinants of the geography of early settlement: the location and frequency of colonies and their towns, the timing of colony and town founding, and the dimensions of urban growth in the first several decades of settlement. I test the proposition that politics, geographical perceptions, faith, and immigration may have been more important than mercantile trade and

4. See, for example, Bernard Bailyn, *The New England Merchants in the Seventeenth Century* (Cambridge, Mass.: Harvard University Press, 1955); Wesley Frank Craven, *The Southern Colonies in the Seventeenth Century, 1607–1689* (Baton Rouge: Louisiana State University Press, 1970), pp. 310–59; Edmund S. Morgan, *American Slavery, American Freedom: The Ordeal of Colonial Virginia* (New York: W.W. Norton & Co., 1975); Gary B. Nash, *Quakers and Politics: Pennsylvania, 1681–1726* (Princeton, N.J.: Princeton University Press, 1968); John E. Pomfret, *Colonial New Jersey: A History* (New York: Charles Scribner's Sons, 1973); and John W. Reps, *Tidewater Towns: City Planning in Colonial Virginia and Maryland* (Williamsburg, Va.: Colonial Williamsburg Foundation, 1972).

5. McManis, *Colonial New England*, pp. 34–35.

6. Carl Bridenbaugh, *Cities in the Wilderness: The First Century of Urban Life in America, 1625–1742* (New York: Ronald Press Co., 1938), p. 6. Boston's population was 2,000 by 1640, according to Darrett B. Rutman, *Winthrop's Boston: Portrait of a Puritan Town, 1630–1649* (Chapel Hill: University of North Carolina Press, 1965), p. 179.

staples for colonial and urban origins. Before I do so, however, a word or two is in order on the unusual cultural significance of towns and cities in the English mind.

Frontier Towns as Indispensable English Institutions

Between 1585 and 1682, the establishment of an English colony and the founding of an urban place, a chief town, were synonymous.[7] Given the varied motives that propelled colonists overseas, this unanimity in settlement policy is peculiar indeed. Puritans, Catholics, Anglicans, and Quakers as well as companies and proprietors endorsed the town as the principal, if not the only, settlement form. Why did they do so? An obvious reason is that the English regarded towns as nodes of commerce, administration, and defense. But that is not quite the heart of the matter. The primacy of colonial towns in the English mind traces back to the pessimism of Elizabethan and Stuart worldviews. According to these views, the earth and nature were in decay, rusting, in senescence; only a thin veneer of culture protected the English from regressing on the great chain of being to the level of the barbarian or, worse, the animal. In the New World, filled as it was with licentious natives and beguiling wildernesses, the veneer of English culture might prove thin indeed. Pessimists could easily imagine how barbaric and wayward colonists might threaten not only the colonial enterprise but the entire fabric of English culture.[8]

English fears of cultural declension were not groundless. Indeed, history seemed to confirm their worst fears. Had not English colonists earlier dispatched to Ireland become seminomadic "barbarians," much like their Irish neighbors? And rumors persisted that lost

---

7. The seventeenth-century English shared the view that a town was a place of concentrated settlement, containing some nonagricultural activity. They differed, however, on its societal role. Winthrop and the Puritans saw the town as the center of an organic, self-sufficient social corporation; others saw it as a marketing nexus between European markets and colonial production areas. In any case, urban places of one kind or another were necessary components of an ideal colony. A full discussion of English views on the indispensability of frontier towns appears in Carville Earle and Ronald Hoffman, "The Urban South: The First Two Centuries," in *The City in Southern History*, ed. Blaine Brownell and David Goldfield (Port Washington, N.Y.: Kennikat Press, 1976), pp. 23–51.

8. Margaret T. Hodgen, *Early Anthropology in the Sixteenth and Seventeenth Centuries* (Philadelphia: University of Pennsylvania Press, 1964), pp. 354–85.

Roanoke colonists now lived like "white Indians" in the wilderness. Some even detected barbarism among the planters in the townless colonies of Maryland and Virginia. Vigilance alone could not prevent the erosion of English culture in the New World; colonists also required institutional support. Toward that end, the English insisted upon the town as the most basic and conservative of frontier institutions. The Carolina proprietors made the point nicely. "We must assure you that it is your and our concern very much to have some good towns in your plantations for otherwise you will not long continue civilized or ever be considerable or secure, there being no place in the world either of these without them."[9] For the English, no colonial business was more important than building a town, a repository of their culture, on an otherwise barbaric frontier.

Monopoly Colonization and the Location of Colonies and Their Towns

If the English agreed about the critical conservative role of towns in colonization, they also shared similar views on the frequency and location of towns. The point is cogently made by contrasting the English strategy of monopoly colonization and the Dutch strategy of free trade. In the case of the English, the Crown granted specifically delimited territorial franchises to colonial companies and proprietors who, in turn, exercised centralized, monopolist powers within their territories. These monopolists founded just one, or at most a few, towns and located them with administrative and cultural centrality in mind. The Dutch, by contrast, pursued a strategy of free trade along the Atlantic Seaboard of North America. Their colonial companies established multiple competing trading posts; Dutch towns thus proliferated in zones of profitable staple trade with native Americans, in line with Vance's mercantile model.[10]

9. W. L. Saunders, ed., *The Colonial Records of North Carolina*, 10 vols. (Raleigh, N.C.: P. M. Hale, Printer to the State, 1886–90), Vol. 1, p. 229. For Puritan attitudes toward the wilderness, see James F. Axtell, "The Scholastic Philosophy of the Wilderness," *William and Mary Quarterly*, 3rd ser., 29 (1972), pp. 335–66.

10. Leiby, *The Early Dutch and Swedish Settlers of New Jersey*; and McKinley, "The English and Dutch Towns of New Netherland," pp. 1–18. The multiple, scattered Dutch towns are appropriately described by the first phase of the urban-transport model developed by Edward J. Taaffe, Richard L. Morrill, and Peter R. Gould, "Transport Expansion in Underdeveloped Countries: A Comparative Analysis," *Geographical Review* 53 (1963), pp. 503–29. Monopoly colonization is an apt term for English colonial policy, provided

The origins of English monopoly colonization lie in the imperial context of the late sixteenth century. In the European scramble for the New World, the English had made a slow start. Preoccupied by political instability and internal strife, England lagged some 70 to 80 years behind the Iberians. Indeed, English interests in colonies were not galvanized until the 1570s, when, owing to political tranquillity, Frobisher's purported discovery of gold on Baffin Island, and Drake's fabulous booty pirated from the Spanish colonies, the English devised a new and distinctive colonial strategy[11]—one that was prodded along further by explosive population growth.

To ease what appears to have been a Malthusian crisis that had swollen the ranks of laborers, craftsmen, and artisans and that had resulted in a precipitous fall in real wages and rampant unemployment,[12] the two Richard Hakluyts proposed that the English embark upon permanent, large-scale colonization of the New World.[13] The cure, though timely, was beyond the financial capability of a penurious monarchy, especially in view of the risky prospect of low or even negative rates of return. Yet the Crown could hardly afford not to involve itself in the intensifying competition for American space, since colonies offered the opportunity to vent surplus population and provide England with a "domestic source" for expensive imported exotic commodities (for example, wine, sugar, and silks). Accordingly, Elizabeth and her Stuart successors devised a scheme that imposed the risks of permanent colonization upon private investors in exchange for grants of sizable colonial territories and extensive pow-

---

that concept embraces differences in degrees of monopoly. Colonial charters varied markedly in political powers and obligations, yet these differences were of small consequence for colonial urban development. Marshall Harris, *Origin of the Land Tenure System in the United States* (Ames: Iowa State College Press, 1953), pp. 141–54.

11. George L. Beer, *The Origins of the British Colonial System, 1578–1660* (New York: Macmillan Co., 1908), pp. 1–9; Theodore K. Rabb, *Enterprise and Empire: Merchant and Gentry Investment in the Expansion of England, 1575–1630* (Cambridge, Mass.: Harvard University Press, 1967); and A. L. Rowse, *The Expansion of Elizabethan England* (New York: St. Martin's Press, 1955), pp. 193–94.

12. Peter Ramsey, *Tudor Economic Problems* (London: Victor Gollancz, 1965), p. 78; F. J. Fisher, "Commercial Trends and Policy in Sixteenth Century England," in *Essays in Economic History*, ed. E. M. Carus-Wilson (3 vols.; London: Edward Arnold, 1954), Vol. 1, pp. 154–72; E. H. Phelps-Brown and Sheila V. Hopkins, "Wage Rates and Prices: Evidence for Population Pressure in the Sixteenth Century," *Economica*, 2nd ser., 24 (1957), pp. 289–306; and Beer, *The Origins of the British Colonial System*, pp. 32–46.

13. E. G. R. Taylor, "The Original Writings & Correspondence of the Two Richard Hakluyts," *Hakluyt Society Series 2*, No. 77 (London, 1935), 2, pp. 327–38.

ers therein—what we have here designated as monopoly colonization.[14] This strategy provided the English with a comprehensive and low-cost model for the occupation and settlement of North America. Using that model, we may replicate rather accurately the locations of the English colonies and their urban settlements.

The model of monopoly colonization may be divided into two stages: (1) evaluation and allocation of colonial lands by the English Crown; and (2) occupation of these lands by monopoly colonizers. The first stage describes the rules by which the Crown evaluated colonial environments and then allocated geographically specific colonial franchises (charters) among applicants of various political and religious persuasions (the monopoly colonizers). These rules, as we shall see, assigned territories in northern latitudes to the Puritans and other dissenting groups, in southern latitudes to Anglicans and royal favorites. The second stage of the model describes the settlement strategies deployed by the newly empowered monopolists. Monopolists in each colony established one chief entrepôt and administrative center located near the center of the colony's coastal boundary, provided that a commodious harbor suitable for seventeenth-century maritime vessels was present in that vicinity. These rules fixed the sites of the early English towns. A third stage in the model—which we will take up later—deals with the viability of these premier settlements in the first several decades of their existence.

In the first stage of monopoly colonization, the English Crown evaluated and then allocated the colonial frontier. In their belated attempt to occupy the New World, the English discovered that much of the land already had been taken. Hemmed in by the Spanish to the south and the French to the north, all that remained for England, short of a frontal strategy on Catholic claims, was a residual territory along the Atlantic Seaboard of North America stretching between the present-day states of Georgia and Maine. Yet even here the English faced competition from the Swedes and the Dutch. The Crown was not to be deterred, however, and set about apportioning territory over which it had neither legal nor effective claim.

Before apportionment began, however, the English first assessed the potentialities of the American environment. And in doing so, they drew upon the prevailing geographical myths about global environments and resources. These myths, derived from Greek the-

14. Rabb, *Enterprise and Empire.*

THE PRINCIPALL
NAVIGATIONS, VOIA-
GES AND DISCOVERIES OF THE
Englifh nation, made by Sea or ouer Land,
to the moſt remote and fartheſt diſtant Quarters of
the earth at any time within the compaſſe
of theſe 1500. yeeres: Deuided into three
ſeuerall parts, according to the po-
ſitions of the Regions wherun-
to they were directed.

The firſt, conteining the perſonall trauels of the Englifh vnto *Iudæa, Syria, A-rabia,* the riuer *Euphrates, Babylon, Balſara,* the *Perſian* Gulfe, *Ormuz, Chaul, Goa, India,* and many Iſlands adioyning to the South parts of *Aſia:* toge-ther with the like vnto *Egypt,* the chiefeſt ports and places of *Africa* with-in and without the Streight of *Gibraltar,* and about the famous Promon-torie of *Buona Eſperanſa.*

The ſecond, comprehending the worthy diſcoueries of the Englifh towards the North and Northeaſt by Sea, as of *Lapland, Scrikſinia, Corelia,* the Baie of *S. Nicholas,* the Iſles of *Colgoicue, Vaigats,* and *Noua Zembla* toward the great riuer *Ob,* with the mightie Empire of *Ruſſia,* the *Caſpian* Sea, *Georgia, Armenia, Media, Perſia, Boghar* in *Bactria,* & diuers kingdoms of *Tartaria.*

The third and laſt, including the Englifh valiant attempts in ſearching al-moſt all the corners of the vaſte and new world of *America,* from 73. de-grees of Northerly latitude Southward, to *Meta Incognita, Newfoundland,* the maine of *Virginia,* the point of *Florida,* the Baie of *Mexico,* all the In-land of *Noua Hiſpania,* the coaſt of *Terra firma, Braſill,* the riuer of *Plate,* to the Streight of *Magellan:* and through it, and from it in the South Sea to *Chili, Peru, Xaliſco,* the Gulfe of *California, Noua Albion* vpon the backſide of *Canada,* further then euer any Chriſtian hitherto hath pierced.

Whereunto is added the laſt moſt renowmed Engliſh Nauigation,
round about the whole Globe of the Earth.

By *Richard Hakluyt Maſter of Artes, and Student ſometime*
of Chriſt-church in Oxford.

Imprinted at London by GEORGE BISHOP
and RALPH NEWBERIE, Deputies to
CHRISTOPHER BARKER, Printer to the
Queenes moſt excellent Maieſtie.

1589.

FIGURE 2.1. A reproduction of the title page of Richard Hakluyt's *The Principall Navigations . . .* (London: George Bishop and Ralph Newberie, 1589). The writings of the Hakluyts, Elder and Younger, recapitulated the history of Euro-pean overseas colonization and defined a locational strategy for English settle-ment of the New World.

ories of climate, held that latitude was the principal climatic and agronomic control.[15] Boldly—and foolishly, as it turns out—the English concluded that mediterranean-like climates would prevail in the latitudes of present-day North Carolina and the Chesapeake while damp and cool maritime climates (like those of old England) would preside over what would be called "New England." The English evaluated these "data" in accordance with emerging mercantilist principles, namely that the most valuable American lands would complement rather than duplicate the climates and products of the mother country. Thus it was that English monopoly colonization designated as optimal those American environs that were located in mediterranean latitudes—from which they expected plentiful exotics such as sugar, oranges, grapes, and silk—and as marginal those lands located in the latitudes of England, that is, of "New England."

The next step in monopoly colonization involved the allocation of territorial franchises. The English Crown applied this simple rule: optimal "mediterranean" environs were apportioned to political friends and religious conformists, marginal lands to dissenting political and religious factions, of which there were several. And in this manner, the Crown gradually allocated all of the land along the Atlantic Seaboard. By the early 1680s—some 70 years after monopoly colonization began—the process was virtually complete. At that point, we find Puritans and Quakers ensconced in the marginal lands of New England and the middle colonies, and Anglicans and royalists in the optimal "mediterranean" colonies to the south. Catholic Maryland might seem an exception, until we recall that George Calvert, the colony's proprietor, was a close friend of the Crown and that his Catholicism, in any event, was not that distant from the high Anglicanism of the Stuarts (Figure 2.2).

This brings us to the second part of the model—to colonization proper and the set of rules governing the distinctive pattern of English settlement. More precisely, these rules specify the location and frequency of the premier administrative and cultural urban centers vital to each colony. These rules require a caveat: they apply only in colonies having presettlement boundaries, namely Massachusetts,

15. Gary Dunbar, "Some Curious Analogies in Explorers' Preconceptions of Virginia," *Virginia Journal of Science*, n.s. 3, 9 (1958), pp. 323–26. H. Roy Merrens, "The Physical Environment of Early America: Images and Image Makers in Colonial South Carolina," *Geographical Review* 59 (1969), pp. 530–56.

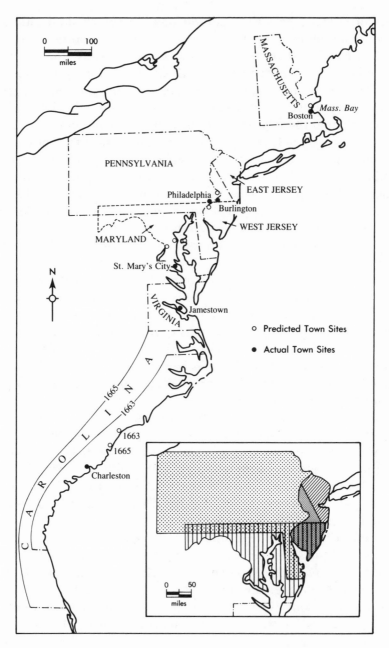

FIGURE 2.2. English Colonial Boundaries and Town Locations in Seventeenth-Century North America. Source: Harris, *Origin of the Land Tenure System*, pp. 71–140.

East Jersey, West Jersey, Pennsylvania, Maryland, Virginia, and the Carolinas; they do not apply in indiscriminately located colonies such as Plymouth, Rhode Island, and Connecticut.

Modeling the settlement component of monopoly colonization involves four steps. The first step consists of mapping presettlement boundaries, as reconstructed in Marshall Harris's classic volume on American land tenure. These boundaries, though vaguely perceived by colonists, formed the spatial frame for the monopoly colonizers' choice of town locations.[16] The second step entails measuring coastal boundaries for each colony and locating expected port sites at the midpoints. In the third step, the model imposes a constraint that precludes port location on emergent, sandy shorelines penetrated by navigable estuaries. This rule excludes ports on the coastal segment from Sandy Hook to Cape Hatteras; in this region, the model positions port sites on the inland estuaries of the Delaware and Chesapeake bays. For complex estuaries such as the Chesapeake Bay, two "coastal" boundaries and port sites may exist. More specifically, the Chesapeake's north-south alignment provides an eastern segment, while southern segments for Virginia and Maryland are created by the northwesterly orientations of the James and Potomac rivers, respectively. Although the locational model might be further refined by identifying favorable harbor and navigational features conducive to port location, the increase in precision is not compensated by an appreciable improvement in site prediction.[17] In the fourth and final step, locations and frequencies of expected port sites are compared to the actual ports (that is, those urban ports and entrepôts established in the first decade of colonization).

The model provides good predictions of town frequency and location. On the matter of frequency, monopolists tended to channel resources and energy into a single port town, a primate urban center. The one-port-per-colony rule is confirmed in Virginia (Jamestown), Maryland (St. Mary's City), and Pennsylvania (Philadelphia). Charles Town in Carolina also fits the one-port model, though it should be noted that the proprietors initially had in mind three settlements, perhaps because of the exceptionally long coastline of more than 600

16. Harris, *Origin of the Land Tenure System*, pp. 71–140.
17. For the problems associated with natural harbor classification, see F. W. Morgan, *Ports and Harbours*, 2nd ed., rev. James Bird (London: Hutchinson University Library, 1961), pp. 26–53; and Guido G. Weigend, "Some Elements in the Study of Port Geography," *Geographical Review* 48 (1958), pp. 185–200.

miles.[18] The one-port model applies less well in the three other colonies. In the first years of settlement, Massachusetts had eight towns; East Jersey, six; and West Jersey, four. The frequency of towns is not as exceptional as it may at first appear.

In East and West Jersey, monopolist proprietors divided their control among numerous submonopolies, wherein the frequency model continued to apply. The six small towns spawned by the colonization of northeastern Jersey between 1664 and 1666 resulted when the proprietors, Lord Berkeley and Sir George Carteret, granted submonopolies to four groups of Puritan associates from Long Island and New England. The associates established just one or two towns in each of their four grants.[19] Similarly, in West Jersey, a syndicate of Quaker proprietors acquired title from Lord Berkeley in 1676 and divided the colony into ten separate territories. Had all gone as scheduled, ten port towns would probably have appeared, one in each submonopoly. As it was, the Quakers established only four towns—Salem, Burlington, Gloucester, and Greenwich—before their scheme for orderly settlement dissolved in 1675 when one of the Quaker shareholders unilaterally carved out his territory on the southwest Jersey coast at Salem. Efforts to reinvoke orderly colonization failed, and town founding came to a halt.[20]

The singularly unimpressive results of Jersey colonization, particularly in the west, raise a question: why did the Jersey monopolists, from Berkeley and Carteret to the Quaker shareholders, pursue a policy of dividing colonies into submonopolies rather than hewing to the authoritative, centrally administered policy that prevailed elsewhere? One plausible explanation is bad timing. The 1660s were times of general prosperity; hence returns on colonial investments may have been lower and migrants fewer, since they probably fared better in England than in the New World. Monopolists therefore lacked the capital to support ambitious schemes and the colonists to

18. Francis Paul Jennings, "Miquon's Passing: Indian-European Relations in Colonial Pennsylvania, 1674 to 1755" (Ph.D. diss., University of Pennsylvania, 1965), p. 89; Craven, *The Southern Colonies*, pp. 316–38; Converse D. Clowse, *Economic Beginnings in Colonial South Carolina, 1670–1730* (Columbia: University of South Carolina Press, 1971), pp. 1–41; and Reps, *Tidewater Towns*, pp. 31–45, 55–58.

19. John E. Pomfret, *The New Jersey Proprietors and Their Lands*, New Jersey Historical Series, Vol. 9 (Princeton, N.J.: D. Van Nostrand Co., 1964), pp. 8–20.

20. John E. Pomfret, "West New Jersey: A Quaker Society, 1675–1775," *William and Mary Quarterly*, 3rd ser., 8 (1951), pp. 493–519.

carry them out.[21] Hoping to salvage something from their colonies, the Jersey monopolists surrendered centralized control to submonopolists who might settle at least a portion of their colonies. The spatial implication of this policy, of course, was an increased frequency of towns per colony.

With the Jersey towns accounted for, what of the remaining exception, Massachusetts? No fewer than eight towns—Boston, Charlestown, Dorchester, Medford, Roxbury, Salem, Saugus, and Watertown—dotted the coast of the Massachusetts Bay colony within two years of initial settlement.[22] For reasons given earlier, Salem may be excluded as inapplicable to the monopolist model: the town was established in 1623 by the Dorchester Company to serve the fishing industry along the coast. Monopoly colonization proper thus did not begin until the 1629 chartering of the Massachusetts Bay Company. The Company's first expedition went to Salem, rejected that site, and moved to the Charles River. There, the Puritans engaged in a dispute over the best site, which they resolved by establishing several towns instead of one.[23] Although independent behavior of this sort was atypical for English colonization—indeed elsewhere it would have been regarded as treasonous defiance of company or proprietary authority— the locational outcome in Massachusetts did not differ significantly from other English colonies.

Perhaps it is natural that Puritan dissenters violated the rule of one town per colony; yet on the matter of location, their several towns clustered near the theoretically expected site. Their choice of the Charles River area in fact placed them within fifteen miles of the coastal midpoint—a locational prediction error of about 15 percent, when the distance separating actual and expected sites is expressed as a proportion of boundary length. For purposes of comparison, the predictive accuracies for the other English colonies are computed in Table 2.1. Locational errors range from as little as 1 percent to almost 28 percent (also see Figure 2.2).[24]

The best and worst estimates apply to the estuarine towns of

21. For economic conditions during the 1660s and 1670s see Charles Wilson, *England's Apprenticeship, 1603–1763* (New York: St. Martin's Press, 1965), pp. 160–84.

22. McManis, *Colonial New England*, pp. 35–39; and Rutman, *Winthrop's Boston*, p. 23.

23. Rutman, *Winthrop's Boston*, pp. 23–28.

24. This locational model assumes the intent of monopolists to occupy central sites. Statements substantiating that intent are rare, perhaps because a central location was so obvious that it did not require comment.

TABLE 2.1

Locational Prediction Errors for the Monopoly Colonization Model

Town and colony[a]	Length of coastal boundary (miles)	Midpoint location (miles)	Distance between actual and predicted location (miles)	Prediction error[b]
Jamestown, Virginia[c]	100	50.0	1.0	1.0%
Boston, Mass. Bay Colony	81	40.5	12.5	15.4%
St. Mary's City, Maryland	342[d]	171.0	95.0	27.8%
Burlington, West Jersey	180	90.0	30.0	16.7%
Cape Fear, Carolina	576	288.0	55.0	7.2%
Port Royal, Carolina	760	380.0	140.0	18.4%
Charles Town, Carolina	760	380.0	62.0	8.2%
Philadelphia, Pennsylvania	298	149.0	25.0	8.4%

[a] The small size of grants in East Jersey precludes the use of the locational model.
[b] The prediction error is calculated by dividing the distance between the actual and predicted location by the length of the coastal boundary.
[c] The Virginia Company grant extended 100 miles inland.
[d] The boundary segment used here is from the Atlantic to the Potomac and west.

the Chesapeake colonies. The Virginia expedition of 1607 located Jamestown almost precisely midway into the colonial grant of 100 miles inland. By contrast, the first Marylanders in 1634 placed St. Mary's City 95 miles downstream from the predicted site near the falls of the Potomac. Indian geography seems to have made the difference. In Virginia, the Company gave pointed instructions precluding settlement among "strong and clean-made" natives who might threaten the colony's safety.[25] The first colonists found the Indians of the lower James unimposing, but just beyond Jamestown Island they encountered a series of powerful tribes who had congregated for spring planting. Adhering to their orders, the expedition dropped downstream to the safety of Jamestown Island, and there established the chief town.[26] The Maryland colonists, like the Virginians, reconnoitered their southernmost river; but unlike the Virginians, who encountered weak tribes for 40 or 50 miles, the Marylanders soon met the formidable Piscataways, made even more awesome by their war regalia. The expedition hastily retreated to the lower Potomac, where they founded St. Mary's City.[27] A central site was preferable, but not at the expense of the colony's security.

25. Alexander Brown, *The Genesis of the United States* (2 vols.; Boston: Houghton Mifflin and Co., 1890), 1, pp. 79–85.
26. "Observations by Master George Percy, 1607," in *Narratives of Early Virginia, 1606–1625*, ed. Lyon Gardiner Tyler (New York: Barnes and Noble, 1966), pp. 20–23.
27. Clayton C. Hall, ed., *Narratives of Early Maryland, 1633–1684* (New York:

The Indians of the Delaware Valley were less of an impediment. When the English established Burlington and Philadelphia in the late 1670s and early 1680s, the Delaware Indians had been pacified and acculturated through a half-century of Dutch and Swedish contact. Indian geography had little bearing on town locations, and consequently the colonists came close to the theoretical sites.[28] Philadelphia overshot the mark by just 8.4 percent; Burlington undershot it by 16.7 percent. The proximity of these two towns suggests that some local advantage took precedence over a purely central site. Indeed, both towns occupied a zone of navigable, fresh water, lying just beyond the inner intrusion of the Delaware estuary. This zone of fresh water offered a resource of inestimable value for seventeenth-century ports, "there being no worm (in the fresh water) that eats the bottoms of the Ships, as is usually done in *Virginia* and *Barbados*, & c. which renders the said Countries very fit for Trade and Navigation."[29] It was also a healthier habitat.

South of Chesapeake Bay, large deepwater estuaries gave out, and accordingly Carolina colonizers established their chief ports along the coast. Charles Town, founded in 1670 on the Ashley River, lay about 65 miles south of the coastal midpoint (an error of 8.2 percent). But there is more to the story. The original proprietors had not foreseen an Ashley River settlement. As noted above, their initial plan called for three equidistant settlements along the 600-mile coastline. When the first Carolina charter was issued in 1663, the proprietors envisioned the Albemarle region, already settled by Virginians, as one core settlement; Cape Fear, about 240 miles south, as a second; and Port Royal, some 200 miles farther south, as a third. The proprietors engaged private adventurers for the colonizations of Cape Fear and Port Royal, but these came to naught. Then, under the vigorous leadership of Ashley Cooper, Lord Shaftesbury, the proprietors organized a Port Royal expedition in 1669–70. Indian hostiles in that vicinity caused the expedition to turn north along the coast toward their ultimate destination on the Ashley River.

Charles Scribner's Sons, 1910), pp. 40–42; Lois Green Carr, "The Metropolis of Maryland: A Comment on Town Development Along the Tobacco Coast," *Maryland Historical Magazine* 69 (1974), pp. 124–45.

28. Jennings, "Miquon's Passing," p. 51.

29. Thomas Budd, *Good Order Established in Pennsylvania and New-Jersey, in America, Being a True Account of the Country; with its Produce and Commodities There Made in the Year 1685*, ed. Edward Armstrong (New York: William Gowans, 1865), p. 77.

Shaftesbury was not disappointed by the centrality of the Charles Town site.[30]

Having clarified the roots of English colonial policy and its implications for colonial town locations and frequencies, let us turn to the issue of urban growth, or the lack thereof, during the first decades in the New World.

Why Some Towns Grew and Others Didn't

The initial English colonial ports had an enormous head start over later competitors, but initial advantage alone did not guarantee population growth or urban dominance. Some towns succeeded beyond expectation—one thinks of Boston, Charles Town, and Philadelphia—whereas others sank into obscurity—Jamestown, St. Mary's City, Elizabethtown, and Burlington come to mind. What caused growth or decline? In the long run, as Vance points out, urban growth depended on staple exports, but as decisive, perhaps, were the early decades of settlement when colonial immigrants provided the urban economic base. On occasion, newly established English colonies and towns were overwhelmed by hundreds and even thousands of English and Western European immigrants, uprooted by hard times and exaggerated promotional literature, but then the European economy would improve and immigration would ebb. Such spurts, though often brief, caused explosive growth in recipient port towns, with Boston and Philadelphia being the classic cases.

Boston mushroomed from a small village to a town of 1,200 persons between 1629 and 1640; and Philadelphia posted a population of more than 4,000 within a decade of its founding in 1682 (see Table 2.2). Space permits only a brief sketch of these immigrant boomtowns. In the 1630s, thousands of Puritans fled English economic depression and religious persecution and migrated to New England. They funneled through Boston, and the merchants there were besieged by heavy demands and short supplies. Prices shot up, and enormous profits awaited the entrepreneurs who assembled and sold English manufactured goods or provisions gathered from the Chesapeake colonies. Immigration and the boom it created waned in

30. In 1678, a new Charles Town was established at the confluence of the Ashley and Cooper rivers, a few miles upstream from the old town. Craven, *The Southern Colonies*, pp. 316–38.

TABLE 2.2

The Population of Colonies and Towns During the First Several Decades of Colonization

Colony and Town	Year	Population	Year	Population	Year	Population	Year	Population
Virginia	1610	350	1617	351	1620	2,200	1624	7,000–10,000[a]
Jamestown	–	–	1617	50	–	–	1624	175
Massachusetts	1630	506	1640	8,932	1650	14,037	–	–
Boston	1631	200	1640	1,200	1650	2,000	–	–
Maryland	1640	583	1650	4,504	–	–	–	–
St. Mary's City	1641	50–60	1650	100	–	–	–	–
New Jersey[b]	1670	1,000	1680	3,400	–	–	–	–
South Carolina	1670	200	1680	1,200	–	–	1690	3,900
Charles Town	–	–	1680	700	1685	900	1690	1,100
Pennsylvania	1680	680	–	–	1690	11,450	–	–
Philadelphia	–	–	1685	2,500	1690	4,000	–	–

SOURCES: Bridenbaugh, *Cities in the Wilderness*, p. 6; Greene and Harrington, *American Population Before the Federal Census of 1790*, p. 144; Carr, "The Metropolis of Maryland," pp. 124–45; Rutman, *Winthrop's Boston*, p. 57; and *Historical Statistics*, Part 2, p. 756.

[a] Immigrants to Virginia, 1607 to 1624.
[b] Estimates of urban population are lacking.

the 1640s, and only then did the earnest search for a staple crop begin.[31]

Some 50 years later the scene was reenacted on a grander scale in Pennsylvania, this time by English Quakers who were fleeing the economic and religious hard times of the 1680s. Merchants did a brisk business provisioning the immigrants and made huge—some thought excessive—profits. Writing to William Penn in January of 1689, Governor Blackwell complained of "the Extensive Extortion (I call it no otherwise) wherewith the poorer sort of people are oppressed by the wealthier traders." Goods worth £100, he railed, were priced at £200 because of inflation, to which was added 50 percent freight, and the retailer added on £100 more, pushing the price to £400. Sawyers did well too, receiving three times the wages paid in England.[32] With profits like these, Philadelphia grew spectacularly, though not quite as Penn had envisioned. By 1690 its 4,000 citizens constituted fully one-third of Pennsylvania's population.[33] The more fragmentary evi-

31. Bailyn, *The New England Merchants*, pp. 16–39; Rutman, *Winthrop's Boston*, pp. 180–86.

32. Governor Blackwell to William Penn, Jan. 25, 1689; cited in Edwin B. Bronner, *William Penn's "Holy Experiment": The Founding of Pennsylvania, 1681–1701* (Philadelphia: Temple University Publications, 1962), p. 85.

33. Bridenbaugh, *Cities in the Wilderness*, p. 6. By 1685, almost 90 ships had delivered about 8,000 immigrants to Pennsylvania. Nash, *Quakers and Politics*, p. 50.

dence for Charles Town in the 1680s suggests a similar process of rapid immigration—there of Barbadian planters, French Huguenots, and English nonconformists—stimulating the town's growth to 1,200 persons by 1690.[34]

More to the point, these boomtowns grew because they attracted predominantly family migrants of modest capital, which they spent in establishing New World households. In New England, according to a study of a sample of immigrants during the 1630s, nuclear family members constituted more than two-thirds of the immigrants, and the families tended toward middling socioeconomic status.[35] Also suggestive of family migration is the balanced sex ratio of 157 males per 100 females among New England ship passengers.[36] The figures are similar for Pennsylvania in the 1680s. Surviving immigration lists indicate that 56 percent of the immigrants arrived in nuclear or extended families and just 33 percent came as servants. Moreover, sex ratios on these two lists ranged from 151 to 163 males per 100 females. And in Carolina, the 1680s immigration sharply lowered adult male-to-female sex ratios from 380 per 100 in 1672 to 153 per 100 in 1703—a figure almost identical to those of 1630s New England and 1680s Pennsylvania.[37]

These several family migrations generated urban growth; however, the quantitative effects varied substantially. Precisely how many immigrants passed through these towns is not known; but assuming a minimum based on their colony's populations in 1640 and 1690, respectively, eight immigrants to Massachusetts during the 1630s yielded one urban dweller, while during the 1680s one of every three immigrants to Pennsylvania and Carolina lived in Philadelphia or

34. Bridenbaugh, *Cities in the Wilderness*, p. 6; Clowse, *Economic Beginnings*, pp. 69–94; Richard S. Dunn, "The English Sugar Islands and the Founding of South Carolina," *South Carolina Historical Magazine*, 72 (1971), pp. 81–93.

35. T. H. Breen and Stephen Foster, "Moving to the New World: The Character of Early Massachusetts Immigration," *William and Mary Quarterly*, 3rd ser., 30 (1973), pp. 189–222.

36. Herbert Moeller, "Sex Composition and Correlated Culture Patterns of Colonial America," *William and Mary Quarterly*, 3rd ser., 2 (1945), pp. 113–19.

37. Evarts B. Greene and Virginia D. Harrington, *American Population Before the Federal Census of 1790* (New York: Columbia University Press, 1932), pp. 172–73; Nash, *Quakers and Politics*, pp. 51–54; "A Partial List of the Families who arrived at Philadelphia Between 1682 and 1687," *Pennsylvania Magazine of History and Biography* 8 (1884), pp. 328–40; and "A Partial List of the Families who resided in Bucks County, Pennsylvania, Prior to 1687, with the Date of their Arrival," *Pennsylvania Magazine of History and Biography* 9 (1885), pp. 223–33.

FIGURE 2.3. The port of Boston in the early 1770s. Boston's eminence derived in part from provisioning the Puritan families who came to the city in the "Great Migration" of the 1630s. Reproduced from *Harper's New Monthly Magazine* 4 (1851), p. 3.

Charles Town.[38] These figures, in addition to underlining the relative importance of these colonial ports, suggest that the Puritans brought less capital to the New World than did the Pennsylvania Quakers or the migrants to Carolina (see Table 2.2).

Considerably less capital was spent in the Chesapeake towns. Immigrants, though numerous, mostly consisted of young men without economic demands for urban goods and services. The typical Chesapeake immigrant—a young man, without family, engaged as an indentured servant or Virginia Company employee—was provisioned by his master or the Company. A 1624/25 Virginia muster reveals the striking contrast with New England. Of 1,218 colonists, more than three-fourths were males; two-fifths were servants; and fewer than two-fifths belonged to nuclear families. A decade later, male immigrants outnumbered females by six to one.[39] All of this meant a slim economic base for the aspiring towns of Jamestown and St. Mary's

38. *Historical Statistics of the United States, Colonial Times to 1957* (2 parts; Washington, D.C.: U.S. Bureau of the Census, 1960), 2, p. 756.

39. Irene W. D. Hecht, "The Virginia Muster of 1624/25 as a Source for Demographic History," *William and Mary Quarterly*, 3rd ser., 30 (1973), pp. 65–92; and Moeller, "Sex Composition," pp. 113–19.

TABLE 2.3

A Chronology of Colonial Charters, Town Founding, and Economic Depressions During the Seventeenth Century

Charter	Town	Depression	Remarks on depression
1584: Patent to Walter Raleigh	1587: City of Raleigh	1586–87	"A sharp crisis"
1606: Virginia Company of London	1607: Jamestown, Virginia	1603	Plague and depression
1606: Virginia Company of Plymouth			
1620: Council for New England		1622	Minor depression
1629: Heath Patent for Carolina		1629	Trade paralyzed, war with Spain and France
1629: Massachusetts Bay Company	1630: Boston (and other Mass. towns noted in text)	1636	Deepening depression
1633: Maryland	1634: St. Mary's City, Maryland	late 1630s	Depression regarded as chronic
		1649	Acute depression
		1659	Bottom of recession, effects felt after 1660, Cromwell's Spanish War
1663: Carolina (first charter)		1664–67	Inflation, Dutch War
1664: Jerseys (to Duke of York who conveyed to Berkeley and Carteret)	1665–66: East Jersey towns (Elizabethtown, Woodbridge, Piscataway, Middletown, Shrewsbury, Newark)		
1665: Carolina (second charter)	1670: Charles Town	1672–74	Inflation, Dutch War
	1675: Salem, West Jersey	1678	
	1677: Burlington, West Jersey	1682–90	Beginning of long depression
1681: Pennsylvania	1682: Philadelphia		

SOURCES: Harris, Origin of the Land Tenure System in the United States, pp. 71–154; and Wilson, England's Apprenticeship, pp. 160–84.

City. In Virginia, between 1607 and 1624, more than 7,000 immigrants came through Jamestown. Had the town grown in proportion to Boston, 900 persons would have resided there, but Jamestown never approached that figure; a population of two hundred seems a generous estimate.[40] Some of the discrepancy results from the high mortality in early Virginia, but a substantial share reflects the immigration of unfree men without capital.

Immigration: Timing, Composition, and Directionality

If initial urban growth was largely a matter of immigrant demand, then what are the mechanisms that determined the timing, composition, and directionality of immigration waves? First, timing and composition: colonization ventures show a close relationship with economic cycles. English colonies were founded in 1584–87, 1607, 1620, 1629–39, 1663–65, and 1681—dates that generally coincided with economic depressions of varying severity (see Table 2.3). Free-family migrations, the kind that generate urban growth, burgeoned during the worst of these depressions in the 1630s and 1680s.[41] Not surprisingly, these difficult decades were accompanied by accelerating religious persecution, aimed at Puritans in the earlier depression and Quakers in the later one. In these two decades, religious refuges were established in Massachusetts, Maryland, and Pennsylvania, and, save for Maryland, they received heavy flows of free-family migrants.

Free-family migrants also went in large numbers to the secularly based colony of Carolina. In the 1680s Carolina attracted a mélange of Barbadian Anglicans fleeing a severe depression in the sugar trade, English nonconformists and Scottish dissenters disgruntled with the Stuarts, and French Protestants evicted by the revocation of the Edict of Nantes.[42] In sum, severe depressions accompanied by religious persecution triggered free-family migration, which in turn stimulated urban growth in the receiving regions. Boston, Philadel-

40. Based on the 1624–25 census, Greene and Harrington, *American Population*, p. 144.
41. Colonial charter dates are from Harris, *Origin of the Land Tenure System*, pp. 71–154. Seventeenth-century economic conditions are described in Wilson, *England's Apprenticeship*, pp. 52, 53, 182; and Ramsey, *Tudor Economic Problems*, p. 78.
42. Clowse, *Economic Beginnings*, pp. 14–22.

phia, and Charles Town were the principal beneficiaries of this process. The one counterexample, when a severe depression failed to stimulate migration and urban growth, occurred in the 1580s with Raleigh's abortive Roanoke Colony. Conditions were ripe for a sizable town on the outer banks of Carolina, but the Spanish Armada and Anglo-Spanish hostilities short-circuited the venture (see Figure 2.2).

In sharp contrast, colonial towns founded during mild depressions (Jamestown in 1607) or amid general prosperity (the Jersey towns and Charles Town in the 1660s and 1670s) grew slowly, or not at all. A buoyant or recovering English economy slowed down the pace of family migration and accelerated the emigration of male laborers to the staple plantation colonies. Thus, when the English economy made a strong showing between 1650 and 1675, the mainland colonies attracted few immigrants, except in the Chesapeake; and there, half or more were servants who provided little stimulus for urban growth.[43] Put succinctly, prosperity directed labor migration to expanding staple regions; severe depression, meanwhile, caused whole families to flee areas of persecution for havens of religious toleration. Colonial urban growth depended on the latter and less frequent waves of migration.

If changing economic conditions governed the timing of English colonization, migration, and town growth, then it becomes important to ascertain the regularity of economic rhythms. Economic depressions during the seventeenth century recurred, on the average, once every 16 years, provided the inflationary periods during the Anglo-Dutch wars of 1664–67 and 1672–74 are excluded (see Table 2.4). The depression interval, however, varied somewhat erratically from 10 to 25 years. More predictable were the intervals between severe or chronic depressions—those that produced heavy family migration and urban growth. These severe depressions recurred at long-swing intervals (or Kondratieffs) of 45 to 60 years, in the 1580s, 1630s, and

43. Wesley Frank Craven, *White, Red, and Black: The Seventeenth-Century Virginian* (Charlottesville: University Press of Virginia, 1971), pp. 15–16, 85–86; Russell R. Menard, "Immigration to the Chesapeake Colonies in the Seventeenth Century: A Review Essay," *Maryland Historical Magazine* 68 (1973), pp. 323–29; *idem*, "The Growth of Population in Early Colonial Maryland, 1631–1712" (unpublished report prepared for the St. Mary's City Commission, Apr., 1972); *idem*, "Immigrants and Their Increase: The Process of Population Growth in Early Colonial Maryland," in *Law, Society, and Politics in Early Maryland*, ed. Aubrey C. Land, Lois Green Carr, and Edward C. Papenfuse (Baltimore: Johns Hopkins University Press, 1977), pp. 88–110; David W. Galenson, *White Servitude in Colonial America: An Economic Analysis* (Cambridge: Cambridge University Press, 1981).

TABLE 2.4

*Recurrence Interval for European Depressions
Between 1586 and 1690*

Sequence of depression years	Interval (in years)
1586–87/1603	17.0
1603/1622	19.0
1622/1634[a]	12.0
1634/1649	15.0
1649/1659	10.0
1659/1684[b]	25.0
Mean	16.3

SOURCES: Wilson, *England's Apprenticeship*, pp. 160–84.
Immanuel Wallerstein, *The Modern World-System II: Mercantilism and the Consolidation of the European World-Economy,
1600–1750* (New York: Academic Press, 1980).
NOTE: The inflationary years of the Dutch wars, 1664–
67 and 1672–74, are not included in the depressions.
[a]Depressions of 1629–39 placed at a mean year of 1634.
[b]Depressions from 1678 to 1690 placed at mean year of
1684.

1680s. The causes of the short cycles and the long swings, though
worthy of careful study, go far beyond the scope of this essay. For the
moment, it is sufficient to note the conjuncture, at half-century intervals, of severe depression, the founding of colonies of religious refuge, the ensuing flows of family migrants, and the rapid growth of
colonial towns (see Figure 2.4).[44]

The destinations of English colonists is a complex issue, but one
that takes us full circle to royal politics. Recall that high Anglican
Stuarts allocated the best lands to Anglicans and Catholics, the worst
to religious nonconformists such as the Puritans and Quakers. The
best colonial lands, according to the analogical geographical theory
of the time, were those in the mediterranean latitudes where wine,
cork, silk, and spices could be produced. The Chesapeake Bay, for
instance, fell within this optimal zone, and accordingly the Crown
granted it to Anglicans and Catholics. Marginal lands from New England to the Delaware Valley were settled by Separatists, Puritans,
and Quakers. Ironically perhaps, the "mediterranean" lands attracted few family migrants, who went instead to religious refuges in

44. P. M. G. Harris, "The Social Origins of American Leaders: The Demographic
Foundations," *Perspectives in American History* 3 (1969), pp. 159–244; Richard A. Easterlin,
Population, Labor-Force, and Long Swings in Economic Growth: The American Experience (New
York: National Bureau of Economic Research, distributed by Columbia University Press,
1968). See also Joseph A. Schumpeter, *Business Cycles* (2 vols.; New York: McGraw-Hill
Book Co., 1939), 1.

the marginal zones of New England, Pennsylvania, and West Jersey or the suboptimal zone of the Carolinas. Consequently, towns flourished in places (and times) where they were least expected by the Crown.[45]

Extension of the Model

In conclusion let us summarize the monopolist-migration model of colonization in English North America and suggest its applicability for certain other frontiers (see Figure 2.4). In the case of seventeenth-century English North America, colonization began with an evaluation of environmental resources along the Atlantic Seaboard followed by the allocation of optimal lands to "friends" of the Crown and marginal lands to religious dissenters (Panel 1 of Figure 2.4). With royal charters in hand, settlement began. English colonizers everywhere regarded towns as indispensable frontier cultural institutions. Colonization was unthinkable without them. In all but two cases, English monopoly colonization yielded one town per colony, centrally located on the coastal boundary (Panel 2 of Figure 2.4). The Dutch policy of free trade, by contrast, fostered multiple, scattered towns (not unlike those observed for nineteenth-century Ghana, Australia, and New Zealand) in periodic trading zones, as posited by Vance's mercantile model.[46] These frontier towns generally followed the trade in staples rather than preceding it. As for the timing of colonial charters, colonization, and town founding, all were governed by English economic depressions, recurring irregularly but at a mean of sixteen years. In turn, urban growth or the lack of it in the initial decades of settlement hinged on the volume of demand generated by free-family immigrants, who were pushed abroad by economic depression and religious persecution. Heavy volumes of family migration occurred during the most severe depressions, recurring at long-swing intervals of about 50 years (Panels 3 and 4 of Figure 2.4).

45. See, for example, Gary Dunbar, "Some Curious Analogies," pp. 323–26; Douglas R. McManis, *European Impressions of the New England Coast, 1497–1620*, University of Chicago Department of Geography Research Paper No. 139 (Chicago, 1972); Merrens, "The Physical Environment of Early America," pp. 530–56; and Charles M. Andrews, *The Colonial Period of American History* (4 vols.; New Haven, Conn.: Yale University Press, 1964), 1.

46. Taaffe, Morrill, and Gould, "Transport Expansion"; and Peter J. Rimmer, "The Search for Spatial Regularities in the Development of Australian Seaports 1861-1961/2," *Geografiska Annaler* 49B (1967), pp. 42–54.

I. Evaluation and Allocation of Colonial Territory

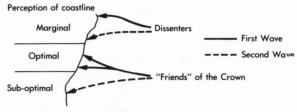

II. Location and Frequency of Initial English Towns

III. Immigrant Destinations in Seventeenth Century

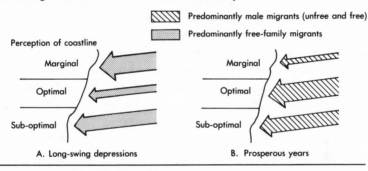

A. Long-swing depressions   B. Prosperous years

IV. Urban Growth in the First Two Decades

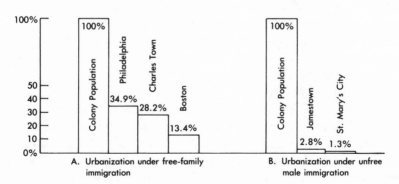

A. Urbanization under free-family   B. Urbanization under unfree
   immigration   male immigration

FIGURE 2.4. The Model of Monopoly Colonization in English North America during the Seventeenth Century. Sources: The urbanization levels shown in Panel 4 are based on estimates of the sizes of cities and colonial populations in Table 2.2 and the sources cited therein.

The destination of these families was as predictable as their timing. Family migrants went to the lands that had been assigned to religious dissenters, and towns flourished where the Crown least expected. These waves of family migration caused rapid urban growth and boomtown conditions. But immigration peaked quickly, and after a decade of urban prosperity, the rate of immigrant flows and expenditures dwindled. Consequently, the immigrant boomtowns of Boston, Charles Town, and Philadelphia required a more enduring economic base. That these towns were able to find such sustenance in staple crops or the carrying trade testifies to an immense initial advantage achieved during the immigrant decades of the 1630s and the 1680s. The other and more obscure early ports of colonial America were victims of bad timing and location. Towns founded during mild recessions received few family migrants, although male laborers often arrived in abundance. Towns located in the mediterranean latitudes also floundered. These were Anglican colonies, and for most of the century the persecution of Anglican families was insufficient to propel them overseas.

Although the monopoly colonization model references the spatial and temporal coordinates of seventeenth-century English expansion, some of its components are applicable on other frontiers. Monopoly colonization and the one-port-per-colony rule may apply in sixteenth-century Ibero-America and among late-nineteenth-century imperialist colonies wherein resources were channeled into pre-eminent and centrally located capital cities.[47] Nineteenth-century frontiers are especially fascinating because the models of monopoly colonization and free trade are frequently overlain. The mercantile model appropriately describes the multiple, scattered ports that developed under competitive free trade in the first half or so of the nineteenth century. Later in the century, imperialism superimposed on this rudimentary urban structure a monopoly colonization model which privileged one port as the administrative-economic center.

This kind of historical layering of political economy and urban pattern is obscured in the well-known but simplistic urban-transport model of Taaffe, Morrill, and Gould.[48] By glossing over the institutional dynamics of European political economy, this spatial-descriptive model assumes a timeless evolutionary inevitability. Their

47. Carville V. Earle, "Reflections on the Colonial City," *Historical Geography Newsletter* 4 (1974), pp. 1–15.
48. Taaffe, Morrill, and Gould, "Transport Expansion."

model, while it may apply in Ghana, fails abysmally in English North America or in the trans-Appalachian West. Had they distinguished monopolist and mercantile principles guiding colonization and urban settlement, their projection of the model to other times and places would have been more measured.

The submodel that specifies immigration as a source of initial urban growth also may prove useful on the post-1700 North American frontier. Although I am reluctant to press an argument beyond 1800, the evidence before that date tends to support the conjunction at 50-year intervals of severe depression, family migration, and frontier boomtowns. For example, the long depression of the 1740s launched heavy migration into the southern piedmont and the Great Valley—the so-called backcountry—and numerous towns arose along the Great Wagon Road, several of them rivaling or surpassing the older coastal plain towns. These boomtowns grew because of immigration, and it was not until the 1750s and 1760s that they became closely integrated into the mercantile orbits of coastal ports. Similarly, the 1790s saw another wave of migration beyond the Appalachians and concomitant expansion in towns such as Louisville, Pittsburgh, Lexington, and Cincinnati.[49] In the end, settlement in North America (or elsewhere) is not reducible to a single model of staple trade, central place, or monopoly colonization; all are essential for unraveling historical processes that are specific to particular times and spaces.

49. Julius Rubin, "Urban Growth and Regional Development," in *The Growth of the Seaport Cities, 1790–1825*, ed. David T. Gilchrist (Charlottesville: University Press of Virginia, 1967), pp. 12–13; Richard C. Wade, *The Urban Frontier: Pioneer Life in Early Pittsburgh, Cincinnati, Lexington, Louisville, and St. Louis* (Chicago: University of Chicago Press, 1967). For the 1740s immigrant boomtowns in the back country of Maryland, Virginia, and the Carolinas, see Chapter 3. The traditional interpretation of frontiers as male dominated seems applicable during times of prosperity and commercial frontier expansion; however, long-swing depressions foster family migration and a more balanced sex ratio. For example, frontier Kentucky in 1790 had a sex ratio of 111.4, a figure resembling those of the 1630s and 1680s migrations on the Atlantic Seaboard. Moeller, "Sex Composition and Correlated Culture Patterns," p. 128. For the traditional view, see Jack R. Eblen, "An Analysis of Nineteenth-Century Frontier Populations," *Demography* 2 (1965), pp. 399–413.

CHAPTER 3

Why Tobacco Stunted the Growth of Towns and Wheat Built Them into Small Cities

Urbanization South of the Mason-Dixon Line, 1650–1790

An urban experience of considerable magnitude transformed the South in the eighteenth century. Where only scattered farmsteads and plantations existed in 1700, hamlets, towns, and cities had developed by 1800 (see Figure 3.1). On the coastal plain and in the zone of falls at the edge of the piedmont, ports had emerged with connecting arteries stretching far westward to the multitude of communities that had proliferated in the backcountry. The Southern environment, once thought inimical to urban civilizations, had spawned Charleston (formerly Charles Town), Norfolk, and Baltimore, cities that constituted worthy rivals of the northern ports. But the geography of Southern urbanization was not uniform; it was, rather, a complex matrix of urban systems, each exhibiting characteristics peculiar to the staples it exported. A triad of distinctive systems had evolved, based on the commodities of wheat, rice, and tobacco, each of which enjoyed expansive markets during most of the century. The exportation of wheat produced a configuration of sizable ports supplied by an array of interior urban places. By contrast, the rice port of Charleston, despite its aggressive growth, did not generate a constellation of supporting hinterland towns. And, lastly, the tobacco towns of the Chesapeake achieved neither substantial size nor integration within a hierarchical urban system.

The original version of this paper was co-authored with Ronald Hoffman.

The issues involved here transcend the early American South, since they focus on a critical phase in the process of economic development in staple regions. Urban systems were indispensable to the evolution of industrial societies and the related achievement of sustained economic growth. Their absence or impoverished state presaged a future blighted by stagnation. Thus the patterns of urbanization, which were the consequences of developmental forces unleashed by particular staples, predisposed production regions to divergent trajectories of long-run economic development.

This problem also transcends disciplinary boundaries. Historians, economists, and geographers have all contributed to a theoretical and conceptual explanation of variations among preindustrial urban systems. The emerging consensus suggests that the nature of these urban systems derived from the backward and forward linkages engendered by a region's staple crop.[1] Most students have concentrated on the backward linkages occasioned by consumer demand. According to the important investigations of Robert E. Baldwin and Douglass C. North, certain staples such as tobacco and cotton, because of their labor-intensive requirements, created societies marked by a distinct disparity between rich and poor. The unevenness of consumer demand, in turn, stunted the development of local urban places.[2] By contrast, these authors reason that capital-intensive staples such as wheat fostered the family farm along with

1. Backward linkages are defined as those impacts on economic activity in the producing region occasioned by consumer demand within that region; forward linkages as those impacts on economic activity created by the movement of staple exports from production sites to consumption sites beyond the region. These definitions reflect interest in export flows and regional economic base. Slightly different definitions are employed in input-output analyses of economic development. Morton Rothstein, "Antebellum Wheat and Cotton Exports: A Contrast in Marketing Organization and Economic Development," *Agricultural History* 41 (1967), pp. 91–100; Charles M. Tiebout, "Exports and Regional Economic Growth," *Journal of Political Economy* 64 (1956), pp. 160–64; Albert O. Hirschman, *The Strategy of Economic Development* (New Haven: Yale University Press, 1958), pp. 98–119. The association of urban development and economic growth is widely known; see, for example, Simon Kuznets, *Toward a Theory of Economic Growth with "Reflections on the Economic Growth of Modern Nations"* (New York: W. W. Norton, 1965); *idem, Economic Growth and Structure: Selected Essays* (New York: W. W. Norton, 1965), pp. 194–212; and Walt W. Rostow, *The Stages of Economic Growth: A Non-Communist Manifesto* (Cambridge: Cambridge University Press, 1960).

2. Robert E. Baldwin, "Patterns of Development in Newly Settled Regions," *Manchester School of Economic and Social Studies* 24 (1956), pp. 161–79; Douglass C. North, "Location Theory and Regional Economic Growth," *Journal of Political Economy* 63 (1955), pp. 243–58; Douglass C. North, "Agriculture in Regional Economic Growth," *Journal of Farm Economics, Proceedings* 41 (1959), pp. 943–51.

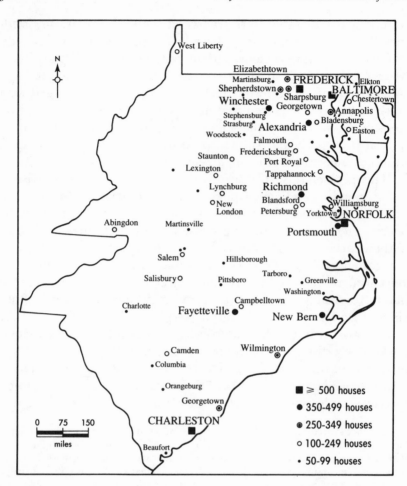

FIGURE 3.1.   Southern Towns and Cities having Fifty or More Houses about 1790. Source: Jedediah Morse, *The American Gazetteer* . . . (Boston: 1797).

an egalitarian wealth-income structure and extensive demand for a wide range of goods provided by urban centers of varying rank and size.

The seemingly logical assumption that towns grew slowly, passively responding to a process of maturing settlement and accumulating demand, is at considerable variance with much of the colonial American experience. Often the opposite occurred, as James Vance has so persuasively argued.[3] On the eighteenth-century southern

3.   James E. Vance, Jr., *The Merchant's World: The Geography of Wholesaling* (Englewood Cliffs, N.J.: Prentice-Hall, 1970).

frontier, urban places arose early and played dynamic roles in organizing the staple export trade. More importantly—and this was a crucial factor for all of the newly settled regions in colonial America—the movement of commodities from farm to market generated employment opportunities and attendant urban systems that varied with the particular staple involved and the marketing requirements that it imposed.

Two historians, Morton Rothstein and Jacob Price, have examined the salient aspects of forward linkages.[4] Rothstein hypothesizes that the flow of antebellum grains created more non-farm employment than did that of cotton and that this accounted for two distinctly different urban systems. His perceptive analysis recognizes that the physical properties of the commodities involved were important for urbanization. Price's study of marketing organization in colonial America convincingly demonstrates that port growth in production regions depended to a large extent on whether staple commodities captured the "entrepreneurial headquarters" of the trade. When regional exports were channeled to a principal market destination abroad, the ports within the receiving zone tended to capture the trade's operating institutions and allied industries at the expense of colonial ports located in the production region. In the tobacco and rice trades, for example, Price argues that the dominance exerted by the English ports retarded urban growth within the Chesapeake and at Charleston. Conversely, he suggests that staples such as wheat, which were exported to diverse markets, encouraged the development of ports and other commercial institutions within the staple-producing region.

From the examinations to date of backward and forward linkages, a comprehensive, although still unrefined, theory of preindustrial urban development has begun to coalesce, even though many of its components remain obscure. This essay focuses primarily on the physical character of the eighteenth-century South's major staples and their attendant impact on forward linkages. These crucial features, which have been largely ignored, accounted for the profile of the South's three regional urban systems. More precisely, the size and

4. Rothstein, "Antebellum Wheat and Cotton Exports," pp. 91–100; Jacob M. Price, "Economic Function and the Growth of American Port Towns in the Eighteenth Century," *Perspectives in American History* 8 (1974), pp. 123–86. Also see Carville Earle and Ronald Hoffman, "Regional Staples and Urban Systems in Antebellum America," in *Géographie du Capital Marchand aux Amériques 1760–1860*, ed. Jeanne Chase (Paris: École des Hautes Études en Sciences Sociales, 1987).

spatial pattern of regional ports and their respective hinterland towns resulted from the staple produced. Because each of the staples differed in bulk, weight, and perishability, each engendered distinctive commodity flows and processing demands, which, in turn, stimulated or retarded a host of urban functions including staple packaging and processing, allied industrial procedures, transportation services, and the provisioning and repair activities associated with freight shipment. All of these interrelated components were integral to the working of the region's preindustrial urban systems. More significantly, they constituted the predictive foundations of future Southern economic development.

From the very beginning of overseas colonization the English sponsors of the various settlement projects urged their people to locate in compact communities—to "plant in towns." The New World was to be a land whose rich economy would be urban-based. The founders of New England, the directors of the Virginia Company, the proprietors of Maryland, New York, the Jerseys, Pennsylvania, and Carolina were of one mind: towns were to form the core of their settlements. In the region ranging from New England to Pennsylvania, the original conception seemed to be borne out as more and more towns, during the course of the century, came to dominate the landscape. A familiar residential pattern of agricultural villages and a few sizable towns emerged, a way of life with which the English could be comfortable.[5]

The Southern experience was altogether different. Here the best-laid plans repeatedly went awry. In Virginia, Maryland, and Carolina the well-ordered visions of the English architects were quickly replaced by a ragged residential pattern of dispersed farmsteads. Virginia's story illustrates the experience of the region. Initially, towns composed of craftsmen and professionals were to be built— their names, "Jamestown," "Bermuda City," "Elizabeth City," and "Charles City," reflecting the English image. But the economic realities of the New World quickly subverted the English conception. The decentralized settlement system that evolved departed radi-

5. For discussion of the seventeenth-century English settlement experience, see Carville Earle and Ronald Hoffman, "The Urban South: The First Two Centuries," in *The City in Southern History*, ed. Blaine Brownell and David Goldfield (Port Washington, N.Y.: Kennikat Press, 1976); and Carville Earle, "The First English Towns of North America," *Geographical Review* 67 (1977), pp. 34–50.

cally from the intended design.[6] Observers in England were bewildered by it since they could not conceive of life—whether commercial or social—existing in an area without towns. Furthermore, they feared that without an urban focus—as the word urbane implies—civilization itself could not endure. I discuss this fear more fully in Chapter 2.

The English did not understand what had transpired in the South. From their perspective the region was a strange land, while the northern colonies reflected a more traditional pattern of development. But in focusing on the spatial dimensions alone, they missed the common denominator that underlay all of the English settlements. In fact, commercial and social life were sustained outside of an urban context much as they were sustained in the towns. The majority of rural settlers combined their farming activities with at least one other rough trade, with the result that those who provided the support services needed to maintain life—coopers, carpenters, cobblers, and tailors, for example—were normally available whether the people lived clustered around a New England common or a Chesapeake estuary. Consequently, in both the northern and southern colonies an occupational mosaic, very similar in its functional structure, prevailed.[7]

In the mid-seventeenth century, however, the tidewater planters began to question the value of their atypical settlement and marketing pattern. Their concern sprang not from a fear of social regression, but rather from their disquietude over a declining tobacco economy. Starting in 1655 the Chesapeake assemblies initiated an unprecedented era of settlement engineering. General town acts passed the Virginia Assembly in 1655, 1662, 1680, 1685, 1690, and 1705. The Maryland Assembly followed suit in 1668, 1669, 1671,

6. For early Virginia, see Sigmund Diamond, "From Organization to Society: Virginia in the Seventeenth Century," *American Journal of Sociology* 63 (1958), pp. 457–75; Irene W. D. Hecht, "The Virginia Colony, 1607–1640: A Study in Frontier Growth" (Ph.D. diss., University of Washington, 1969), pp. 1–62; Edmund S. Morgan, "The Labor Problem at Jamestown, 1607–1618," *American Historical Review* 76 (1971), pp. 595–611; and John W. Reps, *Tidewater Towns: City Planning in Colonial Virginia and Maryland* (Williamsburg, Va.: Colonial Williamsburg Foundation, 1972), pp. 24–91.

7. Joan Thirsk, "Industries in the Countryside," in *Essays in the Economic and Social History of Tudor and Stuart England*, ed. F. J. Fisher (Cambridge: Cambridge University Press, 1961), pp. 70–88; Mildred Campbell, "Social Origins of Some Early Americans," in *Seventeenth-Century America*, ed. J. M. Smith (Chapel Hill, N.C.: University of North Carolina Press, 1959), pp. 63–89; Agnes Leland Baldwin, *First Settlers of South Carolina, 1670–1680* (Columbia, S.C.: University of South Carolina Press, 1969).

1683, 1684, 1686, 1688, 1706, 1707, and 1708. Although the motives and interests in these measures varied, the assemblies sought, above all else, to acquire control over the marketing and distribution of tobacco. By such consolidation they hoped to drive prices upward. But despite juridical directives the town acts failed. By 1710 few of the statutory towns existed as places of commerce. As Governor Francis Nicholson, a man who labored in both Chesapeake colonies, remarked in 1697, "people in these parts have been used to live separately" and "it is very difficult to bring them at once to cohabit, especially by restraint."[8]

Charleston constituted the one exception to the apparent lack of Southern urbanization. Settled in 1670, the town, after an initial period of limited growth, began to expand in the 1680s and 1690s.[9] Carl Bridenbaugh, in his study of early American towns, estimated Charleston's population as 1,110 in 1690–91 and 2,000 in 1700. These figures are surprisingly large and suggest that early South Carolina was heavily urbanized. In 1690 the colony's entire population included only 3,500 to 4,000 people; by 1700 it numbered between 5,000 and 6,000. If these estimates are correct, Charleston contained 25 to 33 percent of South Carolina's total population.[10]

Charleston's early growth, though phenomenal by Southern standards, becomes less impressive on closer inspection. The town's prosperity rested on the heavy, but episodic, immigration of Protestant

8. John C. Rainbolt, "The Absence of Towns in Seventeenth-Century Virginia," *Journal of Southern History* 35 (1969), pp. 343–60. Reps, *Tidewater Towns*, pp. 46–116; Edward M. Riley, "The Town Acts of Colonial Virginia," *Journal of Southern History* 16 (1950), pp. 306–23; Governor Nicholson to Council of Trade and Plantations, Mar. 27, 1697, *Calendar of State Papers, Colonial Series* (London: PRO, 1860–   ), Vol. 15, p. 421; Lois Green Carr, "The Metropolis of Maryland: A Comment on Town Development Along the Tobacco Coast," *Maryland Historical Magazine* 69 (1974), pp. 124–45; Carville V. Earle, *The Evolution of a Tidewater Settlement System: All Hallow's Parish, Maryland, 1650–1783*, University of Chicago Department of Geography Research Paper No. 170 (Chicago, 1975), pp. 62–100.

9. Wesley Frank Craven, *The Southern Colonies in the Seventeenth Century, 1607–1689* (Baton Rouge: Louisiana State University Press, 1970), pp. 310–59; Converse D. Clowse, *Economic Beginnings in Colonial South Carolina, 1670–1730* (Columbia: University of South Carolina Press, 1971), pp. 1–41.

10. Carl Bridenbaugh, *Cities in the Wilderness: The First Century of Urban Life in America, 1625–1742* (New York: Ronald Press Co., 1938), p. 6; *Historical Statistics of the United States, Colonial Times to 1957* (2 parts; Washington, D.C.: U.S. Bureau of the Census, 1960),'Part 2, p. 756; Evarts B. Greene and Virginia D. Harrington, *American Population Before the Federal Census of 1790* (1932; reprint, New York: Columbia University Press, 1932), p. 172.

families during the economically depressed decades of the 1680s and the 1690s. By 1700, this immigration and the urban growth it created had come to an end.[11] Charleston's future expansion was by no means assured. Furthermore, the figures developed for Charleston's early population by Bridenbaugh and others are suspiciously high. Most were derived from extrapolations based on the number of families allegedly living within the city. The figure most commonly cited is that provided by the eighteenth-century historian John Oldmixon, who in 1708 recorded that upward of 250 families resided in Charleston.[12] However, many of the city's residents lived there only in the summer and fall. From the earliest years of settlement, South Carolina had developed a reputation for its unhealthy climate. Most people attributed the epidemics spawned by the malaria-ridden swamps of the Carolina lowlands to the fetid summer air and believed that Charleston's cool ocean breezes offered a protective haven from disease during the perilous summer and autumn months. Actually, the brackish salt water surrounding Charleston accounted for the city's general freedom from malaria, but whatever the reason, all those who could afford the expense built residences within the city. Charleston was also attractive as a temporary settlement because it served as a fort in times of conflict with Spanish raiders or Indian tribes.[13]

Accordingly, Charleston moved into the eighteenth century with its immigrant economic base vastly depleted and its traffic in transient "resorters" and politicians inadequate to sustain a sizable urban community. Charleston's vigorous expansion awaited the rapid growth of the rice and slave trades in the 1730s. Spurred by these commercial developments, Charleston grew to a city of some 12,000 people by the American Revolution. An impressive metropolis, it caused one visitor to observe that it could be "ranked with the first cities of British America and yearly advances in size, riches and population."[14]

11. Clowse, *Economic Beginnings*, pp. 73–76; Earle, "The First English Towns."

12. John Oldmixon, *The British Empire in America* . . . , 2nd ed. (2 vols.; London: J. Brotherton, J. Clarke, 1741), Vol. 1, p. 512.

13. John Duffy, "Eighteenth Century Carolina Health Conditions," *Journal of Southern History* 18 (1952), pp. 289–302; see also St. Julien R. Childs, *Malaria and Colonization in the Carolina Low Country* (Baltimore: Johns Hopkins University Press, 1940).

14. Quoted in Alexander Hewatt, *An Historical Account of the Rise and Progress of the Colonies of South Carolina and Georgia* (London: A. Donaldson, 1779), Vol. 2, p. 289; Price, "Economic Function," p. 176.

Charleston's commercial growth in the eighteenth century was due to a number of related factors. The city's modest early expansion resulted from its role as the center of a vast and highly lucrative Indian trade. The English had intense competition in this trade from the Spanish and French, both of whom enjoyed the geographical advantage of river access from their Gulf settlements to the interior Indian tribes. Yet the British, because of their ability to supply goods to the Indians more cheaply than their competitors, came to dominate the southwestern region. As one commentator noted in 1708, "The English trade for cloth always attracts and maintains the obedience and friendship of the Indians—they affect them most who sell best cheap."[15]

In the beginning the Indian trade consisted essentially of settlers exchanging European manufactured goods with the various tribes for deerskins and furs. As the trade expanded, deerskins became the main commodity exported, and the large numbers involved—from an annual average of around 50,000 to an occasional maximum of over 100,000—created a strong demand for extensive storage facilities. This demand, which coincided with the inland movement of the Indian tribes by the second decade of the eighteenth century, transformed the trade from a secondary pursuit, followed by individual planters, to a capital-intensive industry operated by an exclusive mercantile community. The men who dominated the trade, whether of local origin or from England, needed mercantile correspondents to dispose of the skins and, more important, credit relationships to fund the inland flow of trading goods. Because of their connections, many of these traders were able to achieve commanding positions enabling them to enter the other commercial markets developing in South Carolina, particularly the rice, slave, naval stores, lumber, and provision trades.[16]

South Carolina's economy continued to develop throughout the eighteenth century. Charleston, which was already an active town by 1700, grew during the next decades into an important distribution point for Caribbean trade. Because of the city's role in supplying the West Indies with a wide array of foodstuffs and lumber products, Charleston developed as a reexport center. Governor James Glen, in one account, enumerated 66 items specifically sent to Charleston for

    15. Verner W. Crane, *The Southern Frontier* (Durham: Duke University Press, 1928), pp. 22, 29, 65–67.
    16. Clowse, *Economic Beginnings*, pp. 139, 159, 227, 243.

FIGURE 3.2. A mid-nineteenth-century representation of rice fields, slave labor, and the plantation overseer in the Low Country of South Carolina. Note the flatness of the terrain, the slaves tilling the young rice plants, and, in the distance, the bank of trees lining the ditches that drained the fields of wet rice. The eighteenth-century scene was little different than the one shown here. Reproduced from *Harper's New Monthly Magazine* 19 (1859), p. 723.

reexport to the Caribbean. The commodities ranged from cloth, hats, and linens to metallic goods, furniture, and liquors.[17]

The island trade, though continuing to expand, was vastly overshadowed after the 1730s by dealing in rice. Rice had, in effect, become "king," particularly after Parliament agreed, in 1730, to allow the direct exportation of rice to southern Europe. From 1724

17. Report of Governor Nathaniel Johnson and Council, 1708, quoted in William J. Rivers, *A Sketch of the History of South Carolina, From Its First Settlement in 1670, to the Year 1808* (Charleston, 1856), Vol. 1, pp. 233–38; Chapman J. Milling, ed., "A Description of South Carolina by James Glen," in *Colonial South Carolina, Two Contemporary Descriptions* (Columbia, S.C.: University of South Carolina Press, 1951), pp. 56–58.

to 1774 it accounted for one-half to two-thirds of the total value of South Carolina's exports. The increase in rice production could only be accomplished by an expanding slave population. This, in turn, required the colony, formerly an exporter of provisions, to import, in Governor James Glen's words, "great quantities of bread, flour, beef, hams, bacon and other commodities." Indigo, after its development in the 1740s, came to rank second in value to rice. And following the settlement of the backcountry, the colony was once again able to resume its exportation of grain. By the 1760s the shipment of provisions, especially grain from the backcountry, ranked third.[18]

The exportation of rice and later of grain had a decisive impact on Charleston's eighteenth-century urban development. Until the mid-1740s, rice and slaves were the dynamic ingredients that accounted for the city's impressive expansion. At that point the town's growth rate leveled off as rice production reached a plateau. The raising of irrigated rice was confined to the lowland swamps of the coastal plain, and despite rising prices, no additional acreage remained after the 1740s for augmenting production. Not until the 1760s would Charleston undergo another cycle of expansion as it established the links that facilitated the export of the piedmont's most important crop—wheat.[19] But the settlement of the Carolina backcountry, with

18. Milling, "A Description of South Carolina by James Glen," p. 36; Charles Joseph Gayle, "The Nature and Volume of Exports from Charleston, 1724–1774," in *The Proceedings of the South Carolina Historical Association,* ed. Robert L. Meriwether (1937), p. 25; Henry C. Dethloff, "The Colonial Rice Trade," *Agricultural History* 56 (1982), pp. 231–43; Leila Sellers, *Charleston Business on the Eve of the American Revolution* (Chapel Hill: University of North Carolina Press, 1934), pp. 3–96, 148–77; Peter A. Coclanis, *The Shadow of a Dream: Economic Life and Death in the South Carolina Low Country, 1670–1920* (New York: Oxford University Press, 1989); Lester J. Cappon, ed., *Atlas of Early American History* (Princeton, N.J.: Princeton University Press, 1976), p. 27.

19. Charleston, benefiting from its size and facilities for export and from the southeastern flow of rivers, captured much of the trade of the Carolina piedmont and usurped urban functions from North Carolina coastal and river ports. Similarly, Norfolk encroached from the north; and consequently perhaps two-thirds of North Carolina's exports found markets through South Carolina and Virginia. In addition, North Carolina's sluggish rivers, fronted by a hazardous, shoaly coastline, discouraged navigation and port development. With the exception of Wilmington, none of the other ports— Edenton, New Bern, Bath, Beaufort, New Brunswick—developed into significant trading centers. These developments are thoroughly and perceptively discussed in H. Roy Merrens, *Colonial North Carolina in the Eighteenth Century: A Study in Historical Geography* (Chapel Hill: University of North Carolina Press, 1964), pp. 147–54. Also see J. F. D. Smythe, *Tour of the United States of America* (2 vols.; London, 1785), Vol. 2, pp. 98–99; and Charles Crittenden, *The Commerce of North Carolina, 1763–1789* (New Haven: Yale University Press, 1936), p. 75.

its concentration on grain production, may be traced to economic and political forces that had become predominant in the Chesapeake colonies. There an urban system had developed which partially fulfilled the discredited dreams of the seventeenth-century sponsors of colonization.

In the Chesapeake region the pace of urbanization quickened, particularly in the eighteenth century's second decade, because of changes in the structure of the area's economy. Tobacco continued dominant on the tidewater's western shore and in the piedmont valleys of the Patuxent, Potomac, and James rivers. Along the intricate coastline a number of tobacco towns began to emerge and ultimately flourished as dynamic centers of the tobacco trade, though these communities remained small by the relative standards of the tidewater's political capitals, Williamsburg and Annapolis. In the piedmont, the commercialization of a new tobacco frontier was reflected in the development of a mercantile network which had its foci not in towns but in isolated country stores and crossroads hamlets often operated by Scottish merchants or storekeepers.[20]

These limited moves toward urbanization reflect economic changes of the time that greatly affected the operation of the tobacco trade. Because of the expansion of European markets, particularly the French, the levels of Chesapeake tobacco production rose slowly at first and then dramatically, forcing organizational and marketing improvements in the conduct of the trade. Tobacco's expansion came about in a most unusual manner. The market for tobacco had stagnated in the late seventeenth century. In the average year from 1699 to 1709, the English imported nearly 29 million pounds of tobacco, mostly from Maryland and Virginia. Home consumption generally absorbed 11 million pounds. London's tobacco merchants reexported the rest to Europe, with approximately 45 percent going to Holland for manufacturing and shipping throughout Europe. Before 1713 English merchants tried unsuccessfully to tap new markets in northern Europe and Russia, but, by sheer coincidence, they acquired even better clients among their adversaries, the French. The development of the French tobacco market, as told in Jacob Price's

20. The important role of the Scottish merchants has been set out in Jacob M. Price, "The Rise of Glasgow in the Chesapeake Tobacco Trade, 1707–1775," *William and Mary Quarterly*, 3rd ser., 2 (1954), pp. 179–99. Also see James H. Soltow, "Scottish Traders in Virginia, 1750–1775," *Economic History Review* 12 (1959), pp. 83–98; and Calvin B. Coulter, "The Virginia Merchant" (Ph.D. diss., Princeton University, 1944).

monumental work *France and the Chesapeake* is a case study in paradox. France was England's leading enemy from 1690 to 1713—a period during which the two nations warred for 16 of 23 years. In the
first round of fighting, from 1690 to 1697, the French fleet enjoyed
extraordinary success in capturing scores of English ships, many of
them carrying Chesapeake tobacco, and, inadvertently, the French
consumer acquired a strong preference for the Chesapeake varieties.
With the interlude of peace from 1698 to 1702, the Anglo-French
tobacco trade geared up only to be temporarily interrupted by the
War of the Spanish Succession. But despite the outbreak of hostilities, the English quickly agreed to allow the French trade to continue
by shipping in vessels owned by neutral nations, for the trade's con-
tinuance served their interests as much as those of the French.[21]

When peace returned in 1713 the prospects for an enduring and
unprecedented trade created organizational alterations in England
and the Chesapeake. In Britain the focus of the trade, long centered
in London, began to extend northward and westward as the outports
of Liverpool and Whitehaven and the Scottish port of Glasgow intensified their efforts in the tobacco trade. Each of these cities carved
out regional niches in the Chesapeake. London firms were predominant in the quality sweet-scented tobacco areas between the James
and Rappahannock rivers and in the "bright" tobacco belt located on
Maryland's central western shore. Outport merchants, from Liver-

21. Chesapeake tobacco exports generally stagnated between 1680 and 1710, but
they rose spectacularly after 1713 from about 30 million pounds to over 40 million by 1727
and 50 million after 1741. *Historical Statistics*, Part 2, p. 766; Cappon, *Atlas of Early American
History*, p. 26. For the effects of the French market, see Jacob M. Price, *France and the
Chesapeake: A History of the French Tobacco Monopoly, 1674–1791, and of Its Relationship to the
British and American Tobacco Trades* (2 vols.; Ann Arbor: University of Michigan Press,
1973), Vol. 1, pp. 178–85, 509–30. For British exports on the eve of this expansion, see
Jacob M. Price, *The Tobacco Adventure of Russia: Enterprise, Politics, and Diplomacy in the Quest
for a Northern Market for English Colonial Tobacco, 1676–1722*, Transactions of the American
Philosophical Society, n.s., 51, Part I (1961), p. 6; and Russell R. Menard, "The Tobacco
Industry in the Chesapeake Colonies, 1617–1730: An Interpretation," *Research in Economic History* 5 (1980), pp. 109–77. The attitude of Crown officials and British merchants
toward Chesapeake towns altered dramatically as prospects of expanding tobacco exports
became distinct. Town planning policies evaporated as exports expanded and reinvigorated a mercantilist view that was clearly expressed by the English Commissioners of Customs in 1709: "The Establishing of Towns and Incorporating of the Planters . . . will put
them upon further Improvements which would be of Very Ill consequence, not only in
respect to the Exports of our Woolen and other Goods and Consequently to the Dependence that Colony ought to have on this Kingdom, but likewise in respect to the Importa-
tion of Tobacco hither for the home and Foreign Consumption." Reps, *Tidewater Towns*,
pp. 90–91.

pool and Whitehaven, organized the trade in poorer tobacco regions along Maryland's eastern shore and the southern tip of the western shore. Scottish merchants, who capitalized by exclusively serving the French snuff market, bought up the middling tobaccos grown in the piedmont valleys of the Patuxent, Potomac, and James rivers.[22]

Besides molding specialized zones, the British merchants introduced a number of cost-saving marketing innovations, which, although designed to expedite the turn-around time of tobacco ships, also revised the decentralized settlement system. The British dispatched resident agents, or factors, to conduct their trade in the Chesapeake. Unlike their predecessors, the supercargoes, these factors lived year-round in the tidewater. And in place of the tedious barter system, the factors purchased, collected, and stored tobacco at accessible landings in advance of the fleet's arrival. These practices greatly speeded the loading of tobacco ships and eliminated the need for costly winter layovers.[23]

To facilitate this merchandising process, small towns developed along the entire tobacco coast. Many of these were the statutory towns that had been authorized in the previous century. The towns grew not only in response to the reorganization described above, but also because the British factors specifically decided to cluster together in advantageous commercial locations favored by good navigation and immediate access to distinctive tobacco-producing areas. A description of Oxford, Maryland, before mid-century typifies the bustle along the Chesapeake coast: "Seven or eight large ships, at the same time, were frequently seen at Oxford, delivering goods and completing their landing; nor was it uncommon to dispatch a ship with 500 hogsheads of tobacco in twelve days after its arrival. . . . Men skilled in the article were employed by the merchants or store keepers and called Receivers, to view, weigh, mark and give receipts to planters after which

22. My conclusions on British urban spheres of influence in the eighteenth-century Chesapeake should be regarded as surmises based on the best evidence presently available. Certainly, no merchant group exercised exclusive dominance over large portions of the Chesapeake. Price, "The Rise of Glasgow," pp. 179–99; Robert Polk Thompson, "The Merchant in Virginia, 1700–1775" (Ph.D. diss., University of Wisconsin, 1955), pp. 157–99; Paul G. E. Clemens, "From Tobacco to Grain: Economic Development on Maryland's Eastern Shore, 1660–1750" (Ph.D. diss., University of Wisconsin, 1974), pp. 16–22, 82–84, 96–100; Earle, *Evolution of a Tidewater Settlement System*, pp. 91–92.

23. Earle, *Evolution of a Tidewater Settlement System*, pp. 91–92. For the reduction in port time, see James F. Shepherd and Gary M. Walton, *Shipping, Maritime Trade, and the Economic Development of Colonial North America* (Cambridge: Cambridge University Press, 1972), pp. 78–79, 198.

FIGURE 3.3.   A busy wharf scene from a small tobacco port very much like the scene of Oxford, Maryland, described in the text. Note the slave opening a tobacco hogshead for the tobacco inspection officer. This illustration represents Mary Lee Eggart's enhancement of the original which appears as the cartouche on *The Fry and Jefferson Map of Virginia and Maryland* (London, 1751).

vessels were sent to collect it, when it underwent a pressing and packing preparatory for shipping."[24]

It must be recognized, however, that these towns had a distinctly limited impact on the prevailing settlement pattern. Though extremely important, they were small and performed the singular role of trade. The secondary and tertiary institutions normally associated with town life—a concentration of craftsmen, mechanics, churches, schools, inns, and political functions—were rarely found in these communities. The typical tobacco town contained eight to ten merchants along with an occasional inn or craftsman. The number of merchants present was governed not by chance but by the limited volume of tobacco produced in the small trade area surrounding the tobacco town. In the vast majority of cases this tobacco came from the hinterland contiguous to the town, which, according to the best information, rarely exceeded "a circle of twelve to fourteen miles."[25]

24. Quoted in Oswald Tilghman, *History of Talbot County, Maryland, 1661–1861* (Baltimore: Williams and Wilkins Co., 1915), Vol. 1, p. 351.

25. Coulter, "The Virginia Merchant," p. 29. William Cunninghame to Mr. John Turner, Oct. 6, 1771, *William Cunninghame and Company Letterbooks, 1767–1774* (Scottish Record Office ms., Edinburgh). Within the Chesapeake, there was little interconnection among these insular, distended tobacco towns, contrary to the views expressed by James

These trade areas might have been vastly enlarged—tobacco could withstand long-distance land transport, and indeed it did later in the century—but the dangers of expansion outweighed the gains. Each town built a reputation for integrity in the tobacco trade and for its distinctive tobacco quality or variety, a result of unique local soils or production methods. A town's reputation for tobacco was a fragile thing, especially before careful inspection procedures were legislated, and this trademark could be ruined by mixing tobacco varieties from distant places or by the concealment of trashy tobacco packed in hogsheads by unknown and untrustworthy planters. The choice of small trade areas allowed merchants intimate knowledge of their customers and provided the traders with a measure of control over tobacco's variety, quality, and reputation.

Another factor that limited the growth of tobacco towns was the relatively modest amount of tobacco each production area could generate. At the moderate population densities common to the tidewater (some fifteen laborers per square mile), a hinterland of 6 to 7 miles in radius and 113 to 154 square miles in area would produce annually some 1,695,000 pounds of tobacco—a small amount, perhaps one-sixth the product of grain from an equivalent area. Most merchant factors, meanwhile, handled a minimum of one hundred hogsheads per year; and after the 1740s, two hundred to three hundred hogsheads (about 200,000 to 300,000 pounds of tobacco) constituted a normal year's transactions. At 200,000 pounds per merchant, eight merchants would have been able to operate profitably in the average tobacco town.[26] When the number of traders ap-

---

O'Mara in *A Historical Geography of Urban System Development: Tidewater Virginia in the 18th Century*, Geographical Monographs no. 13 (Downsview, Ontario: York University, 1983).

26. Densities of fifteen laborers per square mile are probably a high estimate for older tidewater areas. In the 1770s, the Virginia counties of James City, Hanover, and Charles City averaged between ten and twelve laborers per square mile. In the early eighteenth century, the number of merchants in the Chesapeake was closely regulated by the volume of tobacco exports, as follows: from 1710 to 1719, tobacco exports were 21,244,000 pounds, and there were 135 merchants engaged in the trade; from 1720 to 1729, tobacco exports were 33,350,000 pounds, and there were 157 merchants; from 1730 to 1739, the figures were 35,351,000 pounds and 168 merchants; and from 1740 to 1749 the figures were 42,688,000 pounds and 224 merchants. My model would predict merchants at the rate of one per 200,000 pounds of exports, or 107, 167, 177, and 213 in the respective decades. C. G. Gordon Moss, "The Virginia Plantation System: A Study of Economic Conditions in the Colony for the Years 1700 to 1750" (Ph.D. diss., Yale University, 1932), pp. 422–30; *Historical Statistics*, Part 2, p. 766. Virginia tobacco exports generally constituted two-thirds of the total for the Chesapeake, and this estimate

proached ten, only one condition could result—intense competition
and prohibitively high prices for tobacco. A Scottish factor specified
this effect in 1740 while discussing with friends the elements of locational strategy: "Mr. Miller has finished his purchase below, and by
what I learn proposed to settle at Hanover Court House (Virginia),
am of opinion it will not be in his power to make any valuable purchase of tobacco in those parts, the place being so crowded with
stores already; there being no less than eight stores mostly pretty
large besides several small ones."[27]

The tobacco towns, though they redirected the tobacco trade, had
a minimal impact on the character of the tidewater settlement system.
All crafts and professional activity remained essentially decentralized, with the exception of those concentrated in Williamsburg and
Annapolis, which attracted luxury craftsmen who catered to the resident British officials and the social elite that visited the capitals during the political season. In the countryside, small planters and small
farmers usually did their own craft and repair work, but on occasion
they had need of the specialized services of carpenters, coopers, tanners, sawyers, or weavers. The smaller planters unable to do the work
contracted with itinerant workers or roughly skilled neighbors. Larger
planters also did this, but more frequently they hired servants or
trained their slave population for home manufactures or repairs. For
more refined goods, the elite sent orders to the capital or their
English merchants.

This inequality among planters fragmented consumer demands,
while the fluctuating price of tobacco made their expenditures er-
ratic. The trend of all planters toward self-sufficiency became especially pronounced as the depressions within the tobacco economy
became more severe during the second and third quarters of the
eighteenth century. Through self-sufficiency they reduced plantation
costs, and thereby coped more effectively with the recurrent swings
of the Atlantic tobacco economy. George Mason captured the com-

---

is used in the table. Margaret Shrove Morris, *The Colonial Trade of Maryland, 1689–1715*,
Johns Hopkins University Studies in Historical and Political Science, 32nd ser., no. 3
(1914), p. 34.

27. Quoted in Coulter, "The Virginia Merchant," pp. 46–47. The functional significance of small tobacco towns is elaborated in Joseph A. Ernst and H. Roy Merrens, "'Camden's Turrets Pierce the Skies!': The Urban Process in the Southern Colonies During the
Eighteenth Century," *William and Mary Quarterly*, 3rd ser., 30 (1973), pp. 549–74.

plexity of this pattern in a description of his father's plantation, which resembled more a small town or village than a rural settlement:

> My father had among his slaves carpenters, coopers, sawyers, blacksmiths, tanners, curriers, shoemakers, spinners, weavers and knitters, and even a distiller. His woods furnish timber and plank for the carpenters and coopers, and charcoal for the blacksmith; his cattle killed for his own consumption and for sale supplied skins for the tanners, curriers, and shoemakers, and his sheep gave wool and his fields produced cotton and flax for the weavers and spinners, and his orchards fruit for the distiller. His carpenters and sawyers built and kept in repair all the dwelling-houses, barns, stables, ploughs, harrows, gates &c., on the plantations and the out-houses at the home house. His coopers made the hogsheads the tobacco was prised in and the tight casks to hold the cider and other liquors. The tanners and curriers with the proper vats &c., tanned and dressed the skins as well for upper as for lowere leather to the full amount of the consumption of the estate, and the shoemakers made them into shoes for the negroes. . . . The blacksmiths did all the iron work required by the establishment, as making and repairing ploughs, harrow, teeth chains, bolts &c., &c. The spinners, weavers and knitters made all the coarse cloths and stockings used by the negroes, and some finer texture worn by the white family, nearly all worn by the children of it. The distiller made every fall a good deal of apple, peach and persimmon brandy. . . . All these operations were carried on at the home house, and their results distributed as occasion required to the different plantations. Moreover all the beeves and hogs for consumption or sale were driven up and slaughtered there at the proper seasons, and whatever was to be preserved was salted and packed away for after distribution.[28]

An extensive slave population accounted for the complexity of the Mason plantation, but it differed from the numerous smaller units more in quantity than in kind. In order to remain competitive in the tobacco economy, practically all Chesapeake planters, rich or

28. Quoted in Edmund S. Morgan, *Virginians at Home: Family Life in the Eighteenth Century* (Charlottesville, Va.: University Press of Virginia, 1963), pp. 53–54. A qualitative statement of plantation adjustments to cyclical prices appears in Louis Morton, *Robert Carter of Nomini Hall: A Virginia Tobacco Planter of the Eighteenth Century* (Charlottesville, Va.: University Press of Virginia, 1964). Statistical evidence for these generalizations appears in Earle, *Evolution of a Tidewater Settlement System*, pp. 101–35.

poor, managed to acquire the requisite services on their own or within their immediate neighborhood. They thus had little need to go to town regularly, and, correspondingly, craftsmen and mechanics had no incentive to cluster in these locales.[29]

Had the Chesapeake colonies remained committed to the exclusive production of tobacco their urban history would indeed have been meager. But during the eighteenth century two additional and distinctly different agricultural regions emerged—one on marginal eastern land, the other in the west along the Great Valley and the Blue Ridge Mountains. And in both regions communities developed that performed a combination of secondary and tertiary functions. To be more specific, they were centers of staple commerce and transport that also served nearby farmers, offering them needed goods and services. In a word, they were towns.

It is somewhat odd that in the Chesapeake poorer soils created conditions conducive to town growth. But no matter how strange, these less productive tobacco lands were among the fundamental ingredients in the swift establishment of towns in two specific tidewater zones. In the bay's eastern sector and near its mouth, planters became diversified farmers during the early eighteenth century as tobacco gave way to a variety of commercial crops including wheat, corn, cattle, and hogs. And with this agricultural transformation gaining momentum, especially in the 1720s and 1730s, small towns and embryonic cities took root.

On Maryland's eastern shore, one of the most vital of these communities, Chestertown, consolidated important portions of the new grain trade and in two short decades came to rival Annapolis, the colony's capital, in size. A visitor to the town exclaimed in the mid-1750s, "For number and neatness of buildings, I esteem it a little if anything inferior to the metropolis of Annapolis."[30] Similarly, Norfolk, at the mouth of the bay, capitalized on the curious combination of a marvelous harbor, extraordinary access to the West Indies, and

29. On the varied activities of small planters not owning slaves, see *ibid.*; Allan Kulikoff, "Community Life in an Eighteenth-Century Tobacco County: Prince Georges County, Maryland, 1730–1780" (paper presented at the Annual Meeting of the Eastern Historical Geography Association, College Park, Maryland, Oct. 26, 1973); and *idem, Tobacco and Slaves: The Development of Southern Cultures in the Chesapeake, 1680–1800* (Chapel Hill, N.C.: University of North Carolina Press, 1986).

30. "Fisher Journal, 1750–1775," *Some Prominent Virginia Families*, ed. Louise Pecquet du Bellet (Lynchburg, Va., 1907), Vol. 3, p. 795.

some of the poorest soils in the Chesapeake. In 1775, the year before its utter destruction by British and American troops, Norfolk ranked as colonial America's fifth largest city. Her merchants drew upon a vast hinterland. From the Dismal Swamp to the south the town received tar, pitch, turpentine, and timber for a thriving shipbuilding industry and staves for West Indian sugar and molasses. Further south and west, drovers from the Carolinas brought sizable herds of cattle and hogs for slaughter. And from all over the bay, sloops and schooners carried corn, wheat, flour, and other provisions to Norfolk's merchants.

A second series of towns appeared in the 1740s and 1750s. These were far removed from the bay's waters. In the west along the Great Valley and amidst the Blue Ridge Mountains, the backcountry towns of Frederick in Maryland and Winchester in Virginia grew at a pace even more accelerated than that of the grain towns of the Chesapeake. The western communities developed because of a combination of stimuli. Three expansionary factors can, however, be isolated as actuating instruments. First, starting in the mid-1740s, thousands of settlers began to funnel down into the Valley and Blue Ridge, and from the beginning towns developed to facilitate their migration. Second, during the 1750s this process intensified as the French and Indian War drove people southward and into towns for safety. And last, the emergence of an extensive and profitable trade with the coastal export centers in wheat, flour, hemp, and flax resulted in the scores of urban clusters, large and small, that dotted the backcountry by the colonial era's end.

A third and final series of towns emerged simultaneously during the mid-eighteenth century as the backcountry became settled. Rather than being central to any specific geographic or economic region, these urban areas—Baltimore, Alexandria, and to some extent Fredericksburg, Petersburg, and Richmond—channeled trade among the mosaic of separate economic regions in Maryland and Virginia. All of these towns shared one crucial element in common— their location in the fall zone near the heads of ocean navigation. Located between the boundaries of two distinctive physical and economic regions, these urban settlements integrated the commercial staples of the backcountry and the eastern coastal plain and forwarded them to Atlantic markets.

By the American Revolution a remarkable urban transformation had occurred in the Chesapeake. During the eighteenth century's second and third quarters, 1725–75, the communities of Norfolk, Baltimore, Alexandria, Fredericksburg, and Frederick rivaled or surpassed the populations of Williamsburg and Annapolis. At the same time an array of villages, hamlets, and crossroads junctions emerged. A number of factors contributed to this expansion—soil, market demand, staple flows and transportation requirements, migration patterns, farm income levels, wars—the elements varied. But the basic cause was clear: the Atlantic world began to run desperately short of food. Above all else this single condition discharged economic forces that swept over and permanently transfigured the Chesapeake settlement system. Established eastern planters, new western farmers, black slaves, merchants, craftsmen, mechanics—all were directly affected.

The shortage appeared initially in the West Indies, then in southern Europe, and eventually in the British Isles. For the first time since the sixteenth century food deficits were severe among the Atlantic nations.[31] In each area where shortages developed, a combination of population growth and regional economic specialization had overtaxed the food supply. Wishing to expand their sugar production, British and French West Indian planters between 1700 and the 1730s doubled their slave population, an overall increase of 240,000.[32] In southern Europe, the population of Portugal, Spain, and Italy collectively expanded from 18 million in 1700 to 30 million by 1800. During the same time span, England, Scotland, and Ireland, while rapidly industrializing, swelled from 9 million to 16 million.[33]

Increasing demographic pressures were already exerting heavy demands on available food supply by the late 1750s. And then the bad European harvests began. Famine became a distinct possibility. For a dozen years after 1759 Europe suffered a cycle of "untoward

31. B. H. Slicher van Bath, *The Agrarian History of Western Europe A.D. 500–1850*, trans. Olive Ordish (London: St. Martin's Press, 1963), pp. 195–206; Joan Thirsk, ed., *The Agrarian History of England and Wales, IV: 1500–1640* (London: Cambridge University Press, 1967), pp. 575–77. The kind of demand shifts described here are not accounted for by staple theory, but that admission is not quite the same thing as ignoring these shifts, as some of the theory's overzealous critics have maintained. See, for example, Coclanis, *The Shadow of a Dream*, pp. 91–94. To turn the tables, their alternative—the theory of comparative advantage—is hardly an adequate account of the cascading European demands for food described here.

32. Philip D. Curtin, *The Atlantic Slave Trade: A Census* (Madison, Wis.: University of Wisconsin Press, 1969), pp. 51–93; Richard S. Dunn, *Sugar and Slaves: The Rise of the Planter Class in the English West Indies, 1624–1713* (New York: W. W. Norton, 1972), pp. 87, 312.

33. Marcel Reinhard, *Histoire de la population mondiale de 1700 à 1948* (Paris: Domat-Montchrestien, 1949), pp. 91–92, 112, 148–50.

seasons as no man living can remember the like, nor probably anyone living will ever see in so long a course again."[34] Southern Europe, as it had in the past, looked to its northern neighbors for aid. But the nations of the north, including England and the great "granary" of Poland, had absolutely nothing.

By the mid-1760s three-quarters of the Atlantic area needed food. Since the 1720s and 1730s a steady, though always reasonable, demand for grain had been felt throughout the North American colonies. Accordingly, wheat and corn production had risen, most especially in the middle colonies and to a lesser degree in the Chesapeake. Suddenly the pressure became overwhelming. In the Chesapeake, planters who had already diversified production decided to break even further with tobacco and concentrate on raising more wheat and corn. A comparison of Virginia export figures for 1740 with figures for 1770 graphically demonstrates the alteration and expansion that occurred. Corn exports to the West Indies soared from 42,212 bushels to 388,298 bushels; wheat to southern Europe from 25,204 bushels to 185,926 bushels; and flour to all destinations from 15 tons to 2,591 tons.[35] Maryland, in just one year, 1769, exported directly abroad 290,000 bushels of wheat, more than 110,000 bushels of corn, and over 2,000 tons of flour. To these figures must be added Maryland's overland transportation to Philadelphia, which amounted to 340,000 bushels of wheat and 100,000 bushels of corn.[36] In sum, the Chesapeake colonies had attained by the 1770s exports of about 2.3 million bushels of grain or grain-equivalent. At European consumption standards this was enough to feed 390,000 people. In the

34. *Considerations on the Policy, Commerce and Circumstances of the Kingdom* (London, 1771), pp. 104–6, quoted in Gaspar John Saladino, "The Maryland and Virginia Wheat Trade from Its Beginnings to the American Revolution" (M.A. thesis, University of Wisconsin, 1960), p. 91.

35. David Klingaman, "The Significance of Grain in the Development of the Tobacco Colonies," *Journal of Economic History* 29 (1969), pp. 268–78. See also Marc Egnal, "The Economic Development of the Thirteen Continental Colonies, 1720 to 1775," *William and Mary Quarterly*, 3rd ser., 32 (1975), pp. 210–14.

36. Maryland's exports for 1769, according to customs lists, amounted to 349,762 bushels of wheat, of which 292,979 bushels went to European markets; 3,461.3 tons of flour destined for Europe and the West Indies; 226,946 bushels of corn, with 113,846 bushels going to Europe and the West Indies, and the rest to the coastwise trade. Customs 16/1, Public Record Office ms. Maryland's overland grain exports to Philadelphia were estimated by Robert Alexander in 1774. Edward C. Papenfuse, Jr., "Economic Analysis and Loyalist Strategy During the American Revolution: Robert Alexander's Remarks on the Economy of the Peninsula or Eastern Shore of Maryland," *Maryland Historical Magazine* 68 (1973), p. 194; Cappon, *Atlas of Early American History*, p. 27.

Caribbean, at the much lower standard of one pint of grain a day, about 840,000 slaves could be maintained.[37] Certainly the Chesapeake alone could not feed the Atlantic nations, but in concert with other American colonies it helped stave off a famine of tragic dimensions. And in the process prosperity and urban growth permanently transformed the tidewater.

While the clamor for food affected the entire Chesapeake, the areas most dramatically restructured were the eastern shore of Maryland, the lower James Valley of Virginia, and the backcountry. Initially, the idea of diversification appealed to people east of the bay and south of the lower James because of their inferior tobacco soils, as I noted earlier. Much of the land was sandy, low-lying, and wet, a combination that gave the tobacco a dark color, a bitter taste, and a poor reputation. On the northern part of Maryland's eastern shore better soils prevailed, but there too the plains of dense, stiff clay were better suited for shallow-rooted grains than the deeper-rooted tobacco plant. The average Virginia planter of the 1720s, for example, tended 4,400 tobacco plants per year, but a planter of the lower James cultivated just 2,110 (or less).[38] Similar conditions existed on Maryland's eastern shore. Before 1750, the typical tobacco producer in Talbot County raised 1,300 pounds or less. Across the bay his counterpart normally expected anywhere from 1,450 to 1,850 pounds.[39] Equally hard was the fact that the price of tobacco in the

---

37. A ton of bread or flour was roughly equivalent to 51.4 bushels of wheat. Klingaman, "The Significance of Grain," p. 272. Robert Alexander estimated European grain consumption per capita at twelve bushels per year. Papenfuse, "Economic Analysis," p. 194. In the Caribbean, each slave received one pint of grain a day and occasionally half a rotten herring. C. M. MacInnes, *England and Slavery* (Bristol: Arrowsmith, 1934), pp. 112–13.

38. With respect to the average number of tobacco plants tended per laborer in 1724, the Virginia counties of Princess Anne, Isle of Wight, Nansemond, and Norfolk, the four counties closest to Norfolk Town, ranked 24th, 25th, 27th, and 28th, respectively, among 28 Virginia counties. Despite these low rankings, over 90 percent of taxable males over 16 years of age tended tobacco. These estimates exclude the labor of boys and the plants they tended. C.O. 5/1319, f. 220, Public Record Office ms.

39. The estimates of tobacco poundage per laborer are from estate inventories. The eastern shore figure of 1,200 pounds is for 1740–50. Western shore estimates are Charles County's 1,466 pounds for 1746 and Anne Arundel County's 1,863 pounds for 1740–47. After 1747, Maryland's tobacco inspection system, by prohibiting the marketing of trash tobacco, sharply reduced yields per laborer. Clemens, "From Tobacco to Grain," p. 47; *idem, The Atlantic Economy and Colonial Maryland's Eastern Shore: From Tobacco to Grain* (Ithaca, N.Y.: Cornell University Press, 1980); Earle, *Evolution of a Tidewater Settlement System*, pp. 24–27; Edward C. Papenfuse, Jr., "Planter Behavior and Economic Opportunity in a Staple Economy," *Agricultural History* 46 (1972), p. 305; Kulikoff, *Tobacco and*

less productive zones ranged from 15 to 50 percent below prices in the more prosperous areas.[40]

As "poor relations," the eastern and southern Chesapeake became the first regions to shatter tobacco's hold. Both began to diversify and, as a consequence, experienced urban growth in the 1720s and 1730s. The influences they responded to were related in character, though different in origin. In Norfolk and the lower James the West Indies market played a direct role in the transition. On Maryland's eastern shore the Indies' market demands were also crucial, but generally these pressures were expressed through the city of Philadelphia. By the second quarter of the eighteenth century wheat was flowing from the eastern shore, much of it under the direction of Philadelphia merchants who for the next 50 years expanded and consolidated their hold over the Delmarva Peninsula.[41] Ultimately the Philadelphians acquired firm control over as much as three-fourths of this grain, though by the end of the colonial era Baltimore's merchants were beginning to provide some competition.[42]

The merchants of Philadelphia channeled the peninsula's grain

---

Slaves, pp. 109–17; Lorena S. Walsh, "Plantation Management in the Chesapeake, 1620–1820," *Journal of Economic History* 49 (1989), pp. 393–406; Mary McKinney Schweitzer, "Economic Regulation and the Colonial Economy: The Maryland Tobacco Inspection Act of 1747," *Journal of Economic History* 40 (1980), pp. 557–65.

40. The lowest prices occurred in the areas of Nansemond County (near Norfolk), the lower Northern Neck, and the eastern shore. For the considerable geographic range in Virginia and Maryland tobacco prices, see Coulter, "The Virginia Merchant," pp. 108, 116, 144. In Maryland, the lowest prices were in St. Mary's and Charles counties on the lower western shore as well as on the entire eastern shore, especially in the southern end. Maryland Hall of Records, Accounts, Liber 9, ff. 118–23.

41. Philadelphia merchants, as early as the second decade of the eighteenth century, provided marketing and shipping services for the eastern shore, but the development of an expansive trade awaited the abrupt rise in wheat prices after 1750. Then, eastern shore farmers discovered that Philadelphia merchants offered prices higher than local merchants. As prices continued their secular rise, large quantities of grain moved toward Philadelphia and its milling satellite of Wilmington, and Philadelphia's hinterland penetrated deeply into the central eastern shore. The interested reader is referred to the appendix for a discussion of the expanding zones of commercial wheat production destined for urban markets. Ronald Hoffman, *A Spirit of Dissension: Economics, Politics, and the Revolution in Maryland* (Baltimore, 1973), pp. 60–80; Saladino, "The Maryland and Virginia Wheat Trade," pp. 73–75; Arthur L. Jensen, *The Maritime Commerce of Colonial Philadelphia* (Madison, Wis.: State Historical Society of Wisconsin, 1963), pp. 77–79; David E. Dauer, "Colonial Philadelphia's Intraregional Transportation System: An Overview," Regional Economic History Research Center, *Working Papers*, Vol. 2, no. 3 (1979), pp. 1–16.

42. Alexander estimated that Baltimore in 1774 drew off about 20 percent (140,000 bushels) and Philadelphia about one-half (340,000 bushels). Papenfuse, "Economic Analysis," p. 194.

in several directions, the most important of which came straight to their city by one of three distinct routes. The first led up the bay to Elkton, where the grain cargoes were shifted for land passage to Christiana Bridge. At Christiana, shallops picked up the wheat and corn for the run to Philadelphia. A second popular method consisted of shipping grain across the eastern shore's many portages. Whenever the heads of two rivers came close to meeting, one flowing into the Chesapeake and the other into the Delaware, traffic developed between them. Heavily used portages were located at the heads of the Elk, Sassafras, Chester, Choptank, and Nanticoke rivers. A third alternative avenue, the most expensive and traveled only during bad weather, consisted of wagon transport directly to Philadelphia.[43]

An enormous volume of traffic flowed along these routes, and everywhere towns and hamlets were created to provision the wagoners, feed their teams, and repair broken wheels, axles, and singletrees. The traffic became especially heavy in the fall after the harvest. Approximately 10,000 wagon trips were required to haul about 223,000 hundredweight of grain, the normal level of trade to Philadelphia for the late colonial period.[44] At prevailing freight rates the income generated from these transport services ranged between £6,900 and £12,500, enough to support 400 to 700 wagoners at a comfortable yearly income of £17.[45] Naturally the wagoners spent much of their

43. Philadelphians traded at many places on the eastern shore, and they probably monopolized the wheat trade at the head of the bay and at the heads of the Sassafras, Chester, and Choptank rivers. Hoffman, *A Spirit of Dissension*, pp. 64–65.

44. Wagons and carts were more frequent on the upper eastern shore and in the west than in any other part of Maryland. Clarence P. Gould, *Money and Transportation in Maryland, 1720–1765*, Johns Hopkins University Studies in Historical and Political Science, 33rd ser., no. 1 (Baltimore, 1915), p. 145. In these calculations, I use Pownall's observation of 1755 that the typical wagon with four horses hauled 22 hundredweight, with one hundredweight equaling 112 pounds. Other contemporary estimates of wagon capacity range from 30 to 50 bushels (16.1 to 25.9 hundredweight). Thomas Pownall, *A Topographical Description of the Dominions of the United States of America*, ed. Lois Mulkearn (Pittsburgh: University of Pittsburgh Press, 1949), p. 134. Saladino, "The Maryland and Virginia Wheat Trade," p. 47. In the typical year between 1770 and 1775, eastern shore farmers sent overland to the Delaware River 282,000 bushels of wheat (at 60 pounds per bushel), 86,000 bushels of corn (at 56 pounds per bushel), and 16,500 barrels of flour (at 196 pounds per barrel), or a total of 222,946 hundredweight, which required 10,134 wagon trips. Calculated from Hoffman, *A Spirit of Dissension*, pp. 64–65.

45. The income figures assume an average portage distance of fifteen miles and freight rates of between .59 pence (ca. 1770) and .9 pence (ca. 1800) per hundredweight per mile. Saladino, "The Maryland and Virginia Wheat Trade," pp. 47, 61–62. James T. Lemon, *The Best Poor Man's Country: A Geographical Study of Early Southeastern Pennsylvania* (Baltimore: Johns Hopkins University Press, 1972), p. 276. For other freight rates, see

income for provisions and repairs along the way. The bill for the two-day trip, including four meals, a night's lodging, and oats and corn for four horses, came to seven shillings, six pence. For all wagons this amounted to a yearly expenditure of approximately £3,800.[46] Because of this commerce a network of inns, ordinaries, and small hamlets emerged connecting Maryland's larger regional towns, Chestertown, Georgetown, and Charlestown, to Philadelphia.

The rapid expansion of Chestertown, located in Maryland's eastern shore county of Kent, vividly demonstrates how grain, unlike tobacco, encouraged urban development. By the 1770s this thriving port exported 130,000 bushels of corn and 5,000 barrels of flour.[47] All of the grain, because of its great bulk, required considerable care in marketing. Chestertown's wheat exports, approximately 7,800,000 pounds, were roughly the output of 1,300 family farms. If these farmers had raised tobacco instead of wheat, their output would have totalled just 1,300,000 pounds, or 16.7 percent of the weight of wheat.[48] Transported from farm to market, the wheat required 3,165 wagon trips; the tobacco, moving by water on twelve-hogshead flats, 108 trips. At Chestertown, wheat took up more storage space than tobacco—161,785 cubic feet to 28,860 cubic feet.[49]

James Weston Livingood, *The Philadelphia-Baltimore Trade Rivalry, 1780–1860* (Harrisburg, Pa.: Pennsylvania Historical and Museum Commission, 1947), pp. 29–30 (.63 pence); Pownall, *A Topographical Description,* p. 134 (ca. 1755, .2 pence, a figure that seems remarkably low). Seventeen pounds represents the annual income of a wagoner who contracted with George Washington in 1756. Worthington Chauncey Ford, *Washington as an Employer and Importer of Labor* (Brooklyn, N.Y.: private printer, 1889), p. 22.

46. Ordinary prices come from the county court, which regulated these prices. By the mid-eighteenth century, Cecil County on the north end of the eastern shore had more ordinaries (12.8) per 1,000 people than any other county in Maryland. Gould, *Money and Transportation,* pp. 147, 150.

47. Virtually moribund before 1730, Chestertown grew to well over 100 houses by the mid-1750s, and to about 200 houses by the Revolution. Reps, *Tidewater Towns,* pp. 111–14; Greene and Harrington, *American Population,* p. 134; "Fisher Journal," p. 795.

48. A typical Pennsylvania family farmer planted about ten acres in winter grain, which yielded 80 to 100 bushels. In these calculations, I take a bushel to be 60 pounds. Lemon, *The Best Poor Man's Country,* pp. 151–56. The output estimate for tobacco is based on yields of 1,000 pounds of tobacco per laborer, which was typical after the enactment in 1747 of Maryland's tobacco inspection system. Earle, *Evolution of a Tidewater Settlement System,* pp. 24–27; Papenfuse, "Planter Behavior and Economic Opportunity," pp. 305–6.

49. The transportation figure assumes that wagons hauled 22 hundredweight. A hogshead of tobacco weighed about 1,000 pounds after the mid-eighteenth century. Lewis Cecil Gray, *History of Agriculture in the Southern United States to 1860* (2 vols.; 1933; reprint, Gloucester, Mass., 1958), Vol. 1, p. 222. Pound for pound, wheat required less storage space than tobacco. One thousand pounds of wheat took up 20.7 cubic feet as compared

Chestertown merchants, no doubt, lacked the necessary storage capacity and housed much of the wheat on farms until the arrival of overseas orders. But once in town the storage of grains demanded utmost care, while tobacco entailed few precautions besides insuring that the hogsheads were not jostled and broken. Because the grain had to be bulk stored, any excessive moisture would cause "heating," a process which endangered the entire crop unless it was immediately and thoroughly dried. "Heating" also created a problem for wheat and corn destined for low-latitude markets since the grains frequently had to be sacked.[50] Even more caution was demanded for the West Indies where the heat and humidity prohibited the shipping of unprocessed grain and necessitated milling the wheat into flour and often even baking the bread before transport.[51]

Grain also demanded more shipping tonnage than tobacco. One hundred and thirty thousand bushels of wheat filled up 3,482 tons of shipping as compared to the 325 tons required for 1,300 hogsheads of tobacco, the equivalent output of a similar number of eastern shore farmers (four hogsheads took up one ton of shipping space). Equally important, much of the wheat, flour, and corn, especially that going to the West Indies, was sent in sloops and schooners of 100 tons or less because of marketing conditions in the Caribbean.[52] This required some 20 to 30 vessels a year. An equivalent amount of tobacco could have been hauled in one or two fair-sized ships. It can safely be surmised that grain attracted ten times more shipping tonnage and 20 to 30 more vessels per year than did tobacco. Furthermore, the grain ships (especially those destined for the West Indies) came throughout the year while the eighteenth-century tobacco fleet rarely remained more than several months. Because of this year-round trading activity, the port of Chestertown and even

to 22.2 cubic feet for a hogshead of tobacco weighing about 1,000 pounds. However, wheat volume was far greater when considered as the labor output of comparable hinterlands. Shepherd and Walton, *Shipping, Maritime Trade, and the Economic Development of Colonial North America*, p. 67.

50. Arthur Pierce Middleton, *Tobacco Coast: A Maritime History of Chesapeake Bay in the Colonial Era* (Newport News, Va.: Mariner's Museum, 1953), pp. 184, 195–96; Saladino, "The Maryland and Virginia Wheat Trade," pp. 53–55; Pamela Satek, "William Lux of Baltimore: 18th Century Merchant" (2 vols.; M.A. thesis, University of Maryland, 1974), Vol. 1, p. 696.

51. Customs 16/1, Public Record Office ms.

52. Middleton, *Tobacco Coast*, p. 184; Saladino, "The Maryland and Virginia Wheat Trade," p. 43. Larger vessels were employed in the southern European grain trade.

some lesser export centers soon developed allied industries in ship-building, repair, and chandlery.[53] In this manner, wheat and corn provided the forward linkages essential for port and inland urban development.

Towns developed in grain-producing regions for yet another reason besides the demands of export marketing and transportation. Wheat farmers, on the average, had more money to spend on urban goods and services than did their counterparts dependent on tobacco. Wheat far surpassed tobacco in profitability, except—and this is a big exception—under a system of labor where slaves were inherited and maintenance costs were low. Because the comparative economics of farming and planting involves numerous assumptions, calculations, and estimates, the formula for deriving net revenues from tobacco and wheat is placed in an Appendix for the interested reader or specialist. Only the final estimates, and their implications, are set forth here.

The net revenues from tobacco and wheat, after 1750, appear in Table 3.1. Wheat earned the highest return on the eastern shore, and wage labor was more efficient than slave labor. In the excellent price years for tobacco (1769) and wheat (1772), the tobacco planter using slave labor on the eastern shore earned net revenues of £1.07 for every pound sterling invested in production; on the western shore, where prices were higher, the return came to £1.49. The grain farmer paying day laborers earned £2.90. During the times of poorest market conditions, tobacco planters on neither shore cleared enough to cover costs, while grain farmers made £.83. In other words, the wheat farmer did nearly as well in his worst year as the tobacco planter in his best. Furthermore, over the period from 1750 to 1775 the grain producer did consistently better. For every pound sterling invested in production the wheat farmer earned £1.61 and the tobacco planter £.95.

Given the poor returns for tobacco planting, it must be asked why wheat culture, wage labor, and urban growth did not spill over into the lower western shore of Maryland and Virginia. Three factors precluded this regional economic change. Tobacco plantations in this

53. Fifteen vessels cleared from Chestertown for foreign destinations in 1769. Nine of these went to southern Europe and six to the British West Indies. Robert L. Swain, "Chestertown as a Colonial Port, 1706–1775," *Washington College Bulletin* 14 (1936), p. 14. Owing to the disparities in staple weight, bulk, and perishability already discussed, the proportion of the wholesale price devoted to marketing (the marketing margin) amounted to about 30 percent in the case of wheat and less than 10 percent in the case of tobacco.

TABLE 3.1

Gross Revenues, Production Costs, and Net Revenues in Wheat and Tobacco in Maryland After 1750

(In pounds sterling)

	Highest Prices			Lowest prices			Aggregate for 1750–75		
	Tobacco[a] (1769)		Wheat[b] (1772)	Tobacco[a] (1755)		Wheat[b] (1757)	Tobacco—western shore		Wheat
	Eastern shore	Western shore		Eastern shore	Western shore		Wage labor	Slave labor	
Gross revenues	7.42	9.29	24.00	2.83	3.54	11.45	158.66	158.66	418.05
Production costs	3.59	3.59	6.20	3.59	3.59	6.26	93.34	81.25	159.90
Net revenues	3.83	5.70	17.80	−.76	−.05	5.19	65.32	77.41	258.15
Net revenues/costs	1.07	1.49	2.90	−.21	−.01	.83	.70	.95	1.61

[a] Produced by slave labor.
[b] Produced by wage labor.

region were competitive with wheat because slave labor had low maintenance costs, because slaves produced non-tobacco revenues, and, most important, because tobacco prices were 25 to 100 percent higher than on the eastern shore. Slave labor was thus the rational economic choice for tobacco planters, especially since the crop required almost daily attendance, although the hours involved in any single day were generally few. The use of wage laborers, always hired by the day rather than by the year, would have been prohibitive. Because of the prevailing wage rates and the number of days required in tobacco production, a day laborer's costs would have greatly exceeded that of an inherited slave, who required no initial outlay and maintenance expenditures of about £3 per year.[54] Tobacco produced by slaves rather than wage laborers, for the period 1750 to 1775, yielded a gain of over one-third in net revenues per unit of input.

The gap between wheat and tobacco revenues narrows even further when other activities such as corn production are credited along with the higher tobacco prices prevailing on the western shore. Assuming that the average slave produced eight barrels of corn in conjunction with 1,000 pounds of tobacco, the net revenues of each pound invested in production would climb to £1.59, a return close to that earned from wheat produced with wage labor.[55] This narrow margin did not justify the abandonment of tobacco and slavery on Maryland's western shore.

For these reasons, prosperous wheat farmers and towns skirted the edge of the tobacco coast. Because of their high levels of expendable income and their more egalitarian distribution of income and wealth, wheat-farming regions linked the farmers all the more tightly to the towns where they sold their grain. After 1750, the average wheat producers accumulated over twice the amount of disposable income attained by tobacco planters. Moreover, because wheat was produced by family and wage labor whose availability put a ceiling on the amount of wheat acreage and farm size, this staple encouraged a more even distribution of farm income and a uniformity of demand unknown in tobacco regions.[56] With their augmented and

54. This is the estimate given in Harry J. Carman, ed., *American Husbandry* (Port Washington, N.Y.: Kennikat Press, 1964), pp. 164, 252. A detailed comparison of the economics of slave and wage labor in the culture of wheat, tobacco, cotton, and corn appears in the Appendix and in Chapter 6.

55. Gray, *History of Agriculture*, Vol. 1, p. 219.

56. On wealth patterns for wheat and tobacco regions, compare Earle, *Evolution of a Tidewater Settlement System*, pp. 114–19; and James T. Lemon and Gary B. Nash, "The

uniform consumption power and their need for staple marketing facilities, Maryland wheat farmers provided brisk demands for imported or locally produced commodities, for transport services, and for the other social and cultural amenities offered in urban places.

In Virginia the shift to grain and diversified commodities resulted in a similar rise of urban places, including one large port, Norfolk. Before the spread of commercial grain culture, Norfolk's early years were singularly unimpressive. Both tobacco traders and the yearly tobacco fleet bypassed Norfolk's commodious deep-water harbor in favor of roadsteads located on the York River in the midst of the high-quality sweet-scented tobacco region.[57] Authorized by an act of the Assembly in 1680, the town recorded few accomplishments distinguishing it from other tidewater communities in its first half century.[58] Because of its location on the Elizabeth River a few tobacco purchasers resided there. As a designated political and social center—a church and court house had been erected by 1700—it attracted a few additional persons, including some craftsmen, mechanics, and traders, by the century's second decade. Still, until 1720 Hampton and Yorktown were definitely more important places of trade.[59]

But then the commercial picture changed swiftly as these ports steadily fell behind Norfolk. Impressed by what he saw in 1728—the town had already extended its boundaries—William Byrd declared that Norfolk "has most the air of a town of any in Virginia. It is not a town of ordinaries and public houses like most in this country, but

Distribution of Wealth in Eighteenth-Century America: A Century of Change in Chester County, Pennsylvania, 1693–1802," *Journal of Social History* 2 (1968), pp. 1–24. Also see Darrett B. Rutman and Anita H. Rutman, *A Place in Time: Middlesex County, Virginia, 1650–1750* (New York: W. W. Norton, 1984); Gloria L. Main, *Tobacco Colony: Life in Early Maryland* (Princeton, N.J.: Princeton University Press, 1982); Alice Hanson Jones, "Wealth Estimates for the Southern Colonies about 1770," (paper presented at the Annual Meeting of the Organization of American Historians, Chicago, 1973), pp. 1–35; *idem, Wealth of a Nation to Be: The American Colonies on the Eve of the Revolution* (New York: Columbia University Press, 1980); and the data, though not always the argument, of Jackson Turner Main, *The Social Structure of Revolutionary America* (Princeton, N.J.: Princeton University Press, 1965), pp. 7–67.

57. Middleton, *Tobacco Coast*, p. 98; Coulter, "The Virginia Merchant," pp. 43–44.

58. Thomas J. Wertenbaker, *Norfolk: Historic Southern Port*, ed. Marvin W. Schlegel, 2nd ed. (Durham, N.C.: Duke University Press, 1962), pp. 5–8.

59. Norfolk in 1705 had 30 to 50 lot-owners and a population of 200 to 300, which probably made it a lesser town than the thriving ports of Hampton and Yorktown. Wertenbaker, *Norfolk*, p. 508; Rogers D. Whichard, *The History of Lower Tidewater Virginia* (3 vols.; New York: Lewis Historical Publishing Co., 1959), Vol. 1, pp. 324–50; Moss, "The Virginia Plantation," pp. 435–36.

the inhabitants consist of merchants, ship carpenters and other useful artisans with sailors enough to manage navigation."[60] At Norfolk wharves he recorded seeing twenty brigantines and sloops unloading West Indian rum and loading flour, beef, pork, and lumber. Byrd had exactly defined the economic base that would characterize Norfolk until the Revolution. Already free of the tobacco economy, the town had turned to the West Indian trade. As Norfolk's population expanded in the 1730s, life and landscape became more complex. In 1736 the town acquired borough status and gained a mayor, a council, aldermen, and representation in the Virginia Assembly. Other changes followed incorporation, including the addition of a market house, school, and borough church. Most important, in 1739 the town's merchants succeeded in having the area's customs collector and deputy naval office transferred from Port Hampton across the James to Norfolk, an obvious recognition of the community's growing importance in Virginia's new commerce.[61] For the next 25 years the town matured steadily; its boundaries were enlarged in 1757 and 1761, and its population by the mid-1760s was in the neighborhood of 3,000.[62]

In 1764 Governor Francis Fauquier nicely conceptualized the relationship between Norfolk's moderate growth and the West Indies grain trade: "The town of Norfolk and James River having almost wholly engrossed the West India and grain trade—but in the whole it does gradually tho not greatly increase."[63] But at the very moment that Fauquier wrote Norfolk verged on a period of dynamic expan-

60. Considerable expansion occurred during the 1720s, when the town gained its first suburban development and swine were prohibited from roaming the streets. Yet the town's precarious existence was dramatized when Byrd's surveying party of 1728 camped at the edge of town, for fear of causing a famine by the arrival of so many people. John Spencer Bassett, ed., *The Writings of Colonel William Byrd of Westover in Virginia, Esqr.* (New York: Doubleday, 1970), p. 28.

61. Probably 1,000 persons lived in town by 1740. Wertenbaker, *Norfolk*, pp. 5–9. In securing a deputy naval office from Hampton, on the north side of the James River, Norfolk townsmen argued that their side of the river owned 30 sloops compared to 3 for the Hampton side. Moss, "The Virginia Plantation," pp. 437–38.

62. Reps, *Tidewater Towns*, p. 216. Whichard, *The History of Lower Tidewater Virginia*, Vol. 1, pp. 371–83. In 1765, Norfolk contained over 400 houses. Lord Adam Gordon, "Journal of an Officer who travelled in America and the West Indies in 1764–1765," in *Travels in the American Colonies*, ed. Newton D. Mereness (New York: Macmillan, 1916), p. 406.

63. "Answers to the Queries sent to us by the right honorable the Lds. Comrs for Trade and Plantation Affairs from Gov. Francis Fauquier," Jan. 30, 1764, Customs 5/1330, f. 265a, Public Record Office ms.

sion. Within ten to twelve years it more than doubled in size. As of 1776 the town contained 1,300 houses, numerous warehouses, a complex occupational structure that emphasized mercantile and shipping industries, and a population of around 6,000 to 6,500. Among the cities of British North America it ranked fifth, and it was the largest city in the Chesapeake.[64]

Norfolk's flourishing condition depended primarily on trade with the West Indies, a market of very specific and exacting requirements. In the Caribbean large volumes of foodstuffs could not be imported because of the extreme perishability of food in the region's tropical heat and humidity. As a result, mainland traders to the Indies dispatched small schooners and sloops on frequent runs throughout the year.[65] Norfolk's critical asset lay, in the words of one observer, in its "centrical position." To be precise, Norfolk's central location on the eastern seaboard near the mouth of the Chesapeake Bay made it a strategic reception point for intelligence regarding market conditions throughout the Atlantic arena.

Because of the town's proximity to the West Indies, Norfolk's merchants normally obtained these reports several days before their competitors in Baltimore, Philadelphia, and New York. Similarly,

64. In the 1776 burning of Norfolk, 1,331 houses, nearly all of the structures in the town, were destroyed. Virginia General Assembly, *Journal and Reports of the Commissioners appointed by the act of 1777, to ascertain the losses occasioned to individuals by the burning of Norfolk and Portsmouth, in the Year 1776* (Document no. 43, Richmond, Va., 1836), pp. 1–23. 1776 population estimates vary between 6,000 and 6,250, which figures rank the town of Norfolk behind Philadelphia, New York, Boston, and Charleston. By some estimates, Norfolk also ranked behind Newport, Rhode Island. The ranking excludes New Haven, Connecticut, which included rural and urban populations within its limits. Wertenbaker, *Norfolk*, p. 47. Carl Bridenbaugh, *Cities in Revolt: Urban Life in America, 1743–1776* (New York: Knopf, 1955), pp. 216–17; William S. Rossiter, *A Century of Population Growth 1790–1900* (Washington, D.C.: GPO, 1909), pp. 11–15.

65. The typical cargo of vessels clearing from the lower James River for the West Indies in March–June 1756 consisted of 31 barrels of pork, 1,878 bushels of corn, and 90 bushels of peas, along with odd lots of lumber products, livestock, beef, and candles. According to the lower James's customs lists for 1730–31 and 1755–56, more than 47 percent of all vessels cleared for the West Indies. Of these, 89 percent or more left Virginia between Christmas and September 24. Spring was the peak quarter for West Indian sailings—about 40 percent left then. In summer sailings fell off, but corn exports remained high. Trade slackened in the autumn quarter, but unpredictable droughts or hurricanes in the Indies occasionally generated a flurry of trade. Customs 5/1443, ff. 58, 66, 85, and Customs 5/1447, ff. 26, 44–46, Public Record Office; Malcolm C. Clark, "The Coastwise and Caribbean Trade of the Chesapeake Bay, 1696–1776" (Ph.D. diss., Georgetown University, 1970), pp. 85–111. On perishability in the West Indies, see Richard Pares, *Yankees and Creoles: The Trade between North America and the West Indies before the American Revolution* (Cambridge: Cambridge University Press, 1956), pp. 84–85.

their vessels generally enjoyed a valuable head start in the race to be first to a volatile market. For the West Indies, where, more than in any other staple market, demand shifted with extraordinary speed, accurate information was imperative. At the start of a week an island's food supply could be perilously short, and yet by its end, if too many ships converged simultaneously, its markets might well become glutted. Those who arrived first made fine profits, while the last vessels, late by only a few days, often had to scurry elsewhere in search of a sale as their cargoes wasted below.[66]

Norfolk enjoyed still another advantage in the Caribbean trade, an ice-free harbor, which gave the city's merchants a near monopoly during the winter quarter. Farther north, in Baltimore and Philadelphia, frequent freezes in December and January brought their West Indies business to a halt, while Norfolk's mercantile men lay ready to ship whenever a demand arose. Because of this condition, traders in both Baltimore and Philadelphia frequently sent flour and other commodities to commission merchants in Norfolk for export in the cold months.[67]

But Norfolk's spectacular success resulted from more than just its mild climate and fortuitous position as a receiving center of commercial intelligence. Located in an economically diverse region, the town drew a wide range of goods demanded in the Caribbean. From sandy, poor tobacco lands to the south and east came tar, pitch, and turpentine. The Dismal Swamp area provided hardwoods, clapboard shingles, staves, and heading. Farther south, from the Albemarle region of North Carolina and from some sectors of Virginia as well, drovers brought herds of livestock for slaughtering, barreling, and shipping. Other commodities flowing into Norfolk from the immediate environs included tobacco, deerskins, beaver, fur hides, tallow, wax, feathers, butter, and cheese.[68] For its most important grain export, corn—by 1770 Norfolk led all mainland ports in shipping this commodity—the town pulled from a wide zone. Almost one-third of

66. The rapid shifts in West Indian markets, and the higher risks entailed in serving them, are detailed in *ibid.*, pp. 65–91; and Jensen, *The Maritime Commerce of Colonial Philadelphia*, pp. 42–56. Norfolk vessels destined for the West Indies had an advantage of one to two days over those from Alexandria and the Potomac Valley. *The Journal of Nicholas Cresswell, 1774–1777* (Port Washington, N.Y.: Kennikat Press, 1968), pp. 30–31.

67. Saladino, "The Maryland and Virginia Wheat Trade," pp. 56–57; Middleton, *Tobacco Coast*, p. 45; Satek, "William Lux," Vol. 1, pp. 321–24. For Lux's dealings with Norfolk merchants, see Satek, Vol. 2, pp. 430, 435, 473–76, 520.

68. Merrens, *Colonial North Carolina*, pp. 134–35, 247. Wertenbaker, *Norfolk*, pp. 34–35.

its corn came from Virginia's eastern shore, the rest from the James River valley and nearby sections of North Carolina.[69] Wheat and flour came from even more distant sources, since Norfolk never developed a large milling industry because the wheat raised in its surrounding area was of poor quality and went for local consumption. Instead, the city's merchants purchased these products from other ports, especially Baltimore and Alexandria. These two towns preferred to ship their grain directly, but in the winter quarter they depended on Norfolk.[70]

Through a combination of persistence, hard work, and an occasional gamble, Norfolk's mercantile community made the city a vital import as well as export center. By the 1760s her merchants distributed a wide variety of West Indian and European goods. To facilitate these flows, regular linkages were established throughout the bay with monthly and even weekly runs to the key ports of Alexandria and Baltimore. As an Alexandria shipper observed, "We have very little intercourse with York. . . . Goods may lay there a year if a vessel is not sent for them . . . but [we] have weekly opportunities of picking up goods at either Hampton or Norfolk."[71]

All of this good fortune abruptly halted with Norfolk's destruction in 1776. The British and patriot fire literally leveled the town. Her merchant property—warehouses, wharves, ships, stores—burned to a cinder. So, too, the shelling ruined Norfolk's second basic industry, shipbuilding and refitting. Norfolk's sizable economic stake in this business sector stretched back over 40 years, having developed in tandem with the West Indies trade. Indeed, these two enterprises, by

69.   Corn exports from the lower James for 1768–72 averaged 286,000 bushels a year compared to Philadelphia's exports of 200,000 bushels or less. In 1768, Norfolk's exports of 330,000 bushels of corn were more than double that of any other Chesapeake port, and exceeded Maryland's total corn export volume. During the early 1770s, an estimated 100,000 bushels of corn exported from Norfolk came from the eastern shore. Customs 16/1, Public Record Office; Papenfuse, "Economic Analysis," p. 194.

70.   The extraordinary volume of corn and wheat going through Norfolk in the early 1770s evidently overtaxed the town's storage facilities, and one merchant, Neil Jamieson, had his outlying factors purchase wheat and corn with the condition that they be stored on the seller's farm until needed in Norfolk. James H. Soltow, *The Economic Role of Williamsburg* (Williamsburg, Va.: Colonial Williamsburg, 1965), pp. 93–94.

71.   John Carlyle of Alexandria, merchant, to George Washington, Sept. 1, 1758, quoted in Coulter, "The Virginia Merchant," p. 61. The frequency of Chesapeake vessels coming to Norfolk translated into lower freight rates, according to Neil Jamieson, and loading was performed there both more cheaply and more speedily than at other Chesapeake ports. Neil Jamieson to Robert Alexander, May 11, 1781, quoted in Soltow, *The Economic Role of Williamsburg*, p. 90.

complementing one another, had propelled the town beyond its urban competitors. The cumulative growth process had begun when Norfolk first entered the Caribbean market. From the beginning that commerce proved ship-intensive, with the amount of tonnage and the number of bottoms demanded by the islands' corn trade far outstripping the comparable needs of tobacco transport. Because of Norfolk's Caribbean traffic, the town attracted 10 times more shipping tonnage and 20 to 30 times more vessels than any of the existing tobacco ports. Naturally, this concentration of vessels stimulated chandlery, refitting, and eventually construction businesses that expanded considerably during the century's second and third quarters. With the destruction of the town in 1776, the total loss sustained by people engaged in shipbuilding and allied occupations fell just slightly below that of the merchants, though the average personal loss was far less since many more persons worked in ship construction and servicing trades.[72]

Norfolk's merchants, having ridden a spectacular wave of prosperity, mourned deeply their town's destruction—the golden age of commerce they had foreseen suddenly laid waste in a hail of fire. But their vision, though seductive, was wrong. In truth, there would not have been a time of enormous riches even if the British had never sailed up Hampton Roads. Norfolk's comparative trade position within the Chesapeake had actually begun to decline a decade or two earlier. Other ports up the bay were cutting deep inroads into the town's commercial zone. Norfolk had, in commanding fashion, appropriated the exportation of corn, but in wheat and flour, commodities of far more value, her position had increasingly worsened. Compared to Norfolk, Baltimore exported two-and-one-half times more wheat and ten times more flour. Chestertown equaled Norfolk in the value of wheat exports and shipped more flour. And Alexandria, a very young port, already by the 1760s matched Norfolk in

72. On the relation of grain volume and shipping, see note 53, this chapter. Norfolk and its environs took an early lead in the shipping industry, and between 1700 and 1750 the area contained 81 percent of Virginia's mariners and about 59 percent of the ship carpenters. Moss, "The Virginia Plantation," pp. 371–72. According to Fauquier, Norfolk-built vessels commonly were sold along with their cargoes in the West Indies. Customs 5/ 1330, f. 265a, Public Record Office ms. After Norfolk's destruction in 1776, the shipping industry accounted for 51.3 percent of the claimants giving their occupation to Customs officials, while merchants accounted for 22.7 percent. The former included 35 mariners, 20 carpenters, 6 ship carpenters, 5 blacksmiths, 4 blockmakers, 4 joiners, 2 sailmakers, a chandler, a coppersmith, and a cooper. Their total property loss (38.5 percent) fell just below the 39.5 percent claimed by the smaller merchant community. Virginia General Assembly, *Journal and Reports*, pp. 1–23.

both wheat and flour.[73] When ordered by the total value of their corn, wheat, and flour exports in the years just preceding the Revolution, Norfolk's value was two-fifths that of Baltimore, about one-and-one-half times greater than Chestertown's, and approximately double Alexandria's.[74]

Several conditions accounted for Norfolk's relative decline in a time when the town, ironically, experienced its most vigorous period of expansion and prosperity. The single most important cause was the enormous European demand for wheat, occasioned by the continent's successively poor harvests. With the establishment of this market, the merchants of Baltimore and Alexandria, who serviced the trade, lost the need for Norfolk's ice-free harbor, since sales to the Continent were regularly conducted during the spring and summer months. Similarly, the time saved by shipping from Norfolk, a major factor in the Caribbean trade, counted for little when dealing with southern Europe.[75]

A second important factor in the erosion of Norfolk's position was the collapse of the beef and pork trade in the 1760s. Traditionally, these exports had been extremely important for the West Indies. During the mid-1740s and early 1750s this commerce possibly carried a value for Virginia second only to tobacco. At the trade's height in the 1740s some 40,000 barrels of beef and pork were shipped annually. Yet by 1768 meat exports had fallen precipitously to just 4,573 barrels valued at less than £11,000.[76] The causes of this surprising reversal are not clear. Perhaps home consumption diverted

73. Norfolk's yearly exports from 1768 to 1772 amounted to 286,000 bushels of corn, 97,000 bushels of wheat, and 1,173 tons of flour. Baltimore in 1774 exported about 240,000 bushels of wheat and 120,000 barrels of flour. In the same year, Chestertown sent out 50,000 bushels of corn, 100,000 bushels of wheat, and 20,000 barrels of flour, and Alexandria exported about 100,000 bushels of wheat and 14,000 barrels of flour. Customs 16/1, Public Record Office ms.; Papenfuse, "Economic Analysis," p. 194; *The Journal of Nicholas Cresswell*, p. 27.

74. The comparative export values, based on Philadelphia wholesale prices in 1770 and the quantities given in note 73, are Baltimore, £148,776; Norfolk, £61,381; Chestertown, £42,366; and Alexandria, £32,099. For prices, see *Historical Statistics*, Part 2, pp. 772–73.

75. On the rapid growth of the enormous southern European grain trade, see Hoffman, *A Spirit of Dissension*, chaps. 2 and 4; Saladino, "The Maryland and Virginia Wheat Trade," pp. 91–122; and Middleton, *Tobacco Coast*, pp. 178–212.

76. During the 1740s, half these exports went to the West Indies and half to Portugal and the Madeira Islands. Gray, *History of Agriculture*, Vol. 1, pp. 209–10. In 1768, the West Indies market was the only important destination for Chesapeake pork and beef. Customs 16/1, Public Record Office. Virginia's beef and pork earnings for the mid-1740s totalled over £80,000.

some of the beef and pork away from export, but a more likely explanation may involve the crisis that struck Southern meat producers
in the 1760s. During that decade a combination of raging cattle dis-
temper and severe, recurrent winter droughts killed vast numbers of
animals, though the precise figures cannot be determined.[77] The immediate implication for Norfolk, a town that enjoyed an excellent
reputation for its high-quality meat, was critical. To reconstitute the
depleted herds would have taken years, and in the interval, if the
corn and commodity trades to the West Indies had suddenly failed,
hard times would certainly have hit Norfolk.[78]

To the north a new and more stable merchant community, Baltimore, had no such worries. If, upon close examination, the Chesapeake's first large port revealed signs of slippage because of a shaky
commercial foundation, its successor enjoyed rock-bottom stability.
Had the war not destroyed Norfolk, Baltimore would still have become the tidewater's leading commercial center, although the war
did accelerate the transformation. Baltimore's location in the fall
zone near the rich western wheat country ensured its ultimate ascendancy. One traveler, J. F. D. Smythe, on the eve of the Revolution
understood this perfectly. Despite substantial surface improvement,
Norfolk, he noted, "was by no means in such a state of increase and
improvement as the more inland towns, at or near the falls of the
great rivers; these being the chief emporiums of trade and commerce
for the large, populous, and extensive back country . . . and, having
also all the advantages of navigation, intercept the inland trade from
Norfolk, which renders it flourishing, yet only so in an inferior
degree."[79]

Baltimore's rise resulted from a series of interrelated factors in-
volving the extension of backcountry settlement, the expansion of the
European wheat trade, and the pattern of competition and cooperation that developed with Philadelphia. From its founding in 1729
until the 1750s, Baltimore, located on the northwest branch of the

77. In one Chesapeake parish during the 1760s, the average household's hog population fell by 47 percent, cattle by 45 percent, sheep by 33 percent, and horses by 22
percent. Earle, *Evolution of a Tidewater Settlement System*, pp. 124–26. For suggestive hints
at the causes of livestock deaths, see *Maryland Gazette*, April 7, 1768, and August 3, 1769;
and Jack P. Greene, ed., *The Diary of Landon Carter of Sabine Hall* (Charlottesville, Va.:
University Press of Virginia, 1965), pp. 290, 293.

78. Norfolk had one more handicap. The town's excellent harbor attracted British
naval vessels, which in turn discouraged smuggling into and out of Norfolk. Satek, "William Lux," Vol. 2, pp. 458–59.

79. J. F. D. Smythe, *A Tour in the United States of America*, Vol. 1, pp. 10–11.

Patapsco River, remained a small, undistinguished town exporting some tobacco and a variety of other standard commodities. As in the case of Norfolk, the area's immediate environs were poorly adapted for commercial agriculture. The paltry soils around the city produced "mean" tobacco and unexceptional wheat. To the north and east a region of treeless "barrens" predominated, which farmers believed were unsuited for cropping and fit only for rearing livestock. At Elkridge, ten to fifteen miles southwest of the town, fine "bright" tobaccos were raised, but these were exported from local landings in that vicinity.[80]

Beginning in the 1740s Baltimore's economic horizons gradually began to improve. The backcountry had begun to fill as families settled with the intention of raising some tobacco, but mainly wheat. Already the price of wheat had started to climb, and from the first years of settlement the farmers raised bumper crops. Soon the rich limestone valleys of western Maryland that bordered along the Monocacy became a commercial wheat zone of considerable importance. In marketing their produce the region's settlers selected from among three tidewater ports—Georgetown on the Potomac, Annapolis on the Severn, or Baltimore. The latter easily prevailed.[81]

During the 1750s and 1760s Baltimore's merchants fashioned a stunning victory over their rivals. Simultaneously they consolidated the wheat trade of the Monocacy with that of central and western Pennsylvania. Also they began vying with Philadelphia for the Delmarva Peninsula trade, and before the Revolution they had managed to capture 15 to 20 percent of that market.[82] Several factors contributed to Baltimore's success. Of the various Maryland ports, its superior location, near Pennsylvania farmers west of the Susquehanna River and adjacent to the western wheat country, enabled the city to attract trade and investment capital. William Lux, a prominent Bal-

80. Hoffman, *A Spirit of Dissension*, chap. 4; Clarence P. Gould, "The Economic Causes of the Rise of Baltimore," in *Essays in Colonial History Presented to Charles McLean Andrews* (New Haven: Yale University Press, 1931), pp. 225–51; J. Thomas Scharf, *The Chronicles of Baltimore* (Baltimore, 1874), pp. 18–51.

81. Gould, "The Economic Causes," pp. 227–32. Aubrey C. Land, "A Land Speculator in the Opening of Western Maryland," *Maryland Historical Magazine* 48 (1953), pp. 191–203. Baltimore grew rapidly after 1752, when there were 25 houses; by 1764, there were 200 houses; by 1768, 350 houses; and by 1774, 564 houses and 5,935 persons. Satek, "William Lux," Vol. 2, p. 768; Arthur E. Karinen, "Numerical and Distributional Aspects of Maryland Population, 1631–1840" (Ph.D. diss., University of Maryland, 1958), pp. 197, 200, 205.

82. Hoffman, *A Spirit of Dissension*, chap. 4; Papenfuse, "Economic Analysis," p. 194.

timore merchant, focused on his locational advantage while courting a prospective buyer in 1767:

> The situation of our town to an extensive back country, which is now well cultivated and from which we draw large quantities of wheat, flour and flaxseed, renders it fair for a place of considerable trade. We have this season loaded many vessels and our prices have been encouraging. We think we can venture to assure you that we can always load these articles on easier terms than at Philadelphia or New York which have heretofore been the principal marts for those commodities. As proof of this we ourselves shipped three cargoes of wheat for a house in London which does not average 4/sterling per bushel. The lateness of the orders and the great increase of shipping has now rendered cargoes difficult to be procured so that at this time [we] could not give you the same dispatch to vessels that they can at Philadelphia. But we think this well compensated by the difference of price.[83]

With the grain trade soaring in the mid-1760s and with investment capital flowing steadily into the city from Philadelphia and abroad, Baltimore rapidly became the foremost flour milling center of the Chesapeake. Mills and millers proliferated everywhere—so many that the town's flour exports totaled over 100,000 barrels by the Revolution.[84] Economic considerations dictated the concentration of flour milling in Baltimore rather than in the producing back-country hinterlands. Simply put, the western farmers earned more by shipping wheat than by having it converted to flour. Even with flour prices higher than wheat, the differences were more than offset by milling, barreling, and wagon costs and the weight losses sustained in conversion (see Appendix). Only in two years, 1741 and 1762, would farmers have found it more profitable to send flour, and then only if they resided at distances from the city of 43 to 48 miles. Otherwise, a coastal milling location was clearly best for farmers. The town's merchants also preferred this pattern since it allowed them more options. They could export the wheat in bulk, mill it locally

83. Satek, "William Lux," Vol. 2, pp. 688–89.

84. In the fall of 1765, Lux observed that Baltimore exported more than 30,000 bushels of wheat and that the mills in the vicinity of Baltimore had "ground near as much." Satek, "William Lux," Vol. 2, pp. 503–4. One estimate claims that Baltimore exported nearly 120,000 barrels of flour by the Revolution, but I suspect this to be a generous estimate. Papenfuse, "Economic Analysis," p. 194.

into flour, or even make it into bread, depending upon the foreign demand.[85]

Baltimore would eventually rival Philadelphia, New York, and Boston in influence. Expanding constantly throughout the Revolutionary War, Baltimore cut deeply into the Delmarva trade zone controlled by Philadelphia, and this pattern, continuing after the conflict, enabled the city to expand substantially. But fundamentally Baltimore's commercial foundation was still the western wheat country. Indeed, before Baltimore could ever begin to grow, the backcountry had to be commercialized and its vast agricultural riches funneled to the coast. And again, in these economic developments, towns—this time backcountry towns—were critically important. Before there could be a Baltimore there had to be a Frederick and a Winchester.

During the 1740s two decades of intensive urban growth got under way. Far from the coast a number of backcountry towns began to develop. In a veritable wilderness they appeared and expanded with great speed until the 1760s, and then their pace of expansion slowed. But almost as if by reflex a similar burst of urban construction commenced eastward. Located along the fall zone, a series of towns servicing the expansive markets of Europe emerged, one of which was Baltimore. And soon the newer communities surpassed their backcountry counterparts, as dozens of western centers were consolidated into recognizable hinterlands.

First the backcountry towns must be examined. From Maryland to South Carolina they grew with unprecedented speed. By the 1750s a series of distinct clusters dotted the migratory corridor known popularly as the "Great Wagon Road." As the migrants and travelers of that decade swung south from Pennsylvania before the lofty Blue Ridge front, they first encountered the fertile Monocacy Valley and Frederick, a community started by early settlers in the late 1740s. "This town," wrote an army officer in 1755, "has not been settled above seven years [it was actually ten years old] and there are about 200 houses and two churches, one English, one Dutch. The inhabitants, chiefly Dutch [in fact they were mostly German], are industrious but imposing people; here we got plenty of provisions and for-

---

85. The locational economics of flour milling and its zones of profitability are discussed in the Appendix. Further information on other economic activities in Baltimore can be found in the appendices of Ronald Hoffman, "Economics, Politics and the Revolution in Maryland" (Ph.D. diss., University of Wisconsin, 1969), pp. 389–441.

age."[86] What the officer might also have noticed was that Frederick was already Maryland's largest town. Baltimore, of course, would soon overtake it, but never Annapolis, the capital city of some 60 years.[87] Farther south into Virginia's Shenandoah Valley, travelers passed through a string of towns all built either in the 1740s or in the 1750s: Mecklenburg, Martinsburg, Winchester, Stephensburg, Strasburg, Woodstock, and Staunton. The most important of these communities, Winchester, after little more than a decade, equaled Williamsburg and was half the size of Norfolk.[88] South of the Great Valley in the Carolina piedmont, another series of smaller towns developed from the late 1740s: Salem, Hillsborough, Salisbury, Charlotte, Camden, and Orangeburg.

The establishment of one of these communities, the North Carolina town of Salisbury, exemplifies most of the critical factors associated with backcountry urbanization. Salisbury, located on the northwest Carolina frontier, was formally created in 1755. Its official founding came a little less than ten years after the first migrants had entered the area. From their initial entry the entire region exploded, as swarms of new settlers arrived each year, many of them possessing capital and diverse skills reminiscent of their seventeenth-century counterparts. Reverend James Maury, while watching many of them pass from Virginia, recorded that "these are not the idler and the vagrant pests of society . . . but the honest and industrious, men of worth and property, whom it is an evil at any time to a community to lose."[89] When Salisbury's survey took place, the wider area already contained a complex and diverse occupational structure.

86. Quoted in Gould, "The Economic Causes," p. 229.
87. Annapolis probably numbered about 150 houses in 1760. Reverend Andrew Burnaby, *Travels through the Middle Settlements in North America in the years 1759 and 1760* . . . , 2nd ed. (Ithaca, N.Y.: Great Seal Books, 1960), p. 46.
88. Winchester grew from a small village of about 60 houses in 1753 to nearly 200 houses by 1760. Frederic Morton, *The Story of Winchester in Virginia* (Strasburg, Va., 1925), p. 85. On other backcountry settlements, see Robert D. Mitchell, "The Upper Shenandoah Valley of Virginia during the Eighteenth Century: A Study in Historical Geography" (Ph.D. diss., University of Wisconsin, 1969), pp. 231–36; and *idem*, *Commercialism and Frontier: Perspectives on the Early Shenandoah Valley* (Charlottesville: University Press of Virginia, 1977). Meanwhile, Williamsburg numbered about 200 houses in 1759. The capital, however, swelled to 5,000 to 6,000 persons during court times. Burnaby, *Travels*, p. 4; "Journal of a French Traveller in the Colonies, 1765," *American Historical Review* 26 (1921), p. 742.
89. "Emigration from Virginia to North Carolina and other Southern Colonies: Letter of James Maury to Hon. Philip Ludwell," *William and Mary Quarterly*, 1st ser., 14 (1905), p. 96.

Within the town's borders specifically, there resided two innkeepers
and a man who combined the professions of a millwright, surveyor,
and attorney. And shortly after the survey's completion, lots were
taken out by more innkeepers, another attorney, a potter, a carpenter, a blacksmith, a surgeon, a miller, a butcher, a tailor, a candle-
maker, and possibly a weaver. Most of these people were apparently
already in the vicinity, probably farming, as were the three school-
masters, one of whom may have held a university degree. Others
moved into Salisbury within the next several years, including a doc-
tor, several merchants and lawyers, a hatter, a tailor, and a wagon-
maker. All of this town settlement occurred, it should be emphasized,
within the short space of fourteen years after the first settler set foot
in the region.[90]

The experience of Salisbury and the entire northwestern Carolina region suggests that some of the more cherished traditional concepts of the colonial frontier may be misleading. Undoubtedly, those
people who came were a tough breed, but they were not the isolated
and rough-hewn yeomen described by Frederick Jackson Turner.
According to the Turnerian explanation, commercial life on the
frontier progressed in stages from woodsmen to livestock drovers to
self-sufficient farmers to commercial agrarians and townsmen. In his
view, during the early stages of settlement, towns were not present,
and hardy frontiersmen sustained themselves in a very self-reliant
manner. But, at least in the Carolinas, the lonely frontiersmen living
apart from all urban contacts never existed in any significant number. Nor were the people of the region necessarily the illiterate rabble
portrayed in the emotional and widely read writings of Reverend
Charles Woodmason. These were families of substance, with a desire
to establish town society on the frontier. One clergyman who visited
the area accurately described its inhabitants as "serious and judicious" people.[91]

Another factor, often ignored and extremely important for the
colonial frontier, was the region's dense population. Frequently the

90. Robert W. Ramsey, *Carolina Cradle: Settlement of the Northwest Carolina Frontier,
1747–1762* (Chapel Hill, N.C.: University of North Carolina Press, 1964), pp. 152, 154,
157–58, 166–69, 171, 190, 195. Ramsey's study, though conceptually unfocused, contains
impressive detail on the character of backcountry settlement.

91. "Journal of Reverend Hugh M. Aden," in Rev. William Henry Foote, ed.,
Sketches of North Carolina . . . , (New York: R. Carter, 1846, reprinted 1965), p. 169. A
similar critique of the Turnerian view appears in Mitchell, *Commercialism and Frontier.*

backcountry has been conceived as sparsely populated, when in reality many of its environs contained a population density surpassing older coastal regions. Invariably most visitors to the Carolina piedmont commented on the numbers present and the rapidity with which it was populated. In the 1760s Reverend Woodmason recorded that the Carolina frontier was "most surprisingly thick settled beyond any spot in England of its extent—seldom less than 9, 10, 1200 assembled of a Sunday."[92] Similarly, one North Carolina governor, Josiah Martin, found settlement in the region "numerous beyond belief."[93]

Several factors help explain what was occurring, not only in Salisbury but throughout the entire Southern backcountry. Certainly, much of the settlement taking place during mid-century proceeded in accordance with some coordinated, though not formally rigid, plan. For the Salisbury area seven major families provided the nuclear foundation. Most were of some means—a few had been minor officials in other colonies—though none were really affluent. They moved to the location almost simultaneously and with the sure knowledge that they in turn would facilitate and profit from the settlers to follow. A majority of these later settlers migrated from well-established communities in Pennsylvania and Maryland and most had resided in the colonies for 30 years. Several nomadic types also came from the Shenandoah Valley, traveling, as it were, always slightly ahead of the larger groups.[94] The growth of their town, Salisbury, and others along the Great Wagon Road's migratory corridor thus resulted because they functioned as way stations for the flows of people moving southward.

Still, to isolate migration as a causal element of urban growth does not adequately explain why these towns emerged so rapidly between 1745 and 1763 or why their development slowed afterward. Before 1745 migration into the backcountry was small and sporadic, but that condition quickly changed as the economic depression of the 1740s hit the American colonies. Pennsylvanians and new immigrants of diverse nationalities and sectarian beliefs, along with tidewater Englishmen, disillusioned with tenancy and poverty in a to-

92. Richard Hooker, ed., *The Carolina Backcountry on the Eve of the Revolution: The Journal and Other Writings of Charles Woodmason, Anglican Itinerant* (Chapel Hill, N.C.: University of North Carolina Press, 1953), pp. 14, 23.
93. Quoted in Merrens, *Colonial North Carolina*, p. 163.
94. Ramsey, *Carolina Cradle*, p. 192; see also pp. 37, 70, 161–62, 173, 178, 201–2.

bacco economy, struck out for new opportunities, sacred and secular, to the south and west.[95] The first wave of settlers took up lands in Maryland and Virginia, and with their coming the towns of Frederick and Winchester were founded. For the next several years the pace of this movement stabilized. Then, in 1754, with the outbreak of the French and Indian War transforming the middle Atlantic backcountry into a terror-stricken battlefront, new settlers by the thousands began fleeing southward. They sought, first, refuge in the young towns and, ultimately, security in the Carolina piedmont, where conditions remained generally calm. During this period Frederick and Winchester sharply increased in size by offering both immediate protection and help in facilitating the southward flow. Nothing as intense as this stream of thousands had occurred in the colonial experience since the founding of Pennsylvania in the 1680s.

In a single week in 1756 "near three hundred persons passed Bedford Court House," read one report. Similarly, during the first nine months of that year, approximately 5,000 had crossed the ferry atGoochland County Court House and "great numbers are daily following and others preparing to follow in the spring."[96] Naturally this concentration spawned a new series of way stations and expanded those towns already established. The migratory stimulus ran long and hard. In 1763, nine years after the early fighting, a compassionate resient of Frederick recorded that "every day for some time past has offered the melancholy scene of poor distressed families driven downwards through this town with their effects, who have deserted their plantations for fear of falling into the cruel hands of our savage enemies."[97]

When the hostilities finally ended in 1763, a matrix of substantial towns—Frederick and Winchester had tripled in size—spanned the Great Wagon Road. Twenty to thirty miles, a day's journey by wagon, separated the larger towns, and tucked in between them were the smaller hamlets and villages that serviced the migrants during the

95. A useful summary of these developments appears in Carl Bridenbaugh, *Myths and Realities: Societies of the Colonial South* (New York: Atheneum, 1967), pp. 119–96.

96. "Emigration from Virginia to North Carolina," p. 95; W. L. Saunders, ed., *The Colonial Records of North Carolina* (10 vols.; Raleigh, N.C.: P. M. Hale, Printer to the State, 1886–90), Vol. 4, p. 1312.

97. T. J. C. Williams, *History of Frederick County, Maryland* (Baltimore: Regional Publishing Company, 1967), p. 40. See also "Reverend James Maury to Mr. John Fontaine, June 15, 1756," in Ann Maury, *Letters of a Huguenot Family*, trans. and comp. Rev. James Fontaine (Baltimore, 1967), p. 403.

day. With this linear urban network in place, migrant flows contracted somewhat and became less frenetic, with the result that these urban communities grew at slower rates. Peace on the frontier paradoxically threatened the economic base of these precocious backcountry towns.[98]

Peace also presaged an expansion of overseas trade that would rapidly mesh the networks of migrant towns into the commercial trading orbits of coastal and fall-zone ports. As wheat prices leapt upward in the 1760s, coastal merchants and backcountry farmers found mutual profit in the exchange of this bulky crop. Western roads were jammed with hundreds of wagons, hauling wheat as well as flax, hemp, and assorted crops. The frontier boomtowns of the 1750s, which had thrived on the westward flow of migrants, now serviced equally heavy eastward staple flows. Town inns and ordinaries bustled, and wagon repairmen flourished.

Frederick and York (Pennsylvania), both tributary to Baltimore, exemplified the new economic base of backcountry towns. Fifteen to twenty percent of their occupations serviced the heavy wagon traffic. York, a town of about 3,000 in 1783, contained nineteen innkeepers and nine blacksmiths, as well as saddlers and singletree makers. Frederick in 1797 was larger but contained a similar occupational array, with the addition of comb makers and wheelwrights. In one crucial respect—the addition of small-scale manufacturing to their urban economic base—these towns differed from other towns further inland. Distillers provisioned the inns. Wagonmaking and tanning firms responded to the brisk demand for vehicles and parts. In turn, the tanners' leather became the raw material for a radically new industry, the manufacture of shoes, boots, and hats for a domestic market of consumers both locally and in towns lower down in the urban hierarchy.[99] Frederick and York were reenacting the series of changes that

98. Neither Frederick nor Winchester appears to have grown appreciably between 1760 and 1775. Frederick contained about 300 houses and 2,000 persons by the early 1780s. Morton, *The Story of Winchester*, p. 85; Johann David Shoepf, *Travels in the Confederation* (Baltimore, 1911), Vol. 1, pp. 313–14. The slower growth of these towns resulted from the continued decentralization of backcountry trade. Mitchell, "The Upper Shenandoah Valley," pp. 426–58; Miles S. Malone, "The Distribution of Population on the Virginia Frontier in 1775" (Ph.D. diss., Princeton University, 1935), pp. 34–35.

99. Calculations are from the lists in J. Thomas Scharf, *History of Western Maryland* . . . (2 vols.; Baltimore: Regional Publishing Company, 1968), Vol. 1, p. 492; George R. Prowell, *History of York County, Pennsylvania* (2 vols; Chicago: J. H. Beers and Company, 1907), Vol. 1, pp. 647–49; and Lemon, *The Best Poor Man's Country*, p. 126. In York,

had earlier transformed their port of Baltimore. Voluminous grain flowshad tripped off a sequence of linked urban activities, initially focused on transport, provision, and repair and soon after on derivative manufacturing. Other linked industries were to follow in the national period, further deepening the gulf between extensive urban systems founded upon grains and those generated by tobacco and cotton.

This suggests another feature of the South's eighteenth-century urban configuration initiated by the emergence of the backcountry as a great zone of commercial wheat production. The commercial ties between these inland towns and coastal or fall-zone ports during the 1750s and 1760s created several extensive urban systems, aligned along wagon roads and focused on a dominant grain port. Baltimore, whose creation has already been discussed, expanded from several hundred families to 6,000 persons by the Revolution. More important, Baltimore achieved autonomy in its overseas trade and assumed the dominant role within its hinterland to the west, north, and east. Other grain ports carved out similar domains. Alexandria, tapping the Shenandoah Valley, rose from an inconsiderable place in 1765 to a town of some 3,000 a decade later. Fredericksburg on the Rappahannock River increased to perhaps 2,000 people by the Revolution as it combined the grain trade with the substantial volume of tobacco that was raised in its market sphere.

Elsewhere in the South, urban systems were less elaborate and autonomous. A new configuration of tobacco towns began to emerge as tobacco production penetrated the piedmont. But unlike the tidewater, where a multitude of small coastal ports handled the tobacco trade, the piedmont's tobacco was exported by a few large centers. Petersburg and Richmond grew to over 2,000 and 1,000 respectively by 1776 because of their role as tobacco warehousing centers for the Virginia and Carolina interior. Within these vast inland trading areas, however, a network of sizable transport towns similar to those of the grain regions did not appear. The low-bulk flows of tobacco stimulated nothing more than country stores and crossroads villages.[100]

---

storekeepers, innkeepers, cordwainers (shoemakers), and tailors were the leading occupations, each representing 5 to 10 percent of the town's occupations.

100. These are rough estimates of population based on several sources. Shoepf, *Travels*, Vol. 1, pp. 359–60; Vol. 2, pp. 42–72; Robert Walter Coakley, "Virginia Commerce During the American Revolution" (Ph.D. diss., University of Virginia, 1949), pp. 23–39. *Colonial Panorama 1775: Dr. Robert Honyman's Journal . . .* , Philip Padelford, ed. (San Marino, Calif.: The Huntington Library, 1939), p. 76. For Virginia in the Confedera-

A major contributing influence to the development of the large tobacco ports of Petersburg, Richmond, and to a lesser degree Baltimore involved the restructuring of marketing patterns that occurred in the quarter century before the Revolution. With the passage of inspection acts in the 1730s and 1740s, tobacco no longer needed to be marketed in a small area in order to ensure quality, and it began to be shipped increasingly long distances for export. This reorientation progressed slowly, but the channeling of tobacco throughout the tidewater into a growing series of consolidated flows to a few major ports was a pronounced feature of the Chesapeake area by the 1770s. This process of convergence greatly accelerated in the post-Revolutionary era as the new method of depersonalized tobacco marketing was permanently established. With this transition completed, the older towns of the tobacco coast, where merchants and planters had operated in an intimate context, ceased to serve as places of international commerce.

Finally, further south in the Carolinas, grain had begun to flow from the piedmont to river shipping centers and to Charleston. But compared to the Chesapeake, the grain movements, traffic, and inland towns were considerably smaller. Rice continued to dominate the Charleston trade and thereby linked that city closely to British ports.[101] This final set of developments represented the completion of the early South's urban systems.

When the eighteenth-century British historian John Oldmixon surveyed the American colonies in 1708, he found few towns worthy of mention in the great swath of territory from the Chesapeake Bay to the Savannah River. Could he have seen Abraham Bradley's 1796 map of the United States, Oldmixon might well have stared in wonder. An astonishing urban transformation had occurred in the South. True, the matrix of urbanization was uneven, with vast areas devoid of any urban place, but, taken collectively, their total number was

---

tion and early national periods, see Peter J. Albert, "The Protean Institution: The Geography, Economy, and Ideology of Slavery in Post-Revolutionary Virginia" (Ph.D. diss., University of Maryland, 1976). Albert's dissertation, although principally a study of the geography and economy of slavery, contains important implications for the method of commercial marketing and the pattern of urbanization. Edward C. Papenfuse, *In Pursuit of Profit: The Annapolis Merchants in the Era of the American Revolution* (Baltimore: Johns Hopkins University Press, 1975), chap. 5.

101. Price, "Economic Function," pp. 161–63.

impressive. From Maryland to South Carolina there existed, by 1790, 262 distinctive cities, towns, and villages. Together they contained 16,000 houses and over 100,000 persons.[102]

To map all of the urban places the South had fostered by the end of the century was not easy. Even a cartographer of Bradley's talent missed many important sites. Fortunately, some estimates for Southern counties can be constructed. The most comprehensive source is Jedediah Morse's *American Gazetteer*, which lists town sizes for the year 1790. As with any compendium, Morse's information has its defects. Certainly some towns were missed, others given archaic names, and a few incorrectly located. More problematic is Morse's convention of either listing town sizes as the approximate number of houses or attaching a qualitative description to a place—"post town" or "small town." These shortcomings notwithstanding, Morse's recordings provide a valuable source for estimating the urban population as a percentage of total population for every Southern county (see Figure 3.4).[103]

By the late eighteenth century economic conditions had created

102. These estimates are based on the number of towns and their houses about 1790 as listed in Jedediah Morse, *The American Gazetteer* . . . (1797 reprint; New York: Arno Press, 1971). Morse lists the number of urban houses for all towns of note and for many towns with as few as ten to twenty houses. Some smaller towns, however, he denotes simply as "post town," "small town," or "village." I assign ten houses to the first two descriptions and five houses to a "village." The usual procedure for converting urban houses to urban population for a town for which the average number of persons per house is unknown is by use of a multiple that is known for other cities and towns in the region, and the most familiar of these multiples is seven persons per house. Morse's gazetteer shows multiples from 3.3 (Beaufort, North Carolina) to 10.17 (Yorktown, Virginia), with a mean of 7.11 for thirteen Southern towns and cities. Greene and Harrington, *American Population*, p. xxiii.

103. The index of urbanization for Figure 3.4 is more specifically defined as the proportion of a county's white male population 16 years and older that resided in urban areas. I use this subpopulation in place of total population in order to exclude dependent populations and thus focus attention on those persons, both rural and urban, whose decisions most affected the growth of towns. The index numerator, the urban population, equals Morse's figure of urban houses in the county multiplied by that county's average number of white males 16 years and older per family. Unfortunately, in the case of Virginia this multiple cannot be derived directly since the state census does not list families or households. Alternatively, I estimate white males 16 years and older in Virginia counties using a regression model. The dependent variable is the number of white males 16 years and older residing in urban areas in Maryland and North Carolina counties, and the predictor (independent variable) is the proportion of a county's population that was slave. The denominator of the urbanization index equals the total number of white males 16 years and older in the county. Morse, *The American Gazetteer*, pp. 198–200, 203–6, 289–91. The base map is from Stephen S. Birdsall and John W. Florin, *A Series of County Outline Maps of the Southeastern United States for the Period 1790–1860*, Map Study No. 2 (Chapel Hill, N.C.: Department of Geography, University of North Carolina, 1973).

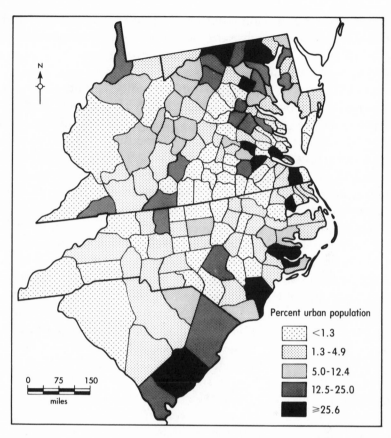

FIGURE 3.4. The Pattern of Southern Urbanization about 1790, by County. Sources: Urban population estimates are based on housing counts provided in Morse's *The American Gazetteer* and a population multiplier of 7 persons per house derived from *ibid.* and Evarts B. Greene and Virginia D. Harrington, *American Population Before the Federal Census of 1790* (Gloucester, Mass.: Peter Smith, 1966), p. 172. See also n. 103. For county populations and boundaries, see W. S. Rossiter, *A Century of Population Growth ... 1790–1900* (Washington, D.C.: GPO, 1909).

a distinctive urban pattern, resembling a horseshoe oriented from northeast to southwest with its open end in the Carolinas and its hollow center in the tobacco coast. The hollow center extended from the northern Virginia piedmont through Virginia's southside and on into North Carolina's piedmont. Contemporary travelers through this area invariably stressed the absence of towns, the abundance of isolated taverns, and the pervasiveness of tobacco culture. In the areas surrounding this zone, however, urbanization rose in varying degrees. The highest levels were located in the eastern coastal zone, where sizable seaport centers linked Southern agriculture to foreign markets. To the west and in the backcountry moderate to high urbanization prevailed, especially from Frederick County, Maryland, south along the Great Wagon Road to the communities of western North Carolina. Significantly, the map's only continuous link from coastal cities to the backcountry occurs along the northern rim in the South's most productive wheat zone. This pattern essentially confirms what other historians and visitors recorded. In sum, the South contained a chiefly rural central zone surrounded by an urbanized periphery along the coast and in the backcountry.

In preindustrial staple economies, the development of extensive urban systems was a precondition for later industrialization and sustained economic growth. With regard to the factors that caused some regions in the Chesapeake in particular and the South in general to urbanize while others did not, scholars have traditionally attributed causation to the physical environment of the region or generalized economic conditions. An alternative explanation, which I have presented here, suggests that staple flows and their linkage effects were the principal determinants of urban development in the eighteenth-century South. In this region, elaborate urban systems emerged when expansionary markets fostered increased staple flows and where the commodities were sufficiently bulky, weighty, and perishable to require forward linkages in the transport, manufacturing, and service sectors. More precisely, the ecological and economic attributes of staples dictated the three major dimensions of urbanization in the colonial South: the timing of its development, the size and location of towns, and their integration into urban systems.[104]

The seventeenth-century South made a shambles of naive visions of an urban colonial society. After English planners recognized that

104.   Critics of staple theory have pointed out that the modest levels of urbanization in the grain lands of early modern Prussia and Poland run counter to the theory. Their critique, however, ignores the fact that urbanization did indeed occur and in amounts not dissimilar from those in the wheat-producing regions of the colonial south. The latter, and not Western Europe, is the relevant comparison. See Immanuel Wallerstein, *The Modern World-System I: Capitalist Agriculture and the Origins of the European World-Economy in the Sixteenth Century* (San Diego: Academic Press, 1974), pp. 320–24; and Marian Malowist, "The Economic and Social Development of the Baltic Countries from the 15th to the 17th Centuries," *Economic History Review*, 2nd ser., 12 (1959), pp. 177–89.

towns would not necessarily develop in the colonies, they attempted to impose an urban network through statutes, instructions, and threats. But the obstacles to town growth were overwhelming. In the Chesapeake, the low relative bulk and weight of tobacco and its minimal processing requirements thwarted forward linkages and urban growth. Trade was conducted by semi-specialized merchant planters or through the periodic visits of supercargoes rather than by full-time resident merchants. Tobacco culture also frustrated backward linkages by limiting consumer demand. The wide dispersion of plantations and the cyclical character of tobacco prices discouraged urban merchants and craftsmen from settling permanently at a particular site. Not until the 1680s and in the lower South alone did an urban place—Charleston—begin to develop. And even this was due to short-term immigration rather than substantive changes in the colony's economy.

In contrast to the limited Southern urbanization of the seventeenth century, the first half of the eighteenth witnessed sustained urban development from the Chesapeake to Carolina. One decisive factor in this process was the increasing demand by the Atlantic community for American commodities, especially tobacco and food. In Europe and the West Indies population growth, economic specialization, and interludes of peace expanded commercial markets. This increased volume of staple flows made profitable the establishment of permanent traders in Southern towns. With the demand for tobacco emanating from the French market, British merchants crowded into the Chesapeake, reorganizing the tobacco trade and activating the listless "paper towns" legislated in the previous century. Elsewhere in this region, where soils were ill-suited for tobacco or transportation costs were prohibitive, planters turned to other staples—wheat, corn, pork, and beef—which could be marketed in the West Indies and southern Europe. Competing for the trade in these commodities, the merchants of Norfolk, Chestertown, and Philadelphia carved out commercial zones in the eastern and southern Chesapeake. Simultaneously, planters in the Carolina low country sent foodstuffs, especially rice, to the same markets. Charleston, capitalizing on its location and size, immediately became the export center for the rice trade, which expanded steadily after 1715 and meteorically after 1730, when London permitted the direct exportation of rice to southern Europe.

The selective growth of coastal ports in the first half of the eighteenth century established the foundation for an extensive development of urban systems after mid-century. Towns and cities multiplied throughout the South, with the most impressive increases occurring in the fall zone and in the west. The backcountry towns were first to prosper. Established by nomadic entrepreneurs who had expected to service a modest number of immigrants, these communities swelled enormously as tens of thousands moved into the Great Valley and the piedmont. Coming from Pennsylvania and the Chesapeake, these migrants were pushed south and west by several powerful forces. Near the coast economic opportunities had deteriorated. Population pressures drove up the price of land, and the long depression of the 1740s encouraged steady migration. The frontier also proved hospitable for evangelicals, seeking refuges for religious convictions awakened in the 1740s. Then followed the French and Indian War, which caused the movement to expand as throngs of frontier settlers retreated briefly to the security of the Maryland and Virginia backcountry towns before dispersing throughout the piedmont. With the return of peace and the establishment of the backcountry towns as centers of local commerce, the focus of urbanization shifted to the fall zone. At various sites, near the heads of navigation in the Chesapeake tidewater, cities and towns grew rapidly. Baltimore, Alexandria, Fredericksburg, and Richmond responded to the chronic food shortages plaguing Europe in the 1760s by tapping agricultural hinterlands in the recently settled western region. Charleston expanded because of similar markets. The level of growth that took place was impressive. Thus, after a half century of urban development preceding the Revolution, the South could claim three of the six largest cities in the new nation.

Just as shifting markets influenced the timing of Southern urbanization, the kinds of staples produced in the region defined the proportions of urban places. The weight and volume of each staple, its requirements for in-transit processing, and its market destinations established the possible limits of urban development in a market economy. The regional economies of tobacco and grains, the major staples of the eighteenth century, shaped two opposite urban patterns. Tobacco towns were small, containing rarely more than 50 houses and normally less than 10 merchants. The scale of these ports and their populations reflected the modest volume of tobacco they handled. Tobacco's output, in weight and bulk, amounted to just one-sixth that of grain from a comparably settled area. Furthermore, these towns drew on smaller hinterlands that were constricted by merchant efforts to ensure the quality and reputation of local to-bacco. The nature of the crop—its low bulk and the fact that the imperishable hogshead required no in-transit processing and mini-mal storage facilities—fostered wide dispersal and consequently small size in its shipment centers. There was little corollary urban growth: artisans and craftsmen did not settle in the tobacco towns for the simple reason that their services were not needed.

The small port typified the tobacco coast until the Revolution, but in the preceding quarter century changes in tobacco marketing were favoring the growth of a few sizable centers for tobacco warehousing. Tobacco inspection legislation, by assuring the maintenance of grad-ing standards over wide areas, shifted responsibility for quality con-trol from the merchants to the colonial government. Certain tobacco traders, no longer tied to local planters and the reputation of their tobaccos, expanded their trading zones. Tobacco was increasingly shipped longer distances to growing coastal ports. This reorientation accelerated rapidly in the post-Revolutionary era as tobacco through-out the tidewater and the piedmont of Virginia and North Carolina converged on Petersburg, Richmond, and Baltimore. Yet in their extensive tobacco hinterlands, the transportation of this low-bulk staple failed to stimulate inland towns comparable to those that had developed in grain regions.

Wheat and corn regions, in contrast to tobacco production zones, created towns and cities of varying size, some with almost 6,000 in-habitants. The flow of these bulky staples generated transport ser-vices and a host of allied industries in towns and coastal ports. Inland towns provisioned wagoners and animals, repaired vehicles, and shod horses. The wagoners' demands encouraged manufactures such as tanning, which, in turn, created the external economies for local con-sumer industries such as boot, shoe, and hat production. The largest of the coastal ports channeled a tremendous volume of grain from their hinterlands and profited immensely from their transshipment functions. These staples required storage facilities, in-transit proces-sing and packaging industries, and shipping services. Flour milling, baking, and shipbuilding diversified the urban economy. Indeed, the development of the grain trade and of manufacturing went hand in hand and produced the most extensive urban systems in the eighteenth-century South.

The rise of Charleston resembled that of the Chesapeake grain ports in some ways, although the South Carolina community's emphasis on rice and slaves imparted a more genteel quality to the city's lifestyle. Like wheat and corn, rice was a bulky grain in great demand in European markets. Charleston's expansion reflected this staple flow and the stimulus it created for transport and warehousing facilities. But the course of urban development under wheat and corn differed in two essential ways from that under rice. First, Carolina rice planters enjoyed profits that far surpassed those possible in wheat and corn regions. In consequence, they spent lavishly when in Charleston. Their buying attracted highly skilled artisans, teachers, musicians, actors, dance instructors, and even a few mystics. Such luxury occupations would have been out of place in the rude, bustling grain ports of the Chesapeake. Second, while Charleston's glitter charmed its many visitors, the city's expansion was restricted by its staple. The exacting ecological requirements of wet rice confined its production to lowland coastal swamps, and the limits of cultivation had been reached by the 1740s. Consequently, staple flows achieved a plateau and Charleston's growth leveled off before mid-century. Accordingly, Charleston's rice hinterland was shallow and it contained few tributary towns of note; in this respect, the city resembled more closely the tobacco ports than the far-flung urban networks of wheat and corn ports. Then, in the 1760s, the development of wheat production in the Carolina piedmont initiated another era of port and urban-system expansion similar to that which was occurring in the Chesapeake grain regions. By the time of the Revolution Charleston's wharves so teemed with grain that the British command believed a blockade of the city would quickly bring the Carolina backcountry to its knees.

Although Southern urban development flourished in grain-producing regions, the fortunes of individual urban centers depended on their locations within the regions. Promising locations had to lie beyond the economic reach of urban competitors. The northern Chesapeake provides a case in point. Chestertown started with excellent prospects because it organized the wheat trade on the eastern shore. But after the sharp price rises of the 1750s, Philadelphia merchants steadily encroached on Chestertown's hinterland, thereby limiting its potential size. At the same time, Baltimore, located beyond Philadelphia's commercial orbit, grew free from any serious outside interference. Further south, North Carolina's ports suffered a strangulation similar to Chestertown's as Charleston and Norfolk enlarged their market spheres at the expense of these coastal towns.

Another dimension of Southern urbanization involved the influence exerted by the region's staples on the integration of urban places into urban systems. Wheat and corn regions generated extensive linear networks of towns focused on a dominant coastal port. Because these staples were produced over a broad range of ecological zones, and because continually rising prices for the commodities permitted long-distance transport to coastal ports, the wheat export centers dominated hinterlands that extended deep into the interior. Consequently, inland transport towns proliferated in number and grew in size in proportion to the grain flows passing through them. By contrast, rice and tobacco ports drew on shallow hinterlands that did not justify an extensive system of tributary transport towns.

The focus of the urban system—the urban dominant—was equally influenced by the staple produced. The urban dominant constituted the major point of exchange for tributary towns in the system and housed the marketing and financial institutions of the staple trade. During the eighteenth century the South produced three patterns of urban dominance, one concentrated in British ports, another split in orientation between these and colonial ports, and the last controlled exclusively by colonial ports. The isolated tobacco towns of the Chesapeake represented the first type. All of them traded primarily with a British city such as London, Glasgow, Liverpool, or any of the smaller outports. These British ports captured the marketing, financing, and processing institutions of the highly channeled tobacco trade. In a word, the Chesapeake tobacco towns were welded firmly into the core of the capitalist world system. Charleston exemplified the second category of split dominance. Although it had largely surrendered control of the northern European rice trade to British ports, Charleston also had a tradition of independent trade in rice with southern Europe after 1730 and in wheat and corn exports beginning in the 1760s. In a sense, the Carolina city reflected at once the features of dependence and autonomy characteristic of tobacco and grain urban systems, respectively. The third form of urban dominance emerged among the autonomous grain ports, which served varied markets overseas and thereby achieved a measure of economic independence. These ports provided commercial foci for their inland towns and fostered indigenous marketing and financial institutions. They also established the foundation for a more diverse economy, less vulnerable to the fluctuations of overseas commercial conditions when the expansionary markets of the eighteenth century receded. Moreover, these grain export centers severed the bonds of colonial economic dependence on Britain in advance of the Revolution, and when political ties were broken in 1776, these ports and their urban systems were more than capable of standing on their own, their distinctive achievement laying the foundation for a modern and semi-autonomous American economy within an expanding capitalist world system.

APPENDIX

This appendix consists of two parts. The first of these addresses the issue of slavery's profitability, the second the locational criteria involved in the decision of whether to market wheat or flour.

The Profitability of Slavery

During the eighteenth century tobacco prices generally remained steady except when poor market conditions forced downward fluctuations. By contrast, wheat prices had risen dramatically by mid-century with the result that many areas formerly devoted to tobacco shifted to wheat production. Yet despite these pressures, tobacco culture retained a firm and profitable foothold in regions with three comparative advantages. All of the Chesapeake's major tobacco areas that continued to thrive after mid-century possessed good soils that yielded a rich supply of high-quality tobacco, a viable riverine transportation system, which facilitated efficient access to market, and an abundant slave labor force that expanded by natural increase during the course of the century. In areas that possessed these attributes, the raising of tobacco continued to provide handsome returns, while elsewhere the shift to wheat reflected a rational response to prevailing market conditions. Because these staples played such large roles in shaping Southern urbanization, a word or two is in order on their comparative profitability in various regions of the South.

The comparison of returns on tobacco and wheat involves the

calculation of gross revenues, production costs, and net revenues for the period 1750 to 1775. For purposes of this analysis, gross revenues equal price multiplied by the output of a single worker. In the case of tobacco, 1,000 pounds of tobacco is the typical output of a Maryland laborer after 1750. Wheat output for the same laborer equals 100 bushels, or 6,000 pounds.[105] Tobacco prices for Maryland's western shore are based on annual averages from Anne Arundel and Prince George's counties. These levels are deflated by one-fifth for eastern shore prices. As for wheat prices, the annual averages that prevailed on the Philadelphia market are accepted as essentially concurrent with prices in Maryland.[106] All prices are converted to sterling using a currency exchange rate series derived from probate materials.

On the cost side, production expenses include labor, land, seed, and taxes. These expenses exclude animal and implement costs because animal costs in tobacco production were normally negligible. In the case of wheat, the steers and oxen used in plowing and tilling added some expenses, but these are omitted here. Implement costs, though probably higher for wheat than tobacco, are assumed to cancel one another out and in fact constituted only a small share of production expenses. The effect of these omissions probably is a marginal increase in the profitability of wheat.

The most important expenses on any eighteenth-century farm or plantation consisted of land, labor, and seed. Land costs depended on the acreage necessary to produce a specified output of wheat or tobacco. In the case of wheat, most agricultural historians of the colonial period accept a figure of 10 bushels of wheat per acre as the average yield and 10 acres as the average amount of land per worker.

105. After 1747, a laborer on Maryland's western shore produced about 1,000 pounds of tobacco. In that year, the passage of a tobacco inspection act, which excluded trash tobacco from the market, caused a substantial drop in labor output. Eastern shore labor yields probably sank below 1,000 pounds. Earle, *Evolution of a Tidewater Settlement System*, pp. 25–26; Papenfuse, "Planter Behavior and Economic Opportunity," pp. 305–6. For further amplification of the economics of slavery and free labor, see Chapter 6. For wheat output, see Lemon, *The Best Poor Man's Country*, pp. 151–57.

106. Tobacco prices for plantations on the western shore appear in Earle, *Evolution of a Tidewater Settlement System*, pp. 14–18, 227–29. Eastern shore tobacco prices are deflated by one-fifth. Also see note 40, this chapter. For wheat prices, see *Historical Statistics*, Part 2, pp. 772–73. The Philadelphia prices, though purportedly wholesale, resemble farm prices in Maryland and Virginia. Compare, for example, the tobacco prices in *Historical Statistics* with those shown in Shepherd and Walton, *Shipping, Maritime Trade, and the Economic Development of Colonial North America*, p. 208.

For our purposes 10 acres were judged necessary to raise 100 bushels of wheat. Similarly, two to three acres were required to produce 1,000 pounds of tobacco.[107] During the eighteenth century rental rates ranged from four to sixteen pence per acre, so rentals for ten wheat acres ran between 40 and 160 pence, while two tobacco acres cost 8 to 32 pence.[108] Had I used landowners (about 50 percent of all households) in my calculations, land costs would have risen, but these costs would have been proportionate to land rentals for wheat and tobacco.

In estimating labor costs it is first necessary to determine the worker-days required to raise a hypothetical quantity of wheat or tobacco. To produce 100 bushels of wheat required about 26.33 worker-days of labor allocated in the following manner: plowing, 6 or 7 days for ten acres;[109] sowing and harrowing, 2 days; reaping and binding, 13.33 days at the rate of 3.4 acres a day;[110] threshing and fanning, 5 days at 20 bushels per day.[111] At the prevailing wage rate of 3 shillings per day I estimate total labor costs for 10 acres of wheat to be 79 shillings or £3.95 sterling.[112]

For tobacco labor costs the most comprehensive set of eighteenth-century estimates is provided by the anonymous author of *American*

107. Estimates of wheat yields per acre vary widely, but agricultural historians tend to agree on about ten bushels per acre as an average figure. Lemon, *The Best Poor Man's Country*, pp. 152–53; R. O. Bausman and A. J. Munroe, eds., "James Tilton's Notes on the Agriculture of Delaware in 1788," *Agricultural History* 20 (1946), p. 184. For tobacco yields, see Middleton, *Tobacco Coast*, pp. 378–79.

108. Estimates of land rent on the western shore range from four to eight pounds of tobacco per acre, or from four to sixteen pence depending on the price of tobacco. The higher rental estimate of sixteen pence is used in the calculation of production costs. Earle, *Evolution of a Tidewater Settlement System*, pp. 210–13.

109. In one day, a single plow turned one to two acres of fallow. Bausman and Munroe, "James Tilton's Notes," p. 184.

110. Gray, *History of Agriculture*, Vol. 1, p. 170.

111. By treading horses or oxen over the grain, probably two acres of grain a day were threshed. *Ibid.*, Vol. 1, pp. 170–71. In the early nineteenth century, flail threshing and winnowing 100 bushels required about 104 hours. William N. Parker, "Productivity Growth in American Grain Farming: An Analysis of Its 19th-Century Sources," in *The Reinterpretation of American Economic History*, ed. Robert W. Fogel and Stanley L. Engerman (New York: Harper and Row, 1971), p. 179.

112. Daily wage rates appear in *Historical Statistics*, Part 2, p. 771. A high rate of 3 shillings is used in these estimates. The lack of a wage rate series for the eighteenth century is unfortunate because wages may have varied substantially, and these variations should be built into cost estimates. For example, labor shortages during the wheat boom of the late 1760s and early 1770s helped drive up daily wages to 5 shillings—a figure that made wage labor less attractive and slavery more appealing. Saladino, "The Maryland and Virginia Wheat Trade," p. 45.

Husbandry.[113] But these calculations are, by any reasonable measure, excessive. I have relied instead on more realistic and tightly reasoned nineteenth-century estimates provided by the Census Bureau, particularly since the production techniques employed were virtually the same in both centuries. The Census estimated a total of 185 worker-hours or 23.1 worker-days of labor in order to raise 1,000 pounds of tobacco on two acres. Using these figures the total free-labor cost for tobacco equaled £3.46 sterling per year, while a slave cost £3 for annual maintenance.[114] Thus, tobacco and wheat demanded roughly equivalent labor inputs and costs to produce comparable output levels. But there was a fundamental difference between the raising of wheat and tobacco, and that distinction is crucial when contrasting the advantages of slave versus free labor. The production of tobacco necessitated almost unrelenting attention during the entire production cycle. It was what I call a multiple-day crop. In some days only a few short hours were demanded; in others, those demands on labor were incessant. To put the matter explicitly, the cultivation of tobacco made the contracting of free labor prohibitively high, since farm

113. The anonymous author gives the labor costs of tobacco production in terms of English wages, and I converted his monetary estimates to worker-days. Carman, *American Husbandry*, pp. 166–68.

114. This Census report cites the dollar cost of producing an acre of tobacco. These costs are converted to worker-hours by dividing them by the daily wage rate of 60 cents. The itemized labor expenditure devoted to two acres of tobacco in the late nineteenth century is: seedbeds, 3.33 hours; weeding seedbeds, 3.33 hours; twice breaking ground (plowing), 10.0 hours; harrowing, marking, and hilling, 10.83 hours; drawing and setting plants, 6.67 hours; cultivating, three plowings, and two hoeings, 17.5 hours; topping, worming, and suckering, 21.67 hours; harvesting and curing, 66.7 hours; taking down, sorting, and stripping, 30.0 hours; and bulking and prizing, 15.0 hours. These tasks closely resemble those described by eighteenth-century chroniclers of tobacco culture. J. B. Killebrew, comp., "Report of the Culture and Curing of Tobacco," in *Agriculture, 1880* (U.S. Bureau of the Census), Vol. 3, p. 212. A twentieth-century estimate of worker-hours in tobacco production may be noted. To produce an acre of flue-cured tobacco requires 400 to 460 hours, with harvesting taking up 165 hours. These estimates of 50 to 67.5 days per acre are not comparable to colonial labor costs. First, tobacco in the colonial Chesapeake was air-cured, and therefore about 60 hours should be subtracted. Furthermore, colonial yields were one-third of present-day yields; assuming that labor costs increased directly with output, to produce an acre of tobacco that met today's yields under colonial conditions would require about 110 to 133 hours, and two acres would require 220 to 266 hours. These figures are more in line with my earlier estimate of 185 hours based on nineteenth-century estimates. Use of a lower-bound estimate for labor costs in tobacco planting has the effect of giving a maximum profit, and thus strengthens the case that tobacco generally proved less profitable than wheat culture, except under conditions of slavery and in excellent tobacco lands. G. Melvin Herndon, *William Tatham and the Culture of Tobacco* (Coral Gables, Fla.: University of Miami Press, 1969), pp. 434–39. Slave maintenance costs are from Carman, *American Husbandry*, pp. 164, 252.

workers were always hired by the day and never by the hour. Tobacco production required as many as 39 separate days of labor, and the hire of day laborers exorbitantly raised annual labor costs to £5.85 as compared to £3 per slave.[115] Wheat, by contrast, was labor-intensive only during the planting and harvesting season and required little in the way of maintenance during the growing period. And, because the harvest of wheat had to be accomplished quickly in the two weeks before the ripened wheat shed its grain, the wheat farmer with a slave in any case had to hire additional labor to help bring the crop in. For the wheat farmer, then, free labor rather than slave was clearly preferable.

Seed costs for the two commodities also differed somewhat. For tobacco these expenses were always negligible, while for wheat the price varied with market conditions. Generally, with applications of one bushel per acre, and at the cost of 3 shillings per bushel, the cost of wheat seed ran to about 30 shillings.[116]

At this point my total estimates may be summed up. The costs for producing 100 bushels of wheat on ten acres (that is, a typical worker's output) were £3.95 for day labor, £0.67 for land, and £1.15 for seed, or a total of £6.2. The comparable costs for producing 1,000 pounds of tobacco on two acres were £3.46 for labor and £0.13 for land or a total of £3.59. Subtracting production costs from gross revenues yields net revenues for a hypothetical planter producing 100 bushels of wheat or 1,000 pounds of tobacco. For those who wish to observe a stricter comparison of profitability, Table 3.1 in the text to Chapter 3 contains estimates of net revenue per unit of production costs for tobacco and wheat. By either measure wheat far exceeded tobacco in profitability when using free labor. But—and again this distinction is crucial—tobacco production remained competitive at western shore prices, and when slave labor was employed no initial capital outlays were necessary. To be exact, the existence of a self-reproducing slave population enabled tobacco profits to rival and surpass those possible in wheat in the Chesapeake regions that contained rich soils and a functional river network—conditions present

115. This is a low estimate of days of labor, derived by counting the separate operations for the cultivation of one acre of tobacco, as given in Carman, *American Husbandry*, p. 167.
116. The thickness of wheat seed application varied from one-half to two bushels per acre, with one bushel the most common application by the second half of the eighteenth century. Gray, *History of Agriculture*, Vol. 1, p. 170; Bausman and Munroe, "James Tilton's Notes," p. 181.

on Maryland's western shore and in Virginia's James River valley, where tobacco culture remained economically viable.

The Extent of the Hinterland for Wheat and Flour Milling

Another set of calculations important to this essay concerns (1) the expanding wheat hinterlands of coastal ports and (2) the localization of flour milling in those ports. As the price for wheat rose it became possible to ship the grain from increasingly long distances and still turn a profit. Expanding grain hinterlands, in effect, set the geographic limits for attendant urban systems. Three critical factors influenced the expansion of the grain production zone: market price of the crop, production costs, and the expenses entailed in transport. These elements have been calculated and the extent of the hinterland in zones of commercial wheat production from 1720 to 1775 appear in Table 3.2 (Column A). This table is based on a hypothetical farmer who produced 100 bushels of wheat for market. The maximum distance of production equals gross revenues (100 bushels multiplied by the Philadelphia price) minus production costs (estimated earlier in this Appendix) divided by the transportation cost to move 100 bushels of grain one mile (for which I use a freight rate of 0.9 pence per hundredweight per mile or 4.02 shillings per 100 bushels per mile).[117]

Actually, the wheat producer who lived some distance from the coastal market had two strategies for selling his crop—he could ship it in bulk or have the wheat milled into flour. Naturally, the farmer chose the alternative offering the greatest return, and on this matter the historical record seems clear: most farmers shipped their wheat to coastal ports for milling, with the result that milling industries developed in or near the coastal towns and contributed to their rapid growth. Some scholars have puzzled over this decision since flour earned much higher prices than wheat. But this practice can be easily explained by the considerable costs of milling, which included milling tolls, weight loss sustained in grinding, and the capital requirement for barreling—expenses that collectively more than offset the comparative price advantage of flour.

117. This is a high estimate of freight rates, and those earlier in the eighteenth century may have been lower by as much as one-third. Distances in the table may be adjusted accordingly. See n. 45, this chapter. These theoretical distances agree very well with the known expansion of the hinterlands of Philadelphia and Baltimore.

TABLE 3.2

Market Zones for Wheat and Flour, 1720–75

Col. A: maximum distance for commercial wheat production, in miles from a coastal market.
Col. B: maximum distance for commercial flour production, in miles from a coastal market.
Col. C: net returns to wheat minus net returns to flour at the farm (in shillings); N = flour not profitable
at any distance.
Col. D: distance at which flour returns become greater than wheat returns.
Col. E: zone of profitable flour milling inland (Col. B minus Col. D, provided that Col. B is larger); NF =
not profitable to mill flour for the market.

Year	Col. A	Col. B	Col. C	Col. D	Col. E
1720	27.8	13.8	86.7	36.3	NF
1721	27.2	9.5	92.3	38.6	NF
1722	25.7	10.4	84.4	35.3	NF
1727	24.4	22.9	56.7	23.7	NF
1728	26.4	10.0	88.0	36.8	NF
1729	31.5	15.6	98.5	41.2	NF
1730	30.5	22.5	81.8	34.2	NF
1731	10.3	0.0	N	N	NF
1732	11.9	0.0	N	N	NF
1733	16.3	0.0	N	N	NF
1735	26.6	15.0	79.7	33.4	NF
1736	19.0	0.0	N	N	NF
1737	27.8	14.1	86.1	36.0	NF
1738	21.8	9.7	70.1	29.3	NF
1739	11.4	0.0	N	N	NF
1740	19.5	0.0	N	N	NF
1741	46.8	46.4	104.1	43.5	43.5 to 46.4
1742	27.0	14.3	82.5	34.5	NF
1743	14.2	0.0	N	N	NF
1744	7.2	0.0	N	N	NF
1745	7.0	0.0	N	N	NF
1746	10.0	0.0	N	N	NF
1747	14.5	0.0	N	N	NF
1748	42.1	38.8	99.0	41.4	NF
1749	51.8	49.2	119.3	49.9	NF
1750	35.8	23.1	102.1	42.7	NF
1751	32.5	17.3	99.5	41.6	NF
1752	35.5	25.9	95.9	40.1	NF
1753	36.5	22.5	105.8	44.3	NF
1754	36.2	32.8	86.0	36.0	NF
1755	36.6	29.5	92.4	38.7	NF
1756	32.8	19.6	96.3	40.3	NF
1757	27.0	11.8	87.1	36.5	NF
1758	30.9	23.6	81.5	34.1	NF
1759	49.9	46.5	116.2	48.6	NF
1760	49.5	45.3	116.8	48.9	NF
1761	42.0	34.3	106.6	44.6	NF
1762	50.3	48.5	114.3	47.8	47.8 to 48.5
1763	57.3	51.4	137.2	57.4	NF
1764	36.5	20.0	110.7	46.3	NF
1765	38.3	25.8	107.3	44.9	NF
1766	56.4	46.4	142.8	59.7	NF
1767	63.7	58.6	150.2	62.8	NF
1768	64.5	56.2	157.5	65.9	NF

TABLE 3.2

(*continued*)

Year	Col. A	Col. B	Col. C	Col. D	Col. E
1769	56.3	47.6	140.2	58.7	NF
1770	65.7	56.8	161.4	67.5	NF
1771	72.0	61.8	177.7	74.3	NF
1772	89.5	88.3	200.0	83.7	83.7 to 88.3
1773	81.5	73.0	195.4	81.8	NF
1774	71.7	62.6	174.9	73.2	NF
1775	55.2	44.2	142.0	59.4	NF

For the last time I return to my hypothetical farmer who converted his 100 bushels of wheat to flour. Milling costs included a toll of ten percent or more[118] and a weight loss of one-third to one-half.[119] The farmer's 6,000 pounds of wheat (100 bushels) after milling was reduced to between 2,700 and 3,000 pounds. In my calculations I use the lower estimate of 2,700 pounds. Next, the flour required 13.78 barrels at a cost of approximately 23 shillings.[120] Using these figures I calculate the geographic limits of commercial flour production by the same method previously employed for wheat: to wit, gross revenues (2,700 pounds of flour multiplied by the Philadelphia price) minus all farm production costs, with the remainder divided by the transport cost of 0.9 pence per hundredweight. The maximum distances for profitable commercial flour milling appear in Column B of my table.

The decision to send wheat or flour depended on the distance to be traveled and the comparative returns for wheat and flour. To determine the distances at which flour afforded a greater return than wheat, I employ the following procedure. First, I establish the difference between the gross returns for wheat and flour at the farm (Col-

118. On milling tolls, see Paul W. Gates, *The Farmer's Age: Agriculture 1815–1860* (New York: Holt, Rinehart and Winston, 1960), p. 158; and William Walter Hening, *The Statutes at Large, being a collection of all the Laws of Virginia* (New York, 1819–23), Vol. 1, pp. 301, 347–48.

119. Sources differ on the weight lost in converting wheat to flour. The percentage loss is given before the source. For superfine flour: 34.7 percent, Edwin Morris Betts, *Thomas Jefferson's Farm Book, with Commentary and Relevant Extracts from Other Writings* (Princeton, N.J.: Princeton University Press, 1953), p. 208; 58.3 percent to 45 percent, Gates, *The Farmer's Age*, pp. 158–59; 33.3 percent, Lemon, *The Best Poor Man's Country*, p. 276; 30 percent, Mitchell, "The Upper Shenandoah Valley," p. 375; 44 percent, Bausman and Munroe, "James Tilton's Notes," p. 184.

120. Lemon, *The Best Poor Man's Country*, p. 276.

umn C). Second, I calculate for varying distances the transport cost of wheat and the barreling and shipping cost for flour. Transport costs of flour are always lower, of course, because of the smaller quantities involved. Third, I identify the distance at which the transport savings for flour equal the higher returns on wheat at the farm.[121] These figures appear in Column D of my table. Beyond these distances flour offered a greater return than wheat. The zone where flour is both profitable and offers a higher return than wheat is determined by subtracting Column D from Column B when the latter is greater. Only in 1741, 1762, and 1772 did such a theoretical zone of inland commercial flour milling exist (Column E). The conclusions to be drawn from these figures seem obvious. Flour, in all but a few years and a few places, offered the farmer lower returns than wheat.

121.   This is accomplished by a linear regression of the difference in barreling and transport costs between flour and wheat (x) on the distance from the market (y). To estimate the distance at which flour offers greater returns than wheat, in the regression equation substitute for (x) the difference in profits between wheat and flour at the farm. At the predicted distance, transport savings to the lower-bulk flour equal the higher revenues to wheat at the farm.

CHAPTER 4

Boston, Vanguard of the American Revolution

This essay offers a locational reinterpretation of the coming of the American Revolution. The argument is straightforward: As a consequence of a series of adversities in the years preceding 1776, one place above all others emerged as the vanguard of revolution. The place, of course, is Boston. That city's prosperous urban economy, predicated uniquely and almost exclusively upon foreland trade and shipping services, was besieged after 1740 by a cumulative process of what I term "spatial relative deprivation," of economic hardships uncharacteristic of the city's earlier history as well as of the good fortune enjoyed by its competitors along the Atlantic Seaboard. Bostonians reeled under the weight of a series of dramatic alterations in the structure of the Atlantic economy during the 1740s and 1750s, followed soon after by British imposition of spatially biased trade policies during the 1760s and 1770s—policies that threatened nothing less than an evisceration of the city's foreland trade. In their vigorous responses to these repeated challenges to the city's welfare, Bostonians eventually provoked the British into egregious overreaction, while simultaneously assembling a set of novel revolutionary repertoires—a model for revolution as it were—for diffusion to the rest of the mainland colonies. Boston's role as the vanguard of revolution was not merely a principled opposition to infringements on republicanism or a paranoiac reaction to moderate British policies; hers rather was a desperate fight for economic survival in the Atlantic economy. And given British refusal to appreciate either the city's tribulations or the spatial biases in their post-1763 trade policies, revolution seems to have been Boston's only recourse.

Boston and the Origins of the American Revolution

My inquiry into the origins of the American Revolution began rather modestly, inspired more by a glaring gap in my lectures on the historical geography of the United States than by burning curiosity about the American Revolution in particular, or revolutions in general. It seemed to me that no course in American historical geography would be complete without at least one lecture on the coming of the Revolution, followed by some obligatory remarks on the war itself. Yet I soon discovered that the historiography of the Revolution, for all of its subtlety, elegance, and nuanced argument, rarely acknowledged locational issues. Geographers went a step further, skipping over the whole affair as little more than a perturbation in American frontier expansion and economic development.[1]

Disappointed with the meager literature on the geography of the American Revolution, I decided to organize my lectures around a crude chronology and chorography of critical events, that is, a plotting of key incidents on maps and timelines in a sort of primitive locational and historical inquiry. Using basic texts in American history, especially Richard Morris's wonderful *Encyclopedia of American History*, I listed and mapped the events leading to the Revolution, beginning rather conventionally with the Parliamentary acts following the French and Indian War.[2] The mapping of these familiar developments—the British neomercantile initiatives, colonial responses, and British counterresponses—demonstrated one overwhelming geographical reality—a pronounced locational clustering in Massachusetts and, more precisely, within a radius of twenty miles

1. There are several notable exceptions to the rule of aspatial historical interpretation, and the ensuing essay draws upon them where appropriate. The urban interpretation of the Revolution perhaps comes closest to the argument presented here. See, for example, Carl Bridenbaugh, *Cities in Revolt: Urban Life in America 1743–1776* (New York: Knopf, 1955); and Gary B. Nash, *The Urban Crucible: The Northern Seaports and the Origins of the American Revolution* (Cambridge, Mass.: Harvard University Press, 1979). More generally, see Jackson Turner Main's *The Social Structure of Revolutionary America* (Princeton, N.J.: Princeton University Press, 1965); his *The Sovereign States, 1775–1783* (New York: New Viewpoints, 1973); Marc Egnal, "The Origins of the Revolution in Virginia: A Reinterpretation," *William and Mary Quarterly*, 3rd ser., 37 (1980), pp. 401–28; and *idem, A Mighty Empire: The Origins of the American Revolution* (Ithaca, N.Y.: Cornell University Press, 1988). Geography's curious omission of the Revolution (and all other American wars, for that matter) has been remedied in part by D. W. Meinig, *The Shaping of America: A Geographical Perspective on 500 Years of History: Vol. 1, Atlantic America, 1492–1800* (New Haven, Conn.: Yale University Press, 1986), esp. pp. 295–323; and Leonard J. Hochberg, "The Geography of Revolution: The Cases of England, the United States, and France" (Ph.D. diss., Cornell University, 1986), chapter 4.

2. Richard B. Morris, ed., *Encyclopedia of American History* (New York: Harper and Row, 1970).

FIGURE 4.1. A mid-nineteenth-century representation of the Boston Massacre on the evening of March 5, 1771. Three Bostonians died immediately after the British volley and two others were mortally wounded. Reproduced from *Harper's New Monthly Magazine* 4 (1852), p. 304.

of the city of Boston. The result of this primitive mapping reminds us that Lexington was but a few miles from Boston, that the Boston Massacre and the Boston Tea Party took place in the same city, and that prerevolutionary American radicalism in general was remarkably concentrated in space (see Figures 4.1 and 4.2). Consider the spatial packing of revolutionary icons into the small confines of eastern Massachusetts between 1770 and 1776: the aforementioned Boston Massacre and Boston Tea Party, the Boston Port Act, Lexington and Concord, and Bunker Hill. Based on my rough count from Morris's *Encyclopedia*, the city and the colony accounted for nearly half of all place references between 1770 and 1776 and for over a third between 1764 and the end of 1775 (see Table 4.1).

But even these impressive statistics understate Boston's role as vanguard of revolution. Bostonians assembled an impressive revolutionary repertoire within months of the passage of the General Revenue Act of 1764. They denounced "taxation without representation" and organized a boycott of selected English imports. And when the Massachusetts House of Representatives, meeting in Boston, autho-

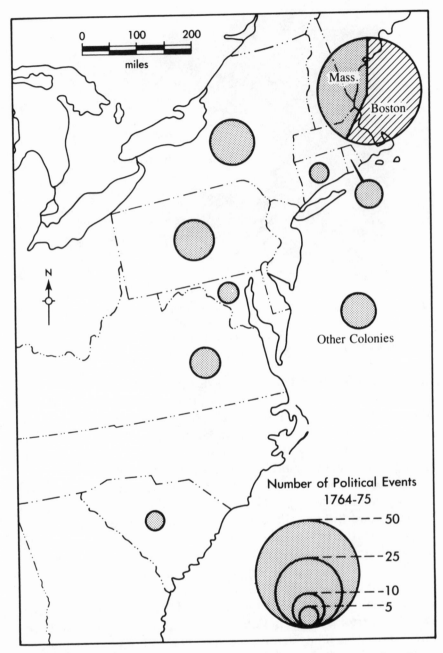

FIGURE 4.2. The Distribution of Political Events prior to the American Revolution, 1764-1775. Source: Richard B. Morris, ed., *Encylopedia of American History* (New York: Harper & Row, 1970).

TABLE 4.1

Distribution of Key Political Events Leading to the American Revolution, 1764–75

Date	Boston	Other Mass.	New York	Penn.	Virg.	R.I.	Conn.	Md.	S.C.	Other	Total
1764	2	1	1		1						5
1765	2	1	3	3	2	2	1	2	1		17
1766			1	1							2
1767	2	1	1	1		1					6
1768	5	1	2		1		1			2	12
1769			1	2	1	2	1	2	1	4	14
1770	2		1							1	4
1771											0
1772	1	1			1	2	1		1	1	8
1773	4	1	2	2					1		10
1774	6	7	2	1	1	1	1	1		2	22
1775	1	5		2	2			1	1	1	13
Totals	25	18	14	12	9	8	5	6	5	11	113

SOURCE: Events were counted from Morris, *Encyclopedia of American History.*
NOTE: The distributional proportions of prerevolutionary events for the period 1764–75 were as follows: Boston, 22.1%; Other Mass., 15.9%; Boston & Other Mass., 38.0%; New York & N.Y. City, 11.5%; Pennsylvania & Philadelphia, 10.6%; Virginia, 8.0%; Rhode Island, 7.1%; Connecticut, 4.4%; Maryland, 5.3%; South Carolina, 4.4%; Other, 9.7%.

rized a committee of correspondence to inform other colonies of the issues and responses, they added organizational structure to their movement. By the summer of 1764 Bostonians had put into place a tripartite model of revolutionary dissent: argument, action, and institutional structure. Later in the summer of 1764 they added the element of violence, when the city's Sons of Liberty burned the records of the Vice-Admiralty Court, ransacked the home of the Comptroller of the Treasury, and looted the house and library of Chief Justice Thomas Hutchinson. And as radicalism begat British response and colonial counterresponse, Boston's revolutionary crusade spread from its tiny hearth in eastern Massachusetts to the other mainland colonies in British North America.

Primitive locational inquiry, of course, raises the question, why Boston? What features peculiar to that city predisposed its citizens toward revolutionary action? The decisive factor, in my view, was the city's geographic structure, which was unlike that of any other city along the Atlantic Seaboard of British North America. Whereas most other colonial port cities coordinated extensive agricultural hinterlands, Boston was an entrepôt without hinterland resources, a bustling commercial center almost entirely dependent for its prosperity upon an overseas and domestic coastal trading foreland: in short, its urban economy was acutely vulnerable to policies that taxed trade and commerce.[3]

Boston's predisposition toward revolutionary politics—and its consequent role as vanguard place—can be traced to geography and, more specifically, to four distinctive locational processes: (1) the city's long-term evolution into an entrepôt with no hinterland, dependent upon a decentralized foreland trade; (2) changes in the Atlantic economy that resulted in spatial relative deprivation in the city's foreland economy after 1740; (3) a further deterioration as the result of spatially biased British neomercantile policies after 1763; and (4) a propitious, if momentary, political coalition of Massachusetts's polar geographic societies in the 1770s. I take these up in turn.

Boston: The Evolution of a Regional System with No Hinterland, 1630–1750

In 1750, Massachusetts's split geographical personality set it apart from all other colonies along the Atlantic Seaboard. The colony was divided into two geographical worlds: the coastal enclaves of Boston and Salem, in which a dynamic mercantile capitalism prevailed, and the inland villages and towns, which fostered a quiet rural subsistence economy. In one world, Boston merchants looked outward to the extensive trade in their maritime foreland; in the other, interior farmers looked inward to the subsistence needs of a burgeoning population. The two groups, despite living "cheek by jowl," rarely intersected. Bostonians had little need for the produce of inland farmers, nor they for the exotic goods and services of Boston.[4]

This juxtaposition of urban capitalism and rural subsistence farming—of polar spatial economies—had deep roots, dating back almost to the founding of Massachusetts in 1629. Initially, city-hinterland relations had been intense, as Boston merchants provisioned the thousands of Puritan migrants streaming through the city on their

3. For an understanding of the term "foreland," critical for interpreting external trade links (and hence positioning within a "world system"), see Guido G. Weigend, "Some Elements in the Study of Port Geography," *Geographical Review* 48 (1958), pp. 185–200.

4. Conceptualizing New England as a "split geographical personality" is the only sensible way of characterizing the regional divergence portrayed by social historians. See note 9, this chapter, for references. Some economists argue for a quickening of economic exchange between coast and interior after 1750; full hinterland integration took place after the Revolution. See Winifred B. Rothenberg, "The Market and Massachusetts' Farmers, 1750–1855," *Journal of Economic History* 41 (1981), pp. 283–314.

way to build new rural communities appropriate to the impending millennium. The merchants sold a bit of everything: corn imported from the Chesapeake, stock and farm tools from England, household wares from Europe. Mercantile profits were generous, and Boston swiftly settled in as the colony's primate city.[5]

But these halcyon days were short-lived. The flow of immigrants dried up following a string of Puritan political victories in England during the Civil War and Cromwell's interregnum, throwing Boston's economy into a stall. The city's merchants desperately sought a more enduring economic base in a staple commodity trade with the interior, but they soon discovered that prospects for this trade were gloomy in this dour land. The colony's thin, glaciated soils and cool, damp climate resulted in meager crop yields; and, in any case, the millennial Puritan farmers reserved their enthusiasm for God rather than the market. Bostonians looked elsewhere for an economic base, in the process sharpening the regional division between two geographical worlds: a mercantile coast and a Puritan subsistence interior.[6]

Forsaking an unpromising hinterland, Boston's merchants instead pursued an aggressive expansion of their maritime foreland into the Atlantic economy. Her merchants and sailors boldly directed their ships into places where others dared not venture—into, for example, the recesses of small and neglected Chesapeake estuaries, or the dangerous shoal waters of Pamlico Sound, or the tiny islands of the West Indies. They built ships and dispatched them to Europe, the coast of Africa, the West Indies, and the other mainland colonies. The city provided maritime services such as freight forwarding and insurance for all takers.

Boston merchants conducted the "triangular trade" in textbook fashion.[7] Producing little themselves, they instead shuffled goods

5. Boston's population growth in the seventeenth century is detailed in Chapter 2. Also see Bernard Bailyn, *The New England Merchants in the Seventeenth Century* (Cambridge, Mass.: Harvard University Press, 1955).

6. The principal exception is the forestry hinterland, which supplied timber for ship construction. Charles E. Clarke, *The Eastern Frontier: The Settlement of Northern New England, 1610–1763* (New York: Knopf, 1970).

7. The new economic history presumes to have demolished the notion of the triangular trade, and it probably has for regions south of New England. Dyadic voyages predominated there because of the emphasis on the direct grain trade, but New England merchants continued working triangular routes while servicing their extensive foreland. For an aspatial interpretation of American trade, see James F. Shepherd and Gary M. Walton, *Shipping, Maritime Trade, and the Economic Development of Colonial North America* (Cambridge: Cambridge University Press, 1972).

around the Atlantic economy, exchanging African slaves, Dismal Swamp staves, and Chesapeake corn for West Indian molasses, which the city's distilleries converted into rum. As mercantile middlemen, they wholesaled European goods in the coastal colonial trade or ferried surplus slaves from busted West Indian sugar planters to eager buyers in the Chesapeake tobacco plantations. Boston so adroitly exploited the manifold opportunities of an Atlantic foreland that by 1740 it ranked as the largest city in British North America and one of the most important cities in the British Empire—an achievement that testified not only to the mercantile resourcefulness of its citizens but also to the considerable freedom they enjoyed in the conduct of trade and commerce, a freedom jeopardized after 1763 by the revival of British mercantilist trade policy.[8]

Just over the hill from Boston, so to speak, was an entirely different world—a world of "peaceable kingdoms," closed-corporate peasant communities, and rural subsistence economies.[9] Here, in the 1630s and 1640s, Puritan farmers had set about creating their millennial "city upon a hill." These were not cities in the modern sense, but more nearly nucleated farm villages surrounded by common open fields. And while the Puritans' communal ideal frequently succumbed to population pressure, land subdivision, and outmigration, the key elements in the system—rurality, subsistence economy, and family, community, and religious focality—endured until late in the eighteenth century. Throughout this time, interior farmers concerned themselves more with the region's rapid natural population increase and the problems of land scarcity than with the functioning of an Atlantic market mediated through Boston.

For these reasons, a distinctive precapitalist mentality flourished within sight of the city. While Boston may have been one of the great cities in the colonial empire, it was largely irrelevant for Massachusetts's interior farmers—a reality most vividly illustrated in Kenneth

8. The varied destinations of Boston's foreland trade circa 1700 are evident in Bernard Bailyn and Lotte Bailyn, *Massachusetts Shipping, 1697–1714: A Statistical Study* (Cambridge, Mass.: Harvard University Press, 1959).

9. In this parochial world, family, land, and community superseded market. See, for example, Sumner Chilton Powell, *Puritan Village: The Formation of a New England Town* (Middletown, Conn.: Wesleyan University Press, 1963); John Demos, *A Little Commonwealth: Family Life in Plymouth Colony* (New York: Oxford University Press, 1970); Kenneth A. Lockridge, *A New England Town, the First Hundred Years: Dedham, Massachusetts, 1636–1736* (New York: W. W. Norton and Co., 1970); Philip J. Greven, *Four Generations: Population, Land, and Family in Colonial Andover, Massachusetts* (Ithaca, N.Y.: Cornell University Press, 1970); and Michael Zuckerman, *Peaceable Kingdoms: New England Towns in the Eighteenth Century* (New York: Knopf, 1970).

Lockridge's wonderful book on rural Dedham from 1630 to 1730. In his account, Lockridge found it necessary to mention Boston just once or twice, despite the fact that the distance from Dedham to the city center of Boston was less than ten miles. One would be hard-pressed to find any more powerful evidence of the split geographical personality of colonial Massachusetts.[10]

In 1740, the two worlds of Massachusetts stood in equipoise. No one thought much about disturbing this balance, since each world functioned effectively in isolation. But three decades later, the situation had changed dramatically. Coalition of these two divergent regional systems became a matter of some urgency; indeed, for Boston, coalition was a precondition for economic survival through political revolution. Why did Boston's survival hinge upon this curious geopolitical union?

The story begins with the gnawing sense of spatial relative deprivation experienced by Bostonians from the 1740s onward. The sources of deprivation were several, but all turned upon the city's unique role as a foreland port and the changing parameters of the Atlantic trade upon which it depended. Two sequential changes were more fundamental than others: first, the economic restructuring of the Atlantic foreland beginning in the 1740s; and second, British neomercantile policies after 1763 and their unwitting spatial biases. Although ingenuity had enabled Bostonians to adapt to adverse economic conditions on previous occasions, the city had never had to cope with the magnitude of changes that cascaded upon it in the middle third of the eighteenth century.

Spatial Relative Deprivation in Boston's Foreland Economy

Spatial relative deprivation extends a familiar sociological hypothesis to geographical inquiry. According to this hypothesis, col-

10. For Dedham, see Lockridge, *A New England Town*. A precapitalist mentality applies for rural villagers in colonial New England, but probably does not apply for market-oriented farmers and planters southward. For the precapitalist, Malthusian interpretation, see James A. Henretta, "Families and Farms: *Mentalité* in Preindustrial America," *William and Mary Quarterly*, 3rd ser., 35 (1978), pp. 3–32; and Daniel Scott Smith, "A Malthusian-Frontier Interpretation of United States Demographic History Before c. 1815," in *Urbanization in the Americas: The Background in Comparative Perspective*, ed. W. Borah, J. Hardoy, and G. A. Stelter (Ottawa: National Museum of Man, 1980), pp. 15–24. For the market thesis (extended to the colonies at large), see John J. McCusker and Russell R. Menard, *The Economy of British North America, 1607–1789* (Chapel Hill: University of North Carolina Press, 1985).

lective expressions of grievance, outrage, and even revolutionary action are caused by relative rather than absolute deprivation in social and economic position. Take the case of poverty. People long mired in the depths of poverty are less likely to rebel than those who, having enjoyed a taste of prosperity, see it slipping away from them as others climb ahead. When these processes converge upon particular places or regions, when economic well-being in one place lags far behind the well-being of other places, we may properly speak of spatial relative deprivation. Indeed, in the spatial version of the hypothesis the collective expression of grievance is usually more volatile owing to the massing of complaint and the multiplicative effects of concentrated action. When spatial relative deprivation accumulates over time, chances are improved for the kind of explosive revolt that rocked Boston and the empire in the 1760s and 1770s—that is, for the creation of a revolutionary vanguard place.[11]

If the possibility for revolution increases in a place when its prosperity deteriorates relative to that of other places, then Boston was a prime candidate for dissent. The city was certainly no stranger to prosperity. For nearly a century, Boston had reigned as America's largest and most influential trading center. The city's extensive foreland trade had helped its population grow to 16,000 by the 1730s, but ill economic winds already had begun to blow. In short order, Boston lost its privileged position in the coastal and West Indian trades, surrendered the rank of leading colonial city to New York and Philadelphia, and watched wistfully as the huge profits from the new direct grain trade to Europe funneled into booming grain ports to the south. Spatial relative deprivation registered promptly on the demographic barometer. The city's population stopped growing in the 1740s, enabling first New York and then Philadelphia to surpass it in the middle and late 1760s. Despite a resurgence on the eve of the Revolution, Boston counted at that date a third fewer people than New York and a fifth fewer than Philadelphia.[12]

11. Analyses of revolutionary collective behavior rarely position it in particular geographic locations; even geographically sensitive scholars focus on group rather than place attributes. See, for example, Charles Tilly, "Revolution and Collective Violence," in *Macropolitical Theory*, ed. Fred Greenstein and Nelson W. Polsby (Boston: Addison-Wesley, 1975), pp. 483–555.

12. For urban populations, see Bridenbaugh, *Cities in Revolt*; Nash, *The Urban Crucible*; and Jacob M. Price, "Economic Function and the Growth of American Port Towns in the Eighteenth Century," *Perspectives in American History* 8 (1974), pp. 121–86.

Boston's slippage may be traced first to a restructuring of the Atlantic economy. Restructuring came in two waves: (1) the rise of competition from the 1680s to the 1730s; and (2) the rise of the direct European grain trade (which Boston could not penetrate) after 1750. The first wave broke with the Glorious Revolution and the European depression of the 1680s and 1690s. These events transformed the geographic structure of the Atlantic economy and British policy toward it. The results—a new liberality toward colonial trade and commerce, the founding of Philadelphia, Charleston, and Norfolk, and the resurgence of the West Indian sugar trade— adversely affected Boston's foreland trade. The new ports challenged Boston's previously uncontested leadership in the coastal and West Indian trades. Philadelphia merchants captured Boston's trade with the corn and wheat farmers in the Delaware Valley and in the marginal tobacco lands of the upper Chesapeake. Norfolk took over the trade in provisions and wood products out of Pamlico Sound and the Dismal Swamp; and Charleston garnered the substantial provisions trade of lower Carolina. Taking advantage of their accessibility to key supply regions and market destinations—and in the case of Charleston, its added advantage of familial and mercantile connections in Barbados and the French West Indies—these youthful ports made deep inroads into Boston's foreland. That the combined populations of Philadelphia, Charleston, and Norfolk by 1730 exceeded Boston's is telling evidence of their achievement and Boston's loss.[13]

But Boston's problems were just beginning. During the three decades between 1740 and 1770, while the cities and regions to the south embarked on one of the most dramatic phases of demographic and economic growth in American history, the population and economy of Boston stagnated. In this "golden age of colonial culture," to use Thomas Wertenbaker's felicitous phrase, prosperity visited almost all Americans, save those with the misfortune of residing in Boston.[14]

The underpinning of this golden age was the spectacular new trade in grain sold directly in European markets. Although the direct

13. For Boston's competitors, see Carville Earle and Ronald Hoffman, "Staple Crops and Urban Development in the Eighteenth-Century South," *Perspectives in American History* 10 (1976), pp. 5–78; and Chapter 3.

14. Thomas J. Wertenbaker, *The Planters of Colonial Virginia* (Princeton, N.J.: Princeton University Press, 1922); also, McCusker and Menard, *The Economy of British North America*.

European trade may be dated as early as the 1730s, when Carolina merchants dispatched rice to southern Europe, the real boom came in the 1750s with the appearance each spring of European food shortages. American wheat provided the margin between starvation and subsistence—a margin that had become dangerously thin because of industrialization, poor weather, and the wartime destruction of European granaries, most notably Poland in the 1750s. The direct trade at first focused on southern Europe; by the 1760s it encompassed Ireland, and in the 1770s England itself. Capitalizing on high prices and profits in the grain trade, New York, Philadelphia, and Baltimore grew rapidly. Bostonians, meanwhile, watched enviously from the sidelines.[15]

Boston was ill-suited for these changes in the Atlantic economy. The new grain trade differed radically from the demanding West Indian and coastal trades in which Boston excelled. These older trades demanded consummate mercantile skill in composing commodity mixes and ship schedules for a vast array of small markets. The new grain trade, by contrast, was simplicity itself—acquire grain from a hinterland; store it at the port; ship it to European markets once a year (in spring, the time of dearth); and backhaul with commodities purchased in European markets. The single prerequisite for success was locational accessibility to a productive agricultural hinterland—which Boston did not have—rather than finely honed mercantile skills, which Boston had in abundance. Excluded from the immense profits of the booming grain trades of New York, Philadelphia, and Baltimore, the merchants of Boston experienced their first pangs of spatial relative deprivation.[16]

Boston's descent was swift. In three decades (1740–70), the city dropped from first to third in population among the cities of British North America. While Boston's population stuck at 16,000, New York's and Philadelphia's each rose from 10,000 in 1740 to 21,000 by 1770. Measuring economic performance by trade or welfare, as Gary Nash has done, reveals that Boston suffered an absolute as well as a relative

15. Earle and Hoffman, "Staple Crops."
16. For the unique demands of the West Indian trade, see Richard Pares, *Yankees and Creoles: The Trade Between North America and the West Indies Before the American Revolution* (Cambridge, Mass.: Harvard University Press, 1956); and for the contrasting simplicity of the European grain trade, see Gaspar John Saladino, "The Maryland and Virginia Wheat Trade from Its Beginnings to the American Revolution," (M.A. thesis, University of Wisconsin, 1960).

deterioration of its once lofty position as the premier city in the American colonies.[17]

The Bias of Neomercantilist Policy

The injuries inflicted by the Atlantic economy, though painful, were at least comprehensible to the Bostonian mercantile mind. It understood the impersonal market forces that restructured the Atlantic economy and resulted in the city's relative deprivation. Such were the costs of doing business in a capitalist economy. What it found incomprehensible, however, was the inequitable spatial bias of British policy after 1763. Neomercantilist taxations on imports and commercial transactions—the two most vital ingredients in Boston's foreland economy—seemed to target Boston, and Boston alone. No other colonial port depended so heavily upon foreland imports, reexports, and commerce; hence no other port shouldered such a disproportionate burden of the tax. Already reeling from aftershocks in a restructured Atlantic economy, Bostonians were unprepared to endure further injury through the caprice of English politicians thousands of miles from their city.

But we are not quite at the heart of the matter. The worst part of British policy was its insensitivity to Boston's heroic efforts to adapt to the Atlantic economy. In the 1750s, Bostonians refashioned their foreland trade, focusing their coastal wholesale-reexport traffic upon the grain ports, where demand was burgeoning for upmarket consumer goods. If Bostonians could not control the profitable grain trade out of New York, Philadelphia, and Baltimore, they at least could benefit from the affluence that it produced. Scouring the marts of Europe, Bostonians imported tea, china, ceramic tableware, cloth, ribbon, lace, cutlery, and fine furniture; and reexported them via the coastal trade to the booming regional systems southward. For most colonials, these delivered goods were superfluity; but for Bostonians, they were the last, best hope for sharing in the general colonial prosperity. By servicing consumers in the "golden age of colonial culture," Boston merchants hoped to revitalize their city's tattered foreland economy.

Boston's revamped strategy seemed to be working. Recent esti-

17. Nash, *The Urban Crucible*, pp. 147–83.

mates of Boston's coastal trade put its value circa 1770 at £300,000 to £400,000—or anywhere from 40 to 55 percent of the city's total trade. In the two decades between 1753–54 and 1772, ship clearances from Boston to other mainland ports more than doubled, an increase that accounted for virtually all of the gain in total clearances. Boston even outstripped its competitors in the coastal trade, though not in overall trade. The 24,500 tons of coastal North American clearances from Boston in 1772 were more than double New York's clearances (11,900 tons, constituting 41.6 percent of total clearances) and were one and a half times those of Philadelphia (15,100 tons, constituting 33.7 percent of total clearances). These figures suggest that Bostonians had made considerable headway in revitalizing the city's trade through coastal reexports of upmarket consumer goods. Conversely, the rest of Boston's foreland trade had stagnated, and despite her impressive gains in the coastal trade, her competitors were coming on strong—New York, for example, had quadrupled its coastal clearances between 1753 and 1772.[18]

More importantly, the spatial bias in British trade policies after 1763 threatened to undo Boston's strategy. The economic burden of these policies fell heavily and disproportionately on the foreland entrepôt.[19] Taxes levied on imports such as paper, ribbon and lace, and tea, as well as on commercial documents ranging from mercantile contracts to ship entries and clearings, imposed a heavy burden on Boston's foreland trade and commerce. Judging from the disproportionate tax burden they bore after 1763, Bostonians had a point when they complained of a geographic bias in British policy. In the case of the Sugar Act of 1764, Boston and Salem paid 25 percent of total taxes collected in 1769 and 34 percent in 1772, as compared to New

18. McCusker and Menard, *The Economy of British North America*, pp. 109, 196. Our knowledge of the volume of the coastal trade is regrettably thin, the consequence of which has been to obscure Boston's unique foreland economy. Shepherd and Walton, *Shipping, Maritime Trade, and the Economic Development of Colonial North America*.

19. In discounting the burden of British policies upon the colonial economy—and thereby undermining a material basis for revolutionary action—economic historians have relied upon aggregate data. While the economic burden may have been modest on average, Boston was anything but average. The impact of British policies was substantially greater for a foreland entrepôt serving multiple markets. For the aspatial thesis, see Robert Paul Thomas, "A Quantitative Approach to the Study of the Effects of British Imperial Policy upon Colonial Welfare: Some Preliminary Findings," *Journal of Economic History* 25 (1965), pp. 615–38; Peter D. McClelland, "The Cost to America of British Imperial Policy," *American Economic Review* 59 (1969), pp. 370–81; and Gary M. Walton, "The New Economic History and the Burden of the Navigation Acts," *Economic History Review*, 2nd ser., 24 (1971), pp. 533–42.

FIGURE 4.3. A mid-nineteenth-century representation of the Boston Tea Party. On the evening of December 16, 1773, Bostonians disguised as Indians boarded *The Dartmouth* and two other vessels and dumped their cargoes of tea into Boston harbor. Reproduced from *Harper's New Monthly Magazine* 4 (1851), p. 1.

York's 18.1 and 15.1 percent and Philadelphia's 17.6 and 17.9 percent. And whereas New York and Philadelphia contributed less than one percent of the revenues collected under the Townshend duties, Boston and Salem paid over 40 percent. Boston also bore a disproportionate share of the fees charged by customs for entering and clearing vessels from the harbor. These fell more heavily upon Boston because among all American cities there was "not one equal it in the Quantity of Shipping it employs." A cautious estimate of Boston's taxes and associated fees in 1772 suggests a burden in excess of £16,000, a little over 2 percent of New England's overseas and coastal trade revenues of £700,000. That was not a trivial amount in a mercantile world in which commission rates, rates of return, and interest rates ranged between 2.5 and 10 percent. And, as if to add insult to injury, the British location of the headquarters of their reorganized customs system in Boston signaled an end to the city's illicit molasses trade with the West Indies.[20]

20. In addition to the sources cited in note 19, see Oliver M. Dickerson, *The Navigation Acts and the American Revolution* (Philadelphia: University of Pennsylvania Press, 1951), pp. 172–207; Lawrence A. Harper, "The Effect of the Navigation Acts on the Thirteen Colonies," in *The Era of the American Revolution*, ed. Richard B. Morris (New York: Columbia University Press, 1939), pp. 3–39; and "The Boston Customs District in 1768," Massachusetts Historical Society, *Proceedings* 58 (1925), pp. 418–45.

Recent estimates of regional accounts underline Boston's especial vulnerability to British taxation policy on the eve of the Revolution. New England's trade account—virtually a synonym for Boston's—generated 62 percent of its revenue from sources that were heavily taxed: invisible earnings from shipping and maritime services (36.5 percent) and the coastal trade, increasingly in upmarket consumer goods (26 percent). The middle colonies, by contrast, earned just 47 percent from these same sources, while a majority of their earnings came from the thriving export of grain—earnings that Bostonians tapped through the coastal trade. That Bostonians bristled at policies that taxed mercantile services, entrepôt wholesaling, and reexport is hardly surprising.[21]

Conversely, policymakers in England were equally short-tempered. Unappreciative of the spatial consequences of their actions, they were irritated by the provincial reaction to policies they regarded as proportionate and judicious. They could not conceive that their tax policies were spatially biased against foreland ports, that these policies gave the appearance of punishing Boston exclusively. That the British did not apprehend differences in the trade geography of American ports is evident in the consignment of stamp paper after the Stamp Act of 1765. The colony of Massachusetts received just 10.2 percent of total paper, which was far below the 25 to 40 percent share of taxes the colony eventually paid. New York and Pennsylvania, in contrast, received 10 to 11 percent of the stamp paper, which was more in line with their tax shares of 15 to 18 percent.[22] Nor did the British appreciate the volatility of Boston's geographic situation, that threats upon its already tattered foreland trade might transform the city into a vanguard of revolution.

Bostonians, meanwhile, were not prepared to endure neomercantile taxation policies that struck at the city's only practical options for economic viability. They reacted bitterly to each policy round. Revolutionary rhetoric grew shrill; violence became commonplace. British measures and countermeasures failed to address the key

21.   Annual estimates of regional accounts for 1768–72 show that on average New England earned £439,000 from commodity exports, £304,000 from the coastal trade, and £427,000 from invisibles; the middle colonies' account stood at £527,000, £220,000, and £250,000, respectively. McCusker and Menard, *The Economy of British North America*, pp. 108–10, 198–99.

22.   Dickerson, *The Navigation Acts and the American Revolution*, p. 192; Edmund S. Morgan, *The Stamp Act Crisis: Prologue to Revolution* (Chapel Hill: University of North Carolina Press, 1953).

issue—Bostonian insistence on a complete elimination of import duties and taxes on the documents of commerce and trade.[23]

Boston led the way in dissenting from British policy during the
1760s, but revolution depended on broadening the base of disaffec-
tion, on winning over other colonial cities and regions whose support
hitherto had been ephemeral and halfhearted. But mobilizing support was not easy; seemingly natural urban alliances foundered. Merchants in other colonial cities episodically joined in Boston's critique,
but only when it suited their interests. They had little stake in opposing
policies that had only a modest impact on their export trade in grain,
tobacco, and rice. Frustrated by the inconstancy of their prosperous
neighbors, Bostonians turned to an unnatural ally closer to home.
By successfully mobilizing the Massachusetts countryside—no mean
achievement given the polarity of the colony's spatial economies—
Bostonians (with a British assist) assured the revolutionary moment.

The Revolutionary Coalition of Spatial
Opposites: Boston and Rural New England

Could 16,000 people, however aggrieved by spatial relative deprivation, have made a revolution? History mooted this question when
the two geographical worlds of Massachusetts—capitalist Boston and
the precapitalist interior—formed a curious revolutionary coalition.
This momentary and unstable union of the mid-1770s deserves somewhat more attention than it has received; and from varied sources,
we may piece together how it happened.

In the 1770s, these two diametrical worlds shared one thing in
common—the vivid memory of Parliament's high-handed disposition of the colony's currency problems in the late 1730s and early
1740s. During these difficult times, the two worlds of Massachusetts
concurred in the view that the colony desperately needed a currency
emission, and a very large one at that. They disagreed, however, on
the emission's purpose and security. Bostonians naturally wanted a
lubricant for economic growth and thus favored an emission secured
by a silver bank. Interior farmers were more concerned with finding

23. Despite a massive literature on Boston's role in the Revolution, no one to my
knowledge has ventured the conclusion that the city's unique economic geography was the
basis for its singularly intense patriotic fervor. But see the revealing volume by John W.
Tyler, *Smugglers & Patriots: Boston Merchants and the Advent of the American Revolution* (Boston: Northeastern University Press, 1986).

a medium of exchange that would ease the pressures caused by population growth, outmigration, and speculation. They preferred an emission secured by a land bank. The controversy over security and the size of the currency emission quickly came under British scrutiny. Parliament summarily settled the issue in 1741; henceforth, emissions of paper currency by the colony of Massachusetts were prohibited. The geographical exclusivity of the statute did not go unnoticed; nor was it forgotten a quarter century later when Parliament once again singled out Boston and Massachusetts.[24]

More than politics was involved in the currency dispute. Bostonians could not escape the conclusion that their economic woes began shortly after the passage of the 1741 statute. The correlation seemed more than coincidence. Although the Crown relaxed the prohibition on currency emissions in wartime, the statute had a chilling effect even then. During the French and Indian War, for example, emissions in Massachusetts were only 13 percent of all New England's emissions, 25 percent of Pennsylvania's, and 36 percent of New York's. Massachusetts' per capita emissions fell from £3–4 in 1730 and 1740 to £0.7 in 1760. In marked contrast, Pennsylvania's in the same period rose from £1.5 to £3.[25]

Currency scarcity in Massachusetts put the colony at a disadvantage. In the countryside, the shortage of paper money retarded the land market and thus exacerbated demographic pressures and speculation. It probably slowed as well the incipient rural commodity markets that had begun stirring in the 1750s. And in Boston, currency shortages handicapped the city's merchants in competing with Philadelphia and New York for wartime shipping, ship servicing, and shipbuilding contracts—contracts that, in combination with their booming grain trade, enabled Philadelphia and New York to surpass Boston during the 1760s.[26]

The smoldering memory of 1741 was by itself an insufficient condition for a revolutionary coalition 35 years later; yet we should not

24. Richard L. Bushman, "Massachusetts' Farmers and the Revolution," in *Society, Freedom, and Conscience: The American Revolution in Virginia, Massachusetts, and New York,* ed. Richard M. Jellison (New York: W. W. Norton and Co., 1976), pp. 77–124, esp. pp. 113–20; Nash, *The Urban Crucible,* pp. 80–87.

25. The size of currency emissions appears in *Historical Statistics of the United States, Colonial Times to 1970* (2 parts; Washington, D.C.: U.S. Bureau of the Census, 1975), Part 2, p. 1199.

26. See especially Nash, *The Urban Crucible,* pp. 99–127; and Bushman, "Massachusetts' Farmers and the Revolution," pp. 77–124.

underestimate its role in the mobilization of interior dissent and the alliance of aggrieved farmers and Bostonians. The statute of 1741 lent historical example to the outraged rhetoric of inland farmers when, in May of 1774, Parliament simultaneously passed the Massachusetts Government Act and the Quebec Act. These joint statutes, as British General Gage understood, galvanized Massachusetts's polar regional systems into a revolutionary force. The people, he wrote, were "numerous, worked up to a Fury and not just a Boston Rabble but the Freeholders and Farmers of the Country."[27]

Parliament accomplished what Boston could not. It extended the geographic bias of British policy from the narrow confines of Boston to the colony at large. The imperial arm muscled its way into the life of quiescent rural towns and villages in inland Massachusetts, threatening their most precious institutions. The Government Act stipulated that henceforth town meetings would require the approval of the royal governor and that town sheriffs were to be appointed by royal representatives rather than by the electorate—a critical matter given the sheriff's role in foreclosure proceedings, which had risen dramatically because of the want of currency. The Quebec Act also flexed British muscle on the frontier, closing off settlement to New Englanders while leaving it open for popish French Canadians. A rural eruption ensued that politically transformed the geographic landscape. The split geographical personality of Massachusetts was suddenly made whole. And with the odd alliance of precapitalist rural farmers and capitalist Bostonians, it was possible at last to conceive of an American Revolution.[28]

A locational reinterpretation of the American Revolution drives home one major conclusion: that the British brought the rebellion upon themselves. Their neomercantile policies after 1763 disregarded at least three fundamental axioms in political geography: first, the axiom of spatial variability of policy impacts; second, that of spatial relative deprivation, with its potential for inspiring revolutionary action; and third, that of the locational concentration of grievance in a revolutionary vanguard place. Although the British

27. Quoted in Bushman, "Masachusetts' Farmers and the Revolution," pp. 81–82. On the missteps in British policy and their exploitation by Bostonian patriots, see Richard D. Brown, *Revolutionary Politics in Massachusetts: The Boston Committee of Correspondence and the Towns, 1772–1774* (Cambridge, Mass.: Harvard University Press, 1970).

28. Bushman, "Massachusetts' Farmers and the Revolution," pp. 77–124; on the sequence of events, strategy, and tactics in forging the coalition, see Brown, *Revolutionary Politics*, pp. 178–209.

remembered the third axiom once the Revolution had begun—as evidenced by their strategy of isolating and attacking the cancerous insurrectionism in New England—it was a case of too little geography, too late.[29]

The preceding interpretation of the American Revolution illustrates the amenability of locational inquiry to what might be termed grand history, the kind that addresses big questions and provokes enduring historiographical controversy. Incorporating a locational perspective into grand history is hardly difficult. It amounts to an admission that location matters; that space is alive, vibrant, and dialectical; and that locational concepts such as scale, regional systems, hinterland, foreland, and spatial relative deprivation have analytic utility. Having acknowledged this, historians will discover in their own work a rich harvest of locational observations and insights that, when rearranged, provide novel perspectives on familiar historiographic debates. Ironically, however, these locational insights are rarely preserved in the ethereal realm of grand history. Large generalizations covering heterogeneous areas characteristically gloss over behavioral variations that are spatially specific. And it is precisely this locational inattentiveness that perpetuates historiographic controversy rather than resolves it. The geographer's strong suspicion is that much of this controversy—the stuff of grand history—could be reconciled by a proper specification of events in time and space.

29. See Lawrence Henry Gipson, "The American Revolution as an Aftermath of the Great War for the Empire, 1754–1763," *Political Science Quarterly* 65 (1950), pp. 86–104. Gipson brilliantly sketches the British policy dilemma after 1763, but he makes too little, perhaps, of the alternatives that might have been chosen. A colonial quota system for the sharing of the tax burden, considered by Grenville in 1764, would have been a more equitable spatial policy than trade duties and fees. Conversely, one could argue, based on the distribution of stamp paper, that British policy mistakenly assumed a relatively homogeneous distribution of trade among the various colonies, and hence an equitable tax incidence. The British demonstrated a better geographical grasp of the situation once the Revolution had begun. The first stage in British military strategy aimed at isolating New England's radicalism. See John Shy, "The American Revolution: The Military Conflict Considered as a Revolutionary War," in *Essays on the American Revolution*, ed. Stephen G. Kurtz and James H. Hutson (Chapel Hill: University of North Carolina Press, 1973), pp. 121–56.

CHAPTER 5

The Industrial Revolution as a Response to Cheap Labor and Agricultural Seasonality, 1790–1860

A Reexamination of the Habakkuk Thesis

T he advent of industrialization and the emergence of the industrial city during the last three centuries have fundamentally transformed human society; no other combination of developments has equaled their importance. In the Anglo-American world, where the transition to industrialization first occurred, scholars have emphasized that the high cost of labor played a critical role in the sequence of economic expansion. Indeed, so uncontested has been the traditional account of the decisiveness of labor costs in the process of industrialization that its basic premises have gone almost unexplored. The classic interpretation, represented most fully in H. J. Habakkuk's *American and British Technology in the Nineteenth Century* (1962), ascribes the introduction of manufacturing technologies into the United States to a shortage of labor in a nation that contained a modest population and abundant land.[1] Habakkuk contends

The original version of this paper was co-authored with Ronald Hoffman.

1. For a recent summation of the decisive and continuing influence of H. J. Habakkuk's *American and British Technology in the Nineteenth Century: The Search for Labour-Saving Inventions* (Cambridge: Cambridge University Press, 1962), see Paul Uselding, "Studies of Technology in Economic History," *Research in Economic History: Supplement 1* (1977), pp. 159–219, esp. pp. 207–8: "In many respects Habakkuk's work is like John Hicks' celebrated *Value and Capital* in that it has a kaleidoscopic quality. Certain changes in perspective reveal an endless variety of possibilities for viewing technological events, their causes and consequences. Economists are fond of saying 'It's all in Adam Smith,' and one is tempted to remark that for economic historians concerned with technological events, 'It's all in Habakkuk.'"

that between 1810 and 1840 would-be entrepreneurs adopted new technologies to increase the productivity of scarce labor. His thesis rests on the assumption that the number of American laborers was very limited and, hence, that labor was high-priced. Yet a close comparison of the relationship of industrial labor costs to seasonal agricultural employment during the first half of the nineteenth century in three distinctive economies—the grain belt of the Mid-Atlantic states and the Old Northwest, the cotton South, and the English countryside—suggests that this argument needs to be revised. The results of such a comparative analysis indicate that industrialization and the growth of the industrial city were more easily achieved when labor was cheap, facilitating industrial investment, than when it was expensive, necessitating such investment (a pattern exemplified by the notably rapid industrialization that took place in Philadelphia during the 1820s).

In all of the regional economies examined, the nature of staple production was the principal regulator of the cost and availability of urban labor and, therefore, of the level of industrialization and urbanization. More precisely, in both the United States and England during the period 1800–1860, the production of regional agricultural staples, by determining the amount rural laborers earned, governed the processes of economic development, urbanization, and industrialization. The three regions possessed remarkably different seasonal demands for agricultural labor, and in each, the cost of unskilled urban labor was a function of rural labor's earnings: where rural laborers did poorly, urban labor was cheap; where they did well, urban labor was expensive.

The Old Northwest, for example, featured a wheat, corn, and livestock economy with a production schedule that required heavy labor inputs for only four months of the year, with the greatest demand arising between corn tillage and wheat harvest. Consequently, most rural wage earners could anticipate full employment for only one-third to one-half of a year at best. Because their annual earnings were correspondingly low, these workers could be induced into urban employment easily and inexpensively. In England and the cotton South, however, crop seasons ranged from eight to twelve months. In these economies, the yearly earnings of rural workers were higher, and therefore the costs of attracting rural labor to city jobs also increased substantially. Although the nearly full-year employment created by England's diversified and intensive agricultural economy did not hinder migration to the cities, it did raise the expense of hiring urban workers to a level that prevented extensive investments in machine technology. In the cotton South, aspiring urban entrepreneurs confronted labor costs that were truly prohibitive. The escalating price of cotton in the 1850s easily enabled non-slaveholders to earn high annual incomes in a variety of rural occupations—as small planters, plain farmers, overseers, or even tenants—and thus materially diminished any possible attractions of city life.

The grain economy of the Mid-Atlantic states and the Old Northwest and the cotton economy of the South represented the extremes. In the Old Northwest cities of the 1850s (as in the Philadelphia region of the 1820s), labor was cheap, a condition that encouraged both urbanization and the diffusion of machine technology. Conversely, the high cost of labor (whether free or slave) in the cotton South stymied any movement toward industrialization and urbanization. Finally, labor costs in England during the early decades of the nineteenth century represented an intermediate situation in which the price of both skilled and unskilled labor retarded the diffusion of machine technology but allowed substantial urbanization to occur.

What follows is a comparative analysis of the availability and cost of labor in the grain belt of the North, the cotton South, and the English countryside, along with a development of the implications of these data for industrialization in the three regions. Included are a review of the literature on scarce and expensive American labor as a cause of technological change; the presentation of an alternative model of development based on low-priced labor, resembling in structure Sir Arthur Lewis's theory of development with an unlimited supply of labor, but—unlike Lewis's—incorporating the mechanism of agricultural seasonality and its market imperfections; and, to test this model, an examination of labor costs as determinants in the processes of capital accumulation, urbanization, and industrialization.

The Habakkuk Thesis:
Dear Labor and Industrialization

Neoclassical economists have claimed that both labor and capital benefited from American economic development, at least in the northern United States. Labor received increasingly higher wages and larger shares of its products' value added. In other words, wages accounted for a greater percentage of the total value of production exclusive of the cost of materials. The theoretical underpinning for this belief is the contention that both skilled and unskilled labor were scarce and, therefore, commanded premium wages and earnings. In rural areas, the scarcity of labor allegedly encouraged the payment of high wages equal to labor's marginal product, defined here as the value of increased output acquired by the application of additional labor. High farm wages, in turn, meant that, in order to attract rural labor, urban employers had to pay a transfer wage that exceeded the value of urban labor's marginal product. To do this, urban capitalists were compelled to elevate labor's marginal product to the level of wages, and they made this adjustment by adding machine technology. Over the long term, capital investment in mechanization increased output per worker, and labor's share of product value added remained steady. This argument, generally referred to as the "Habakkuk thesis" after its principal proponent, contains a number of logical and evidentiary problems. Although economic historians have nibbled at the edges of this thesis, they have avoided challenging the central proposition of labor scarcity.[2]

2. Economic historians have assumed an odd stance on the Habakkuk thesis. On the one hand, it has received nearly universal acclaim; on the other, it is in practice just as often ignored, and nowhere is that more evident than in contradictory interpretations of manufacturing retardation in the nineteenth-century South. For that region, proponents of Habakkuk's thesis should have explored cheap regional labor as the critical determinant of retardation, but in fact economic historians have ignored labor costs altogether and focused instead upon (1) noneconomic factors such as the institution of slavery, elite hegemony, and a rural ethos anathema to manufacturing; (2) the comparative advantage of plantation slavery; (3) capital scarcity, albeit usually without a suitable explanation for the absence of internal finance or external capital flows; or (4) the old chestnut of inegalitarian consumer demand. Habakkuk's theory of labor costs silently recedes from the historiographic accounts. See, for example, Fred Bateman and Thomas Weiss, *A Deplorable Scarcity: The Failure of Industrialization in the Slave Economy* (Chapel Hill: University of North Carolina Press, 1981); Gavin Wright, *Old South, New South: Revolutions in the Southern Economy Since the Civil War* (New York: Basic Books, 1986); idem, *The Political Economy of the Cotton South: Households, Markets, and Wealth in the Nineteenth Century* (New York: W. W. Norton, 1978); Stanley L. Engerman, "A Reconsideration of Southern Economic Growth, 1770–1860," *Agricultural History* 49 (1975), pp. 343–61; idem, "Some Economic Factors in Southern Backwardness in the Nineteenth Century," in *Essays in Regional Economies*, ed. J. F. Kain and J. R. Meyer (Cambridge, Mass.: Harvard University Press, 1971); Heywood Fleisig, "Slavery, the Supply of Agricultural Labor, and the Industrialization of the South," *Journal of Economic History* 36 (1976), pp. 572–97; Glenn Porter and Harold Livesay, *Merchants and Manufacturers: Studies in the Changing Structure of Nineteenth-Century Marketing* (Baltimore: Johns Hopkins University Press, 1971); David Meyer, "The Industrial Retardation of Southern Cities, 1860–1880," *Explorations in Economic History* 25 (1988), pp. 366–86; Roger Ransom and Richard Sutch, "Capitalists Without Capital: The Burden

Peter Temin, the most forthright critic of the Habakkuk thesis, has focused on capital and its availability for technological investments in the 1850s and has argued by implication that American labor must have been nearly as cheap as British labor. Temin observed that American and British capital were equally scarce—a fact suggested by the countries' similar interest rates. Accordingly, British and American firms, having access to similar technologies, would have industrialized at equal rates if labor costs, like capital costs, were identical. But most American industries used demonstrably more machinery than equivalent British industries.[3] Although a logical deduction from Temin's evidence would be that American labor was cheaper than British labor, this possibility has met with considerable resistance on the part of economists. Regarding low-priced American labor as an impossible proposition, they have tried instead to sustain Habakkuk's thesis by constructing elegant, if implausible, models suggesting the abundance of American capital and hence its cheapness vis-à-vis labor, proposing dual scarcities of capital and labor, or positing a three-factor situation wherein the abundance of American raw materials permitted waste in processing and hence the use of inefficient machines and expensive labor.[4] Temin's critics have one thing in common: they deny out of hand the possibility of an inexpensive labor supply.

Habakkuk's views on technological innovation during the first three decades of the nineteenth century, when American manufacturers began investing capital in the new machine technologies while

of Slavery and the Impact of Emancipation," *Agricultural History* 62 (1988), pp. 133–60; and John E. Moes, "The Absorption of Capital in Slave Labor in the Ante-Bellum South and Economic Growth," *American Journal of Economics and Sociology* 20 (1961), pp. 535–41.

3. Peter Temin, "Labor Scarcity and the Problem of American Industrial Efficiency in the 1850's," *Journal of Economic History* 26 (1966), pp. 277–98; Alexander J. Field, "Land Abundance, Interest/Profit Rates, and Nineteenth-Century British Technology," *Journal of Economic History* 43 (1983). Economic historians continue to be perplexed by Temin's paradox; see William N. Parker, "New England's Early Industrialization: A Sketch," in *Quantity and Quiddity: Essays in U.S. Economic History*, ed. Peter Kilby (Middletown, Conn.: Wesleyan University Press, 1987), pp. 17–46, 36–37.

4. D. L. Brito and Jeffrey G. Williamson, "Skilled Labor and Nineteenth-Century Anglo-American Managerial Behavior," *Explorations in Economic History*, 2nd ser., 10 (1972), pp. 235–51; Paul A. David, "Labor Scarcity and the Problem of Technological Practice and Progress in Nineteenth-Century America," *Technical Choice Innovation and Economic Growth: Essays on American and British Experience in the Nineteenth Century* (London: Cambridge University Press, 1975), pp. 19–91. Also see Robert Fogel, "The Specification Problem in Economic History," *Journal of Economic History* 27 (1967), pp. 283–308.

English manufacturers lagged behind, have also been disputed. As with Temin's critique for the 1850s, the accumulating evidence for this earlier period reveals more similarities in than differences between English and American wages, thus weakening the explanatory power of labor costs. Don Adams's careful compilation of American and English wages for 1790–1830 contradicts Habakkuk's thesis on almost every essential. Specifically, Adams demonstrates that American agricultural wages were comparable to those of England and that the wage differential between skilled and unskilled labor, though similar in both countries, was generally wider in the United States. And Nathan Rosenberg's research on the cotton textile industry in the mid-1820s reveals a parallel pattern. His evidence also shows that wage differentials between the skilled workers (mule spinners and hand-loom weavers) and the unskilled were, if anything, wider in the United States than in England.[5] Had American capitalists applied Habakkukian logic, they should have used their relatively cheaper unskilled labor more intensively and thus slowed the pace of machine diffusion. Since they did not pursue such a course, their behavior remains unexplained.

The objections raised by Temin, Adams, and Rosenberg have approached a low-cost labor interpretation of the antebellum United States, but each has stopped short of explaining its causes. Equally important, their work has not accounted for industrialization—that is, the United States's preoccupation with machine technology in the years after 1800. The thrust of their criticism has been largely negative: it has obliterated ideas of substantial differences in American and English wage rates and seriously undermined Habakkuk's thesis that American labor was expensive, but it has left us without an interpretation of comparative industrialization. Indeed, if wage rates in England and the United States were virtually the same, then Habakkuk's logic would lead us to expect similar factor combinations of labor and capital in the two countries. If these were the controlling economic realities, then the capital intensity of American industry

5. Don Adams, "Wage Rates in the Early National Period: Philadelphia, 1785–1830," *Journal of Economic History* 28 (1968), pp. 404–26; *idem*, "Some Evidence on English and American Wage Rates, 1790–1830," *Journal of Economic History* 30 (1970), pp. 499–502; Nathan Rosenberg, "Anglo-American Wage Differences in the 1820s," *Journal of Economic History* 27 (1967), pp. 221–29. For a dissenting view, suggesting narrower skilled-unskilled margins on Pennsylvania iron plantations, see Jeffrey F. Zabler, "Further Evidence on American Wage Differentials, 1800–1830," *Explorations in Economic History*, 2nd ser., 10 (1972), pp. 109–17.

FIGURE 5.1. A mid-nineteenth-century reproduction of the wheat harvest. The laborers in this scene are using the scythe which, though still common in the 1850s, was being replaced by the cradle and the mechanized reaper. On large farms, wheat harvest typically entailed mobilizing a score or more laborers from the surrounding community. Reproduced from *Harper's New Monthly Magazine* 15 (1857), p. 307.

would remain impervious to rational analysis. The wage rates deployed by proponents of Habakkuk's thesis are highly misleading, however—and that is particularly true in the case of agricultural employment. A careful examination of American agriculture and its English counterpart shows that the doctrine of American labor scarcity misconstrues the evidence on wages and misinterprets the role of labor costs in the early stages of industrialization.

Agricultural Seasonality and Urban Wage Determination

Antebellum agriculture was seasonal, unlike manufacturing, which customarily operated most of the year. The agricultural season and the demand for labor varied remarkably from one staple region to another, with the length of the crop season determining whether laborers were hired for a few days, a few months, or the entire year. Thus, it is often misleading to use daily or monthly wage rates as indicators of rural earnings when comparing farming systems so radically different from each other as those under discussion, for the convention of calculating farm labor earnings by multiplying monthly wage rates by twelve (or daily wage rates by 311 working days) seriously distorts fundamental differences in contrasting systems. Agricultural labor's earnings are more accurately determined by multiplying the number of days or months a typical laborer worked by the daily or monthly wage rate.[6]

In the Middle Atlantic and midwestern states, grain farming was the principal business—and it was a seasonal one indeed. Yearly contracts for labor were rare, except when farms were opened, sod was busted, and timber was cleared. From the mid-eighteenth century until 1860, farm labor was seasonal. In wheat areas, farm boys were hired for ten days to two weeks during harvest. Sometimes the urgency to locate labor produced a sense of panic as farmers confronted the potential disaster of having much of their crop overripen and disperse before it could be harvested. Once ripened, wheat required harvesting within a maximum of ten days to two weeks. Notices such as the following, which appeared on the front page of

---

6. For this point, see Carville V. Earle, "A Staple Interpretation of Slavery and Free Labor," *Geographical Review* 68 (1978), pp. 52–65; and Chapter 6. I am gratified that my arguments on the decisive role of agrarian seasonality have been conceded (albeit sometimes grudgingly) by the mainstream of economic history. See, for example, Gavin Wright, "American Agriculture and the Labor Market: What Happened to Proletarianization?" *Agricultural History* 62 (1988), pp. 182–209, esp. p. 208. See also Claudia Goldin and Kenneth Sokoloff, "The Relative Productivity Hypothesis of Industrialization: The American Case, 1820 to 1850," *Quarterly Journal of Economics* (Aug. 1984), pp. 461–87; and Alexander J. Field, "Sectoral Shift in Antebellum Massachusetts: A Reconsideration," *Explorations in Economic History* 15 (1978), pp. 146–71.

the *Chicago Press and Tribune*, were typical: "Laborers wanted. We learned that farmers just now are greatly in need of laborers to gather their crops. Here is a chance for every idle man in the city. Take almost any road west, south, or north and in a single day, every man who wants work can find it." Similarly, in mixed grain areas, labor customarily worked ten weeks to four months, usually in the period from plowing and corn planting in the spring through corn tillage and on to the July harvest of small grains. Four months constituted the usual term for farm laborers in the grain belt, and during the rest of the year they were underemployed or unemployed.[7]

Similar circumstances prevailed wherever wheat and corn had become major commercial staples. Just before the Civil War, a small farmer explained to Frederick Law Olmsted how this labor system operated. The "poor white people" and "rural mechanics," he related, "hardly ever worked on farms except in harvest, when they usually received a dollar a day, sometimes more. In harvest-time, most of the rural mechanics closed their shops and hired out to the farmers at a dollar a day.... At other than harvest-time, the poor white people, who had no trade, would sometimes work for the farmers by the job; not often at any regular agricultural labor, but at getting rails or shingles, or clearing land."[8] Obviously, if labor's earnings were principally confined to several months, then annual earnings amounted to substantially less than the amount that could be earned in other farming systems employing labor year-round.

By contrast, English agriculture in the early nineteenth century was labor-intensive, with farm laborers employed most of the year in the tasks of marling, manuring, plowing and tilling the arable soil, and tending livestock. The English agricultural historian Eric L. Jones has admirably described the increasing demand for labor on English farms as the agricultural work year was extended:

> The seasonal work-rhythm in agriculture was most evident on the larger arable farms. The crop-year meant brisk activity sowing the cereals in autumn and spring, frantic haste and urgency

7. See Allan G. Bogue, *From Prairie to Cornbelt: Farming on the Illinois and Iowa Prairies in the Nineteenth Century* (Chicago: Quadrangle Books, 1968); David E. Schob, *Hired Hands and Plowboys: Farm Labor in the Midwest, 1815–1860* (Urbana: University of Illinois Press, 1975); and Paul W. Gates, *The Farmer's Age: Agriculture, 1815–1860* (New York: Holt, Rinehart and Winston, 1960). Also see other sources cited in Earle, "A Staple Interpretation," pp. 52–65.

8. Frederick L. Olmsted, *A Journey in the Seaboard Slave States* (New York: Dix and Edwards, 1856), pp. 82–83.

at harvest, and comparative somnolence in between. Threshing was virtually the only winter task of any importance. During the eighteenth and nineteenth centuries the starkness of this rhythm was tempered by the new rotations which gained ground. Of these, the Norfolk four-course was the arch-typal but by no means the sole pattern. Its tight sequence of wheat, turnips, barley, clover, then wheat again, its arable flock and its yarded bullocks suggest the directions in which most of the new systems created jobs. Sowing, hoeing and singling the root crops, hurdling the sheep, feeding the fatting bullocks through the winter went some way toward the evolution of a farming system in which work was available, in a series of short bursts, most of the year through.[9]

9. Eric L. Jones, *Seasons and Prices: The Role of the Weather in English Agricultural History* (London: Allen and Unwin, 1964), pp. 60–61. In studying the agricultural history of England from the mid-eighteenth century, certain fundamental factors must be kept in mind. First, between 1750 and 1840 the population of England and Wales more than doubled, while the increase in the home production of cereals, through dramatic, was slightly less than twofold. Second, because substantial imports from outside the United Kingdom were not possible, the nation remained largely dependent on its indigenous agricultural economy for sustenance. Third, and most important for our argument, the era of Parliamentary enclosure, which began in 1750, did not produce a decline in rural population. On this point there is some consensus, and few scholars would seriously quibble with Eric L. Jones, who has claimed that England's agricultural labor supply grew from 1.7 million in 1801 to 2.1 million in 1851. Similarly, geographer J. A. Yelling recently concluded: "What is certain is that the general effect of parliamentary enclosure on village population totals was far from catastrophic; and that although certain aspects of the process favored economy of labour, the broad package of land-use changes that occurred in most parishes continued to support a high level of employment. It would be fair to add that this occurred at a time of rapid upsurge in rural populations when employment was expanding in common-field parishes, also, and in neither case is it easy to see precisely how the extra jobs were found." Yelling, *Common Field and Enclosure in England, 1450–1850* (Hamden, Conn.: Archon Books, 1977), p. 226. Yelling's observation is well taken—no one can yet say in any definitive fashion how England's rural population maintained itself. Several excellent studies, however, do suggest how the agricultural work year and its concomitant labor requirements expanded markedly between 1750 and 1840. Two factors are stressed as fundamental in creating the economic foundation that emerged in the English countryside: the physical process involved in enclosure and the introduction of new crops. In two important essays, J. D. Chambers has demonstrated how the enclosure effort dramatically increased the amount of land under cultivation, a development that, he emphasized, required substantial additional work to bring the virgin soil into production. Chambers has also suggested how a pattern of high, year-round employment was instituted by the introduction and spread of turnip cultivation and green fodder crops and the heightened concentration on livestock, all of which "called for labour throughout the year in field, barn and stockyard." Chambers, "Enclosure and Labour Supply in the Industrial Revolution," *Economic History Review*, 2nd ser., 5 (1953), pp. 319–43; and *idem*, "The Vale of Trent, 1670–1800," *Economic History Review*, Supplement 3 (1957), pp. 2–63. In a prize-winning essay examining England's farm economy in the period, C. Peter Timmer has

In some areas of England, laborers worked on lengthy contracts of six months or a year; in others, particularly in the south of England, rural workers stitched together employment from day work, piece work, and harvest work; but, in virtually all of England, the average farm laborer found employment for most, if not all, of the year.[10] Thus, in the 1820s, English farm workers probably earned

---

advanced convincing quantitative support for Chambers' general arguments. Specifically, Timmer contends that England's augmented agricultural production resulted from the diversification created by growing turnips and grasses and by the accompanying attention paid to husbandry. But he observed that—and this is absolutely critical—the new agricultural form did not include a corresponding expansion in worker output: "Even if a 50 percent increase in yield was achieved on the new farm," he wrote, "the increase in output *per worker* was nearly nil. The English agricultural revolution increased land, not labor, productivity." In essence, the growth in commodity production resulted from an increase in the amount of arable land and the number of agricultural laborers. To substantiate his interpretation, Timmer provides a comparison of the labor requirements on English farms that did and did not practice the new agriculture. The significance of his conclusion is clear: "The new farm needed two-fifths more labor on a year-round basis, *but it did not put any added pressure on labor supplies in the critical harvest period.*" Timmer, "The Turnip, the New Husbandry, and the English Agricultural Revolution," *Quarterly Journal of Economics* 83 (1969), pp. 375–95, esp. pp. 392, 394.

10. From the perspective of the agricultural laborer, of course, the basic importance of the changing economy of the English countryside involved two related considerations: how secure were the prospects for employment and what level of annual income could be expected? These are indeed complex issues. The years 1790–1840 were, as E. J. Hobsbawm and George Rude describe in *Captain Swing* (New York: W. W. Norton, 1968), a time of transition and tension in rural England as the old system of annual labor contracts was replaced by a new one under which labor was hired daily, weekly, or monthly. Examples of both practices abound in the literature of the period. In Scotland, Wales, and the north of England both comtemporaries, such as James Caird in *English Agriculture in 1850–51* (1852; reprint, New York: Kelley, 1967), and modern scholars, such as Christabel S. Orwin and Edith W. Whetham in their *History of British Agriculture, 1846–1914* (London: Archon Books, 1964), have recorded the continuation of annual and semiannual contracts specifying much of the payment in kind—a situation that may or may not have worked to the laborer's benefit. By contrast, England's richer agricultural regions introduced a bewildering array of new hiring methods. Some workers functioned under the older arrangements. Others, by preference or coercion, labored under a wage-rate system that varied by season and task. Still others worked exclusively on a piece-rate basis. The employment patterns differed not only between regions but within regions and even within counties. One investigation completed in 1838 reveals, for example, that in each of Bedfordshire's 26 parishes a different wage-rate system existed; see G. R. Porter, "Agricultural Queries, with Returns from the County of Bedford," *Journal of the Statistical Society of London* 1 (May 1838), pp. 89–96. But, again, the important issue to be addressed is what this variegated labor market meant in terms of the incomes of agricultural laborers and the availability of reliable employment. Several conclusions seem clear. First, rural workers adjusted reasonably well and were not impoverished—at least not until the mid-1840s, when the flight from the countryside began. Second, they found virtually year-round work—R. A. C. Parker's study of the wheat, barley, turnip, and livestock farms contains clear evidence that labor

about $170 and board for the year, while American laborers in grain-farming districts counted on about $40, out of which they had to deduct room and board for the off eight months.[11] Presumably, many found some additional work; but clearly labor in the American grain belt was cheap, and it did not take a very high urban salary to induce these unskilled workers from rural to permanent urban employment. Here was a vast source of inexpensive labor convenient for exploitation by American entrepreneurs.

Urban wages were thus tightly enmeshed with the regional agricultural economy. The key mechanism determining urban wages, as elucidated by development economists, is the transfer wage. Simply put, the transfer wage indicates the wages for unskilled urban labor (or what amounts to the same thing—its cost) for a particular farming region and represents the annual wage that will induce rural labor to seek unskilled urban jobs. That wage may be found by solving the following formula for unskilled urban wages: $W_u - W_r = C_u - C_r$, where W_u is the annual urban wage or earnings, W_r is the amount of rural earnings, and C_u and C_r are the living costs in city and coun-

---

was hired for 48 weeks of the year; see Parker, *Coke of Norfolk: A Financial and Agricultural Study* (Oxford: Clarendon Press, 1975). Third, and this point is essential to determining annual family income, the hiring of labor was not restricted to the male heads of households; women and children were also employed. The results of this practice, particularly in the major agricultural centers of England (the southern and eastern counties), were substantial, and one investigation of the moderately rich counties of Norfolk and Suffolk in the 1830s underscores its importance. Single men or families where the wife did not work had annual incomes of $120 to $130. By contrast, families with one or more children above the age of ten who worked—and in this sample there were a sizable number, 273 of 539, or 50.6 percent—earned from $140 to $200. See James Phillips Kay, "Earnings of Agricultural Labourers in Norfolk and Suffolk," *Journal of the Statistical Society of London* 1 (1838), pp. 179–83. As a writer from Dorsetshire observed somewhat later (and in a far more depressed agricultural period), any discussion of the income of a farm laborer must at least take into account "whether his children living with him do not earn nearly or entirely their own maintenance"; see "Wages in Dorsetshire," *Journal of the Statistical Society of London* 22 (1859), pp. 521–22. With virtually all available evidence pointing to a lack of extensive emigration or "flight" from the countryside to year-round employment and satisfactory annual incomes, it is apparent that from 1800 to 1840 the rural English agricultural laboring family had a viable economic position. Also see A. L. Bowley, "The Statistics of Wages in the United Kingdom during the Last Hundred Years: Part I: Agricultural Wages," *Journal of the Royal Statistical Society* 61 (1898), pp. 702–22.

11. On British labor and wages, see Adams, "Some Evidence on English and American Wage Rates," pp. 505–6; H. C. Carey, *Essay on the Rate of Wages* (Philadelphia: Carney, Lea, and Blanchard, 1835), p. 91; and Eric L. Jones, *Agriculture and the Industrial Revolution* (New York: Wiley, 1974). On the high incidence of yearly contracts, see Hobsbawm and Rude, *Captain Swing*.

try. When urban earnings were greater than the sum of the living costs in the city and the rural earnings, less the living costs of the countryside (when, that is, $W_u - W_r > C_u - C_r$), migration from rural to urban jobs became more attractive. Just how great this inequality had to be is problematic, because the non-pecuniary income attached to rural life increased substantially the value of rural wages— that is, W_r was usually higher than the cash value of rural earnings by 30 to 40 percent.[12] For purposes of clarity, the transfer wage without non-pecuniary income as part of the calculation will be denoted as W_u and the wage with non-pecuniary rural income will be given as W_u'.

The transfer wage is a product of labor markets and their imperfections. Although antebellum rural labor markets in the crop season were competitive, with the conditions of supply and demand largely responsible for setting the cost of labor, they were in the off-season frequently imperfect, with either more buyers or more sellers, as Stanley Lebergott has observed.[13] Imperfections were especially common in seasonal farming districts like the American grain belt. In effect, the rural labor market constituted a hybrid that was perfectly competitive during the crop season and oligopsonistic or even monopsonistic during the off-season. In the farm season, farmers (buyers) and laborers (sellers) were numerous, demand was inelastic, and daily wages were high. Conversely, the off-season market was glutted with underemployed laborers and few buyers. This hybrid rural labor market in turn fixed the supply curve for urban labor at the transfer wage. On the demand side, the handful of urban entrepreneurs in the labor market exerted considerable influence on industrial wage determination. These firms paid wages that were not only low but also less than marginal product, thereby causing exploitation in the form

12.   The model is similar to the formula for the slavery-free labor inequality devised by Evsey Domar; see Domar, "The Causes of Slavery or Serfdom: A Hypothesis," *Journal of Economic History* 30 (1970), pp. 18–32. On non-pecuniary income, see W. Arthur Lewis, "Reflections on Unlimited Labour," in *International Economics and Development: Essays in Honor of Raul Prebisch*, ed. Luis Eugenio DiMarco (New York: Academic Press, 1972), pp. 75–96; Gerald M. Meier, *Leading Issues in Economic Development*, 3rd ed. (New York: Oxford University Press, 1976), p. 158; and especially A. J. Fonseca, *Wage Issues in a Developing Economy: The Indian Experience* (Bombay: Oxford University Press, 1975), pp. 1–30. Note that the transfer wage operates within both perfect and imperfect labor markets, and its operation affects the incomes of all who seek urban work, native or immigrant.

13.   Stanley Lebergott, *Manpower in Economic Growth: The American Record since 1800* (New York: McGraw-Hill, 1964), pp. 164–90. Also see the informative observations on labor markets in Richard A. Lester, *The Economics of Labor* (New York: Macmillan, 1946), pp. 93–127.

of a producer's surplus.[14] The producer's surplus equaled the sum of money saved by the employer through the payment of a wage less than that which would be required in a perfectly competitive urban labor market—that is, a market where the demand for labor that existed during the crop season prevailed throughout the entire work year.

The fact is that rural labor in the United States rarely worked in a twelve-month employment cycle. The norm was nine to ten months in the South and four to six months in many of the Mid-Atlantic and midwestern states. Our purpose in using a year-round, perfectly competitive rural labor market as a benchmark is to illustrate the critical interrelationship of rural earnings and urban wage rate determination: unskilled urban wages were determined by the earnings of rural labor, which were in turn established by the seasonality of employment and the market imperfections that existed during the off-season. If the crop year was extended, the level of annual income necessary to employ unskilled urban labor rose and, conversely, if the crop year was shortened, the annual wages offered urban laborers declined. The disparity, therefore, between what rural laborers could have earned if employed for twelve months and their rural earnings for four, six, or ten months—what we have defined as the degree of exploitation resulting from seasonality—was critical in establishing the upper bound of the urban wage rate, which, in most cases, was paid on the basis of twelve months of employment. In the long run, it should be noted, exploitation diminished. It did so precisely because, as new firms entered the urban labor market to take advantage of low-cost labor, they eventually created an autonomously competitive year-round labor market, with numerous firms competing for idle rural labor. Or, expressed differently, the level of exploitation dwindled as urban labor markets themselves became perfectly competitive.[15]

14. For a graphical representation of this situation, see Figure 5.4. See also Paul A. David, "Learning by Doing and Tariff Protection: A Reconsideration of the Case of the Ante-Bellum United States Cotton Textile Industry," in *Technical Choice Innovation and Economic Growth: Essays on American and British Experience in the Nineteenth Century* (London: Cambridge, University Press, 1975), p. 147. David, however, has attributed market imperfections to year-round monopsony of a single firm in an isolated labor market. The seasonal imperfections suggested here are more general in their operation.

15. The notion of exploitation as a function of seasonality, since it departs from standard usage in economics, requires a brief explanation. Here, the term focuses on the labor market that permitted entrepreneurs to pay low wages because of the unequal demands for labor in rural and urban sectors. The cost of labor in the urban sector is determined by the work requirements of agriculture. More specifically, the annual income

Within the hybrid labor market established by seasonal agriculture, the transfer wage was the main, though not the exclusive, strategy used by urban firms to attract laborers. It was the preferred strategy for firms that wanted a permanent, year-round labor force, which they could acquire by offering annual urban wages at a level only slightly above that of seasonal rural earnings. Alternatively, firms in seasonal industries favored a second strategy. Operating primarily during the fall and winter, when an imperfect labor market prevailed, they could push wages down toward subsistence. A third strategy was noneconomic in nature. For reasons of paternalism or equity, some firms paid wages that were greater than subsistence or transfer wages. Each strategy, nevertheless, involved some degree of exploitation, as the following hypothetical examples make clear. Consider the case where farm laborers earned $10 per month during a four-month crop season. Suppose also that the year-round urban firm attracted rural workers by paying them a transfer wage of $60. Had perfect labor markets existed throughout the year, the firm would have paid labor $120. The absolute difference of $60 was the producer's surplus, and the relative difference of 50 percent was the degree of exploitation caused by market imperfections. Consider now the subsistence wage strategy of the firm that hired only temporary labor during the fall and winter seasons. Meat packers, wood-

---

earned by rural labor—a product of seasonality—is the prime determinant of urban wages and, therefore, yearly urban earnings. Some neoclassical economists undoubtedly will object to this method of calculating exploitation on the basis of year-round work. Their argument is that, since seasonality was a normal condition during the nineteenth century, labor markets were perfectly competitive. Moreover, by denying the impact of seasonality, they contend that neither market imperfections nor exploitation commonly occur in developing staple economies. It is obvious, however, that this neoclassical interpretation does not coincide with the reality of labor market functioning during the nineteenth century, when the key determinant was rural incomes rather than "marginalist" economics. Unskilled urban workers were paid not according to their productivity but in accordance with what they could have earned in their chief alternative employment—namely, rural labor. When seasonality truncated these earnings, the result was an urban labor market that served both to exploit labor and to create a producer's surplus that was used as a subsidy for industrialization. For further thoughts and reservations on the marginalist model of wage determination, see the sources and evidence cited in n. 18 of Chapter 11 below. The persistent role of the transfer wage is implied in the earnings parity of agricultural and manufacturing laborers until the "shock" of the Great Depression and federal policy interventions which advantaged wages in the manufacturing sector. See Lee J. Alston and T. J. Hatton, "The Earnings Gap Between Agricultural and Manufacturing Laborers, 1925–1941," *Journal of Economic History* 51 (1991), pp. 83–99.

lot operators, and iron millers, for example, frequently paid little more than the cost of subsistence in the glutted labor market. Suppose the monthly subsistence wage was $3; then the producer's surplus equaled $7 per month and exploitation amounted to 70 percent. In theory, firms that paid wages in excess of subsistence or the transfer wage did so for noneconomic reasons. They reduced their potential profit while lowering labor's exploitation. But unless they raised their yearly wages to the amount that would have been paid in a perfect labor market, some degree of exploitation still existed. Precisely which strategy firms pursued is a matter for empirical determination. The following discussion focuses on the transfer wage as the main strategy used in the reshaping of the antebellum American economy.[16]

The Midwest and the South in the 1850s

When considering the effects of the transfer wage, it is important at the outset to underscore the distinctly confined impact exerted by immigration on the operation of the antebellum American labor market. During the first half of the nineteenth century, the immigration of some four million people to New England and the Middle Atlantic and North Central states certainly contributed to the expansion of the cheap labor pool in those sections. But the major mechanism of seasonality strictly limited the range of potential market consequences. Immigrants went mainly to cities, presumably because of the better employment opportunities afforded by year-round work as opposed to seasonal rural labor. Most of them made their original destination an urban center or moved to the city shortly after their arrival in a rural area, thereby increasing in some sections the already ongoing rural to urban movement. This pattern had the effect of depressing the cost of urban labor, although clearly it did not reduce it to the level where rural employment became a viable or attractive alternative. Conversely, and significantly, if immigration had not occurred, urban wages would not have risen appreciably. The deter-

16.   Lester, *The Economics of Labor*, pp. 93–127; Joan Robinson, *The Economics of Imperfect Competition* (London: Macmillan, 1933). For thinking on the effects of seasonality on economic development in the European context, see Franklin F. Mendels, "Proto-Industrialization: The First Phase of the Industrial Process," *Journal of Economic History* 32 (1972), pp. 241–61.

minant of seasonality would have continued to establish the level of compensation that rural employers could afford to extend. The urban entrepreneurs would still have been likely to offer relatively low wages—wages only somewhat higher than total rural income—to induce migration from the countryside. Expressed succinctly, the low wage standards set by rural labor's seasonality were by themselves enough to keep urban wages low, so the effect of immigration was minimal.[17]

The transfer wage during the nineteenth century varied considerably among American regions. The greatest difference existed between the northern grain belt and the cotton South. For illustrative purposes, the grain-farming regions in northern and central Illinois and the cotton-planting agriculture of Alabama during the 1850s may be compared: Illinois rural earnings reflected the seasonal underemployment of farm labor, while Alabama earnings represented year-round rural employment. In Illinois, farmers hired labor for short terms of ten weeks to four months. Hiring peaked in the period from spring plowing and corn planting in April through corn tillage in May and June and the harvest of small grains in July. A typical laborer's season brought wages of $14 to $18 per month for four months, or annual earnings of $56 to $72. During the remainder of the year, sporadic and unpredictable labor demands lowered wages and increased prospects for unemployment. Rural workers also faced steep living costs. Although they received room and board for the four months they were employed, they found themselves paying out about $48 of their summer earnings in the course of the remaining eight months.[18] Costs of living in the urban areas of the region were higher than rural expenses. Most evidence suggests that it cost

17. A caveat is in order before proceeding to the regional comparisons. Mine is a model of regional wage determination for unskilled laborers; it should not be confused with a model of migration. A fully specified model of migration obviously must take into account the larger unit of the household, its earnings, and its cost of maintenance. Chapter 8 in this volume develops such a model, one that resolves the seeming paradox of migration to the low-wage Midwest rather than to the high-wage South.

18. Schob, *Hired Hands and Plowboys*, p. 188; Paul A. David, "The Mechanization of Reaping in the Ante-Bellum Midwest," in *Industrialization in Two Systems: Essays in Honor of Alexander Gerschenkron by a Group of His Students*, ed. Henry Rosovsky (New York: Wiley, 1966), pp. 3–39; Earle, "A Staple Interpretation," p. 60; James Penn, "Land, Labor, and Class in the Old Northwest: A Geographic Perspective" (Ph.D. diss., University of Wisconsin, 1983); Jeremy Atack and Fred Bateman, *To Their Own Soil: Agriculture in the Antebellum North* (Ames: Iowa State University Press, 1987); Wright, "American Agriculture and the Labor Market," pp. 182–209.

a single male \$165 to live in the region's cities. Entering these figures into the formula for ascertaining the transfer wage ($W_u - W_r = C_u - C_r$), we find that the transfer wage based on earnings alone (W_u) was roughly \$173 to \$189, while the transfer wage based on earnings plus non-pecuniary income (W_u') was roughly \$190 to \$211—that is, $W_u = \$165 - \$48 + (\$56 \text{ to } \$72) = \$173 \text{ to } \$189$; $W_u' = \$165 - \$48 + 1.3 (\$56 \text{ to } \$72) = \$190 \text{ to } \$211$. Rural to urban migration was theoretically attractive, then, when the midwestern urban wage was above \$190.[19]

In the South, cotton established a more demanding regimen and a higher transfer wage. The crop required sustained attention during the long growing season, and this made free labor prohibitively expensive. White labor costing over \$100 per year simply could not compete with slaves costing \$50 to \$60.[20] But rural life had attractions for young white men capable of driving slaves and overseeing plantations. These year-round jobs promised rapid capital accumulation and economic mobility. Annual pay was substantial for an overseer in the cotton belt of Alabama and Mississippi, where the average wage was about \$400 and the range from \$200 to \$1,000. Assuming a starting pay of \$300, along with fringe benefits covering living costs ($C_r = 0$), the first-year overseer did well.[21] The bidding level for urban firms seeking labor was exorbitantly high. Southern merchants and manufacturers had to offer a starting pay of \$300 plus an additional sum of perhaps \$150 to cover living costs in the town or city. These costs placed the transfer wage (W_u) at \$450 and, to overcome

19. Figures for living costs are based on those for an adult in eastern manufacturing cities in 1860 and adjusted for regional costs of living. See *Report of the Special Commissioner of the Revenue for the Year 1868*, 40th Cong., 3rd sess., 1869, H. Exec. Doc. 16, p. 122; and Philip R. P. Coelho and James F. Shepherd, "Differences in Regional Prices: The United States, 1851–1880," *Journal of Economic History* 34 (1974), pp. 551–91. Non-pecuniary income is not a residual measure; rather, it is based on empirical observation by development economists. The theoretical basis for the ratio of non-pecuniary income to rural earnings is well established; presumably, its level is set by comparative rates of return in rural and urban areas. See Lewis, "Reflections on Unlimited Labour," pp. 75–96; and Meier, *Leading Issues in Economic Development*, p. 158.

20. On cotton generally, see Lewis Cecil Gray, *History of Agriculture in the Southern United States to 1860*, 2 vols. (1933, reprint, Gloucester, Mass.: Peter Smith, 1958). For the seminal work on slave costs, see Alfred H. Conrad and John R. Meyer, "The Economics of Slavery in the Ante-Bellum South," in *The Reinterpretation of American Economic History*, ed. Robert W. Fogel and Stanley L. Engerman (New York: Harper and Row, 1971), pp. 342–61.

21. William Kauffman Scarborough, *The Overseer: Plantation Management in the Old South* (Baton Rouge: Louisiana State University Press, 1966), pp. 3–66.

FIGURE 5.2. A mid-nineteenth-century representation of cotton picking. Although slaves are depicted here, the tasks were the same for small planters and their families. The rarity of illustrations showing whites in the cotton fields is a commentary on the skewed northern perceptions of the cotton South. Reproduced from *Harper's New Monthly Magazine* 8 (1854), p. 456.

the non-pecuniary income attached to rural earnings, the adjusted transfer wage (W'_u) at \$540.[22] In sum, unskilled labor was less expensively induced out of the countryside in Illinois than in Alabama; or, to put it in different terms, urban labor was twice as expensive in the South as in the North because of the protracted demands of the cotton economy.

The overseers were not atypical; their considerable earnings accurately reflected the equally good fortune of the lesser planters and

22. The cost of living in southern cities is estimated at \$150 by adjusting the cost in eastern manufacturing cities (\$165) by regional price indices from Coelho and Shepherd, "Differences in Regional Prices," p. 570.

non-slaveholding whites during the 1850s. These small planters accounted for over 80 percent of the cotton South's heads of households. Like the large planters, these small producers derived their earnings primarily from growing cotton. Throughout the cotton belt, 75 to 80 percent of the non-slaveholders raised cotton, and in the Black Belt of Alabama and Mississippi over 90 percent did so.[23] Almost every white family participated in the gamble of cotton, and conditions favored their success. Although slave prices had spiraled beyond the reach of these small producers, the costs of land, family labor, and capital were minimal, especially when cotton prices pushed above 10 cents per pound. For labor, the small planter used himself and members of his family. As Frederick Law Olmsted observed, "I have, in fact, seen more white native American women at work in the hottest sunshine in a single month, and that near midsummer, in Mississippi and Alabama than in all my life in the free States, not on account of an emergency, as in harvesting either, but in the regular cultivation of cotton and of corn, chiefly of cotton."[24] The small planter obtained land by leasing it or buying it as cheaply as $2 an acre. For capital, he needed only a one-horse plow, which was primitive in the extreme and of little expense, and a horse or mule, which was expensive but could be purchased on a year's credit, with payments beginning after the sale of the first crop. By driving himself and his relations, the aspiring planter raised a good crop of cotton, perhaps as much as ten bales and certainly as much as eight bales. At 10 cents per pound, the small planter's gross revenue ranged roughly from $320 to $400.[25] Incomes of this magnitude show quite clearly why overseers' earnings were high. They also explain the deep attachment of "poor whites" to the country rather than the city.

The transfer wage, theoretically, was the mechanism that determined urban wages. What is more, the transfer wage established regional bidding floors for unskilled and semiskilled labor that were low in the Midwest and high in the South. In Chicago, for instance,

23. On the cotton production of non-slaveholders, see Gavin Wright, *The Political Economy of the Cotton South*, chaps. 2 and 3.

24. Frederick Law Olmsted, *A Journey in the Back Country* (New York: Mason Brothers, 1860), p. 298.

25. Olmsted is informative on every point made here, but also see Robert R. Russel, "The Effects of Slavery upon Nonslaveholders in the Ante-Bellum South," *Agricultural History* 15 (1941), pp. 112–26; and Charles S. Davis, *Cotton Kingdom in Alabama* (Montgomery, Ala.: State Department of Archives and History, 1939), pp. 67, 154–55. On mules, see Robert B. Lamb, *The Mule in Southern Agriculture*, University of California Publications in Geography, No. 15 (Berkeley: University of California Press, 1963), pp. 17–29.

unskilled labor working for the McCormick Reaper Company in the late 1850s earned 6 cents per hour for ten hours a day, six days a week, or $186.60 for the year's work. Indeed, this figure falls within the lower range of the transfer wage and suggests that non-pecuniary income in rural areas was of very little significance during the late 1850s. Certainly the depression of 1857 and the several lean years thereafter made farm labor unattractive and capital accumulation unlikely. Similarly, the Illinois Central Railroad drove wages down to 80 cents per day ($248.80 per year), and the company made every effort to reduce wages further at decade's end.[26]

The low transfer wage not only in Illinois but throughout the Midwest involved a considerable degree of economic exploitation. Indeed, exploitation was inherent in a markedly seasonal staple economy with imperfect labor markets in the off-season. Compare, for instance, the actual earnings of unskilled urban labor with those earnings that workers would have received under competitive conditions such as those prevailing during the crop season. Monthly wages of $14 to $18 from spring planting to summer harvesting would have yielded annual incomes of $158 to $216 had employment been year-round. Adding in board at $6 per month or $72 per year, workers would have earned $230 to $288 in perfectly competitive markets. In practice, entrepreneurs paid somewhat less for year-round labor. The degree of exploitation by our rough measure was 18.9 to 35.2 percent for the McCormick Company and from 0.0 to 13.6 percent for the Illinois Central. The lower level of exploitation on the Illinois Central is attributable, perhaps, to the workers' ability

26. Robert Ozanne, *Wages in Practice and Theory: McCormick and International Harvester, 1860–1960* (Madison: University of Wisconsin Press, 1968), pp. 3–21. The company usually boosted wages in the spring, when in competition with farmers, and dropped wages in the fall after harvest. For other examples of the smallness of unskilled labor's wages, see Bessie Louise Pierce, *A History of Chicago, Volume 2: From Town to City, 1848–1871* (New York: Alfred A. Knopf, 1940), p. 500; and David L. Lightner, *Labor on the Illinois Central Railroad, 1852–1900: The Evolution of an Industrial Environment* (New York: Arno Press, 1977), pp. 22–29, 76–89, esp. pp. 88–89. For the contrary view that the Chicago labor market of the 1850s was more autonomous, that unskilled wages in manufacturing were regulated by employment opportunities in urban construction, see Paul A. David, "Industrial Labor Market Adjustments in a Region of Recent Settlement: Chicago, 1848–1868," in *Quantity and Quiddity: Essays in U.S. Economic History,* ed. Peter Kilby (Middletown, Conn.: Wesleyan University Press, 1987), pp. 47–97. David concedes, however, that his argument "scarcely implies" that in situations in which "hired and family workers were released from agriculture *en masse*, unskilled laborers' wages (and construction) would not have been generally much lower"—a situation that routinely occurred, of course, at the end of every crop season. *Ibid.*, p. 80.

to resist the wage cuts urged by company officials. McCormick, the Illinois Central, and other year-round firms were not the sole beneficiaries of low-cost labor. Equally important were those off-season industries that sought temporary labor between fall and spring. At these times labor was even cheaper, and, theoretically, firms could have driven wages down toward subsistence. Such a strategy was feasible because the labor market contained few buyers and a glut of idle farm hands who drifted about the countryside and into the cities, where they hoped to find work.

The sheer dimension of the army of rural laborers reentering the labor market in late summer and fall has not been fully appreciated. Census takers in 1860 recorded over 240,000 farm laborers in the Midwest—a number more than double the population of Chicago at the same date. In grain-growing rural areas, somewhere between 8 and 18 percent of the population were farm laborers, and they made up an even larger share of the labor force.[27] In wheat-raising Genoa Township in DeKalb County, Illinois, farm laborers accounted for 35 percent of the adult male labor force.[28] As the crop season ended in July and August, laborers remained in the country, hoping for work as teamsters for the crops they had just harvested, but by fall they began drifting into the cities and towns. They came to the cities, as Horace Greeley later remarked, "under a vague, mistaken impression that there must be work at some rate where so much is being done and so many require service, and squander their means and damage their morals in fruitless quest of what is not there to be had. When Spring at length arrives, they sneak back to the rural districts, ragged, penniless, debauched, often diseased, and everyway deteriorated by the Winter plunge."[29]

Demobilization of the rural labor force was thus an immense social problem for the cities of the Midwest. Cincinnati, for instance, reportedly sheltered 7,500 common laborers, or 6.5 percent of its total population, far more than could find work, during the winter of 1851. Earlier, in the 1840s, their numbers exceeded even the demand from the rapidly growing winter business of hog-slaughtering and pork-packing. Consequently, the city organized the Cincinnati

27. Schob, *Hired Hands and Plowboys*, pp. 250–72.

28. U.S. Census Office, Eighth Census of the United States, 1860, Manuscript Census Returns, DeKalb County, Illinois, Population Schedule, National Archives, Washington.

29. Horace Greeley, *What I Know of Farming: A Series of Brief and Plain Expositions of Practical Agriculture as an Art Based upon Science* (New York: G. W. Carleton, 1871), p. 303; Wright, "American Agriculture and the Labor Market," pp. 182–209.

Fire Wood Company specifically to make work for jobless laborers.[30] Chicago had its problems, too, and the *Tribune*, expressing relief at the arrival of the 1860 harvest season, advised unemployed laborers to strike out into the countryside to the nearest wheat farm. What was a social problem for the cities was often a financial crisis for the laborer, whose grim winter prospects a Wisconsin youth nicely summarized: "I have not found a place for the winter yet for it is rather hard to hire out to work by the month through the winter season. Though I have not hired out for the winter I have worked about a month . . . and shall work some more either by the month or chopping some cordwood."[31]

The glutted labor market was a windfall for firms operating mainly during fall and winter, as exemplified by the lumber industry of Michigan during the 1850s. Several thousand of Michigan's 35,000 farm hands moved into the pineries during the logging season between mid-November and mid-March. The logging firms offered wages that were generally lower than those of competitive markets. Unskilled loggers earned $10 to $16 per month instead of the $14 to $18 per month they earned during the farm season. Adding in the value of winter board raised the woodsman's wages to $16 to $22 versus $20 to $24 in the crop season. Here, however, exploitation was less than might be expected in a glutted market. Theoretically, if wages had been pushed down to subsistence, roughly equivalent to the $6 cost of board, exploitation would have amounted to 70 percent; in practice, the rough figures suggest a range from 0 to 25 percent. As the crop season approached, the lumberjacks went back to the farms, but some undoubtedly remained to work as unskilled hands in the sawmills. For those who stayed, wages shot up abruptly to between $20 and $26.50. These rates created wages that were virtually identical to those for farm workers at the same time. In sum, winter wages in the Michigan pineries were less than competitive market wages, yet they were also considerably above the subsistence wages that seem to have been offered in Cincinnati in the late 1840s and early 1850s.[32]

30. Schob, *Hired Hands and Plowboys*, pp. 157–58. For similar conditions in St. Louis, see Jeffrey S. Adler, "Vagging the Demons and Scoundrels: Vagrancy and the Growth of St. Louis, 1830–1861," *Journal of Urban History* 13 (1986), pp. 3–30.

31. Lucian Enos to his parents, Lafayette County, Wisconsin, Oct. 31, 1843, Wisconsin Territorial Letter Collection, as quoted in Schob, *Hired Hands and Plowboys*, p. 150.

32. For this industry I have drawn extensively from the excellent study by Barbara E. Benson; see her "Logs and Lumber: The Development of the Lumber Industry in

FIGURE 5.3. A mid-nineteenth-century reproduction of winter logging—hauling the logs—typical of Upper Michigan. Loggers customarily migrated between summer employment in the grain belt to winter work in the pineries of Michigan—and, at a later date, Wisconsin and Minnesota. Reproduced from Eminent Literary Men, *One Hundred Years' Progress of the United States* (Hartford, Conn.: L. Stebbins, 1872), p. 92.

The Michigan pineries also reveal another general feature of labor costs—namely, the effect on the transfer wage of lengthening the work season. Farm workers who supplemented their work in the crop season with work in pineries, iron furnace collieries, or packing houses raised their rural earnings and thereby pushed the transfer wage upward. In Michigan, the laborer earned $64 on the farm ($16 per month for four months) and $52 in the lumber camps ($13 per month for four months), while board was covered for all but four months. With these figures in the formula, the transfer wage (W_u) equals $257: $W_u - \$116 = \$165 - \$24$. Thus the theoretical transfer wage was considerably higher in Michigan than in Illinois. This difference was, in fact, reflected in actual urban wages. The prevail-

Michigan's Lower Peninsula, 1837–1870" (Ph.D. diss., Indiana University, 1976). Also see George Barker Engberg, "Labor in the Lake States Lumber Industry, 1830–1930," (Ph.D. diss., University of Minnesota, 1949).

ing wage for unskilled urban labor in Detroit, according to *DeBow's Review*, was 87.5 cents per day, or $272 per year, in 1860. In Illinois, however, where off-season work opportunities were decidedly limited, daily wages were 60 to 80 cents per day, or $186 to $249 annually.[33] Too much ought not to be made of one case, but the evidence is consistent with the theory that implies an increase in the transfer wage as rural earnings were stretched longer over the year. Thus, Illinois seems to have been the lowest labor-cost state in the Midwest, a region where urban unskilled labor was generally inexpensive. (Compare the wages in Chicago with those of other midwestern cities in Table 5.1.)

Conversely, the high costs of Southern urban labor reflected the region's higher transfer wage, and observers of the South often commented on "the great deficiency of tradesmen and mechanics" as well as unskilled white workers. The problem of the railroads symbolized the exorbitant cost of Southern free wage labor. In Louisiana, the state's railroad construction projects paid unskilled workers $26 to $30 per month ($312 to $360 per year), carpenters $50 to $60, and supervisors $100 or higher. Nonetheless, a dearth of labor frustrated that state's efforts and all of the South's railroad building programs. Despite the comparatively high wages offered, they failed to attract the region's native white labor. In some cases these shortages forced builders to forfeit their contracts, while in most instances the firms involved resorted to the expedient of importing large numbers of white workers from the North or from Europe.[34]

Other industries also illustrate the South's high transfer wage. Steamboat crewmen along southern rivers, for example, annually earned an average of $360 in 1850 and perhaps $430 in 1860. At the same time, white workers on Louisiana's canals earned $35 a month including board, or $420 per year. By contrast, midwestern boatmen on the Illinois and Michigan Canal earned from $112 to $144 annually in the mid-1850s.[35] Moreover, all of Mississippi's fourteen cot-

33. "Mechanics and Laborers' Wages North and South," *DeBow's Review* 29 (1860), p. 381. Also see Table 5.1.

34. Olmsted, *A Journey in the Seaboard Slave States*, p. 566; Merl E. Reed, *New Orleans and the Railroads: The Struggle for Commerical Empire, 1830–1860* (Baton Rouge: Louisiana State University Press, 1966); U. B. Phillips, *A History of Transportation in the Eastern Cotton Belt to 1860* (New York, 1908), pp. 126, 160, 245–51.

35. G. W. Morse, "Railroad and Water Communication," *DeBow's Review*, 19 (1855), pp. 193–201; Eric F. Haites, James Mak, and Gary M. Walton, *Western River Transportation:*

TABLE 5.1

Mechanics and Laborers' Wages North and South

	Painters	Bricklayers	Stone Masons	Carpenters	Plasterers	Laborers
	$	$	$	$	$	$
Southern States						
New Orleans	2.00 to 2.50	2.50 to 3.50	2.00 to 3.00	2.25 to 2.50	2.25 to 2.50	1.25 to 1.50
Richmond	1.75 to 2.25	2.00 to 3.00	2.00 to 2.50	1.50 to 2.00	1.75 to 2.25	1.00 to 1.50
Louisville	1.75 to 2.00	2.50 to 3.00	1.75 to 2.00	1.75 to 2.50	2.00 to 2.25	1.00 to 1.25
Galveston	1.75 to 2.00	2.75 to 3.00	2.00 to 3.00	2.00 to 3.00	1.75 to 2.25	1.25 to 1.50
Charleston	1.75 to 2.00	2.50 to 3.50	2.00 to 2.50	2.50 to 2.75	2.00 to 2.50	1.00 to 1.50
Little Rock	2.50 to 3.50	2.00 to 3.00	2.00 to 2.50	2.00 to 3.00	2.50 to 3.00	1.00 to 1.25
Norfolk	1.75 to 2.00	2.00 to 2.50	2.25 to 2.50	1.50 to 2.00	1.75	1.00 to 1.25
Memphis	2.00 to 2.50	2.00 to 3.00	2.00 to 2.50	2.25 to 2.50	1.75 to 2.50	1.00 to 1.50
Nashville	2.25 to 2.50	2.50 to 3.00	2.00 to 2.50	2.25 to 2.50	2.00 to 2.50	1.00 to 1.25
Northern States						
Chicago	1.50 to 1.75	1.75 to 2.00	1.50 to 2.00	1.25 to 1.75	1.50 to 2.00	.50 to 1.00
Pittsburgh	1.50 to 2.00	1.75 to 2.00	1.50 to 1.75	1.25 to 1.75	1.50 to 1.75	.75
Cincinnati	1.50 to 1.75	2.00 to 2.50	1.25 to 1.50	1.00 to 2.00	1.50 to 1.75	.75 to 1.00
Detroit	1.50	2.00	1.50	1.75	1.50	.88
Columbus, O.	1.50	2.00	1.50	1.50 to 2.00	1.75 to 2.00	.75 to 1.00
Buffalo, N.Y.	1.50 to 2.00	1.50 to 2.00	1.50 to 1.75	1.00 to 1.50	1.50 to 1.75	.50 to .75
Lowell, Mass.	1.00 to 1.75	1.50 to 1.75	1.50 to 2.00	1.25 to 1.75	1.00 to 1.50	.75 to 1.00
Bangor, Me.	1.50 to 2.00	1.50 to 2.00	1.50 to 2.00	1.50 to 2.00	1.25 to 2.00	.75 to 1.00
Madison, Wis.	2.00	2.00	1.50	2.00	2.00	.50 to .75

SOURCE: *DeBow's Review*, XXIX (1860), p. 381.

ton mills were constructed with cheap, imported northern labor, and the only really profitable cotton factory was operated at the state's penitentiary.[36] Travelers justifiably lamented the high costs of labor in southern cities—a point clearly revealed in the table of wages in northern and southern cities published in *DeBow's Review* in 1860 (see Table 5.1). With scarcely an exception, southern wages for unskilled and skilled workers were higher than those of northern cities. In a cotton port such as Galveston, unskilled laborers earned $1.25 to $1.50 per day, while the reported wages for Chicago were $0.50 to $1.00 per day, with most receiving $0.80 or less, according to the evidence presented above. Expressed as annual income, the laborers of Galveston earned $388 to $455, and those of Chicago $155 to $249. Galveston and Chicago represented the extremes of regional differences in urban wages because cotton and grains decisively influenced the level of the transfer wage in Texas and Illinois. Clearly labor was expensive in southern cities and cheap in northern cities.

The composition of the southern free labor pool also underlines the advantageous position of those southern whites who chose to remain in planting rather than migrate to towns and cities. The skilled urban trades, whether in coastal ports or interior towns, were largely dominated by persons of northern or foreign birth who moved in large numbers into the South's urban centers during the 1850s.[37] Similarly, the pool of unskilled free labor largely comprised foreign-born persons, free Negroes, and northern laborers looking for work in the winter. Southern cities generally resembled Olmsted's unflattering and characteristically bigoted remarks about Richmond, which housed "a considerable population of foreign origin, generally of the least valuable class; very dirty German Jews, especially, abound,

---

The Era of Early Internal Development, 1810–1860 (Baltimore: Johns Hopkins University Press, 1975), pp. 170–77; Lebergott, *Manpower in Economic Growth*, p. 325. Wages for steamboat operators are adjusted from 1850 to 1860 levels by following Stanley Lebergott, "Wage Trends, 1800–1900," in *Trends in the American Economy in the Nineteenth Century*, ed. William N. Parker, National Bureau of Economic Research, Studies in Income and Wealth, No. 24 (Princeton, N.J.: Princeton University Press, 1960), pp. 449–99, esp. pp. 465.

36. Walter Carey Hearn, "Towns in Antebellum Mississippi" (Ph.D. diss., University of Mississippi, 1969), pp. 113–30. The backwardness of Southern manufactures is generally accepted, even in recent revisionist work stressing similarities between southern and western manufacturing; see Fred Bateman and Thomas Weiss, "Comparative Regional Development in Antebellum Manufacturing," *Journal of Economic History* 35 (1975), pp. 182–208.

37. Ira Berlin and Herbert G. Gutman, "Slaves and Freeworkers, and the Social Order of the Urban South," Davis Center, Princeton University, 1976.

and their characteristic shops ... are thickly set in the narrowest and meanest streets, which seem to be otherwise inhabited mainly by negroes."[38]

For would-be southern entrepreneurs the region's high transfer wage established barriers that were virtually insurmountable. Rural opportunities and year-round employment had so elevated the transfer wage and the bidding floor for unskilled southern white labor that employers, unwilling to pay out a minimum of $400 for white workers, increasingly experimented with lower-cost slaves. Yet shifting slaves from the plantation to the factories, canals, and railroads also added costs. A rural slave generally cost his owner $50 to $60 per year, while the expense of maintaining an urban slave may have tripled or quadrupled total costs. Slaves were excluded, moreover, from those jobs requiring even minimal reading and reckoning abilities as well as from much factory work, because pro-slavery ideologues had poisoned entrepreneurial faith in slave competence.[39]

Cheap Labor as a Subsidy for Economic Development

Sharp regional variations in the transfer wage proved decisive for the course of economic development. By creating a cheap labor pool that could count on farm work only during the four-month crop season and faced an imperfect off-season labor market, grain farming established a favorable setting for urban merchants and manufactur-

38. Olmsted, *A Journey in the Seaboard Slave States*, p. 51.

39. The transfer of slaves from the urban to the rural sector reflected the elasticity of urban demand and the high returns to cotton, especially in the 1850s, according to Claudia Goldin, *Urban Slavery in the American South, 1820–1860: A Quantitative Study* (Chicago: University of Chicago Press, 1976). For a discussion of attempts to adapt slaves to nonagricultural tasks, see Robert S. Starobin, *Industrial Slavery in the Old South* (New York: Oxford University Press, 1970). Starobin has argued that industrial slaves in small towns were provisioned at about the same levels as plantation slaves, and this implies that their maintenance costs would have been as low as $20 to $30 per year. Richard Wade, however, noted that slaves in larger cities had high maintenance costs. *Ibid.*, pp. 146–89; Wade, *Slavery in the Cities: The South, 1820–1860* (New York: Oxford University Press, 1964), p. 134, and chaps. 3 and 5. Our estimates of slave costs are on the conservative side. Robert Evans, Jr., has shown a hire rate of $197 for the lower South for 1856–60, which with urban labor costs added on puts the cost of slaves at $362; see his "The Economics of American Negro Slavery," in Universities-National Bureau Committee for Economic Research, *Aspects of Labor Economics* (Princeton, N.J.: Princeton University Press, 1962), pp. 185–243, esp. p. 216.

ers. Farmers did not have much latitude in raising wages: they were limited by commodity prices and the short crop season, while their competitors hired for a twelve-month period. This condition, which applied with special force to the wheat belt, sometimes created a context at variance with the normal operation of the law of supply and demand; rural labor began to grow scarce, but its price, instead of rising, held steady. In the Old Northwest an emerging scarcity of rural labor in the 1850s was countered by mechanizing the small grain harvest, a process that helped hold down and ultimately stabilize rural wages. Urban employers continued to be the chief beneficiaries of low farm wages. These employers at once offered laborers better wages than they could earn on the farm and gained a labor force at a cost considerably below labor's average product.

Consider the situation of urban midwestern firms. During the off-season they had access to unlimited supplies of cheap labor—that is, the supply curve was infinitely elastic and wages were set at a low level by the transfer wage. These firms exercised a marked influence on wage determination because, given the ability of oligopsonistic buyers of labor to pay wages less than marginal product, the market had become less perfect on the demand side. Labor could be hired up to the point where labor's marginal costs equaled its marginal product; however, the annual wages paid to labor, or the transfer wage, fell below this intersection. Such a situation is illustrated in Figure 5.4, and the shaded area shows the extent of the producer's surplus and exploitation. Sir Arthur Lewis has argued that such a model is applicable to much of the underdeveloped world, but is applying a labor surplus model to the antebellum Midwest justifiable? Yes, provided that Lewis's hypothesis is revised so as to incorporate seasonality as the determinant of market imperfections and low transfer wages—or, what is the same thing, of cheap labor. The producer's surplus then becomes an important source of internal finance for northern economic development.[40]

The South was quite different. Urban wages were fixed at considerably higher levels, so the producer's surplus from labor was converted into a producer's deficit. In the southern case illustrated in Figure 5.5, the firm operates inefficiently because the marginal product of labor exceeds both the wage and the average product; firms in such situations were reluctant to hire unskilled white labor.

40. Lewis, "Reflections on Unlimited Labour," pp. 75–96; also see the excellent summary of Lewis's work in Meier, *Leading Issues in Economic Development*, pp. 157–63.

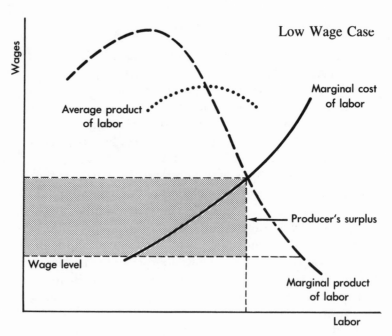

FIGURE 5.4. Urban Wages and Producer's Surplus in the Grain Belt.

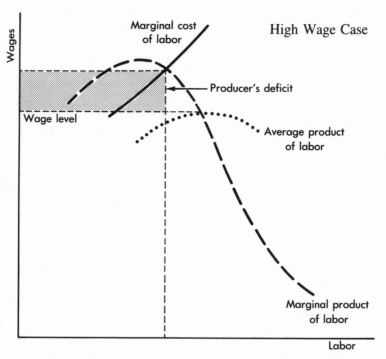

FIGURE 5.5. Urban Wages and Producer's Deficit in the Cotton Belt.

One way around this problem—and one widely used in the South—was to employ white skilled labor in clerical jobs, which elevated the curve of labor's marginal product and positioned wages below average product. Under these conditions, industrialization in the South was rare. The halting steps toward manufacturing in the 1850s were aimed not at inducing white labor to the factories but at adapting slave labor to the factory regime.[41]

Figures 5.4 and 5.5 indicate the labor situation faced by midwestern and southern firms. Midwestern employers had a strong inducement to use cheap labor, thereby earning a producer's surplus. Conversely, southern firms needed to avoid unskilled labor, except for slaves, and tried instead to raise the marginal productivity of white labor in mercantile and related activities.[42] The southern case exemplifies Habakkuk's argument for the scarcity of American labor. Were Habakkuk correct, the South should have witnessed a widespread diffusion of machines and industrialization. In fact, that did not happen. The experience of the United States in the antebellum era thus provides very little verification for the thesis of labor scarcity and high wages as the cause of technological change and urban industrial development, and it points to some theoretical weaknesses in the Habakkuk model. First, the model implies that in the preindustrial period firms were operating inefficiently with high-cost labor; but, assuming that entrepreneurs were rational, they would have avoided such a position. Second, the source of investment capital is problematic in Habakkuk's model, given the presence of high interest rates and the absence of a producer's surplus. Third, his theory of technological change fails to explain the impressive shifts into service-sector employment that had, at least since the mid-eighteenth century, proceeded apace, unaided by new technology and increased productivity.

A much stronger case may be made for inexpensive labor subsidizing American economic development—a case that explains the shifts both to capital-intensive manufacturing and to labor-intensive service industries (a topic which is the focal point of Chapter Eight).

41. Southern cities were preeminently places of commerce, whereas in northern cities warehousing and storage, transport, and manufacturing rivaled the commercial sector. See Carville Earle and Ronald Hoffman, "Regional Staples and Urban Systems in Antebellum America," in *Géographie du Capital Marchand aux Amériques, 1760–1860*, ed. Jeanne Chase (Paris: École des Hautes Études en Sciences Sociales, 1987), pp. 151–81.

42. There was considerable debate about the social effects of industrializing slaves; see Starobin, *Industrial Slavery in the Old South*, pp. 190–232.

Cheap labor meant that midwestern firms hired labor at half the cost of southern firms. Low midwestern wages contributed to a producer's surplus, which in turn provided internal capital for firm expansion. As the scale of operation expanded and the labor market remained imperfect, labor's marginal product effectively rose while the urban transfer wage remained relatively unchanged. These changes augmented the producer's surplus, until urban labor markets themselves became perfectly competitive. Thus, labor's share of value

TABLE 5.2

Wages, Value Added, and Wage Shares in Manufacturing, 1860

Region and state	Wages	Value added	Wage share[a]
Middle American Grain Belt	*$204,982,000*	*$459,075,000*	*44.1%*
Delaware	1,704,000	3,428,000	49.7
Illinois	7,638,000	19,818,000	38.5
Indiana	6,318,000	14,185,000	44.5
Iowa	1,922,000	4,779,000	40.2
Kansas	880,000	2,826,000	31.2
Kentucky	6,021,000	14,015,000	43.0
Michigan	1,080,000	2,424,000	44.6
Minnesota	712,000	1,278,000	55.7
Missouri	6,670,000	15,444,000	43.2
New Jersey	16,277,000	31,363,000	51.9
New York	65,447,000	150,226,000	43.6
Ohio	22,303,000	47,307,000	47.1
Pennsylvania	60,369,000	135,119,000	44.7
Tennessee	3,371,000	7,417,000	45.4
Wisconsin	4,269,000	9,446,000	45.2
South Atlantic and Gulf Coast	*$32,838,000*	*$66,885,000*	*49.1%*
Alabama	2,133,000	4,371,000	48.8
Florida	620,000	1,424,000	43.5
Georgia	2,925,000	6,068,000	48.2
Louisiana	3,955,000	8,277,000	47.8
Maryland	7,191,000	14,383,000	50.0
Mississippi	1,618,000	3,093,000	52.3
North Carolina	2,689,000	5,700,000	47.2
South Carolina	1,380,000	2,966,000	46.5
Texas	1,163,000	2,948,000	39.4
Virginia	8,544,000	17,657,000	48.4
New England	*$104,169,000*	*$202,478,000*	*51.5%*
Connecticut	19,026,000	37,368,000	50.9
Maine	8,304,000	14,877,000	55.8
Massachusetts	56,963,000	109,869,000	51.9
New Hampshire	8,111,000	15,185,000	53.4
Rhode Island	8,760,000	18,911,000	46.3
Vermont	3,005,000	6,269,000	47.9

SOURCE: U.S. Bureau of the Census, *Manufactures of the United States in 1860* (Washington, D.C.: Government Printing Office, 1865).
NOTE: Value added is net, derived by deducting raw material costs and capital depreciation, uniformly estimated at 8 percent of capital's value, from value of output.
[a]Wage share equals wages divided by value added times 100.

added was low in the early stage of urban labor market development and improved only after the removal of market imperfections.[43]

Wage shares in American manufacturing support this hypothesis. In New England, for example, textile-mill wage shares deteriorated from 1820 to 1840 as the new factory system displaced artisanal production. Wages constituted about 48 percent of value added in the 1820s but only 40 percent between 1830 and 1860.[44] The manufacturing census of 1860 (Table 5.2) provides further corroboration. It shows that wage shares of value added were lowest in the grain belt (44.7 percent) from the Mid-Atlantic states through the Midwest. The chief exception was in Minnesota, where high wage shares reflected an immature frontier economy. The same source reports, as expected, higher labor shares in the deep South (49.1 percent), particularly in the Gulf and Atlantic Coast states, despite the use of cheap slave labor in factory production. The highest wage share occurred in New England (51.5 percent). This pattern is not particularly surprising. Labor's share had doubtlessly fallen earlier in the century, a point suggested by the textile industry, and, by 1860, labor supply was both less elastic and better organized. Accordingly, wage shares in New England increased at the expense of the producer's surplus. Rising wage shares are also suggested by Edward C. Budd's examination of factor shares after 1850.[45]

Such changes in wage shares seem to be intimately connected with economic development in its early stages. Lewis has suggested that wage shares traditionally follow a uniform pattern as economic

43. This argument closely resembles Sir Arthur Lewis's model of economic development with unlimited supplies of cheap labor. Wages rose later in the century, but whether because of perfect competition or as a result of labor's struggle for an increased share of the product remains an empirical issue. American rural labor became less elastic as it found off-season employment, thereby raising rural earnings and, hence, the transfer wage. Rural income on the Dakota frontier, for example, rose in the late nineteenth century, and higher labor costs probably hindered the region's urban growth; see John C. Hudson, "Migration to an American Frontier," *Annals of the Association of American Geographers* 66 (1976), pp. 242–65.

44. Robert Zevin, "The Growth of Cotton Textile Production after 1815," in *The Reinterpretation of American Economic History*, ed. Robert W. Fogel and Stanley L. Engerman (New York: Harper and Row, 1971), pp. 122–47.

45. *Manufactures of the United States in 1860, Compiled from the Original Returns of the Eighth Census* (Washington, D.C.: U.S. Bureau of the Census, 1865); and Edward C. Budd, "Factor Shares, 1850–1910," in *Trends in the American Economy in the Nineteenth Century*, ed. William N. Parker, National Bureau of Economic Research, Studies in Income and Wealth, No. 24 (Princeton, N.J.: Princeton University Press, 1960), pp. 365–98.

development takes place, with labor's share starting small and then growing larger as the process accelerates. Is it coincidence, for example, that the wage share of Illinois in 1860 resembles that of the developing nation of Venezuela in the 1950s?[46] Lewis's model would suggest not. Rather, his argument posits an evolutionary process wherein labor subsidizes capital investment for a time but then labor's position improves as labor supply becomes less elastic and, we would add, as seasonal market imperfections are removed. Wage shares as indicators of development, however, must be used cautiously, and, in this regard, middling wage shares are particularly difficult to interpret. They may indicate two different courses of economic development: (1) they may reveal, as Lewis suggests, development through the progressive erosion of the producer's surplus as the labor supply becomes less elastic; or (2) they may indicate a situation of economic stagnation caused by initially high wages and earnings for labor that allow a negligible producer's surplus and, hence, very little "plowback capital" for development. The second situation arose in the American South, where the long crop season created high rural wages, and it has also emerged in underdeveloped countries, where minimum wage legislation or related policies have artificially raised the transfer wage. In both instances, that of the antebellum South and that of contemporary underdeveloped countries, the effect on economic development has been an appreciable retardation of the industrialization process.[47] Industrialization and labor exploitation, it appears, have proceeded hand in hand.

In sum, the reasonably low-cost labor that existed in the American Midwest was indispensable for that region's economic advance, although the position of labor within that process was an unenviable one. In the grain belts of the United States, the exploitation of labor persisted until economic growth established a more competitive labor market in increasingly autonomous urban areas.

Rural Labor and Industrialization in the Middle States, 1790–1840

Low-cost labor was used in the Midwest in the 1850s as it had been earlier in New England and the Mid-Atlantic states. In each of

46. Lewis, "Reflections on Unlimited Labour," pp. 89–90.
47. Bateman and Weiss, "Comparative Regional Development," pp. 182–208. On underdeveloped countries, see various essays in Meier, *Leading Issues in Economic Development*.

these areas, cheap labor provided the stimulus not only for industrial growth but also for the process whereby skilled labor was replaced by a combination of machine technology and unskilled labor. The Philadelphia region in the early nineteenth century illustrates this development. This area combined mixed grain farming, impressive urban growth, and an early start in manufacturing and the factory system.[48] Here, inexpensive labor was the decisive inducement for the mechanization of cotton textile production.

Between 1800 and 1830 Philadelphia's merchants and manufacturers had solid reasons for using low-cost agricultural labor in urban jobs. By the turn of the century, the city's extensive hinterland had matured into perhaps the preeminent mixed-farming region in the nation. High yields of wheat and corn from southeastern Pennsylvania as well as the upper half of the Delmarva Peninsula were channeled into Philadelphia as they had been for much of the eighteenth century. Rural labor was abundant as early as the 1750s. At the end of that decade, laborers made up 15 percent of the taxpayers in Lancaster County, Pennsylvania, and small tenants and sharecroppers, also part of the available harvest force, constituted another 10 to 15 percent. These proportions remained the same for at least the next two or three decades. In Chester County, through the start of the nineteenth century, laborers (noted in the tax lists as inmates) constituted from 15 to 23 percent of taxable persons, and another 10 percent were tenants. The abundance of unskilled rural labor permitted a York County farmer to mobilize over one hundred harvesters in 1828. Pennsylvania thus bore a striking resemblance to the Midwest of the 1850s, and this similarity extended also to the seasonal work schedule. Farm workers toiled mainly in the harvest. Although some laborers may have worked seven or eight months of the year on diversified farms close to Philadelphia, the overwhelming majority worked mainly between April and July. This was a sore point for the property owners of the town of Lancaster, who complained as early as 1767 that "quitrents could never be collected from the poor of the town, who were idle for 'want of employment,' except during harvest time."[49]

48. For two especially relevant studies, see James T. Lemon, *The Best Poor Man's Country: A Geographical Study of Early Southeastern Pennsylvania* (Baltimore: Johns Hopkins University Press, 1972); and Diane Lindstrom, *Economic Development in the Philadelphia Region, 1810–1850* (New York: Columbia University Press, 1978).

49. Lemon, *The Best Poor Man's Country*, pp. 12, 96, 234; James T. Lemon and Gary B. Nash, "The Distribution of Wealth in Eighteenth-Century America: A Century of Change in Chester County, Pennsylvania, 1693–1802," *Journal of Social History* 2 (1968),

In the Delmarva portion of the hinterland, the labor pattern was similar. Farm account books there clearly reveal the preference of grain farmers for hiring day laborers frequently, one- or two-month laborers occasionally, and longer-term laborers rarely, if at all. On the mixed-grain Dixon farm between 1821 and 1824, day laborers were preferred. They constituted seven of the eight laborers hired in 1821, eight of the twelve in 1822, fifteen of the eighteen in 1823, and eight of the ten in 1824. Of the ten workers hired on other terms, six were hired for two months or less, two for eight months, and two for a year. Hired help was required for grain harvesting and haying in late June and July and, except for a hand or two, was unnecessary for the rest of the year. Even the one- and two-month hands were taken on for the June and July work peak.[50] In short, the grain economy in the rural zone around Philadelphia had created by the 1780s, and perhaps earlier, a permanent pool of rural day laborers. Their work was confined mainly to the harvest season (to an even greater degree than that of midwestern laborers in the 1850s), and their annual earnings were, of necessity, very small.

Rural labor became even cheaper for Philadelphians between 1815 and 1830. The region's export staples of wheat, corn, and derivative commodities stagnated following the Napoleonic Wars and the recession of 1819. Rural farm wages and earnings followed the downward course. In 1818, 1826, and 1830—critical years for technological innovation in Philadelphia—farm wages fell from $11.00 to between $9.00 and $9.50 per month. Paralleling the wages of farm hands, the wages of unskilled workers on eastern Pennsylvania iron

---

pp. 1–24; Stevenson Whitcomb Fletcher, *Pennsylvania Agriculture and Country Life, 1640–1840* (Harrisburg, Pa.: Historical and Museum Commission, 1950), pp. 119–20; Lucy Simler and Paul G. E. Clemens, "The 'Best Poor Man's Country' in 1783: The Population Structure of Rural Society in Late-Eighteenth-Century Southeastern Pennsylvania," *Transactions of the American Philosophical Society* 113 (1989), pp. 234–61.

50. Julia Ann Dixon, Farmer, Private Accounts, Delaware State Archives, Dover, Del. For other useful private accounts, see those of Isaac Gurwell, 1791–1808; Joseph Evans, 1785–1805; and Bennett Downes, 1793–1814; Delaware State Archives, Dover, Del. These combinations of seasonal and annual workers compare favorably with those on the bonanza farms of the Great Plains after the Civil War. On one of the largest of these farms, which employed up to 250 laborers, only 8 percent of the laborers worked for ten to twelve months, while 92 percent worked five months or less. These figures are calculated from data in Fred A. Shannon, *The Farmer's Last Frontier: Agriculture, 1860–1897* (New York: Harper and Row, 1945), p. 159. Allan G. Applen, "Labor Casualization in Great Plains Wheat Production," *Journal of the West* 16 (1977), pp. 5–9.

plantations fell from \$15 to between \$12 and \$13.[51] This synchronous movement of wages suggests that farm laborers and unskilled ironworkers supplied the same market and thus experienced the same economic pattern of recession and recovery.

The phenomenon of urban industrial growth during recessions, though paradoxical, is precisely what happened in Philadelphia during the 1820s. Albert Fishlow has noted a connection between depression, increased labor inputs, and import substitution in the economic growth of Brazil during the 1930s, and a comparable situation occurred more than a century earlier in the Philadelphia region.[52] The fall of wages between 1818 and 1826 expanded the demand for unskilled urban labor at the expense of farm labor. Changes in agriculture and urbanization are certainly compatible with this labor shift. Farm wages fell because of a marked slowdown in the trade of farm products, as evidenced by Philadelphia's grain receipts. Exports tailed off during the 1820s, as did grain, flour, and meal inspections. Wheat, flour, and corn inspections either lessened or grew at modest annual rates of up to 1.48 percent. As the farm commodity trade declined, so did farm earnings and the level of the transfer wage. Laborers moved to the towns and cities in the region, as Diane Lindstrom has clearly shown. Philadelphia, for example, grew by nearly 38 percent between 1820 and 1830, a decade in which there was little foreign immigration; this growth rate was about double that of its hinterland.[53] Laborers were induced to go to the city even though wages were falling rapidly because city life had a compensating feature, the declining cost of living. Wholesale prices had fallen by as much as 80 percent from peaks reached during the War of 1812, and by the 1820s, prices had fallen to 1790 levels. The recession after the War of 1812 thus meant lower labor costs for urban entrepreneurs and declining living costs for new migrants to the city.[54]

In brief, the recession merely mobilized an already abundant and inexpensive labor force. As farmers retrenched with the slowdown

51. Lebergott, *Manpower in Economic Growth*, p. 539; Zabler, "Further Evidence on American Wage Differentials," pp. 109–17.

52. Albert Fishlow, "Origins and Consequences of Import Substitution in Brazil," in *International Economics and Development: Essays in Honor of Raul Prebisch*, ed. Luis Eugenio DiMarco (New York: Academic Press, 1972), pp. 311–65.

53. Lindstrom, *Economic Development in the Philadelphia Region*, pp. 170–74. On the importance of rural to urban migration for a later time, see John Modell, "The Peopling of a Working-Class Ward: Reading, Pennsylvania, 1850," *Journal of Social History* 5 (1971), pp. 71–95.

54. Adams, "Wage Rates in the Early National Period," p. 424.

of trade, rural laborers were attracted to cities and towns to which they had often drifted during the off-season. But this time many laborers remained permanently, because the city offered steadier employment at slightly higher wages accompanied by declining living costs. Urban work was created by the entrepreneurs of Philadelphia and its region who accurately understood how they might use the cheap unskilled labor force available to them. Some firms, such as the iron furnaces, with their enormous demand for woodcutters, provided winter work for these laborers. More ingeniously, other firms borrowed British technology and, by using the machine, tapped the pool of cheap labor and endowed it with extraordinary skills.[55]

The motive behind capital investment in machines was a simple one—to convert cheap unskilled labor into cheap skilled labor. Habakkuk's argument notwithstanding, there is little evidence that entrepreneurs envisioned machines as increasing the productivity of unskilled labor. Quite the opposite: they regarded machines, along with division of labor, as allowing them to maintain roughly the same output while drastically cutting labor costs. In this spirit Eli Whitney claimed that interchangeable parts would "substitute correct and effective operations of machinery for that skill of the artist which is acquired only by long practice and experience; a species of skill which is not possessed in this country to any considerable extent." Whitney did not emphasize the machine's ability to increase physical product but rather how the shortage of skilled labor could be overcome by the combination of machines and unskilled labor. Some years later, James Montgomery succinctly stated entrepreneurial motives from the cost side. "The great object with all manufacturers in this country," he claimed, "is to pay their help just such wages as will be a sufficient inducement for them to remain at the work. Hence the greater the quantity of work produced, the higher the profits, because paid at a lower rate of wages."[56] Philadelphians understood the language of Whitney and Montgomery, and they put it to prac-

55. For the story of efforts to secure British textile technology, see David J. Jeremy, "British Textile Technology Transmission to the United States: The Philadelphia Region Experience, 1770–1820," *Business History Review* 27 (1973), pp. 24–52.

56. William P. Blake, "Sketch of the Life of Eli Whitney, the Inventor of the Cotton Gin," *Papers of the New Haven Historical Society* 5 (New Haven, Conn.: New Haven Historical Society, 1894), p. 122, as quoted in Habakkuk, *American and British Technology*, p. 22. James Montgomery, *Practical Detail of the Cotton Manufactures of the United States of America and the State of the Cotton Manufactures of That Country Contrasted with That of Great Britain* (Glasgow: J. Niven, 1840), pp. 97–98.

tice. By using machines and low-priced labor, they could produce the same output, at a slightly lower cost, as by using skilled high-priced workers. In so doing, they undermined the status of skilled laborers, pushing them down toward the level of the unskilled workers.

One of the great advances in the American industrial revolution was the application of machines in the cotton textile industry. Philadelphia and New England were in the front ranks in adopting this technology during the decade and a half after the War of 1812. In both regions, machine-made cloth of coarse but sturdy quality rapidly displaced the domestic plaids, ginghams, and checks produced by the highly skilled mule spinners and hand-loom weavers. Local yarn mills, supplying local weavers and household looms, gave way to integrated mills combining the new technologies of throstle spindles, filling frames, roving machines, and power looms.[57] David J. Jeremy has detailed a number of basic organizational and technological innovations that expanded American textile production from 1814 to 1840.[58] Larger machines were introduced that increased the number of spindles per operator from 64 to 166. Similarly, the speeds at which the machines operated were accelerated by over 100 percent, and virtually all stages of production were mechanized and featured, by 1840, automatic fault detection systems. In another important decision, the manufacturers narrowed the range of goods they produced for the middle- and lower-quality mass markets. This step simplified operating procedures, shortened the learning period for the untrained worker, and allowed the use of less complex machinery. Finally, as happened at Waltham, manufacturers initiated the process of vertical integration to concentrate "unskilled teenage females as the nucleus of a labor force," whose physical weaknesses and lack of skill were compensated for by "maximum mechanical work."

57. Zevin, "The Growth of Cotton Textile Production," pp. 122–47; Caroline F. Ware, *The Early New England Cotton Manufacture: A Case Study in Industrial Beginnings* (1931; reprint, New York: Houghton Mifflin, 1966), pp. 3–118; William A. Sullivan, *The Industrial Worker in Pennsylvania, 1800–1840* (Harrisburg, Pa.: Historical and Museum Commission, 1935), pp. 17–27; Jeremy, "British Textile Technology Transmission," pp. 24–52. See Cynthia J. Shelton's insightful study of the archetypal case in the Philadelphia region, *The Mills of Manayunk: Industrialization and Social Conflict in the Philadelphia Region, 1787–1837* (Baltimore: Johns Hopkins University Press, 1986). Shelton identifies the 1820s as the initial decade for Manayunk's introduction of the power loom and maintains (with somewhat less evidence) that immigrants constituted the mass of unskilled workers—neither of which contradicts the theoretical argument presented here.

58. David J. Jeremy, "Innovation in American Textile Technology during the Early Nineteenth Century," *Technology and Culture* 14 (1973), pp. 40–76.

The same substitution occurred in the Philadelphia region; but there unskilled men and boys were the cheap input, and they were employed disproportionately.[59] James Montgomery, in calculating the results of these changes, estimated in 1840 that a British mill of 128 looms produced 35,000 yards of cloth in two weeks, while its American equivalent made some 51,300 yards in the same period.[60]

Rural Labor and Textile Industrialization: Philadelphia and England Compared

The decisive victory of the machine in American textile manufacturing stands in marked contrast to the sluggish diffusion of machine technology in Britain. The difference may be explained by contrasting labor supplies. In comparing the economics of using the hand-loom weaver or the power-loom operator in Philadelphia and Britain, two points become apparent. First, the transfer wage was lower in Philadelphia than in Britain, so American costs for unskilled labor and power looms were lower than the costs of hand-loom weavers; conversely, British hand-loom weavers were generally cheaper than unskilled laborers using the new technology. Second, the output of hand and power looms were very much the same, so productivity did not figure as a motive for machine investment.

In the Philadelphia region, cheap labor and textile machinery proved less costly than skilled textile operators, and, accordingly, manufacturers pursuing the "great object" of low wages adopted the new textile technology. Unskilled urban labor was inexpensive because of the low transfer wage occasioned by the sizable number of

59. Women were considerably more numerous in the textile industry in New England (New Hampshire, Rhode Island, and Massachusetts) than in the mills located in the grain belt of the Middle Atlantic states (New Jersey, Delaware, Maryland, and the Eastern District of Pennsylvania). The 1822 census of manufactures discloses that women constituted 33.3 percent of all employees in New England mills but only 16 percent in those of the Mid-Atlantic states. Excluding children, who constituted about half of the employed in both regions, women comprised 63.5 percent of the employees in New England. See U.S. State Department, *Digest of Accounts of Manufacturing Establishments in the United States, and of Their Manufactures* (Washington: Gales and Seaton, 1823). For further detail on New England's industrialization and the role of labor, see Field, "Sectoral Shift in Antebellum Massachusetts," pp. 146–71. Although Shelton contends that the gender composition of Manayunk and New England mills of the 1830s were similar, her statistical grouping of women and children does not permit substantiation of the case. Shelton, *The Mills of Manayunk*, pp. 62–63.

60. Jeremy, "Innovation in American Textile Technology," pp. 40–76.

farm laborers, the problem of seasonality, and the duress of the Mid-Atlantic agricultural economy after the War of 1812, which led to a decline in rural wages. Meanwhile, skilled labor was quite costly. Skilled workers continued to command high wages despite the economic slowdown after 1815, and, as a consequence, the differential between their wages and those of the unskilled widened and reached a maximum in 1822.[61]

The low transfer wage in the hinterland of Philadelphia reflected the acute seasonality of the region's rural economy. Rural wages amounted to about $10 per month, so earnings (using an employment estimate generously set at four months) amounted to $40 per year. Rural subsistence costs in the off-season consumed about $26 to $27 of labor's earnings.[62] Rural life offered little promise, especially in areas wracked by depression, where little land was available and population pressure made land acquisition improbable. In this context, the city offered an attractive alternative. Urban living costs were about $55 for a single adult male, which implies a transfer wage (W_u) of about $68 to $69. The compensation for rural non-pecuniary income, however, appears to have been quite large. The intangible income of rural life, judging from the $110 per year earned by unskilled workers on the Pennsylvania Canal, was about double farm wages.[63] A high non-pecuniary income is not unreasonable for a low

61. Zabler, "Further Evidence on American Wage Differentials," pp. 109–17. The differential remained substantial even after 1822; see Table 5.1. Using literary evidence on the post-1815 glut of skilled weavers in the Philadelphia region, Shelton infers that their wages fell. My suspicion, however, is that skilled wage rates had recovered by 1820 when power looms were introduced. Shelton, *The Mills of Manayunk*, pp. 48–53.

62. Board is estimated at one-third the monthly wage. Lebergott, *Manpower in Economic Growth*, pp. 257–72, esp. p. 262; Nicholas Biddle, "Address by Nicholas Biddle, Esq., 15 January 1822," in *Sketch of the History of the Philadelphia Society for Promoting Agriculture* (Philadelphia, 1939), pp. 49–50.

63. M. Carey, *Appeal to the Wealthy of the Land, Ladies as well as Gentlemen, on the Character, Conduct, Situation, and Prospects of Those Whose Sole Dependence for Subsistence Is on the Labour of Their Hands*, 3rd ed. (Philadelphia: L. Johnson, 1833), pp. 8–9. Living costs are based on estimates for a family of two adults and two children (equated as one adult). I thus divide family living costs by three to get an individual laborer's expenses. Although unskilled urban wages were low, steady employment frequently compensated—a point made by James Ronaldson, an employer located in the manufacturing district of Rockdale in southeastern Pennsylvania, who observed in 1832, "I know that, in consequence of our men losing no time from bad weather, want of jobs, and at fifty cents per day, the old men and youths thrive better than on a farm or at laboring work and job work. Indeed, in this establishment, one family whose father is a mason, and another family whose father is a country carpenter, has been supported by them all last winter: the men were out of em-

TABLE 5.3

Daily, Weekly, and Annual Wages of Labor in England and the United States,
Old and New Technologies

(*In dollars*)

	England			United States		
	Daily	Weekly	Yearly	Daily	Weekly	Yearly
Old Technology						
Common mule spinners						
in cotton mills	1.02	6.12	318.24	1.24[b]	7.44	386.88
Weavers on Handlooms	.74	4.44	230.88	.90	5.40	280.80
New Technology						
Boys 10 or 12 years of age						
(spindles)	.22	1.30	67.60	.25	1.50	78.00
Women in cotton mills						
(power looms)	.33	1.96	101.92	.42	2.50[c]	130.00
Farm Labor (board included						
and expenses deducted)	—	—	170.00[a]	—	—	13.31[d]

SOURCES: Farm labor wages are as estimated in text, with board and expenses deducted for periods of unemployment. Otherwise wages are adapted from Zachariah Allen, *The Science of Mechanics* (Providence, R.I.: Hutchens and Cory, 1829), p. 347, and reprinted in Nathan Rosenberg, "Anglo-American Wage Differences in the 1820s," *Journal of Economic History*, 27 (1967), 221–29, Table 1.

NOTE: The yearly wage is based on 312 working days.

[a] See text.
[b] Mean of the range of $1.08 to $1.40 per day.
[c] Mean of the range of $2.00 to $3.00 per week.
[d] $40 minus $26.69.

income, preindustrial economy; however, its size may be slightly exaggerated by underestimation of off-season employment. Supposing that $110 indicates the annual wage at which rural labor would have migrated to urban jobs, we may compare this wage to those prevailing in the textile industry during the 1820s (see Table 5.3).[64]

---

ployment." Ronaldson to Mathew Carey and Clement C. Biddle, in U.S. Department of the Treasury, *Documents Relative to the Manufactures in the United States Collected and Transmitted to the House of Representatives in Compliance with a Resolution of January 19, 1832*, Vol. 3 (Washington: Secretary of the Treasury, 1833), pp. 212–14. For further details on Ronaldson's mill, see Anthony F. C. Wallace, *Rockdale: The Growth of an American Village in the Early Industrial Revolution* (New York: Knopf, 1978).

64. The estimates presented here suggest that unskilled men and women received comparable annual earnings in the textile industry, and this may account for the disproportionate employment of men in the Mid-Atlantic region. By contrast, in New England the wages of unskilled men seem to have been considerably higher than those of women, thus giving the latter a competitive advantage. Parenthetically, the lower wages paid to New England women may reflect the region's high ratio of women to men in the general population. For New England, see Thomas Dublin, *Women at Work: The Transformation of Work and Community in Lowell, Massachusetts, 1826–1860* (New York: Columbia University Press, 1979), p. 65; Howard Gitelman, "The Waltham System and the Coming of the

Consider the firm choosing between the old and new technologies. Its costs for the old technology were the wages paid to skilled hand-loom weavers, whose average earnings were $280 per year. If a firm wished to replace hand-loom weavers with power looms and unskilled workers and if physical outputs and cloth values were equal and canceled productivity differences, unskilled labor would have been cheaper, provided machine costs fell under $170.80, which they usually did. Power looms in the period from 1815 to 1825 varied in price, ranging from $125 for the expensive Waltham loom to as little as $70 for other models.[65] As most operators handled two looms, machine costs were doubled, and total costs for machines and unskilled labor amounted to $250 to $360. Loom costs, however, would have depreciated over their useful lives, and, hence, annual costs were considerably below these figures. Paul A. David has shown that looms installed in the 1830s had an average life of 37 years, but this is surely too long for the first power looms installed in the 1810s and 1820s.[66] The risks of technological obsolescence and rapidly falling machine prices warrant an accelerated depreciation schedule. Five years seems a maximum, given market and technological uncertainties, and such a short useful life has the effect of making the cost of the new technology more expensive.[67] Annual machine costs, then, amounted to $28 to $50, and, adding in labor ($110), total costs came to between $138 and $160. When the hand-loom operator cost $280 (the weaver bore the cost of his or her loom), textile manufacturers stood to save $120 to $142 per operator by turning to the power loom and low-priced, unskilled labor.

Irish," *Labor History* 8 (1967), pp. 227–53; and Jonathan Prude, *The Coming of Industrial Order: Town and Factory Life in Rural Massachusetts, 1810–1860* (Cambridge, Mass.: Harvard University Press, 1983).

65. Although the argument made here focuses on the introduction of the power loom, a similar case can be made for the rationality of adopting other new machines in the textile industry and in other industries as well. George Sweet Gibb, *The Saco-Lowell Shops: Textile Machinery Building in New England, 1813–1949* (Cambridge, Mass.: Harvard University Press, 1950), pp. 39–50, esp. p. 42.

66. Paul A. David, "The 'Horndahl Effect' in Lowell, 1834–56: A Short-Run Learning Curve for Integrated Cotton Textile Mills," in *Technical Choice Innovation and Economic Growth: Essays on American and British Experience in the Nineteenth Century* (London: Cambridge University Press, 1975), p. 177.

67. Rental rates of $10 to $15 a year for looms that the Boston Manufacturing Company sold at $125 imply a useful life of eight to twelve-and-a-half years; thus, the estimate of five years certainly gives an upward bias to machine costs. Gibb, *The Saco-Lowell Shops*, pp. 42–43.

Habakkuk has argued that machines were adopted not to cut costs but to raise labor productivity. No evidence points to gains in physical productivity, however, until long after the introduction of machines, and these gains may be attributed to technical improvements and organizational efficiencies unanticipated by the innovators. New technologies frequently involved no clear gains in productivity. A case in point was Oliver Evans's grain mill, which increased output by perhaps as little as 10 percent; more importantly, his mill enabled the use of boys and unskilled men, both employable at low wages.

The physical output of the power-loom operators initially seems to have been about the same as that of the hand-loom weavers. Although the claim has been made that the power-loom operator of the 1830s turned out seven times the cloth produced by the skilled weaver, this estimate presents the power loom in the most favorable light.[68] Perhaps the most efficient mills of New England in about 1830 had achieved this level of advantage. In these elite mills, an operator tending two power looms fed by 70 spindles produced 33,708 yards of cloth (of relatively low thread count) per year. By contrast, expert Philadelphia hand-loom weavers turned out 18 yards per day and, therefore, 5,598 yards during the conventional working year of 311 days.[69] This sixfold advantage of New England over Philadelphia was unusual in 1830 and is grossly out of line for the period from 1815 to 1825, when the new technology was introduced. A more likely figure for the majority of mills is based on American cloth output in 1831, and the assumption that there were 15 spindles feeding each power loom. Each power-loom operator would have turned out only 5,561 yards of cloth—a figure almost identical to that of hand-loom weavers.[70] At earlier dates, the spindle-to-loom ratio was closer to the lower estimate. In 1827, an integrated mill at

68. The sevenfold advantage reputedly occurred on British steam looms, with operators tending two looms each; Edward Baines, *History of the Cotton Manufacture in Great Britain* (London: H. Fisher, R. Fisher, and P. Jackson, 1835), pp. 239–40.

69. The New England estimates are calculated from spindle counts and cloth output figures in David, "Learning by Doing and Tariff Protection," pp. 95–173, and from ranges of spindle-to-loom ratios suggested in Zevin, "The Growth of Cotton Textile Production," p. 141. For the suggestion of low productivity for power looms in Britain in 1819, see S. J. Chapman, *The Lancashire Cotton Industry* (Manchester: University of Manchester Press, 1904), p. 31. On hand-loom production in Philadelphia, see Sullivan, *The Industrial Worker in Pennsylvania*, p. 39.

70. David, "Learning by Doing and Tariff Protection," pp. 95–173; Zevin, "The Growth of Cotton Textile Production," p. 141.

Manayunk, near Philadelphia, was set up with a spindle-to-loom ratio of 21.4 to 1. Philadelphia mills in 1819 had a ratio of 8.4 to 1. In New England the first sale of textile machinery by the Boston Manufacturing Company to the Poignard Plant & Company had a ratio of 6.3 to 1; and Boston Manufacturing's sales and grants of rights to use their equipment between 1817 and 1823 indicate 14 spindles for every loom. These low ratios of spindles to power looms suggest that the early mills were far less productive than the elite mills of New England in the 1830s and imply a cloth output of about 5,600 yards per power-loom operator. There was, therefore, no immediate appreciable gain in physical productivity with the shift to power looms.[71]

Although the outputs of hand and power looms were roughly the same, cloth woven on the hand loom commanded a higher price, and price differences may have narrowed the advantage of the new technology. Some idea of the price spread is apparent in wholesale prices of high quality checks and coarse sheeting in Philadelphia. In 1819, hand-loom checks brought a margin of 2.12 cents per yard over power-loom sheetings.[72] This price spread meant that the hand-loom weaver earned the firm about $118 more than the power-loom operator; these higher revenues, however, did not offset the lower costs of the power loom and unskilled labor. On the cost side, the new technology had an advantage of $120 to $142 per worker, which more than compensated for the higher value of cloth produced by the hand-loom weaver. The power loom's advantage was even greater when hand-loom weavers turned out less than the eighteen yards per day which was the standard for expert weavers.

The case of the power loom underscores the characteristic feature of American capitalism—namely, the use of cheap, instead of expensive, inputs, provided any differences in productivity are overcome. As firms introduced the new technology, their productivity remained stable, but they gained cost advantages by substituting low-cost, unskilled labor for expensive, skilled labor. Machines endowed

71. Sullivan, *The Industrial Worker in Pennsylvania*, pp. 17–23; Gibb, *The Saco-Lowell Shops*, pp. 40–47; Jeremy, "British Textile Technology Transmission," pp. 24–52. For a recent report of similar outputs for English hand and power looms about 1810, see John Stephen Lyons, "The Lancashire Cotton Industry and the Introduction of the Power-Loom, 1815–1850," *Journal of Economic History* 38 (1978), pp. 283–84.

72. These price spreads give a rough idea of the advantage of hand-loom weavers; but the prices generally represent imported goods, so conclusions on this matter must remain tentative. The Bezanson prices must serve until we have a price series for domestic cloths: Anne Bezanson et al., *Wholesale Prices in Philadelphia, 1784–1861: Part II: Series of Relative Monthly Prices* (Philadelphia: University of Pennsylvania Press, 1937), pp. 30, 196.

unskilled workers with the ability to make a simple, coarse fabric. Although worker productivity at a later date underwent vast expansion because of technical and organizational efficiencies, to assert that American firms introduced machines for the purpose of elevating labor's physical productivity is to read history backwards.

On the other side of the Atlantic, industrialization followed a different course. English textile manufacturers were relatively slow in adopting the new technology. Skilled laborers continued running the hand looms and the mules despite the availability of power looms, throstle frames, and related machinery. The explanation for the slow pace of British technological diffusion is merely the reverse of that used for the United States.

In England the old technology remained more profitable than the new, largely because skilled workers were cheaper and more abundant and unskilled workers were more expensive than their American counterparts. During the mid-1820s, English hand-loom weavers earned $230, about $50 less than American weavers.[73] The lower costs of skilled labor precluded a massive influx of unskilled English farm labor into the city. English rural labor, unlike American, was expensive; estimates put a laborer's earnings at about $170 annually, board included.[74] These high incomes reflected nearly year-round employment. English farming was much more diversified than American farming, integrating crops and livestock in greater variety, placing emphasis on labor-intensive activities such as raising

73.   Rosenberg, "Anglo-American Wage Differences in the 1820s," pp. 221–29.
74.   H. C. Carey, *Essay on the Rate of Wages*, p. 91; Adams, "Some Evidence on English and American Wage Rates," pp. 505–6; Hobsbawm and Rude, *Captain Swing*, pp. 23–55. As noted earlier, rural earnings varied markedly from place to place and among farm laborers' families. Our estimates are, however, consistent with the comprehensive survey of Norfolk and Suffolk laborers in the 1830s undertaken by James Phillips Kay, who demonstrated that the average yearly earnings for laborers in families amounted to $173. The range varied from $120 per year for single laborers to a family income of $216 for families with several children over ten years of age. Kay's survey of 539 laborers also underlines employment opportunities during the lengthy farm year characteristic of English agriculture. Kay, "Earnings of Agricultural Labourers in Norfolk and Suffolk." Equally instructive is the importance of marriage and the family. Among the 539 laborers surveyed by Kay, 93.3 percent were married and 81.4 had children. If opportunities were severely limited in the English countryside, such widespread household and family formation would have been much less prevalent, particularly since children constituted a clear economic burden until they reached the age of ten. The English pattern contrasts sharply with that of the American Midwest at the same time; Schob's survey of townships in 1860 shows that 25 percent or less of the laborers were married; Schob, *Hired Hands and Plowboys*, pp. 268–72. In short, rural laborers in the American grain belt did not form families in the countryside as did their English counterparts.

FIGURE 5.6. Mid-nineteenth-century representations of textile weaving using the old technology of the hand loom and the new technology of the power loom. Note that the power loom operator is attending four machines; earlier in the century, when power looms were first introduced, operators usually attended just two machines. Reproduced from Eminent Literary Men, *One Hundred Years' Progress of the United States* (Hartford, Conn.: L. Stebbins, 1872), p. 277.

potatoes and turnips along with grains, and providing daily attention to livestock. Land improvements—notably draining, marling, manuring, and pasture making—also commanded the laborer's attention during the year. Annual labor contracts were not uncommon, and the seasonal unemployment endemic to American grain farming was generally absent in the English landscape. Year-long employment often included board, and hence subsistence costs were low for the English farm laborer.[75]

The English worker contemplating a move to the city certainly faced living costs as high as those in the United States ($55). The transfer wage ($W_u$) equalizing city and country earnings then amounted to an urban wage of $225. Including non-pecuniary income, estimated here as 30 percent of rural earnings, the transfer wage (W_u'), required to move the unskilled laborer permanently from farm to city, becomes $276: remembering that $W_u = C_u - C_r + W_r$ and that $W_u' = C_u - C_r + 1.3(W_r)$, we see that $W_u = \$55 - \$0 + \$170$, while $W_u' = \$55 - \$0 + 1.3(\$170)$. Thus, $W_u = \$225$ and $W_u' = \$276$.[76]

75. On continued use of yearly contracts and the rural hostility aroused in 1830 by attempts to put labor on a wage-rate basis, paying by the day or by the month, see Hobsbawm and Rude, *Captain Swing*, pp. 23–55. The drive to put English farm labor on a wage-rate basis would have made English laborers much more like their American counterparts, although the labor intensity of English agriculture would have precluded the long periods of seasonal unemployment that typified American grain-farming regions; see J. D. Chambers and G. E. Mingay, *The Agricultural Revolution, 1750–1880* (New York: Schocken Books, 1966), esp. pp. 133–34; and Jones, *Agriculture and the Industrial Revolution*, pp. 211–33. Subsistence costs may have been higher in the south of England, where six-month or yearly contracts gave way to day work, piece work, and harvest wages and where the laborer usually provided his own room and board. We may estimate an extreme lower bound for rural net income by using the earnings ($120) of a single laborer finding his own room and board except during the harvest and haymaking season of 11 weeks; subsistence costs then had to cover the remaining 41 weeks. Jelinger Cookson Symons estimated that it cost 30 shillings per week to maintain a family of five (including two children over fifteen years of age) residing in or near a country town; Symons, *Art and Artisans at Home and Abroad with Sketches of the Progress of Foreign Manufacturers* (Edinburgh: W. Tait, 1839). Subsistence costs for a single laborer would then be about one-fourth that sum, 7.5 shillings per week, or $73.80 for 41 weeks. Net rural earnings would thus amount to $46.20 ($120—$73.80). For Symons's work, see the compilation by Paul Uselding, "Wage and Consumption Levels in England and on the Continent in the 1830s," *Journal of European Economic History* 4 (1975), pp. 501–13. A higher estimate of perhaps 9 shillings per week seems justified for larger cities; see T. R. Gourvish, "The Cost of Living in Glasgow in the Early Nineteenth Century," *Economic History Review*, 2nd ser., 25 (1972), pp. 65–80. The fact that day workers usually received payments in kind equal to an additional 15 percent of their money earnings is consistent with the argument presented here. See Glenn Hueckel, "English Farming Profits during the Napoleonic Wars, 1793–1815," *Explorations in Economic History* 13 (1976), pp. 331–45.

76. If a lower bound is preferred, we may use Kay's data showing a single laborer's earnings of $120, from which maintenance costs of $73.80 are deducted, leaving net rural earnings of $46.20. Adding non-pecuniary income of $36 pushes this total up to $82.20. On the matter of urban living costs, Symons's evidence suggests about 7.5 shillings per week, or $93 dollars per year; adding this to net rural earnings gives a lower bound of the transfer wage at $175, a figure still considerably above the American level. Also, for wages of unskilled men in the textile industry, Symons indicated a weekly wage of $4.32, which converts to annual earnings of $216—a figure close to our theoretical estimate of $225.

English manufacturers rightly saw little reason to introduce machines and tap the pool of rural labor, since rural laborers were more expensive than skilled hand-loom weavers ($230) and less productive. Adding in the costs of power looms made the new technology a losing proposition. Although cotton manufacturers used women on power looms and children on throstle spindles, they could not utilize unskilled rural male labor like their counterparts in the American grain belt.[77] Accordingly, before 1840 the generally beneficent English countryside provided substantial earnings that encouraged rural population growth and discouraged the introduction of the new textile technology. These favorable employment opportunities in rural England were further underscored by the pattern of emigration and immigration. It is important to note that English society sent few emigrants to the low-wage United States. And, for that matter, Irish migrants preferred settlement in high-wage England rather than in the United States.[78]

Uselding, "Wage and Consumption Levels," pp. 501–13. Symons's evidence further sustains my view of the cheapness of English skilled labor. Comparing England and France on the differential wage between skilled workers in various industries and unskilled men in the textile industry shows that the English exhibited a lower differential for machine makers, iron founders, and blacksmiths. Thus, it would appear that the low wages paid to skilled laborers would be a central issue in English economic history. Yet aside from a brilliant essay by E. J. Hobsbawm, this problem has received slight attention; see Hobsbawm, "Custom, Wages, and Work-Load in Nineteenth-Century Industry," in his *Labouring Men: Studies in the History of Labour* (New York: Weidenfeld and Nicolson, 1964), pp. 244–70. On the continuing importance of cheap skilled labor in nineteenth-century industrialization, see D. K. Harley, "Skilled Labour and the Choice of Technique in Edwardian Industry," *Explorations in Economic History* 9 (1974), pp. 391–414.

77. The sex composition of the English cotton textile industry in 1835 resembled that of New England but contrasted sharply with that of the Mid-Atlantic grain belt. Exclusive of children, the work force in England in 1835 consisted of 55.4 percent women; in New England in 1822, 63.5 percent women; and in the Mid-Atlantic states in 1822, just 34.5 percent women; see Phyllis Deane and W. A. Cole, *British Economic Growth, 1688–1959: Trends and Structure*, 2nd ed. (Cambridge: Cambridge University Press, 1967), pp. 182–92; and U.S. State Department, *Digest of Accounts of Manufacturing Establishments in the United States and of their Manufactures* (Washington: Gales and Seaton, 1823). The English preference for employing women with the new textile technology was thoroughly grounded in wage differences between unskilled men and women. Unskilled English women in textiles earned just 33.3 percent of the wages paid to their male counterparts, whereas women earned 70 percent of male wages in France, 57 percent in Switzerland, and 50 percent in Austria and Prussia. Once again, as in the case of cheap skilled English labor, the low wage scale for English women has received surprisingly little attention. For the wage comparisons, see Uselding, "Wage and Consumption Levels," p. 505; and Ivy Pinchbeck, *Women Workers and the Industrial Revolution, 1750–1850* (London: F. S. Crafts, 1969).

78. Various commentators upon this work have suggested that emigration from En-

Labor costs in England and the American grain belt were precisely the reverse of Habakkuk's claim. The Middle Atlantic states
contained low-cost, unskilled rural labor and expensive, skilled urban
labor; firms there introduced machines to tap the supply of inexpensive labor, to cut costs, and to earn a producer's surplus. In England,
skilled labor was comparatively cheap, and firms neglected the new
technology unless inexpensive child and female labor was available.
The subsidy of low-priced labor thus offers a logical and plausible
explanation for the introduction of machines; where unskilled labor
was moderately expensive, as in England, machine technology advanced but slowly, and where it was extremely expensive, as in the
cotton South, machines did not advance at all.

The immediate consequence of the success of the machine in

---

gland contradicts the argument for generally high rural earnings in that nation. In fact,
emigration from the English countryside was decidedly limited during the period under
discussion—a central point in Arthur Redford's classic study, *Labour Migration in England,
1800–1850*, ed. W. H. Chaloner, 3rd ed. (Manchester: Manchester University Press,
1976). Scholars who claim that English migration to the United States was large have been
misled by the aggregation of English, Scottish, and Irish data. In fact, the English contribution to American immigration was negligible between 1820 and 1845. During these
years, England contributed just 31,922 persons, or 2.7 percent of the immigrants to the
United States. Nor does Irish migration to the United States contradict my view. In the
period 1820–33, Irish migrants to this country numbered 38,384. Far more Irish went to
England, though in the absence of official lists I must rely on Irish population estimates
for these figures. As of 1833, native-born Irish accounted for nearly 60,000 people in the
Lancashire cities of Manchester and Liverpool, with at least 30,000 more in that county's
countryside. Another 60,000 lived in London, and many other Irish immigrants were scat-
tered in the smaller cities and towns of England and Scotland. As the author of an 1836
Parliamentary report on the state of the Irish poor in Great Britain remarked: "They are
to be found in greater or less strength in every manufacturing or commercial town from
Aberdeen, Dundee, and Greenock to the central counties of England and the metropolis.
There are also many Irish in the Isle of Man, the Island of Guernsey, and at Sheerness.
Their roaming and restless habits appear to have carried them to every place where there
was any prospect of obtaining profitable employment." House of Commons, *Report on the
State of the Irish Poor in Great Britain, Parliamentary Papers*, Vol. 34 (London, 1836), p. 433.
To these permanent emigrants should be added the seasonal migrant workers, who num-
bered over 57,000 in 1841 according to official, and probably conservative, estimates. In
all, before the famine of the mid-1840s, the Irish moved predominantly to high-wage
England rather than to the low-wage United States. See William J. Bromwell, *History of
Immigration to the United States Exhibiting the Number, Sex, Age, Occupation, and Country of Birth
of Passengers Arriving from Foreign Countries by Sea, 1819 to 1855*, reprint ed. (New York:
Arno Press, 1969); and *Report on the State of the Irish Poor*, pp. 427–642. Also see Oliver
MacDonagh, "The Irish Famine Migration to the United States," *Perspectives in American
History* 10 (1976), pp. 357–446; and E. J. T. Collins, "Migrant Labour in British Agricul-
ture in the Nineteenth Century," *Economic History Review*, 2nd ser., 29 (1976), pp. 38–59,
esp. pp. 40–50.

American textile production was that firms reaped a producer's surplus and labor was exploited. Granted, rural labor improved its income by migrating permanently to urban jobs: annual incomes of unskilled urban workers were better than they would have been in the country because of steady, year-round employment. From the standpoint of the urban firm, however, the level of wages was not the main issue. More important was the share of value added going to labor, and on that score it appears that, even though wages eventually rose, labor's share of value added fell during the phase of initial industrialization. The explanation is simple. As George Gibb understood so well, textile firms achieved this result by hiring disproportionately large numbers of low-cost laborers at the relative expense of skilled positions. Unskilled wages did rise, but because they began at such a low base, workers earned little more than subsistence.[79]

Mathew Carey was particularly outraged by the inadequate incomes earned by workers in Philadelphia during the 1820s and 1830s. Carey understood that these low incomes reflected a structural problem in the economy—what is here labeled as imperfect labor markets occasioned by agricultural seasonality.[80] In the seasonal farm economy of Pennsylvania, the unskilled laborer was part of a vicious cycle. Idle much of the year in the country, he left for the city and there discovered that his wages and earnings were also small because they were determined by what he had made in the countryside. In the short term, Carey's remedy for the urban poor was the compassionate charity of Philadelphians; in the long run, the vicious cycle was smashed by the emergence of more perfectly competitive markets. By 1860, labor's share of value added in manufacturing had risen appreciably in New England and in all probability in the Middle Atlantic states. Thus, development based on cheap labor contained a self-correcting mechanism, so that, as more firms entered the labor market, wages were determined increasingly by supply and demand in urban areas rather than by the transfer wage based on seasonal rural earnings. Simultaneously, however, the asset of cheap labor

79. Gibb observed that the decline in wage shares "did not come about as a result of individual pay cuts, but because of a general shift toward employment of new help at lower rates. . . . This shifting downward of wage rates seems to indicate that machine-building techniques were being systematized to permit the replacement of highly skilled mechanics by lower-paid, more specialized, and less skilled men." Gibb, *The Saco-Lowell Shops*, pp. 54–55.

80. M. Carey, *Appeal to the Wealthy of the Land*, pp. 3–36; Sullivan, *The Industrial Worker in Pennsylvania*, pp. 29–157.

passed on to midwestern wheat and corn states, which rapidly reenacted the course of events that had occurred a half century earlier in
the Mid-Atlantic states, as exemplified by the case of Philadelphia.

Although it is currently fashionable to discount the importance
of staple theory, our research has confirmed the central role of these
commodities in the processes of economic growth, urbanization, and
the transition from preindustrial to industrial economies.[81] From
1800 to 1860 the character of agriculture and the costs of labor in
the United States and England provided the foundation for the development of these countries' respective modern industrial systems.
In each country the physical nature of the staples established the
levels of labor required for their cultivation and, as a corollary, the
income that could be earned by rural laborers. Where labor requirements were seasonal, as in the grain belt of the United States, annual
rural earnings were low. Therefore, the urban transfer wage was correspondingly low, and the pool of low-priced labor arising from the
staple economy could be used in conjunction with the new technology by urban entrepreneurs seeking to reduce the costs of manufactures. By contrast, the cotton economy of the southern United
States created year-round labor requirements and offered high rural
earnings, which would-be urban entrepreneurs were unable to match.
Southern cotton thereby retarded the processes of urbanization and
industrialization that were made possible by the seasonality of northern grains. Finally, in England, the intensification of the agrarian
system did not preclude urbanization, but, by raising the transfer
wage and the cost of unskilled urban labor, it removed a critical incentive for investments in machine technology and preserved a niche
for skilled artisans and craftsmen.[82]

81. For an extended examination of the colonial economy, see Carville Earle and
Ronald Hoffman, "Staple Crops and Urban Development in the Eighteenth-Century
South," *Perspectives in American History* 10 (1976), pp. 5–78; and Chapter 3.

82. The structure of the American and British labor markets also had profound
effects on the politics of labor and the nature of the working class. The social tensions
caused by the displacement of the American skilled artisan by the machine and the unskilled worker were mitigated in England by the relatively high costs of unskilled workers
and the slower pace of technical change. Despite repeated efforts at creating a unified
American working class, such a coalition was doomed by the wide differential in the wages
of the skilled and the unskilled, by the divergence of their economic interests, and by the
recurrent threat of displacement by the machine. These deep-seated divisions in the American labor movement repeatedly undermined working-class alliances during the nineteenth and early twentieth centuries. For elaboration, see Chapter 11 in this volume. The
working-class experience at the Manayunk mills in the 1830s offers an object lesson in the
fragility of these alliances, once we have cleared away the romantic illusion of enduring
class harmony. Shelton, *The Mills of Manayunk*, esp. pp. 134–73.

Staple theory thus offers a compelling interpretation of preindustrial economic development as a precursor of industrial economies as well as an explanation of the transition to industrialization. By clarifying the functional interdependence of rural and urban labor markets and the operation of the transfer wage, staple theory affords a new interpretation of technological change and the origins of industrial economy as well as a prelude to the schismatic predispositions within the American working class.

CHAPTER 6

To Enslave or Not
to Enslave

Crop Seasonality, Labor
Choice, and the Urgency
of the Civil War

The American enslavement of massive numbers of Africans
was not, recent scholarship concludes, an unthinking decision. Enslavement was a deliberate, rational, and purposive
response to dramatic reconfigurations in labor markets and agrarian
systems in the late seventeenth century. In the course of a generation, southern planters abandoned white indentured servants and replaced them with imported African slaves—a labor force that was less
costly and more efficient for embryonic agrarian systems in the Chesapeake and the Carolinas. By 1720, the rational transformation of
the southern labor force was complete; African slaves had been installed as the plantation's primary source of labor and as the region's
largest ethnic minority.[1]

But the decision to enslave (or not to enslave) did not end with
the mass enslavement of Africans between 1680 and 1720. From that
point until the abolition of slavery in 1865, rational agrarians reenacted this decision-making process again and again. Rational choice—
by definition—entails perennial reassessment of labor efficiencies
(slave or free) amidst a context of changing labor markets and inno-

I am indebted to Allan Bogue and the late Franklin Mendels for their comments and
suggestions, and to David Donald for his skepticism.
1. Russell R. Menard, "From Servants to Slaves: The Transformation of the Chesapeake Labor System," *Southern Studies* 16 (1977), pp. 355–90. David W. Galenson, *White
Servitude in Colonial America: An Economic Analysis* (Cambridge: Cambridge University Press,
1981).

vations in agrarian practice. Neither farmers nor planters, northern or southern, could evade the decision to enslave or not to enslave until slavery as a viable labor choice was abolished once and for all, until it was removed from the domain of acceptable alternatives within the labor market.

The question of slavery was especially relevant in an expansive national economy such as the United States. Agrarians soon discovered that the terms of labor's employment (the very basis of rational choice) were in constant flux, ever shifting as a result of volatile labor markets and relentless agrarian innovations. Comparative labor force efficiencies, in consequence, were rarely fixed for long. Conditions that in one period made slavery profitable and viable might just as readily disappear in another; and conversely, slavery's rational advantage in one place might just as easily spill over to another. Enmeshed in this dynamic and unpredictable context, rational agrarians had little choice but to be constantly vigilant, continually checking and rechecking the comparative profitabilities of slavery, servitude, and free hired hands, and entertaining always the prospect of abandoning one mode of labor for another.

This paper explores the perennial choice (one is tempted to say dilemma) that a dynamic capitalism imposed upon rational agrarians during the century and three-quarters between the mass enslavement that took place around the 1680s and slavery's abolition in 1865. The discussion privileges regions and times that experienced sudden changes in the terms of labor's employment, where the pressure to choose between slavery and freedom was extraordinarily acute and where, after rational evaluation, agrarians abandoned (or considered abandoning) one labor supply for another. Attention focuses on two regions, one that abandoned slavery—the eastern shore of Maryland during the second half of the eighteenth century—and another that proposed its adoption—the lower midwestern corn belt on the eve of the American Civil War.

Through the lens of these heightened regional experiences, we observe in microcosm the lives of all American agrarians and the recurrent, difficult, and often tormented decisions imposed upon them by a dynamic capitalism and a credo of rational economic calculation. Let us turn to these agrarians' perennial dilemma of choosing between slavery or free labor and examine the rationality that usually informed their momentous and far-reaching decisions.

FIGURE 6.1. A mid-nineteenth-century reproduction of slave quarters on a southern plantation. The individual on horseback is probably the overseer of the plantation. Reproduced from *Harper's New Monthly Magazine* 19 (1859), p. 730.

A Staple Interpretation of Slavery and Free Labor

The economic interpretation of rural labor choices offers a powerful explanation of the geography of slavery and free labor in antebellum America.[2] Although critics of this thesis have mounted an assault during the past three decades, I shall contend that they have erred in (1) their application of the economic model of labor choice, (2) their conclusion that slavery was the most efficient agrarian labor system in all of North America, and (3) their inference that the North rejected slavery for ideological and moral reasons rather than economic ones. Economic rationality was more pervasive than this ar-

2.   The economic interpretation of slavery and free labor has been sustained more by argument than by substantive evidence of labor efficiency. The best statement connecting plantation crops and slavery appears in Lewis Cecil Gray, *History of Agriculture in the Southern United States to 1860* (2 vols., 1933; reprint, Gloucester, Mass.: Peter Smith, 1958), Vol. 1, pp. 462–80. Also see Robert E. Baldwin, "Patterns of Development in Newly Settled Regions," *Manchester School of Economic and Social Studies* 24 (1956), pp. 161–79; and Douglass C. North, "Agriculture in Regional Economic Growth," *Journal of Farm Economics, Proceedings* 41 (1959), pp. 943–51. A cogent review of the issues is Stanley L. Engerman, "Some Considerations Relating to Property Rights in Man," *Journal of Economic History* 33 (1973), pp. 43–65.

gument allows. When these critics assume that slave- and free-labor efficiencies should be compared on a yearly basis, they unwittingly place wage labor in an untenable position. Wage labor could never compete with slavery on an annual basis; hired labor was competitive, however, for a portion of the year. Farmers who needed labor for a few days, weeks, or months found the use of hired labor decidedly cheaper and more efficient than slaves. The decisive factor in the farmer's choice of either slave or free labor came down to the annual labor requirements of his staple crop: crops such as wheat, which required only a few weeks of attention, lent themselves to wage labor; whereas crops such as tobacco or cotton, which demanded sustained attention during a long growing season, lent themselves to slave labor. The introduction of appropriate free-labor costs into a labor efficiency model reveals that the geography of antebellum slavery and free labor conforms well with economic theory. Farmers and planters used the economically rational labor supply; and more specifically, northern farmers rejected slavery not because it was morally or ideologically repugnant, but because it was less efficient than free labor in the production of small grains.

The causal link between staple crops and choice of labor supply is clearest in regions shifting between few-day and multiple-day staples. Accordingly, this essay examines instances of staple change in two regions: the tobacco-to-wheat transition on the eastern shore of Maryland during the eighteenth century and the wheat-to-corn transition in the antebellum lower Midwest. On Maryland's eastern shore, tobacco produced by slaves prevailed until the 1750s; but as wheat took hold, hired labor proved more efficient and gradually replaced slaves. Privately manumitted slaves swelled both the free black population and the general wage-labor force. Matters were reversed in the emerging corn belt of southern and central Ohio, Indiana, and Illinois. Wheat was the initial staple, produced by wage labor and family members. But owing to the expansion of corn production in the 1840s and 1850s, to the demanding cultivation requirements of corn as compared with wheat, and to rising wage rates, hired labor was steadily pushed into economic competition with slaves. The corn-hog region gave increasingly vocal support to pro-slavery politics and legislation that imposed severely restrictive state laws—laws that curtailed the civil rights of free blacks and led them toward servitude if not enslavement. Slavery was headed northward in the wake of a corn economy; the only way to halt the laws of economics and pre-serve northern free labor was to destroy the "peculiar institution" in a civil war.

The economic interpretation of labor systems is controversial, and the wise course is to proceed cautiously. Following a brief review of the economic model of labor choice and the critique of a purely economic interpretation, I turn to the refined staple model of labor choice and to the two regions where it came into play.

Slave or Free Labor: The Economic Interpretation and Its Detractors

Interpretations of slavery and free labor, whether economic or noneconomic, begin with the same process: the calculation of relative labor efficiencies. The rational capitalist farmer, faced with a choice of slavery or free labor, chooses in accordance with Evsey Domar's model of labor profitability.[3] The farmer compares outputs and costs of slaves and freemen and uses the labor supply that offers the greatest return. Stated more specifically, the farmer prefers free labor when $P_f - P_s > W_f - W_s$, where P_f is the net average productivity of free labor, P_s is the net average productivity of slave labor, W_f is the cost of free labor, and W_s is the cost of slaves, properly discounted, and their subsistence. The model is simplified when slave and free-labor outputs are shown as equivalent or nearly so, in which case labor choice becomes a matter of least cost, and free labor is used when $W_s > W_f$. Domar, though he does not test his model with data from the United States, speculates that such a test would probably show slavery to have been the most efficient labor supply for the entire nation. Therefore, he concludes, northern rejection of slavery must be interpreted on noneconomic grounds. Yet Domar is ambivalent. As an economist, he knows that if his hunch proves correct, it will seriously undermine economic rationality as a general model of behavior.

3. Evsey Domar, "The Causes of Slavery or Serfdom: A Hypothesis," *Journal of Economic History* 30 (1970), pp. 18–32. Economic historians have acknowledged Domar's contribution, but they have given too much attention to the land-labor ratio as a determinant of wage rates while disregarding empirical tests of the labor efficiency model. Wage labor can be used in societies with high land-labor ratios provided that the agricultural regime is acutely seasonal. Paul A. David, *Technical Choice Innovation and Economic Growth: Essays on American and British Experience in the Nineteenth Century* (London: Cambridge University Press, 1975).

I know of two tests of Domar's model, albeit crude ones. Each sustains his hunch about slavery's economic superiority. In 1967, Arthur Zilversmit presented a double-barreled argument for slavery's economic advantage as a source of northern labor before 1800.[4] First, he concluded that slave and free-labor outputs were similar, thus casting doubt on the assumption that the incentive of freedom re-sulted in greater productivity than slavery. Independently, John Hicks has arrived at the same conclusion on theoretical grounds.[5] Having determined that productivities were equal, Zilversmit turned to the cost side, compared slave prices with white servant prices and annual free wage rates, and concluded plausibly that slaves, when costs were discounted over their useful lives, were much less expensive than either wage labor or servant labor. Although more refined economic calculations might increase slave costs, these revisions in Zilversmit's estimates would not alter his conclusions that slavery was the most efficient labor system for the North and the South and that its aboli-tion in the North, therefore, was rooted in ideology and ethics. North-ern agrarians thus seemed to have been irrational economic actors.

Domar and Zilversmit weakened the economic interpretation of regional labor systems, but the most damaging blow was delivered much earlier. William Strickland in 1795 tried to prove that slavery was a poor economic choice in Virginia, but despite his efforts the Englishman's evidence showed just the opposite: slaves cost less than free labor not only in Virginia but in all of the United States as well. Strickland's method was straightforward. He believed the Virginia planters' lament that slaves entailed excessive costs and low returns, and he set out to prove it. Confident that slaves were more expensive than free labor, he tried to verify these complaints by examining la-bor prices. Using records of construction costs on the James River Canal, Strickland calculated slave costs at £18 a year, which consisted of annual hire rates for adult male slaves of £9 plus maintenance costs of £9. He then computed daily slave cost at 1 shilling, 2 pence, and compared this figure with Chesapeake free-labor day rates. Much to Strickland's disappointment, slaves seemed to cost the plan-ters less than free whites, who hired out at 1 shilling, 6 pence a day.

4. Arthur Zilversmit, *The First Emancipation: The Abolition of Slavery in the North* (Chi-cago: University of Chicago Press, 1967), pp. 33–53. Also see Leon F. Litwak, *North of Slavery: The Negro in the Free States, 1790–1860* (Chicago: University of Chicago Press, 1961), pp. 3–29.

5. John Hicks, *A Theory of Economic History* (Oxford: Clarendon Press, 1969), pp. 122–40.

In fact, the cost advantage to slavery was even greater, owing to Strickland's biased accounting. Specifically, his slave maintenance estimate of £9 was very high, and a more realistic figure on the order of £3 to £6 a year drives down daily slave costs to between 9.4 and 11.7 pence per day. If these figures are correct, then slaves cost less than either free Negroes or free whites. Slavery was cheaper in Virginia and also in the northern states, where free labor received 1 to 2 shillings per day according to Strickland's own estimates.[6]

But Strickland persisted in pressing his thesis of slavery's economic inferiority. Having lost on the cost side, he launched a vicious (and racist) attack on slave output—Domar's productivity. Slaves were depicted as inert, recalcitrant, slovenly, and prone to willful destruction and pilfering. Given these traits, Strickland concurred with "the received opinion of the country, that slave-labor is much dearer than any other; and that the price paid for the time of a slave, by no means shows the amount of value of his labor; it certainly is much higher than it appears to be; though not knowing the quantity of labor performed by slaves in general in a given time, in a sufficient number of instances, I have not data whereon to calculate the exact value."[7]

This tactic belies economic reality. Low slave productivity cannot be inferred from Strickland's exaggerated stereotype of black behavior. Slaves may have been at times lazy, slovenly, and subversive in the fields, but the evidence we have from colonial America suggests that white freemen behaved in similar ways;[8] and furthermore, measures of physical productivity thus far assembled show no appreciable differences in output between white and black, or slave labor and free labor. For instance, Chesapeake tobacco growers between 1660 and 1770 consistently produced between 1,500 and 2,200 pounds per year per laborer, and slaveholding planters produced more tobacco per laborer than those planters without slaves.[9] Nor is there any com-

6. William Strickland, *Journal of a Tour in the United States of America, 1794–1795, With a Facsimile Edition of William Strickland's "Observations on the Agriculture of the United States of America,"* ed. J. E. Strickland (New York: New York Historical Society, 1971), pp. 31–36.

7. *Ibid.,* pp. 33–34.

8. See, for example, David Bertelson, *The Lazy South* (New York: Oxford University Press, 1967); and Edmund S. Morgan, *American Slavery, American Freedom: The Ordeal of Colonial Virginia* (New York: W. W. Norton, 1975).

9. Carville V. Earle, *The Evolution of a Tidewater Settlement System: All Hallow's Parish, Maryland, 1650–1783,* University of Chicago Department of Geography Research Paper No. 170 (Chicago, 1975), pp. 24–27.

pelling reason for believing that free labor produced more corn than did slaves per unit of labor input.[10] In short, Strickland's invective against the productivity of slaves must be dismissed. The rest of his argument, demonstrating the lower costs of slave labor, supports the Domar-Zilversmit thesis, which maintains that northern farmers who hired free labor chose an inefficient labor force.

The economic interpretation of American slavery and free labor, long sustained by tradition and faith, has been eroded as a result of these studies of northern irrationality. The suggestion that northern farmers were irrational, that they used an inefficient labor supply, has subtly shifted the attention of economic history and historical geography from South to North and from economic to noneconomic explanations of northern free labor. The issue is not why the South used slaves but why the North did not use them.[11] In the remainder of this essay, I address the borderlands between North and South, where both slaves and free labor were accessible. Careful consideration of these borderland regions reveals flaws in the revisionist inefficiency thesis, while refining and clarifying the role of staples and the rational economic basis of labor choice, that is, of choosing slavery in the South and free labor in the North.

A Further Exploration of the Staple Economic Interpretation of Labor Systems

Domar's labor efficiency model will explain the geography of agrarian labor, provided that the labor inputs of freemen and slaves are compared fairly. Returning to that model, let us assume that slave and free-labor outputs are equivalent—a point suggested by the evidence cited above. Entrepreneurs select their labor supply by comparing costs and choosing the least expensive, so that they use slaves

10. "I have a hard time believing that slaves could not be used in the mixed farming of the North; much food was produced on southern farms as well, most of the slave owners had very few slaves, and many slaves were skilled in crafts." Domar, "The Causes of Slavery or Serfdom," p. 30.

11. Domar urged this refocusing in 1970, but so far the "new" economic history has disregarded the problem of slave-free labor efficiencies under the same crops and instead has directed attention to the comparative efficiencies of farms and plantations. These are not the same, as is forcefully pointed out in Paul A. David and Peter Temin, "Slavery: The Progressive Institution?" in *Reckoning with Slavery*, ed. Paul A. David, Herbert G. Gutman, Richard Sutch, Peter Temin, and Gavin Wright (New York: Oxford University Press, 1976), pp. 165–230, reference on pp. 202–3.

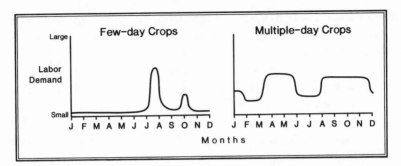

FIGURE 6.2. Hypothetical Labor Regimes for Few-day and Multiple-day Staple Crops before 1860.

when $W_s < W_f$ and free labor when $W_f < W_s$. All this is easy enough; the tough problem is assessing the comparable costs. Heretofore, slave-labor and free-labor costs have been assessed as though each source of labor was employed for a whole year. Such a procedure, while appropriate for slaves as permanent fixtures, has the effect of vastly inflating the costs of hired labor, customarily employed by the day or for several weeks or months but rarely by the year. Seasonal hired labor was competitive with slave labor so long as the number of days of hired labor employment multiplied by the daily wage rate was less than the annual cost of a slave.

It is precisely at this point that staples played the decisive role of regulating the number of days of labor required for production. Staples, of course, varied remarkably in their daily demands for labor during the growing season. The time-honored distinction between plantation crops and small grains reflects these differences in labor requirements (see Figure 6.2). Plantation crops, such as tobacco, cotton, and wet rice, are so called because they were planted separately and commanded individual attention by labor during the growing season, especially during cultivation.[12] Their frequent and steady demand for labor throughout the crop year invariably drove wage-labor costs above slave costs. By contrast, broadcast grains such as wheat demanded labor in concentrated applications. Although wheat labor worked sunup to sundown during fall planting and midsummer harvest, no labor was required between these periods.[13] The eco-

12. Gray, *History of Agriculture*, Vol. 1, pp. 462–80; Baldwin, "Patterns of Development," pp. 161–79.
13. "Our winter crops of wheat, barley, & c. also the oats flax & buckwheat are so disposed of as to require no further care [until harvest] after the seeds are put into the

nomically rational antebellum wheat farmer almost always employed wage labor because the cost of the few days of labor required usually fell below the annual cost of slaves.

The plantation/small-grain dichotomy, though traditional, confuses the main issue: how many days of attention a staple required during the crop season. The appropriate dichotomy is actually between few-day and multiple-day crops rather than plantation crops and small grains. For instance, dairy farming, though never regarded as a plantation activity, demanded labor during the entire year and was thus as much a multiple-day staple as plantation cotton or tobacco. Might this fact not explain the otherwise anomalous use of slaves in the dairying zone of colonial Narragansett, Rhode Island?[14] To cite another example, corn required a number of labor days intermediate between the extremes of wheat and cotton or dairying. The extensive labor demands of corn during the three- to four-month period of plowing and tillage made it adaptable to slaves or freemen, depending on wage rates and slave costs.[15] Using the "required-days" approach suggested here, we may achieve a more realistic assessment of the labor costs that faced the farmer who chose between slaves and freemen.

A caveat is in order. Staple labor days are not to be confused with labor intensity. For example, two crops using equivalent acreage and requiring identical labor inputs of 300 worker-hours may have different allocations of labor during the growing season. One crop may be tended in just 30 days, for ten hours a day, while the other requires 75 days at four hours a day. Given prevailing wage rates and slave costs in pre-1860 America, the former favored free labor, the latter slaves.[16]

---

ground." R. O. Bausman and A. J. Munroe, eds., "James Tilton's Notes on the Agriculture of Delaware in 1788," *Agricultural History* 20 (1946), pp. 176–87, quote on p. 181. See also Peter Kalm, *Travels into North America* (Barre, Mass.: The Imprint Society, 1972), p. 77; and John H. Klippart, *The Wheat Plant: Its Origin, Culture, Growth, Development, Composition, Varieties, Diseases, etc., etc. Together with a Few Remarks on Indian Corn, Its Culture, etc.* (Cincinnati: Moore, Wilstach, Keys, 1860), pp. 475–78.

14. Percy Wells Bidwell and John I. Falconer, *History of Agriculture in the Northern United States, 1620–1860* (New York: Peter Smith, 1941), pp. 106, 109–10.

15. Bausman and Munroe, "James Tilton's Notes," p. 181; Robert Russell, *North America, Its Agriculture and Climate; Containing Observations on the Agriculture and Climate of Canada, the United States, and the Island of Cuba* (Edinburgh: A. and C. Black, 1857), pp. 81–82; Allan G. Bogue, *From Prairie to Cornbelt: Farming on the Illinois and Iowa Prairies in the Nineteenth Century* (Chicago: Quadrangle Books, 1968), pp. 132–33.

16. Economists generally have regarded labor inputs in terms of intensity (man-

At this point, we may refine Domar's model by specifying more precisely free-labor costs and by restricting comparison to similar staples. For a given staple, farmers will choose free labor when $W_r D_l < W_s$, where W_r is the wage rate of free labor and D_l represents the labor days required by the staple.

Staples and Labor in the Colonial Chesapeake

Staple change and labor adjustments in the eighteenth-century Chesapeake lend empirical support to this theoretical discussion. Between 1720 and the Revolution, wheat supplemented and then replaced tobacco as the staple of Maryland's upper eastern shore. The outline of changes in staples and labor is fairly clear.[17] The clayey soils of that region produced a poorer quality tobacco that was less valuable than western shore crops. As grain prices rose after 1720, reflecting demands from southern Europe and the West Indies, slave-owning tobacco planters of the upper eastern shore rationally shifted to grains, especially wheat. This new few-day staple also entailed adjustments in the labor supply. Some slaves were hired out for short terms; others functioned as sharecroppers; and still others were emancipated by their owners. Manumission was abetted, of course, by Quaker abolitionists and revolutionary egalitarianism, but the rock-bottom cause was economic. Wheat was produced more efficiently with free labor than with slaves.[18]

An example may clarify the economic pressures on the average planter during the middle of the eighteenth century. On the typical

---

hours or man-days); hence systematic data on the more critical labor input of required days are lacking. These data are available, however, in sensitive accounts by agricultural historians. See Bogue, *From Prairie to Cornbelt*, pp. 132–33; Gray, *History of Agriculture*, Vol. 1, pp. 462–80; and Paul W. Gates, *The Farmer's Age: Agriculture, 1815–1860* (New York: Holt, Rinehart and Winston, 1960).

17. This discussion of economic change on the eastern shore derives from many sources, too numerous to be listed here. See especially Carville Earle and Ronald Hoffman, "Staple Crops and Urban Development in the Eighteenth-Century South," *Perspectives in American History* 10 (1976), pp. 7–78; Paul G. E. Clemens, "From Tobacco to Grain: Economic Development on Maryland's Eastern Shore, 1660–1750" (Ph.D. diss., University of Wisconsin, 1974); and *idem, The Atlantic Economy and Colonial Maryland's Eastern Shore: From Tobacco to Grain* (Ithaca, N.Y.: Cornell University Press, 1980). On Chesapeake slavery, see Richard S. Dunn, "Black Society in the Chesapeake, 1776–1810," in *Slavery and Freedom in the Age of the American Revolution*, ed. Ira Berlin and Ronald Hoffman (Charlottesville: The University Press of Virginia for the United States Capitol Historical Society, 1983), pp. 49–82.

18. On manumission and free blacks on the eastern shore, see the impressive study

tobacco plantation, one laborer produced 1,000 pounds of tobacco on three acres. Total labor input was about 185 worker-hours, or 23 worker-days. From the standpoint of labor choice, the more decisive figure was the number of days of labor attendance required by tobacco—a figure which amounted to as many as 75 days spread over the January-to-November cropping season. The planter who hired free labor at a wage rate of 3 shillings a day paid out the handsome sum of £11 5s.[19] The use of slaves instead effected a considerable savings. A prime male slave field hand cost £5 10s. a year (calculated by using an average slave price of £50 discounted over a useful life of twenty years, or £2 10s. a year, plus annual maintenance costs of £3).[20] Tobacco planters chose slaves for the simple reason that they cost less than half of the price of free labor.

Conversely, the advantage shifted to free labor when wheat became more profitable and planters turned to grain farming. In the case of wheat, a slave prepared and sowed ten acres in August and

---

by Ira Berlin, *Slaves without Masters: The Free Negro in the Antebellum South* (New York: Vintage Books, 1974), pp. 15–78. Also see Kenneth L. Carroll, "Religious Influences on the Manumission of Slaves in Caroline, Dorchester, and Talbot Counties," *Maryland Historical Magazine* 56 (1961), pp. 176–97; and *idem*, "Maryland Quakers and Slavery," *Maryland Historical Magazine* 45 (1950), pp. 215–25. These studies emphasize religion and revolutionary ideology as the chief causes of manumission and the growth of the free black community; yet these interpretations fail to explain the strength of pro-slavery sentiment among tobacco-producing Quakers on Maryland's western shore as well as manumission activity that began before the Revolution. In 1790, the proportion of free Negroes to all Negroes was highest in the upper bay counties of Maryland. *Return of the Whole Number of Persons within the Several Districts of the United States, According to 'An Act Providing for the Enumeration of the Inhabitants of the United States,' Passed March the First, One Thousand Seven Hundred and Ninety-One* (Philadelphia: Childs and Swaine, 1791), p. 47. On slave hire and hire rates, see Strickland, *Journal of a Tour*, pp. 31–36; and "Letters of Father Joseph Morley, S.J., and Some Extracts from His Diary (1757–1786)," *Records of the American Catholic Historical Society* 17 (1906), pp. 180–210, 289–311, esp. p. 300.

19. These estimates, their sources, and a preliminary statement of the argument made here appear in Earle and Hoffman, "Staple Crops," pp. 36–39, 68–78.

20. Slave prices appear in Clemens, "From Tobacco to Grain," p. 171; *Historical Statistics of the United States, Colonial Times to 1970* (2 parts; Washington, D.C.: U.S. Bureau of the Census, 1975), Part 2, p. 1174; Allan Kulikoff, "Tobacco and Slaves: Population, Economy and Society in Eighteenth-Century Prince George's County, Maryland" (Ph.D. diss., Brandeis University, 1976), pp. 485–88; and Harry J. Carman, ed., *American Husbandry* (Port Washington, N.Y.: Kennikat Press, 1964), p. 164. Twenty years as the useful life for adult male slaves for discounting purposes is suggested in Carman, p. 164; and Clemens, "From Tobacco to Grain," pp. 47–53. However, calculating slave life expectancy is an intractable problem. Among Prince George's County whites in the eighteenth century, life expectation at age 20 was 27 additional years. Kulikoff, pp. 38–41. Maintenance costs are from Carman, p. 164.

September, and harvested 100 bushels the following July. Although wheat's labor input of about 25 worker-days resembled that of tobacco, wheat required a mere 25 days in attendance, one-third the attendance requirement of tobacco. Whereas slave costs in wheat were the same as in tobacco, £5 10s., hired labor costs, for 25 days at 3 shillings per day, fell to £3 15s. For the wheat farmer, wage labor was 30 percent cheaper than slaves.[21]

These cost savings resulted in substantial productivity gains for free labor in wheat. A farmer who invested his savings of £1 15s. in additional day labor could hire another 12 days' worth of labor during wheat harvest. The farmer, in other words, could expand wheat output from 100 bushels to nearly 150 bushels—a gain of 50 percent over slave output. Free labor's superior productivity in wheat was a direct consequence, therefore, of the cost savings to free labor that resulted from the opportunity of hiring free workers in small daily increments. This productivity had little or nothing to do with output incentives mythically attached to the condition of freedom.[22]

The unique harvest regimen of wheat conferred another advantage on a divisible labor supply—that is, a labor supply able to be hired by the day. Wheat's maturation allowed only about ten days for the July harvest. Once the grain had passed through the short dough or harvest stage, the seeds became dead ripe, shattered, and fell to the ground as reaped. In this narrow harvest window, a slave reaping at the maximum rate of an acre a day was hard-pressed to finish ten acres of wheat. Conversely, the employment of wage laborers assured that the harvest would be completed on time. The farmer, instead of hiring one laborer for ten days, might hire two workers for five days, thus minimizing the loss of grain by overripening and shattering.[23]

Slaves and wheat made an unhappy marriage on Maryland's eastern shore. Slaves were more expensive and less productive than wage labor, and planters becoming farmers were under increasing pressure to shift from slaves to hired labor. After 1750, slave owners pur-

---

21. Earle and Hoffman, "Staple Crops," pp. 68–78.

22. The belief that freedom was a production incentive and resulted in productivity gains over slavery probably rests on free labor's superior output in broadcast grain production—a superiority I have attributed to the few required days of labor and the divisibility of free labor. The alleged incentive of freedom disappeared in tobacco production, where a slave doubled the output of freemen of equivalent cost.

23. Klippart, *The Wheat Plant*, pp. 475–78; Leo Rogin, *The Introduction of Farm Machinery and Its Relation to the Productivity of Labor in the Agriculture of the United States During the Nineteenth Century* (Berkeley: University of California Press, 1931), p. 78.

FIGURE 6.3. A mid-nineteenth-century representation of wheat and the implements used in planting and harvesting from the colonial period to the 1850s. Reproduced from *Harper's New Monthly Magazine* 15 (1857), p. 301.

sued several alternatives: they hired out slaves by the day or week during the harvest bottleneck, proposed sharecropping schemes that might reduce slave maintenance costs while keeping available the harvest labor force, or privately manumitted slaves. Although these were the most important accommodations to the new agrarian system, the range of solutions was limited only by the ingenuity of individual planters as they sought to match the new staple with the most appropriate labor supply.[24]

The transformation from slaves to free labor on the eastern shore was excruciatingly slow; yet we have no reason to expect instantaneous labor adjustment to the economic model. In the first place, although slaves had become decidedly inefficient, they nonetheless involved a heavy sunk cost not easily recouped. More decisively, a wholesale change in labor force involved the risk of a sudden reversal in relative labor costs or in staple production technology. For instance, slaves might have produced wheat at less cost than free labor if any of the following conditions had prevailed: an extension of the wheat harvest by rescheduling of planting, a rise in free wage rates, or a fall in slave costs. The first of these, crop rescheduling, appealed to George Washington, and doubtless eastern shore farmers tried it too. By planting wheat at staggered intervals in the fall or by sowing several varieties, farmers hoped to make the fields mature at different times and thus spread the harvest over more than the customary ten days. Washington then saw how slaves could be used to advantage: "If Wheat of different kinds are sowed so as to prevent the Harvest coming on at once, it is my opinion that hirelings [wage labor] of all kinds may be dispensed with."[25] Recall my earlier calculations in which free labor tended fourteen to fifteen acres and slaves ten; successful crop scheduling could reverse this situation. By extending the wheat harvest beyond fifteen days, farmers would have created a clear-cut advantage for slave labor. Fortunately for northern free labor, Washington's cropping scheme was never successfully implemented, as John H. Klippart observed nearly a century later.[26] Indeed, almost two centuries passed before Warren Thornthwaite worked out the intricacies of the crop calendar.

24. Berlin, *Slaves without Masters*, pp. 15–78; Carroll, "Religious Influences," pp. 176–97; "Letters of Father Joseph Morley," p. 300; Strickland, *Journal of a Tour*, pp. 31–36.

25. George Washington, *The Diaries of George Washington, 1748–1799*, 4 vols., ed. J. C. Fitzpatrick (Boston: Houghton Mifflin Co., 1925), Vol. 1, p. 338, cited in Gray, *History of Agriculture*, Vol. 1, p. 550.

26. Klippart, *The Wheat Plant*, pp. 475–78.

A second condition that would have favored slave-produced wheat was a rise in wage rates. In 1769, while Washington toyed with crop scheduling, wheat was in great demand, prices were high, and bumper crops drove wages up. Day wages for skilled harvesters rose from a norm of 3 shillings to 5 shillings a day.[27] At that rate, ten acres of wheat harvested by wage labor cost £6 5*s.* compared with £5 10*s.* for a slave. Slave owners were understandably reluctant to free their slaves until they could be assured of a steady, abundant, and low-cost supply of free labor. The year 1769 was atypical, however. Although similar wage peaks occurred sporadically through 1860, the costs of wage labor generally remained lower than slave costs. When the situation occasionally reversed, farmers supplemented their supply of free labor with marginal lower-cost laborers such as convicts or free Negroes.[28]

A third way wheat farmers might profitably have used slaves is if slave costs had fallen; indeed, theory implies such an adjustment and the mechanisms responsible. In an isolated wheat-producing region, the demand curve for slaves would shift downward as slave inefficiencies in wheat production were perceived. As the market lowered slave prices, and hence discounted costs, slave masters simultaneously could have reduced maintenance costs by cutting expenditures for food, health care, clothing, and shelter.[29] In practice, however, such cost-reducing adjustments by markets and masters seem to have been blunted by external regional demand for slaves. Prices for Chesapeake slaves rose rather than fell, suggesting that lower slave demand on the eastern shore was compensated by augmented demand from the expanding tobacco economy of the western shore. The existence of this neighboring market for slaves proved to be decisive in propping up eastern shore slave prices and costs, despite slave inefficiencies in wheat. Freedom on the eastern shore, somewhat ironically, was contingent on the existence of slavery in a nearby region. Although the market failed to make slaves competitive with free labor, masters may have moved in that direction by lowering slave costs, either by reducing medical care, housing, and clothing of

27. Gaspar John Saladino, "The Maryland and Virginia Wheat Trade from Its Beginnings to the American Revolution" (M.A. thesis, University of Wisconsin, 1960), p. 45; Bidwell and Falconer, *History of Agriculture*, pp. 117–18; *Historical Statistics*, Part 2, p. 1196.
28. In the antebellum Midwest, free Negroes were used principally during bumper harvests. David E. Schob, *Hired Hands and Plowboys: Farm Labor in the Midwest, 1815–1860* (Urbana: University of Illinois Press, 1975), pp. 83–87.
29. This argument appears in Richard Sutch, "The Profitability of Ante Bellum Slavery—Revisited," *Southern Economic Journal* 31 (1965), pp. 365–66.

slaves or by affording quasi-freedom via sharecropping and eventual manumission.[30]

Slavery lost out on the wheat-producing eastern shore precisely because none of these three conditions—harvest extension through crop scheduling, rising wage rates, or declining slave costs—seems to have been met. For these reasons, a few-day crop such as wheat fostered the development of a labor force that was free, flexible, and divisible in its inputs.

Staples and Labor in the Antebellum Midwest

Slavery decayed, albeit slowly, on Maryland's eastern shore with the change from tobacco to wheat. But what of the reverse situation, where few-day wheat gave way to a multiple-day crop? Would farmers in this case attempt to install the "peculiar institution?" The test case here comes from the antebellum Midwest and deals with the transition from wheat to a corn-hog complex that took place just before the Civil War. This staple change, as we shall see, posed a momentous threat to northern wage labor in particular and to society in general. I begin, however, at a more mundane level by comparing the costs of slave labor and free labor under wheat and its successor, Indian corn. Having demonstrated slavery's superior efficiency in corn production, I turn to the pro-slavery politics that accompanied these midwestern agrarian changes.

Antebellum labor costs provide the basic economic information for my model of labor choice. Slave costs are from Alfred H. Conrad and John R. Meyer's estimate of $51 as the annual cost of a slave between 1830 and 1850. They arrive at this figure by first discounting the price of a twenty-year-old male slave ($900 to $950) over a useful life of thirty years (the annual cost is thus $30) and second adding yearly maintenance costs of $21.[31] Farm-labor wages come

30. On slave prices, see Clemens, "From Tobacco to Grain," p. 171; *Historical Statistics*, Part 2, p. 1174; and Kulikoff, "Tobacco and Slaves," pp. 485–88. These prices are not entirely satisfactory, for we need a series specifically for the eastern shore after 1750. However, rather high slave prices are suggested in "Letters of Father Joseph Morley," p. 300. Slave clothing allowances, as an indicator of maintenance costs, seem to have remained the same from the 1720s to the Revolution, but the evidence is fragmentary. Clemens, "From Tobacco to Grain," pp. 47–53, 175.

31. Alfred H. Conrad and John R. Meyer, "The Economics of Slavery in the Ante-Bellum South," in *The Reinterpretation of American Economic History*, ed. Robert W. Fogel and Stanley L. Engerman (New York: Harper and Row, 1971), pp. 342–61, esp. pp. 345–47. The farmer who was considering the adoption of slavery would probably have purchased

from Stanley Lebergott's wage series for the various states under consideration.[32] Comparison of slave and wage costs from these sources shows that wage labor when hired by the year was expensive and could not compete with slaves. For example, in 1830 the average monthly wage in the United States of $8.85 totaled $95.20 for twelve months—almost double the cost of a slave.[33] These figures cast serious doubt on Clarence H. Danhof's belief that freemen were commonly hired for eight to ten months during the cropping season; eight months of labor in 1830 cost more than $70, still far in excess of slave costs.[34] Long labor contracts of this sort were used selectively, notably during the first years of farm making and sod busting; but otherwise the eight-to-ten-month laborer cost too much. Other students of rural labor suggest that midwestern farmers preferred short-term hires, ranging from a number of days to several months at a time; and their impressions and evidence conform remarkably well with the hypothesis of labor costs presented here.[35] Given the prevailing wage rates in midwestern states in 1850, three to five months was the theoretical maximum for wage-labor hire; beyond that time, slaves became cheaper than freemen. Parenthetically, we may note that free labor had improved its competitive economic position vis-à-vis slaves between 1750 and 1850. The annual cost of a slave in 1750 equaled about 36 days of wage labor as compared with 65 days of hired labor in 1850 Ohio.

Wheat was the initial commercial staple of the Midwest, and its labor requirements fell easily within the economic range of free labor. The link between day labor and wheat should be clear from the

---

a prime male field slave rather than an infant or child; hence the appropriate costs are given by slave market prices rather than the considerably lower costs of slave reproduction and rearing. For the latter costs, see Yasukichi Yasuba, "The Profitability and Viability of Plantation Slavery in the United States," *Economic Studies Quarterly* 12 (1961), pp. 60–67.

32. Stanley Lebergott, *Manpower in Economic Growth: The American Record since 1800* (New York: McGraw-Hill, 1964).

33. Monthly wages are with board included; *ibid.*, p. 539.

34. Clarence H. Danhof, *Change in Agriculture: The Northern United States, 1820–1870* (Cambridge: Harvard University Press, 1969), pp. 73–78. This criticism should not impugn the remainder of this excellent and essential book.

35. Bogue, *From Prairie to Cornbelt*, pp. 182–87; Merle Curti, *The Making of an American Community: A Case Study of Democracy in a Frontier County* (Stanford, Ca.: Stanford University Press, 1959), pp. 145–49; Paul W. Gates, "Frontier Estate Builders and Farm Laborers," in *The Frontier in Perspective*, ed. Walker D. Wyman and Clifton B. Kroeber (Madison: University of Wisconsin Press, 1957), pp. 143–64; Schob, *Hired Hands and Plowboys*, pp. 69, 103–4, 258.

earlier discussion of the Maryland case. However, subtle changes in nineteenth-century wheat production conferred even greater advantages upon day labor in the Midwest. While the harvest labor bottleneck of ten days to two weeks persisted into the nineteenth century, it became even more constricted because output per acre increased from the colonial norm of ten bushels per acre to twenty to thirty bushels or more. Accordingly, time spent in harvesting and gathering wheat (despite some efficiencies introduced by the cradle and the flail) increased from 60 percent of total labor time to about 83 percent in the nineteenth century until the introduction of the reaper. Harvesting and getting in an acre of wheat, according to Leo Rogin, required about five days instead of one or two.[36] That meant that a slave could harvest only two to three acres of wheat, while divisible day labor, hired at the 1850 Ohio wage rate for the equivalent of a slave's cost and allocating five-sixths of its work to harvest, handled ten or eleven acres of wheat. In other words, the cost of slave labor was $17.00 to $25.50 per acre, while the cost of free labor was $4.64 to $5.10 per acre if hired on a daily basis and $11.00 to $16.50 per acre if hired on a monthly basis.[37] As long as wheat persisted as the midwestern staple, day labor was economically superior to both slaves and monthly hired hands. Nor did the superiority of the day hand diminish with increased scale of operation—a point demonstrated later in the century in the bonanza wheat farms of the Red River Valley, where day laborers hired at the critical periods vastly outnumbered laborers hired by the month or season.[38]

Pressures to adjust the labor supply intensified with the transformation of the midwestern staple economy in the decade or two before the Civil War. Wheat crops in the south central portions of

36. Rogin, *The Introduction of Farm Machinery*, pp. 229–43; Gates, *The Farmer's Age*, pp. 156–69. See also Paul A. David, "The Mechanization of Reaping in the Ante-Bellum Midwest," in *Industrialization in Two Systems: Essays in Honor of Alexander Gerschenkron by a Group of His Students*, ed. Henry Rosovsky (New York: Wiley, 1966), pp. 3–39.

37. The discussion, of course, concerns pre-reaper harvest technology. I have used the 1850 Ohio daily hire rate, without board, of 78 cents and the monthly hire rate, with board, of $11. My calculation of the costs of monthly labor presumes the hiring of two laborers for three months at the 1850 Ohio rate. They would have harvested four to six acres of wheat at a total cost of $122. Lebergott, *Manpower in Economic Growth*, p. 539; Schob, *Hired Hands and Plowboys*, p. 259. Somewhat higher daily rates of $1.27 for 1849–53 have been recorded in Illinois, particularly for harvest cradlers. David, "The Mechanization of Reaping," pp. 35–37.

38. Fred A. Shannon, *The Farmer's Last Frontier: Agriculture, 1860–1897* (New York: Harper and Row, 1945), pp. 155–61.

Ohio, Indiana, and Illinois suffered from disease and high humidity; and as wheat became less attractive and the demand for hogs and pork increased, farmers initiated the transition to a corn-hog staple economy. Wheat was supplemented and then displaced by these new regional staples.[39] Corn production imposed a new seasonal regime upon the region. From the standpoint of labor requirements, corn lay intermediate between the few days required by wheat and the multiple days required by tobacco and cotton. In choosing the most efficient source of labor for corn—the classic American example of an "intermediate-day" crop—farmers were often ambivalent. Comparative calculations of the costs of slave and free labor sometimes favored one system, sometimes the other.

Like cotton, corn was a row crop. It was planted and tended individually and technically we might speak of it as a "plantation crop."[40] But unlike cotton, corn's agronomic demands for labor were concentrated in just one-third of the year—what midwesterners called the "crop season." The four-month season lasted from April through July. Workers planted corn in the spring, cultivated it during the tedious phase of tillage (lasting roughly 60 days, usually in May and June when the corn rows were weeded three times or more), and, after corn was "laid by" around the fourth of July, harvested small grains and did some haying. At the end of July, the work load slackened abruptly and most hired hands were cut loose. Relatively few hands were required for the harvest of the corn, which went on into the dead of winter. Harvest progressed casually, conducted principally by family labor or by hogs let loose to mow down the fields.[41]

Corn farmers thus sought labor for the "crop season," the three

39. Midwestern economic change is thoroughly discussed in J. E. Spencer and Ronald J. Horvath, "How Does an Agricultural Region Originate?" *Annals of the Association of American Geographers* 53 (1963), pp. 74–92. See also Carville Earle, "Regional Economic Development West of the Appalachians," in *North America: The Historical Geography of a Changing Continent*, ed. Robert Mitchell and Paul Groves (Totowa, N.J.: Rowman and Littlefield, 1987), pp. 172–97; Bogue, *From Prairie to Cornbelt*, pp. 156–72; and John G. Clark, *The Grain Trade in the Old Northwest* (Urbana: University of Illinois Press, 1966), pp. 147–71, 197–211. Regional boundaries were hazy. Although the lower Midwest continued to produce wheat, corn and hogs became the main staples. But toward the Great Lakes, wheat remained dominant and the corn-hog complex penetrated more slowly. See the maps of corn and wheat production in Charles O. Paullin, *Atlas of the Historical Geography of the United States*, ed. John K. Wright (Washington, D.C.: Carnegie Institute of Washington and the American Geographical Society of New York, 1932), Plate 143.
40. A laborer in corn tended about 25 acres and invested perhaps 850 hours per year. Shannon, *The Farmer's Last Frontier*, p. 143.
41. Russell, *North America*, pp. 81–82; Bogue, *From Prairie to Cornbelt*, pp. 132–33.

to four months from April or May through July. Rural laborers were typically engaged on short-term contracts ranging between ten weeks and four months.[42] The increase in labor costs that resulted from corn's longer crop season brought free labor into competition with slavery. (It makes no difference that state legislatures and referenda had outlawed slavery in the Midwest in the first quarter of the century.) For instance, an Illinois farmer who hired a four-month laborer with board in 1850 spent $12.55 a month and $50.20 for four months, whereas a slave would have cost the farmer $51.00. A decade later, the pressure for a labor supply adjustment intensified as rising wages increased the cost of a four-month laborer to $54.00.[43] These wage rates, I might add, are conservative estimates; David Schob has indicated that the monthly rate may have been as high as $13.00 to $18.00 rather than $12.55.[44] By the mid-1850s, slave labor probably cost less than free labor in the production of corn, an intermediate-day staple crop.[45] To make matters worse, slaves had long since mastered the techniques of corn production, and they employed these in Kentucky, just across the river from freedom.

The corn farmers' dilemma thus becomes apparent. The economic advantage of slavery or free labor could swing one way or another depending on the relative costs of slaves and the monthly hire rates for a crop season. But during the 1840s and 1850s, the

42. "The general practice in Central Illinois is to hire about the 1st of April for the crop (corn) season, or until after harvest, which includes wheat, oats, hay, & c." *The Merchants' Magazine and Commercial Review* 41 (1859), p. 760. The small grain harvest was in July, so the author meant that labor was hired from April to the end of July, or for four months. Also see Russell, *North America*, p. 539.

43. Lebergott, *Manpower in Economic Growth*, p. 539. The labor problem was most severe between 1854 and 1857, when wage rates peaked. David shows that Illinois common laborers received $1.25 a day then compared to $0.85 a day in 1849–53—an increase of 35 percent. Adjusting monthly rates according to this percentage increase, we find that monthly wages would have risen from $12.55 in 1850 to $16.94 in 1854–57, making total wages $67.75 for four months. Slave costs fell below this. David, "The Mechanization of Reaping," p. 36.

44. Schob, *Hired Hands and Plowboys*, p. 104.

45. Slave costs rose during the 1850s, but at a less rapid rate than free-labor costs. Slave prices moved up to $1,306 between 1856 and 1860. Discounting this price over thirty years and adding $21.00 for annual maintenance puts slave costs at about $64.50 per year—or $3.00 less than the four-month hire rate for free labor, as calculated in note 43. For slave prices, see Yasuba, "The Profitability and Viability of Plantation Slavery," pp. 60–67. During the 1850s, midwestern real wages generally exceeded those of all other regions except the East South Central states, thus compounding the pressure on free labor in this region. Philip R. P. Coelho and James F. Shepherd, "Regional Differences in Real Wages: The United States, 1851–1880," *Explorations in Economic History* 13 (1976), pp. 203–30.

trend favored the use of slave labor. In 1850, hiring a free laborer for the season cost about the same (roughly $50) as purchasing and maintaining a slave; during the ensuing decade, as wage rates were driven up by competition from railroad and canal construction, the cost of the hired hand exceeded the costs of the slave. Or, as expressed more pungently by one midwesterner, the superiority of free labor, at least for corn farmers in the lower Midwest, "is a mere humbug."[46]

The political implications of this analysis are far-reaching. As slavery became more efficient than free labor, we should and do find an acceleration of pro-slavery advocacy and legislation emanating from the central and lower midwestern corn belt during the 1840s and 1850s. Slavery was headed north. If corn farmers had their way, the threat was nothing less than the impending dissolution of northern society based on free labor. The issue of slavery assumed a new urgency, and its enemies, in such disarray before 1850, molded a unified opposition on the northern margins of the corn belt. Their choice was simple: allow slavery to survive anywhere in the United States and corn farmers eventually would adopt the institution; destroy slavery completely and this labor supply would be removed as a competitor with freemen. The efficiency of slaves in corn culture affords a new vantage point for interpreting the otherwise baffling political behavior of antebellum midwesterners.

In a series of referenda in the first quarter of the nineteenth century, the midwestern states had prohibited the institution of slavery. This made economic sense because slavery was already a dead letter for the majority of farmers, who produced wheat and used more efficient free labor. But the referenda prohibiting slavery posed an ominous threat: if laws could prohibit slavery, they could also introduce the peculiar institution if and when it became profitable.[47] That day was not far off. As economic change swept over the lower Midwest and as corn-hog farming supplemented or displaced wheat dur-

46. These are the words of Dumas Van Deren, as cited in Arthur Charles Cole, *Lincoln's "House Divided" Speech: Did It Reflect a Doctrine of Class Struggle?* (Chicago: University of Chicago Press, 1923), pp. 32–33.

47. Eugene H. Berwanger, *The Frontier Against Slavery: Western Anti-Negro Prejudice and the Slavery Extension Controversy* (Urbana: University of Illinois Press, 1967), pp. 7–29; Theodore Calvin Pease, *The Story of Illinois* (Chicago: A. C. McClurg, 1925), pp. 96–113; Jacob P. Dunn, *Indiana: A Redemption from Slavery* (New York: Houghton, Mifflin, Boston, 1888); Paul Finkelman, "Slavery, the 'More Perfect Union,' and the Prairie State," *Illinois Historical Journal* 80 (1987), pp. 248–69; *idem*, "Slavery and the Northwest Ordinance," *Journal of the Early Republic* 6 (1986), pp. 343–70.

ing the 1830s and 1840s, the differential between the costs of slaves and free labor narrowed. Accordingly, the emerging corn belt of the lower Midwest gave little support to anti-slavery politicians; the opponents of slavery found more fertile ground for their abolitionist societies, anti-slavery newspapers, and third-party efforts in the wheat-producing counties of the upper Midwest. This sectional rift was apparent in the elections of the late 1840s and early 1850s, when the northern counties of Illinois and Indiana cast increasingly larger votes for anti-slavery third parties, while the nascent corn-belt counties voted overwhelmingly for the regular parties, particularly the Democrats (see Figure 6.4).[48]

The upper Midwest's opposition to slavery was galvanized, however, by the addition of a new and powerful argument against it—an argument that becomes more reasonable when placed in the context of the increasing efficiency of slavery in the lower Midwest. Salmon Chase and the Free-Soil Party adopted all of the standard arguments about the immorality of slavery and the wisdom of excluding it from the territories, but they went a step farther. Northern society, they proclaimed, faced the grave danger of an inexorably expanding slave power or slavocracy. In threatening free labor, slavery attacked the underpinnings of northern civilization.[49] Chase's argument has been treated unkindly, however, by political historians. Should we accept their verdict that he and his supporters were paranoid, grossly distorting the dangers of slave encroachment in the North, or crassly political, manipulating issues and voters through the use of exaggerated rhetoric and playing on the racial fears of midwesterners?[50]

48. Theodore Clarke Smith, *The Liberty and Free Soil Parties in the Northwest* (New York: Russell and Russell, 1967), pp. 325–31; Paullin, *Atlas of the Historical Geography of the United States*, Plates 105, 114, 115; and Arthur Charles Cole, *The Era of the Civil War, 1848–1870* (Springfield: Illinois Centennial Commission, 1919), pp. 101–201.

49. See the perceptive examination of Chase in Eric Foner, *Free Soil, Free Labor, Free Men: The Ideology of the Republican Party before the Civil War* (London: Oxford University Press, 1970), pp. 73–102. Chase and other anti-slavery advocates are cast as irresponsible fanatics in Avery Craven, *An Historian and the Civil War* (Chicago: University of Chicago Press, 1964). Benson has suggested that Chase and men of his persuasion were guilty of overblown campaign rhetoric and reckless demagogy which got out of hand in the late 1850s. I disagree. See Lee Benson, *Toward the Scientific Study of History: Selected Essays of Lee Benson* (Philadelphia: J. B. Lippincott Co., 1972), pp. 225–340, esp. pp. 297–303; and Eric Foner, "The Causes of the American Civil War: Recent Interpretations and New Directions," *Civil War History* 20 (1974), pp. 197–214.

50. Foner's thesis that northern fears of an aggressive, expanding slave power played a decisive role in the coming of the war is pursued by Larry Gara, "Slavery and the Slave Power: A Critical Distinction," in *Beyond the Civil War Synthesis: Political Essays of the*

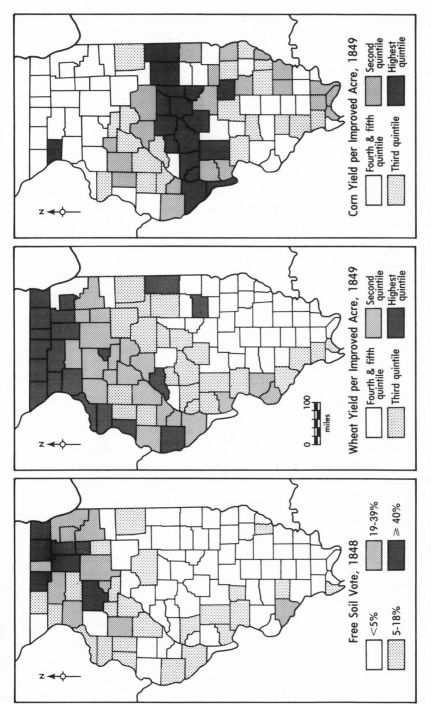

FIGURE 6.4. Antislavery Politics and Agricultural Production in Illinois during the late 1840s. Sources: For agricultural production, see U.S. Census Office, *The Seventh Census of the United States: 1850* (Washington, D.C.: Robert Armstrong, 1853). Voting returns are from the *Tribune Almanac and Political Register for 1848* (New York, n.d.).

Quite the opposite if the economic analysis presented here is correct. Chase was on solid ground; if he was guilty of anything, it was of detecting the threat of slavery to the North before more ordinary men and of placing blame on a conspiracy of expansionist-minded southern slaveowners rather than where it belonged—on economic developments that advanced the corn staple and pushed up wage rates in the late 1840s and 1850s.

Chase's argument did not immediately win the day. His fear of slave expansion into the Old Northwest was not shared by his natural allies in northern Illinois, Indiana, and Ohio. They faced a more pressing problem—control of an expanding free Negro population. Their anti-Negro attitudes, racism by another name, led them into an uneasy coalition with pro-slavery advocates in the corn belt. This coalition in the late 1840s and early 1850s voted repeatedly against free Negroes, excluding fugitive slaves and free Negroes from these states and circumscribing the civil and political rights of those who were already there. African colonization for midwestern free Negroes also held broad appeal.[51]

The cement of racism began to crack in the mid-1850s. Upstaters who detested Negroes and wanted to get rid of them perceived that downstaters wanted to strip free Negroes of their rights only in order to enslave them or else facilitate the introduction of slavery. The subtle schemes of pro-slavers were laid bare in an 1855 committee report of the Indiana legislature: the idea of African colonization, it claimed, originated "in the basest motives and most mercenary considerations. It is one of the offspring of slavery . . . intended to remove the free blacks from the country in order to increase the value and . . . security . . . of slaves."[52] Even more drastic action had been taken by

---

Civil War Era, ed. Robert P. Swierenga, Contributions in American History No. 44 (Westport, Conn.: Greenwood Press, 1975), pp. 295–308. A leading advocate of corn culture, the midwestern Yankee Solon Robinson, produced a lengthy apologia for slavery in *DeBow's Review* in 1849. The timing of his conversion, coming as it did when corn culture was expanding into the lower Midwest and wage rates were rising, seems more than coincidental. Solon Robinson, "Negro Slavery at the South," in *Solon Robinson: Pioneer and Agriculturalist*, 2 vols., ed. Herbert Anthony Kellar (Indianapolis: Indiana Historical Bureau, 1936), Vol. 2, pp. 253–307.

51. Berwanger, *The Frontier Against Slavery*, pp. 30–59. For a slightly different view of midwestern racism, see John M. Rozett, "Racism and Republican Emergence in Illinois, 1848–1860: A Re-evaluation of Republican Negrophobia," *Civil War History* 22 (1970), pp. 101–15.

52. Quoted in Emma Lou Thornbrough, *The Negro in Indiana: A Study of a Minority* (Indianapolis: Indiana Historical Bureau, 1957), p. 86.

pro-slavers in Illinois. The legislature of 1853 put through a law that compelled free Negroes new to the state to pay a fine of $50 plus court costs; Negroes unable to pay this exorbitant sum were hired out for six months to the highest bidder. Indiana carried a similar law on the books, and efforts to strengthen its provisions were narrowly defeated in 1851.[53] That these laws favored black servitude, and potentially permanent bondage, did not escape the opponents of slavery. A delegate to Indiana's constitutional convention of 1850 clearly understood the implications of the attack on the free Negro:

> If I am not mistaken the favorite proposition, and it has been already avowed and advocated here, is, that all persons in whose blood negro descent shall be detected, shall be arrested and sold for six months to the highest bidder and the proceeds applied to the operations of the Colonization Society: And what a spectacle will Indiana in that attitude present to the civilized world? We reprobate slavery and the slave trade, denounce the one as inhuman and the other as piracy punishable with death. And yet what is it proposed to do. Nothing less than to erect shambles at every county seat, enjoin it upon officers to sell, not slaves, but those who are confessedly free, into slavery, differing only from the Southern States, as to its duration.[54]

Identical concern surfaced in Illinois, where many regarded the law of 1853 permitting court-appointed sale of free Negroes as a harbinger of slavery.[55]

Pro-slavery efforts became more blatant as pressures for a more efficient labor supply accumulated in the corn belt. Dumas Van Deren succinctly summarized the corn farmers' interests in 1854. He and other Illinoisans were

> prepared to pronounce openly our full and candid preference in favor of slave labor in agricultural business. . . . We have dis-

53. N. Dwight Harris, *The History of Negro Servitude in Illinois and of the Slavery Agitation in that State, 1719–1864* (Chicago: A. C. McClurg, 1904), pp. 188, 235–36; Cole, *The Era of the Civil War*, pp. 224–29; Thornbrough, *The Negro in Indiana*, pp. 58–59.

54. *Report of the Debates and Proceedings of the Convention for the Revision of the Constitution of the State of Indiana, 1850* (2 vols.; Indianapolis, Ind.: A. H. Brown, 1850), Vol. 1, pp. 457–58.

55. Harris, *The History of Negro Servitude*, pp. 237–38; Gustave Koerner, *Memoirs of Gustave Koerner, 1809–1896*, 2 vols., ed. Thomas J. McCormack (Cedar Rapids, Iowa: Torch Press, 1902), Vol. 2, pp. 29–32; Finkelman, "Slavery, the 'More Pefect Union,' and the Prairie State," pp. 248–69.

covered that the novelty of free labor is a mere humbug. . . . We have been endeavoring to learn the sentiments of our people upon this subject, and have been astonished to see with what unanimity they express themselves in favor of the introduction of slave labor. I have conversed with many of our best farmers who were raised in the eastern States, and they will give their hearty cooperation in effecting this object.[56]

By about mid-decade, upper midwesterners comprehended that the immediate threats to civil society were not free Negroes but slavery, and not southern expansionists but corn farmers in the lower Midwest. Chase was vindicated, and his fear of the slave power carried justifiable weight in the emerging Republican party.

National events magnified the regional anxieties and geopolitical tensions that crisscrossed the Midwest. With the myth of slavery's "natural limits" in disarray, the defenders of free society pinned their hopes on "unnatural limits" defined by national law.[57] But these were crumbling as well. First, by approving the Compromise of 1850, Congress had violated the traditional territorial boundary between slavery and freedom (the parallel of 36 degrees, 30 minutes) that had been enshrined in the Missouri Compromise. Second, in the very same year that Van Deren trumpeted the cause of midwestern slavery, Congress did away with the Missouri Compromise altogether, repealing it in Stephen Douglas's Kansas-Nebraska Act of 1854. Henceforth in the territories, slavery or freedom was to be decided by majority vote.

By the mid-1850s, anti-slavery midwesterners felt besieged, hemmed in by the crumbling boundaries of free society on the national scale and the pro-slavery rhetoric (and real sentiments) of downstaters at the state level. With their position deteriorating rapidly, a political response was inevitable. Shortly after the passage of the Kansas-Nebraska Act, a storm of anti-slavery protest swept over the upper Midwest. Wheat farmers and their urban neighbors mobilized their forces, radicalized anti-slavery politics, and lent their

56. Cited in Cole, *Lincoln's "House Divided" Speech*, pp. 32–33.

57. The "natural limits" thesis achieved its fullest historiographic expression in Charles W. Ramsdell, "The Natural Limits of Slavery Expansion," *Mississippi Valley Historical Review* 16 (1929), pp. 151–71. The powerful influence of this static and deterministic environmental thesis upon historiography is everywhere apparent. See, for example, Robert McColley, *Slavery and Jeffersonian Virginia* (Urbana: University of Illinois Press, 1964), p. 181. A more dynamic interpretation of slavery's range appears in the works of Paul Finkelman cited in note 47.

support to the rise of the Republican party—their last, best hope for preserving "unnatural limits" on the extension of slave society.[58]

The Supreme Court also engendered deep fears among midwestern Republicans. The ramifications of the Court's decision in the Dred Scott case in 1857 went far beyond the narrow issue of the legal status of slaves in free territories. By providing slavery with a constitutional justification, the Court had effectively prevented even free states from barring slavery in their jurisdictions. "Does the Constitution make slaves property?" queried one Ohio Republican. "If so, slavery exists in Ohio today, for the Constitution extends over Ohio, doesn't it?" Radical Republicans thus feared that the debate over slavery and freedom had been sealed by the Taney Court's decision in Dred Scott; it had made slavery national, freedom purely local.[59]

Of course other interpretations were possible. Indeed, most Americans, north and south, discounted the political significance of Dred Scott. Not only did they disagree with the radicals' reading of the case, but they condemned the notion of slavery's nationalization as injudicious and irresponsibly inflammatory rhetoric. Historians, almost without exception, have joined in the popular critique of radical Republican behavior. Even the most sympathetic scholar of northern anti-slavery politics has concluded that Republicans exaggerated the dangers of slavery's northern advance, overreacted to events of the 1850s, and were unnecessarily apocalyptic in their vision of free society's impending doom. The historiographic critique thus accents a paranoid style in northern anti-slavery politics. The entire argument, however, is premised on one dubious assumption: that radical Republicans were desperately fearful of something that did not exist—a southern conspiracy to advance slavery through national leg-

58. For the role of the Midwest, see Foner, *Free Soil, Free Labor, Free Men*; and William E. Gienapp, *The Origins of the Republican Party, 1852–1856* (New York: Oxford University Press, 1987).

59. *Cincinnati Gazette*, September 3, 1860, quoted in Foner, *Free Soil, Free Labor, Free Men*, pp. 101–2. In the course of the Lincoln-Douglas debates in 1858, Lincoln pointed out on many occasions that the greatest danger from slavery was close at home rather than in the South. At Ottawa, he asked: "What is necessary for the nationalization of slavery? Is it simply the next Dred Scott decision? Is it merely for the Supreme Court to decide that no State under the Constitution can exclude it, just as they have already decided that under the Constitution neither Congress nor the territorial legislature can do it?" Cited in David Potter, *The Impending Crisis, 1848–1861*, completed and edited by Don E. Fehrenbacher (New York: Harper and Row, 1976), pp. 328–55. Also see Roy P. Basler, ed., Marion Dolores Pratt and Lloyd A. Dunlap, asst. eds., *The Collected Works of Abraham Lincoln* (8 vols.; New Brunswick, N.J.: Rutgers University Press, 1953–55), Vol. 2, p. 467.

islation, administrative action, and legal interpretation—the so-called slave power conspiracy. While it may be true that midwestern radical Republicans had fabricated a mythical slave power conspiracy, the real danger for free society lay not in the South, but rather within the ranks of free society itself—in the corn belt economy of the lower Midwest. By divorcing anti-slavery politics from its local and regional contexts, modern historiography has unjustly tarnished anti-slavery politicians who better understood the gravity of events in the American Midwest.[60]

Let us look more closely at the politics of slavery in its midwestern context, circa 1858. The future of free society was problematic and had been so for nearly a decade. All of the traditional restraints on slavery—the natural limits and the unnatural limits—seemed to have fallen by the wayside. What then remained to halt slavery's inexorable advance into the corn belt, and then the Middle West, and then free society at large?

The prospect of slavery in the lower Midwest made the Civil War inevitable and irrepressible; more importantly, the impending threat of slavery's expansion made the issue a matter of some urgency.[61]

60. Radical Republicans have not fared well even among historians sympathetic to their cause, as evidenced by Foner's observation that the radicals "may be charged with overreacting to the events of the 1850s, but they were articulating fears which ran deep in the northern mind on the eve of the Civil War." Foner, *Free Soil, Free Labor, Free Men*, pp. 101–2. Foner believes that Republican fears of slave expansion arose out of a mythical slave power conspiracy rather than a genuine perception of changes in staple crops and their economic imperatives in a market society. On that point, Barbara Fields has contended that my argument reduces the coming of the Civil War to microeconomic calculations. She is partially correct. If nothing had changed—if the war had not occurred, if slavery had not been abolished, and if wage rates and slave costs had persisted in the same relationship after 1860—I believe that the pressures to adopt slavery would have been inexorable. I disagree with Fields, however, in her contention that my thesis invariably privileges material over ideological-moral interests. On the contrary, my admiration is highest for those men and women who, like Abraham Lincoln and many southern unionists, rose above regional and material interests. I concede, regrettably, that their kind is too few in the annals of American history. Barbara J. Fields, *Slavery and Freedom on the Middle Ground: Maryland During the Nineteenth Century* (New Haven, Conn.: Yale University Press, 1985), p. 211.

61. A quantitative study of the causes of the Civil War concludes that "northern preferences to eliminate slavery were more than twenty times as strong as those to preserve the Union." Gerald Gunderson, "The Origin of the Civil War," *Journal of Economic History* 34 (1974), pp. 915–50. This finding is consonant with the argument presented here: if the North had allowed the South to secede peacefully or if they had compromised on the issue of slavery in order to preserve the Union, slavery would have persisted and shortly thereafter would have expanded into the lower Midwest, thereby upsetting the delicate geo-

With every cent that free wages increased and with each farmer who adopted corn as his staple, the potential for slavery became stronger. Democracy, which had preserved the North for free labor, now threatened to be its undoing. Northern morality would never hold the line against slavery because, according to one southern critic, this morality was only superficial: "Once persuaded to consider this question [of slave labor] . . . it is not apprehended that moral qualms will hinder their action. It requires the least rudimental knowledge of Yankee nature, and no argument at all to show, that where a real interest, and a question of abstract morality conflict in a Yankee's mind, abstract morality will sustain a grievous overthrow."[62]

This jaundiced southerner understood well the moral fragility of the North, but he seriously misinterpreted its political geography, that is, that in its "real interest" the lower Midwest departed sharply from its northern neighbors. Among the latter, slavery constituted an alien and inefficient labor system contributing nothing to society except the problem of the free Negro. The northern wheat belt counties became bastions of free labor, free soil, and anti-slavery sentiment in the late 1850s.[63] Citizens of these counties argued that excluding slavery from the territories or confining it to the South did not go far enough. It had to be destroyed forever in order to remove temptation from the "real interest" of corn-growing midwesterners. Such was the unequivocal course of action laid out by Abraham Lincoln on June 16, 1858:

> In my opinion, it [slavery agitation] *will* not cease, until a *crisis* shall have been reached, and passed. A house divided against itself cannot stand. I believe this government cannot endure, permanently *half* slave and *half* free. I do not expect the Union to be dissolved—I do not expect the house to *fall*—but I do ex-

---

political balance that had been constructed during the preceding half century. In this context, the extermination of slavery, either peacefully or forcefully, was the only course open to the upper Midwest and the Republican Party. Contrary to some historians, I see no irony in northerners, notwithstanding their lack of interest in emancipating slaves, fighting a war for slavery's abolition. See, for example, Roger L. Ransom, *Conflict and Compromise: The Political Economy of Slavery, Emancipation, and the American Civil War* (Cambridge: Cambridge University Press, 1989).

62. This essay carries the ominous title "African Slavery Adapted to the North and North-west," *DeBow's Review* 25.(1858), pp. 378–95.

63. Cole, *The Era of the Civil War*, pp. 101–201.

pect it will cease to be divided. It will become *all* one thing or *all* the other. Either the opponents of slavery, will arrest the further spread of it, and place it where the public mind shall rest in the belief that it is in course of ultimate extinction; or its *advocates* will push it forward, till it shall become alike lawful in *all* the States, *old* as well as *new—North* as well as *South*.[64]

Lincoln was hardly paranoid about the problem of slavery's extension into "old" states; quite the reverse actually. He was in truth a ruthless geographical realist, who knew intimately the state of Illinois, its people, and their all-too-human frailties. And most of all, he knew the corn belt as only a native son could. Cognizant of the intense conflict between "real interest" and "abstract morality" that was being played out in the Midwest, he invested his energies and his life in ensuring that abstract morality would not suffer "a grievous overthrow." A paranoid, then, Lincoln was not; more accurately, his was the messianic vision of a native son setting forth to rescue his people from themselves. Just over two years later, he was given the chance.

The senatorial election of 1858 introduced Abraham Lincoln to the nation, and in 1860, he turned his earlier defeat by Stephen Douglas into a narrow presidential victory. Winning the presidency was important because it bought time. Slavery's progress could at least be stalled momentarily by the forces of anti-slavery. But the victory did nothing to change the reality of slavery's economic superiority in the antebellum corn belt. Lincoln understood that efforts to legalize slavery in the Midwest would persist until either relative labor costs shifted in favor of free labor (which was unlikely any time soon) or the institution of slavery was put on the road to ultimate extinction. As long as slavery existed in the nation, corn farmers would be tempted to use it. For the union and free society to endure, slavery had to be put where it would not disturb the public mind; that is to say, it had to be abolished once and for all.[65]

64. Basler, ed., *The Collected Works of Abraham Lincoln, 1848–1858*, Vol. 2, pp. 461–62.

65. Lincoln, above all else, was a man of his place, a product of the emerging corn belt of the lower Midwest. This former rail-splitter and seasonally employed rural laborer understood the implications of corn production for labor systems and politics. See, for example, Eric Foner, "The Causes of the American Civil War," p. 201. The geography of the 1858 election reaffirmed Republican fears. As Bruce Collins has demonstrated, this election's voting patterns are poorly explained by ethnocultural associations; he urges more attention to economic factors—among which, I would add, staple crop production and labor choice should be at the head of the list. Bruce Collins, "The Lincoln-Douglas

By 1860, the economic geography of corn culture, rising wages, and incipient slavery in the lower Midwest had brought the nation to its greatest impasse. The delicate geopolitical balance constructed out of assorted compromise in the first half of the century was in disarray; Lincoln was preparing to make his way toward Washington; and southerners spoke of secession rather than sufferance to an anti-slavery president. They rightly feared the new president, but they never quite understood the man or the basis of his radicalism: that the vanguard of slavery was not some mythical southern slavocracy but rather the "real interest" of corn-belt farmers in the American Middle West.

In this essay, I have tried to show that moral fiber cannot explain the geography of slavery and free labor and that the economics of staple crops and labor costs can. Before 1860, slavery was neither good nor bad, it was merely efficient or inefficient—and labor decisions were made accordingly. We can no more extol the principles of slave emancipators on Maryland's eastern shore or the Republicans of the upper Midwest who brought the issue of slavery to war than we can denigrate as unprincipled the pro-slavery advocates in the midwestern corn belt. They all subscribed to and acted on the same set of economic principles. The thesis that moral superiority motivated anti-slavery northerners must be shown for what it is: a comfortable liberal myth that obviates examination of the basic amorality of the antebellum American economic system.

Contest of 1858 and the Illinois Electorate," *Journal of American Studies* 20 (1986), pp. 391–420.

CHAPTER 7

The Myth of the Southern Soil Miner

Macrohistory, Agricultural Innovation, and Environmental Change

The differentiation of life is in part a matter of environmental adaptation, in part a question of cultural growth and diffusion. The origin and spread of ideas and skills is of course not to be thought of as taking place by any evolutionary sequence. There are no stages of culture; there are only inventions that make their way out into a wider world.

—*Carl O. Sauer* [1]

When conservationists of the 1930s wanted examples of destructive occupance of the American landscape, the South provided them with their most dramatic horror stories. Photographs of worn-out soils, gullied fields, and streams choked with sediment offered graphic evidence of the region's environmental abuse. Regional histories inspired by the unkind critiques of European visitors and native agrarian reformers lent further weight to an indictment of the South as an archetype of destructive occupance. These histories, and others since, told of over three centuries of chronic environmental exploitation; of an agrarian cycle of soil exhaustion and erosion, land abandonment, and frontier migration; and of an ecological myopia embedded within southern culture.

The criticism was unsparing and relentless, if not always consistent. It represented part of a larger critique of American society ini-

1. Carl O. Sauer, with a commentary by Martin S. Kenzer, "Regional Reality in Economy," *Association of Pacific Coast Geographers' Yearbook* 46 (1984), pp. 35–49, 45.

tiated earlier in the century by Progressives and reinvigorated by the Great Depression. Few regions were better suited to the Progressive critique. The South was filled with ambiguities and immense ironies; so too was Progressive thought. Few regions offered more ample room for the play of their discordant ideals and goals. One wing of Progressive thought could criticize southerners for an excess of capitalism and wanton exploitation of land and people, while another wing accused them of infidelity to capitalist principles of efficient resource use and management. One suspects that only in the inscrutable South could such contrapuntal themes have been brought into harmony. At the empirical level, highly contradictory philosophies of economy and environment came out sounding the same. From often radically different premises, historians, geographers, conservationists, sociologists, economists, and agronomists alike came to the same conclusions about southern wastefulness. They discredited past agricultural practices and blamed the region's environmental problems on a distinctively southern agrarian trilogy—plantation economy, slavery (and its legacies), and row crop cultivation.[2] The consensus historiography roundly scorned the agent of destructive occupance, the southern planter, as lazy, slovenly, and single-minded in pursuit of short-term profit. One provocative analogy, which I borrow for this essay's title, compared the southern planter to a "soil miner"— digging out the fertility from the soil, sifting it for short-term gains, and depositing the waste in a spoil bank of degenerate old fields. Such imagery—a legacy of the Progressive and New Deal critique of American society—has become an integral part of southern regional history.[3]

2. Hugh H. Bennett, *Soil Conservation* (New York: McGraw-Hill, 1939); *idem, Soils and Southern Agriculture* (New York: Macmillan, 1921); Lewis Cecil Gray, *History of Agriculture in the Southern United States to 1860* (2 vols., 1933; reprint, Gloucester, Mass.: Peter Smith, 1958); Carl O. Sauer, "Theme of Plant and Animal Destruction in Economic History," *Journal of Farm Economics* 20 (1938), pp. 765–75; *idem, Land and Life: A Selection from the Writings of Carl Ortwin Sauer,* ed. John Leighly (Berkeley: University of California Press, 1967); Avery O. Craven, *Soil Exhaustion as a Factor in the Agricultural History of Virginia and Maryland, 1606–1860* (Urbana: University of Illinois Press, 1926); Stanley W. Trimble, "Perspectives on the History of Soil Erosion Control in the Eastern United States," *Agricultural History* 59 (1985), pp. 162–80; Howard W. Odum, *Southern Regions of the United States* (Chapel Hill: University of North Carolina Press, 1932); Rupert Vance, *Human Geography of the South* (Chapel Hill: University of North Carolina Press, 1932). On Progressive environmental views, see Samuel P. Hays, *Conservation and the Gospel of Efficiency: The Progressive Conservation Movement, 1890–1920* (Cambridge, Mass.: Harvard University Press, 1959).
3. For the "miner" metaphor, see Warren C. Scoville, "Did Colonial Farmers Waste Our Land?" *Southern Economic Journal* 20 (1953), pp. 175–81, esp. p. 178. Scoville also cites

One senses, however, that the history of the southern soil miner is overdrawn, that the theme of unrelieved destruction has assumed mythic proportions. Reconsideration of this bleak historical interpretation seems advisable for at least two commonsense reasons. First is the matter of economic plausibility; that is, why did southerners persistently destroy the soil that nurtured them? The familiar rejoinder of free land on the frontier is inadequate, of course, because migration to fresh lands was not costless. It entailed expenses for sale, purchase, travel, land clearance, and settlement creation. These cost burdens suggest that southern planters would have at least occasionally implemented strategies of soil maintenance as an alternative to outmigration. The second consideration that casts doubt on the environmental history consensus is the rather one-dimensional caricature of the southern planter that emerges from it. Could anyone have performed this badly all of the time? Contradicting the invariant historical image of the soil miner is a variety of evidence documenting southern sensitivity to agronomic practice and soil conservation. Were these environmental sensitivities always episodic or tangential to the main business of making profits from tobacco, cotton, and other plantation staples?[4]

To these commonsensical reservations about the myth of the southern soil miner, we may add a doubt about the overly simplistic equation of environmental abuse with southern slavery. The persona of the southern soil miner fits too neatly into a morality play that juxtaposes southern evil and northern virtue. In this drama, southern soil abuse derived naturally from the evils of the region's plantation slave economy; the north, by contrast, enjoyed the virtues of family farms, free labor, and ecologically wise mixed farming systems. These neat regional caricatures, however, are as unjust to northern farmers as they are to southern planters. Northern farming, as we know, has not been immune to environmentally destructive occupance, as evidenced by the spectacles of the mud-filled Mississippi and the wind-eroded Great Plains. Nor was southern

numerous postwar economic histories that incorporate the New Deal conservation critique. Other metaphors include land butchers, robbers, and killers.

4. The impotence of southern conservation efforts, which came "in sporadic dribbles," is a principal theme in Trimble, "Perspectives on the History of Soil Erosion Control," p. 163; in Trimble's view, matters did not improve until the advent of the Soil Conservation Service under the New Deal.

planting always and everywhere hell-bent on short-run profit to the exclusion of environmentally adaptive agronomic systems. Planters neither thought nor acted in so disjunctive a mode.[5]

A judicious reconsideration of southern environmental history, therefore, is contingent on acknowledging three possibilities for the planters of the region: occasional sensitivity to soil abuse, implementation of ameliorative agronomic strategies, and attempts to achieve compatibility between the institution of slavery and wise agro-ecological practice. Insofar as this discussion reintroduces a sense of the problematic into southern environmental history, this essay will have served its purpose.

Fifteen years of studying American agricultural history have persuaded me that southern planters occasionally employed agronomic practices that were ecologically as well as economically sound. On at least two occasions, southern experimentation resulted in agronomic strategies that maintained soil fertility and minimized erosion losses. These adaptive strategies emerged out of cyclical economic crises in the 1680s Chesapeake and the 1840s cotton belt. Planters responded to these depressions by engaging in a great deal of agricultural experimentation; in the ensuing economic upswing, innovations devised during the depression diffused slowly at first and then with increasing speed throughout the Chesapeake tobacco coast (circa 1680–1740) and the cotton belt (circa 1840–80). Although similar in process and intent—to maintain soil fertility and profits—the specific innovations differed strikingly in agronomic practice. The Chesapeake tobacco system maintained soil fertility through recyclic land rotation in conjunction with slave labor and the by-product of diversified crops. The antebellum cotton system, in contrast, preserved soil fertility via crop rotation of cotton and corn intercropped with leguminous, nitrogen-fixing cowpeas. Although land rotation and crop rotation systems differed radically in agronomic organization, both maintained soil productivity, retarded soil erosion, and maximized plantation profits. In

5. The thesis linking slavery and destructive soil abuse is usually associated with Eugene D. Genovese, *The Political Economy of Slavery: Studies in the Economy and Society of the Slave South* (New York: Vintage Books, 1967), pp. 85–105. But the argument is older, as Genovese acknowledges. See John Taylor, *Arator: Being a Series of Agricultural Essays, Practical and Political*, 2nd ed. (Georgetown, D.C., 1814); Chester W. Wright, *Economic History of the United States*, 2nd ed. (New York: McGraw-Hill, 1947); and Trimble, "Perspectives on the History of Soil Erosion Control."

both cases, capitalist profit and constructive environmental occupance coexisted.[6]

These wise agro-ecological systems, however, did not endure,
and therein lies one of the principal ironies of southern history. Both
land rotation and crop rotation systems were discredited and abandoned as bad times resettled over their respective regions—much
as the Progressive-New Deal critique discredited previous agrarian
practices. A new wave of agrarian experimentation, innovation, and
diffusion swept over southern landscapes. "Bookish" and scientific
agrarian reform, first in the 1780s Chesapeake and later in the eastern cotton belt during the 1870s and 1880s, introduced continuous
cultivation, straight rows, clean-tilled fields, plows, and fertilizers—
all of which initiated an unprecedented period of environmental
destruction. When we view southern agricultural history in this cyclical context, the notion of a southern soil miner driven inexorably
toward destructive occupance of the landscape can be seen to be, at
least partially, a myth. The myth is clearly inappropriate to long periods of southern history; and even when it seems to apply, it misinterprets environmental intentions that were well-meaning, if sadly
uninformed.

Agricultural Innovation, Macrohistorical Rhythms, and Environmental Change

The linear conception of history that underlies the myth of the
southern soil miner is indefensible from the standpoint of modern
historical analysis. Three centuries is simply too long and too diverse
a time for which to postulate unchanging human behavior toward
the environment. Historical time is quite different. It ebbs and flows;
it is differentiable into homogeneous periods of stasis and recurrent
cycles of change. A heuristic paradigm that accommodates a dynamic
environmental history and the recurrence of agricultural innova-

6. Space precludes extensive documentation of these cases. The relevant citations
may be found in Carville Earle, *The Evolution of a Tidewater Settlement System: All Hallow's
Parish, Maryland, 1650–1783*, University of Chicago Department of Geography Research
Paper No. 170 (Chicago, 1975); and *idem*, "Tillage Capacity and Soil Maintenance in the
19th-Century Cotton South: A New Theory of Crop Choice," *Working Papers of the Social
Science History Workshop*, Paper 86–7 (Minneapolis: University of Minnesota Department
of History, 1986).

tion is the by now familiar 45- to 60-year "long wave" associated with capitalist economies. This macrohistorical rhythm, identified first by N. D. Kondratieff and popularized by Joseph Schumpeter, has been traced back to the 1790s and the early phases of the industrial revolution. Each of the waves—there have been four since 1790—consists of several distinguishable internal phases of economic growth (see Figure 7.1). These are, in sequence, depression or bad times, takeoff, acceleration, and deceleration. Although various names have been applied to these phases, quibbling over them is less important than understanding their cyclical integrity and the context they establish for agricultural innovation and environmental change.

The Theory of the Long Wave

The long wave argument, of course, is controversial, but skepticism has to do more with weak theory than with insecure evidence. A brief review and critique of the theory of long waves points up certain affinities with capitalist environmental history. Long waves were discovered, if that is the word, in the 1920s by the Russian N. D. Kondratieff, but he offered little guidance as to their generation. Shortly thereafter, Joseph Schumpeter's classic work on business cycles effectively introduced the long wave to an English-speaking audience. Schumpeter is best known for his emphasis on entrepreneurial innovation in the genesis of long waves; his at times prolix style of exposition, however, obscured the central problems of long-wave theory: the wave's consistent 45- to 60-year duration and its clocklike recurrence.[7]

Schumpeter's insights, however, constituted the foundation for later theoretical statements, of which Walt Rostow's offers perhaps the most sophisticated and cogent views on macrohistorical rhythms.[8] His thesis, desperately compressed, is that long economic cycles are

7. N. D. Kondratieff, "The Long Waves in Economic Life," *Review of Economic Statistics* 17 (1935), pp. 105–15; Joseph Schumpeter, *Business Cycles: A Theoretical, Historical, and Statistical Analysis of the Capitalist Process* (2 vols.; New York: McGraw-Hill, 1939). But see evidence of even earlier discovery of this rhythm by the Dutch scholar J. van Gelderen. Ger van Roon, "Long Wave Trends and Economic Policies in the Netherlands in the XIXth and XXth Century," *Journal of European Economic History* 12 (1983), pp. 323–37.

8. Walt W. Rostow, *The World Economy: History and Prospect, Part Three* (Austin: University of Texas Press, 1978); Walt W. Rostow and Michael Kennedy, with the assistance of Faisal Nasr, "A Simple Model of the Kondratieff Cycle," *Research in Economic History* 4 (1979), pp. 1–36.

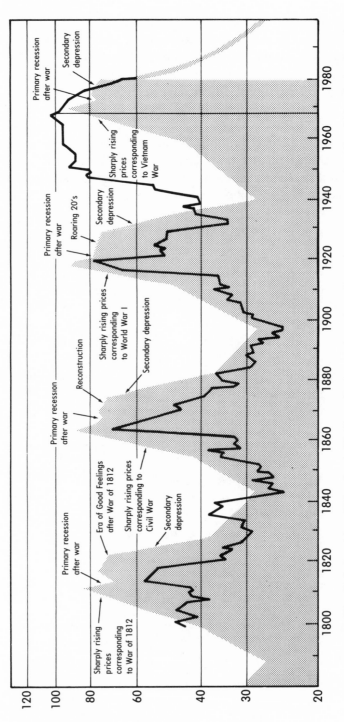

FIGURE 7.1. The Relationship of Kondratieff's Four Cycles to American Experience, 1790–1980. The U.S. wholesale price index (1967 = 100) is shown as a solid line. Kondratieff's long-wave cycles are shown in gray. Source: John A. Agnew, *The United States in the World-Economy: a Regional Geography* (Cambridge: Cambridge University Press, 1987), p. 22.

historically specific to industrializing capitalist societies, with their dramatically increased scale of innovations and investments in basic foodstuffs and raw materials and with the lengthening lag they face between an economic innovation and its productive installation. The long wave, in Rostow's view, had its inception in Western Europe in the last half of the eighteenth century and soon spread across the Atlantic to the United States. Innovations entailed quantitative and qualitative changes in investment; railroads, mines, and oil fields required massive infrastructural inputs, long lags between investment and installation, and levels of capital mobilization unavailable before the industrial revolution.

Rostow's explanation of 45- to 60-year rhythms is keyed to the lengthening lag between innovations and their full installation. The large scale of innovations and investments meant long delays between a depression innovation and its diffusion into full-capacity production. A lag of 15 to 25 years became commonplace in industrializing capitalist economies. Rostow maintains that this lag, by introducing a sharp discontinuity into the economy, was responsible for long-wave generation. In the first half of the long wave, the economy's output "undershot" demand or optimal capacity because the infrastructural investments for new innovations were incomplete. Accordingly, prices rose and economic growth slowly accelerated. The tide turned in the second half of the long wave when innovations were finally in place. Output exceeded or "overshot" optimal capacity, prices fell, and economic growth decelerated toward a long-wave depression. The entire process unfolded over 45 to 60 years and, owing to the discontinuous investment lag, produced an S-shaped or logistic curve of economic growth. The wave commenced with depression innovation, rose slowly during the period of investment gestation, accelerated as infrastructure was put in place, and decelerated as production exceeded optimal capacity. After a half century or so, the economy fell again on difficult times. And once again, entrepreneurs sought out new innovations that would eliminate economic stagnation and lift the economy into the next long wave.

Rostow's theory of long waves, albeit a major advance, is overly restrictive in its application. It is confined to one type of society, industrializing capitalist; to one class of innovations, discontinuous large-scale investments; and, by omission, to one type of environ-

mental consequence, ecological neutrality. It skips over a host of capitalist innovations that were not linked directly to industrialization
and that were smaller in scale, more continuous in their diffusion,
and non-neutral in their environmental impacts. I refer, of course,
to the ample record of capitalist agrarian innovations made by farmers and planters from the sixteenth century to the present.

Long-Wave Theory, Agricultural Innovation Diffusion, and Environmental Change

A somewhat more liberal theory of long waves would acknowledge these innovations and their bonds with environmental change
and macrohistorical rhythms. Three strands of evidence encourage
theoretical reconsideration. First is the remarkable symmetry in the
trajectories of agrarian innovation diffusion and long waves.[9] Both
are described by continuous, S-shaped, logistic curves. By way of contrast, Rostow's curves are mismatched. His long-wave curves are continuous logistic, while his curves of innovation-investment diffusion
are discontinuous. His step-like diffusion model has a hard time explaining why accelerated economic growth regularly took place prior
to the installation of massive infrastructures.[10]

A second strand of evidence is the 45- to 60-year simultaneity of
long waves and the diffusion of agricultural innovations. To cite just
a few examples (see Table 7.1 later in the chapter for others), the
English diffusion of clover and turnips circa 1680–1740 matches
closely with its long wave, as does the diffusion of hybrid corn and
cotton harvesters in the United States or combine harvesters in
England circa 1930–1980. Similarly, the improvements in English
wheat yields circa 1580–1640 document a close correspondence in
agricultural diffusion and the long wave.[11] Such logistic symmetry
and simultaneity seem more than fortuitous.

9. As noted later in the text, the correlation of agrarian diffusion and long-wave
processes has gone undiscerned by both diffusionists and economists. See for example,
Rostow's work cited above and Everett M. Rogers, *Diffusion of Innovations*, 3rd ed. (New
York: Free Press, 1983).

10. Rostow's theory describes discontinuous investment, yet his statistical modeling
introduces continuous investment assumptions during the first 15 to 25 years of the long
wave. Rostow and Kennedy, "A Simple Model of the Kondratieff Cycle," pp. 1–36.

11. In presenting these examples, I do not imply that these are the only innovations
devised and diffused in the period or that inventions as distinct from innovations cluster
in long-wave depressions. Mark Overton, "The Diffusion of Agricultural Innovations in
Early Modern England: Turnips and Clover in Norfolk and Suffolk, 1580–1740," *Institute*

The final strand of evidence is a more tentative observation on long-wave environmental interaction. The diffusion of innovation was accompanied by unanticipated, non-neutral environmental change. This change had two immediate effects. First, destructive occupance became evident in the deceleration phase of long waves and initiated a critique of prevailing agrarian practice. Second, the degree of environmental abuse conditioned the severity of the long-wave depression that ensued. The classic American example, of course, is the Great Depression, the extensive destructive environmental occupance of its preceding logistic, and the Progressive-New Deal critique of American agricultural practice. A comparable historical case, as I will show, is destructive occupance in the long wave that began in 1790 and culminated in the deep depression of the 1830s and 1840s.

This provisional evidence seems to implicate agricultural innovation and diffusion in an explanation of long-wave economic rhythms. The implications, of course, are far-reaching. Instead of four long waves, we may be dealing with as many as eight. Instead of regarding long waves as a product of late industrial capitalism, we may be dealing with a process inherent to the entire history of capitalist societies. Instead of regarding discontinuous, large-scale corporate investments as the prime mover of long waves, we more accurately may be dealing with the small-scale, continuous investments of farm households. And instead of ecologically neutral innovation, we may be dealing with impacts sufficient to govern the magnitude of long-wave crises.

A theory of agricultural innovation and long-wave economic growth is not, therefore, unrelated to environmental history—indeed, that is the whole point of interest here. Every agrarian innovation has consequences for the use or abuse of land and resources, and these consequences, in turn, reverberate upon ensuing innovation, diffusion, and long waves. Sketching these theoretical

---

of British Geographers, Transactions, n.s. 10 (1985), pp. 205–21; *idem*, "Agricultural Revolution? Development of the Agrarian Economy in Early Modern England," in *Explorations in Historical Geography: Interpretative Essays*, ed. Alan R. H. Baker and Derek Gregory, (Cambridge: Cambridge University Press, 1984), pp. 118–39; Zvi Griliches, "Hybrid Corn and the Economics of Innovation," *Science* 132 (July 29, 1960), pp. 275–80; David Grigg, *The Dynamics of Agricultural Change: The Historical Experience* (New York: St. Martin's Press, 1983). See Chapter 12 in the present volume for additional references on agrarian innovation and diffusion.

ties will bring us full circle to our main theme, the myth of the southern soil miner. My sketch consists of three interlocking propositions, which are provisional, despite their declarative form: (1) long-wave depression begets agricultural experimentation and innovation; (2) the diffusion of these innovations begets long-wave curves; and (3) the attendant diffusion of unanticipated environmental impacts begets, in part, long-wave depressions and a new round of agrarian innovation.

The Source of Agricultural Innovation: Long-Wave Depressions

The most critical, and certainly the most interesting, phases of capitalist agricultural history are the recurrent depressions of long waves. These are times of great difficulty and hardship, yet of remarkable creativity, experimentation, and innovation. In a process that has rendered capitalism so remarkably successful and at the same time so deeply mysterious, the adversity of falling prices, rising unemployment, and stagnating economic growth triggers an array of agricultural experiments and speculations. Deceleration of the long wave invites critique of prevailing practice; depression demands solutions. Experimentation aims at ending economic malaise through what Schumpeter termed "creative destruction." It seeks to replace current technologies and practices, suffering from diminishing returns and low profits, with more productive alternatives.[12] Experimentation embraces the entire society, from the microscale of farm and plantation households to the mesoscale of local, state, and regional institutions to the macroscale of nation-state political economies. At the microscale, experiments draw upon the entire reservoir of agrarian knowledge and experience. The

12. Innovations may be more productive in a variety of ways: by using resources more efficiently, e.g., using idle labor time to produce subsistence crop supplements to staple crop production; by improving quality of output; by regulating through cooperative efforts commodity supply; or by switching from one staple crop to another. The process of sorting from among these alternatives should be better understood if we are to develop a satisfactory theory of innovation. The risks and uncertainties of innovation in earlier times are nicely described in Margaret W. Rossiter, "The Organization of Agricultural Improvement in the United States, 1785–1865," in *The Pursuit of Knowledge in the Early American Republic: American Scientific and Learned Societies from Colonial Times to the Civil War*, ed. Alexandra Oleson and Sanborn Brown (Baltimore: Johns Hopkins University Press, 1976), pp. 279–88.

depression is a time of reconsideration, revision, and reconfiguration—what Thomas Kuhn called, in a different context, a paradigm shift.[13]

It is, moreover, an exhilarating, heady time. The phase of depression-experimentation is filled with creative as well as crackpot ideas, with interesting speculations, with useless inventions suddenly made practical, with unlikely innovators—I think of the contributions of slaves to the emergence of wet rice culture in late seventeenth-century South Carolina—and with innovations of varying long-term utility. It is a time, however brief, for those humanistic versions of history that celebrate "the great man (or woman)," the entrepreneurial genius, and the creative inventor. It stands in brilliant contrast to the ensuing period, when the more prosaic diffusion logistic takes over and routinely plays out the plot established during the creative phase of long-wave depression, experimentation, and innovation.

Agricultural innovations have a long history of association with capitalist macrohistorical cycles. It is possible to trace the clustering of these innovations in the depression phases of eight long waves encompassing the years between 1580 and 1980.[14] The types of innovations vary from simple tools or machines to fundamental reorganizations of agrarian practice. The list in Table 7.1 is selective rather than exhaustive and includes a number of familiar innovations alongside some less familiar ones that are discussed herein. A word about the list: The macrohistorical cycles are numbered from earliest to latest; dates refer to the depression commencement of the cycle and the end of the last deceleration phase. The listed in-

13. To reiterate, the issue here is innovation and not invention. Indeed, inventions may be more likely in the upswings of the long wave or in the early phases of the downswings. Innovation in long-wave depressions frequently draws upon premature inventions, revises or reconfigures them, and then applies them in new social and economic contexts. See, for example, Willis Peterson and Yoav Kislev, "The Cotton Harvester in Retrospect: Labor Displacement or Replacement?" *Journal of Economic History* 46 (1986), pp. 199–216, esp. pp. 202–4. The analogy between the processes of innovation in long-wave depressions and paradigmatic revision in science is pertinent; the accumulation of anomalous findings in science prompts theoretical revision in the same fashion that the diminishing returns to innovations compel agrarians to seek new solutions. Thomas S. Kuhn, *The Structure of Scientific Revolutions* (Chicago: University of Chicago Press, 1962).

14. For systematic documentation of innovation clustering in long-wave phases of deceleration and depression, see Raymond S. Hartman and David R. Wheeler, "Schumpeterian Waves of Innovation and Infrastructure Development in Great Britain and the United States: The Kondratieff Cycle Revisited," *Research in Economic History* 4 (1979), pp. 37–85.

TABLE 7.1

Selected Agrarian Innovations, 1580–1980

---

1 (1580s–1630s) unspecified improvements in English wheat production nearly doubling
  per acre yields in the first half of the seventeenth century; Hakluyt and Stuart colonization
  schemes aimed at venting surplus population and tapping colonial agricultural
  productivity.
2 (1630s–1680s) Chesapeake tobacco yield per worker triples as a probable consequence of
  innovations in topping the plant and in housing (curing) the tobacco.
3 (1680s–1730s) English incorporation of clover and turnips into crop rotation systems;
  Chesapeake adoption of land rotation in tobacco production and its integration with slave
  labor and crop diversification.
4 (1740s–1780s) agricultural policy innovations, most notably Chesapeake tobacco inspection
  systems.
5 (1790s–1830s) cotton gin, steamboat and canals, and "high farming" reform.
6 (1840s–1880s) reaper, railroads, southern crop rotation system (cotton, corn, cowpeas).
7 (1880s–1920s) commercial fertilizers, tractors, threshers.
8 (1930s–1970s) hybrid corn; combine harvesters (England).

SOURCES: These innovations and their diffusions are documented by various sources. See especially
the previously cited works for the indicated long waves: Overton (1 and 3); Earle (3, 4, 6, and 7); Griliches
(8); and Hartman and Wheeler (5–8). On English overseas enterprise and colonization (1), see Theodore
K. Rabb, *Enterprise and Empire: Merchant and Gentry Investment in the Expansion of England, 1575–1630*
(Cambridge, Mass.: Harvard University Press, 1967). On tobacco topping and curing (2), Russell R.
Menard, "The Tobacco Industry in the Chesapeake Colonies, 1617–1730: An Interpretation," *Research
in Economic History* 5 (1980), pp. 109–77. On the Chesapeake tobacco inspection system (4), Earle, *The
Evolution of a Tidewater Settlement System*; Mary McKinney Schweitzer, "Economic Regulation and the
Colonial Economy: The Maryland Tobacco Inspection Act of 1747," *Journal of Economic History* 40 (1980),
pp. 551–69. On transport innovations (5), see Hartman and Wheeler above, and on their diffusions,
John R. Borchert, "American Metropolitan Evolution," *Geographical Review* 57 (1967), pp. 301–32. On
midwestern reapers and cultivators (6), see Allan Bogue, *From Prairie to Cornbelt* (Chicago: University of
Chicago Press, 1963); Paul David, *Technical Choice Innovation and Economic Growth: Essays on American and
British Experience in the Nineteenth Century* (Cambridge: Cambridge University Press, 1975), pp. 195–223.
On fertilizers (7), Richard A. Wines, *Fertilizer in America: From Waste Recycling to Resource Exploitation*
(Philadelphia: Temple University Press, 1985). On tractors and threshers (7), John T. Schlebecker, *Whereby
We Thrive: A History of American Farming* (Ames: Iowa State University Press, 1975). Tractors display two
sequential logistics in waves 7 and 8; see Allan Bogue, "Changes in Mechanical and Plant Technology:
Corn Belt, 1910–1940," *Journal of Economic History* 43 (1983), pp. 1–26. Bogue also discusses combines,
corn pickers, and hybrid corn. On cotton harvesters (8), Peterson and Kislov, "The Cotton Harvester in
Retrospect," pp. 199–216.

novations emerged, of course, during the period of depression-
experimentation—a period that lasted usually for a decade plus or
minus several years.

The impressive list of innovations in Table 7.1 illustrates the significance of experimentation during recurrent macrohistorical depressions. Among the host of experiments, the successful ones became practical economic innovations that were subsequently diffused
to and integrated within the rural economy during the 45- to 60-year
logistic. The temporal regularity in the diffusion of these critical innovations is remarkable. The logistic curve of the diffusion of Chesapeake slavery and diversified output (tobacco along with corn, peas,

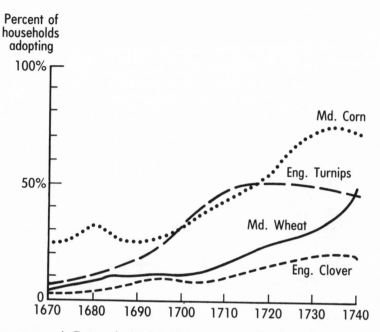

FIGURE 7.2. A Comparison of the Diffusion of Selected Agricultural Innovations, 1670–1740, in England (Clover and Turnips) and Maryland (Corn and Wheat). Sources: Overton, "The Diffusion of Agricultural Innovations in Early Modern England," pp. 205–21. Earle, *The Evolution of a Tidewater Settlement System,* pp. 122–23.

beans, and small grains), circa 1680 to 1740, matches almost precisely the simultaneous English diffusion of clover and turnips (see Figure 7.2). And these logistics replicate the post-1930 diffusion curves for American hybrid corn and English combine harvesters. It is to these diffusion processes and their affiliation with long waves that we now turn.

The Source of Long Waves: Agricultural Innovation Diffusion

My second theoretical proposition is that capitalist long waves take their shape from the recurrent periods of diffusion of agricultural innovations. This proposition has emerged from the tantalizing correlations between the curves of agrarian diffusion and long waves in the economy. Yet despite a massive literature on diffusion processes, these correlations have not been discerned by diffusionists—an indication, I believe, of their neglect of macrohistorical context as well as their unwillingness to distinguish critical innovations from trivial ones.[15] Thus, while numerous studies have demonstrated a natural history in rural innovation diffusion in the United States and Britain, none has recognized that the diffusion curves of critical innovations fit approximately the 45- to 60-year time-frame of long-wave economic growth. Nor do the reports of S-shaped or logistic curves of diffusion acknowledge their remarkable symmetry with long-wave curves. The undiscerned parallels extend even down to the language used in categorizing phases. Diffusionists speak of four phases of adoption: innovators, early majority, late majority, and laggards—categories that in number and timing resemble the language used in describing long-wave economic growth. And when diffusion is described as a continuous logistic process—beginning slowly, accelerating, leveling off, and then decelerating—the description mimics precisely the continuous changes in the curve of long-wave economic growth.[16]

To get at the reasons for diffusion's leisurely half-century pace as well as its S-shaped curve is to move closer to an explanation of long-wave economic growth. These reasons are hardly arcane. The slow pace of agricultural diffusion results from the imperatives of face-to-face communication, diffusion by demonstration, and individual rural households as the fundamental unit of adoption. The shape of the diffusion logistic, meanwhile, arises from rural conservatism with respect to the economic risks of introducing new technologies. Risk is especially high when innovations are incubating during long-wave depressions. When few have adopted an innovation (that is, when sample size is small), rural households calculate the probabilities of economic success with great difficulty. The proverbial wisdom, and

15.   The closest anyone has come is a statement of need: "Linking cycle studies with spatial diffusion remains as a challenge to human geographers and economists alike. Cycles appear to be an endemic aspect of economic processes, as does diffusion." Don Pakes and Nigel Thrift, *Time, Spaces, and Places: A Chronogeographic Perspective* (Chichester: John Wiley, 1980), p. 415. Also see Rogers, *Diffusion of Innovations*; and Lawrence Brown, *Innovation Diffusion: A New Perspective* (London: Methuen, 1981). The diffusion literature tends to lump innovations irrespective of their significance for economic history. But when critical innovations have been identified, little attention has been paid to their correlations with the shape and timing of long waves. A useful critique of diffusionism, congenial to the views expressed here, is J. M. Blaut, "Diffusionism: A Uniformitarian Critique," *Annals of the Association of American Geographers* 77 (1987), pp. 30–47.

16.   Rogers, *Diffusion of Innovations*, pp. 163–209, 241–70; Rostow and Kennedy, "A Simple Model of the Kondratieff Cycle," pp. 1–36.

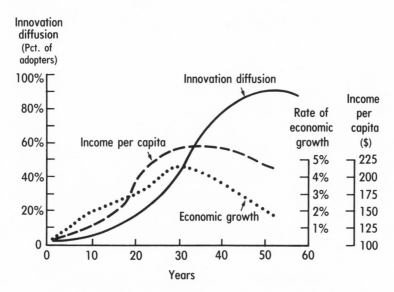

FIGURE 7.3. A Schematic Representation of the Effect of the Diffusion of an Agricultural Innovation on Economic Growth and Per Capita Income Across a Kondratieff Long-wave Cycle.

rightly so, is that innovators are a bit odd or foolhardy. But the basis for assessing economic risk improves as the innovation diffuses. Sample size increases and probabilities of economic success or failure are more firmly grounded.

Once under way, diffusion meshes with long-wave economic growth; the two increase simultaneously (see Figure 7.3). Economic growth is continuous because "innovators" and "early majority" earn preemptive profits or "adoption rents" from early adoption—thus improving income per capita. They also benefit from rising prices—a consequence of the partial diffusion of productive capacity and the resultant undershooting of optimal capacity. About midway into the logistic, however, economic growth rates dwindle as innovation diffusion spreads to the "late majority" and then to the "laggards." Their incremental output causes productive capacity to overshoot optimal capacity; prices fall, economic growth sags, and diffusion comes to a halt. ("The market is saturated" is the preferred expression in the diffusion literature.) Bad times return to the region, but the cycle begins anew as agrarians search out innovations that might provide new sources of profit and economic growth in the next long wave.[17] In this manner, the routine diffusion of agrarian innovations generates recurrent long waves in capitalist economies.

The Ecological Consequences of Innovation Diffusion

It is a short step from macrohistorical rhythms and agricultural innovation diffusion to the problems of environmental history. The simple but not obvious point is that agrarian innovations have environmental consequences. Indeed, one of the principal aims of agrarian innovation is environmental improvement, for example, restoring, maintaining, or improving soil fertility. The innovator's dilemma, however, is that these consequences are usually unknowable. A priori or even incremental assessment of these impacts is extremely difficult because of the peculiarly long lags separating an innovation's adoption and feedback on its environmental effects. The insidious effects of soil exhaustion and soil erosion, for example, are often imperceptible for long periods. Similarly, a particular variety of fertilizer may increase yields in the short run, but an unsuspected nutrient deficiency in the fertilizer mix may impoverish soil in the long run—this is precisely what happened in the eastern cotton belt during the 1870s and 1880s. In sum, the environmental impacts of depression innovations are known only in retrospect. By the time environmental information is fed back—usually not until the decelerating phase of the diffusion logistic—the destructive or constructive impacts on the landscape are virtually unstoppable.

In this context of uncertainty, innovating farmers and planters of the periods under study were all at sea. They could not calculate long-run environmental (and economic) risk. Nor could they calculate the short-run economic risks at the outset of an innovation since the mathematical probabilities of ecological success or failure were simply unknown and incalculable. Impotent to come up with rational solutions, yet compelled to innovation by economic circumstance, rural innovators behaved in classically Weberian fashion— they relied upon non-rational sources of legitimation. Historically, these sources arose from one of two contending agrarian epistemologies: one derived knowledge from the practical, empirical experi-

17. My interpretation of long-wave growth is more complex than this summary allows. Of particular importance is the inextricable relationship of post-depression international war and its contribution to rising agricultural prices and innovation diffusion. A full exposition appears in Chapter 12.

ence of local agrarians (one is tempted to refer to them as folk capitalists); the other derived knowledge from the theory, inference, and speculation of scientists and agrarian reformers conveyed through books, scientific treatises, and correspondence. Although an undercurrent of tension ran perennially between these two epistemologies, the tension surfaced dramatically when stakes were high, that is, in the critical phase of long-wave depression, experimentation, and innovation. The two sets of ideas and their agents contended vigorously for the hearts and minds of rural folk. In some depressions, innovators relied on the practical advice of respected neighbors—what contemporaries called "the testimony of practice"; in other depressions, they accepted the counsel of bookish and theoretical agrarian reformers who offered "the testimony of science." To some extent, the debate has intensified in this century as "true science" has sought to discredit both "uninformed" practice and ill-conceived scientific "quackery."[18]

We do not know for sure why one epistemology prevailed over another in any particular period. But it is fairly obvious that a principle of alternation was at work. The victorious epistemology of one long wave was usually discredited in the deceleration and depression that inevitably followed. And so the field was cleared for the hegemony of the contending epistemology, its innovations, and its agents in the ensuing long wave. The environmental consequences of this debate between science and practice were paradoxical. The more adaptive ecological innovations emanated from the practical advice of local planters; and conversely, innovations that wreaked havoc on the southern landscape emanated from agrarian reformers and their not always reliable "testimony of science." When "science" prevailed, destructive occupancy marked by soil exhaustion, erosion, and sedimentation attended the diffusion logistic and intensified the ensuing long-wave crash. Such was the case in the tobacco South between 1790 and 1840 and in parts of the cotton South between 1880 and

18. Richard A. Wines, *Fertilizer in America: From Waste Recycling to Resource Exploitation* (Philadelphia: Temple University Press, 1985), pp. 41, 156–57, 167, 170; Asa Gray, "Practice and Science Agree," *American Agriculturalist* 34 (1875), p. 140. See also Margaret W. Rossiter, *The Emergence of Agricultural Science: Justus Liebig and the Americans, 1840–1880* (New Haven: Yale University Press, 1975), pp. 116–17. For the "true science" critique, see Bennett, *Soils and Southern Agriculture*, preface. Neglect of the contentious nature of innovation diffusion in its early stage (as well as its basis in class) has resulted in the stagnation of diffusion theory. See Derek Gregory, "Suspended Animation: The Stasis of Diffusion Theory," in *Social Relations and Spatial Structures*, ed. Derek Gregory and John Urry (New York: St. Martin's Press, 1985), pp. 296–336.

1930. The severity of these environmental and economic crises called for extreme remedial solutions.[19]

Macrohistory and Southern Agricultural Practice

Macrohistorical analysis thus makes two points of significance for students of southern agricultural innovation and environmental change. First, the recurrence of bad economic times stimulated agricultural experimentation at multiple scales ranging from the folk to the nation-state. Second, ensuing innovation diffusion was accompanied by economic risk and environmental uncertainty. The former largely accounted for the S-shaped configuration of the logistic curve; the latter for unintended destructive environmental consequences. While agrarians preferred innovations that maintained soil fertility and ecological equilibrium, their evaluation of new developments was handicapped by the long time it took to receive adequate feedback. Lacking unequivocal evidence on the impact of their innovations, planters and farmers based their adoption decisions on either the local wisdom of practice or the extra-local wisdom of "science."

These points place innovation and environmental change in a dynamic, and more problematic, macrohistorical context. Therein, we may reconsider the historiographic myth of the southern soil miner. What emerges is a new southern planter—adaptive to economic change, attentive to problems of soil exhaustion and erosion, and contemplative of economic risk and environmental uncertainty—and a new history of the southern landscape that is sensitive to the cyclical alternation between constructive and destructive occupance.

My reconsideration of southern environmental history examines

19. The undistinguished environmental record of agricultural science and agrarian reform was the consequence in part of theoretical speculation uninformed by empirical method—the basis of practical farming—and in part of complex prescriptions that were an invitation to selective and partial adoptions by farmers and planters. By the turn of this century, however, agricultural scientists were adopting more empirical methods and ensuring their full dissemination via state and local agricultural agents. Environmental catastrophes, though not improbable, have become less likely. Rossiter, *The Emergence of Agricultural Science*; Wines, *Fertilizer in America*, pp. 167, 170. For an example of the detrimental effects of scientific research on hybrid corn, see Allan Bogue, "Changes in Mechanical and Plant Technology: Corn Belt, 1910–1940," *Journal of Economic History* 43 (1983), pp. 25–26. Also see Wendell Berry, *The Unsettling of America: Culture and Agriculture* (San Francisco: Sierra Club Books, 1977).

FIGURE 7.4. A mid-nineteenth-century reproduction of tobacco production. The slaves are tilling the weeds from among the rows of tobacco plants. In the case of planted crops, the phase of tillage in late spring and early summer exerted the heaviest demands on slave labor. The practice of using hoes and axes in tillage had changed little since the colonial period. Reproduced from *Harper's New Monthly Magazine* 11 (1855), p. 8.

two cases that, in retrospect, have a remarkable dramaturgical symmetry. Each begins with local agricultural experiments during a long-wave depression; each is followed at first by logistic diffusion of innovations that are profitable and environmentally constructive and later, in ensuing bad times, by the abandonment of these innovations in favor of "scientific" reforms and, ironically, destructive occupance. As if to reinforce their historical symmetries, in each case the ecologically adaptive innovations, arising out of the experience of local planters, have been misunderstood and distorted by contemporaries and scholars alike.

The first case comes from the plantation tobacco economy of the colonial Chesapeake, 1680–1790. Constructive environmental innovations were introduced in the long depression of the 1680s and endured for two macrohistorical cycles. The critical innovation, a system of land rotation, succumbed to the "primitivist" critique of postrevolutionary agricultural reformers. The reformed system of plowing, clean tillage, continuous cultivation, and rude fertilizers hastened the destructive processes of soil exhaustion and erosion—all of which was faithfully recorded in the travel narratives of the period.

The second case is that of the southern cotton belt, 1840–1890. Its environmental macrohistory closely recapitulates the experience of the colonial Chesapeake. During the depressed 1840s, the vicious cycle of worn-out soils, land abandonment, and outmigration that had prevailed on the booming cotton frontier was replaced by an imaginative local innovation in agricultural practice. The new system of crop rotation cleverly combined cotton, corn, and leguminous cowpeas so as to maintain both profits and soil fertility. This agrarian system diffused throughout the cotton belt both before and after the Civil War; indeed, it endured in some parts of the South until after the turn of the century. But in one subregion, the eastern cotton belt, the crop rotation system was eliminated through the efforts of scientific and corporate reformers. In the long, downward slide to the depression of the 1880s, planters followed the advice of reformers and converted from crop rotation to cotton specialization and liberal fertilizer application. The economic consequences showed up first, as early as the 1880s, in the form of debt peonage; the environmental consequences soon followed in the form of worn-out land and deeply gullied cotton fields—a scene graphically portrayed in the photographs of conservation textbooks in this century.

The Chesapeake Tobacco Economy, 1680–1790

The perfidious tobacco economy in the seventeenth-century Chesapeake provided two opportunities for agrarian experimentation and innovation. Long-wave depressions in the 1630s and 1680s drove tobacco prices so low that the viability of the economy was in doubt. In terms of price history, the 1630s were the worst of times. Prices fell to 36 times below the levels that had prevailed in the boom times between tobacco's introduction (1612?) and the mid-1620s; in the boom period, tobacco brought three shillings for a pound, and ordinary men, producing 500 pounds of tobacco each, earned seven times as much as their English counterparts. The sharp fall in prices, *ceteris paribus*, should have ended commercial tobacco production, but planter experimentation and agricultural innovation salvaged the economy. Although the evidence is fragmentary, we know that while prices plummeted between 1630 and 1650, tobacco output per worker tripled or quadrupled (from 500 pounds to between 1,500 and 2,000 pounds per worker). Tobacco scholars make a plausible case that productivity growth had its source in several innovations, including the new practice of topping the plant, which channeled plant nutrients from the seed to the leaves, and improvements in housing, curing, stripping, and packing the harvested leaf. These productivity innovations just barely compensated for the dramatic decline in tobacco price. Although the earnings of Chesapeake workers dropped to the level of English earnings, the innovations prevented them from dropping below that level, which would have induced small planters to consider return migration to England. In short, these innovations preserved the viability of the Chesapeake tobacco economy.[20]

Long-Wave Depression and the Reappraisal of Agrarian Practice

This story of bad times and agricultural experimentation was replayed in the 1680s. A steadily declining tobacco price hit bottom in the 1680s and early 1690s, dropping below a penny a pound. The crisis prompted a reevaluation of prevailing production practices. A visitor to Virginia in the 1680s provided a window on traditional practices and the problem of soil fertility. Planters, he observed, used a primitive crop rotation system supplemented by animal manures. A few acres were devoted to tobacco (usually three acres per worker) and a few other acres were planted in corn. On these fields, which seem to have been continuously cultivated or at best subject to very

20. Russell R. Menard, "The Tobacco Industry in the Chesapeake Colonies, 1617–1730: An Interpretation," *Research in Economic History* 5 (1980), pp. 109–77; Edmund S. Morgan, *American Slavery, American Freedom: The Ordeal of Colonial Virginia* (New York: W. W. Norton, 1975).

short fallow, planters coped with declining soil fertility by "forcing the land" with animal manures. Vestiges of this simple rotation system survived until well into the eighteenth century.[21]

The traditional system, however simple, had certain advantages in a society that was labor-scarce and relied principally on servants for supplemental plantation labor. Servants were especially valuable because their land clearance contributed directly to plantation capital formation. Over the course of their four- to seven-year contracts, servants cleared a modest amount of land for tobacco and corn. When a servant's term expired, planters used these capital improvements in land for the continuous cultivation of tobacco and corn. Successful planters perhaps purchased another male servant to do the cultivation and to make additional land improvements.

This expansion path, however, became more difficult in the last quarter of the century when the supply of servants declined and their price rose. In the absence of servant laborers' clearance of fresh land, lands were continuously cultivated, soils wore out, and yields declined. Planters combated soil exhaustion by applying animal manures, but the ecological disadvantages of continuous cultivation were evident by the 1670s and 1680s. Yields declined in long-settled areas. Buyers complained that manures fouled tobacco's taste—an observation confirmed by twentieth-century science—and this lowered its price. If the tobacco economy was to endure, the Chesapeake planter required an alternative and superior agronomic system.[22]

Chesapeake Land Rotation, 1680–1780

The crisis of the 1680s and 1690s triggered several creative experiments. Some planters called for propping up prices by a statutory stint on tobacco production; others wanted a more efficient, urban-based marketing system; and still others proposed a thorough restructuring of the region's agricultural system.[23] The last of these won out. In a classic illustration of local innovation and diffusion,

21. On cowpenning tobacco in the 1680s, see William Byrd to Father Hormonden, June 5, 1686, "Capt. Byrd's Letters," *Virginia Historical Register and Literary Advertiser* 2 (1849), p. 81. Lewis Cecil Gray, *History of Agriculture*, Vol. 1, p. 217; and Earle, *Evolution of a Tidewater Settlement System*, pp. 28, 129. On the persistence of this old technology into the late 1750s, see Richard Corbin's letter cited in Aubrey C. Land, ed., *Bases of the Plantation Society* (New York: Harper and Row, 1969), pp. 140–43, esp. p. 141.

22. Earle, *Evolution of a Tidewater Settlement System*, pp. 24–30. On servant supply and prices, see David W. Galenson, *White Servitude in Colonial America: An Economic Analysis* (Cambridge: Cambridge University Press, 1981), pp. 134–68.

23. John J. McCusker and Russell R. Menard, *The Economy of British America, 1607–1789* (Chapel Hill: University of North Carolina Press, 1985).

Land Rotation (Recycled in Shifting Cultivation), 1680's-1790's

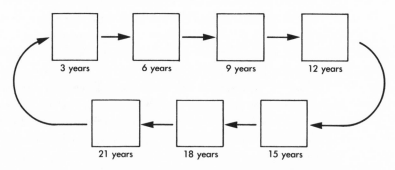

FIGURE 7.5. The Chesapeake Cycle of Land Rotation in Tobacco Production, 1680s–1790s. A typical worker cultivated a three-acre parcel of tobacco for three successive years, at which point production was relocated to a new parcel and the abandoned field was turned into crops and fallow in the following sequence: corn (3 years); wheat (1 year); fallow old fields (20 years).

Chesapeake planters introduced a complex system that combined recyclic shifting cultivation (or land rotation), slave labor, and diversified crops (tobacco along with corn, beans, peas, and small grains). The new system was profitable as well as ecologically efficient, and it diffused widely in the region by 1740. This new system was something of an ethnic amalgam, borrowing elements from Indian, Afro-American, and European sources. The crux of the system was the Indian practice of shifting cultivation or land rotation; its indispensable source of labor was the perpetually bound Afro-American slave; and its diversified mix of crops was a rude imitation of contemporary English innovation (that is, in the English case, clover, turnips, and small grains).

But then again, the Chesapeake's agrarian system was new and it departed in several ways from its sources of inspiration. Although the new system mimicked Indian shifting-cultivation systems, it differed from Indian practice in its regular recycling of land back into production after approximately a twenty-year fallow.[24] The Chesapeake system took full circle the vicious cycle of cultivation, exhaustion, abandonment, and outmigration, but instead of outmigration,

24. The conventional attribution of shifting cultivation to American Indians invites reconsideration. African slaves who provided the labor for the new system brought with them a long experience with shifting cultivation systems. Their contributions to Chesapeake agriculture may have been more substantial than is usually imagined. For slave contributions to wet rice agriculture farther south, see Peter H. Wood, *Black Majority: Negroes in Colonial South Carolina from 1670 through the Stono Rebellion* (New York: Alfred A. Knopf, 1975).

Chesapeake planters put their land in fallow and reclaimed it after sufficient time had elapsed for "natural" renovation.

The land rotation system worked as follows (also see Figure 7.5). Beginning with fertile, virgin land, a typical worker haphazardly cleared three acres. Trees were girdled and left to die in a field littered with stumps and roots. In the first year, raw or "strong land" was planted in corn or beans or both. Tobacco followed during the next two to three years, depending on the inherent fertility of the soil. In the fourth through seventh years, corn was intercropped with peas and beans and the whole cultivation cycle was finished off with a modest crop of small grains like wheat or rye. Thereafter, the worn-out parcel was abandoned to "old field" colonization. During the next two decades, a succession of grasses, shrubs, pines, and hardwoods restored soil fertility. When the restoration was complete—a time indicated usually by second-growth forest—the laborer cleared the renovated old fields and the cultivation cycle started anew. Perpetual land clearance thus was a prerequisite of the system of shifting cultivation. Every three or four years, "new" tobacco lands were cleared. And as tobacco rotated onto renovated land, planters knocked down their wooden tobacco houses and reassembled them near the new fields.[25]

The ecological genius of this system of land rotation was easily misunderstood. Eighteenth-century travelers in the tidewater Chesapeake universally misinterpreted what they saw. Unaware of the ecological functions of this mobile agrarian system, they hastily condemned the cosmetic appearance of the Chesapeake landscape—its unkempt fields littered with dying trees and stumps and hummocked by mini-excavation pits (the result of row crop "hilling"), its ragged fallow land in various stages of restoration, and its ramshackle tobacco houses in miscellaneous states of decay. To be sure, the tobacco landscape after 1700 was not pretty, but it was highly functional in economy and ecology. Tobacco yields ceased their decline; soil fertility was maintained; erosion was retarded by the chaotic drainage system of typical tobacco fields, filled as they were with the numerous check dams of stumps, roots, hills, and pits. To borrow a cliché from the contemporary world of sports, the colonial system of shifting cultivation amounted to "winning ugly."

25. Earle, *Evolution of a Tidewater Settlement System*; Lois Green Carr and Russell R. Menard, "Land, Labor, and Economies of Scale in Early Maryland: Some Limits to Growth in the Chesapeake System of Husbandry," *Journal of Economic History* 49 (1989), pp. 407–18.

The innovation of land rotation was not unrelated to the concurrent introduction of slave labor on a massive scale into the Chesapeake. Indeed, the transformation of the Chesapeake labor force from servants to slaves was accomplished during this macrohistorical cycle. The proportion of slaves in the population rose from less than 5 percent in the 1670s to 30 percent or so in the first decades of the next century to nearly 50 percent by the 1740s. Meanwhile, indentured servants virtually disappeared, except for those employed in skilled tasks. Scholars have provided varying interpretations of this labor transformation. The principal arguments have focused on planter displeasure with irascible, undisciplined servants or, alternatively, relative price changes that favored slaves over servants.[26] Neither interpretation, however, is sufficient since in dealing exclusively with the transformation they neglect the matter of slavery's continuing viability. Reconsideration of slavery's competitive advantage in the emerging agrarian system of shifting cultivation at once addresses the issues of labor transformation and the viability of slavery.

The efficient functioning of Chesapeake land rotation was contingent on a perpetually bound labor force. Slavery offered the perfect complement to an agrarian system that demanded periodic clearance of land. In the new system of land rotation, slaves cleared tobacco land as needed (usually every three to four years), and when they became superannuated, their sons assumed the task, followed by their sons. Conversely, use of temporary servant labor was inefficient in this system since land improvement was perpetual and continued long after the expiration of the servant's contract. More specifically, this new system fundamentally redefined the meaning of land—and labor costs—in the Chesapeake. Henceforth, improved land was ephemeral in status. It entered briefly into the capital stock of the plantation, and then it was "destroyed" in long fallow. Land thus shifted from being a stock resource under the innovation of the previous system of continuous cultivation to being a flow resource under recyclical shifting cultivation.[27] This redefinition of land forced a revision in the planters' accounting procedures and in their

26. Morgan, *American Slavery, American Freedom*; Russell R. Menard, "From Servants to Slaves: The Transformation of the Chesapeake Labor System," *Southern Studies* 16 (1977), pp. 355–90; Galenson, *White Servitude in Colonial America*.

27. The link between slavery and land rotation is strengthened by Hugh Jones's observation that tenants "forced" (manured) their lands. Lacking labor for perpetual clearing, tenants persisted in the practice of continuous cultivation. Hugh Jones, *Present State of Virginia, 1724* (New York: Sabin's Reprint, 1865), pp. 53–54.

labor preferences. Amortization schedules were reconfigured with adverse effects on servant labor costs. In the old system, planters amortized over the indefinite life of continuously cultivated, improved land; in the new system, they amortized servant costs over a useful life of seven years or less—the amount of time that cleared land was in productive use before being placed in long fallow. Consequently, because of the shorter useful life of improved land, servant costs increased while slave costs remained unchanged.

Slavery's competitive advantage on the demand side received an added boost from the supply side. Relative prices for slave and servant labor came to favor slaves during the long-wave depression of the 1680s and 1690s. While servant prices were rising, perhaps because of the slow growth in English population as well as planter dissatisfaction with servant productivity, slave prices fell sharply. As the depression of the 1680s swept over the sugar islands in the West Indies, debt-stricken West Indian planters wholesaled their surplus slaves in an effort to make remissions on overextended credit. Many slaves were transported to the Chesapeake, where they were eagerly purchased and integrated into the emerging land rotation system. By 1700, the Chesapeake had virtually abandoned servant labor in favor of slaves.

But supply-side explanations alone are insufficient to explain the ongoing viability of slavery, especially after 1720, when prices favored servants over slaves. What guaranteed slavery's persistence was its lower cost in the recyclical system of shifting cultivation. One might say, without risk of exaggeration, that Chesapeake slavery was more a consequence of plantation agrarian practice than a cause of it.

The diffusion of this new agricultural system followed the logistic or S-shaped curve. Its adoption may be observed in the diffusion of slavery, the principal source of labor in the land rotation system. Slaves increased from a trivial proportion in 1680 to nearly 50 percent of the region's population 60 years later. Diversified output followed a similar trajectory. My study of Maryland's All Hallow's Parish reports a steady increase in the frequency of corn, peas, beans, and small grains—crops that preceded and succeeded tobacco on the rotating fields. Although we lack direct statistical evidence on the diffusion of shifting cultivation itself, the scornful accounts of an atrophied and ugly landscape by Chesapeake sojourners offer compelling corroboration. And finally, of course, there is evidence of worker productivity; as the land rotation system diffused and soil fertility was maintained, the decline in tobacco output per worker halted and yields edged modestly upward.[28]

The viability of recyclic shifting cultivation is attested to by its survival through two macrohistorical cycles (1680–1740, 1740–1780). Despite the fall of tobacco prices to historic lows in the long-wave depression of the 1740s, Chesapeake planters preserved the land rotation system. But they experimented with other components of the tobacco economy. The most notable result of this experimentation was the policy innovation of a tobacco inspection system aimed at improving tobacco's quality and its price.

Agrarian Reform and Destructive Occupance in the Chesapeake, 1780–1840

The land-rotation system, however, did not survive into the third macrohistorical cycle, which began in the 1780s. The system came under withering attack in the postrevolutionary depression. Agrarian reformers, motivated by hard times, population pressure, and nationalist sentiment (Americans were acutely sensitive to European critiques of the American landscape, as Jefferson's *Notes on Virginia* attest), discredited "primitive" agricultural methods and advocated their abandonment in favor of modern "high farming" systems. The intensification arguments of John Beale Bordley, John Taylor of Caroline, and others were persuasive in full or in part. Chesapeake agriculture was transformed. Plows rapidly replaced hoe-and-axe cultivation; fields were put in good order as stumps and other rubbish were removed from them; and a more continuous system of cultivation, using fertilizers such as plaster of paris and animal manures, displaced the "primitive" land rotation system. Improving planters thus imposed order on an unkempt, unruly landscape.[29]

28. Earle, *Evolution of a Tidewater Settlement System*; Edward C. Papenfuse, Jr., "Planter Behavior and Economic Opportunity in a Staple Economy," *Agricultural History* 46 (1972), pp. 297–311; Henry M. Miller, "Transforming a 'Splendid and Delightsome Land': Colonists and Ecological Change in the Chesapeake, 1607–1820," *Journal of the Washington Academy of Science* 76 (1986), pp. 173–87.

29. For a balanced view of agrarian reform, see Curtis P. Nettels, *The Emergence of a National Economy, 1775–1815* (New York: Harper and Row, 1962), pp. 243–51, and sources therein. That reformers successfully converted "rank-and-file" farmers and planters is illustrated, for example, by the diffusion of plows nearly to the bottom of the agricultural ladder in an area relatively isolated from reformist activities: Among tenants in Charles County, (southern) Maryland, the proportion of inventoried households owning plows increased from 21 percent before 1776 to 73 percent by 1820. Lorena S. Walsh,

The tragedy of these Enlightenment-inspired agricultural reforms is that they unleashed an epoch of devastating destructive occupance in the tobacco economy of the upper South. Clean-tilled
fields accelerated erosion. Erosion stripped away vital plant nutrients
and hastened soil exhaustion. Sediment flowed into Chesapeake
streams, creeks, and estuaries, clogging them up and disrupting navigation. The twin evils of erosion and exhaustion forced many planters back into the vicious cycle: selling off their depleted tidewater
plantations and migrating west to fresh lands in the piedmont. But
there, owing to the piedmont's steeper slopes, destructive occupancy
proceeded with even more intensity.[30]

For some time students of Chesapeake history have had their suspicions about the ecological abuses of postrevolutionary agrarian reform. New physical evidence about these abuses seemingly clinches
the case. Recent studies of sediment cores from Chesapeake estuaries
document sharp increases in the rates of sedimentation and pollen
accumulation in the late eighteenth and early nineteenth centuries.
Annual rates of sediment accumulation rose twofold to twentyfold
over rates prevailing during the colonial period, when the ecologically adaptive system of land rotation was in place. This dramatic rise
in sedimentation, as well as in port and navigation siltation, was the
consequence of new agricultural practices introduced in the long-
wave depression of the 1780s and 1790s and diffused in the ensuing
logistic.[31]

By the end of this macrohistorical cycle, circa 1840, the Chesapeake tobacco economy had sunk into an impoverished state. Although the depression stimulated a new group of agricultural reformers, including Edmund Ruffin, their attempt to reverse the

---

"Land, Landlord, and Leaseholder: Estate Management in Southern Maryland, 1642–
1820," *Agricultural History* 59 (1985), pp. 373–96, esp. p. 385; and *idem*, "Plantation Management in the Chesapeake, 1620–1820," *Journal of Economic History* 49 (1989), pp. 393–
406.

30. Miller, "Transforming a 'Splendid and Delightsome Land,'" pp. 173–87. In addition, a good deal of evidence on the destructive occupance that resulted from agrarian
reform is unknowingly supplied by proponents of the "soil miner" thesis. See Craven, *Soil
Exhaustion as a Factor in the Agricultural History of Virginia and Maryland*; and Louis C. Gott-
schalk, "Effects of Soil Erosion on Navigation in Upper Chesapeake Bay," *Geographical
Review* 35 (1945), pp. 219–38.

31. Grace S. Brush, "Geology and Paleoecology of Chesapeake Bay: A Long-term
Monitoring Tool for Management," *Journal of the Washington Academy of Science* 76 (1986),
pp. 146–60.

vicious cycle was impotent. The region was beyond agricultural and environmental salvation. Consequently, the most popular depression experiments dealt not with agronomic practice but rather with radical political economy. These radical ideologies confronted an almost overwhelming set of regional problems—worn-out and worn-down land; a dual economy of poor whites and threadbare planter elites; and a bewildering mix of plantation slaves, hired slaves, and free Negroes created by slaveowners trying to cut costs by manumitting or hiring out slaves. Ideological experimentation led at one extreme to George Fitzhugh's prescription for a paternal, feudal order. He advocated enslaving all men, black and white, under the authority of a natural planter elite. At the opposite, though equally radical, extreme, Hinton Rowan Helper blamed the poor whites' problems on slavery. His racist tract urged immediate removal of all blacks from the region and the nation. Such were the twisted and deformed ideologies that emerged from the tobacco South following one long cycle of extremely destructive environmental occupance.[32]

In retrospect, Enlightenment agrarian reform in the upper South eliminated an ugly landscape in exchange for the ugliest set of regional ideologies that this nation has yet created. The region and the nation might have been better served by the persistence of the "primitive" colonial system of land rotation. That adaptive ecological system, though dependent on slave labor, had at least the redeeming values of maintaining soil fertility and retarding soil erosion. Ironically, the system's success proved to be its undoing. That "primitive" agronomic system was the point of departure for an enlightened, republican ideology—an ideology embarrassed by landscape appearances, dedicated to agrarian reform, and, in retrospect, implicated in the ascent of the southern soil miner.[33]

32. On Fitzhugh, see his writings and their interpretation (with which I demur) by Eugene D. Genovese, *The World the Slaveholders Made: Two Essays in Interpretation* (New York: Vintage Books, 1969), pp. 118–224. Hinton Rowan Helper, *Compendium of the Impending Crisis of the South* (New York, 1860). Also see William M. Mathew, *Edmund Ruffin and the Crisis of Slavery in the Old South* (Athens: University of Georgia Press, 1988).

33. Morgan has pointed out the irony of republican ideology arising out of slavery; the irony is deeper still since slavery was contingent on agrarian systems and agrarian systems were contingent on ideology. To oversimplify the causal chain, land rotation led to slavery, which led to republican ideology which led to reform in agrarian practice, which led to destructive environmental occupancy, which led, in the end, to the twisted racist and quasi-feudal ideologies of Helper and Fitzhugh, respectively. At some point herein, when we come to expect the succession of ideological opposites, irony ends and dialectics begins. Morgan, *American Slavery, American Freedom.*

The Southern Cotton Belt, 1840–1890

The erosional cycle (1780–1840) that plagued the upper South also swept across the emerging cotton belt. Following the invention of the cotton gin, a sharp rise in cotton prices ignited a half century of destructive occupance. The vicious cycle of clearing, planting, abandonment, and migration to virgin frontier lands was extended from coastal Georgia and South Carolina to the Mississippi. The legendary profits from cotton made planters oblivious to the landscape they left in their wake. In this macrohistorical cycle, the myth of the southern soil miner was reality.[34]

Crop Rotation in the Antebellum Cotton Belt

The collapse of cotton prices during the 1830s and 1840s gave pause to headlong expansion and destructive occupance. A new round of agrarian reflection and experimentation commenced. Potential solutions for cotton's problems proliferated. Ideas ranged from regional cooperative controls on supply to railroad building, from economic diversification to applications of Peruvian guano.[35] Although these solutions cluttered the pages of the popular press, the innovation that was to have the greatest impact began without fanfare in local experiments with crop rotation systems. The geographic origins of these experiments are particularly difficult to pin down, but the fragmentary evidence points toward planters in northern and central Mississippi and Alabama. Perhaps aware of the discovery in 1838 that leguminous plants fixed nitrogen from the air, cotton planters devised a crop rotation system that combined the cotton staple with corn and soil-renovating leguminous cowpeas.[36]

This diversified agrarian system, which replaced staple monoculture and its vicious cycle, was organized as follows (also see Figure 7.6). Each planter or slave was allocated, on average, eighteen acres

34. The most eloquent statement on this topic remains W. J. Cash, *The Mind of the South* (New York: Knopf, 1941).

35. Genovese, *The Political Economy of Slavery*; Harold D. Woodman, *King Cotton and His Retainers: Financing and Marketing the Cotton Crop of the South, 1800–1925* (Lexington: University of Kentucky Press, 1968).

36. Here and below, see sources cited in Earle, "Tillage Capacity and Soil Maintenance." While I concur with William Cooper's thesis that southern planters in the 1850s were optimistic about cotton's productivity on existing lands in the South (that is, expansion beyond the region was not imperative), I do not share his view that fertilizers constituted the basis for this optimism. The costs of fertilizer were exorbitant prior to the opening of South Carolina's phosphate mines in 1868. William J. Cooper, Jr., "The Cotton Crisis in the Antebellum South: Another Look," *Agricultural History* 49 (1975), pp. 381–91.

A) The "Vicious Cycle" of Linear Shifting Cultivation, 1790's-1840's

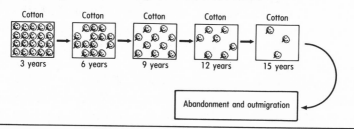

B) Cotton/Corn-Cowpeas Crop Rotation, 1840's-ca. 1900

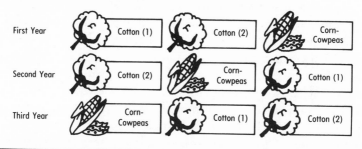

C) Cotton Monoculture and Fertilizers, Eastern Cotton Belt post-1870; Alabama and Mississippi post-1890

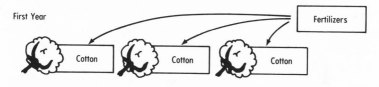

Second Year . . . Tn

FIGURE 7.6. Three Systems of Land Management in the Cotton South: the "Vicious Cycle" of Linear Shifting Cultivation, Crop Rotation (Cotton-Corn-Cowpeas), and Fertilizer-based monoculture. A typical worker cultivated 18 to 20 acres of row crops. Under the first and third systems, virtually all of these acres went into cotton; under crop rotation, roughly 12 acres were allocated to cotton and six acres to corn intercropped with cowpeas.

for row crop production. This relatively fixed amount of land was determined by the slow rates of row-crop tillage and the short two-month cultivation period each spring. Under the old monocultural system, virtually all of the eighteen acres went into cotton; but under the new system, best practice called for twelve acres in cotton and six in corn intercropped in July with leguminous cowpeas. As cotton depleted the soil of plant nutrients, especially nitrogen—usually after two years—cotton land was rotated into fields renovated by nitrogen-fixing cowpeas intercropped with corn. The latter crops gave an added twist to the new system, allowing it to integrate swine-raising and pork production. Following the corn harvest, planters put their hogs upon the corn fields, where the animals mowed down the cowpeas, vines, and corn stalks.[37]

This tight crop rotation scheme accomplished four plantation objectives: Soil fertility was maintained; profits equaled or exceeded those from cotton monoculture; corn met most of the plantation's grain subsistence needs; and swine, fed on corn stalks and cowpea vines, satisfied most of the pork needs. Given these virtues, this local innovation of a cotton-corn-cowpeas rotation diffused rapidly. The new agrarian system seems to have spread widely through the antebellum South during the 1840s and 1850s. Literary evidence and plantation account books document a consensus in the cotton belt that the ratio of two units of cotton land to one of corn and cowpeas yielded the best results. Although the ratio varied slightly in accordance with local soils (fertile soils had higher ratios), rainfall, and tillage implements (mules and plows versus hoes), these variances all fell within a narrow range, for example, 9:5; 10:5; 11:6. Census figures provide further confirmation of diffusion during the 1850s. These report an increasing output of corn and hogs from the cotton belt relative to areas that had traditionally supplied these subsistence commodities. The new crop rotation system thus had the effect of providing the bulk of regional subsistence needs while reducing cotton-belt dependence on provisions from the upper South (Kentucky and Tennessee) and the Midwest.[38]

Perhaps the most dramatic example of the interregional impact of the new plantation economy comes from Cincinnati. As late as the 1840s and early 1850s, that city shipped most of its provisions trade downriver; by 1857, virtually everything was dispatched upriver to

37. The best guides to this agrarian system are John Hebron Moore, *Agriculture in Antebellum Mississippi* (New York: Bookman Associates, 1971), pp. 59–60, 123–27; and Sam Bowers Hilliard, *Hog Meat and Hoe Cake: Food Supply in the Old South* (Carbondale: Southern Illinois University Press, 1972).

38. Genovese, *The Political Economy of Slavery*, p. 97, writes that the only rotation practiced on a large scale was that of cotton and corn, and even an enlightened planter such as M. W. Philips generally ignored legumes. But Philips, speaking in 1846, said: "I plant thin land two years in corn and cowpeas and one in cotton and feel well-assured that with peas I improve my land." *Southern Cultivator* 4 (1846), pp. 78–79. On good land, Philips switched the ratio to the more usual two in cotton and one in corn—doubtless intercropped with cowpeas. Also see "The Cost of Raising Cotton," *The Vicksburg Whig* 17 (August 18, 1855), p. 1.

FIGURE 7.7. A late-nineteenth-century representation of cotton picking supervised by the overseer on horseback. Reproduced from Alex Everett Frye, *Frye's Complete Geography* (Boston: Ginn and Company, 1895), p. 51.

Pittsburgh or Wheeling. Eastern railroads contributed to the reorientation of Cincinnati's trade, but their role, though necessary, was not sufficient. Two decades of cotton-belt crop rotation and attendant crop diversification had nearly eliminated Cincinnati's traditional southern market for provisions. Corn and hog farmers in Kentucky and Tennessee also felt the squeeze. This new agrarian system thus hastened the disengagement of southern and midwestern trade—a disengagement with portentous sectional overtones on the eve of the American Civil War.[39]

39. Carville Earle, "Regional Economic Development West of the Appalachians, 1815–1860," in *North America: The Historical Geography of a Changing Continent*, ed. Robert

The subtlety and intelligence of antebellum crop rotation has been regrettably overlooked by students of southern history. The leading geographer of the southern environment, Stanley Trimble, assumes that agricultural practices were unchanging. In his view, soil destruction accelerated in conjunction with slavery, cotton production, and the "land-killing technology" of use, exhaustion, and abandonment.[40] More appreciative of the fundamental change in southern agriculture are the new economic historians, but even they have been baffled by the unlikely phenomenon of plantation diversification during a period of rapidly rising cotton prices. Their best-known examination of crop choice seriously misinterprets the reasons for planting corn along with cotton.[41] According to this thesis, planters fearful of the cotton market and staple specialization behaved in peasant-like fashion. They averted market risk, provided for subsistence first, and treated cotton as a production residual after corn and pork needs had been met. Although the argument is new, its portrayal of southern planters is stereotypical. Planters take the role of passive reactors to a world market beyond their control; ignored are their contributions to one of the South's most brilliant agrarian innovations.

Both geographers and economic historians have missed the main point of diversified production, namely that corn, swine, and cowpeas were integral elements in a radically new agrarian system—one that was at once ecologically and economically superior to its predecessor. As I have suggested above and document elsewhere, diversification sprang not from a fear of the market, but rather from a conjuncture of capitalist motive, environmental sensitivity, and local innovation during the macrohistorical depression of the 1830s and 1840s.

A New Agrarian System: Fertilizer and Cotton Specialization in the Postbellum Eastern Cotton Belt

The innovation of a cotton-corn-cowpeas crop rotation survived the Civil War and persisted, with one subregional exception, partway

---

D. Mitchell and Paul A. Groves (Totowa, N.J.: Rowman and Littlefield, 1987), pp. 172–97; Sam Bowers Hilliard, *Atlas of Antebellum Southern Agriculture* (Baton Rouge: Louisiana State University Press, 1984), pp. 47, 49, 50, 64–67, 73.

40. Trimble, "Perspectives on the History of Soil Erosion Control," pp. 162–80; *idem, Man-Induced Soil Erosion on the Southern Piedmont, 1700–1970* (Ankeny, Iowa: Soil Conservation Service of America, 1974).

41. Gavin Wright, *The Political Economy of the Cotton South: Households, Markets, and Wealth in the Nineteenth Century* (New York: W. W. Norton, 1978).

into the next macrohistorical cycle (that is, 1880–1930). The exception was the eastern cotton belt states of Georgia and South Carolina, wherein planters adopted a new cropping system with fateful environmental consequences. During the long depression of the late nineteenth century, eastern cotton planters abandoned the cotton-corn-cowpeas rotation in favor of higher profits from cotton specialization and intensive fertilizer application. In this system, soil fertility was maintained by commercial fertilizers instead of the botanic solution of a cowpeas rotation. Agrarian reformers and "the testimony of science" were mobilized on behalf of the new system. State scientists and the agents of fertilizer companies recommended highly the adoption of monoculture and fertilizers. The new system revolutionized the region's agrarian economy and environment in five ways. First, cotton specialization expanded rapidly. Second, market dependency for provisions of corn and pork increased as diversified output was abandoned. Third, following an early spike, yields and profits experienced a long decline. Fourth, as profits declined, credit dependency, crop liens, and debt peonage ensued. And fifth, soil exhaustion and soil erosion were accelerated by deficient fertilizers and perennially exposed soils. A regional tragedy of destructive social and environmental occupance thus unfolded.[42]

The victory of cotton and fertilizers depended on a particular set of circumstances in time and space, in macrohistorical cycle and mesoregional conditions, boosted along by well-intentioned scientific reformers. With respect to time, the so-called guano craze that swept Georgia and South Carolina in the 1870s and 1880s coincided with the long-wave decline in cotton prices. By now it should be evident that the onset of bad times increased the propensity for agrarian experimentation and the predisposition to innovation adoption. With respect to space, the specific innovation—cotton specialization and fertilizer—was contingent upon mesoregional economic and environmental conditions. Two were significant in localizing innovation diffusion in the eastern cotton belt. First was the spatially specific factor of relatively low-cost fertilizers. Fertilizer in Georgia, for example, was twelve to fifteen dollars cheaper per ton than it was further west. Proximity to phosphate rock mines opened in 1868 in coastal South Carolina and to the manure manufacturers clustered

42. My attention was first alerted to the peculiar agrarian changes in the eastern cotton belt by Peter Temin, "Patterns of Cotton Agriculture in Post-Bellum Georgia," *Journal of Economic History* 43 (1983), pp. 661–74.

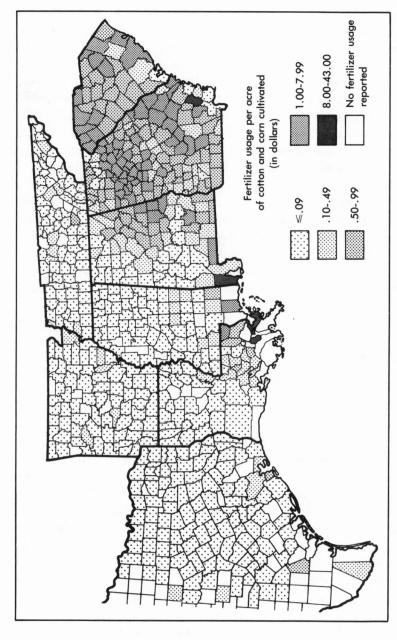

FIGURE 7.8. Money Spent on Fertilizer in the Cotton South, 1880. Note that since fertilizer tended to be cheaper in the cotton belt, this figure probably understates actual fertilizer use there. Source: U.S. Census Office, *The Tenth Census of the United States: 1880, vol. 3, Report on the Productions of Agriculture* (Washington, D.C.: GPO, 1883), pp. 104–40.

Fertilizer usage per acre
of cotton and corn cultivated
(in dollars)

≤ .09

.10–.49

.50–.99

1.00–7.99

8.00–43.00

No fertilizer usage
reported

around this basic raw material meant lower fertilizer prices for the eastern cotton belt.[43] Second was the ecological factor of fertilizer efficiency. The region's heavier spring rains, which hastened chemical activation of fertilizers, combined with a natural soil deficiency in phosphorus assured maximum improvements in yields when phosphorus-rich fertilizers were applied. When state scientists reported that fertilizers improved cotton yields by anywhere from 25 to 60 percent, the argument for adoption of the new system was complete and ineluctable (see Figure 7.8).[44]

The misnomered guano craze ensued. But what initially seemed a foolproof, riskless agrarian system devolved swiftly into an economic and ecological crisis. The mysteries of soil chemistry and fertilizer-plant exchange had eluded planter and scientist alike. Although phosphorus-rich fertilizers produced an initial increase in cotton yields, these declined after a few years of continuous cultivation. Fertilizer deficiencies in nitrogen—the most important plant nutrient for cotton—took their toll.[45] Planters, tenants, and croppers responded by applying even more of the deficient fertilizer; cotton yields decreased further; and debts spiraled out of control. To service their mounting debts, planters attached liens to their cotton crops, which locked them into cotton monoculture.

L. W. Jarman, a local witness to the devastation wrought by fertilizer and monoculture, summarized the situation so perceptively that his words deserve full quotation:

> Who said fertilizer? Well, that's just it. Every farmer says it, every tenant says it, every merchant says it, and even the bankers must speak of it at times. . . . The trouble is that in times past the easy purchase and use of fertilizer has seemed to many of our

43. Wines, *Fertilizer in America*, pp. 112–61, and sources therein.

44. Earle, "Tillage Capacity and Soil Maintenance." For scientific claims on fertilizer's effects on yields, see David F. Weiman, "The Economic Emancipation of the Non-Slaveholding Class: Up-Country Farmers in the Georgia Cotton Economy," *Journal of Economic History* 45 (1985), pp. 71–93, esp. p. 87.

45. Cotton is not an especially exhaustive crop, but soils do require nitrogen replacement either through legumes or nitrogen-enriched fertilizers. B. A. Waddle, "Crop Growing Practices," in *Cotton*, ed. R. J. Kohel and C. F. Lewis, Agronomy Series, No. 24 (Madison, Wis.: American Society of Agronomy, Crop Science Society of America, and Soil Science Society of America, 1984), pp. 233–63, esp. p. 244. At the time, however, critics of excessive fertilizer usage approvingly described fertilizer mixes overloaded with phosphorus relative to nitrogen. Charles W. Burkett and Clarence H. Poe, *Cotton: Its Cultivation, Marketing, Manufacture, and the Problems of the Cotton World* (New York: Doubleday, Page and Co., 1906), pp. 109–46.

Southern farmers a short cut to prosperity, a royal road to good crops of cotton year after year. The result has been that their lands have been cultivated clean year after year, their fertility has been exhausted, . . . their soils have largely washed away, and much land that formerly would make good crops without fertilizer now makes but poor returns with fertilization. . . . [Fertilizers] have caused them to fall into a system of all cotton farming that looked alone to present gain, and not to the improvement of the soil. To say the least of it, the use of commercial fertilizer has not been an unmixed blessing to the Southern farmer. Like all other good things, it can be abused. It has enriched thousands of good farmers . . . on the other hand, it has caused thousands of poor farmers to fall into a system of farming that impoverished them and their lands as well.[46]

By the 1890s, debt peonage was diffusing in the wake of the new agricultural system. Moreover, the signs of destructive occupance spread beyond the region into Alabama and Mississippi.[47] In Georgia and South Carolina, meanwhile, years of deficient-fertilizer application and cotton monoculture had worn out the land. Erosion made matters worse. Unlike the old crop rotation system, with its periodic respite from erosion when fields were intercropped with corn and cowpeas, the clean-tilled fields of Georgia and South Carolina were subject to constant soil wash, stripping, rilling, and gullying. Descrip-

46. L. W. Jarman, "About Fertilizers," in *Southern Crops: As Grown and Described by Successful Farmers and Published from Time to Time in the Southern Cultivator*, comp. G. F. Hunnicutt (Atlanta: The Cultivator Publishing Co., 1911), pp. 370–73. Agricultural chemists strenuously debated the scientific methods and results of fertilizer analyses. State chemists tended to support farmer interests, industry chemists to support the interests of their firms. On this interesting controversy, which reveals a Kuhnian view of science, see Alan I. Marcus, "Setting the Standard: Fertilizers, State Chemists, and Early National Commercial Regulation, 1880–87," *Agricultural History* 61 (1987), pp. 47–73.

47. On the westward diffusion of fertilizer by 1900—probably accompanying the opening of phosphate mines in Tennessee—see Roger L. Ransom and Richard Sutch, *One Kind of Freedom: The Economic Consequences of Emancipation* (Cambridge: Cambridge University Press, 1977), pp. 188–89. I, of course, disagree with their view that fertilizers ameliorated (however mildly) the crushing exploitation by merchants. Nor do I share Gavin Wright's position that war debts were the cause of debt peonage; the planters' volitional abandonment of crop rotation and their overzealous acquisition of fertilizers for the profits of monoculture are sufficient causes. Gavin Wright, *Old South, New South: Revolutions in the Southern Economy Since the Civil War* (New York: Basic Books, 1986), pp. 30–31, 107–15. In a vein similar to Wright's, see Steven Hahn, "The 'Unmaking' of the Southern Yeomanry: The Transformation of the Georgia Upcountry, 1860–1890," in *The Countryside in the Age of Capitalist Transformation*, Steven Hahn and Jonathan Prude, eds. (Chapel Hill: University of North Carolina Press, 1985), pp. 179–203.

tions of erosion and sedimentation in the Georgia piedmont suddenly became commonplace in the 1880s, and the worst effects were associated with planters rather than croppers and tenants.[48] Compounding the regional erosion problem were spring rains 10 to 20 percent higher than those of the western cotton belt in the 1870s. The eastern cotton belt thus provided textbook horror stories for the conservationists who wrote during the downswing of the 1880–1930 macrohistorical cycle—and who, while discrediting these agrarian practices, gave rise to the myth of the southern soil miner.

Southern Environmental History in Macrohistorical Context

Neither history in general nor environmental history in particular is linear. That is not to say that history is everywhere and always recurrent, for it may just as easily consist of short random bursts up and down or steplike ascents and descents. Whatever the historical tempo appropriate to specific times and places, environmental history benefits from a keen sensitivity to changing economic and social conditions. In the case of the southern soil miner, the linear myth of three centuries of destructive occupance eliminates most of what is interesting about the behavior of southerners in that period. The presumption that ten generations of southerners committed one environmental blunder after another obscures their environmental acuity and sensitivity as well as aspects of their ignorance and naïveté.

The story of southern environmental history, therefore, is much richer than is usually allowed by regional historiography. It is full of irony, uncertainty, experimentation, and paradox (for example, the contrasting environmental achievements of practical and "scientific" innovations). One means of re-creating the wit and folly of southern environmental history, though not the only means to be sure, is to structure that experience within the paradigm of macrohistorical

48. Stanley W. Trimble's master's thesis carefully demonstrates the lack of destructive occupance in the Georgia piedmont before the 1880s. And his evidence suggests that after large-scale soil erosion commenced, areas of tenancy and of erosion were not associated—evidence he seems to have ignored in his later writings. All of which suggests that the costs of fertilizer, however low, may have prevented tenants from adopting cotton monoculture on a wide scale and thus spared them from its worst effects. Trimble, "Culturally Accelerated Sedimentation on the Middle Georgia Piedmont" (M.A. thesis, University of Georgia, 1969).

rhythms in the American past. Although these 45- to 60-year rhythms are controversial (much less so today than a decade ago) and their dating is approximate, their macrostructure has the heuristic virtue of helping synthesize an array of otherwise disparate evidence and arguments. These long rhythms simplify the complexity of the American past and differentiate good economic times from bad ones, periods of creative experimentation and innovation from those of routine diffusion, and cycles of local innovation from those of scientific innovation. The macrohistorical paradigm offers a refreshing perspective on southern environmental history, but the merits of this reinterpretation remain to be judged. A succinct summary of the reinterpretation seems a fitting way of closing this essay.

Viewed from the perspective of macrohistory, our survey of three centuries of southern environmental history identifies two symmetrical cycles of local innovation and constructive occupance followed by cycles of scientific reform and destructive occupance. The constructive phases were initiated in cyclical bad times (the 1680s and 1840s). In the ensuing cycle, agrarian innovations that emerged from depression experimentation diffused in accordance with the S-shaped logistic curve. As proof of the economic and ecological viability of local innovations based on practice, they endured through two entire cycles until succumbing finally to the depression innovations of scientific reform.

More specifically, these cycles of constructive landscape occupance occurred in the colonial Chesapeake (1680–1790) and in the nineteenth-century cotton belt (1840–1930?). Both of these long epochs of benign environmental impact were initiated by folk agricultural innovation and diffusion. Although the macrohistorical structures of these two cases are identical, the particular sets of innovations were distinctive to the regions. The colonial tobacco planters devised a system of land rotation; the cotton planters, in contrast, established a system of crop rotation. In the Chesapeake, tobacco planters maintained soil fertility through an intricate system that integrated shifting cultivation, slavery, and crop diversification. Renovating their worn-out fields through natural ecological succession, planters later recycled these old fields back into tobacco production. Equally subtle and creative were the folk innovations of antebellum cotton planters. Their crop rotation system restored soil fertility by rotating cotton with corn intercropped with nitrogen-fixing cowpeas. Corn and pork were profitable by-products of this complex agricultural system. In both cases, soil fertility was maintained and the vicious cycle of land abandonment was broken. Erosion too seems to have been retarded in both systems, though perhaps more effectively in the chaotic fields of the colonial Chesapeake. And for both times and places, the notion of a southern soil miner is an unfounded myth.

The myth has foundation, however, in the macrohistorical cycles that succeeded the constructive occupancy just described. From the standpoint of the southern environment, the most destructive agricultural innovations emerged from scientific agrarian reform in macrohistorical depressions circa the 1790s in the Chesapeake and the 1870s and 1880s in the eastern cotton belt. In the former, advocates of "high farming" damned as primitive the prevailing system of land rotation. In its place, they helped install an environmentally destructive system of clean tillage, plowing, and limestone-based fertilizers. The erosional consequences were severe. A similar story unfolded in the eastern cotton belt a century later. Scientists, fertilizer companies, and agrarian elites argued persuasively on behalf of cotton specialization, which was linked to fertilizers. Neither they nor the adopting planters perceived the nitrogen deficiencies in these fertilizers or the devastating economic consequences (debt peonage) and ecological consequences (worn-out soils, eroded lands, and falling yields) of using them. In these sad times, the myth and the reality of the southern soil miner were one.

The great paradox of southern environmental history is, of course, that practical wisdom was invariably superior to science as a guide to the future environmental consequences of agricultural innovation. The southern soil miner, then, was the product not of plantation economy and slavery (or their legacies), but of misguided epistemologies of scientific agrarian reform. Fortunately, these destructive cycles of occupance did not last. In succeeding cycles, when the practical wisdom of local experience prevailed, the environmental impacts of southern agrarian innovations were benign. And given these cyclical changes in the region's exploitation of the landscape, what then remains of the myth of the southern soil miner? It is in truth a semi-myth, the reality of which is always contingent on proper specification in time and space.

CHAPTER 8

A Tale of Two Cities

The Ecological Basis of the Threefold Population Differential in the Chicago and Mobile Urban Systems, Circa 1860

The development of towns and cities in the antebellum United States resulted from the interplay of a complex of forces. In the broadest perspective, urbanization involved fundamental structural changes in American society: population movements, the reorganization of work, and the transition from preindustrial to industrial culture. It is well known that this transformation was uneven, proceeding vigorously in the North and slowly in the South. The North by 1860 had developed an urban economy and landscape, with large cities linked by transport and trade to a hierarchy of tributary towns. The experience of the South was different. Its cities were smaller, except on the periphery; its towns, usually entrepôts for cotton and tobacco, were energized during the marketing season and quiescent during the rest of the year (Figure 8.1).[1]

One aspect of this complex transformation that needs further study is the sheer difference in the magnitudes of northern and southern urbanization. Put simply, why were northern cities large and southern cities small? Addressing this question through a con-

1. James E. Vance, Jr., *The Merchant's World: A Geography of Wholesaling* (Englewood Cliffs, N.J.: Prentice-Hall, 1970); David Ward, *Cities and Immigrants: A Geography of Change in Nineteenth-Century America* (New York: Oxford University Press, 1971); Allan R. Pred, *The Spatial Dynamics of U.S. Urban-Industrial Growth, 1800–1914: Interpretive and Theoretical Essays* (Cambridge: Massachusetts Institute of Technology Press, 1966); idem, *Urban Growth and the Circulation of Information, 1790–1840* (Cambridge: Harvard University Press, 1973); Cees D. Eysberg, "The Origins of the American Urban System: Historical Accident and Initial Advantage," *Journal of Urban History* 15 (1989), pp. 185–95.

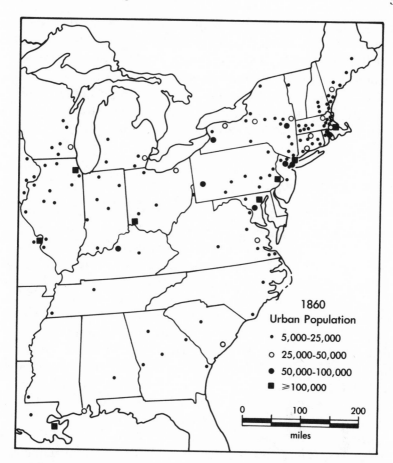

FIGURE 8.1. A Comparison of Urbanization, North and South, 1860. The small dots represent towns and cities with 5,000 to 25,000 population; the circles and squares are cities of more than 25,000. There were 30 of the latter shown in 1860, all but four in northern and border states. Source: U.S. Bureau of the Census, *U.S. Census of Population: 1950*, vol. 2 (Washington, D.C.: GPO, 1953).

trolled comparison of the cities of Chicago and Mobile and their tributary urban systems in the 1850s, this essay seeks to evaluate the relative contributions to urban growth of three factors: (1) the regional economic base for urban employment, consisting of earnings in the several economic sectors (staple marketing, manufactures, and services); (2) the costs of urban labor, as determined by rural earnings and staple seasonality; and (3) the opportunities for family income maximization. The first two of these—economic base and labor costs—jointly regulate the levels of employment in urban systems; the third—family income—regulates the level of the dependent population. Although the conventional wisdom is that the fortune of cities hinges on their economic bases, that was not the case for antebellum Chicago and Mobile. The critical difference, as we shall see, lay in the costs of labor and the employment opportunities available to women and adolescent children.

Chicago and Mobile in 1860

On the eve of the American Civil War, the cities of Chicago and Mobile seemed to have little in common. Chicago ranked as one of the wonders of the world, a city that all travelers were advised to see. Rising spectacularly from a swampy lake plain on the edge of Lake Michigan, the city had a population of over 100,000 by 1860, and railroads from fifteen directions funneled crops and goods into its warehouses. The Gulf Coast city of Mobile seemed lethargic by comparison. This city of not quite 30,000 was almost somnolent in the summer; and even though the tempo quickened a bit with the arrival of inland cotton via steamboats and the one railroad that served the city, Mobile cut a decidedly inferior figure next to Chicago.

Yet if these cities differed greatly in mass and vitality, they also shared many characteristics that enable them to serve as test cases for the theory of urban systems development. Both cities and their hinterlands grew rapidly during the 1850s; both relied on staple commodities (the Chicago system handling grains and livestock, the Mobile system handling cotton); both held second rank after New York and New Orleans as sectional staple markets; and both entrepôts commanded comparable hinterlands of trade and commerce.[2]

What they did not have in common was the sheer size of their urban system populations. Chicago alone contained over 109,000 people as compared to Mobile's 29,000—a threefold to fourfold differential (3.76 to be precise). This pattern was repeated in the tribu-

2. Carville Earle and Ronald Hoffman, "Regional Staples and Urban Systems in Antebellum America," in *Géographie du Capital Marchand aux Amériques, 1760–1860*, ed. Jeanne Chase (Paris: École des Hautes Études en Sciences Sociales, 1987), pp. 151–81; Harriet E. Amos, *Cotton City: Urban Development in Antebellum Mobile* (Tuscaloosa: University of Alabama Press, 1985); and William Cronon, *Nature's Metropolis: Chicago and the West, 1848–1893* (New York: Norton, 1991).

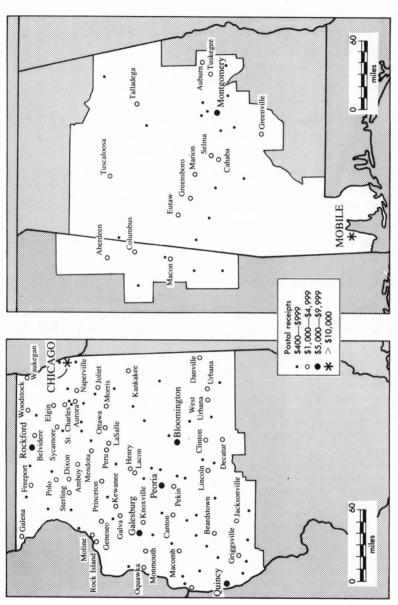

FIGURE 8.2. A Comparison of Postal Revenues in the Urban Systems of Chicago and Mobile, 1858–59. Postal revenues serve as a surrogate for urban populations, since the two are highly correlated (usually .8 or higher). Source: *Register of Officers and Agents, Civil, Military and Naval in the Service of the United States, on the Thirtieth September, 1859* (Washington, D.C.: Department of the Interior, 1859). See also notes 3 and 4.

tary towns and cities of these urban systems, or so it would appear from estimates of urban population based on post office revenues (see Figure 8.2). Postal records for 1858–59 show that post offices in the Chicago system took in $351,217, more than triple the revenues of the Mobile system ($111,268).[3] By this measure, the number of urban dwellers in the Chicago system was 3.16 times the number of urban dwellers in the Mobile system. Mobile fared somewhat better if we limit attention to workers alone. My best estimate is that Chicago's urban system counted nearly 132,000 urban workers (technically, all persons within the boundaries of the system giving occupations in secondary and tertiary industries) as compared to Mobile's 61,787. Thus while Chicago's system had over three times as many urban dwellers as Mobile's system, it had only twice as many in the urban labor force.[4] The distinction is worth remembering.

The First Tale: Demand-Led Urban Theory

One might imagine that such dramatic differences in urban demography would stir the hearts of ardent urban theorists. But the truth of the matter is that urban theory has avoided this empirical

3. Population figures are from *Population of the United States in 1860 . . .* (Washington, D.C.: U.S. Bureau of the Census, 1864). This census, unfortunately, contains very few entries for cities and towns. As an alternative, I use postal revenues as a surrogate for town size. Comparison of town size and postal revenues reveals very high correlations, usually of .8 or higher. The best fit occurs when postal revenues are defined as the sum of net returns, postmaster's compensation, and payments to clerks. *Register of Officers and Agents, Civil, Military and Naval in the Service of the United States, on the Thirtieth September, 1859* (Washington, D.C.: Department of the Interior, 1859); Richard W. Helbock, "Postal Records as an Aid to Urbanization Studies," *Historical Methods Newsletter* 3 (1969), pp. 9–14.

4. For the hinterland boundaries of Mobile, see J. D. B. DeBow, *The Industrial Resources, Statistics, etc. of the United States, And more particularly of the Southern and Western States . . .* (3 vols.; New York: A. M. Kelley, 1854), Vol. 1, pp. 57–59. For Chicago, see John G. Clark, *The Grain Trade in the Old Northwest* (Urbana: University of Illinois Press, 1966); Michael P. Conzen, "A Transport Interpretation of the Growth of Urban Regions: An American Example," *Journal of Historical Geography* 1 (1975), pp. 361–82; and George R. Taylor and Irene D. Neu, *The American Railroad Network, 1861–1890* (Cambridge: Harvard University Press, 1956). The urban labor forces of the Chicago and Mobile urban systems are estimated in two steps. First, the populations in the hinterland counties of Chicago and Mobile are summed in order to determine their proportion to the state populations in each area. For Chicago I use the state of Illinois, for Mobile the states of Alabama and Mississippi. Second, each system's proportion of state population is applied to the summary state table of occupations (excluding nonurban jobs, i.e., fishing, lumbering, mining, farming, planting, overseeing, and so forth). Since the Mobile system's labor force does not include slaves, I have increased my estimate of urban work force by 37 percent—the proportion of slaves in the population of Mobile County.

engagement, preferring instead to invoke a general covering law for all urban systems. According to this law, the prime determinant of the size of urban systems is the aggregate demand of consumers within the bounds of these systems. Perhaps the best-known theory in this genre is the theory of central places. It postulates that the kinds of demographic differentials we observe in antebellum Chicago and Mobile arise from endogenous accumulations of consumer demand. As population densities increase and as incomes rise, the demand for consumer goods and services piles up, satisfying one retailing threshold after another and drawing more and more people into the urban vortex. Stripped to the essentials, demand-led urban theory says roughly the following: in a given space, more population begets more income, which begets more demand, which begets more retailing, which begets more retailing employment, which begets more urban population. The chain of reasoning is hardly inspiring and, worse than that, it is for our purposes probably wrong.[5]

A demand-led theory of urban systems, however useful it may be elsewhere, encounters repeated difficulties when applied to antebellum America. In the first place, the theory does not allow for industrialization, which was a vigorous new source of antebellum urban employment and population growth; nor does it accommodate the spectacular volumetric expansion in the staple commodity trades consequent to the transport revolution. But setting aside these theoretical omissions, demand-led theory must tack against a great deal of contrary evidence contained in recent studies on the antebellum economy. Take the case of regional incomes and income densities in the trans-Appalachian west. Richard Easterlin has documented modest differences in regional farm incomes per capita in the North and

5. Walter Christaller's theory of central place is conveniently summarized in Brian J. L. Berry, *Geography of Market Centers and Retail Distribution* (Englewood Cliffs, N.J.: Prentice-Hall, 1970). Central place theorists maintain that as towns and cities emerge from the accumulation of endogenous consumer demand, they develop a characteristically hexagonal arrangement and a hierarchical structure. Vance dissents vigorously from this view. He counters that large towns appear in the earliest stages of urban-system evolution and function by servicing the long-distance extra-regional trade rather than local consumer demands. As a result, the urban system is linearly arranged along axes of transportation. Central place patterns are, according to Vance, a late addition, grafted as it were onto the mercantile urban system. Vance, *The Merchant's World*. Vance's alternative thesis of long-distance trade nonetheless shares with central place theory the assumption of demand-led urban growth. Also see David F. Weiman, "Urban Growth on the Periphery of the Antebellum Cotton Belt: Atlanta, 1847–1860," *Journal of Economic History* 48 (1988), pp. 259–72.

South. When incomes in 1860 are expressed as densities (the relevant measure for urban system demand), a difference of just 6 percent separates income densities in the North Central states ($2,000 per square mile) from those in the East South Central states ($1,882 per square mile, counting free persons only).[6] Such a minor difference in income densities cannot account for the twofold difference in the labor forces of northern and southern urban systems. This evidence invites misgivings about the capacity of demand-led theory for explaining the cases at hand.

Good theory, of course, always has a fall-back position, and in this case demand theorists shift attention to income distribution or welfare. William Parker makes the point cogently in the antebellum context: If the level of southern "farm income per capita appears to be at least as high as that in the North then the deficiency—if from the demand side—must have lain in the distribution rather than the level of that income."[7] The economics of Parker's position are straightforward. Income inequalities fragment consumer demand, compartmentalizing the various wants of rich and poor and invoking, in the case of the rich, Engels's inverse law of consumption. Accordingly, an allegedly inegalitarian region such as the southern cotton belt should have sustained a much smaller urban population than did an egalitarian farm economy such as the Middle West.

This thesis, though impeccable in logic, runs counter to evidence of widespread inequalities in antebellum wealth and income. Inequality was endemic in the North as well as the South, in the city as well as the country. Various studies of wealth distribution suggest that regional differences in inequality were small. For example, in 1860 wealth distribution was slightly more unequal among the farmers of Wisconsin—a premier wheat-producing state with a close resemblance to Chicago's hinterland—than among planters in the southern cotton belt. Their gini coefficients (a measure of inequality in which 1 represents complete inequality and 0 complete equality) were .690 and .678, respectively.[8] Differing levels of inequality thus

6. Richard A. Easterlin, "Interregional Differences in Per Capita Income, Population, and Total Income, 1840–1950," in *Trends in the American Economy in the Nineteenth Century,* ed. William N. Parker, National Bureau of Economic Research, Studies in Income and Wealth, No. 24 (Princeton, N.J.: Princeton University Press, 1960), pp. 73–140; William N. Parker, "Slavery and Southern Economic Development: An Hypothesis and Some Evidence," in *The Structure of the Cotton Economy of the Antebellum South,* ed. William N. Parker (Washington, D.C.: The Agricultural History Society, 1970), pp. 115–25.

7. Parker, "Slavery and Southern Economic Development," p. 119.

8. Lee Soltow, *Patterns of Wealthholding in Wisconsin Since 1850* (Madison: University

seem an unlikely cause of the twofold differential in urban employment in the Chicago and Mobile urban systems of 1860. In sum, neither income inequalities nor income densities were sufficiently large
to explain the population differences in the Chicago and Mobile urban systems.

The Second Tale: Supply-Side Urban Theory

It is time to thicken the plot in our tale of two cities, to move
beyond the confines of demand-led urban theory. Urban systems deserve a more inclusive theoretical perspective, one that incorporates
a much wider range of causal factors and accommodates the principal components of urban demography—the workers and their dependents. The theory I have in mind divides the rest of this paper
into two parts: one deals with the determinants of urban system employment in Chicago and Mobile, the other with urban system
dependency.

Chapter 1: Why Chicago's Labor Force was Twice as Large as Mobile's

Why is it that some urban systems have many workers while others have very few? I want to venture the proposition that the expla-

---

of Wisconsin Press, 1971), p. 49; *idem, Men and Wealth in the United States, 1850–1870* (New
Haven: Yale University Press, 1975), esp. p. 103. On city and country comparisons, see
Robert E. Gallman, "Trends in Size Distributions of Wealth in the Nineteenth Century:
Some Speculations," in *Six Papers on the Size Distribution of Wealth and Income*, National Bureau of Economic Research, Studies in Income and Wealth, No. 33 (Princeton, N.J.:
Princeton University Press, 1969), pp. 1–30. Although Soltow's data report considerable
intra-regional variation, the inequality differences between North and South are rather
small. For evidence that wealth inequality was notably less in the cotton South and in that
region's best lands (located, in large measure, in the Mobile urban system) as compared to
the rest of the South, see Albert W. Niemi, Jr., "Inequality in the Distribution of Slave
Wealth: The Cotton South and Other Southern Agricultural Regions," *Journal of Economic
History* 37 (1977), pp. 747–53. Gavin Wright, *The Political Economy of the Cotton South:
Households, Markets, and Wealth in the Nineteenth Century* (New York: W. W. Norton, 1978),
pp. 26, 30, contends that inequality was much greater in the cotton South than in the Old
Northwest, but the differences probably reflect divergent sampling techniques (i.e., using
an agricultural region for the South and a state region for the Northwest) that have the
effect of reducing inequalities in areas such as the wheat belt. A similar critique applies to
the distributional arguments forwarded by Roger L. Ransom, *Conflict and Compromise: The
Political Economy of Slavery, Emancipation, and the American Civil War* (Cambridge: Cambridge University Press, 1989), pp. 62–65.

nation has to do with the relation between employment and two key determinants—the base of regional income available for urban labor (what we shall call the employment base) and the level of urban wages. This triad stands in arithmetic relation, such that urban system employment is directly proportional to the employment base and inversely proportional to the level of urban-system wages. The largest urban labor forces, in other words, occur in systems with large economic bases and low urban wages, the smallest in systems with small economic bases and high wages. These interrelations constitute the main ingredients in my model of urban employment. The model may be expressed more generally as $U = E / W$, when U represents the size of the urban system labor force, E the system's employment base (the sum of consumer expenditures, manufacturing earnings, and commodity marketing margins, i.e., the economic base, all adjusted by labor's share), and W the average urban wage. For ease of exposition, I refer to the model's numerator as the demand side of urban employment and its denominator as the supply side.

Defining the Employment Base

Stating the arithmetic theory of urban system employment is easy; defining its components is a bit harder. In deference to demand-led theory, the discussion begins with the concepts of economic base and its subordinate, employment base. Economic base constitutes the source of energy that drives the urban system. Consisting of the net product of the entire range of urban economic activity (manufacturing value added, marketing margins on staple commodities, and service sector earnings), the economic base circulates through the economy and returns as payments to the various factors of production—as, for example, interest on capital, rent on land, profits to entrepreneurs, and wages to urban labor. Factor payments to labor, in turn, define the employment base of an urban system (the numerator in my model).[9]

9. In this paper, the notion of the urban employment base refers to that portion of income that provides wages and salaries for urban workers. This includes wages paid to workers in manufacturing and in staple marketing. Workers offering services and goods to consumers are sustained, in turn, by the expenditures of workers in manufacturing, staple marketing, and farming. Although these estimates of the employment base are crude, they nonetheless constitute an important step toward more refined measures. Naturally, I do not share the pessimistic views of Eric Lampard and Allan Pred, who doubt that local income data and multipliers can be reconstructed. Eric E. Lampard, "The History of Cities in the Economically Advanced Areas," *Economic Development and Cultural Change* 3 (1954–55), pp. 81–136, esp. p. 123; Pred, *The Spatial Dynamics of U.S. Urban-Industrial*

Estimating the size of the employment base is unusually complicated because it draws from all sectors of the regional economy—
manufacturing, staple marketing, and services. My estimations involve three steps: first, I estimate economic base for each sector;
second, I determine labor's share of sectoral economic bases; third,
I sum the latter across all sectors. Manufacturing estimates are the
easiest of the three sectors since the published census provides the
data for calculating employment and economic bases. Estimates for
the other sectors are more difficult. In the case of staple marketing,
economic base estimates involve compilation of commodity receipts
for Chicago or Mobile and multiplication seriatim by their respective
staple marketing margins—the difference between the price of the
staple at the farm and its price in the Chicago or Mobile wholesale
markets. Using these figures and applying industry estimates (e.g.,
estimates from railroads, warehouses, and the like) of labor's share
of economic base yields the employment base for each of the staple
marketing industries in the urban economy. Service-sector estimation is even more difficult, owing to the extraordinary variety of firms
within this sector. Given the diversity of this sector, it is necessary to
make certain simplifying assumptions about consumer expenditures
and factor payments to labor in the service sector.

The first assumption is that consumers spend their entire income
on consumption—an assumption that may not be too far off the
mark given traditionally low savings rates in the United States. Under
this assumption, service-sector economic base consists of all incomes
earned (and spent) in all other sectors—manufactures, staple marketing, and farming.[10] The second assumption is that the service sec-

---

Growth, p. 32; Charles M. Tiebout, "Exports and Regional Economic Growth," *Journal of
Political Economy* 64 (1956), pp. 160–64; Ralph W. Pfouts, "An Empirical Testing of the
Economic Base Theory," *Journal of the American Institute of Planners* 23 (1957), pp. 64–69.

10. On savings rates, see Lance E. Davis, Jonathan R. T. Hughes, and Duncan M.
McDougall, *American Economic History: The Development of a National Economy* (Homewood,
Ill.: Dorsey Press, 1965), pp. 179–87; and Raymond Goldsmith, *A Study of Savings in the
United States* (Princeton, N.J.: Princeton University Press, 1955). In the case of farming, I
use estimates of agricultural service income, which the Bureau of Agricultural Economics
defines as the "sum of all farm products sold, traded, or consumed as food or fuel by the
farm family, net farm rents and farm mortgage interest payments received by persons
living on farms, and the imputed net rental value of owner-occupied farmhouses minus
all production expenses except labor expenses." I deduct expenses from gross earnings in
the proportions indicated by Paul Munyon—for the Midwest, a deduction of 32 percent,
for the South, 41 percent. The greater deduction for the South reflects the fact that slave
labor was not remunerated. See Paul Glenn Munyon, "A Critical Review of Net Income
from Agriculture for 1880 and 1900: New Hampshire, a Case Study," *Journal of Economic*

tor's entire economic base constitutes a factor payment to labor in that sector. This may at first seem a dubious assumption, but considering that the majority of these occupations (laborers, domestics, servants, washerwomen, and a great many artisans) entailed disproportionately large labor inputs, it may not be unreasonable.[11]

Summing the sectoral employment bases in an urban system—manufactures, staple marketing, and services—yields the aggregate employment base (E), the numerator in our labor-force model.

Estimates of Economic and Employment Bases

Provisional estimates—and they could not be otherwise—of employment bases in the Chicago and Mobile urban systems appear in Table 8.1. The table's bottom line shows that Chicago's employment base had a mere 6.9 percent advantage over Mobile's—a differential insufficient to explain the twofold differences in labor force size.

Table 8.1 reveals a further similarity in the ordering of sectoral contributions to the employment bases of these two systems. Staple marketing contributed the least to employment base (just 6.6 percent in Chicago and 4.2 percent in Mobile); manufacturing contributed slightly more (17.0 percent in Chicago and 5.6 percent in Mobile); and the service sector contributed the most (some 77 percent in Chicago and 90 percent in Mobile).

Sector contributions differed, however, in important fashions. The Chicago system was more diversified. Nearly a quarter of its employment base originated in manufacturing and staple marketing—a reflection, of course, of the region's staple commodities and their imperatives for processing, storage, transport, and transshipment. Mo-

---

History 37 (1977), pp. 634–54, esp. p. 639. Although the procedure for estimating farm income is rough, it should be noted that the bias runs in favor of higher incomes in the Midwest, thus strengthening a demand-income interpretation of urban systems.

11.   A more refined estimate of the urban employment base should determine labor's share of value added in the distribution of consumer goods and services. We would then be able to estimate the multiplier effect in subsequent rounds of expenditures by these workers. The task is not an easy one because of the great diversity of jobs encompassed by consumer services and the hence considerable variability of labor's earnings. A beginning may be made with Harold Barger, *Distribution's Place in the American Economy Since 1869* (Princeton, N.J.: Princeton University Press, 1955); and his "Income Originating in Trade, 1869–1929," in *Trends in the American Economy in the Nineteenth Century*, ed. William N. Parker, National Bureau of Economic Research, Studies in Income and Wealth, No. 24 (Princeton, N.J.: Princeton University Press, 1960), pp. 327–33. Also see Theodore Marburg, "Income Originating in Trade, 1799–1869," pp. 317–26 of the same volume.

TABLE 8.1

Regional Economic Base in 1860

	Mobile urban system	Chicago urban system
1. Staple marketing		
(a) Value added	$ 3,679,612	$ 5,638,790
(b) Labor's share	$ 1,397,109	$ 2,391,589
2. Manufactures		
(a) Value added	$ 4,548,427	$17,136,220
(b) Labor's share	$ 1,867,650	$ 6,074,035
3. Consumer goods and services		
(a) Income from staple agriculture	$26,786,054	$19,287,532
(b) Labor's share of staple marketing	$ 1,397,109	$ 2,391,589
(c) Labor's share of manufacturing	$ 1,867,650	$ 6,074,035
(d) Total expenditures for consumer goods and services	$30,050,813	$27,753,156
4. Total employment base [1(b) + 2(b) + 3(d)]	$33,315,572	$36,218,780

NOTES: Value added in staple marketing [1(a)] equals commodity receipts at Chicago (wheat, corn, rye, oats, barley, flour, hogs, dressed hogs, live cattle) and at Mobile (cotton) times entrepôt price minus farm price. Lacking plantation prices for cotton, I used Woodman's estimate of a marketing margin of 7.5 percent and applied it to the value of Mobile's cotton receipts in that city's prices for 1859–60. See text and footnotes for sources. Technically, the value added figures should deduct for the value of materials consumed in the marketing of staples, but I have not deducted these costs. The effect is not large and should be nearly the same in Mobile and Chicago.

Labor's share in staple marketing [1(b)] is calculated in three steps: value added is allocated to the several marketing agencies (mercantile, storage-warehousing, and transport); for each of these marketing agencies, labor's share of value added is estimated from a variety of sources; these several estimates of labor's earnings are summed.

Manufactures' value added is from the Census of Manufactures for 1860 and equals the value of product minus the cost of raw materials.

Labor's share of manufactures, also from the published census, equals the wages paid to labor. This figure probably does not include "wages" paid to slaves in the Mobile urban system.

Income from staple agriculture consists of payments to labor on the farm. I begin with the gross value of staple crops valued at farm prices. This sum is reduced to labor's share (or the agricultural service income) using proportions suggested by Munyon. Gross staple value is reduced to 68 percent for the Midwest and 59 percent for the Cotton South. See text and footnotes for further clarification. Paul Glen Munyon, "A Critical Review of New Income from Agriculture for 1880 and 1900: New Hampshire, a Case Study," *Journal of Economic History* 37 (1977), pp. 634–54, esp. p. 639.

bile was one-dimensional by comparison. Allotting more than 90 percent of the employment base to the service sector, Mobile hooked its fortune to the retailing of goods and services in the rural plantation districts and thus displaced urban employment from her merchants to those in hinterland towns. The extent of this displacement was implied in earlier data that reported that Chicago's population was 3.76 times that of Mobile, while the population of Chicago's urban system was just 3.16 times that of Mobile's urban system. Insofar as these figures are a guide to urban dominance, Mobile seems to have exercised lesser influence over its hinterland towns than did Chicago. These observations lend credence to the often alleged alliance of

small cotton-belt towns and rural planters (who resided in and dominated these towns) against the coastal entrepôt.[12]

A closer look at sectoral employment bases helps clarify the character of these two urban systems.

Staple marketing

Staple marketing, though truly the raison d'être for the Chicago
and Mobile urban systems, had negligible effects on urban employment. In the case of Chicago, the vast quantities of grain and livestock received in the city grossed the handsome sum of $34,002,809
in 1860 prices, but 84 percent of it was returned to farmers in the
hinterland; just 16 percent ($5,638,790)—the average marketing
margin on all of Chicago's staples—went to marketing firms operating between the farm and the Chicago market.[13] And only about 42
percent of that amount, some $2,391,589, wound up in labor's pock-
ets.[14] King cotton channeled even less to the middlemen in Mobile's

12. The significance of small-town ruralization and local political power is suggested
in Weymouth Jordan, *Ante-Bellum Alabama: Town and Country* (Tuscaloosa: University of
Alabama Press, 1987).

13. The gross value of Chicago's staples is the sum of nine staples—wheat, corn,
barley, rye, oats, flour, live hogs, dressed hogs, and cattle. The gross value of the trade is
arrived at by calculating for the nine staples the product of monthly receipts at Chicago
and the monthly prices at Chicago. Prices and receipts are from Chicago Board of Trade,
Annual Statement of Trade and Commerce of Chicago for the Year Ending December 31, 1860
(Chicago, 1861). Also see Earle and Hoffman, "Regional Staples and Urban Systems." Marketing earnings are the middleman charges between the farm and the Chicago market.
These earnings are tabulated on the basis of monthly receipts at Chicago and monthly
price spreads between farm and market. For farm prices, I use those of Wisconsin for
several reasons: they are already compiled; the state was adjacent to Illinois and in 1860 it
produced crops of the same kind and quality; and Chicago and Milwaukee wholesale
prices are very similar, suggesting similar farm prices. W. P. Mortensen and others, *Wisconsin Farm Prices, 1841 to 1933*, Wisconsin Agricultural Experiment Station, Research Bulletin 119 (Madison, Wisc., 1933).

14. Labor's share of staple marketing (42.4 percent) is determined as follows: the
earnings from staple marketing are allocated amongst transport (50 percent), warehousing
and storage (31 percent), and mercantile functions (19 percent). For each of these industry
groups, labor's share of earnings is apportioned according to the following sources. In the
case of transport, the labor share of 30 percent comes from Albert Fishlow's figures for
railroads, corroborated by numerous annual reports of Chicago railroads in the Baker
Library of Harvard University. While labor's share on canals was even higher than on
railroads, canals contributed a small portion of earnings to staple marketing. As for warehousing and storage, a labor share of 35 percent is based on twentieth-century census data
on public warehousing. Finally, for mercantile services, I follow Barger and estimate labor's share as 66 percent of earnings. Adding labor's share from these three sectors yields
a wage total of $2,391,589, or 42.4 percent of gross earnings. Albert Fishlow, *American
Railroads and the Transformation of the Antebellum Economy* (Cambridge, Mass.: Harvard Uni-

urban system. Though her cotton trade grossed over $49,000,000 in 1859–60[15] (a figure half again as large as the gross in Chicago's staple trade), Mobile's urban system earned a marketing margin of only about 7.5 percent, or $3,679,612.[16] Labor's portion came to $1,397,109 (38 percent of gross earnings).[17] The point is that staple marketing, however vital it was for the urban economy, contributed modestly to the economic and employment base of northern and southern urban systems. Farmers and planters were the big winners in the staple trade.

Manufacturing

Manufacturing provided a somewhat larger base for urban employment, but in neither system did this sector contribute more than 18 percent to employment base. Chicago manufactures held a commanding lead, quadrupling the contribution of Mobile manufactures

---

versity Press, 1965), pp. 123–24. See also the annual reports for the Chicago, Burlington, and Quincy Railroad, 1859–60, and the Galena and Chicago Union Railroad, 1860, in the Baker Library. Barger, "Income Originating in Trade, 1869–1929," pp. 327–33; *idem, Distribution's Place in the American Economy*.

15. Mobile cotton receipts and prices are for the crop year beginning September 1, 1859. In that year, Mobile received 843,596 bales of cotton, averaging 518 pounds and valued at 11.2 cents per pound and $58.13 per bale. "Commerce of Mobile," *Hunt's Merchants' Magazine* 43 (1860), pp. 480, 632; "Commerce of Mobile," *DeBow's Review* 29 (1860), pp. 664–67; "Cotton Crop of the United States," *Hunt's Merchants' Magazine* 45 (1861), pp. 497–501; Amos, *Cotton City*, pp. 18–47.

16. Cotton margins were lower than grain and livestock margins because the former afforded easier handling owing to lesser bulk, weight, and perishability. Chicago received 1,149,474 tons of grain and livestock as compared to 218,652 tons of cotton received at Mobile. Marketing margins on cotton ranged from 6 to 10 percent. This range was the result of variations in freight rates charged by steamboats—the principal carrier of Mobile cotton. River rates were very high in dry years or dry seasons, thus pushing the margin up toward 10 percent; margins were low during years of high river discharge. River conditions seem to have been normal in 1859–60, and accordingly I use a margin of 7.5 percent. See the fine study by Harold D. Woodman, *King Cotton and His Retainers: Financing and Marketing the Cotton Crop of the South, 1800–1925* (Lexington: University of Kentucky Press, 1968), p. 25.

17. The computations, though elaborate, are similar to those described in note 14. The earnings from staple marketing in Mobile are distributed as follows: transport, 53 percent; mercantile services, 36 percent; and storage, 11 percent. For more detail, see Earle and Hoffman, "Regional Staples and Urban Systems." Labor's share of staple marketing earnings is lower in Mobile than in Chicago, mainly because southern railroads and steamboats paid smaller shares to labor than did northern railroads. See the annual reports for the Mobile and Ohio Railroad, 1858 and 1860. Also see Eric F. Haites, James Mak, and Gary M. Walton, *Western River Transportation: The Era of Early Internal Development, 1810–1860* (Baltimore: Johns Hopkins University Press, 1975).

FIGURE 8.3. A mid-nineteenth-century representation of a slave hauling cotton to a river landing and an awaiting steamboat. Note that the wagon hauled eight bales of cotton, or roughly the output of one worker. Reproduced from *Harper's New Monthly Magazine* 8 (1854), p. 460.

to the economic base (manufacturing value added of $17,136,220 and $4,548,427, respectively) and tripling their contribution to the employment base ($6,074,035 to $1,867,650).[18]

Consumer Goods and Services

Consumer expenditures constituted the overwhelming majority of the employment base in both systems, providing nearly $28 mil-

18. *Manufactures of the United States in 1860, Compiled from the Original Returns of the Eighth Census* (Washington, D.C.: U.S. Bureau of the Census, 1865), pp. 2–14, 83–113, 285–94.

lion in the Chicago urban system and just over $30 million in the Mobile system. Farmers and planters naturally spent the most, followed distantly by workers in manufacturing and staple marketing.[19]

After all estimates are in, the astonishing fact becomes clear that two urban systems so unlike in size and divergent in character functioned on employment bases that were remarkably alike in value. The one, regarded by many as the eighth wonder of the world, sustained a labor force of perhaps 130,000 on an employment base of a little over $36 million. The other, scarcely noticed even by the sojourners who visited her, sustained just half that many (61,000) on an employment base of some $33 million, that is, about 90 percent of the sum available to its vastly larger counterpart. Even allowing a fairly wide berth for estimation error, the parity in the urban employment bases of these two urban systems should suspend belief in a demand-led theory of urban growth in the antebellum United States in particular and developing economies in general. For a sufficient theory of urban systems, we must turn in our tale of two cities to the subject of labor and its costs.[20]

Regional Wages as the Sufficient Condition for Urban Systems Employment

Economic base and consumer demand are necessary but insufficient theoretical explanations of mid-nineteenth-century urbanization: necessary in the sense that the very existence of Chicago and Mobile depended upon these factors, but insufficent in their capacity to account for comparative urban-system labor force differentials. This brings us back to our arithmetic model of urban-system employment: $U = E / W$. Having discounted the explanatory power of the numerator, we must shift our attention to the denominator, to considerations on the supply side and to regional variations in urban wages and their determinants.

I begin with a paradox of unusual significance for a supply-side theory of urban systems in antebellum America: namely, that an underdeveloped southern economy paid its urban workers so well that their wages not only rivaled northern wages, but surpassed them by a substantial margin.[21] This inverts our expectations and baffles us

19. See note 10 above.
20. On this point see Parker, "Slavery and Southern Economic Development," pp. 115–25.
21. Stanley L. Engerman, "A Reconsideration of Southern Economic Growth,

into asking, what peculiar economic logic is responsible for so bizarre a wage geography? and if that geography is real, is it also a sufficient explanation of twofold employment differentials in the antebellum urban systems under review?

The regional geography of antebellum wages is bizarre only if one presumes that labor markets are competitive and that wages are determined by marginalist economic principles. However useful these models are today, they are less appropriate when applied in the economic context of developing regions and nations. Labor markets in developing economies—of which the antebellum United States was one—operate differently from those in modern market economies. Wage determination derives from competition between labor markets rather than within a single market, that is, between markets operating in a large rural sector and markets operating in a small urban one.[22] In this context, wages in the small urban sector are determined by earnings in the larger rural sector and mediated through the transfer wage—the annual wage sufficient to induce rural workers to shift to unskilled urban employment.[23] All other things being equal, rural workers will transfer to urban work when

---

1770–1860," *Agricultural History* 49 (1975), pp. 343–61. Stanley Lebergott, *Manpower in Economic Growth: The American Record since 1800* (New York: McGraw-Hill, 1964), pp. 539–45; Philip R. P. Coelho and James F. Shepherd, "Regional Differences in Real Wages: The United States, 1851–1880," *Explorations in Economic History* 13 (1976), pp. 203–30.

22. The literature bearing on this model is voluminous, although there is often some confusion on whether the model is one of wage determination or rural-to-urban migration. My main purpose in using it is to clarify wage and earnings levels. Especially useful is the work of W. Arthur Lewis, "Economic Development with Unlimited Supplies of Labour," *The Manchester School* (1954), pp. 139–91; *idem*, "Unlimited Labour: Further Notes," *The Manchester School* (1958), pp. 1–32; and *idem*, "Reflections on Unlimited Labour," in *International Economics and Development: Essays in Honor of Raul Prebisch*, ed. Luis Eugenio DiMarco (New York: Academic Press, 1972), pp. 75–96. Michael Todaro has forwarded a refined migration model wherein migration is contingent on wages and the probability of urban employment over some horizon. His model does not, however, predict the levels of urban wages or annual earnings. Michael P. Todaro, "A Model of Labor Migration and Urban Unemployment in Less Developed Countries," *American Economic Review* 59 (1969), pp. 138–48.

23. On the transfer wage, see Chapter 5. Paul A. David has recently argued that agricultural opportunities provide a floor for unskilled urban wages; increases above that level, he believes, are a reflection of labor demands within the city. See his "Industrial Labor Market Adjustments in a Region of Recent Settlement: Chicago, 1848–1868," in *Quantity and Quiddity: Essays in U.S. Economic History*, ed. Peter Kilby (Middletown, Conn.: Wesleyan University Press, 1987), pp. 47–97.

the net incomes they could earn in the city exceed those they currently earn in the country. More formally, the transfer wage is found by solving for urban wages (W_u) in the following formula: $W_u - C_u = W_r - C_r$, where W_u is annual urban wage or earnings, that is, the transfer wage; W_r is annual rural earnings, adjusted by the value of nonmonetary income associated with rural life;[24] and C_u and C_r are living costs in city and country, respectively.[25]

In a two-sector labor market, urban wage determination begins in the countryside with the annual earnings of relatively unskilled rural workers. Their earnings, whether in Illinois, Alabama, or elsewhere, are constrained by a variety of factors, but two are fundamental: the seasonal regimes of staple crops and agrarian labor demands and the range of off-farm and off-season work opportunities. Agrarian seasonality, of course, varies remarkably from one staple region to another, with the result that rural earnings (and the transfer wage) are usually very low in acutely seasonal regimes such as the grain belt of the antebellum Midwest and very high in protracted cropping regimes such as the cotton belt of the deep South. As we shall see, young men in the Midwest fared much worse as seasonal hired hands than did their counterparts in the South, who entered quite readily into year-round yeomanry and overseeing.

Midwestern farming was the most seasonal of businesses. As a consequence, agrarian demands for rural labor were highly skewed. In Illinois, farmers hired labor for short terms lasting from ten weeks to four months. Hiring peaked in the "crop season," that hectic four-month period from spring plowing and corn planting in April through tillage in May and June to the close-order harvest of wheat, barley, rye, and oats in July. The rest of the year, farm laborers were either unemployed or underemployed. Seasonal hiring in the midwestern grain belt of the 1850s translated into modest annual incomes for rural youth. Their earnings turned on the very good money they earned between April and July and the small change they picked up in odd jobs during the slack months between August and the end of March. The hired hand in 1860 Illinois could count

24. Non-pecuniary income equal to 30 percent of rural earnings is indicated in Gerald M. Meier, *Leading Issues in Economic Development*, 3rd ed. (New York: Oxford University Press, 1976), p. 158.

25. See, for example, Edith Mae Land, *The Effects of Net Interregional Migration on Agricultural Income Growth: The United States, 1850–1860* (New York: Arno Press, 1975), pp. 98–103.

on earning between \$56 and \$72 (W_r) for four months' work; the rest of the year they were at considerable risk.[26]

But even these earnings were not unfettered gain, since hired hands had to cover subsistence costs. Although "crop season" contracts usually included room and board, rural laborers paid for their own subsistence when they were out of contract. And with room and board costs running at about 20 cents per day, the underemployed farm hand had little left after paying out some \$48 in room and board (C_r) during the eight-month off-season.[27]

But what of the city? To be sure, midwestern country boys regarded the dynamism of city life with a certain wonder, and a decision to go there involved more than a rational accounting of comparative net incomes. Yet the shrewdness of young men accustomed to seasonal hiring, low annual wages, and tight budgets for three-fourths of the year should not be underestimated. The city might offer them better pay, but it also cost a great deal more. For northern Illinois farmhands in the 1850s, the city of opportunity was Chicago, and life there was expensive indeed. Annual subsistence probably cost as much in Chicago as in the cities along the northeastern seaboard, where in 1860 and 1861 a single adult living without extravagance spent \$174 on food, clothing, and lodging.[28]

With this estimate of urban living costs (C_u) in hand, we may solve for the transfer wage (W_u) in the Chicago urban system. A transfer wage of \$182 to \$198 equalizes net unskilled earnings in city and country.[29] When annual wages in the Midwest rose above \$200, the wonderment of the city was transformed into hard economic reality. To be sure, the transfer wage typically received a boost from non-pecuniary income associated with rural life—perhaps as much

26. See Chapter 5, as well as Allan G. Bogue, *From Prairie to Cornbelt: Farming on the Illinois and Iowa Prairies in the Nineteenth Century* (Chicago: Quadrangle Books, 1968); David E. Schob, *Hired Hands and Plowboys: Farm Labor in the Midwest, 1815–1860* (Urbana: University of Illinois Press, 1975); and Paul W. Gates, *The Farmer's Age: Agriculture, 1815–1860* (New York: Holt, Rinehart and Winston, 1960).

27. Schob, *Hired Hands and Plowboys*, p. 188.

28. *Report of the Special Commissioner of the Revenue for the Year 1868*, 40th Cong., 3rd Sess., H. Exec. Doc. 16, p. 122. Regional cost-of-living indices for 1860, with the national level set at 100, show the West North Central region at 107, nearly as high as New England (109) and greater than the Middle Atlantic states (97). Philip R. P. Coelho and James F. Shepherd, "Differences in Regional Prices: The United States, 1851–1880," *Journal of Economic History* 34 (1974), pp. 551–91.

29. Specifically, for low rural wages, (W_u—\$56) = (\$174—\$48); and for high rural wages, (W_u—\$72) = (\$174—\$48).

as 30 percent of rural earnings according to empirical estimates in the development literature; but even these intangibles were neutralized by an urban wage offer of $194 to $222, which doubled the net earnings of rural hired hands. We may be fairly confident that in Chicago's hinterland, an annual wage in excess of $200 was sufficient inducement for rural-to-urban migration and sectoral employment shift in the urban-system economy. More importantly for urban systems, the midwestern transfer wage established low wage levels for unskilled urban labor as well as a reservoir of cheap labor for the urban entrepreneurs who benefited from its exploitation.

At the same time, 800 miles away in the deep South of Alabama and Mississippi, young men found compelling reasons to stay in the countryside. Although a great deal has been written about the allegedly blighting effect of slavery on white labor, rural earnings in the cotton belt belie any such devastation.[30] Doubtless slavery was responsible for eliminating the demand for hired hands, but at the same time the peculiar institution created in the task of overseer a ready-made and even more lucrative market for tough, aggressive young men on the move. The business of overseeing slaves and plantation operations, though enough to make northerners blanch, was in the South a respected occupation pursued by nearly 38,000 southerners in 1860. Alabama and Mississippi alone employed 8,000.[31]

Obviously every young man of ordinary circumstance did not become an overseer, but the possibility always existed. Overseers were usually young (29 or 30 was the average age) and upwardly mobile, and their success in moving beyond the job left vacancies that were eagerly filled. Why? For the simple reason that cotton-belt overseers earned anywhere from $200 to $1,000 per year; along with food, lodging, and other fringe benefits. The scholarly authority on the overseer indicates $450 as the average pay, but since we are interested in entry-level pay, an income of $300 seems more appropriate. A competent overseer, however, could expect hefty annual raises.[32]

Other southern boys went directly into the ranks of the cotton-planting yeomanry during the 1850s. A hard-driving planter and his wife, though they might never afford the exorbitant price of a slave,

30. In this regard, Genovese's call for a reexamination of the southern yeomen—a task begun by the Owsley school—is long overdue. Eugene D. Genovese, "Yeomen Farmers in a Slave-holders' Democracy," *Agricultural History* 49 (1975), pp. 331–42.
31. William Kauffman Scarborough, *The Overseer: Plantation Management in the Old South* (Baton Rouge: Louisiana State University Press, 1966), pp. 3–66.
32. *Ibid.*

produced with their own labor anywhere from eight to ten bales of
cotton earning them $320 to $400 each year. Their expenditures for
land and capital, meanwhile, were small. With rewards of this sort,
virtually every small planter in the black belt of Alabama and Mississippi took the gamble of cotton in the 1850s. Few of them worried
overmuch that they would never own slaves or rise into the planter
elite; nor were these achievements necessary since the yeomen did
quite well for themselves in the prosperous cotton districts surrounding Mobile.[33]

When the countryside held out $300 plus expenses for a full
year's work, urban-sector competitors were in trouble. To induce
white unskilled workers into Mobile and her tributary towns, urban
entrepreneurs had to offer that amount plus an additional sum covering urban living costs. How much it cost to live in Mobile and other
southern cities can only be guessed. But if costs were similar to Chicago's ($165), then our wage model ($W_u - \$300 = \$165 - \$0$) yields
a transfer wage of $465 per year. Nor would this picture change very
much if we lowered our estimates of urban living costs by half; a
southern transfer wage of $385 is still substantially higher than its
midwestern counterpart ($200). Making an allowance for rural non-
pecuniary income only increases the southern transfer wage by another $90 or so—a prospect that surely provoked a wince from ur-
ban entrepreneurs already hard-pressed by the high costs of southern labor.[34]

The transfer wage is not merely an empty theory of regional
wage determination. A fair amount of evidence supports the view
that unskilled labor was considerably cheaper in the Midwest than
in the cotton South. In Chicago, for example, laborers averaged just
75 cents a day, or $233 per year. Laborers working for Chicago's
McCormick Reaper Company in the 1850s earned even less, about
60 cents per day, or $187 per year. And workers on the Illinois Cen-

33. On yeomen, see Frederick Law Olmsted, *A Journey in the Back Country in the
Winter of 1853–54* (2 vols.; New York: G. P. Putnam, 1907), Vol. 2, pp. 65–67; Robert R.
Russel, "The Effects of Slavery upon Nonslaveholders in the Ante-Bellum South," *Agricultural History* 15 (1941), pp. 112–26; and Charles S. Davis, *Cotton Kingdom in Alabama* (Montgomery, Ala.: State Department of Archives and History, 1939), pp. 154–55. Also, though
we differ in our interpretation of yeoman behavior, see Gavin Wright, *The Political Economy
of the Cotton South*, esp. chapters 2 and 3.

34. One index of regional prices in 1860 puts East South Central prices 13 percent
below the national average. That implies a Mobile cost of living of $151 (if the northeastern
states' cost of living was $165) and a transfer wage of $451. Coelho and Shepherd, "Differences in Regional Prices," p. 570.

tral Railroad earned about 80 cents a day ($249 per year) during the 1850s. The empirical evidence of low wages thus compares favorably with the regional transfer wage predicted by our two-sector model of wage determination.[35]

Southern wages offer further confirmation for the transfer wage model. Wages in the cotton South, as theorized, were sharply higher than those of the Middle West. In the cotton port of Galveston, unskilled laborers averaged $1.38 per day, or $429 a year. Similarly, crewmen on steamboats serving the Mississippi River and its tributaries earned about $360 per year in 1850 and perhaps $450 by 1860.[36] High wages also prevailed in Louisiana. White workers doing menial canal work in 1851 and 1853 earned alarmingly high wages, or so it seemed to the state engineer. "Thirty-five dollars . . . per month for white labor," he observed, "cannot be too high an estimate, including cost of board." When unskilled canal workers received annual earnings of $420, it is small wonder that the superintendent insisted on using slaves costing half as much ($192).[37]

He was not alone. Throughout the cotton belt during the 1850s southerners experimented with slave labor in a variety of nontraditional tasks on railroads and canals and in factories. Trumpeting the virtues of slave labor became a minor journalistic industry during the decade, but in the end—despite the high costs of white labor—there were practical limits to these experiments. One constraint on industrial slavery was ideological. For southerners to deploy slaves in urban employment while fending off northern anti-slavery critiques with arguments of white paternalism and black incompetence smacked of hypocrisy. Another constraint was economic. The simple and incontrovertible truth was that slaves planting cotton offered a

35. Robert Ozanne, *Wages in Practice and Theory: McCormick and International Harvester, 1860–1960* (Madison: University of Wisconsin Press, 1968), pp. 3–21; David L. Lightner, *Labor on the Illinois Central Railroad, 1852–1900: The Evolution of an Industrial Environment* (New York: Arno Press, 1977), pp. 22–29, 76–89; *DeBow's Review* 29 (1860), p. 381; Bessie Louise Pierce, *A History of Chicago, Volume 2, From Town to City, 1848–1871* (New York: Knopf, 1940), p. 500.

36. Haites, Mak, and Walton, *Western River Transportation*, pp. 170–77. The wages of steamboat operatives in 1860 are 1850 wages adjusted to 1860 levels after Stanley Lebergott, "Wage Trends, 1800–1900," in *Trends in the American Economy in the Nineteenth Century*, ed. William N. Parker, National Bureau of Economic Research, Studies in Income and Wealth, No. 24 (Princeton, N.J.: Princeton University Press, 1960), pp. 449–99, esp. p. 465.

37. *DeBow's Review* 29 (1860), p. 385; G. W. Morse, "Railroad and Water Communication," *DeBow's Review* 19 (1855), pp. 193–201. Wages of about $1.60 per day for unskilled whites exceeded the wages paid for many skilled jobs in Chicago.

far better return on investment than slaves working in southern shops and factories.[38]

The role of the transfer wage was not limited, however, to mediating the level of unskilled urban wages in the antebellum Midwest and cotton South. It also established a regional baseline for the wages of skilled urban workers. Skilled wages stood in arithmetic relation to the regional datum established by the transfer wage. Urban artisans north and south earned wage premiums 1.5 to 2.5 times the prevailing regional transfer wage for unskilled labor (see Table 8.2). Deploying this principle of regional wage-basing, urban entrepreneurs in a developing economy acknowledged the scarcity of skilled labor and resolved it by offering wage inducements that were urban-system specific.[39]

The regional basing principle helps explain certain otherwise curious interregional wage variations. Take the case of the Chicago carpenter earning $466 a year—an income substantially higher than the transfer wage earned by common laborers in the city. But when compared to the common laborer in Mobile making $400 a year, our midwestern carpenter looks much less prosperous indeed. He looks even worse when compared to southern artisans. In the middle and late 1850s, when Chicago artisans (including carpenters, painters, plasterers, stonemasons, and bricklayers) averaged $529 per year, their fellow artisans in the cities of the lower South earned $750 for the same jobs.[40] But after all, travelers to the South had been telling us this for some time. Their travelogues bristled with complaints of outrageous prices charged for mending clothes or hats, shoeing horses, and the like. The root of urban gouging, as many of these sojourners understood, lay deep within the rural cotton economy.

38. Recent arguments to the contrary, the high rates of return to southern manufacturing vis-à-vis the Northwest may be an artifact of ambiguity in the definition of slave inputs. The high returns to manufacturing probably reflect the inclusion of slaves as capital stock rather than labor. In calculating profitability, this definition has the effect of increasing net returns in the numerator in disproportion to the small increment contributed by discounted slave capital in the denominator. For the curiously high returns of southern manufacturing, see Fred Bateman, James Foust, and Thomas Weiss, "Profitability in Southern Manufacturing: Estimates for 1860," *Explorations in Economic History* 12 (1975), pp. 211–32. If returns to manufacturing were as high as they suppose, it is difficult to explain the considerable elasticity of urban slave demand discovered by Claudia D. Goldin, *Urban Slavery in the American South 1820–1860: A Quantitative History* (Chicago: University of Chicago Press, 1976).

39. *DeBow's Review* 29 (1860), p. 381. Also see David, "Industrial Labor Market Adjustments," pp. 85–97.

40. *DeBow's Review* 29 (1860), p. 381.

The evidence is indisputable. The seemingly bizarre geography of antebellum wages was indeed a reality. Cities in the cotton belt invariably paid higher wages than did cities in the midwestern grain belt. But is this striking divergence in regional wages a sufficient explanation of the twofold differentials in their urban system labor forces? A test of the hypothesis requires an estimate of average urban wage, the denominator in our model of labor-force size. To arrive at that estimate, I partition the urban wage into its principal components, skilled and unskilled, and average them using appropriate weights (see Table 8.2). An average wage for an urban system, though something of a fiction, is useful provided that the average is appropriately weighted, judiciously applied, and cautiously interpreted.

For our purposes, the urban wage in a particular region is equal to the average of skilled and unskilled wages weighted by their shares in the urban system labor force. More precisely, the unskilled wage in the denominator equals the transfer wage, the skilled wage equals the average wage of the five artisan groups in Table 8.2, and both wages are weighted by the proportion of unskilled and skilled workers in Illinois or Alabama as reported in occupational summaries of the 1860 census. In order to simplify an already complex procedure, no allowance is made for discriminatorily lower wages paid to women or for slave labor costs (slave hire and maintenance). Estimation biases are discussed fully below, however.

The results: Chicago's average urban system wage equals $371. It represents the average of unskilled wages of $200 weighted at .48 and skilled wages of $529 weighted at .52. Mobile's urban system wage equals $617. It consists of unskilled wages of $400 weighted at .38 and skilled wages of $750 weighted at .62 (see Table 8.2 for skilled wages).

Estimates of this sort are first approximations; error and bias, though unintended, are unavoidable. My guess is that the wage estimates err on the high side given the exclusion of female wages and slave "wage compensation" (note, however, that I have consistently included slaves in labor force counts for the Mobile system). In the case of women, the bias may cancel out since their proportions in the unskilled labor force were roughly the same in the North and the South—32.4 percent in Illinois and 33.2 percent in Alabama (see Table 8.2). As for the exclusion of slave labor's "compensation," the net effect on regional wages is negligible once we allow for slave hire rates of $120 and urban maintenance costs of $165. Assuming a

TABLE 8.2A

Wages and Annual Earnings of Skilled and Unskilled Workers, ca. 1860

(Dollars)

Cities	Skilled workers					Skilled workers (mean)	Laborers
	Painters	Bricklayers	Stonemasons	Carpenters	Plasterers		
New Orleans	2.25(700)	3.00(933)	2.50(788)	2.38(740)	2.38(740)	(778)	1.38(429)
Galveston	1.88(585)	2.88(896)	2.88(896)	2.50(778)	2.00(622)	(841)	1.38(429)
Memphis	2.25(700)	2.50(778)	2.25(700)	2.38(740)	2.13(662)	(716)	1.25(389)
Three lower South cities mean	2.13(662)	2.79(868)	2.54(790)	2.42(753)	2.17(675)	(750)	1.34(417)
Chicago	1.63(507)	1.88(585)	1.75(544)	1.50(467)	1.75(544)	(529)	.75(233)

SOURCE: *DeBow's Review* 29 (1860), p. 381.
NOTE: The first column entry is daily wage; the figure in parentheses is annual earnings based on a work year of 311 days.

TABLE 8.2B

Ratio of Skilled to Unskilled Wages, ca. 1860

	Painters	Brick-layers	Stone-masons	Carpenters	Plasterers	Mean
Three lower South cities	1.58	2.08	1.90	1.81	1.62	1.80
Chicago	2.17	2.51	2.33	2.00	2.33	2.27

SOURCE: *DeBow's Review* 29 (1860), p. 381.
NOTE: The unskilled wage used in the denominator is the wage of laborers in the relevant area.

TABLE 8.2C

Occupational Weights for Regional Wage Estimate, 1860

	Illinois		Alabama	
	No.	Pct.	No.	Pct.
Unskilled	90,086	47.9%	18,528	38.6%
Females	29,144	15.5	6,133	12.8
Laborers	60,942	32.4	12,395	25.8
Skilled	98,002	52.1%	29,477	61.4%
Artisans	55,358	29.4	12,773	26.6
Clerks	11,226	6.0	4,779	10.0
Merchants	13,690	7.3	4,367	9.1
Professional	15,137	8.1	6,727	14.0
Transport	2,591	1.4	831	1.7
Total	188,088	100.0%	48,005	100.0%
Occupational weights				
Unskilled		.48		.38
Skilled		.52		.62

NOTE: The weights are calculated from summary occupational tables at the state level. Although states and urban systems are not identical regions, they are sufficiently similar to permit the rough weighting of skilled and unskilled wages.

lower bound estimate of $200 for slave costs, average southern regional wage declines from $617 to $589—which suggests that the bias from slave exclusion is no more than 5 percent of the Mobile wage estimate.[41]

With these estimates of urban-system wages in hand, the labor force model, $U = E / W$, is fully operational. Doing the arithmetic

41. On slave hire rates, I use a low estimate of $120. Evans reports a much higher rate of $197 for the lower South for 1856–60; with urban living costs added on, the cost of hiring a slave amounted to $362. Robert Evans, Jr., "The Economics of American Negro Slavery," in Universities-National Bureau Committee for Economic Research, *Aspects of Labor Economics* (Princeton, N.J.: Princeton University Press, 1962), pp. 185–243, esp. p. 216.

TABLE 8.3A

Urban System Labor Force Estimates

	Labor's share of regional income		Employment estimate[a]	
	Chicago	Mobile	Chicago	Mobile
Staple marketing	$2,391,589	$1,397,109	6,446	2,264
Manufacturing	$6,074,035	$1,867,650	16,372	3,027
Consumer goods and services	$27,753,156	$30,050,813	74,806	48,705
Total	$36,218,780	$33,315,572	97,624	53,996

[a] Employment estimate equals labor's share of regional income (employment base) divided by the mean regional wage, weighted for skilled and unskilled. Labor's share of regional income may be found in Table 8.1.

TABLE 8.3B

The Accuracy of Urban Labor Force Employment Estimates

	Chicago system			Mobile system		
	Estimate	Actual	Estimate accuracy	Estimate	Actual	Estimate accuracy
Manufacturing	16,372	17,985	91.0%	3,027	6,606	45.8%
Service sector[a]	81,252	113,936	71.3%	50,969	55,181	92.4%
Hidden workers[b]	19,682	—	—	5,845	—	—
Total	117,306	131,921	88.9%	59,841	61,787	96.9%

[a] Includes staple marketing and consumer goods and services.

[b] Part-time workers and unpaid family members are estimated as 15 percent of the actual labor force. In the South, the proportion of these "hidden" workers was applied to the free labor force, or 15 percent of 38,926. It should be noted that occupational listings in the census included these part-time workers and unpaid family members; they are, however, masked in our economic calculations. For sources, see text and footnotes.

for the two systems yields the following results (also see Table 8.3): The model accounts for 74 percent of the labor force in the Chicago urban system (97,624 of the 131,921 workers) and 87.4 percent of the labor force in the Mobile system (53,996 of the 61,787 workers).

These results are good, but not perfect. One problem is that the model excludes part-time workers and unpaid family members. As matters now stand, the contribution of these workers is obscured because our model assumes that workers are paid and work full-time. Their omission is not trivial. The authority on these "hidden" workers has estimated that they amounted to at least 15 percent of the labor force in the service sector.[42] If we adjust our labor force esti-

42. Barger, *Distribution's Place in the American Economy*, pp. 16–18, 101–5. Barger's estimates of "hidden" workers actually are somewhat higher than the proportion used here—24 percent of employees in distribution in 1939 and 20 percent in 1948.

TABLE 8.4

Size Disparities, Actual and Estimated, in the Urban Labor Forces of the Chicago and Mobile Urban Systems

	Actual labor force	Manu-facturing estimate	Staple marketing estimate	Consumer estimate	Hidden workers	Total estimate	Residual
Number of workers	70,134	13,345	4,182	26,101	13,837	57,465	12,669
Percent of actual disparity	100.0%		62.2%		19.7%	81.9%	18.1%

NOTE: The size disparity or spread in the actual labor forces of the two urban systems is based on Chicago's urban labor force of 131,921 and Mobile's of 61,787. The disparity accounted for by the estimates of urban labor forces is based on the data in Table 8.3A, Employment estimates.

mates by that proportion, the Chicago urban system adds 19,682 "hidden" workers, bringing the predicted labor force to 117,306 workers, 88.9 percent of the actual labor force; the Mobile system adds 5,845 "hidden" workers, bringing the predicted labor force to 59,841, 96.9 percent of the actual labor force (see Table 8.3).

What conclusions may be drawn from these provisional estimates of the labor forces in the antebellum urban systems of Chicago and Mobile? First, the model seems to account for most of the labor force differential in the two systems. Second, the model identifies the level of urban-system wages as the decisive factor controlling this differential. Whereas demand-side factors (the numerator in our model) account for just 6.1 percent of the employment differential in the two systems, supply-side factors (the denominator in our model) account for 82 percent—62 percent coming from differences in urban-system wages and 20 percent from "hidden" workers in the service sector. The balance of 18 percent is unexplained residual (see Table 8.4).

The implications of these findings extend far beyond American historical geography, applying also to urban systems that are today emerging from the matrix of developing economies. These urban systems, as those of antebellum Chicago and Mobile, are regulated as much by urban labor costs as by economic base, as much by factors of supply as by those of demand, and as much by agrarian seasonality, rural opportunity, and the transfer wage as by endogenous urban labor markets.

The arithmetic model of urban-system labor force thus lends itself to more extensive application, but certain caveats should be borne in mind when applying it. Aside from all the usual warnings about the perils of economic and demographic estimation, let me emphasize that the model constitutes a theory of the middle range. Middle-range theory takes much for granted and it assumes a great deal that eventually must be proven. Consider briefly what the model does not do. On the demand side, it offers no predictions of regional prices or of the portion of economic base that is allocated to labor (the employment base). These are givens. Similarly, on the supply side, the model offers very little guidance on skilled wage determination—save for the regional-basing principle; nor does it explain the mix of skilled and unskilled workers—a mix essential for weighting urban system wages. But if the theory falls short of a general equilibrium ideal, it nonetheless advances our understanding of developing economies and clarifies the decisive role of the transfer wage in mediating between asymmetric but inextricably interrelated labor markets in country and city. To continue thinking of urban and rural as separate spheres is to have missed the point.

Chapter 2: The Dependent Population

Our tale of two cities is not yet complete. We have told only one side of the story of urban-system demography—the workers' side; the other side of that story—the vast numbers of dependent women, children, adolescents, aged, and infirm—deserves equal time. The sensitivity of the new social history toward these populations notwithstanding, urban inquiry on the whole has paid little attention to dependents, preferring instead to dwell upon adult males in the urban economy. The problem with that approach is that it does not get us very far in explaining the enormous differentials in urban systems' populations. Consider again our comparison of antebellum Chicago and Mobile. Recall that while Chicago's labor force was twice as large as Mobile's, its population was over three times as large. The unexplained disparity—which amounts to nearly 75 percent of the demographic differential in the two urban systems—is attributable to dependent, nonworking populations.

How large were the dependent populations in the Chicago and Mobile urban systems? Since the published Census of 1860 does not report these figures, I have estimated them using dependent-labor-force ratios based on manuscript-census counts from a sample of urban places in the two systems. The Chicago system, as represented by a sample of six places ranging from small towns to the largest city, averaged 2.24 dependents for every member of the labor force. In con-

TABLE 8.5

Dependent Populations in the Cities of Chicago and Mobile, 1860

	Chicago	Mobile
1. Total dependents	71,931	13,994
a. Children 0–14 years	43,183	7,383
b. Adults 60+ years	2,938	467
c. Residual Dependents	25,810	6,144
d. Women 15–59 years	30,685	5,445
e. Working women (d−c)	5,055	0
f. Dependent women (d−e)	25,630	5,445
g. Dependents unaccounted	190	699
2. Labor force	37,270	8,077
Dependency Ratios		
3. Children 0–14 years/labor force	1.158	.914
4. Dependent women 15–59 years/labor force	.688	.674
5. Adults 60+ years/labor force	.079	.058
6. Totals	1.925	1.646
7. Actual dependency ratio	1.930	1.730

NOTE: Unless otherwise indicated, the source of information is the published population data for Cook County, Illinois, and Mobile County, Alabama, adjusted to the populations of the cities of Chicago and Mobile. The actual ratio of dependents to labor force comes directly from the Federal Population Census Manuscripts for 1860. I used a 10 percent sample for Chicago, while for Mobile I used the complete count of workers kindly provided by Ira Berlin and Herbert Gutman. I have assumed that children less than 15 years of age and adults 60 years and older were dependents. Their numbers are counted by the census and they appear as 1a and 1b. Dependent women must be estimated indirectly (1f). The procedure for estimating them is as follows: from total dependents, deduct children (1a) and elderly adults (1b); from the remaining dependents (1c), deduct the number of women 15–59 years; the surplus remaining equals working women (1e). Dependent women then equal the total number of women 15–59 less the working women in that age group. It should be noted that the Mobile figures are for the free population only.

trast, the Alabama cities of Selma and Mobile averaged 1.65 dependents (free population only). Multiplying these ratios by the number of workers in each urban system yields dependent estimates of 295,550 for the Chicago system and 101,949 for Mobile and total population estimates of 427,471 and 163,736, respectively. The population differential in the two urban systems thus amounts to 263,735 persons. Of this differential, urban labor force accounts for only 70,134 persons, or 26.6 percent, while dependents account for 193,588, or 73.4 percent. Obviously urban dependents played an important role in differentiating antebellum urban systems.[43]

43. The ratio of dependents to labor force (those persons listing an occupation in the manuscript census) are as follows (population figures given in parentheses): for the Chicago system, Chicago 1.93 (109,000), Peoria 1.98 (14,400), Elgin 2.25 (3,073), Freeport 2.06 (2,613), Geneseo 2.37 (1,815), and Griggsville 2.86 (1,360); for the Mobile system, Mobile 1.73 (29,258), Selma 1.57 (3,177). Southern dependency ratios are calculated on the basis of free population only. Federal Population Census Manuscripts, 1860. Note that

Who were these dependents? And what peculiar attraction did Chicago have for them that Mobile did not? Urban dependents may be divided into three groups: children, nonworking women, and the elderly. Table 8.5 reports dependency ratios for each of these groups in the cities (not the urban systems) of Chicago and Mobile. The table assumes that everyone under 15 and over 60 years of age is dependent and that the residual consists of nonworking women dependents. The principal point to be made is that the dependency ratios for the two cities differ significantly in only one category of numerical consequence—children under 15 years of age. Chicago thus contained more children than Mobile; it also had a slight edge among dependent women, but the advantage in this case accrued to the towns in the hinterland of the midwestern metropolis.

Fertility and Adolescent Employment Opportunity

Why did Chicago get more children? The answer lies in the realms of domestic family economy and adolescent employment opportunities. Chicago provided a variety of unskilled jobs for adolescents, jobs that contributed income to the family economy and reimbursed some of the costs of child rearing. Opportunities for work as a laborer or a domestic in Chicago were simply more plentiful than in Mobile, where urban slaves preempted these unskilled tasks. Insofar as rational considerations of adolescent labor markets inform fertility decisions, the advantage in antebellum America would seem to have favored Chicago.

Prospective parents in the Midwest and the cotton South certainly had a sense of employment probabilities in the adolescent labor market, having been in it themselves a few years previously. Illinoisans did not need the census to tell them that unskilled positions were abundant in Chicago's urban system, though they may not have

---

the 2.61 differential in the system's population estimates is less than would be expected based on the 3.16 differential implied by postal revenues. This discrepancy could be accounted for by introducing a modest change in the dependency ratios. If the dependency ratios estimated from the manuscript census are decremented by 10 percent in the case of Mobile and incremented by 10 percent in the case of Chicago, the population differential in the two systems increases from 2.61 to 2.96—a figure that is quite close to the population differential suggested by postal revenues in the two urban systems. Thus, a small change in the dependency ratio may have large effects on population estimation. But whatever the true dependency ratios, the critical point remains the same—dependents constituted the overwhelming number of persons in the antebellum urban systems of Chicago and Mobile.

known that these jobs constituted exactly 48 percent of the system's labor force in 1860. Nor did Alabamians, already acutely aware of the scarcity of unskilled work, need precise statistical confirmation that these jobs made up only 38 percent of the urban labor force in the Mobile urban system—or that many of them were performed by slaves.[44]

But even these statistics on the unskilled labor market do not convey the true scarcity of adolescent opportunity, particularly in the South. To be sure, adolescent job prospects everywhere were confined to menial occupations—common labor for the boys, domestic or household work for the girls; but it was in the urban South that job scarcity was most acute. Indeed, in the entire Mobile urban system, the only bright spot in the adolescent labor market was in the city itself. And even that market was confined to young white boys who competed for work as laborers—an occupation that made up 17 percent of the city's free-labor force. Further down the urban hierarchy, in the Selmas, the Wetumpkas, and the Elytons, prospects were gloomier still. In these tributary towns, white laborers simply vanished from local labor markets.[45] And young white southern girls faced even worse circumstances. The tasks of domestic and household servant, the kinds of work routinely performed by young white girls in northern cities, were so thoroughly monopolized by slave women that these jobs virtually disappeared from the occupational listings in the manuscript census of 1860. The upshot is that in the domestic economy of the urban South, children did not pay for themselves, except perhaps in the case of parents who both had a son and resided in the city of Mobile. The disincentives for white urban fertility in a slave society were substantial.

The Midwest offered a setting more conducive to adolescent work. Boys did especially well, finding employment as unskilled laborers, day laborers, and, in the country towns, farm laborers—occupations that constituted 10 to 20 percent of the labor forces in the smaller towns and the larger cities. Girls did well too, though in their case the labor market was geographically asymmetric. Their best opportunities for employment were in the large cities, where servants and domestics constituted 10 to 15 percent of the work force. Small-town girls had a harder go of it, however. Families in these towns rarely

44. *Population of the United States in 1860*, Vol. 2, pp. 104–5.
45. Federal Population Census Manuscripts, 1860. See Table 8.8 for the occupational structures of these towns.

hired on domestics and household servants; consequently, young girls who wanted work packed their bags and migrated upward in the urban hierarchy to Peoria or Chicago. Chicago seems to have been particularly attractive for many young women from the hinterland and areas beyond it. The fact that females constituted 52 percent of Chicago's population aged 15 to 30 in 1860 might not seem evidence of female in-migration until we compare it with data for Mobile, where females made up just 41 percent of this same age group.[46] The Chicago urban system thus provided an adolescent employment niche that was unavailable in the cities of the cotton (and slave) South. But did this midwestern niche translate into higher fertility and, concomitantly, higher child dependency ratios? And similarly, did it translate into higher rates of family immigration?

Fertility decisions, of course, are not derivatives of some strict economic calculus, but neither are they made in complete disregard of child-rearing costs and adolescent income potentialities. Even the most romantic of married couples thinks at some time or other of the impact of children on the domestic budget. This vague rationality may apply with even greater force in developing economies in which children are reasonably expected to enter the labor force at an early age and contribute to the household economy. In making fertility decisions, prospective parents reckoned with probabilities: What was the likelihood of their children's obtaining jobs on reaching adolescence? How much income would they contribute to the domestic economy? Would their earnings recoup some or all of child-rearing costs? Immigrants asked the same sorts of questions, but in their case fertility decisions had already been made and the questions were framed geographically: Given the number and sex of children in an immigrant family, which American city would maximize adolescent earnings and total family income?

Consider these questions through the slightly distorted lens of the rational actor. In matters of fertility, the rational choice is one that maximizes net returns for the domestic economy, that best covers all of the costs of children and turns a profit to boot. One choice, of course, is to have no children; another is to have a child hoping that genetic luck will produce a child of the "right" sex, that is, the sex with the highest probability of gainful and lucrative adolescent employment. Rational fertility decisions are thus a game of chance.

46. *Population of the United States in 1860*, pp. 2–8, 78–85. Also see Tables 8.7 and 8.8.

TABLE 8.6A

Employment Probabilities for the Cities of Chicago and Mobile, 1860

	Chicago	Mobile
Servants	4,490	3
Girls 15–20 years	6,553	668
Girls' employment probability	.685	.004
Laborers	6,430	1,406
Boys 15–20 years	5,551	1,521
Boys' employment probability	1.000	.924

NOTE: Servants and laborers are direct counts from the manuscript census. Boys and girls 15–20 years are from the published census for Cook and Mobile counties, adjusted to the city populations.

TABLE 8.6B

Net Economic Returns of Adolescents, Chicago and Mobile, 1860

	Chicago	Mobile
Boy annual	$ 50.00	$ 169.60
Girl annual	$ 5.25	−$ 148.97
Net returns between age 15–20		
Boys	$300.00	$1,017.60
Girls	$ 31.25	$ 893.82
Net returns to age 21		
Boys	$ 14.00	$ 731.60
Girls	−$254.75	−$1,179.82
Net returns on first child with sex probability of .5	−$120.38	−$ 219.11

NOTE: Net returns are calculated as per text. Employment probabilities are those in Table 8.6A above. Laborer's annual income equals $200 in Chicago and $400 in Mobile. Servant income amounts to $1.46 a week in Chicago and $2.08 in Mobile, board included. Living costs for boys and girls 15–20 amount to $150 per year, except in the case of employed servants. Servant earnings for 1860 are based on figures in Stanley Lebergott, *Manpower in Economic Growth: The American Record Since 1800* (New York: McGraw-Hill, 1964), p. 542. Rearing costs 0–15 years of age equal $286; see n. 47.

Probabilities intrude at every turn: What is the sex-specific probability of adolescent employment or unemployment? What is the probability of children surviving into their majority? and so on. Arriving at the rational choice requires a mass of information, a maze of calculations, and a modicum of faith.

Table 8.6 walks us through the arithmetic of fertility as it bore upon married couples in the cities of antebellum Chicago and Mobile. The arithmetic is premised on certain assumptions about the life cycle prior to a child's majority: there is a 50–50 chance of having a boy or a girl; the child will reside with his or her parents until majority (21 years); and the child will depend entirely on parental support until adolescence, at which point (I use age 15 for the practical reason of consistency with census reporting categories) the child will seek unskilled employment (as a domestic or servant in the case of girls and as a laborer in the case of boys) and, if employed, will contribute income into the domestic economy. In order for children to "pay off," there must be a high probability that the income they will earn in late adolescence is sufficient to offset the costs of child rearing prior to that point.

The rational couple begins by estimating sex-specific employment probabilities of late adolescents in Chicago or Mobile. For girls, the probability of employment (E_f) equals S / A_f, where S is the number of servants in the urban labor force, and A_f is the number of adolescent females 15 to 20 years of age in the urban population. Unemployment probability for girls (U_f) equals 1.00—E_f. Male employment and unemployment probabilities are of the same form, differing only in the substitution of laborers (L) for servants (S). Table 8.6A reports the results. Adolescent employment prospects were excellent for boys in Chicago (1.000) and Mobile (.924); good for Chicago girls (.685); and miserable for the young ladies of Mobile (.004).

But did they earn positive net returns? Table 8.6B summarizes the results of a variety of equations and calculations designed to estimate the probable net returns for one child in 1860 Chicago or Mobile. The critical equation in its most general form is $R_s = [E_s (W_s - C_s) - U_s C_s] t_6 - Y$, where R equals the probable net returns to children; E and U are the probabilities of adolescent employment and unemployment, respectively; W is the annual earnings of an adolescent youth; C is the annual cost; t is the time over which adolescents seek gainful employment; Y is the cost of rearing a child to age 15; and the subscript s is the sex of the child.[47]

Running this equation for boys and girls in Chicago and Mobile tells us the following: net returns were highest for boys in Mobile ($731.60) followed by boys in Chicago ($14.00), girls in Chicago (-$254.75), and, dead last, girls in Mobile (-$1,179.82). If rational

---

47. I estimate child-rearing costs using the research on slave child-rearing expenditures, though doubtless these are too low for white children. The costs of raising a slave child to 14 years of age equal $190, and compounding them at an annual rate of 6 percent gives a total cost of $286. Alfred H. Conrad and John R. Meyer, "The Economics of Slavery in the Ante-Bellum South," in *The Reinterpretation of American Economic History*, ed. Robert W. Fogel and Stanley L. Engerman (New York: Harper and Row, 1971), pp. 342–61, esp. p. 350.

couples could have willfully determined the sex of their offspring, their choices would have been obvious; but nature (at least in antebellum times) dealt them equal probabilities. The birth of a girl, who would earn negative returns, was just as likely as the birth of a boy, who promised positive returns. Applying these probabilities to sex-specific returns shows that having a child probably did not pay. Moreover, the probable loss for parents in Mobile (-$219.11) was substantially greater than for parents in Chicago (-$120.38).

For the extreme rationalist, children were a mixed blessing in Chicago and Mobile. If pure economic rationality had prevailed in fertility behavior, households in both cities would have avoided children altogether. But if rationality was tempered somewhat by the desire for offspring, a risk taker would recognize that the probability of positive returns on a first child was 50–50, the probability of having a boy. But beyond one child, the probabilities of continuing the string of positive returns deteriorated multiplicatively: .25 for a second boy, .125 for a third, and so on.

Under these circumstances, the preferred fertility strategy in antebellum Chicago and Mobile probably consisted of having one child only. Elementary game theory suggests that the optimal strategy would involve having a boy as the first child 62 percent of the time in Mobile and 50 percent of the time in Chicago. But since sex at birth is equiprobable, it would appear that Chicago couples should have had roughly 12 percent more children than couples in Mobile.[48]

These rational fertility strategies imply an antebellum fertility rate of about 1,000 children per 1,000 women 15 to 44 years of age, adjusted for a 12 percent differential favoring Chicago over Mobile, which would give a rate of 1,120 in the former and 1,000 in the latter. In fact, the fertility rates in both cities are quite close to these expectations. In the first instance, Chicago's rate of 1,225 children per 1,000 women and Mobile's of 1,083 exceed predicted fertility by just 10 and 8 percent, respectively; in the second, their fertility differential of 13 percent is almost precisely what game theory would suggest.[49] Chicago's higher fertility rate, in turn, explains about half

48. A concise account of strategies and game theory application, in the form used here, appears in Peter R. Gould, "Man Against His Environment: A Game Theoretic Framework," *Annals of the Association of American Geographers* 53 (1963), pp. 290–97. I use a two-by-two payoff matrix using the strategies of having a boy or a girl and the associated net returns.

49. *Population of the United States in 1860*, pp. 2–8, 78–85. The fertility rate employed here is identical to that used by Yasukichi Yasuba and Don Leet. Yasukichi Yasuba,

of the interurban differential in dependent child ratios—on the order of 26 percent for children fifteen years of age and under.

That is not to say that children were a more attractive investment
in Chicago than Mobile; more correctly, they were less unattractive.
Chicago's extensive employment opportunities for adolescent boys
and girls afforded parents the opportunity of minimizing their most
serious losses—girls. In Mobile, by contrast, the birth of a child invited feast or famine. Parents there might profit handsomely from
the birth of a son, but woe awaited the parents of a baby girl. As she
grew into adolescence, employment opportunities were virtually nil
in a society that assigned the tasks of domestic service to slave women.
Because of slavery, Mobile's daughters constituted an unmitigated
drain on the family budget. Sons probably suffered the same fate in
the interior towns, where most of the unskilled urban occupations,
especially those of the laborer, were preempted by male slaves.

Immigration and Adolescent Employment Opportunity

Fertility explains only about half of the Chicago-Mobile differential in child dependency; the balance probably is attributable to
differential domestic in-migration and foreign immigration. The
logic of the immigrant, like that of the prospective parent, is rooted
more or less in economic returns. A completely rational migrant will
move to the location that maximizes the household's rate of return.
The preferred location, however, varies with family size and composition. An antebellum immigrant with a family of girls and boys was
best served by migrating to a northern city such as Chicago where
jobs were available for adolescent children of both sexes. Conversely,
the unattached male immigrant (or even a family with a male surplus) maximized income by moving to a southern city like Mobile
(though not perhaps to its hinterland towns).

The proposition that urban immigrants preferred locations that
maximized household income is perfectly sensible. Moreover, it helps
to explain, without resort to immigrant racism, why immigrants
avoided the South—unless they came there as single men. If my

---

Birth Rates of the White Population in the United States, 1800–1860: An Economic Study (Baltimore: Johns Hopkins University Press, 1962); Don R. Leet, "Interrelations of Population
Density, Urbanization, Literacy, and Fertility," *Explorations in Economic History* 14 (1977),
pp. 388–401.

proposition is correct, we should find that immigrant flows to North American cities varied substantially in sex composition, that is, that single men went to southern cities and that families and single women went to northern cities. Immigrant sex ratios for the years 1849 to 1855 confirm these suspicions. In this period of general prosperity, Mobile received half again as many male immigrants per female (2.3 males per female) as ports in the northeastern United States (1.5 males per female).[50]

Chicago's age-sex structure likewise indicates sex-selective immigration. Although the city's overall sex ratio is nearly equal (1.06 males per female), the balance tips decidedly in favor of females in the 15-to-30 age bracket. The ratio of males to females falls to .85 for the adolescent age group 15–20 and remains below 1.0 (.94 to be exact) for young adults 21–30. Mobile looked very different indeed. This was a man's city with an overall ratio of 1.23 males per female and ratios of .98 and 1.46 for the age groups 15–20 and 21–30, respectively. These contrasting demographic structures lend themselves to the following interpretation: fertility maintained balanced sex ratios in both cities until age 14 or so, but in the age group between 15 and 20 in-migration reduced Chicago's male-to-female sex ratio by 20 percent while Mobile's hardly changed at all. That the transition in Chicago occurred in this particular age group suggests that these girls came to Chicago alone rather than in family groups. In the age bracket between 21 and 30 years of age, women maintained their advantage in Chicago, but that same cohort experienced a sharp reversal in Mobile, where the male-to-female sex ratio rose by nearly 50 percent. And after 30 years of age, while men formed the majority in both cities, Chicago consistently reported lower male-to-female sex ratios than did the cotton port (see Table 8.7).[51]

I can think of no other set of processes that makes sense of these patterns and trends in urban demographic structure. They were the

---

50. Tabulated from William J. Bromwell, *History of Immigration to the United States Exhibiting the Number, Sex, Age, Occupation, and Country of Birth of Passengers Arriving from Foreign Countries by Sea, 1819 to 1855* (1856; reprint, New York: Arno Press, 1969), pp. 141–72. Immigrants indeed came to southern towns, but doubtless they came as single men rather than in family groups. On the southern city and its immigrants, see Herbert Weaver, "Foreigners in Ante-Bellum Towns of the Lower South," *Journal of Southern History* 13 (1947), pp. 62–73; Thomas Walker Page, "The Distribution of Immigrants in the United States Before 1870," *Journal of Political Economy* 20 (1912), pp. 676–94; Amos, *Cotton City*, pp. 80–113; and William L. Miller, "Slavery and the Population of the South," *Southern Economic Journal* 28 (1961), pp. 46–54.

51. *Population of the United States in 1860*, pp. 2–8, 78–85.

TABLE 8.7

White Sex Ratios (Males/Females)
for Cook and Mobile Counties, 1860

Age groups	Chicago	Mobile
0–9	1.03	1.00
10–14	1.02	.96
15–19	.85	.98
20–29	.94	1.46
30–39	1.28	1.45
40–49	1.38	1.70
50–59	1.13	1.64
Total population	1.06	1.23

SOURCE: *Population of the United States in 1860* . . . (Washington, D.C.: U.S. Bureau of the Census, 1864), pp. 2–8, 78–85.

result of sex-selective and age-selective migration—in the case of Mobile among males 21 to 30 years of age and in the case of Chicago among females aged 15 to 30—in response to the differential employment opportunities provided by these two quite distinctive cities.

Translating sex ratios and fertility rates into dependency ratios is an inexact and messy business. The best that can be said is that Chicago's economy encouraged the differential in-migration of families, young women, and adolescent girls (either alone or in families) as well as higher rates of fertility, while Mobile's encouraged in-migration of young men on the make. Surely female migration to Chicago helped boost the city's dependency rate since, as we have seen, the employment probability for young women was only about .7. Perhaps a third of them at any one time may have been unemployed and dependent. That was not true for young men in Chicago or Mobile; virtually all of them could find unskilled (or better) occupations. Adolescent male dependency in either city was unlikely. The crucial factors accounting for Chicago's dependents lie elsewhere, however—namely in the city's higher rate of fertility and its attraction for immigrants with families.

Dependency in the Hinterland Towns

And what of dependency in the subordinate cities and towns in the Chicago and Mobile urban systems? In the Chicago hinterland, dependency rates varied inversely with employment probabilities and town size. In smaller midwestern towns, the low employment probabilities for young girls and women boosted the rates of depen-

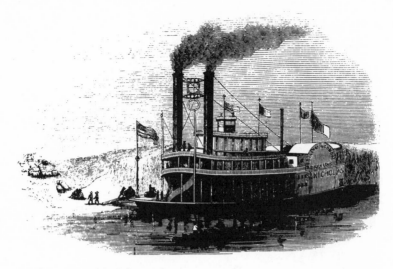

FIGURE 8.4. A mid-nineteenth-century representation of slaves loading cotton onto a river steamboat. Note that the cotton depot is located on the bluff above the river landing. Reproduced from *Harper's New Monthly Magazine* 18 (1858), p. 12.

dency. The town of Geneseo, Illinois, illustrates the point. This agricultural service town of 1,800 persons provided few job opportunities for women, and consequently the town's dependency ratio of 2.38 exceeded Chicago's by nearly 30 percent. If, however, we hypothetically introduce a female servant population equal to Chicago's (12 percent of its labor force), Geneseo's dependency ratio plummets to 1.98 as compared to Chicago's 1.93—a difference of nearly 30 percent reduces to a mere 2 to 3 percent. In a larger city such as Peoria, servant jobs became more numerous (roughly 12 percent of the labor force) and the dependency ratio was 1.98—a level that resembled Chicago's ratio as well as Geneseo's adjusted ratio. All of which suggests a migration flow of adolescent boys and girls from hinterland towns to the larger cities in the Chicago system where the labor market permitted them to achieve a greater degree of "independency."[52]

Matters were reversed in the cotton South. Dependency rates were higher in the city of Mobile (1.73) than in an interior river port such as Selma (1.57). In Selma, as well as Aberdeen, Mississippi, slave labor had effectively expelled unskilled whites, boys and girls, from the labor force and the dependent population as well. In Selma,

52. Above, see note 43.

TABLE 8.8

Occupational Structure in the Chicago and Mobile Urban Systems, *1860: Sample Towns*

(Percents)

	Commerce			Consumer goods and services				Artisans and manufacturers						Agric.	Others
	Merchants	Clerks	Transport	Prof.	Servants	Retail and others	Gov't.	Wood	Grain	Leather	Mechan.	Other	Laborers		
Chicago system															
Chicago (109,000)	8.4%	6.7%	9.2%	3.8%	12.1%	12.4%	1.0%	13.8%	.9%	2.1%	2.2%	1.1%	17.3%	.3%	.8%
Peoria (14,400)	8.3	6.1	7.3	3.8	11.6	11.9	1.2	17.8	3.0	1.8	2.2	1.1	17.3	.3	.8
Elgin (3,073)	7.9	4.1	2.5	7.7	15.9	7.2	.6	12.0	2.2	4.8	1.1	1.8	14.0	1.3	.5
Freeport (2,613)	10.0	4.6	4.6	6.3	10.7	7.9	1.1	15.9	2.0	3.2	2.3	1.2	13.3	8.6	.3
Geneseo (1,815)	10.8	4.1	1.7	7.4	3.0	7.3	.7	18.9	2.0	4.7	1.1	.1	20.5	3.8	.4
Griggsville (1,360)	7.4	3.1	4.5	11.1	3.4	5.1	1.2	17.9	1.7	4.3	1.7	.3	20.7	10.5	0.0
Mobile system															
Mobile (29,000)	—	15.5	—	—	.04	—	—	—	—	—	—	—	17.4	—	—
Selma (1,823 free)	11.1	15.5	3.9	8.6	.4	16.4	1.4	16.6	.4	3.7	5.0	1.1	1.0	4.7	1.4
Wetumpka (1,000 free)	14.4	13.8	1.9	7.4	0.0	5.8	.6	5.4	.3	1.9	.3	0.0	3.2	38.1	4.5
Elyton (603 free)	6.5	2.2	0.0	10.8	6.5	2.2	1.4	0.0	0.0	1.4	8.6	0.0	5.8	51.1	1.4

NOTE: For sources and an explanation of categories, see opposite.

white domestic servants and laborers constituted just 1.4 percent of the free labor force, and in Aberdeen they constituted just 2.6 percent. Just how nasty life could be for unskilled whites in the smaller cotton belt towns is dramatized by the hard plight of women in Aberdeen. They were preempted in domestic service by slave women; and though a few white women found work as teachers, seamstresses, and midwives, the leading occupation among Aberdeen's women was prostitution (4.7 percent).[53] Nor, in sharp contrast with their midwestern counterparts, were their prospects for employment improved by migration to Mobile.

Need we wonder about the lack of urbanism in the antebellum South? One can hardly imagine a more depressing place than the small town of the cotton belt. It offered nothing in the way of opportunities for unskilled yet ambitious white youths. Why, they might have wondered, should they live in a place in which slaves occupied all of the unskilled jobs, where living costs were exorbitant, and where, in the case of young women, their morality was too often compromised? But to ask the question was to answer it. For the unskilled immigrant as well as the rural white—especially those with families—avoiding the entrapment of life in these small towns and in the city of Mobile was the wisest and most rational course of action. It is

53. Federal Population Census Manuscripts, 1860. Also see Table 8.8. The theme of the limited opportunities for urban women in the South needs further development. Equally important is the limited number of positions open for women in small midwestern towns.

NOTE TO TABLE 8.8: Occupations are taken from the Federal Population Census Manuscripts, save for the partial data for Mobile provided by Herbert Gutman and Ira Berlin. For Chicago, I used a 10 percent sample; for Peoria, 20 percent; for Freeport, 50 percent; and for the remaining towns, 100 percent. The job classification is straightforward. Beginning from left to right: Commerce and Consumer Services could be aggregated to form an estimate of the service sector. Within these groups, merchants consisted of dealers, speculators, land agents, bankers and the like as well as merchants proper. Transport included teamsters, railroad men, drovers, steamboatmen and so forth. The category Retailing and others includes mainly retail and wholesale operations though it also includes services that did not fit into any other group. Artisans and Manufacturers are classed by the principal raw material with which they worked. Wood includes the construction industry as well as wagon makers, carpenters, ship carpenters, and so on. Laborers include day laborers but not farm laborers, who are placed under Agriculture. Servants include domestics, but not washerwomen and seamstresses who were placed in Retailing and Other. Once again, Mobile jobs are for the free population. Slave jobs are not recorded by the census. It appears that slaves filled jobs as servants and laborers, judging from the small proportion of freemen occupying these positions. For further detail on Mobile's occupational structure, see Amos, *Cotton City*, pp. 48–113.

in this depressing context of meager adolescent opportunity that the low ratio of dependents to labor force in the cities and towns of the cotton belt must be understood (see Table 8.8).[54]

Reflections

As children of an urban age, we have witnessed a geographic transformation of unprecedented proportion. Metropolitan areas are now home for eight of every ten Americans; farming is a distant and exotic way of life; and rural environs are quaint reminders of a world we have lost. Imagining what life was like before—when towns and cities were mere islands surrounded by a vast rural sea, when urban was subordinate to rural—is no mean feat.

Yet it is a feat worth undertaking for at least two reasons. The first is that in the history of the American city lies the origin of our urban age. The second is that historical restoration strips away all of the complexities of a modern society and exposes an America as vulnerable and as problematic as the developing economies of the contemporary third world. The spectacular growth of American cities in the nineteenth century is at once a preamble to our distinctive modern urban age and a humble postscript to our rather prosaic rural origins and our unusual good luck.

What we think about the nineteenth-century American city has been conditioned by our experiences with its successor. The conventional wisdom of an urban (and Keynesian) age is, of course, that the modern city originated in the wellsprings of an insatiable and accumulative consumer demand. Urban theory implicitly assumes that because, as Keynes claimed, consumer demand was the prime mover in the economic growth of nation-states, it must also have been the crucial factor in the growth of cities and urban systems. Riding Keynesian coattails, demand-led urban theory has swiftly achieved hegemony. But this theory has overextended its grasp; it presumes what should be proven. Assuming the condescending posture of metatheory, it stands above mere empirical tests and applies its arguments indiscriminately across time and space.

In the days before Robert Fogel and Stanley Engerman, Richard Easterlin, and Carl Degler, antebellum American history lent itself to the seductions of urban theory. Antebellum America, in those times,

---

54. Occupational structures in Table 8.8 are very similar, except in the categories of laborers and servants—jobs that were preempted by slaves in the southern urban system.

was a much simpler place. Scholars divided the nation into two contrasting geographical parts. The North was free, prosperous, and dynamic; the South was yoked to slavery, impoverished, and stifled by rampant inequality. These regional caricatures were ready-made for a demand-led theory of urban systems. They implied sizable regional variations in consumer demand, which in turn explained why northern cities, surrounded by high farm incomes and egalitarian income distributions, were large, while southern cities, blanketed by plantation poverty and inequality, were small.

Times and historical interpretations change. The new social and economic histories have blurred the old caricatures of antebellum North and South. They demonstrate more similarities than differences between these two regions—similarities in income, inequality, and capitalist motivation. Urban theory, meanwhile, seems to have marked time. Having insinuated its views into historical thought on antebellum economic development and urbanization circa the 1960s, demand-led urban theory has now come to seem a bit dated, overdrawn, and out of touch with the empirical data.

The increasing dissonance between urban theory and historical evidence has prompted a test of the sufficiency of demand-led theory in the antebellum urban context. The results, I believe, suggest the need for rethinking antebellum urbanization in particular and urban theory for developing economies in general. My inquiry on antebellum urbanization frames an explicit test of urban theory's sufficiency. Does that theory have the capacity to explain interregional differences in the size of cities and urban systems within a developing economy; or, in the antebellum context, does it explain why northern cities were large and southern ones small? A controlled comparison of the demography and economy of the urban systems of Chicago and Mobile circa 1860 demonstrates the insufficiency of mainstream urban theory. Statistical reconstruction of the two systems reveals similarities in incomes, income densities, wealth distributions (both were inegalitarian in that respect), and economic and employment bases. In none of these demand-side variables does the regional difference exceed 10 percent; indeed, in some variables, the direction of the evidence contradicts logical deductions from demand-led theory. Differences of this magnitude are insufficient as explanations of the twofold differentials in urban system labor forces and of the threefold differences in urban population.

Supply-side considerations offer a more powerful explanation of labor force differentials in the antebellum United States. There, as in developing economies generally, unskilled wages varied from one urban system to another as a consequence of economic opportunities in their tributary rural economies. The seasonal production rhythms of regional staples established distinctive regimes governing the demand for farm laborers and their earnings during the year. These earnings, in turn, served as the principal determinants of the transfer wage, which urban entrepreneurs were required to match in order to entice workers from seasonal employment in the country to year-round employment in the city. These regimes of rural opportunity varied considerably across the agrarian regions of antebellum America. In the Midwest, rural earnings were seasonal, confined principally to the four-month "crop season." Rural earnings thus were modest, and unskilled urban labor was correspondingly cheap. Southern urban labor, by contrast, was perhaps twice as expensive owing to the lengthier agricultural work season and the impressive rural opportunities for yeomen and overseers. Midwestern cities and towns thus were beneficiaries of an agricultural economy that created a cheap, easily mobilized labor force for deployment throughout Chicago's urban system. Precisely the opposite occurred in the cotton South, where the rural sector provided young men with an ample work year, unparalleled opportunities for economic advance, and little enthusiasm for life in southern towns and cities despite the high wages paid there.

Contrary to urban theory, it is supply-side factors that account for the large labor-force differentials in urban systems in the antebellum United States. Regional wage differentials alone account for 63 percent of the difference in the labor forces of Chicago and Mobile's urban systems; part-time and unpaid family workers "hidden" in the service sector account for another 20 percent. Demand contributes just 6 percent, while the rest (11 percent) is unexplained variance.

Our modern urban age traces its origins to rural America and to the cheap labor that certain of its regions supplied for the urban process. But antebellum urbanization equally involved the amassing of a vast dependent population of children, nonworking women, and the elderly. Indeed, of the total demographic differential in the urban systems of Chicago and Mobile, dependents accounted for three-fourths and the labor force only one-fourth. Chicago's attraction for dependents seems to have arisen from the ample opportunities it provided for adolescent employment and family income maximization. These in turn encouraged higher rates of fertility and in-migration of families with younger children, thus increasing rates of dependency among children below 15 years of age. This pattern of adolescent and family opportunity did not exist in the towns and cities of the cotton South. Urban slavery in the Mobile urban system stripped away the unskilled job market from white adolescents, increased the economic burden of child rearing, and discouraged native fertility and family in-migration. Southern urban systems thus confronted a double-barreled problem: labor costs were exceedingly high and adolescent employment opportunities were desperately low. The former constrained the growth of the labor force, the latter the growth of a dependent family population.

This tale of two cities has a larger moral. It is that urbanization in developing economies is a vastly more complex process than mainstream urban theory usually allows. Rethinking that process requires a revision of demand-led theory and reconsideration of oft-neglected factors on the supply side: of urban wage levels and their rural determinants in developing economies; of labor supply, adolescent employment opportunities, and family income maximization; and of derivative decisions on migration, fertility, and immigration. If this essay initiates that sort of rethinking, this tale of two cities will have served its purpose.

CHAPTER 9

The Split Geographical Personality of American Labor

Labor Power and Modernization in the Gilded Age

The American economy had entered a new and embattled age of industrial relations—or so it seemed to the U.S. Bureau of Labor in 1887. What most impressed the Bureau about this new age was neither the founding of the American Federation of Labor nor the vigorous expansion of the Knights of Labor; rather, it was the industrial strife and violence that had shattered any semblance of tranquility in relations between labor and capital. "The industrial disturbances which have been so frequent in this country since 1877," the youthful Bureau observed, "really establish the period as one of strikes and lockouts." These weapons of industrial conflict were not new, but what made them so notable was labor's use of them on an unprecedented scale and over a wide geographical range. The old age of labor relations had coped with dozens of strikes in a single year; the new age was perplexed by hundreds of conflicts, and then thousands, spreading across the map like some mysterious contagion. A nation enveloped in the strife between labor and capital can perhaps be excused for overlooking subtle geographical variations in industrial conflict.[1]

Nor were these variations a pressing matter for historians intent, with some justification, on capturing the contours of labor history until Herbert Gutman forcefully pointed out the consequences of

The original version of this chapter was co-authored with Sari Bennett.

1. *Third Annual Report of the Commissioner of Labor, 1887: Strikes and Lockouts* (Washington, D.C.: Government Printing Office, 1888), p. 9.

divorcing the labor movement from its roots in locality and community. In one of his most provocative, controversial, and pessimistic essays, he argued that labor power was inseparable from community and that both were diminished by the inexorable course of Gilded Age industrialization. Setting aside the institutionalists' concern with formal labor organization, Gutman discerned the foundations of labor power in the social structure of preindustrial communities. In times of strife, workers were sustained by the shared values that cut across the social classes of these communities. But change was relentless and less than benign. Industrialization, modernization, and urbanization ripped apart the fabric of preindustrial culture and, in so doing, set in motion the declension of labor power.[2]

Gutman's hypothesis of an inverse relationship between modernization and labor power encourages a systematic and long-overdue examination of the relations between power and place. Testing his proposition for the northeastern United States using the extraordinary strike reports compiled by the U.S. Bureau of Labor for the years 1881 to 1894 reveals that Gutman was only partially correct. Labor power was indeed lost, but it was also regained. His inverse rule applies in the smaller communities of the Northeast, but the decline of labor power halted and began to reverse in communities of 80,000 to 100,000 persons. That is to say that labor power was reconstituted in the region's larger industrial cities, a reversal that underlines the divergent worlds of labor in the Gilded Age. Of course, this model does not completely explain the local bases of labor power; the influence of additional structural variables on the exercise of labor power—labor organization, government, and capital—must be taken into account.[3]

2. Herbert G. Gutman, "The Workers' Search for Power: Labor in the Gilded Age," in *The Gilded Age: A Reappraisal*, ed. H. Wayne Morgan (Syracuse, N.Y.: Syracuse Univ. Press, 1963), pp. 38–68; *idem, Work, Culture and Society in Industrializing America* (New York: Knopf, 1976). For an extension of Gutman's ideas, see David Gordon, "Capitalist Development and the History of American Cities," in *Marxism and the Metropolis: New Perspectives in Urban Political Economy*, ed. William K. Tabb and Larry Sawers (New York: Oxford Univ. Press, 1978), pp. 21–63. Although Gutman reinvigorated the study of labor history by shifting attention from formal to informal sources of power, his theses proved unsettling to many scholars who shared his perspective on the new labor history. Particularly disturbing was the pessimism of a thesis that chronicled the loss of labor power and offered slim hope for its resurrection in the modern industrial milieu. For appreciation and critique, see David Montgomery, "Gutman's Nineteenth-Century America," *Labor History* 19 (1978), pp. 416–29; and David Brody, "The Old Labor History and the New: In Search of an American Working Class," *Labor History* 20 (1979), pp. 111–26.

3. *Third Annual Report of the Commissioner of Labor*, esp. p. 9; *Tenth Annual Report of the Commissioner of Labor, 1894: Strikes and Lockouts* (2 vols.; Washington, D.C.: Government

The strike reports of the Bureau of Labor are critical for the analysis of labor power in the Gilded Age. In their original form, these reports are of little geographical value. Although the Bureau paid attention to geography, reporting the locality of every strike, the utility of the reports is diminished by the Bureau's hierarchical classification of strikes by state, year, and industry. Strike localities, as a result, are scattered in many separate entries throughout the reports. For the present analysis, the strike records are reorganized according to specific locality (city or town) and county. The reorganization identifies 1,585 strike localities within the northeastern quadrant of the United States. Of these, I have determined the county for 1,511 and the population for 1,099 places. It is important for purposes of analysis to link strike records with a broad array of social and economic statistics. In this regard, the county offers a decisive advantage over the town or city as the unit of data collection. As the chief census unit of data collection, the county affords the opportunity of linking

---

Printing Office, 1896). On the establishment of the Bureau of Labor and precedent state bureaus, see *The First Annual Report of the Commissioner of Labor, March 1886: Industrial Depressions* (Washington, D.C.: Government Printing Office, 1886), pp. 5–8. Fifteen state bureaus were in existence in 1886; the first was established in Massachusetts in 1869. Jonathan Grossman, *The Department of Labor* (New York: Praeger, 1973); James Leiby, *Carroll Wright and Labor Reform: The Origin of Labor Statistics* (Cambridge, Mass.: Harvard Univ. Press, 1960); John I. Griffin, *Strikes: A Study in Quantitative Economics*, Columbia University Studies in History, Economics, and Public Law, No. 451 (New York: Columbia Univ. Press, 1939), pp. 15–36. Strike reports have been used at an aggregate rather than a local community level. The neglect of a geographic perspective on American labor reflects scholarly reliance upon trade-union views and sources, and it is apparent that the American Federation of Labor violently opposed the Knights of Labor's practice of organizing labor along geographical lines. Samuel Gompers declared his position in unequivocal terms: "During the early part of the year my attention was called to the fact that there was an effort being made to divide the labor movement of the country on geographical lines. This was studiously fomented and afterwards openly avowed. Steps were immediately taken to counteract the consummation of this suicidal policy, and it is a source of gratification to be enabled to state, that, at least for the time being, the evil sought to be accomplished has been laid at rest, let us hope, never again to be revived. The employing class, the wealth possessors, the corporate power of our country, allow no geographical lines to interfere with the recognition of the identity of their interests. In everything that affects them they stand like a unit. They do not allow mountains, mountain passes, or oceans to divide them. They recognize the identity of their interests, as attested by the unity of their direction, the solidarity of their action. . . . Our efforts and our hopes should not be circumscribed by cities, states, or geographical divisions of our country; our aim should be to unite the workers of our continent, and to strive to attain the unity, solidarity, and fraternity of the workers of the world." *Report of the 17th Annual Convention of the American Federation of Labor*, held at Nashville, Tenn., December 13–21, 1897. For an excellent bibliography on strikes, see the monumental study by Edward Shorter and Charles Tilly, *Strikes in France: 1830–1968* (New York: Cambridge Univ. Press, 1974).

strike data with population, manufacturing, occupation, and other socioeconomic information. Since these data are essential for interpreting variations in strike behavior, strikes are grouped by county.[4]

The Geography of Strikes: The Northeastern United States, 1881–94

In the two decades after 1875, Americans witnessed an unprecedented explosion of worker unrest; strikes multiplied from a mere handful to several thousand in a single year. The northeastern states alone reported 14,455 strikes between January 1881 and June 1894. Although worker protest seemed to sweep the nation, the geography of strikes resembled more nearly a patchwork. Some areas were strikeless; others reported sporadic strikes; and a small but important corpus of places reported disturbances so consistently and with such great frequency as to warrant the label strike-prone (see Figure 9.1).[5]

Strikeless areas were more numerous than might be supposed, encompassing nearly half of all northeastern counties. But the distribution of strikeless counties within the Northeast was uneven. In the area's eastern parts, in general, there were few strikeless counties—they comprised no more than 10 to 20 percent of the counties in the lower New England states, New York, and Pennsylvania. Westward, however, the proportion of strikeless counties increased to 38

4. This analysis is confined to the years 1881 to 1894 because an exceptionally detailed record of strikes by locality exists for those years. Thereafter, the Bureau streamlined the records and abandoned the practice of reporting strikes by locality. Furthermore, the analysis is confined to the northeastern United States—roughly a rectangle with corners at Maine, Maryland, Missouri, and Minnesota. This choice reflects the fact that 90 percent of the strikes that occurred between 1881 and 1894 took place within these bounds. Finally, at the risk of masking temporal changes, strikes have been aggregated for the period in order to ensure a sufficient number of strikes for the statistical analysis of a large number of localities. The use of the county as the principal unit of analysis is a compromise. The unit has the virtue of allowing linkage to a wider array of explanatory structural data. This virtue outweighs the principal disadvantage of the county—that it obscures intra-county variations, particularly in counties containing several cities, such as those in New England. Scholars interested in strikes elsewhere in the nation should begin with *Historical Atlas of the United States* (Washington, D.C.: National Geographic Society, 1988), pp. 160–61.

5. A strike is defined as a work stoppage occurring within a particular locality—a definition that is consistent with the Bureau of Labor's usage and its data collection procedures. On these procedures, see *Third Annual Report of the Commissioner of Labor*, pp. 9–33; and *Tenth Annual Report of the Commissioner of Labor*, Vol. 1, pp. 9–32. According to David Montgomery, "the strike statistics collected by the U.S. Commissioner of Labor for the years 1881 to 1905 are, on the whole, both comprehensive and reliable." See his "Strikes in Nineteenth-Century America," *Social Science History* 4 (1980), pp. 81–104, esp. p. 86.

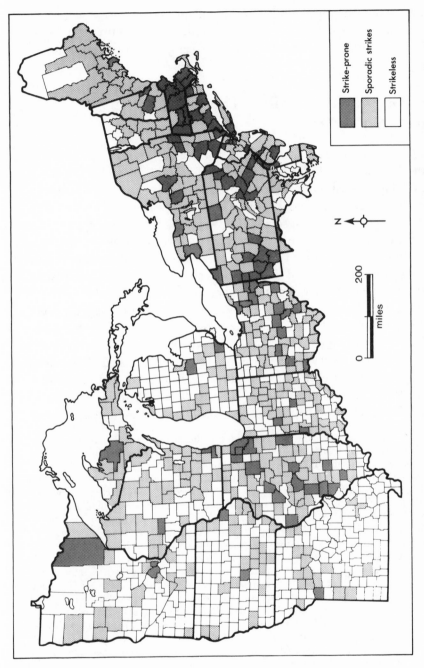

FIGURE 9.1. A Typology of Strike Frequency by County in the Northeastern United States, 1881–94. Strike-prone counties report strikes in nine or more years in the period. Sources: *Third Annual Report of the Commissioner of Labor, 1887*; *Tenth Annual Report of the Commissioner of Labor, 1894*.

percent in Ohio; approached 50 percent in Indiana, Illinois, and Wisconsin; and exceeded 70 percent in the remainder of the Midwest. Between the extremes of strikeless and strike-prone areas were those sections of the Northeast in which strikes occurred sporadically. Two-fifths of the region's counties experienced some form of strike action in eight or fewer of the fourteen years covered by this essay. Collectively, these 400 or so counties contributed only 15 percent of the region's strikes. At the final extreme were 112 strike-prone counties, which, although they accounted for little more than 10 percent of all northeastern counties, reported 85 percent of all strikes between 1881 and 1894 (see Figures 9.1 and 9.2). Indeed, nearly half of all strikes took place in just eight large urban counties. The boroughs of New York City led the way with 23 percent of the region's strikes, followed by Cook County (Chicago), Kings County (Brooklyn), Allegheny County (Pittsburgh), Philadelphia County, Essex County (Lynn, Massachusetts, and others), Suffolk County (Boston), and Hamilton County (Cincinnati).[6]

The geography of strike-prone areas closely corresponds with concentrations of population and industry in the northeastern states. These areas of recurrent worker protest stretched over the industrializing regions of lower New England, New York City, northern New Jersey, and eastern and western Pennsylvania. They extended also into the iron and steel district of eastern Ohio. Scattered strike-prone patches appeared almost everywhere else, especially along the Hudson-Mohawk corridors and in the Midwest, where strike-prone counties tended to occupy isolated urban centers and mining communities.

Industrial conflict, if not ubiquitous, was certainly widespread. Strikes took root to some degree in about half of the counties of the Northeast, and the rapidity with which they spread implies the presence of conditions conducive to strikes. In the areas engaging in strike actions, protest diffused in three waves (see Figures 9.3 and 9.4). Saturation—when strike actions had diffused to 80 percent or more of a state's striking counties—occurred by 1884 in southern New England; between 1886 and 1890 in northern New England, Pennsylvania, and New York; and between 1890 and 1894 in the remainder of the Northeast.

These diffusion waves differed in timing, but in each wave strikes

6. Space precludes presentation of the complete list of localities and counties and their strike records; a short list of strike-prone counties, however, appears in Appendix Table 9A.

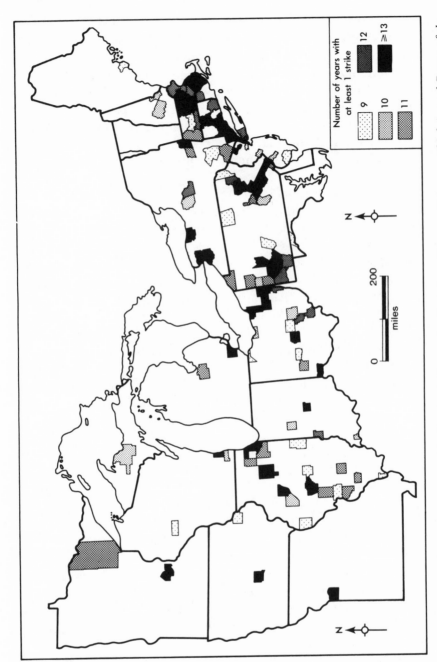

FIGURE 9.2. Annual Frequency of Strikes in Strike-prone Counties, 1881–94. Sources: *Third Annual Report of the Commissioner of Labor, 1887; Tenth Annual Report of the Commissioner of Labor, 1894.*

Number of years with at least 1 strike

9
10
11
12
≥13

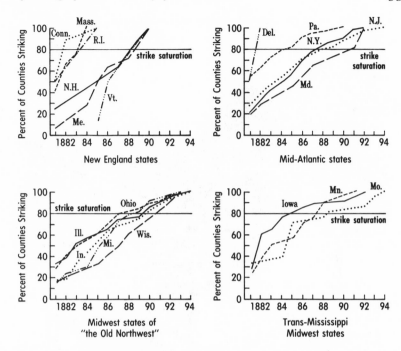

FIGURE 9.3. Strike Diffusion and Strike Saturation in the Northeastern United States, by Region and State, 1881–94. Sources: *Third Annual Report of the Commissioner of Labor, 1887*; *Tenth Annual Report of the Commissioner of Labor, 1894.*

spread in the same three ways: via the urban system, via contagion (the spread of strike behavior from initial strike sites to adjacent counties), and via unique local conditions (see Figure 9.5). Strike diffusion through the urban system seems to have been especially rapid. Of 95 northeastern counties containing cities of 20,000 or more, 62 percent registered strikes in the first year of record (1881) and 85 percent did so by 1883 (which suggests broadly similar structural conditions throughout the urban Northeast). The large city thus was a particularly congenial location for worker protest. Strikes occurred there rapidly and with some spontaneity. The correlation between strikes and cities weakens noticeably, however, below a population level of 20,000. Whereas 99 percent of all large cities (with populations exceeding 20,000) reported strikes at some time between 1881 and 1894, the proportion dropped to 91.6 percent among cities of 10,000 to 20,000; to 68 percent for towns of 5,000 to 10,000; and to just 38 percent for towns of 2,500 to 5,000 (see Table 9.1). If strikes did not fully penetrate the lower reaches of the urban hierarchy, they did achieve some surprising successes in America's

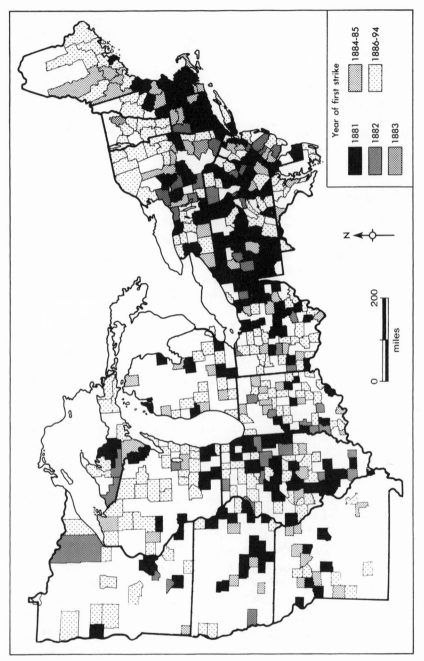

FIGURE 9.4. The Spatial Pattern of Strike Diffusion in the Northeastern United States, 1881–94. Strike actions came earliest and were most widespread in the New England and Mid-Atlantic regions as well as in eastern Ohio and Illinois. Sources: *Third Annual Report of the Commissioner of Labor, 1887; Tenth Annual Report of the Commissioner of Labor, 1894.*

Year of first strike

1881
1882
1883
1884-85
1886-94

N

0   200
miles

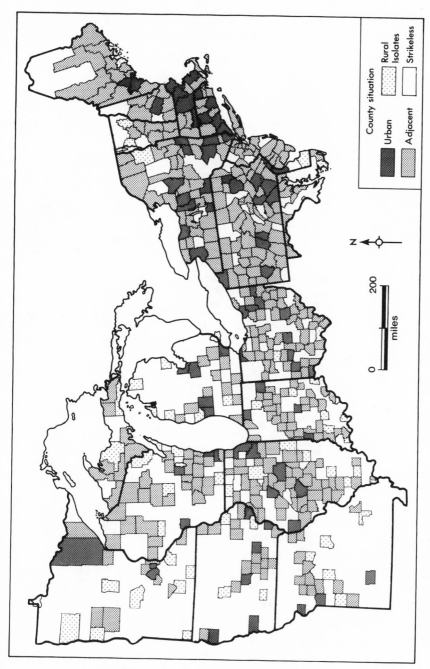

FIGURE 9.5. Probable Channels of Strike Diffusion in the Northeastern United States, 1881–94. Urban settings and contagious diffusion of protest from them to adjacent counties account for three-fourths of all counties reporting strikes. Sources: *Third Annual Report of the Commissioner of Labor, 1887; Tenth Annual Report of the Commissioner of Labor, 1894.*

County situation

Urban

Adjacent

Rural
Isolates

Strikeless

N

0   200

miles

TABLE 9.1

Percent of Towns Having Strikes, by Population Size Classes: Northeastern States

	1890[a] Urban Population Classes				All Towns
	2,500–5,000	5,000–10,000	10,000–20,000	20,000+	
Northeastern States	37.1(596)	68.9(289)	91.6(143)	99.2(121)	58.4(1,149)
Maine	24.2 (32)	76.9 (13)	100.0 (2)	100.0 (2)	40.7 (59)
New Hampshire	50.0 (18)	66.7 (6)	100.0 (3)	100.0 (1)	57.1 (28)
Vermont	12.5 (16)	33.3 (6)	50.0 (2)	0.0 (0)	20.8 (24)
Massachusetts	42.9 (77)	69.7 (33)	89.5 (19)	100.0 (20)	62.4 (149)
Rhode Island	25.0 (8)	33.3 (9)	50.0 (2)	75.0 (4)	39.1 (23)
Connecticut	36.8 (38)	77.8 (18)	87.5 (7)	100.0 (5)	58.0 (69)
New York	38.5 (52)	85.7 (35)	82.4 (18)	100.0 (18)	67.2 (122)
New Jersey	38.1 (21)	90.1 (11)	100.0 (9)	100.0 (7)	70.8 (48)
Pennsylvania	45.3 (75)	77.8 (36)	93.3 (15)	100.0 (16)	64.8 (142)
Delaware	50.0 (2)	0.0 (0)	0.0 (0)	100.0 (1)	66.7 (3)
Maryland	25.0 (8)	50.0 (2)	100.0 (2)	100.0 (1)	46.2 (13)
District of Columbia	0.0 (0)	0.0 (0)	0.0 (0)	100.0 (1)	100.0 (1)
Ohio	42.9 (56)	51.7 (29)	100.0 (13)	100.0 (10)	58.5 (106)
Indiana	25.8 (31)	83.3 (18)	87.5 (8)	100.0 (6)	57.1 (63)
Illinois	47.7 (44)	81.3 (16)	93.3 (15)	100.0 (6)	67.1 (82)
Michigan	29.0 (31)	55.6 (18)	77.8 (9)	100.0 (6)	50.0 (64)
Wisconsin	43.5 (23)	80.0 (15)	100.0 (8)	100.0 (4)	68.0 (50)
Minnesota	50.0 (12)	66.7 (6)	100.0 (2)	100.0 (3)	65.2 (23)
Iowa	22.2 (26)	50.0 (8)	100.0 (5)	100.0 (6)	44.4 (45)
Missouri	17.9 (28)	18.2 (11)	100.0 (3)	100.0 (3)	29.5 (44)

[a] Numbers in parentheses indicate the number of towns in the stated size class.

towns. The states of New Hampshire, Massachusetts, Pennsylvania, Ohio, Illinois, Wisconsin, and Minnesota reported strikes in more than 40 percent of their small towns (those with a population of less than 5,000). New Jersey reported strikes in over 90 percent of its larger towns of 5,000 and 10,000.

Whereas strikes appeared early and spontaneously in cities and large towns, worker protest spread more slowly into adjacent counties—a pattern that geographers label "contagious diffusion." In 340 counties, strikes were reported only after a neighboring county had engaged in a strike action (see Figure 9.5). In the remaining 154 counties, neither urban influence nor contagion operated. The independent origins of their strikes warrant classifying them as isolated from the diffusion process.

In summary, strikes erupted in three distinct geographic contexts. Sixteen percent of all strike counties contained cities of 20,000 or more, which suggests an urban setting for strike behavior; 58 percent involved contagious diffusion from adjacent strike areas (usually urban); and 26 percent were isolated from the influences of large

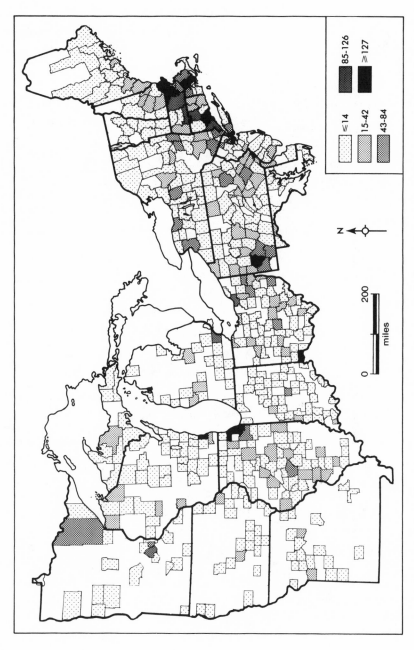

FIGURE 9.6. Strike Frequency in the Northeastern United States, by County, 1881–94. Note the high correlation between worker protest and industrial-urban centers especially in New England and the Mid-Atlantic states. Sources: *Third Annual Report of the Commissioner of Labor, 1887; Tenth Annual Report of the Commissioner of Labor, 1894.*

≤14

15-42

43-84

85-126

≥127

N

200

0

miles

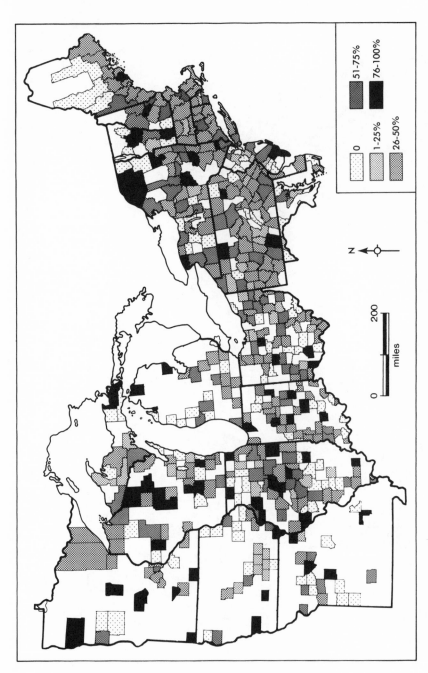

FIGURE 9.7. Fully and Partially Successful Strikes as a Proportion of all Strikes in the Northeastern United States, by County, 1881-94. Strike actions in large urban-industrial centers were moderately successful; strikes more often achieved their goals in rural or modestly urban counties. Sources: *Third Annual Report of the Commissioner of Labor, 1887*; *Tenth Annual Report of the Commissioner of Labor, 1894*.

0

1-25%

26-50%

51-75%

76-100%

N

200

0

miles

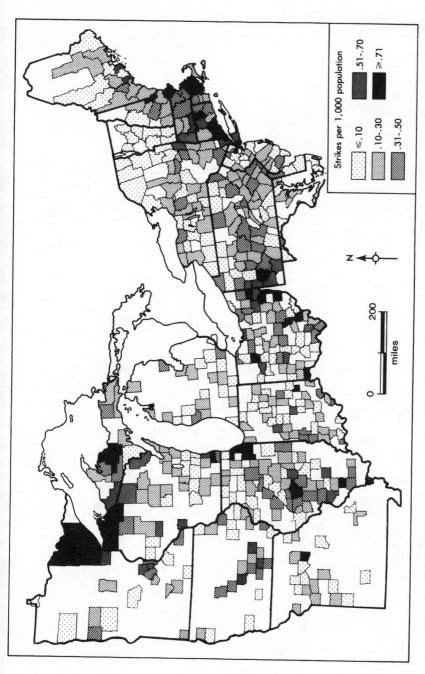

FIGURE 9.8. Strike Rates per 1,000 persons in the Northeastern United States, by County, 1881–94. Unlike the count of strike frequency, a strike rate permits comparison across counties by holding population constant. The strike rate is positively correlated with urbanization, though not as closely as is the case for strike frequency reported in Figure 9.6. Sources: *Third Annual Report of the Commissioner of Labor, 1887*; *Tenth Annual Report of the Commissioner of Labor, 1894*.

Strikes per 1,000 population

≤.10   .51–.70
.10–.30   ≥.71
.31–.50

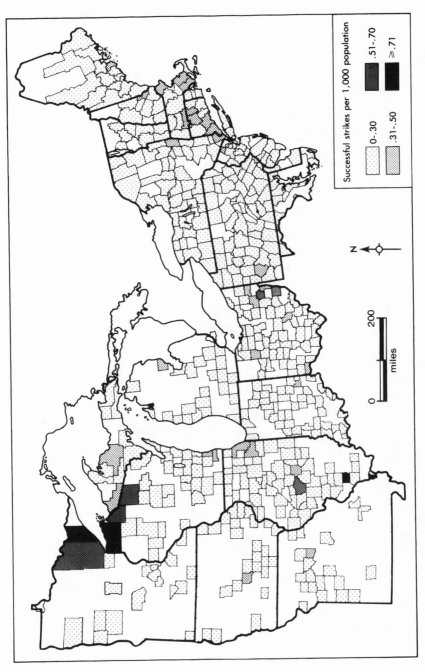

FIGURE 9.9. Successful Strike Rates per 1,000 persons in the Northeastern United States, by County, 1881–94. Although most counties report a low rate of successful strikes, counties which reported a high rate of strikes (Figure 9.8) tended to be more successful. Sources: *Third Annual Report of the Commissioner of Labor, 1887*; *Tenth Annual Report of the Commissioner of Labor, 1894*.

Successful strikes per 1,000 population

0–.30
.31–.50
.51–.70
≥.71

cities or contagious diffusion—most of these occupying scattered locations such as the coal mining areas of southern Illinois and south central Iowa or the metallic mining districts of Michigan, Wisconsin, and Minnesota.

If the pattern of strike diffusion is fairly straightforward, the reverse is the case with respect to patterns of strike frequency, relative strike success, and rates of striking and strike success. These patterns defy easy description. But the maps in Figures 9.6–9.9, along with the preceding discussion of strike diffusion, do suggest two points about worker protest: that strikes were associated with population, or what might be called "the scale of community"; and that strikes were unusually concentrated in large urban counties. These rudimental relationships between power and place, between strikes and the scale of community, lend themselves to analysis by linear regression. This statistical model offers, in addition to a concise description of these relationships, a rigorous empirical test of Gutman's inverse rule of labor power and preindustrial culture.

A Test of Gutman's Inverse Rule of Labor Power

The Gutman hypothesis suggests that labor power varies inversely with modernization. His inverse rule can be tested if an agreement is reached on operational measures for these concepts. In his discussion of modernization, Gutman contrasts preindustrial and industrial communities. Preindustrial communities preserved a more traditional set of values concerning worth and society. Despite a class structure typical of capitalist economies, these communities were more conducive settings for the exercise of labor power. Because they were relatively small, their life was more intimate, and their heterogeneous mixture of residences and workplaces muted class differences to the extent that the several classes concerned themselves as much with community welfare as with the exclusive well-being of their particular class. All of these factors allegedly contributed to the power of the worker. But as these small towns and cities grew into larger industrial centers, the expanding scale of community isolated workers, hardened class lines, and weakened workers' influence over their jobs and communities.[7]

The test of Gutman's inverse rule requires operational measures

7. Gutman, "The Worker's Search for Power," pp. 31–54.

TABLE 9.2

Correlation Coefficients of Strikes with City Size

(all places with recorded population)

	City Size					
	≤ 2,500	2,500–5,000	5,001–10,000	10,001–25,000	25,000–50,000	>50,000
Strike frequency	.157(412)**	.159(235)*	.148(194)*	.258(160)**	.162(47)	.852(45)
Successful strike frequency	.093(412)	.081(235)	.157(194)*	.228(160)**	.084(47)	.813(45)
Strike rate	.425(412)	.034(235)	.084(194)	.093(160)	.088(47)	.357(45)
Successful strike rate	.275(412)**	.032(235)	.041(194)	.017(160)	.138(47)	.475(45)

NOTE: Number of observations are in parentheses. Two asterisks indicate the F-ratio is significant at the one percent level, one asterisk at the five percent level. Successful strikes include both successful and partly successful strikes.

for his concepts of modernization and labor power. In the first instance, modernization is synonymous with industrialization, which, in turn, is highly correlated with population (or scale). Community scale, therefore, serves as an appropriate proxy for Gutman's notion of modernization. In the second instance, Gutman's discussion of labor power is consistent with the definition commonly used in the social sciences. Power, an elusive concept, involves the capacity to influence others and to effect outcomes favorable to those who exercise it. The standard ways of measuring community power by examining local decisions or community ratings of influential persons are impractical for a historical study of hundreds of communities. A simpler and more efficient measure of labor power—and one that is consistent with Gutman's discussion—is community strike behavior. This surrogate for labor power is not unambiguous, however. Imagine a community in which labor has so much power that it exercises influence without resorting to the strike. In this situation, the number of strikes would give a false impression of labor's power. But cases of this sort are rare. The covert exercise of power is the exception rather than the rule in the history of American labor. If strikes truly underestimated labor power, the effects would have been most noticeable in the smaller preindustrial communities. Our results do not show this to have been the case; indeed, they suggest precisely the opposite conclusion.[8]

On the assumption that strike behavior is indicative of labor power in the Gilded Age, we can proceed to a test of Gutman's inverse rule. It seems clear to me that Gutman was not concerned with the sheer frequency of strikes. Numerous tests have demonstrated the obvious and trivial conclusion that strike frequency increases with population. In the northeastern United States, the correlation coefficient between strike frequency and size of place is very strong ($r = .85$) for cities of 50,000 or more and resembles Shorter and Tilly's findings for French strikes. Below that level, relationships are weak and insignificant (see Table 9.2). Virtually the same results apply when successful strike frequencies are analyzed as the dependent variable ($r = .81$).[9]

8. Gutman's equation of labor power with strikes is suggested by David Montgomery, who observes that Gutman's early work "moved from the question of *power* (*who won the strike?*) to that of culture (what values made people stand with or against the industrial capitalists?)" (my emphasis). Montgomery, "Gutman's Nineteenth-Century America," p. 419.

9. Successful strikes here include completely and partly successful work stoppages; the latter are included as successful because even partial success constituted a victory for labor. On scale effects in French strikes, Shorter and Tilly present a correlation coefficient

Gutman envisioned a more sophisticated notion of labor power—one based upon relative rather than absolute measures, upon rates rather than frequencies. He had in mind a concept of labor power that could be compared across communities of various sizes; the use of strike rates per 1,000 persons permits such a comparison for the smallest and largest places. But the results of correlating strike rates and community size tend to run counter to Gutman's inverse rule. First, the signs of the coefficients are positive, rather than negative as Gutman's rule predicts. And second, the correlation coefficients are moderately strong for cities of more than 50,000 and towns of less than 2,500, but they are insignificant for intermediate towns (see Table 9.2). The modesty of the regression coefficients further implies a great deal of unsystematic variation in the strike-rate data, very little of which seems to be explicable by community-scale effects. The inclusion of thousands of small places with infrequent strikes occurring in a random fashion tends to wash out systematic relationships. The "noise" introduced by strikeless and sporadic-strike areas can be reduced by restricting analysis to the 112 strike-prone counties.

The Scale Reversal of Labor Power in the Gilded Age

A new relationship, and one that salvages some of Gutman's insights, emerges from the examination of only the strike-prone counties. The association between population and strike rates in these counties is curved rather than linear. Strike rates vary inversely among small counties—as Gutman theorized—to an inflection point at a population level of about 85,000, at which point strike rates reverse their decline and increase directly with population. For convenience of analysis, the curve has been broken into two segments—small and large places—and the simple linear regression results are presented in Table 9.3. The table shows that both strike rates and success rates vary inversely among the smaller counties (less than 85,000 people), with strike rates having a stronger association with scale. For the larger counties, the association of scale and strike rates is positive and considerably stronger than the small-county association. In addition, the rate of successful strikes is more closely correlated with scale than is the strike rate.

---

of .84 between strike frequency and the size of the industrial labor force—an indicator of scale. Shorter and Tilly, *Strikes in France*, pp. 284–305.

TABLE 9.3

Correlation Coefficients of Strikes with County Size, Strike-Prone Counties

	Counties ≤ 85,000 pop.			Counties > 85,000 pop.		
	r	r^2	n	r	r^2	n
Strike frequency	+.330*	.109	58	+.852**	.726	54
Successful strike frequency	+.304*	.092	58	+.804**	.646	54
Strike rate	−.485**	.235	58	+.617**	.381	54
Successful strike rate	−.334*	.112	58	+.657**	.432	54

NOTE: Two asterisks indicate the F-ratio is significant at the one percent level, one asterisk at the five percent level. Successful strikes include both successful and partly successful strikes.

This "scale reversal" of strike rates at the level of 85,000 has important implications for social history and for amendments in Gutman's inverse rule of labor power. The curvilinear trajectory suggests that labor power was weakest among intermediate-size cities and counties (with populations of about 85,000). In Gutman's terms, these transitional places seem to have been suspended between two cultures—between a smaller, intimate preindustrial era and an impersonal industrial age. As the scale of community increased, the preindustrial cultural foundations of labor power began to crumble. Then, at the critical point of inflection, labor power reemerged as cities moved toward metropolitan status and as labor power drew strength, presumably, from increasing numbers of workers and union organization. This hypothesis—that modernization and its concomitants were responsible for the breakdown of preindustrial labor power and its reformation through formally organized institutions in urban industrial centers—offers a plausible explanation for the scale reversal in labor's power in the Gilded Age, and it has the added virtue of reconciling the institutional and societal interpretations of American labor history. Yet the argument invites more rigorous tests.[10]

Structural Determinants of Labor Power

Although simple regression models identify an important scale reversal of labor power during the Gilded Age, the variations in power are sufficiently complex that a single variable (in this case population) provides very limited explanatory power. Other factors were involved and a comprehensive interpretation must allow for the

10.   The scale reversal of strike rates is discernible, albeit less clearly, in the French strike rate data for 1910–14. Strike rates were lowest in cities of 50,000 to 75,000. Shorter and Tilly, *Strikes in France*, p. 277.

interplay of a variety of intervening structural variables. Four classes of variables are germane: the role of formal labor organizations; labor market characteristics; capital; and government. The ensuing multiple regression analysis incorporates these factors in the form of eighteen structural variables. While space precludes a detailed discussion of these variables, in every case plausible arguments can be made for their inclusion in an analysis of labor power. (See Appendix Table 9B for a detailed list of the independent variables.) The dependent variable in the multiple regression model, of course, is labor power as measured by the surrogate of strike rates. The empirical tests are conducted with data from 111 strike-prone counties (Washington, D.C., is omitted because of insufficient data on all variables) for the years 1881 to 1894. Since this analysis seeks clarification of the processes underlying the scale reversal of labor power, the study is conducted in two parts: one covers small preindustrial communities of fewer than 85,000, the other large industrial places of over 85,000 (see Table 9.4).

These analyses improve our explanation of the dual nature of labor power in the Gilded Age. The model is most effective for the industrial society of the Northeast, where it accounts for 65 percent of the variance in labor power, as compared with about 50 percent for the preindustrial communities. Moreover, the model nicely discriminates between these two worlds of American labor.

Among large industrial cities, four variables emerge as significant determinants of labor power: population, manufacturing wages, industrial concentration, and skilled-unskilled wage ratios, in that order. Population and manufacturing wages exercise the most impact, doubling the effects of the other significant determinants. That labor power increased with population and wages is hardly surprising. The connection with population merely reaffirms, in a multivariant context, the scale reversal identified earlier. As for the favorable effect of high wages on labor activism, that association has been amply documented for other times and places.[11] Well-paid workers, per-

11. See Robert N. Stearn, "Intermetropolitan Patterns of Strike Frequency," *Industrial and Labor Relations Review* 29 (1976), pp. 218–35; Peter Schmidt and Robert P. Strauss, "The Effects of Unions on Earnings and Earnings on Unions: A Mixed Logit Approach," *International Economic Review* 17 (1976), pp. 204–12; Lung-Fei Lee, "Unionism and Wage Rates: A Simultaneous Equations Model with Qualitative and Limited Dependent Variables," *International Economic Review* 19 (1978), pp. 415–43; Lawrence M. Kahn, "Unionism and Relative Wages: Direct and Indirect Effects," *Industrial and Labor Relations Review* 32 (1979), pp. 520–32; and Barry T. Hirsch, "The Determinants of Unionization: An Analysis of Interarea Differences," *Industrial and Labor Relations Review*, 33 (1980), pp. 147–61.

TABLE 9.4

Multiple Regressions
Strike-Prone Counties, 1881–94

(*Dependent variable = strike rate per 1,000 population*)

Counties with >85,000 Population		(n = 53[a])
Variables[b]		
	Intercept −0.064	
WG	.485[†]	
PP	.476[†]	
CN	.255[†]	
WR	−.193*	
Multiple *R*		.806
Multiple *R²*		.649
Counties with <85,000 Population		(n = 58)
Variables[b]		
	Intercept 1.616	
WG	.734[†]	
PP	−.480[†]	
KL	.325[†]	
EMGE	.307[†]	
WVA	−.306[†]	
Multiple *R*		.700
Multiple *R²*		.490

NOTE: Coefficients with an asterisk are significant at the 5 percent level; those with a dagger are significant at the 10 percent level.

[a] Due to incomplete data, Washington, D.C. was omitted from the analysis.

[b] Variables include: WG = wages per manufacturing employee, 1890; PP = county population, 1890; CN = percentage of manufacturing labor force employed in largest industry, 1880; WR = ratio of skilled to unskilled wages, 1880; KL = Knights of Labor membership (1883) as a percentage of manufacturing labor force, 1880; EMGE = average number of employees per manufacturing establishment, 1880; WVA = wages as a percentage of value added by manufacturing, 1890. See Appendix Table 9B for a complete list of variables used in the multiple regressions.

haps because they have secure savings and because they are essential for uninterrupted factory operation, are more likely to engage in strikes than are workers on the margin of subsistence.

The role of industrial concentration (the proportion of workers employed by the leading industry) as a determinant of strike propensity is also confirmed by the literature on strikes. My conclusion that labor power tended to rise with industrial concentration during the Gilded Age echoes the findings of Clark Kerr and Abraham Siegel in their famous paper on strike propensity in the twentieth century. Industrial concentration, they theorize, isolates workers within a particular industry, and the commonality of experience and the cohesion that it produces foster an increase in strike propensity. Yet I am reluctant to impose this modern thesis on the past, at least without some qualification. Gilded Age workers rarely constituted an "isolated mass" in the sense meant by Kerr and Siegel. Levels of industrial concentration almost always fell below 50 percent and a single company rarely dominated a city's employment. A more plausible interpretation is that industrial concentration, in addition to guaranteeing shared grievances among a substantial number of workers, increased their leverage and their willingness to strike. If workers were fired for striking, they readily found employment with another community firm in the same industry (provided, of course, that firms did not blacklist workers).[12]

The final determinant of urban labor power is the wage ratio of skilled and unskilled labor. Power increased when the wage ratio was low, which suggests that a convergence of the economic interests of skilled and unskilled labor created a broad and more united front for labor unrest. Although the gap between skilled and unskilled wages was typically wide in the nineteenth-century United States, the ratio tended to narrow during the 1870s and 1880s, and this convergence of wages and class interests significantly augmented labor power in the industrial cities of the northeastern United States.[13]

Counterpoised to these determinants of worker protest are certain conspicuous variables that had surprisingly trivial effects on the exercise of labor power in industrial cities. Prominent among these insignificant variables is formal labor organization. Although one would expect that organized labor would have augmented labor power during the Gilded Age, my analysis runs counter to that expectation. Neither union organization, as measured by the proportion of strikes ordered by unions, nor Knights of Labor membership contributed significantly to labor power in large cities. If anything, the negative sign attached to the regression coefficient of union organization suggests that organized labor was a handicap to worker power in industrial cities. Why was this so? A provisional line of argument, consistent with much current work on the labor move-

12. Clark Kerr and Abraham Siegel, "The Interindustry Propensity to Strike: An Interpretation," in Arthur Kornhauser, Robert Dubin, and Arthur M. Ross, eds., *Industrial Conflict* (New York: McGraw-Hill, 1954), pp. 189–212. See also Shorter and Tilly, *Strikes in France*, pp. 284–95.

13. The wage ratio in the United States was considerably larger than the British ratio. I suspect that the greater convergence in Britain contributed significantly to class consciousness and to the emergence of a labor party. For discussion of the sources of these international differences, see Chapter 5. For later periods, see E. H. Phelps-Brown, *A Century of Pay: The Course of Pay and Production in France, Germany, Sweden, the United Kingdom, and the United States of America, 1860–1960* (London: Macmillan, 1968), pp. 46–48. For further discussion of the impact of the wage ratio on labor power, see Chapter 11, as well as Gerald Friedman, "Strike Success and Union Ideology: The United States and France, 1880–1914," *Journal of Economic History* 48 (1988), pp. 1–25.

ment, is that formal labor organizations in the 1880s encountered considerable opposition from employers as strike issues shifted from wages to the organization of workers and work rules. Unions temporarily sacrificed the immediate gratification of exercising labor power over wage issues to achieve the long-run objective of recognition as the representatives of various craft and industrial workers. Consequently, while the labor movement in the Gilded Age offered a hint of modern industrial relations, the exercise of labor power was not yet synonymous with union power.[14]

The impacts of government (police expenditures by municipal governments per capita) and ethnicity (the proportion of foreign-born) on labor power were also statistically unimportant. Historians' preoccupation with formal labor organization, government institutions, and ethnicity in the discussion of labor power during the Gilded Age is, therefore, a matter of misplaced emphasis. The decisive determinants of urban labor power resided, as we have seen, within the labor market (wages and wage ratios) and the workplace (city size and industrial concentration).

Elsewhere, in the preindustrial communities of the northeastern United States, the sources of labor power were quite different. Power diminished as these communities modernized and approached populations of about 85,000. This declension in labor power was offset, however, by certain key structural factors. Workers preserved a mod-

14. Assessing the role of union organization for labor power is made particularly difficult by the qualitative shift in the nature and causes of strikes during the mid-1880s. See Jon Amsden and Stephen Brier, "Coal Miners on Strike: The Transformation of Strike Demands and the Formation of a National Union," *Journal of Interdisciplinary History* 7 (1977), pp. 585–616. The dissociation between unions and labor power that my analysis suggests may obscure this qualitative change in the nature of strikes. A thorough analysis of these changes is beyond the scope of this paper, but the reader can consult another study that bears on this issue. That study attempts to compare labor power before and after 1887, when the causes of strikes shifted proportionately from wages to union recognition. Unions during the earlier "wages" period were modestly associated with labor power (the zero-order correlation coefficient being .298). The relationship was weak, except in large midwestern cities, where the coefficient rose to nearly .800. After 1887, when union issues rose to prominence, the overall relationship between unions and power remained about the same, but the midwestern association weakened while the eastern association grew stronger. The existence of regional variations suggests the possibility that unions in the eastern cities initially took up the tough battle of union recognition while those in midwestern cities focused on the easier wage issues. The eastern unions thus might have laid the groundwork for later successes that eluded the labor movement in the Midwest. The timing is consistent with the post-1886 strategy of the American Federation of Labor discussed in Chapter 10 and the divergence of wages discussed in Chapter 11. See also Sari Bennett and Carville Earle, "Labour Power and Locality in the Gilded Age: The Northeastern United States, 1881–1894," *Histoire Sociale—Social History* 15 (1982), pp. 383–405.

icum of power in communities where manufacturing wages were high and the wage share of value added in manufacturing was low; where firms were large; and where the Knights of Labor were active. In this preindustrial world, labor power was on the wane; yet even as power was lost, labor was able to muster strength where wages were good and where large firms paid labor a small share of overall output. The small wage share in particular served as an important rallying issue during the Gilded Age and was used with some success by the Knights of Labor. Aiming their campaign at all wage earners, the Knights repeatedly emphasized the inequities of wage shares and income distribution in a capitalist society. Their argument held a special appeal for the working class in preindustrial America.

Gilded Age industrialization thus split the American laboring classes into two distinct geographical worlds. In one world, workers gained power from the increasing complexity and scale of the industrial city; in the other, they surrendered power as their small communities were inundated by successive waves of industrial expansion. In the world of big cities, formal labor organizations counted for little; in small towns and communities, the Knights of Labor salvaged a measure of power for labor in decline. In big cities, labor benefited from industrial concentration; in small places, large firms facilitated similar ends. In large cities, the convergence of wages and economic interests fostered strike activity; while in small cities, the inequity in labor's share of income augmented labor power. Workers seeking power thus were compelled to come to grips with the contrarieties of their two worlds. That they ultimately failed to resolve these differences in a united working-class politics is testament to the immensity of their task.

Labor power was lost and regained in the transformation of the United States from a preindustrial to an industrial nation. During the Gilded Age, that transformation created a dual society in the northeastern United States, where industrialization advanced most vigorously. Inevitably, the American labor movement reflected this duality. In the smaller cities and towns, the Knights of Labor presided over the dismantling of preindustrial society; at best, they mitigated the inexorable declension of labor power in a modernizing America. In the other society of vast industries and burgeoning cities, labor power was regained. But labor's accomplishment was hardly of a sort that could be called modern. In this reconstitution of labor power, modern union organization played an inconsequential role; more critical were structural conditions in the labor market and in the workplace. The modern nexus between union power and labor power lay some distance in the future; the exercise of labor power in the Gilded Age was more informal, more spontaneous, more popular, and more securely grounded in the nature of labor markets in the industrial cities of the Northeast.[15]

In light of these analyses, Herbert Gutman's bleak intimations on the fate of American labor in the Gilded Age seem somewhat overdrawn. To be sure, Gutman correctly and brilliantly perceived the declension of labor power in preindustrial communities, and he even hinted at the palliative role in this declension of the Knights of Labor and later the Socialists. But Gutman was only half right, which accounts perhaps for his undue pessimism. He did not perceive (nor perhaps could he have) the dramatic reconstitution of labor power that was under way in the alien world of the large industrial city. He would be pleased to know that, insofar as statistics are a useful guide, this reconstitution seems to have had little to do with the organizational and strategic efforts of the trade unions, that its sources resided instead with the workers themselves—with their convergent economic and political interests, on the one hand, and their struggle against industrial concentration, on the other. Statistics do not, of course, tell the whole story—indeed, a great deal of the variance in labor power remains to be explained—but they do suggest that industrial workers in the large cities of Gilded Age America had not "sold out" to high wages or to "pure and simple" trade unionism. Until 1894, at any rate, modern urban labor seems to have derived its power in remarkably traditional ways. Gutman, I believe, would have been pleasantly surprised.

15. My analysis indicates an association between the Knights of Labor and the preindustrial community. For the relationship of small towns and radical labor politics, see James R. Green, "The Salesmen-Soldiers of the 'Appeal' Army: A Profile of the Rank-and-File Agitators," in *Socialism and the Cities*, ed. Bruce M. Stave (Port Washington, N.Y.: Kennikat Press, 1975), pp. 13–40; James Weinstein, *The Decline of Socialism in America: 1912–1925* (New York: Monthly Review Press, 1967); and Leon Fink, "The New Labor History and the Powers of Historical Pessimism: Consensus, Hegemony, and the Case of the Knights of Labor," *Journal of American History* 75 (1988), pp. 115–36. For discussion of the strike as a conservative and modernizing strategy, see Peter Stearns's remarks in Harvey Mitchell and Peter N. Stearns, *Workers and Protest: The European Labor Movement, the Working Classes and the Origins of Social Democracy, 1890–1914* (Itasca, Ill.: F. E. Peacock, 1971), pp. 164–81.

APPENDIX TABLE 9A
Summary Data for Strike-prone Areas

Geographic areas	Population, 1890	Successful strikes/total strikes			Percentage of successful strikes			Total strike rate, 1881–94	Successful strike rate, 1881–94
		1881–86	1887–94	1881–94	1881–86	1887–94	1881–94		
Connecticut									
Fairfield	150,081	39/57	18/50	57/107	68.4%	36.0%	51.1%	.71	.38
New Haven	209,058	38/78	48/135	86/213	48.7	35.5	40.3	1.02	.41
Hartford	147,180	30/50	18/43	48/93	60.0	41.9	51.6	.61	.11
New London	76,634	3/9	14/24	17/33	33.3	58.3	51.5	.41	.22
Delaware									
New Castle	97,182	5/20	8/18	13/38	25.0	44.4	34.2	.39	.13
District of Columbia	230,392	22/43	7/13	29/56	51.2	53.8	51.8	.24	.13
Illinois									
Adams	61,888	6/9	2/7	8/16	66.7	28.6	50.0	.26	.13
Sangamon	61,195	11/27	13/21	24/48	40.7	61.9	70.8	.78	.55
Alexander	16,563	8/19	3/3	11/20	47.1	100.0	50.0	1.20	.66
Macon	38,083	5/9	8/12	13/21	55.6	66.7	61.9	.55	.34
Macoupin	40,380	6/9	4/9	10/18	66.7	44.4	55.6	.45	.25
Madison	51,535	4/11	1/5	5/16	36.4	20.0	31.3	.31	.10
Marion	24,341	0/11	1/5	1/16	0.0	20.0	6.3	.66	.04
Peoria	70,378	5/12	12/23	17/35	41.7	52.2	48.6	.50	.24
Perry	17,529	15/30	4/5	19/35	50.0	80.0	54.3	2.00	1.09
St. Clair	66,571	7/21	9/16	16/37	33.3	56.3	43.2	.56	.24
Vermilion	49,905	0/5	7/12	7/17	0.0	58.3	41.2	.34	.14
Will	62,007	4/9	21/36	25/45	44.4	58.3	55.6	.71	.40
Cook	1,191,992	227/502	273/533	500/1035	45.2	51.2	48.3	.87	.42
Fulton	43,110	2/5	4/15	6/20	40.0	26.7	30.0	.46	.14
Kane	65,061	1/9	0/8	1/17	11.1	0.0	5.9	.26	.02
Lasalle	80,798	8/15	12/16	20/31	53.3	75.0	64.5	.38	.25

APPENDIX TABLE 9A (continued)

Geographic areas	Population, 1890	Successful strikes/total strikes			Percentage of successful strikes			Total strike rate, 1881–94	Successful strike rate, 1881–94
		1881–86	1887–94	1881–94	1881–86	1887–94	1881–94		
Indiana									
Marion	141,156	11/23	22/50	33/73	47.8	44.0	45.2	.52	.23
Tippecanoe	35,078	6/13	2/5	8/18	46.2	40.0	44.4	.51	.23
Vanderburgh	58,809	3/8	7/20	10/28	37.5	35.0	35.7	.48	.17
Vigo	50,195	2/8	9/15	11/23	25.0	60.0	47.8	.46	.22
Iowa									
Dubuque	49,848	8/11	3/6	11/17	72.7	50.0	64.7	.34	.22
Polk	65,410	14/28	7/10	21/38	50.0	70.0	55.3	.58	.32
Maine									
Knox	31,473	2/6	8/12	10/18	33.3	66.7	55.5	.57	.32
Maryland									
Allegheny	41,571	0/9	1/8	1/17	0.8	12.5	5.9	.41	.02
Baltimore City	434,439	23/30	49/93	72/123	76.7	52.2	58.5	.28	.16
Massachusetts									
Berkshire	81,108	2/6	8/26	10/32	33.3	30.8	31.1	.39	.12
Bristol	186,465	23/51	66/139	89/190	45.0	47.4	46.8	1.02	.48
Essex	299,995	19/35	111/238	130/273	54.3	46.6	47.6	.91	.41
Hampden	135,713	17/25	25/68	42/93	68.0	36.7	45.2	.69	.31
Hampshire	51,589	1/4	2/9	3/13	25.0	22.2	23.1	.25	.06
Middlesex	431,167	26/45	55/144	81/189	57.8	38.2	42.9	.44	.19
Norfolk	118,950	14/21	29/48	43/69	66.7	60.4	62.3	.58	.36
Plymouth	92,700	10/23	29/57	39/80	43.5	50.9	48.8	.86	.42
Suffolk	484,780	16/30	143/237	159/267	53.3	60.3	59.6	.55	.23
Worcester	280,787	18/43	36/82	54/125	41.9	43.9	43.2	.45	.19
Michigan									
Marquette	39,521	1/2	12/29	13/31	50.0	41.4	41.9	.78	.33
Saginaw	82,273	5/12	5/7	10/19	41.7	71.4	52.6	.23	.13
Wayne	257,114	31/65	11/37	42/102	47.7	29.7	41.2	.40	.16
Minnesota									
Hennepin	185,294	17/42	25/51	42/93	40.5	49.0	45.2	.50	.23
Ramsey	139,796	14/29	25/48	39/77	48.3	52.1	50.6	.55	.28
St. Louis	44,862	5/16	26/46	31/62	31.3	56.5	50.0	1.38	.69

APPENDIX TABLE 9A (*continued*)

Geographic areas	Population, 1890	Successful strikes/total strikes			Percentage of successful strikes			Total strike rate, 1881–94	Successful strike rate, 1881–94
		1881–86	1887–94	1881–94	1881–86	1887–94	1881–94		
Missouri									
Jackson	160,510	9/20	8/17	17/37	45.0	47.1	45.9	.23	.11
St. Louis City	451,770	57/101	48/112	105/213	56.4	42.9	49.3	.47	.23
New Hampshire									
Merrimack	49,435	3/8	7/13	10/21	37.5	53.8	47.6	.41	.20
Strafford	38,442	5/11	10/17	15/28	45.5	58.8	51.6	.71	.39
New Jersey									
Camden	87,687	1/3	0/9	1/12	33.3	0.0	8.1	.14	.01
Cumberland	45,438	3/8	1/8	4/16	37.5	12.5	25.0	.35	.09
Essex	256,098	33/82	88/141	121/223	40.2	62.4	54.1	.87	.47
Hudson	275,126	12/21	43/74	55/95	57.1	58.0	57.9	.35	.20
Mercer	79,978	1/4	2/11	3/15	25.0	18.2	20.0	.19	.04
Passaic	105,046	11/27	24/42	35/69	40.7	57.1	50.7	.66	.33
Union	72,467	2/4	14/23	16/27	50.0	60.9	59.3	.37	.22
New York									
Albany	164,555	29/37	18/41	47/78	78.4	43.9	60.0	.47	.29
Erie	322,981	13/23	28/52	41/75	56.5	53.8	54.7	.21	.13
Kings	838,547	140/226	433/661	573/887	61.9	65.5	64.6	1.06	.82
Monroe	189,586	6/12	33/58	39/70	50.0	56.9	55.7	.37	.18
New York	1,515,301	485/728	1802/2551	2287/3279	66.6	70.6	69.7	2.16	1.51
Oneida	122,922	2/6	10/16	12/22	33.3	62.5	54.5	.18	.10
Onondaga	146,247	3/4	25/41	28/45	75.0	61.0	62.2	.31	.19
Orange	97,859	1/3	23/45	24/48	33.3	51.1	50.0	.49	.25
Queens	128,059	3/6	41/73	44/79	50.0	56.2	55.7	.62	.34
Rensselaer	124,511	31/37	20/42	51/79	83.8	47.6	64.6	.63	.41
Ulster	87,062	3/4	8/18	11/22	75.0	44.4	50.0	.25	.13
Westchester	146,772	15/25	31/57	46/82	60.0	54.4	56.1	.56	.31

APPENDIX TABLE 9A (continued)

Geographic areas	Population, 1890	Successful strikes/total strikes			Percentage of successful strikes			Total strike rate, 1881–94	Successful strike rate, 1881–94
		1881–86	1887–94	1881–94	1881–86	1887–94	1881–94		
Ohio									
Athens	35,194	5/10	5/19	10/29	50.0	26.3	34.5	.82	.28
Belmont	57,413	19/28	11/24	30/52	67.9	45.8	57.7	.91	.52
Clark	52,277	0/2	14/27	14/29	0.0	51.9	48.3	.55	.27
Columbiana	59,029	6/13	3/14	9/27	46.2	21.4	33.3	.46	.15
Cuyahoga	309,970	21/37	36/64	57/101	56.8	56.2	56.4	.33	.18
Erie	35,462	2/5	3/15	5/20	40.0	20.0	25.0	.56	.14
Franklin	124,807	8/14	14/39	22/53	57.1	35.9	41.5	.43	.18
Hamilton	374,573	82/162	47/108	129/270	50.6	43.5	47.8	.72	.34
Jefferson	39,415	5/13	12/21	17/34	38.5	57.1	50.0	.86	.43
Licking	43,279	7/8	3/8	10/16	87.5	37.5	62.5	.37	.23
Lucas	102,296	2/6	10/31	12/37	33.3	32.3	32.4	.36	.12
Mahoning	55,979	17/24	8/20	25/44	70.8	40.0	56.8	.79	.45
Montgomery	100,852	9/18	4/6	13/24	50.0	66.7	54.2	.24	.13
Muskingum	51,210	6/6	6/11	12/17	100.0	54.5	70.6	.33	.23
Perry	31,151	4/14	10/21	14/35	28.6	47.6	40.0	1.12	.45
Stark	84,170	29/37	3/15	32/52	78.4	20.0	61.5	.62	.38
Summit	54,089	7/12	3/12	10/24	58.3	25.0	41.7	.44	.18
Pennsylvania									
Allegheny	551,959	94/204	182/350	276/554	46.1	52.0	49.8	1.00	.50
Armstrong	46,747	5/11	0/7	5/18	45.5	0.0	27.8	.39	.11
Beaver	50,077	2/5	8/23	10/28	40.0	34.8	35.7	.56	.20
Berks	137,327	17/39	10/28	27/67	43.6	35.7	40.3	.49	.20
Cambria	66,375	2/8	10/22	12/30	25.0	45.5	40.0	.45	.18
Dauphin	96,977	4/8	0/7	4/15	50.0	0.0	26.7	.15	.04
Delaware	74,683	1/9	8/17	9/26	11.1	47.1	34.6	.35	.12
Erie	86,074	7/13	8/14	15/27	53.8	57.1	55.6	.31	.17
Fayette	80,006	8/16	13/34	21/50	50.0	38.2	42.0	.63	.26
Lackawanna	142,088	4/10	8/20	12/30	40.0	40.0	40.0	.21	.08
Lawrence	37,517	5/17	1/10	6/27	29.4	10.0	22.2	.72	.16
Lucerne	201,203	6/20	20/45	26/65	30.0	44.4	40.0	.32	.13

APPENDIX TABLE 9A (continued)

Geographic areas	Population, 1890	Successful strikes/total strikes			Percentage of successful strikes			Total strike rate, 1881–94	Successful strike rate, 1881–94
		1881–86	1887–94	1881–94	1881–86	1887–94	1881–94		
Mercer	55,744	6/12	10/15	16/27	50.0	66.7	55.6	.48	.29
Montgomery	123,290	5/14	8/21	13/35	35.7	38.1	37.1	.28	.11
Northumberland	74,698	5/15	8/11	13/26	33.3	72.7	50.0	.35	.18
Philadelphia	1,046,964	132/240	89/240	221/480	55.0	37.1	46.0	.46	.21
Schuylkill	154,163	6/10	7/16	13/26	60.0	43.8	50.0	.17	.09
Tioga	52,313	9/15	6/9	15/24	60.0	66.7	62.5	.46	.29
Washington	71,155	14/24	7/19	21/43	58.3	36.8	48.8	.46	.29
Wayne	31,010	4/7	2/5	6/12	57.1	40.0	50.0	.60	.29
Westmoreland	112,819	11/26	13/28	24/54	42.3	46.4	44.4	.39	.20
Rhode Island								.48	.21
Providence	255,123	6/16	22/62	28/78	37.5	35.5	35.9	.31	.11
Wisconsin									
Eau Claire	30,673	2/8	4/8	6/16	25.0	50.0	37.5	.52	.20
Milwaukee	236,101	27/46	48/101	75/147	58.7	47.5	51.0	.62	.32
Racine	36,268	4/10	8/24	12/34	40.0	33.3	35.1	.94	.33

SOURCES: Third Annual Report of the Commissioner of Labor, 1887: Strikes and Lockouts (Washington, D.C.: Government Printing Office, 1888); Tenth Annual Report of the Commissioner of Labor, 1894: Strikes and Lockouts, 2 vols. (Washington, D.C.: Government Printing Office, 1896).

NOTE: Successful strikes, by my definition, includes both successful and partly successful strikes. The total strike rate and success rate are defined as the number of strikes per 1,000 population in strike-prone counties.

APPENDIX TABLE 9B

County Variables Used in Multiple Regression Analyses

1. County population, 1890
2. Strike rate/1,000 population (1890)
3. Percentage of county population foreign-born, 1890
4. Wages as a percentage of value added by manufacturing, 1890
5. Skilled wages, 1880
6. Unskilled wages, 1880
7. Ratio of skilled to unskilled wages, 1880
8. Knights of Labor membership (1883) as a percentage of the 1880 manufacturing labor force
9. Value added per manufacturing employee, 1890
10. Average wage per manufacturing employee, 1890
11. Capital investment per manufacturing employee, 1890
12. Capital/labor ratio, 1890
13. Average number of employees per manufacturing establishment, 1880
14. Average number of employees per manufacturing establishment, 1890
15. Police expenditure per capita in principal city of the county, 1890
16. Percentage of manufacturing employment in nondurable industries, 1880
17. Percentage of manufacturing in largest industry, 1880
18. Percentage of total strikes union ordered, 1881–94

CHAPTER 10

The Last Great Chance for an American Working Class

Spatial Lessons of the General Strike and the Haymarket Riot of Early May 1886

E ighteen eighty-six was a year of unusual significance in American labor history—it offered labor's last great chance for a unified working class. In a year filled with dramatic moments, perhaps the best known are those associated with Haymarket: a drama that began with a violent and deadly clash between labor radicals and police on a rainy Chicago evening in early May, unfolded in the spectacle of a trial that electrified the nation, and climaxed with the grim sentencing to death of seven rioters (four of whom were eventually executed in 1887).[1]

But a great deal more occurred in 1886. On May 1, three days before Haymarket, trade unionists organized one of the few general strikes in the nation's history. Following the lead of the Federation of Organized Trades and Labor Unions (FOTLU), 100,000 American workers—skilled and unskilled, immigrant and native, in big cities and in small towns—went out on strike for an eight-hour working

1. Henry David, *The History of the Haymarket Affair* (New York: Russell and Russell, 1958); Paul Avrich, *The Haymarket Tragedy* (Princeton: Princeton Univ. Press, 1984); Eric L. Hirsch, *Urban Revolt: Ethnic Politics in the Nineteenth-Century Chicago Labor Movement* (Berkeley: Univ. of California Press, 1990), pp. 43–85. The seminal nature of the Haymarket riot for the development of the American labor movement is stressed in Leon Fink, "The New Labor History and the Powers of Historical Pessimism: Consensus, Hegemony, and the Case of the Knights of Labor," *Journal of American History* 75 (1988), pp. 115–36, esp. pp. 131–36. Also see Samuel Yellen, *American Labor Struggles* (New York: Harcourt, Brace, 1936).

day. Although Haymarket violence dampened enthusiasm for the general strike in some quarters, the stoppage persisted in many locales well into the summer of 1886.[2]

In early December of 1886, seven months and one week after Haymarket, a third event of historic significance entered the annals of the labor movement. Trade unionists meeting at Columbus, Ohio, reconstituted the FOTLU into a new, more powerful, and more exclusive institution and bestowed upon it the title of the American Federation of Labor (AFL). In a series of bold and schismatic actions, the founders of the AFL rejected the inclusive labor strategy they had recently deployed in the general strike. They committed themselves instead to the pursuit of the sectarian interests of trade and craft unionists, to what has been called "pure and simple trade unionism." The Columbus meetings thus were auspicious in a dual sense: they marked, on the one hand, the birth of a great (albeit exclusivist) institution and, on the other, the death of the socialist dream for a unified American working class. Ironically, just seven months earlier, in the euphoria and solidarity of parading May Day strikers, that dream had seemed near realization. In this swift and, as it turns out, catastrophic reversal of labor's expectations, I believe, lies the unusual significance of 1886.[3]

The three events of 1886—the general strike, Haymarket, and the founding of the American Federation of Labor—profoundly changed the course of American labor history. By year's end, trade unionists felt compelled by events to make a decisive break with the mass of American workers, to abandon inclusive working-class strategies, and to pursue the narrower interests of their membership. Such a momentous decision was not undertaken lightly. Clearly events in 1886 had revealed new truths to trade unionists, truths painfully learned from their chastening experience in organizing the general strike and smoothing over the disruptive effects of Haymarket.

Although trade unionists learned well the lessons of the general

2. David, *History of the Haymarket Affair*; Norman Ware, *The Labor Movement in the United States, 1860–1895: A Study in Democracy* (Gloucester, Mass.: Peter Smith, 1959). On labor's quest for the eight-hour day, see Martha Ellen Shiells, "Collective Choice of Working Conditions: Hours in British and U.S. Iron and Steel, 1890–1923," *Journal of Economic History* 50 (1990), pp. 379–92; Robert Whaples, "Winning the Eight-Hour Day, 1909–1919," *Journal of Economic History* 50 (1990), pp. 393–406.

3. Philip Taft, *Organized Labor in American History* (New York: Harper and Row, 1964), pp. 123–35.

strike and Haymarket, what they learned has been muddied by labor historiography. The reasons for this confusion are not particularly sinister; rather, they are the result of a natural inclination toward the sensationalism of Haymarket violence and retribution. Preoccupation with Haymarket, while it has produced several wonderfully interesting histories, has obscured the more critical role of the general strike in deepening the schism in the American labor movement. Even when historians have examined the general strike, their interest in it has almost always been tangential to their study of the Haymarket drama. The typical inquiry rarely progresses much further than the question, what were the effects of Haymarket on the general strike? Aside from trivializing the general strike, questions of this sort overlook what the strike has to tell us about the 100,000 or so participants who followed the trade unionist's call; about the places in which they resided; about the intensity of their commitment to the strike; and about the implications of these factors for ensuing trade unionist strategy and policy. To answer these questions is to relearn the lessons taught to the trade unionists in 1886 and, in so doing, to comprehend why at the end of that fateful year they decided to go it alone, to pursue the narrow interests of skilled workers in America, and to leave to history the last great chance for an American working class.[4]

The general strike taught trade unionists two important lessons, both of a spatial nature. The first of these is that the general strike was *not* general in geographical distribution. That fact could hardly have been lost on trade unionists. Even a cursory knowledge of strike

4. Among labor historians, perhaps Samuel Yellen comes the closest to appreciating the schismatic role of events in early May 1886. Yet even his sensitivity is directed toward the effects of violence on the labor movement rather than toward the lessons trade unionists learned from the general strike. Yellen writes that after the Haymarket affair "anarchism as a theory and a tactic never regained its hold on the labor movement in the United States. Workmen turned to the more conservative American Federation of Labor, which was able to point back with some satisfaction to the energetic part it played in the eighthour movement and to the resolution it passed for the release of the eight condemned men. But the Noble Order of the Knights of Labor, both because of its official treachery in the strike and its official refusal to petition for the pardoning of the condemned men, was abandoned." I would merely point out that workers repelled by the Knights' behavior were not always welcomed by increasingly sectarian trade unionists. They had the misfortune of falling into the no-man's-land between the bankrupt and decaying Knights of Labor and a parochial trade unionism. Such has been, and remains, the fate of many American workers. Yellen, *American Labor Struggles*, p. 71. Note also Fink's appeal for greater attention and sensitivity to seminal events in labor history generally and to 1886 in particular. Fink, "The New Labor History," pp. 131–36. His plea, however, exaggerates the role of Haymarket and discounts the more critical role of the general strike.

geography would have reminded them of the thinness of their geographical base of support. The reality was that the impressively large number of general strikers (100,000) were concentrated in a depressingly small number of northeastern cities. That is to say that the general strike was parochial in geographical distribution. The second lesson is that episodic violence (in this case provoked at Haymarket) had modest effects upon strike actions in other locations. As the map of general-strike dissipation will suggest, trade unionists effectively warded off the adverse effects of Haymarket nearly everywhere except at the locus of violent confrontation (Chicago).

These spatial lessons of the general strike—its concentrated geographical distribution and the contained effects of episodic violence upon it—had important implications for ensuing trade unionist policy. Chastened by their failure to mobilize a broadly based working-class protest, trade unionists soon after rechanneled their energies into the parochial interests of constituencies that the general strike had defined with unusual clarity, that is, fellow trade unionists located in the large urban centers of the northeastern United States. But the strike also taught trade unionists something about the nature of the American spatial system. The effects of violence, they discovered, were extremely localized in the insular society of late nineteenth-century America—a fact that argued strongly in favor of a decentralized organizational structure so as to further insulate a national trade unionist movement from the extremes of local violence.

The provocative connections between the general strike and the ensuing redirection in trade union policy and strategy have been largely missed by labor historians preoccupied with Haymarket's drama and aggregative, aspatial analyses. The remarkable paradox of sectarian trade unionists organizing a general strike on behalf of the entire working class in May and within eight months withdrawing into the sectarian philosophy of pure and simple trade unionism consequently persists. Geography, I believe, will prove to be instrumental in the explication of this schismatic reversal in trade unionist philosophy and strategy.

The heart of this chapter consists of a statistical reconstruction of the geography of the general strike and its dissipation as reported by the U.S. Bureau of Labor.[5] This reconstruction in four parts seeks to

5. *Third Annual Report of the Commissioner of Labor, 1887: Strikes and Lockouts* (Washington, D.C.: Government Printing Office, 1888). The accuracy and reliability of this re-

resurrect the kind of information that was available to trade unionist organizers following the general strike and upon which they subsequently would act. Part one sketches the historical context that evoked the general strike. Part two delineates the structure of the general strike in the several days before the Haymarket riot. The description characterizes the geographical and industrial composition of the strikes and thus the constituencies responding to the FOTLU's call for a general strike. Part three traces the dissipation of the strike during the weeks and months after Haymarket violence. The spatial variability of dissipation suggests that while violence and other events surrounding Haymarket were damaging to the general strike in Chicago, their effects diminished with increasing distance from the locus of violence. Part four deals with the implications of the general strike for trade unionist policy. The general strike, I submit, provided trade unionists with two invaluable pieces of information: the first on their proper geographical and industrial constituencies, the second on the negligible effects of local labor violence on less militant forms of worker protest in other areas. What they learned was not inconsistent with policies that soon unfolded, namely a parochial, pure and simple trade unionism lodged in big cities, a decentralized organizational structure, and an eschewal of violent protest—policies that were embodied in the chartering of the American Federation of Labor.

The Context of the General Strike

The general strike of May 1, 1886, addressed an issue of long standing in the American labor movement—the length of the work day. Workers had sought a reduction in hours as early as the 1820s. Demands for a shorter day accelerated immediately after the Civil War, and in 1868 federal legislation mandated the eight-hour day for all federal workers. The victory was largely symbolic, however, because the law does not seem to have been enforced and thus few workers were affected by it. As of 1886, although nineteen states and one territory had passed legislation reducing the length of the work day, lax enforcement and legal maneuvering continued to blunt the

---

port is confirmed by David Montgomery, "Strikes in Nineteenth-Century America," *Social Science History* 4 (1980), pp. 81–104.

force of law. The enactments notwithstanding, the typical worker in the 1880s toiled for ten hours a day and sixty hours a week. Frustrated by these "paper reforms," workers considered alternative strategies for achieving the eight-hour day.[6]

The turning point came in the early 1880s. Workers employed the strike—an old and familiar protest tactic—with new vigor. In 1880 alone, workers called over 760 strikes, a sevenfold increase over the previous year and an unprecedented number for industrial nations. The principal reason for protest in 1880, as well as during the four succeeding years, was wages. Confronted by a deteriorating economy, workers throughout the Northeast struck to maintain or improve their wages. By mid-decade, the economy had recovered somewhat, but strike activity remained at a high level. Strikes over the issue of wages were supplemented by strikes for reduced working hours and union organization.[7]

In the forefront of the struggle for a shorter work day was the Federation of Organized Trades and Labor Unions—a loose affiliation of six craft unions founded in 1881. The leadership of the FOTLU proposed in 1884 that its members take unspecified actions designed to implement the eight-hour day. The secretary of the FOTLU, Frank Foster, declared it was time for the Federation to "assume the initiative in a national movement for the reduction of the hours of labor. Sporadic attempts of individual trades in certain localities have met with varying degrees of success, but there is little doubt that a universal, centrally directed advance would prove both practical and triumphant. . . . This much has been determined by the history of the eight-hour law—it is useless to wait for legislation in this matter."[8] Foster's appeal was endorsed in the following year when the FOTLU's annual convention called for explicit action—a general strike on behalf of the eight-hour day to commence on the first day of May 1886. Although the proposal for a general strike of all workers was rejected by the FOTLU's principal rival, the Knights

6. *Tenth Annual Report of the Commissioner of Labor, 1894: Strikes and Lockouts* (2 vols.; Washington, D.C.: Government Printing Office, 1896); Taft, *Organized Labor in American History*, pp. 123–35.

7. Sari Bennett and Carville Earle, "The Geography of Strikes in the United States, 1881–1894," *Journal of Interdisciplinary History* 13 (1982), pp. 63–84; *idem*, "Labour Power and Locality in the Gilded Age: The Northeastern United States, 1881–1894," *Histoire Sociale–Social History* 15 (1982), pp. 383–405; Montgomery, "Strikes in Nineteenth-Century America." Also see Chapter 9.

8. *Report of Proceedings of Federation of Organized Trades and Labor Unions of the United States and Canada* (1884).

of Labor, the trade unionists proceeded with plans for a nationwide general strike.[9]

The First Days of the General Strike

The general strike commenced on the appointed day. Between May 1 and May 3, workers called 357 separate strikes for a reduction in working hours. The number of strikers, according to some estimates, reached 190,000, but the more reliable tabulations from the federal strike report indicate a figure of about 100,000.[10] Work stoppages began on Saturday, when 204 strikes were called, followed by 11 more strikes on Sunday and 142 on Monday. Only a handful of strikes for reduced hours were initiated in succeeding days. By the evening of May 3—a full day before Haymarket—the general strike had reached its apogee. The protest garnered 60,000 strikers on Saturday and another 37,000 on Monday—numbers that made it the largest single work stoppage in the history of American labor. Even more indicative of the magnitude of the strike are the facts that the 98,000 general strikers came close to matching the annual totals of strikers between 1881 and 1884 and that they accounted for nearly a quarter of all strikers in 1886.[11]

But attrition had already begun to settle in. By Monday evening, three days into the general strike, thousands of sympathy strikers had made their point and were returning to work. Over 10 percent (29) of the 204 strikes and almost one-third of the strikers (22,500) had ended their protest by May 3. Of these sympathy strikers, New York City's cigar makers constituted the largest group, with nearly 15,000 participants. As loyal members of the FOTLU the cigar makers supported the general strike even though most members of their union had achieved significant hourly reductions before the strike.

At the peak of the general strike on Monday, May 3, 328 strikes remained in effect and 76,174 workers persisted in their protest for

9. Taft, *Organized Labor in American History*, pp. 123–35; Ware, *The Labor Movement in the United States*; Yellen, *American Labor Struggles*, pp. 39–44; Avrich, *The Haymarket Tragedy*, pp. 181–96.
10. The general strike is defined as all strikes seeking a reduction in working hours and commencing between May 1 and May 3, 1886. In assessing the number of strikes and strikers, previous scholars have relied almost exclusively on impressionistic contemporary estimates. These estimates substantially exaggerate the actual number of workers who participated in the general strike. See sources cited in text.
11. *Third Annual Report of the Commissioner of Labor*.

an eight-hour day. Although the extent of worker mobilization was impressive by Gilded Age standards, the general strike was not in fact a general phenomenon. The FOTLU's general strike organizers, though hoping for widespread worker support, succeeded in mobilizing a mere .5 percent of the nation's 19.3 million workers. As this small fraction suggests, the general strike appealed to a highly selective geographical and industrial constituency.

If the general strike failed to mobilize large masses of workers, it nonetheless drew substantial support in the large urban centers of the northeastern United States (see Figure 10.1). Of the 357 separate strikes, 346 occurred in cities with populations of 10,000 or more. The small towns, mining camps, and mill villages, which had figured so prominently in the worker protest of the early 1880s, played little part in the general strike.[12] Within the urban Northeast, general strike actions were concentrated in five large cities: Chicago, New York City (though not Brooklyn), Cincinnati, Pittsburgh, and Philadelphia, which collectively accounted for 81 percent of the strikes and 76 percent of the strikers. Of the five cities, Chicago and New York accounted for 66 percent of the strikes and 70 percent of the strikers. Chicago alone contributed almost half of the strikes (175) and slightly more than two-fifths of the strikers (42,696). New York City ranked second with 60 strikes and 26,105 strikers, followed by Cincinnati with 29 strikes and 4,104 strikers, Pittsburgh with 14 strikes and 1,552 strikers, and Philadelphia with 12 strikes and 589 strikers. In addition, the cities of Boston; Baltimore; Washington, D.C.; Newark, N.J.; Detroit; Minneapolis-St. Paul; and St. Louis reported over 1,000 strikers each. Outside of the urban Northeast, the general strike received little support except in the cities of Richmond, Louisville, and Covington (Kentucky). The general strike thus defined the selective geographical constituencies of the trade union movement in the 1880s. These constituencies were almost exclusively urban and northeastern; they constituted only a small fraction of the entire American working class.

Within these geographical domains, what kinds of workers supported the FOTLU's call for a general strike? The federal strike re-

12. Bennett and Earle, "The Geography of Strikes," pp. 63–84; *idem*, "Labour Power and Locality," pp. 383–405; Herbert G. Gutman, "The Workers' Search for Power: Labor in the Gilded Age," in *The Gilded Age: A Reappraisal*, ed. H. Wayne Morgan (Syracuse, N.Y.: Syracuse Univ. Press, 1963), pp. 38–68; *idem, Work, Culture and Society in Industrializing America* (New York: Knopf, 1966).

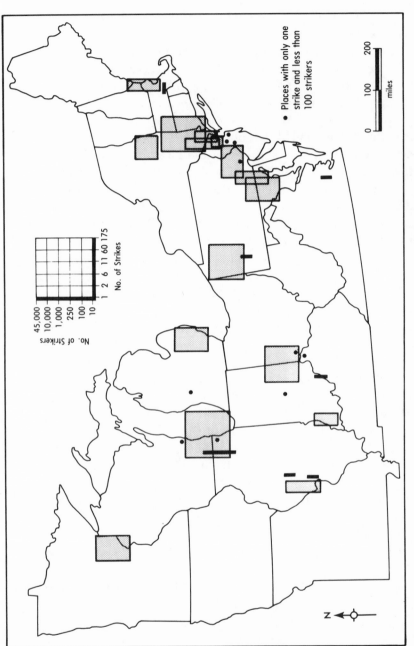

FIGURE 10.1. The Distribution of the General Strike of May 1, 1886: Component Strikes and Striking Participants, by City. The variable intensity of the General Strike at its maximum extent is shown by columns and quadrilaterals drawn to a modified logarithmic scale. Columns depict cities reporting only one strike, but more than 100 strikers; quadrilaterals, cities reporting more than one strike. The map highlights the concentration of the General Strike in the heavily urbanized industrial areas in the northeastern quadrant of the United States. Source: *Third Annual Report of the Commissioner of Labor, 1887.*

TABLE 10.1

Industrial Composition of the General Strike

Places	Number of strikes	Proportion of strikes by industry	
Chicago	176	Wooden goods	28.4%
		Metal goods	19.3%
		Furniture	14.8%
		Machine shops	13.1%
New York	60	Furniture	48.3%
		Machine shops	21.7%
		Clothiers-fur	18.3%
Other cities	86	Furniture	40.7%
		Building trades	27.9%
		Metal goods	10.5%
Other places	35	Building trades	30.6%
		Furniture	19.4%
All places	357	Furniture	26.8%
		Wooden goods	15.6%
		Metal goods	12.8%
		Building trades	10.9%
		Machine shops	10.3%

SOURCE: *Third Annual Report of the Commissioner of Labor, 1887: Strikes and Lockouts* (Washington, D.C.: Government Printing Office, 1888).

NOTE: The "other cities" category includes Cincinnati, Pittsburgh, Philadelphia, Detroit, Baltimore, Washington, D.C., Boston, Minneapolis-St. Paul, and St. Louis.

port tells us that unions initiated virtually all the strikes. Although the report does not reveal the specific unions involved, it does identify the industries in which the strikes occurred. The industrial composition of the general strike suggests that several of the FOTLU's affiliates—the iron and steelworkers, the molders, the cigar makers, and the carpenters—played a key role. Over three-fourths (77 percent) of the general strikes were conducted in just five industries (see Table 10.1). The furniture industry led the way with 27 percent of all strikes, followed by wooden goods (16 percent), metal goods (13 percent), the building trades (11 percent), and machine shops (10 percent). FOTLU affiliates were active in each of these industries: carpenters in building trades, furniture, and wooden goods; molders and iron and steelworkers in metal goods and machine shops. To these we may add the large sympathy strike conducted by the FOTLU's affiliated cigar makers in New York City. Conversely, Federation printers and glassmakers were conspicuously absent from the ranks of general strikers.

The industrial mix of the general strike varied considerably among northeastern cities. In Chicago, for example, the wooden goods and metal goods industries contributed 48 percent of the city's general strikes. In New York, by contrast, the furniture industry accounted for one-half of all strikes. In other cities (excluding Chicago) furniture accounted for two-fifths of the strikes. The building trades, though of modest importance in Chicago and New York, contributed about a quarter of the strikes in all other places. Only one industry, furniture, was an important common denominator across all cities.

The general strike represented a test of trade unionist sentiment. That sentiment was strongest in large urban centers of the northeastern United States and, more specifically, among workers making furniture, wooden goods, or metal goods, or engaged in the building trades. The sympathy support of the cigar makers identified them as a large and friendly constituency. The same could not be said for the inexplicable reticence of trade unionists in printing and glass manufactures. The geographical and industrial composition of the general strike thus taught several lessons for future trade unionist strategy. We will return to these after an examination of the general strike's dissipation on the heels of Haymarket violence.

Haymarket and Its Effects on the General Strike

The eruption of violence in Chicago's Haymarket Square on the evening of May 4 posed a severe challenge to the general strike. Interpretations of the riot's impact conflict, however. One interpretation argues that the effects were paralytic, the other that they were inconsequential. The paralytic interpretation is presented most cogently in *Brief History of the American Labor Movement*:

> The Chicago Haymarket riot, in which one policeman was killed and several others were wounded, aroused public opinion against unionism and radicalism and for several years stopped the movement for the 8-hour day. The meeting in Haymarket Square had been called as a peaceful protest against the killing of four strikers and wounding of others during the strike for the 8-hour day.[13]

This assertion by a new labor historian is similar: "Combined with already existing tensions . . . within the labor alliance, Haymarket

13. *Brief History of the American Labor Movement*, U.S. Department of Labor Statistics, Bulletin 1000 (Washington, D.C.: Government Printing Office, 1976), pp. 80–81.

FIGURE 10.2. Late nineteenth-century representation of Chicago's Haymarket Riot on the evening of May 4, 1886. Called by radical leaders in Chicago's labor movement, the rally in Haymarket Square was only loosely connected with the General Strike of May 1, which had been organized by the Federation of Organized Trades and Labor Unions. Reproduced from John Kouwenhoven, *Adventures of America, 1857–1900: A Pictorial Record from Harper's Weekly* (New York: Harper and Brothers, 1938), n.p.

and its aftermath of antilabor reprisals checked the forward momentum of the Knights of Labor and the hopes for coordinated, national industrial action."[14]

The second interpretation discounts the effects of violence on the general strike. Henry David concludes that even a casual inspection of federal strike statistics makes it "clear that the eight-hour movement was not a complete failure, and that it resulted in some gains. From the dates of the duration of the May strikes no correlation can be made, when all other factors are taken into consideration, showing that the bomb-throwing directly caused the abandonment of strikes for a shorter day." While David concedes that Haymarket probably dampened labor's spirits and that it offered a powerful weapon to the opposition, he argues that the overall impact on the general strike

14. Fink, "The New Labor History," p. 132, esp. n. 33 and sources therein. For ' Chicago, see Hirsch, *Urban Revolt*, pp. 43–85.

was modest.[15] Philip Taft's assessment of Haymarket's benign effects contains even fewer qualifications: "The effect of the Haymarket tragedy on the labor movement was not great. The labor movement was not directly involved, although many organizations and leaders spoke out against the executions. Nor did the throwing of the bomb have any effect on the eight-hour movement."[16]

The fact is that these conflicting interpretations constitute aspatial half-truths. A geographic reconstruction of the general strike's dissipation reveals that in some places Haymarket's effects were paralytic; in others, they were inconsequential. More to the point, trade unionists who understood this spatial variability gleaned valuable insights into the means by which they might minimize the disruptive effects of violence in the future.

As a prelude to the geographic reconstruction, I begin with a review of the independent origins of the strike and the riot in the months preceding these events. The riot traces its beginnings to a specific labor-management dispute at a specific Chicago firm several months before Haymarket. On February 16, after months of contention, workers at Chicago's McCormick Harvester Company struck for the right to unionize. Sporadic confrontations erupted during the next two months. Concurrently, and independently, the FOTLU made preparations for the declaration of a general strike on May 1. In April, the diverse elements that made up Chicago's labor movement mobilized support for the eight-hour-day protest. As the strike date approached, city officials and the press voiced apprehensions about violence. But their fears were misplaced. The day passed without incident as 80,000 workers marched peacefully through the heart of the city. Sunday was also quiet. But the peace was shattered on Monday, though not by general strikers. At an afternoon rally near the McCormick plant, a clash between strikers and company "scabs" resulted in the death of one McCormick striker and the wounding of several others. In response, several Chicago radicals, marginally associated with the general strike, called a protest rally for Tuesday evening in Haymarket Square. The rally of several thousand was disappointingly small in comparison to the huge turnout for the general strike march just three days earlier. Indeed, the rally might have passed without notice had it not been for the explosion

15. David, *History of the Haymarket Affair*, pp. 539–40.
16. Taft, *Organized Labor in American History*, p. 135.

of a dynamite bomb and the ensuing riot. A meager rally was suddenly transformed into a national spectacle.

It would have been easy, and perhaps understandable, for impassioned observers to have presumed a conspiracy between the general strikers and the rioters. Remarkably enough, that association was not made. The independence of these events was preserved even in the highly unsympathetic national press accounts of the riot. Although the press attacked radicals and called for the rooting out of anarchists, it generally steered clear of illogical and unproven assertions implicating general strikers in the violence. The dissociation of general strike and riot in journalistic rhetoric had its counterpart in strike behavior. The violence at Haymarket notwithstanding, the general strike endured for weeks outside of the penumbra of Chicago. Americans in the Gilded Age, it seems, possessed a refined ability to discriminate between cause and effect and between local context and national scene.[17]

Claims that Haymarket violence paralyzed the general strike are greatly exaggerated. Far from being a paralytic event, with a characteristically gamma-shaped dissipation curve, Haymarket had quite modest effects on the general strike. A week and a half after the riot, 45,000 workers remained on strike. A month later, 12,000 held fast, and a month and a half later, 5,000 were still on strike for the eight-hour day. The dissipation of the general strike thus was a lengthy process; it began before Haymarket and continued long after it. On Monday evening, before Haymarket, the dissipation rate stood at 10 percent of the strikes and 25 percent of the strikers. The number of strikes had fallen from 357 to 328 and the number of strikers from 98,000 to 76,000. The pre-Haymarket decline continued on Tuesday. Strike actions fell by another 5 percent and striking workers by 10 percent. This pre-riot trajectory provides a statistical benchmark of sorts for assessing Haymarket's effects in the succeeding weeks and months: as arrests were made (May 5), the grand jury impaneled (May 17), indictments presented (May 27), and the trial begun (June 21). Figure 10.3 describes the complete trajectory of the general strike from the start of the strike on May 1 to June 20, the day before the Haymarket trial. The several curves depict daily totals of general-strike participants in Chicago, the rest of the country, and the nation as a whole.

17. Avrich, *The Haymarket Tragedy.*

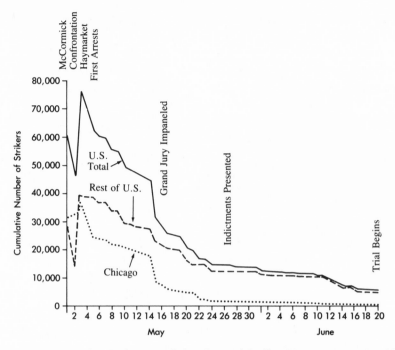

FIGURE 10.3. The Trajectory of the General Strike, May 1–June 20, 1886. The daily totals of general strikers involve subtraction of general strikers who had concluded their strike from the total number of general strikers who began their protest between May 1 and May 3. Source: *Third Annual Report of the Commissioner of Labor, 1887.*

The national curve documents the poor connection between Haymarket events and general-strike dissipation. In the first place, dissipation rates before Haymarket exceed those after the riot. In the second, the sharpest post-Haymarket decline does not occur until May 15, a full eleven days after the riot, and this drop probably owes as much to the interruptive effects of the weekend as to the forthcoming impaneling of the grand jury on Monday, May 17. After another week of moderate decline, the curve flattens out until mid-June, when the trial began.

The aggregate national curve, therefore, lends support to the Taft-David view that Haymarket violence had inconsequential effects on the general strike. The national curve, however, papers over important spatial variations in strike duration. As the second and third curves suggest, while Haymarket effects were relatively neutral in most of the country, they were adverse in the locus of violence. In the case of Chicago, the violence at the McCormick plant on Monday, May 3, triggered a sharp decline in strike support. On May 4, the day after this confrontation, Chicago's general strikers dwindled by almost 17 percent. The decline in the rest of the nation, by contrast, was under 3 percent. This spatial difference persisted after the riot. On May 5, the day after Haymarket, Chicago suffered a 22 percent attrition in striking workers; elsewhere the loss was a mere .6 percent. Even allowing for lags in information diffusion, strike dissipation rates in the rest of the nation indicate little or no effect from the violence in Chicago. Daily dissipation rates during the week following Haymarket declined modestly; even the highest rates of 9 to 12 percent elsewhere were half or less of the comparable rates in Chicago (see Figure 10.4).

Haymarket's divergent spatial effects are perhaps best illustrated by strike figures for May 15, eleven days after the riot. In Chicago, the number of general strikers had fallen from a peak of 36,788 to 8,330—a dissipation rate of 77 percent. Outside of Chicago, the comparable dissipation rate was just 42 percent. Haymarket notwithstanding, 22,807 workers around the nation persisted in the general

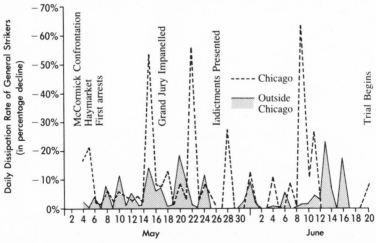

FIGURE 10.4. Daily Dissipation Rates of General Strike Participants, May 1–June 20, 1886. This rate equals the daily reductions in general strikers divided by the total number of daily strikers at the end of the preceding day, the quotient multiplied by 100. Note that Chicago's rate of dissipation exceeds the rest of the nation in all but 8 of the 43 days between May 1 and June 12, when the strike was essentially finished in Chicago. Source: *Third Annual Report of the Commissioner of Labor, 1887.*

strike as of May 15. The dissipation of strikes followed a similar trend, with strikes falling by 59 percent in Chicago as compared to 40 percent elsewhere.

These patterns continued as the trial approached. In the week after the impaneling of the grand jury (May 17), Chicago's strike participation dropped by another 70 percent, nearly double the decline (37 percent) in the rest of the nation. Outside of Chicago, the single effect of Haymarket seems to have been a relatively high dissipation rate (19 percent) on May 20, three days after the impaneling of the grand jury. Conversely, the indictments handed down on May 27 made scarcely a ripple outside of Chicago. In the city, however, general strikers dropped a further 28 percent. By the end of May the general strike in Chicago was effectively dead; elsewhere, it remained viable, with the only substantial losses coming on Monday, June 14—after a weekend. By that date, the general strike had been in effect for a month and a half—considerably longer than the average strike duration for the period 1881 to 1886.

From that point on, the dissipation of general-strike support had more to do with the exceptional length of the protest and the exhaustion of worker resources than with any adverse effects from Haymarket. A Cincinnati furniture worker made this point with a measure of wit: "The first week out, married men received six dollars in strike benefits, single men three. The second week was not so good. Married men received three dollars and single men nothing. And the third week out all were placed on the basis of American equality, everybody got nothing."[18]

Haymarket's modest impact on the general strike, save in Chicago, is underlined by comparing strike durations. In the aggregate, the general strike averaged 18.7 days; Chicago's, however, lasted just over two weeks (14.7 days), while the rest of the country averaged over three weeks (22.5 days). When we compare these figures with the average strike duration of 20.9 days for all strikes in 1886, it becomes apparent that Haymarket violence had little or no effect on the duration of the general strike outside of Chicago. But in that city, local violence seems to have reduced strike duration by about two-fifths. To underline the point, Chicago workers called off half of their strikes within ten days of Haymarket; workers elsewhere called off only about one-fourth.

18. Thomas Brooks, *The Road to Dignity: A Century of Conflict: A History of the United Brotherhood of Carpenters and Joiners of America, AFL-CIO, 1881–1981* (New York: Atheneum, 1981), pp. 42–43.

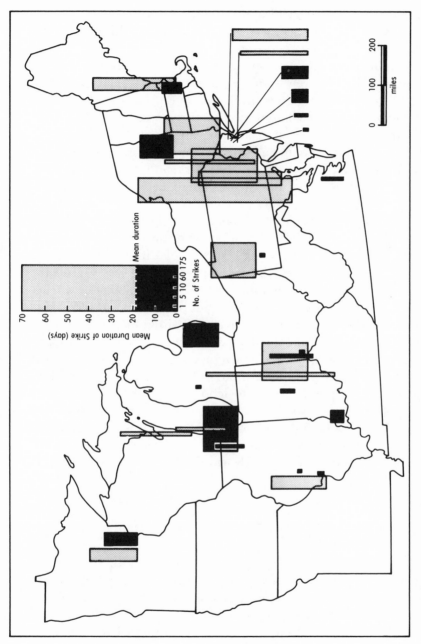

FIGURE 10.5. The Duration and Frequency of the General Strike of 1886 in the United States. Among cities with five or more general strikes, protest tended to be of shorter duration in Chicago and its Midwestern penumbra. Source: *Third Annual Report of the Commissioner of Labor, 1887.*

The division between Chicago and other places oversimplifies the geography of the general strike. By mapping the duration of the general strike in places reporting two or more strikes, we discern three roughly elliptical duration zones (Figure 10.5). In the center is Chicago with its relatively short strikes of two weeks' duration. In zone two—a ring extending from Detroit to Pittsburgh to Cincinnati to Minneapolis—strikes lasted two to three weeks. And in zone three—the northeastern cities and St. Louis—strike duration exceeded three weeks (and, in one case, two months). Exceptions to this elliptical zonation are few—Troy, New York, and the cities of northern New Jersey, where a few strikes lasted between one and two weeks.

In sum, the geographical zonation of strike duration indicates that the adverse effects of Haymarket diminished rapidly with distance from the locus of violence. Outside of Chicago, the general strike averaged three weeks in duration—a figure identical to the average for all strikes initiated between 1881 and 1886. The disruptive effects of Haymarket violence cannot be demonstrated for general strikes outside of Chicago. Conversely, within that city, Haymarket contributed to a dramatic dissipation in general-strike support. Chicago's general strikes lasted an average of just two weeks, and half of these strikes ended within ten days of the Haymarket riot. This sharp spatial divergence seems to lend support to Robert Weibe's thesis that American society in the late nineteenth century was characterized by a high degree of insularity. That is to say that systemic impulses of social behavior—in this case, the reaction to industrial labor violence—were weakly transmitted from one place to another.[19]

Lessons of the General Strike

My purposes in reconstructing the geography of the general strike are two: the lesser of these is to assess Haymarket's impact upon the strike itself; the higher purpose is to reconstruct the informational context available to trade unions following the general strike. What lessons were implied by this geography of general strike adoption and duration? What effects did these lessons have upon

19. Robert Weibe, *The Search for Order, 1877–1920* (New York: Hill and Wang, 1967); Bennett and Earle, "The Geography of Strikes," pp. 63–84.

ensuing trade union strategy and action? One lesson is that the general strike was not general; it was, on the contrary, highly selective in its spatial and industrial distribution. Although it ranked as the nation's largest strike to that date, the general strike managed to mobilize a mere .5 percent of the American industrial labor force. Workers in rural areas and small towns largely disregarded the FOTLU's call for a general strike. Over 90 percent of the 357 component strikes occurred in cities, and the vast majority of these took place in Chicago, New York, Cincinnati, Pittsburgh, and Philadelphia. The industrial composition of the general strike was similarly concentrated. Five industries—furniture, wooden goods, metal goods, building trades, and machine shops—accounted for three-fourths of all strikes. Within these industries, union organizations (principally affiliated with the FOTLU) invoked most of the strikes. The lesson for trade unionists was fairly clear: mobilizing a broad base of working-class support for a general strike or for even more ambitious ends was an exercise in futility. The optimal trade unionist strategy, highlighted by the results of the general strike, involved a narrowing of scope to the large northeastern cities and the industries therein that already had been penetrated by loyal trade union constituencies.

A second and equally important lesson concerned the unusually localized effects of violence upon worker protest. Many in the labor movement understood that the eruption of violence often disrupted local strike objectives. What they did not know was the extent of the ripple effects of violence in the case of a nationwide general strike. Haymarket offered ample evidence that these effects could be confined to the locus of violence. Following Haymarket, the dissipation rate of general strikers was considerably higher in Chicago than in other parts of the nation, and half of the city's general strikes, as compared with a quarter elsewhere, ended within a week of Haymarket. Moreover, the average duration of general strikes in Chicago was only two-fifths that of general strikes elsewhere. The lesson of Haymarket violence thus consisted of two parts. The first was that violence had substantial local effects, the second that systemic diffusion (the ripple effects) of local violence seemed to be extremely weak. Strikers elsewhere were relatively unaffected by the violence at Haymarket and its association, however oblique, with Chicago's general strike.

These highly localized effects of violence underline the peculiar

insularity of American society in the Gilded Age. Americans perceived violence as enmeshed in local rather than national contexts
and in particularistic rather than conspirational terms. These sophisticated perceptions of behavioral context mitigated against simplistic
theories that presumed the ineluctability of worker violence and
working-class protest. One fears that a century later our mass society
has somehow lost the Gilded Age's refined sense of local context and
replaced it with a pernicious tendency to generalize local effects to
regional and national scales. Were the events of the general strike
and Haymarket to occur today, given our propensity for instantaneous judgments in a world of instantaneous communications, it is
hard to imagine that we would have the capacity to distinguish local
contexts from national scene. The judicious reflection that seems
to have characterized the Gilded Age, when communications were
slower and geographic events were distanced by time, seems enviable
indeed.

If the insular society of the Gilded Age was a more reflective society than our own, it follows that trade union interests were best
served by decentralization, that is, by strategies and structures appropriate to local context and capable of localizing the disruptive effects
of unanticipated violence. Precisely such a strategy was envisaged in
the FOTLU's circular letter of November 1886 calling for a national
conference of trade unions for the purpose of establishing a new
federation. The letter spelled out an agenda for the new federation
that incorporated what had been learned from the general strike and
Haymarket. The letter declared that the new organization would develop trade assemblies, councils, and central labor unions *in every city
in America*; that it would found state assemblies or congresses to influence state legislation; and that it would recognize the autonomy of
each trade, while assisting all of them to *influence legislation and public
opinion by "peaceful and legal means."* (my emphasis).[20] The decentral-
ist, nonviolent, and parochial lessons learned seven months earlier
were now on the table.

The general strike offered trade unionists a self-study of sorts:
their strength, according to that survey, lay in big cities rather than
small towns, with selected trade unions rather than with the mass of
the working class, with nonviolent strikes rather than militant confrontation, and with a decentralized organizational structure appro-

20. Ware, *The Labor Movement in the United States*, pp. 294–95.

priate to an insular rather than a systemic mass society. The lessons learned, when translated into trade unionist strategy, contributed directly to the deepening schism in the American labor movement and the eventual supremacy of the FOTLU's successor, the American Federation of Labor. This loose confederation of trade unions pursued the narrow interests of its constituents. Its practice of pure and simple trade unionism and nonviolent worker protest in the industrial cities of an insular society boded ill for a unified American working class. The general strike, though slighted and forgotten, had provided one last trade union experiment that confirmed the wisdom of "going it alone."[21]

21.   I concur with Leon Fink's assessment of the significance of events in 1886 for the future course of the American labor movement. Conversely, I demur from his counterfactual argument that places the "blame" for labor's schism on Haymarket rather than where it belongs—on the general strike and the fatal tactical error of the Knights of Labor in refusing to support it. That is, the general strike constituted the seminal event for the ensuing schism in the working class engineered by trade unionists in the FOTLU. Haymarket and its aftermath were events of secondary significance for the future of the American labor movement. Fink, "The New Labor History," pp. 131–36.

CHAPTER 11

Spoiling the "Roast Beef and Apple Pie" Version of American Exceptionalism

The Agricultural-Geographic Origins of Working-Class Division and the Failure of American Socialism

A merican labor politics have always seemed perverse to the European mind. Here, above all places, in the showcase of industrial capitalism, labor and capital should have been fierce antagonists; here, labor should have contested capital's right to private property; here, labor should have fought valiantly for the lion's share of what it produced; here, in short, we should have had socialism or, at the very least, a political party representing the class interests of American labor. But something went awry in America. Dreams of a socialist millennium and a labor party, dreams that seemed to verge on reality at the beginning of the twentieth century, were never to be.

What went wrong? Why did socialism and class politics fail so thoroughly? These questions of American exceptionalism perennially nag at historians who are sympathetic to socialist philosophies or disenchanted with the sterility of two-party politics. It is fair to say that these questions have beguiled and baffled some of the great minds in the history of social science, yet their genius notwithstanding, history is far from achieving any consensus on the causes of socialism's failure in the United States. What we have are assorted schools of opinion, at least three of which have achieved sufficient notoriety to qualify as competing explanations.

The original version of this chapter was co-authored with Sari Bennett.

The first of these schools regards the American environment as inhospitable to socialist ideologies and politics. Werner Sombart, perhaps the best-known expositor of this position, maintained that socialism failed because American workers enjoyed considerable material prosperity during the nineteenth century. Their economic success, he argued, led to an affirmation rather than a critique of American industrial capitalism—a view that since has been called, for obvious reasons, the "roast beef and apple pie" interpretation of socialism's failure.[1] John Laslett has amplified the Sombart thesis, albeit with somewhat more sophistication and greater fidelity to the historical record. Laslett points out that the socialist critique of capitalism, while appealing initially to a wide variety of trade unionists, lost vitality as unions achieved economic, social, and political gains at the end of the nineteenth century. Radicalism succumbed to a trade unionist accommodation with capitalism.[2] These views may be subsumed under the larger argument that finds the causes of multi-class labor politics in the fluidity of American social and political conditions and the durability of liberal ideology. "In both Canada and the United States," writes the leading proponent of this position, "relatively egalitarian status structures, achievement-oriented value systems, affluence, the absence of a European aristocratic or feudal past, and a history of political democracy prior to industrialization have all operated to produce cohesive systems that remain unreceptive to proposals for major structural change."[3] In this view, the material

1. Werner Sombart, *Why is There No Socialism in the United States?* (1906; reprint, White Plains, N.Y.: M. E. Sharpe, 1976). An excellent introduction to the debate over socialism is John H. M. Laslett and Seymour Martin Lipset, *Failure of A Dream? Essays in the History of American Socialism* (Garden City, N.Y.: Anchor, 1974). Our discussion of the various explanations of socialism's failure in America should mention at least two other views not fully discussed here. The first is Michael Harrington's contention that the agenda of the late-nineteenth-century socialists has been largely achieved under the cover of bourgeois rhetoric and institutions. See his *Socialism* (New York: Saturday Review Press, 1972). Also accenting the positive in the labor movement is Karen Orren, "Organized Labor and the Invention of American Liberalism in the United States," *Studies in American Political Development* 2 (1987), pp. 317–36. The second view is Lawrence Goodwyn's cynical argument that the defeat of populism at the hands of a new American orthodoxy, resting on a hierarchical, well-financed, and well-advertised two-party system, spelled the end for subsequent movements, such as that of the socialists, that sought structural democratic reform. This kind of fatalism does an injustice to socialist successes and papers over the repression aimed at them. See his *The Populist Movement: A Short History of the Agrarian Revolt in America* (New York: Oxford Univ. Press, 1978), esp. pp. 290–92.

2. John H. M. Laslett, *Labor and the Left: A Study of Socialist and Radical Influences in the American Labor Movement, 1881–1924* (New York: Basic Books, 1970).

3. Seymour Martin Lipset, "Marx, Engels, and America's Political Parties," *Wilson Quarterly* (1978), pp. 90–104. For a critique of the findings of the new labor history and a

prosperity of and opportunities open to American workers flatly contradicted the tenets of socialism.

A second school of thought looks to the darker side of American social psychology for its explanation of socialism's failure. The enthusiastic reaction against and repression of socialism, according to this argument, had its sources in a deeply rooted American intolerance for heterodox ideas and behaviors.[4] An ingrained prejudice against the politically exotic or bizarre facilitated the corporate state's vigorous repression of Socialists during World War I. Coming on the heels of hundreds of Socialist electoral victories in 1911 and 1912, state repression savaged party ranks and destroyed an organization that had sought nothing more than the transformation of American capitalism through the "civilized means" of the ballot.[5]

A third school of thought places the blame for socialism's failure squarely on the socialists themselves. Socialists were, in Daniel Bell's judgment, more religious than political; they sought to be in the world but not of it.[6] Seeking a world more pure, they abstained from the kinds of political compromises that a mass political strategy required.[7] Echoing Bell's thesis of sectarian socialism and anticipating Jackson Lears's recent argument about the ambivalence and intellectual incoherence within the labor movement, Gabriel Kolko excoriates the self-flagellation and doctrinal division that have characterized the American left. In a biting and introspective essay, Kolko laments the unceasing sectarian disputes that have sapped the strength of the left. In his view, these were as much to blame for the failure of socialism as were structural conditions of opportunity, intolerant social psychologies, or the hegemonic power of the corporate state.[8]

---

restatement of the thesis of consensus with somewhat more cynicism, see John Patrick Diggins, "Comrades and Citizens: New Mythologies in American Historiography," *American Historical Review* 90 (1985), pp. 614–38.

4. Kenneth McNaught, "American Progressives and the Great Society," *Journal of American History* 53 (1966), pp. 504–20.

5. James Weinstein, *The Decline of Socialism in America: 1912–1925* (New York: Monthly Review Press, 1967). Also see his *The Corporate Ideal in the Liberal State* (Boston: Beacon Press, 1968).

6. Daniel Bell, *Marxian Socialism in the United States* (Princeton, N.J.: Princeton Univ. Press, 1967). Also see Warren Susman, *Culture as History: The Transformation of American Society in the Twentieth Century* (New York: Pantheon, 1984), pp. 86–97.

7. For a dissenting view on Bell's thesis, see Melvyn Dubofsky, *Industrialism and the American Worker, 1865–1920* (New York: Crowell, 1975), pp. 95–101.

8. Gabriel Kolko, "The Decline of Radicalism in the Twentieth Century," in *For a New America: Essays in History and Politics from Studies on the Left, 1959–1967*, ed. James Weinstein and David W. Eakins (New York: Random House, 1970), pp. 197–220; T. J.

All of this commentary by some of our most skilled interpreters of the American past serves to remind us just how varied, complex, and interrelated are the causes of socialism's failure in America. One senses also in this historiography an inconclusive tone, giving the impression that while each of the several interpretive schools has glimpsed some of the truth, none has seen it whole.

What, then, can geographers contribute to the perennial discourse on the failure of American socialism and class politics? A great deal, I believe. At the outset, geographical inquiry expresses reservations about the "roast beef and apple pie" interpretation, and more specifically about its assertion that American workers gave allegiance to multi-class politics because of the high wages that they earned. A geographical interpretation contradicts this assertion. It demonstrates that unskilled workers were not well paid in the antebellum or Gilded Age economies. Indeed, the cheapness of unskilled labor constituted the rock upon which a modern industrializing economy was erected.[9] The failure of class politics, then, must be explained on grounds other than those of the alleged prosperity of American workers.

A geographical approach to the failure of American socialism also discerns certain schismatic tendencies within the ranks of American labor, tendencies that were embedded in deeply seated structural divisions in nineteenth-century economy and society and that lent impetus to internal sectarianism, on the one hand, and external repression, on the other. The first of these divisive tendencies was a product of the American labor market and the historically large differential in skilled and unskilled wages. In a society where skilled labor was dear and unskilled labor was cheap, where the material interests of workers were more often divergent than convergent, labor solidarity was difficult to achieve. Because of the wide differential in American wages, labor coalitions were notoriously unstable. While socialists valiantly attempted to patch over these schisms and unite all workers—and on momentary occasions, when the wages and interests of skilled and unskilled labor converged, succeeded in doing so—the structural odds in the long run were against them. These odds favored trade unionism. Although trade unionists frequently proclaimed the brotherhood of all workers, they usually acted in ac-

---

Jackson Lears, "The Concept of Cultural Hegemony: Problems and Possibilities," *American Historical Review* 90 (1985), pp. 567–93.

9. See Chapter 5.

FIGURE 11.1. The lead article in *Frank Leslie's Popular Monthly* offers a sympathetic account of "socialistic movements." The article appeared in May of 1886, the same month as the General Strike and the Haymarket Riot. Note especially the orderliness and decorum of the strikers depicted here. Reproduced from *Frank Leslie's Popular Monthly* 21, no. 5 (1886), cover page.

cordance with the material interests of their skilled constituency. Far from aiming to destroy a system that had amply rewarded them, they sought merely to secure their privileged position within a capitalist society through the exercise of "pure and simple" trade unionism.

The American labor movement was fractured further by fissures in the sociogeography of the Gilded Age. The intrusion of massive industrialization in the last quarter of the nineteenth century divided the nation into two geographical worlds: large industrial cities and smaller preindustrial cities and towns. In these contrasting worlds, labor's experiences were so remarkably different that they reinforced and deepened even further the schisms between skilled and unskilled workers, trade unionists and socialists, and conservative and radical labor politicians. Giant industrial cities, those with populations of over 100,000, fell under the domain of the skilled, conservative trade unionists; smaller communities, meanwhile, constituted havens for the radical labor politics of the Knights of Labor and later the Socialist Party of America. This curious dualism in labor's sociogeography and its dispiriting implications for American socialism are matters of central concern in the essay that follows.

These geostructural divisions in wages and sociogeography constitute a point of departure for a reconsideration of the inherent instability and schism within the American labor movement. They define the structural context in which labor, capital, and the state found themselves in the late nineteenth and early twentieth centuries. How these parties chose to act within this context and what strategies underlay their choices were critical factors in socialism's American failure.

This essay begins with American labor's deepest and most enduring source of schism—the sizable differential in the wages of skilled and unskilled workers. My point is that the origins of the American wage differential (and the divergent interests entrained) were quite old, lodged in the geography of antebellum labor markets and their peculiar manner of determining wages. Following a brief review of these markets and their societal legacy, the essay reviews their impacts in labor's golden age between 1865 and 1920. The oscillations in labor solidarity, I submit, display an uncanny correlation with temporal and spatial swings in the wage differential between 1865 and 1920. The essay describes how wage convergence in the 1880s and again on the eve of World War I fostered labor solidarity and radical labor politics; how wage divergence and an emerging sociogeographic division in the 1890s undermined them; and how, despite a dramatic convergence in the wage structure after 1907, an entrenched urban trade unionism, abetted by cultural intolerance toward heterodoxy and the repressive arm of the state, succeeded in crushing its radical adversary once and for all. The story's theme, if one is necessary, is that American socialism never really endangered American society and that its destruction seems to have been the overzealous and hyperbolic act of small, mean, and frightened men. The extraordinary geostructural divisions in labor's material interests and bases of operation were more than ample restraints on socialism's ideological and political progress.

Labor and the Labor Market in Industrializing America

A geographic perspective on American labor begins with a reassessment of the optimistic evaluations of labor's welfare voiced by Werner Sombart, Seymour Lipset, and others. I will argue that industrialization did not benefit the American worker nearly as much as the "roast beef and apple pie" version of the labor experience seems to imply. Contrary to that version of American history—a version reinforced by the economists' doctrine of labor scarcity and high wages—American industrialization before and after the Civil War was predicated on the use of cheap, unskilled labor in the northern United States. The wages of unskilled industrial workers in the Northeast were low compared to unskilled wages in either the antebellum South or England; only when juxtaposed against the exceedingly low earnings of seasonal rural workers in the region could they be judged high. Herein lies the principal source of the wide differential in American wage structures.

That is not to argue that American industrialization was ruinous for the unskilled worker, however. The spectacular growth and development of the American economy—subsidized as it was by the entrepreneurial exploitation of cheap labor—did eventually improve unskilled industrial wages in the second half of the nineteenth century. Three factors—the emergence of competitive urban labor markets; the expansion of more intensive agriculture, which increased the competition for urban workers; and labor's aggressive use of strikes and other tactics—combined to force wages upward. But these advances in the late nineteenth century are merely a coda to a story that properly begins with the antebellum origins of cheap labor and the reasons why previous interpreters have been misled about the alleged prosperity of the unskilled American worker.

That the American economy was benevolent toward labor is a long-established and widely shared view, dating back at least to the marginalist revolution in the second half of the nineteenth century. According to neoclassical economic doctrine, American workers were equitably rewarded by an economy in which labor was exceedingly scarce—the result of a favorable land-labor ratio. The unvarnished theory of labor scarcity implied that all American workers earned high wages, and in order to confirm this deduction, scholars trotted out a good deal of supporting evidence. They pointed to farmers' repeated complaints about the high wages commanded by farm laborers and to industrialists' laments over the rarity, expense, and willful independence of skilled workers. When anecdotal evidence of this sort comported so nicely with abstract theory, it was only natural that scholars came to the conclusion that American labor was uniformly scarce and expensive. Labor, it followed, reaped its fair share as the American economy grew.

This rosy view of American labor history has served as the foundation for some of our most important interpretations of the American past. Frederick Jackson Turner's frontier thesis, perhaps the most influential of all interpretations in American history, maintained that free land on the frontier served as a "safety valve" for workers in eastern cities. Opportunities on the frontier reduced the supply of urban labor, increased urban wages, and alleviated class tension and conflict in one stroke. Although historians have challenged virtually every corollary of the frontier thesis, Turner's central axiom—the sanguine view that the urban wage earner was well paid—persists unscathed. Turner's beneficent land-labor ratio also served as the underpinning for H. J. Habakkuk's highly regarded interpretation of American industrialization. The position of American labor was an enviable one, in Habakkuk's view. In a labor-scarce economy, urban entrepreneurs were required to pay exceptionally high wages for unskilled labor. In order to pay high wages and remain profitable at the same time, they were compelled to economize on labor and increase productivity through the introduction of machine technology. Technology thus was critical for raising labor's marginal productivity to the already high level of wages. In this benevolent view, America got industrialization and workers retained their high wages.[10]

Although the doctrine of labor scarcity has triumphed in history and economics, certain evidence contradicts this benign interpretation of the American economy. The plausibility of this account of high wages and the absence of class conflict notwithstanding, the labor-scarcity interpretation is at odds with numerous studies documenting high levels of social and economic inequality in city and country. Nor does the thesis square with trends in nineteenth-century factor shares. Edward Budd, for one, has shown that labor's share of output was quite low in the antebellum United States, rose during the course of the nineteenth century, and did not stabilize until the early twentieth century. Trends in labor's share of value added in manufacturing raise further suspicions about well-paid American workers. This evidence, circumstantial though it may be, hints that antebellum American wages may not have been as high as has been supposed. Furthermore, the doctrine of high wages and labor scarcity has been challenged on theoretical grounds by Peter Temin. His purely deductive analysis arrives at the seemingly paradoxical conclusion that American wages in the antebellum period probably were lower than wages in Britain.[11]

What we require is a new theory that reconciles the ambiguities in the wage evidence with the failure of class politics in the industrializing United States. Neoclassical theories of labor scarcity, whatever their other virtues, are inappropriate to labor markets and wage determination in developing economies such as the United States. Nineteenth-century observers more faithfully captured the essence of the American labor market—an essence that departed radically from notions of competitive labor markets and marginalist wage de-

10. The literature on labor scarcity is voluminous and I limit my citations to the two seminal works. Frederick Jackson Turner, *The Frontier in American History* (New York: H. Holt, 1922); H. J. Habakkuk, *American and British Technology in the Nineteenth Century: The Search for Labour-Saving Inventions* (Cambridge: Cambridge Univ. Press, 1962).

11. Edward C. Budd, "Factor Shares, 1850–1910," in *Trends in the American Economy in the Nineteenth Century*, ed. William N. Parker, National Bureau of Economic Research, Studies in Income and Wealth, No. 24 (Princeton, N.J.: Princeton Univ. Press, 1960), pp. 365–98; Peter Temin, "Labor Scarcity and the Problem of American Industrial Efficiency in the 1850s," *Journal of Economic History* 26 (1966), pp. 277–98; *idem*, "Labor Scarcity in America," *Journal of Interdisciplinary History* 1 (1970–71), pp. 251–64. Melvyn Dubofsky takes a rare and skeptical view of the economists' claim of high wages and labor scarcity for the period between the Civil War and World War I in his *Industrialism and the American Worker*, pp. 13–22.

termination held by neoclassical economists. James Montgomery, an authority on the antebellum cotton industry, came closer to the truth when he observed that in America capital was motivated by the "great object" of paying "their help just such wages as will be a sufficient inducement for them to remain at the work. Hence the greater the quantity of work produced, the higher the profits, because paid at a lower rate of wages."[12]

Montgomery's point is simple—cheap rather than expensive labor was the great object of American industry. But what were the sources of cheap labor to which Montgomery alluded? These sources were hardly a mystery, since they had been identified as early as the 1790s by none other than Alexander Hamilton in his classic *Report on Manufactures*.

It is one of history's small ironies that Hamilton's concern with labor economics has been overlooked by students of economic thought. Hamilton understood that any persuasive argument for American industrialization first had to disarm the theoretical critique of American labor by contemporary political economists. That critique maintained that cheap labor and the wage fund were indispensable conditions for economic development, that the American economy of labor scarcity and high wages failed to satisfy these conditions, and that, ergo, industrialization there was practically impossible. Hamilton took considerable pains to demolish this myth of American labor scarcity. Unskilled labor in the United States, he submitted, was not nearly as dear as political economists had supposed. He identified four sources of cheap American labor—women, children, immigrants, and farmers and farm workers idled by the seasonality of agricultural labor—which, in his view, nullified the critique of political economists and provided theoretical justification for American industrialization.[13]

American entrepreneurs also knew of these sources of cheap unskilled labor, and they effectively exploited them during and after the War of 1812. Firms in the cotton textile industry installed the most sophisticated machinery, including the power loom and the throstle frame, and deployed cheap, unskilled operatives—women

12. James Montgomery, *Practical Detail of the Cotton Manufactures of the United States of America and the State of the Cotton Manufactures of That Country Contrasted with That of Great Britain* (Glasgow: J. Niven, 1840), pp. 97–98.

13. Samuel McKee, Jr., ed., *Alexander Hamilton's Papers on Public Credit, Commerce and Finance* (New York: Columbia Univ. Press, 1934), pp. 177–276, esp. pp. 206–8.

and children in New England; women, children, and men in the middle states—in the manufacture of coarse, inexpensive cloth.[14]

Here was the template for American industrialization. And what more logical place to combine machines with cheap, unskilled labor than in the rural "suburbs" of the great mercantile cities of the early nineteenth century, near a supply of seasonally unemployed rural labor. Industrial entrepreneurs pursued this locational strategy in the Boston suburbs of Waltham and Lowell, in Philadelphia's Manayunk, and in Baltimore's Hampden and Ellicott City. In addition to providing ready access to cheap supplies of rural labor, these peripheral locations effectively sealed off a naïve unskilled labor force from the contaminating political influences of the central city and skilled artisans who might have provided articulate labor leadership and political savvy. The effects of this geographical segregation of skilled and unskilled workers on the direction of labor politics during the 1820s and 1830s were profound. While workers' political parties and unions flourished among skilled trades in the central cities, these institutions scarcely touched the lives of unskilled workers residing several miles away in these first industrial satellites.[15]

Unskilled workers, generally speaking, had neither leverage nor power in the new suburban factories. Their ease of replacement by other unskilled workers rendered them weak and vulnerable, and it should come as no surprise that they were in attitude docile, politically apathetic, and malleable—ideal traits, of course, for subordination to the factory's disciplined rhythm. To compound their dilemma, factory operatives garnered only modest support from their seemingly logical allies, the skilled workers. Although they resided in different worlds, skilled and unskilled workers directly competed with each other. In industry after industry, the new technologies of machines, factories, and unskilled operatives threatened skilled artisans with job displacement, loss of income, and erosion of status. Nor would these divisions in the ranks of labor disappear so long as there

14. See the argument and sources cited in Chapter 5.

15. Students of the antebellum urban economy, generally speaking, have ignored the geographical separation of the skilled urban workers in the city center from the unskilled workers in the industrial "suburbs." An example of this truncated view of urban structure occurs in Edward Muller and Paul Groves, "The Emergence of Industrial Districts in Mid-Nineteenth Century Baltimore," *Geographical Review* 69 (1979), pp. 159–78. A broader focus on the geography of labor in the urban economy is required, and hints toward that end may be found in Bruce Laurie, "The Working People of Philadelphia, 1827–1853," (Ph.D. diss., Univ. of Pittsburgh, 1971), pp. 22–70.

existed a wide differential in the wages of the skilled and the un-skilled. The labor market as it was provided entrepreneurs with a powerful inducement for substituting the new technology of machines and unskilled labor for the old technology based on skill alone. It was these ancient divisions in wages and location that set the house of labor against itself and that undermined repeated attempts to create a united and radical working class.[16]

The peculiar geography of nineteenth-century labor markets offers a point of departure for this reconsideration of the failure of American socialism and class politics. From the outset of the nineteenth century, these markets had created a pool of cheap unskilled labor that served simultaneously as an inducement (and subsidy) for industrialization and a disincentive for labor solidarity. But what were the causes of cheap labor in a nation of abundant land? And how did antebellum labor markets yield this paradoxical result? An outline of the functioning of these labor markets, however spare and compressed, is prerequisite to understanding the schismatic nature of working-class politics before and after the Civil War.[17]

In a developing economy such as the antebellum United States, labor markets divide into two sectors—a large rural sector and a small but growing urban sector. In this context, urban wage determination results from the interaction of these two sectors and their respective labor markets. These markets are mediated by the transfer wage, or the annual wage necessary to draw unskilled workers from

16. See Chapter 5. The wide spread in the wages of the skilled and the unskilled remained evident at the beginning of the twentieth century, particularly in comparison with British wages. See E. H. Phelps-Brown, *A Century of Pay: The Course of Pay and Production in France, Germany, Sweden, the United Kingdom, and the United States of America, 1860–1960* (London: Macmillan, 1968), pp. 47–48.

17. See Chapter 5. As the labor movement accelerated during the Gilded Age and the Progressive Era, the divergent interests of the skilled and the unskilled continually introduced tensions. Samuel Gompers was wary of trying to organize unskilled workers because of their high turnover and the ease with which "scabs" could replace them. He moved with extreme caution on the matter of industrial unionization, despite considerable pressure from some of the unions affiliated with the American Federation of Labor. Conversely, the radical position was stated flatly by Big Bill Haywood in 1905: "I do not care the snap of my finger whether or not the skilled workman joins this industrial movement. When we get the unorganized and unskilled laborer into this organization, the skilled worker will of necessity come here for his own protection." Quoted in Philip S. Foner, *History of the Labor Movement in the United States* (4 vols.; New York: International, 1935); Vol. 4, p. 37. On Gompers, see Bell, *Marxian Socialism in the United States*, pp. 42–43; and William M. Dick, *Labor and Socialism in America: The Gompers Era* (Port Washington, N.Y.: Kennikat Press, 1972), pp. 83–110.

rural to urban employment. Urban entrepreneurs must pay a wage that generates annual net urban incomes that equal or exceed annual net rural incomes. This is expressed by the formula $(W_u—C_u) = (W_r—C_r)$, where W_u is the transfer wage, W_r is rural earnings, and C_u and C_r are the costs of living in city and country, respectively. The urban entrepreneur must, then, pay a wage (W_u) that is determined principally by rural employment opportunities and the seasonality of rural production.[18] In regions where rural earnings are low, urban wages will be low; where they are high, urban wages will be high.

In one important antebellum region, the grain belt of the northern United States, the transfer wage was especially low. The acute seasonality of wheat and corn production severely constricted rural employment opportunities and the annual earnings of labor. Wheat farmers, for instance, usually hired labor for ten days to two weeks at harvest time, while corn farmers took on labor for the "crop sea-

18.   Precisely when and why wage determination shifted from the transfer wage to marginal productivity remains unclear; indeed, the poor agreement between marginal productivity theory and contemporary wage levels suggests that the shift may never have occurred. In theory, the transformation should have taken place during the Gilded Age with the emergence of more nearly perfect competitive urban labor markets and the breakdown of customary wage-setting practices inherited from the antebellum labor market. Somewhat ironically, the labor unrest of the 1880s can be seen as an opening salvo aimed at reducing labor's economic exploitation, dislodging the low-wage structure that had long been customary (particularly for the unskilled), and putting wage determination on a marginal productivity basis. The turbulence of labor-capital relations in the 1880s and 1890s indicates that capitalists staunchly opposed in practice what their academic apologists claimed was in theory the new marginalist mechanism of wage determination. For evidence of wage exploitation in the antebellum economy (wages less than marginal product), see the curious essay by Richard K. Vedder, Lowell E. Gallaway, and David Klingaman, "Discrimination and Exploitation in Antebellum American Cotton Textile Manufacturing," *Research in Economic History* 3 (1978), pp. 217–62. The essay's peculiarity rests with the authors' claim that exploitation was minimal although their evidence suggests precisely the opposite. Note their offhanded discussion of adult male wages in 1832: "In the case of adult males, their marginal productivity is significantly greater than their unadjusted wage in five of six cases, suggesting some degree of exploitation of male labor." Indeed! Male workers' wages averaged $327 per year, while their marginal product, depending on several assumptions, ranged anywhere from $500 to $700. For evidence of the continuing importance of the transfer wage until the 1930s, see Lee J. Alston and T. J. Hatton, "The Earnings Gap Between Agriculture and Manufacturing Laborers, 1925–1941," *Journal of Economic History* 51(1991), pp. 83–99. For additional skepticism on marginal productivity, see Lawrence Klein and R. F. Kosobud, "Some Econometrics of Growth: Great Ratios of Economics," *Quarterly Journal of Economics* 75 (1961), pp. 173–98; Lester Thurow, "Disequilibrium and the Marginal Productivity of Capital and Labor," *Review of Economics and Statistics* 50 (1968), pp. 23–31; and Peter T. Gottschalk, "A Comparison of Marginal Productivity and Earnings by Occupation," *Industrial and Labor Relations Review* 31 (1978), pp. 368–78.

son" lasting from planting and tillage in April through the harvest of wheat and hay in early July. Rural laborers, who occasionally amounted to 20 to 30 percent of rural adult males, typically secured farm work for about a third of the year and were unemployed or underemployed for the rest of the year. Their annual earnings under these seasonal agrarian regimes, as a consequence, were modest indeed.

The rural laborer's plight was the urban entrepreneur's windfall. The market that provided this windfall of cheap labor functioned in the following manner. Urban entrepreneurs in the grain belt bid against farmers in a hybrid rural labor market—one that was perfectly competitive in the spring and early summer and imperfectly competitive during the remaining eight months of the year. Urban entrepreneurs in the region thus were dealt a low transfer wage. That is to say that unskilled urban labor came cheap in a region stretching from Pennsylvania to Illinois between 1800 and 1860. During the 1820s, for example, Philadelphians hired unskilled urban labor for about $110 to $150 per year, while English firms in the Midlands and in Lancashire paid about $225. Similarly, during the 1850s, entrepreneurs in Chicago paid unskilled workers about $190 per year while their counterparts in southern cities paid out $400 or more. In each case, regional wages were rooted in agrarian systems' seasonality and rural employment opportunities.

If unskilled urban labor in the American grain belt was cheap and readily available from farms or foreign immigration, the same was not true for the skilled labor force. Skilled labor was consistently scarce and expensive. Eli Whitney underscored the rational consequences of the large wage differential that resulted. Interchangeable parts, he observed, would "substitute correct and effective operations of machinery for that skill of the artist which is acquired only by long practice and experience; a species of skill which is not possessed in this country to any considerable extent."[19] Whitney, like Alexander Hamilton before him and James Montgomery after, understood that the sizable differential in the cost of labor (high for skilled labor and low for unskilled) constituted the fulcrum for American industrialization.

By combining unskilled labor with the "correct and effective op-

19. William P. Blake, "Sketch of the Life of Eli Whitney, the Inventor of the Cotton Gin," *Papers of the New Haven Colony Historical Society* 5 (1894), p. 122.

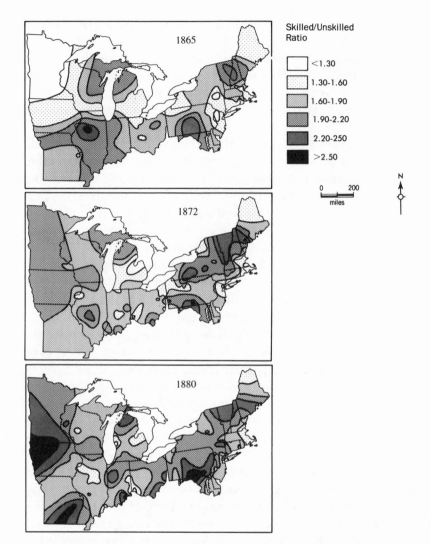

FIGURE 11.2 Ratio of Skilled and Unskilled Wages in the Northeastern United States, 1865, 1872, and 1880. Skilled wages are represented by the daily wages of machinists; unskilled wages, of common laborers. These maps accent the considerable spatial variability of the wage ratio following the Civil War. While the progressive darkening of the map indicates a trend toward wage divergence, note the advance or persistence of small wage ratios in many parts of the Midwest and along the Atlantic Seaboard in 1880. Source: United States, Congress, House of Representatives, *Report on the Statistics of Wages in Manufacturing Industries with Supplementary Reports*, by Joseph D. Weeks, House Misc. Doc. 42, vol. 13, part 20, 47th Congress, 2nd Sess. (Washington, D.C.: GPO, 1886).

erations of machinery," grain-belt entrepreneurs could manufacture a reasonably sophisticated product at costs lower than those of the skilled artisan. A case in point is the differential diffusion of the power loom in the United States and England. In the United States diffusion proceeded rapidly. Although the productivity of the new technology (the power loom) and the old artisanal technology (the hand loom) were about the same in the American case, the costs of the new machine, appropriately discounted, plus the unskilled operative were substantially less than the wages of a skilled weaver. Precisely the opposite occurred in England, where the high costs of unskilled labor (a reflection of the intensity of English agriculture, its longer season, and the consequent higher annual earnings of English rural laborers) retarded the diffusion of the power loom and enabled skilled hand-loom weaving to persist.

At the precise moment when the antebellum labor market in the United States was encouraging industrialization through the introduction of machines and factories, it was also fomenting division in the ranks of the wage-earning classes. Skilled and unskilled workers found themselves in constant opposition as industrialization progressed. Whitney's rational strategy of replacing scarce artisans with machines and cheap, unskilled operatives posed a continuing threat to skilled workers. The interests of American workers thus diverged sharply. In England, conversely, the much narrower wage differential facilitated working-class solidarity, first by reducing the threat to skilled workers of displacement by unskilled workers, second by structuring a convergence rather than a divergence of material and class interests.

On the eve of large-scale industrialization, circa 1865, the American labor market may be characterized as one of cheap unskilled labor, expensive skilled labor, and a wide wage differential—all of which predisposed the economy on the one hand toward rapid industrialization and labor politics, and on the other toward fragmentation and division. The regional geography of wages was somewhat more complex, however, than this caricature allows. Wage ratios in 1865 were especially large in grain belt areas such as south central Pennsylvania, Illinois, western Indiana, and southern portions of Michigan and Wisconsin. Lower ratios prevailed along the Atlantic Seaboard from Philadelphia to Albany and east to Boston, as well as in the upper Midwest (see Figure 11.2). Fifteen years later, the geography of wage ratios had changed considerably. Wages diverged in many places—a situation not altogether unexpected given the depressed conditions during the 1870s and 1880s. But it was the exceptions to the rule that would prove critical for solidarity and ferment in the ranks of American labor during the 1880s. Areas of convergent wages included the seaboard cities from Philadelphia to Boston, much of Illinois, southern Ohio, and Indiana. Most significant in that regard was the Midwest, which had experienced a remarkable convergence of wages between 1865 and 1880.[20]

While the causes of these trends in the wage ratio are elusive, what is clear is that in many areas of the Midwest—in Illinois, southern Ohio, and Indiana—unskilled wages rose while skilled wages held steady or declined modestly. The result was a sharp lowering of midwestern wage ratios. Seaboard cities also reported a narrow wage differential in 1880, but in their case, the result reflected persistence rather than convergence in wage structures between 1865 and 1880.

On the eve of the spectacular eruption of American worker protest, the geography of wages and wage differentials had assumed a configuration of unusual political significance for the labor movement. For a moment, in the turbulent 1880s, convergent wages in a few strategic regions invited heady visions of labor solidarity and, for some, a working-class millennium. But that was not to be. A decade later, the divergence in the wages and material interests of workers, among other factors, would dash these visions and others that followed.[21]

20. In Figure 11.2, skilled wages are represented by machinists, unskilled wages by common laborers. The ratio is based on daily wage payments. Observations are limited to urban places in the northeastern United States; the greater complexity of the 1880 map reflects an increase in the density of place-specific wage data as compared to earlier years. An aggregate time series of the wage ratio, using carpenters as skilled and common laborers as unskilled, appears in Table 11.2. The source for Figure 11.2 is Joseph D. Weeks, *Report on the Statistics of Wages in Manufacturing Industries with Supplementary Reports*, 47th Cong., 2nd sess., 1886, H. Misc. Doc. 42, Vol. 13, pt. 20.

21. Although economists have given considerable attention to the wage ratio or, as it is sometimes called, the wage differential, social historians have been unappreciative of its conceptual significance for the variabilities in material interests and class coalition. It is worth noting that the American wage ratio historically has been high in comparison to that of Britain or continental European nations. See Phelps-Brown, *A Century of Pay*, pp. 47–48; Paul Uselding, "Wage and Consumption Levels in England and on the Continent in the 1830s," *Journal of European Economic History* 4 (1975), pp. 501–13; Harry Ober, "Occupational Wage Differentials, 1907–1947," *Monthly Labor Review* 67 (1948), pp. 127–34; Harold Lydall, *The Structure of Earnings* (Oxford: Clarendon Press, 1968),

The Labor Movement, Worker Protest, and Structural Division in the Gilded Age, 1865-94

The progress of socialism and working-class politics, of course, was bound up in a vastly larger labor movement. Within that movement, socialists worked tirelessly on behalf of an American working class, one that was organized in itself and for itself, that was unified by material conditions as well as by consciousness of labor's interests and the interests of its capitalist adversary. Although the socialist moment never arrived in the United States, this radical philosophy made considerable inroads into the labor movement in the half century after the Civil War. These came in two great surges. The first surge attended the rise of the Knights of Labor during the strife-torn 1880s. This semi-secret order, founded in 1869 for the purpose of unifying all wage earners in opposition to capital, saw its influence peak in 1886. The decline was equally rapid; by the early 1890s, the Knights amounted to little more than a hollow shell of an organization. Socialism's second surge came at the turn of the century in the form of the Socialist Party of America. Unlike the Knights, who eschewed partisan politics in favor of labor organizing and education, the Socialist party lodged its faith in political organization and the ballot. But by 1920, partisan politics also had failed and the party had all but slipped from the scene of American politics. The American encounter with socialism and working-class politics had at last ebbed away. Despite the Knights' enrollment of more than 700,000 members and the Socialist party's election of over 1,000 public-office holders and garnering of nearly 900,000 votes in 1912, these attempts at remaking America in the socialist image were history, as it were, by the 1920s.

But every failure has its successes. The hundreds of communities, towns, and cities that supported the Knights of Labor and the Socialists offer a window on socialism's appeal. They reveal the kinds of places that were congenial for socialism and, as importantly, those

---

pp. 163–80, 182–85; and Paul A. David, "Industrial Labor Market Adjustments in a Region of Recent Settlement: Chicago, 1848–1868," in *Quantity and Quiddity: Essays in U.S. Economic History*, ed. Peter Kilby (Middletown, Conn.: Wesleyan Univ. Press, 1987), pp. 47–97.

that were not. I begin with the Knights of Labor and the context of worker protest that they shaped—and were shaped by—during the turbulent 1880s.

Friedrich Engels had high hopes for American socialism during the Gilded Age, and he premised his optimism on the Knights. "The Knights of Labor," he wrote in 1887,

> are the first national organization created by the American working class as a whole; whatever be their origin and history, whatever their platform and their constitution, here they are, the work of practically the whole class of American wage-earners, the only national bond that holds them together, that makes their strength felt to themselves no less than to their enemies, and that fills them with the proud hope of future victories. . . . To an outsider it appears evident that here is the raw material out of which the future of the American working-class movement, and along with it, the future of American society at large, has to be shaped.[22]

Engels, like many others who dreamt of a socialist millennium, was caught up in the flood tide of the American labor movement. Never before had Americans, or Europeans for that matter, witnessed such an outpouring of labor unrest. American work stoppages in the form of strikes or lockouts had risen from a handful per year to nearly a thousand, and the conflict between labor and capital, once confined to the older Atlantic port cities, now spread throughout the industrializing Northeast. It is hard to imagine the significance of the 1880s unless its turbulence is put in the context of just how far the labor movement had come during the preceding eight decades.

The nineteenth century was truly the century of the strike. Although workers in western Europe and, to a lesser extent, the United States, had employed the strike in the eighteenth century, this strategy was neither widespread nor effective. The course of strike history, however, shifted gears after 1800. In the United States, the number of strikes climbed steadily until 1880, when strike actions escalated to unprecedented heights. Although 1877, the year the railroad strikes broke out, is conventionally considered to be the start

22. Frederick [Friedrich] Engels, *Conditions of the British Working Class in 1844* (London, 1887), preface.

of the upswing in labor unrest, the strike curve suggests that the inflection in worker protest actually occurred a decade or so earlier. The critical period seems to have been between 1865 and 1880 (see Figure 11.3).[23]

The Civil War constitutes a great divide in the American labor movement. Before the war, strikes occurred only sporadically. The number of strikes fluctuated from year to year, but rarely were there more than fifteen in any one year. The pace accelerated to about twenty strikes per year during the war and then rose to over fifty per year between 1867 and 1877. The railroad strikes of 1877, however galvanizing for the American labor movement, do not mark a sharp discontinuity with preceding strike activity. The sharpest increases occurred in 1880, when strike actions surpassed 700, and again in 1886, when strikes topped the 1,000 mark.

The foundation for the turbulent 1880s seems to have been laid in the years between the Civil War and 1875—a decade characterized by agitation for the eight-hour day, by severe depression in the early 1870s, and by efforts at forming national labor organizations. This decade witnessed the establishment of 26 new national unions to go along with the six already in existence. Most of these were trade unions, but at least one attempted to establish a more broadly based national organization. The National Labor Union, though organized for all workers, appealed in fact to only a few; for all practical purposes, it had expired by 1870. The Knights of Labor constituted a more durable product of this critical decade. Established in 1869, the Knights had made modest inroads into the labor movement by the late 1870s.[24]

Following a decade of heady expansion (1865–75), the labor movement stalled briefly. The movement that had produced over thirty labor unions and some 300,000 members rapidly lost ground. By 1878, just eight or nine national unions survived and, according to Samuel Gompers's estimate, trade union rolls had declined to

---

23. The strike curve presented here should be regarded as provisional since it is based on fragmentary historical data compiled by the Bureau of Labor in the 1880s. Until we have a comprehensive study of pre-1880 strikes using local records, the Bureau of Labor's list serves as a rough approximation of the tempo of strike activity. *Third Annual Report of the Commissioner of Labor, 1887: Strikes and Lockouts* (Washington, D.C.: Government Printing Office, 1888), pp. 1029–1108.

24. John Commons et al., eds., *History of Labour in the United States* (1918; reprint, New York: Macmillan, 1966), Vol. 2, pp. 42–48; David Montgomery, *Beyond Equality: Labor and the Radical Republicans, 1862–1872* (New York: Knopf, 1967).

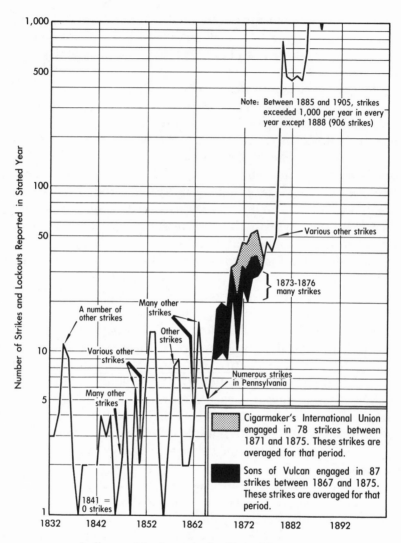

FIGURE 11.3. Strikes and Lockouts in the United States, 1832–85. Note that strike data before 1880 are incomplete; I have graphed the numbers of those of which I am certain, but additional strikes are known to have occurred throughout the pre-1880 period. Sources: *Third Annual Report of the Commissioner of Labor, 1887*; and *Tenth Annual Report of the Commissioner of Labor, 1894*.

about 50,000—a sixfold decrease in the space of six years.[25] Paradoxically, this sudden collapse of the trade unions had little effect on the pace of strike activity, which continued unabated, nor on the Knights of Labor, who stood poised for their finest hour. The labor movement, for perhaps the first time, had bypassed the mediating role of trade unions and infected directly the unskilled and unorganized workers in the Northeast.

The downward trend in union influence persisted until the late 1880s. Barely half of the strikes reported between 1881 and 1887 were conducted under union auspices. Unions experienced a resurgence after 1887, however, and over the next seven years they conducted 60 to 70 percent of all strikes in the Northeast. These trends lend support to David Montgomery's observation that the role of unions in strike activity varied inversely with wage issues. When wages were cut (and wage ratios converged) during the depressed years between 1873 and 1879 and again in 1883 and 1884, trade unions fared poorly. Unions offered little support for unorganized workers in their resistance to wage reductions, perhaps because unions were strapped for finances and because their skilled-worker constituencies suffered smaller wage reductions than did other workers.[26] In sum, in the two decades after the Civil War, the American labor movement experienced a profound shift. Formal labor organizations were in the ascendant until the depression of 1873. But as wage issues became paramount from 1873 to the mid-1880s and as wages converged in many locales, the movement staked out a larger front. It broadened its appeal to all workers, thus abetting the cause of the Knights of Labor and offering a portent of the socialist moment.

The curve of strikes tells about history; the map of strike locations adds a spatial dimension to the story of the American labor movement. And once again, the Civil War stands out as a divide. Before the war, strikes were concentrated in a few older cities, notably Philadelphia, Boston, and Pittsburgh. The singular exception to this pattern was Massachusetts, with its scattering of strikes in numerous textile and shoemaking towns. The geography of strikes intensified during the 1850s, but the basic pattern remained unchanged until the 1860s. In that decade, strike actions accelerated in

25. Commons, *History of Labour*, Vol. 2, pp. 175–81.
26. David Montgomery, "Strikes in Nineteenth-Century America," *Social Science History* 4 (1980), pp. 81–104.

New York City, and, for the first time, in the anthracite regions of northeastern Pennsylvania, home of the Molly Maguires. Strike actions dotted the lower Midwest at Cincinnati and St. Louis. These additions to the strike map, though modest, prefigured an explosion in strike locations during the 1870s. In that decade, strikes filled up the map of Massachusetts with Fall River, New Bedford, and Lynn appearing prominently. Worker protests also spread into the bituminous-coal mining and iron centers of western Pennsylvania and eastern Ohio. And the number of strikes in Cincinnati and St. Louis increased (see Figures 11.4–11.6).[27]

Although the pre-1881 strike data are suspect from the standpoint of completeness, they capture the coarse patterns of spatial change in strike activity. The maps in Figures 11.4–11.6 underline two important geographical trends: first, the concentration of localized strikes in the seaboard cities of the Northeast during the 1850s and 1860s; and second, the spatial expansion of strike activity in the 1870s. Strike actions had become more numerous and more widespread by 1880. Worker protest constituted a familiar part of the American social landscape, from the smallest mining camps and midwestern towns to the largest industrial cities.

The 1880s perpetuated the trend toward the geographical expansion of labor unrest. In that decade, strikes spread westward into Indiana, Illinois, and Iowa, and southward into West Virginia and Kentucky. The strike, if not yet a national phenomenon, was firmly implanted in the industrializing northeastern quadrant of the nation. In the next fourteen years, strikes were reported in 99 percent of all northeastern cities with 20,000 or more people, in 58 percent of all towns and cities above 2,500, and in over 50 percent of the region's 973 counties. While eastern seaboard cities persisted as an important locus of industrial conflict, the geographic center of worker protest had moved into the Midwest. (See Chapter 9 for a detailed examination of strike geography.)

The geography of strikes in the 1880s highlights the connections among several elements in our interpretation of the American labor movement. In the first place, the labor unrest of the 1880s was ac-

27. Based on an examination of pre-1881 strike reports in Pennsylvania, David Montgomery detects a turning point more nearly at mid-century, when strikes spread geographically, penetrated into new industries, and focused increasingly on wage issues. Viewed from a national perspective, these changes are more evident following the Civil War. Montgomery, "Strikes in Nineteenth-Century America," pp. 86–89.

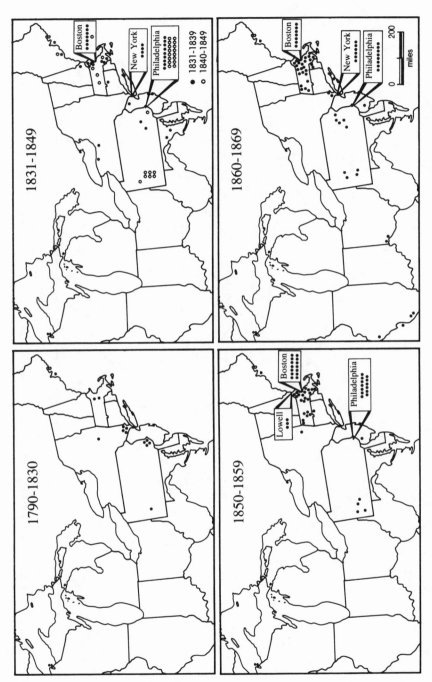

FIGURE 11.4. The Location of Strikes, 1790–1869. Each dot or circle represents one strike. Sources: *Third Annual Report of the Commissioner of Labor, 1887; Tenth Annual Report of the Commissioner of Labor, 1894.*

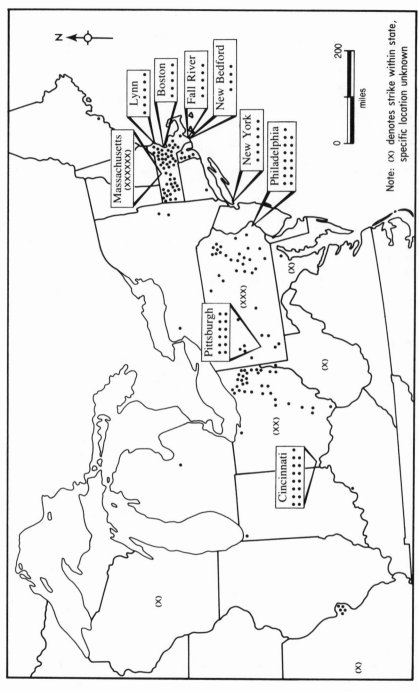

FIGURE 11.5. The Location of Strikes, 1870–79. Note the increased frequency of strike actions in the Midwest as compared to previous decades (Figure 11.4). Sources: *Third Annual Report of the Commissioner of Labor, 1887; Tenth Annual Report of the Commissioner of Labor, 1894.*

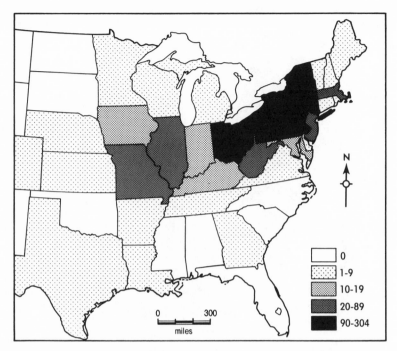

FIGURE 11.6. Strikes by State in 1880. Source: *Third Annual Report of the Commissioner of Labor, 1887.*

companied by rapid growth in the Knights of Labor; this was the first occasion in which a socialist philosophy had enjoyed mass appeal (see Figures 11.7 and 11.8).[28] Second, thanks to the detailed strike record compiled by the federal government, we may tease out the interplay between strikes, the Knights of Labor, union activity, and the material interests of labor. My analysis of that record explores the spatial variations in labor power (as measured by strike rates per 1,000 population) and its relation to four sets of structural determinants: labor markets, labor organizations, capital, and government. Here I summarize the main points of an analysis which appears in full in Chapter 9.

28. Figures 11.7 and 11.8 are based on the Knights of Labor's membership in 1883—perhaps the most suitable year from the standpoint of the comprehensiveness of the organization's membership records. Knights of Labor, *Proceedings of the General Assembly, 1883.* For a thorough geographical examination of the Knights of Labor, see Jonathan E. Garloch, "A Structural Analysis of the Knights of Labor: A Prolegomenon to the History of the Producing Classes" (Ph.D. diss., Univ. of Rochester, 1974).

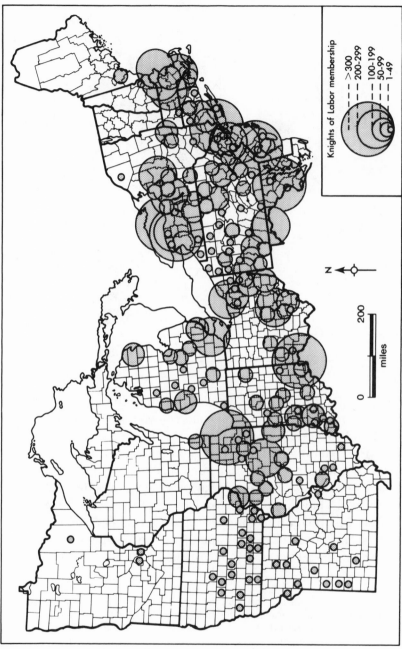

FIGURE 11.7. Knights of Labor Membership, by County, in 1883. Note the widespread distribution of the Knights near the peak of their influence on the American labor movement. Source: Knights of Labor, *Proceedings of the General Assembly of the Knights of Labor* (1883); and the membership compilations in the appendixes of Jonathan E. Garloch, "A Structural Analysis of the Knights of Labor: A Prolegomenon to the History of the Producing Classes," (Ph.D. diss., University of Rochester, 1974).

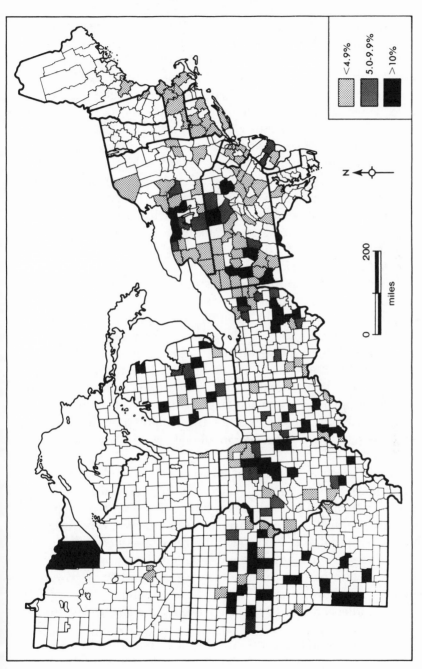

FIGURE 11.8. Knights of Labor Membership in 1883 as a Percent of the Labor Force in Manufacturing in 1880. This map makes two points: the Knights' membership was proportionally larger in the Appalachians and westward and in rural communities and smaller towns than in large urban-industrial centers. Sources: *Proceedings of the General Assembly of the Knights of Labor* (1883); Garloch, "A Structural Analysis of the Knights of Labor"; U.S. Census Office, *Report on the Manufactures of the United States at the Tenth Census: 1880* (Washington, D.C.: GPO, 1883).

The geography of worker power in the Gilded Age reveals patterns of concentration and division in the distribution of worker protest. Concentration is evident in the northeastern United States, where 112 counties, or 11 percent of all counties, accounted for 85 percent of the region's strikes. These "strike-prone" counties experienced at least one strike in nine or more years between 1881 and 1894. Division is manifested in the curiously curvilinear relationship between power and place size. Labor power in strike-prone counties declines in small communities (85,000 or less), and then inflects sharply upward in larger industrial cities. This "scale reversal" of labor power divides the labor movement into two worlds. Moreover, it contradicts prevailing labor historiography, which posits an inverse relation between labor power and community scale. Herbert Gutman's famous proposition of a declension in labor power as industrialization invades the American economy is only half right. Labor power may have been lost in the preindustrial community, but it was reconstituted in the industrial city.[29]

What factors might account for this geographical division in the exercise of labor power? One obvious consideration is the role of organized labor. The rapid growth of the Knights of Labor and the formation of the American Federation of Labor during the 1880s certainly hint that formal labor organizations facilitated the reconstitution of labor power in the larger cities. But this hypothesis, though plausible, is wrong. Neither the Knights nor the trade unions exerted significant influence on labor power in large, industrial cities.

Far more decisive were structural conditions in urban labor markets. Convergence in the wages of skilled and unskilled labor in the Midwest during the late 1870s was followed by a burst of strike activism previously confined mainly to large cities in the East, which suggests that the material and ideological interests of skilled and unskilled workers came into alignment and broadened the popular base of labor unrest. This pattern of wage convergence and labor power established in the Midwest spread eastward after 1886 into the large cities of the middle states and New England. By the late 1880s, the

29. The scale reversal of labor power necessitates a revision in Herbert Gutman's thesis attributing the declension of labor power in the Gilded Age to the diffusion of modernization. Gutman's argument is partially correct, but labor power was reconstituted in the large industrial cities and the key question is why. Herbert Gutman, "The Workers' Search for Power: Labor in the Gilded Age," in *The Gilded Age: A Reappraisal*, ed. H. Wayne Morgan (Syracuse, N.Y.: Syracuse Univ. Press, 1963), pp. 31–53.

locus of labor power had shifted again to the large eastern cities, where narrow wage differentials had prevailed since the Civil War.[30] In this mimetic process, the Midwest provided the pattern for the exercise of labor power.

The principal source of labor power in the Gilded Age lay in the convergence of wages and material interests within the ranks of labor and not with formal labor organizations such as the trade unions or the Knights of Labor. The power of the Knights was confined almost exclusively to the small, preindustrial cities and towns of the Midwest, and after 1886 they had little influence even there. The Knights made very few inroads into industrial America, for reasons that will soon become apparent. What may be fairly said is that the Knights helped to ease the painful transition to modern society, but the organization was of small consequence for labor power. In retrospect, what seemed a golden opportunity for class politics and socialist advance turned out to be, like the age itself, merely gilding.

As we learn more of the turbulent 1880s, the unimpressive role of formal labor organizations in large cities necessitates consideration of other factors affecting labor power, factors such as the labor market and conditions in the workplace, as well as the countervailing influences of capital and government intervention. Addition of these variables increases the complexity as well as the statistical robustness of our labor power model. The refined multivariate model of labor power in large cities identifies four significant factors: population, a low wage ratio, high wages in manufacturing, and industrial concentration. The respective roles of population and wage ratios have already been discussed in some detail—the larger the city and the smaller the wage ratio, the higher the strike rate. With respect to wages, a great deal of research has documented that better-paid workers exhibit a higher propensity to strike, because presumably their larger earnings enabled them to weather strikes more effectively than low-paid workers.

Industrial concentration, the fourth determinant of urban-industrial labor power, recalls Clark Kerr and Abraham Siegel's famous hypothesis on strike propensity and the effects of industrial isolation.[31] Their notion of worker isolation is not quite the same, how-

---

30. Sari Bennett and Carville Earle, "Labour Power and Locality in the Gilded Age: The Northeastern United States, 1881–1894," *Histoire Sociale—Social History* 15 (1982), pp. 383–405.

31. Clark Kerr and Abraham Siegel, "The Interindustry Propensity to Strike: An

ever, as industrial concentration in the Gilded Age. Kerr and Siegel had in mind the dominance of a community by a single firm or industry, for example, a mining or "company" town geographically and socially segregated from other industries. Industrial concentration in the Gilded Age was rarely so monolithic, especially in large cities. Seldom did a single industry employ more than 40 or 50 percent of the workers in any one city. These levels of industrial concentration nonetheless offered workers unique opportunities for the exercise of labor power. In these cities, workers were willing to strike not because they were isolated but because, in the event that they were fired for strike activity, they could find work with another firm in the same industry. Paradoxically, perhaps, industrial concentration provided protesting workers with more leverage and power. To sum up, the decisive factors in the exercise of labor power in large industrial cities—the economic security of high wages, a convergence of the material interests of skilled and unskilled workers, and job mobility—all flowed from the characteristics of urban labor markets. The role of formal labor organizations, it should be noted, was statistically insignificant.

Labor's sources of power were quite different in the preindustrial world of small cities and towns in the northeastern United States. Strike rates varied inversely with community size, and labor power diminished as the curvilinear inflection point (a population level of 85,000) approached. In this context of decline, workers in some communities exercised more power than those in others. Four determinants were decisive. Labor augmented its power in communities where labor received a smaller share of manufacturing value added, where firms (employees per firm) were larger, where the Knights of Labor were more active, and where wages were higher. Of these determinants, only one—the wage level—operated in larger cities as well. This underlines the point that, in fact, we are dealing with two qualitatively distinct geographical worlds.

Perhaps the most interesting aspect to emerge from the analysis of these preindustrial communities is the statistical association between labor power, wage shares, and the Knights of Labor. Interesting because labor's small share of income and profits was one of the

---

Interpretation," in *Industrial Conflict*, ed. Arthur Kornhauser, Robert Dubin, and Arthur M. Ross (New York: McGraw-Hill, 1954), pp. 189–212. For the complete list of variables used in the analysis, see note 32.

principal issues raised by the Knights of Labor. The Knights repeatedly drove home the message of inequity in capital's relations with labor. Recall that no issue rallied more support to the socialist perspective than the issue of unfairness in the way that capitalism apportioned the fruits of labor. The Knights seem to have delivered this message with special effect in preindustrial, small-town contexts, where labor's meager wage share was more readily perceived.

Labor power in the Gilded Age reflected, in sum, the transitional nature of the late nineteenth century—an age suspended, however briefly, between the preindustrial and the industrial worlds. Although preindustrial communities mitigated somewhat the declension of labor power by voicing grievances about capitalist inequity and mobilizing opposition through the Knights of Labor, the declension of labor power was inexorable, a result of the awesome, overwhelming, and intrusive dynamic of industrialization, urbanization, and modernization, that is, of a maturing capitalism. But among industrial cities, labor power was reconstituted. That revitalization of labor power, however, had little to do with formal labor organizations. More decisive were high wages, industrial concentration (and the prospect for job mobility), large populations, and convergence in the wages of skilled and unskilled workers. Structural economic factors, rather than formal labor organization, government intrusion, and ethnicity, facilitated labor's exercise of power in the Gilded Age.[32]

Which brings us back to the question of the socialist program of the Knights of Labor—the first such program having broad appeal. It enjoyed modest, if transitory, success during the early years of the Gilded Age. The Knights displayed surprising strength in some un-

32. This analysis of labor power considers seventeen independent variables; the determinants cited in the text are statistically significant at the 5 or 10 percent level. Among large cities, the multiple regression model accounts for 65 percent of the variation in labor power; in the smaller communities, it accounts for 50 percent. The independent variables are: county population, 1890; proportion foreign-born, 1890; wage share of value added in manufacturing, 1890; skilled wages (machinists), 1880; unskilled wages (common laborers), 1880; ratio of skilled to unskilled wages, 1880; Knights of Labor membership as a proportion of the 1880 labor force in manufacturing; value added per manufacturing worker, 1890; average wage per manufacturing employee, 1890; capital investment per manufacturing employee, 1890; capital-labor ratio, 1890; employees per manufacturing establishment, 1880; employees per manufacturing establishment, 1890; police expenditures per capita in the principal city within the county, 1890; proportion of manufacturing employment in nondurable industries, 1880; proportion of manufacturing employment in the largest industry, 1880; and proportion of strikes ordered by unions, 1881–94.

usual places, notably the small towns and cities of the Midwest, and enlistments there helped to increase the membership to over 700,000 by 1886 and to buoy up the socialist movement. Yet the Knights lost control of the labor movement soon after 1886—a consequence, in part, of strategic miscalculations in that year (including failure to support the general strike and silence at the harsh verdict in the Haymarket trial) and, equally as much, of structural divisions in the labor market and the sociogeography of American industrialization. By the late 1880s, the organization was headed swiftly toward oblivion. Engels's vision of the Knights as "the raw material out of which the future of the American working-class movement . . . has to be shaped" had ended badly. But the legacy of socialism endured, to be carried forward into the Progressive Era by political parties such as the Socialist Labor Party and the Socialist Party of America.

Socialism Through the "Civilized Means" of the Ballot, 1895-1920

Unlike the Knights, who disdained politics in favor of inculcating class consciousness, Socialist leaders openly embraced partisan politics. They aimed at undoing American capitalism through the "civilized means" of the ballot. In 1892, the Socialist Labor party put forth its first national ticket, and in 1896, under Daniel DeLeon, the party received .3 percent of the presidential vote—its best showing ever. The Socialist Party of America, founded in 1901, enjoyed somewhat more success. Gaining momentum from the elections of 1904 and 1908, the party and its perennial presidential candidate, Eugene Debs, gathered 6 percent of the popular vote in the election of 1912. And the party did even better at the local level, electing over 1,200 office holders, including 79 mayoral candidates.

Debs's showing in 1912, though modest at the national level, was quite strong in various parts of the northeastern states. His vote tally exceeded the regional mean in western Pennsylvania, eastern and southwestern Ohio, southwestern Indiana and Illinois, and northern portions of Michigan, Wisconsin, and Minnesota (see Figure 11.9). And in the congressional campaign of 1912, the Socialist party, along with the Public Ownership party in Minnesota and the Social Democrats in Wisconsin, polled surprisingly well. The party won over 15 percent of the congressional vote in Schenectady, parts of New

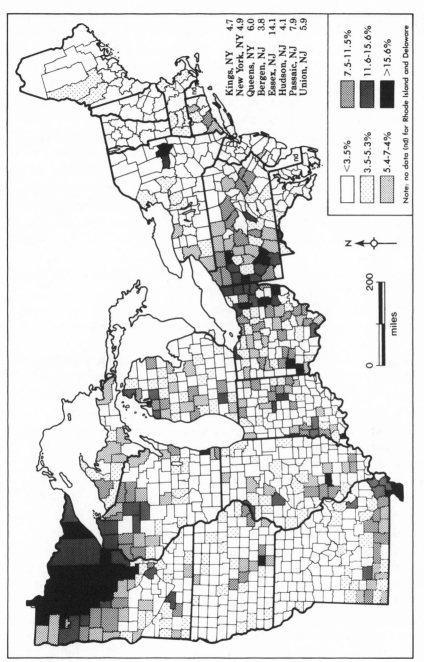

Kings, NY	4.7
New York, NY	4.9
Queens, NY	6.0
Bergen, NJ	3.8
Essex, NJ	14.1
Hudson, NJ	4.1
Passaic, NJ	7.9
Union, NJ	5.9

<3.5%

3.5-5.3%

5.4-7.4%

7.5-11.5%

11.6-15.6%

>15.6%

N

200

0

miles

Note: no data (nd) for Rhode Island and Delaware

FIGURE 11.9. The Socialist Vote in the Presidential Election of 1912. Source: Edgar Eugene Robinson, *The Presidential Vote, 1896–1932* (New York: Oxford University Press, 1970, originally published 1947), pp.380–98.

York City, and westward in Pittsburgh, Chicago, Terre Haute (Debs's hometown), Dayton, and Columbus. In the upper Midwest, Socialist candidates won over 30 percent of the vote in Milwaukee, about 17 percent in Minneapolis, and about a third of the vote in the bonanza wheat country of the Red River Valley, the Minnesota votes being received by the Public Ownership party (see Figure 11.10).[33]

Contemporaries and historians of the Progressive Era's Socialist Party have rightly discerned numerous continuities with the labor movement of the Gilded Age. Engels clearly envisaged the Knights of Labor as a forerunner of socialism if not socialism itself. Nor was it coincidence that the Knights of Labor drew support from the small preindustrial communities of the Midwest—precisely the kind of place where Eugene Debs was raised. To be sure, the Knights and the Socialist Party differed radically in their strategies for undoing capitalism, but they shared both an abiding commitment to the gradual destruction of that system through "civilized means" and a geography that rendered that commitment problematic.

Exploring the Gilded Age antecedents of the Socialist Party seems, then, a fitting way of concluding this inquiry into the failure of American socialism. I discern these continuities through a multiple regression model of Socialist Party voting (presidential) in 1912 using the seventeen independent variables deployed in the previous analysis of labor power in the Gilded Age. Based on that analysis, I offer some provisional thoughts on the failure of socialism as a consequence of industrialization, diverging wages, and the superiority of a trade unionist strategy informed by these geographical realities.

The sharp lines that divided preindustrial and industrial American communities in the Gilded Age are softened somewhat in this analysis of socialism's antecedents. In all but one case, variables that played significant roles in the exercise of labor power in the Gilded Age—wage ratios, industrial concentration, wages, the wage share of value added in manufacturing, and the Knights of Labor—vanish from the regression model of the 1912 Socialist vote. That vote, in large cities and small, varies directly with union organization and the proportion of manufacturing employment in durable goods produc-

33. The presidential votes are compiled from various state sources, most of which are cited in Edgar Eugene Robinson, *The Presidential Vote, 1896–1932* (1947; reprint, New York: Oxford Univ. Press, 1970), pp. 380–98. The congressional vote comes from *Congressional Quarterly's Guide to U.S. Elections* (Washington, D.C.: Congressional Quarterly, 1975). The congressional district boundaries are from Michael J. Dubin for his compilation of the Atlas of U.S. Congressional Districts, 1788–1963.

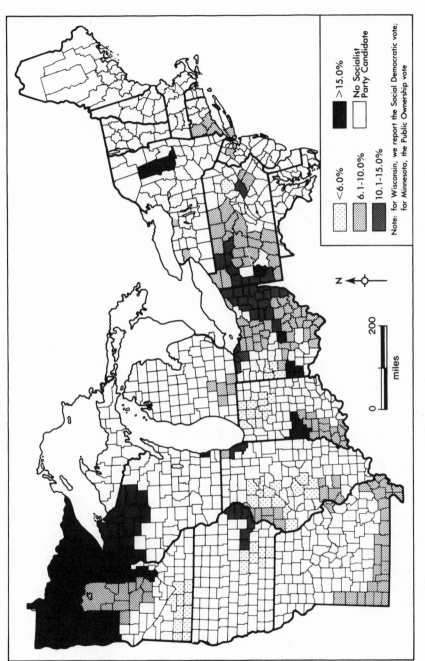

FIGURE 11.10. The Socialist Vote in the Congressional Election of 1912, by Congressional District. Sources: *Congressional Quarterly's Guide to U.S. Elections* (Washington, D.C.: Congressional Quarterly, 1975). Congressional district boundaries are from Michael J. Dubin (personal correspondence).

<6.0%

6.1-10.0%

10.1-15.0%

>15.0%

No Socialist Party Candidate

Note: for Wisconsin, we report the Social Democratic vote; for Minnesota, the Public Ownership vote

N

200

0

miles

TABLE 11.1

Continuities Between the Gilded Age and the Progressive Era:
Multiple Regressions of Selected Variables for Strike-Prone Counties, 1881–94,
and the Socialist Vote for President in 1912

Counties with < *85,000 Population* (n = 58)			*Counties with* > *85,000 Population* (n = 51)[a]		
Variables[b]			Variables[b]		
Intercept	−74.09			Intercept	−35.67
PP	.266‡		ND	−.740*	
ND	−.442*		PP	−.383‡	
UO	.245†		UO	.306‡	
	Multiple R	.684		Multiple R	.599
	Multiple R^2	.468		Multiple R^2	.358

NOTE: Coefficients marked * are significant at the 5-percent level; those with † are significant at 10 percent, and those with ‡ at 15 percent.

[a] Providence, Rhode Island; New Castle, Delaware; and Washington, D.C. were omitted from the analysis owing to incomplete data.

[b] PP = County population, 1890; ND = Percentage of manufacturing employment in nondurable industries, 1880; UO = Percentage of total strikes union ordered, 1881–94.

tion. This evidence of homogenization notwithstanding, the Gilded Age division between industrial and preindustrial America is reaffirmed with respect to the scale of community. In what amounts to the mirror image of the exercise of labor power in the Gilded Age, Socialist support varies directly with the size of preindustrial communities and inversely with the size of industrial cities (see Table 11.1)

The "scale reversal" of labor power in the Gilded Age thus persists in the socialist politics of the Progressive Era. But unlike the Gilded Age, when labor power was weakest in communities of about 85,000, in the Progressive Era these transitional places provided Socialists with their greatest support. The Socialist Party agenda, it seems, held a special appeal for communities experiencing the greatest stress in the awkward transition to modern society. Socialists, in other words, did not merely replace the older Knights of Labor— that correlation is very weak. Whereas the Knights were securely anchored in the small towns of a preindustrial world, Socialist victories were concentrated in cities of intermediate size on the hinge of an older preindustrial world and the newer world of industrialism, communities in the no-man's-land, if you will, between *gemeinschaft* and *gesellschaft*.

It would be presumptuous to press these conclusions too far, since my analysis of the continuities and changes in Amerian socialism is intended as suggestive rather than definitive. What does seem clear, however, is that American labor radicalism, whether in the

1880s or in 1912, enjoyed its greatest successes in the small towns and medium-sized cities of preindustrial America; and that its geography was dynamic, the locus of radicalism having shifted dramatically in just three decades from the small-town setting of the Knights of Labor in the 1880s to the intermediate cities in crisis that were the Socialist Party's stronghold after the turn of the century. Precisely how and why this geographical realignment of socialism took place, of course, will require much additional analysis. Our preliminary inquiry nonetheless leaves little doubt that Herbert Gutman and Robert Weibe were correct in drawing sharp contrasts between the cultures, societies, and economies of preindustrial and industrial worlds.[34] From that perspective, labor radicalism served mainly as an ephemeral social bond in a world coming unglued, a palliative for painful structural change, and a voice for the unempowered in their awkward transition from one way of life to quite another. And given the meteoric growth of American cities and the ceaseless infiltration of modernization into preindustrial America, radical philosophies such as socialism were destined for a brief but useful life.

If socialism flourished briefly in preindustrial America, its failures were almost absolute in the industrializing cities of the northeastern United States. Socialist success among industrial cities of over 100,000 was confined to one city, Milwaukee, where the Party won 27 percent of the presidential vote in 1912. The problem in larger cities was that trade unionists effectively challenged the Socialist strategy of unifying all workers. Urban trade unions were firmly entrenched by 1900, having experienced a dramatic expansion after the founding of the American Federation of Labor in 1886. In 1900, the AFL reported that 32.5 percent of all local labor unions were located in large cities (with population of over 100,000)—a figure that surpassed the mark attained by the Knights of Labor in 1883, when 26.5 percent of their assemblies were in large cities. Trade union membership data for Illinois in 1901 further demonstrate the large city's congeniality for trade unions. Chicago, though reporting just 24 of the state's 169 AFL locals, contained nearly 116,000 trade unionists—82 percent of the state total (also see Table 11.2).[35]

34. Herbert Gutman, "The Workers' Search for Power," pp. 31–54; *idem*, *Work, Culture and Society in Industrializing America* (New York: Knopf, 1976); Robert Weibe, *The Search for Order, 1877–1920* (New York: Hill and Wang, 1967). See also the studies of urban socialism for further confirmation of the argument made here. Bruce M. Stave, ed., *Socialism and the Cities* (Port Washington, N.Y.: Kennikat Press, 1975).

35. The Knights of Labor calculation is based on Garloch, "A Structural Analysis,"

Socialist disappointment over the big-city triumphs of conservative trade unionism was assuaged somewhat by the success of industrial unionism in other parts of the nation. Socialists looked favorably upon industrial unions that pursued the inclusivist strategy of uniting all workers—skilled and unskilled—within a place-specific industrial complex. The Socialist Eugene Debs regarded this distinction among unions as of the utmost significance for radical labor politics. He trusted that workers "once united in one great industrial union will vote a united working class ticket." Like most other Socialists at the time, Debs believed "that industrial unionism . . . as opposed to craft unionism then prevalent, was prerequisite to class unity."[36]

The validity of these views—if only in communities on the hinge of preindustrial and industrial worlds—has been suggested by a study of industrial unionism and the presidential elections of 1908 and 1912 in transitional New York counties—those communities having populations of 52,000 to 100,000. The vote for the Socialist Party, that study reports, varied directly with union membership and inversely with the number of unions—a variable combination that implies industrial unionism. In the 1912 regression model, these two variables explain over 90 percent of the vote for Eugene Debs and the Socialist Party. But when larger industrial counties (and cities) are added in, the model's explanatory power falls to just 56 percent. All of which recalls a by now familiar geographical juxtaposition: the alliance of radical labor politics and industrial unionism among communities in transition to the modern world, and the failure of that alliance when butting up against entrenched trade and craft unions in the large industrial cities. In New York State, and perhaps in the nation at large, trade unions and industrial unions worked at geopolitical cross-purposes. The former allied with the traditional two-party, multi-class political system, the latter with that system's antagonist, class-based and radical labor politics.[37]

---

p. 119. For the AFL, I used *List of Organizations Affiliated with the American Federation of Labor* (Washington, D.C.: American Federation of Labor, 1900), pp. 9–32; and *Twelfth Biennial Report of the Bureau of Labor Statistics of the State of Illinois 1902* (Springfield, Ill., 1904), Table 3, p. 312-lG.

36.   Arthur Schlesinger, Jr., ed., *Writings and Speeches of Eugene V. Debs* (New York: Hermitage Press, 1948), p. 332; James Weinstein, *Ambiguous Legacy: The Left in American Politics* (New York: New Viewpoints, 1975), p. 5; Dick, *Labor and Socialism*, pp. 83–110.

37.   Sari Bennett, "Continuity and Change in the Geography of American Socialism: The Presidential Elections, 1900–1912," *Social Science History* 7 (1983), pp. 267–88.

The origins of this geopolitical juxtaposition may be traced to strategic decisions made some fifteen to twenty years before. Drawing upon the lessons of the general strike in the spring and summer of 1886, trade unionists in the American Federation of Labor deliberately abandoned the working class. Instead of organizing all workers across the nation, they concentrated their energies and organizational efforts among loyal constituencies, that is, among trade and craft unionists in large industrial cities. Concurrently, labor radicals conceded (unwittingly perhaps) to trade unionists the urban-industrial terrain and ministered instead to the wounds of a bloodied preindustrial America in its transition to the modern world. The consequences of these strategic choices were decisive. By 1900, trade unionists had secured an insurmountable advantage in the rapidly growing cities of the Northeast and Midwest.

When in 1896 and 1900 Socialist politicians returned to the large industrial city in search of votes, they received an unusually chilly welcome. Campaigners for DeLeon and then Debs swiftly discovered that their adversaries in the labor movement had not been idle. Trade unionists had set in motion in 1886 an urban strategy that effectively preempted the popular base of Socialist electoral support. With trade unionists serving one portion of the urban population and machine politicians another, about all that was left for the Socialists was the mass of immigrants. Mobilizing these nonvoters, of course, offered nothing in the way of immediate, practical gain for a party committed to transforming America through the "civilized means" of the ballot. In this bleak context, the Socialist strategy of victory through electoral politics seemed doomed and forlorn from the start.

Bad strategy (or more properly bad geographical strategy) plays a large part in the story of socialism's failure in America, but it is hardly the entire story. Strategy is, after all, contingent on material conditions and the accuracy of strategic appraisals of those conditions. Indeed, structural conditions may exert such overwhelming power on what we do that strategy—no matter how clever, no matter how adroit the strategists, and no matter how great the energy and resources at their command—is impotent. In the case of American socialism, one structural condition proved devastating to radical labor politics, though not always and not everywhere. That condition was the historically large differential in the wages (and, in consequence, the material interests) of skilled and unskilled workers.

Recall that during the turbulent 1880s this historically divisive structure was thrown into reverse. Wages converged rapidly, especially in the Midwest; convergence in turn fostered class solidarity and facilitated the exercise of labor power. But this conjuncture of structure and socialist interest did not long endure, nor should it have. In a rapidly growing industrial economy, wages and wage differentials are by definition dynamic, varying in accordance with the volatility and rhythms of capitalist labor markets. That dynamism played a decisive role in the nature of the American labor movement in the half century between the Civil War and the end of World War I—by which time socialism as a force in American institutional life was, for all practical purposes, dead.

The dynamism of the American economy is revealed in the cyclical procession of the wage differential (or, what is the same thing, the skilled-unskilled wage ratio) between 1865 and 1920. Recall that the wage ratio passed through two cycles, the first lasting from late antebellum times to 1890, the second from 1890 to 1918–20 (see Table 11.2). In the first cycle, the antebellum wage ratio, which surpassed that of every industrializing nation in western Europe, shrank appreciably between 1865 and the late 1880s; in the second cycle, it grew as wage divergence reached a maximum between 1903 and 1907 and then shrank again (and rather sharply) until 1918–20. Consider the possibility that convergent wages (for example, in the 1880s and 1910s) induce comparable convergences in the political interests and solidarity of skilled and unskilled workers (and conversely, of course, for divergent ratios). It then follows that cyclical changes in wage ratios should anticipate the oscillations in radical and trade unionist labor politics.[38]

A certain symmetry in the cycles of wages and labor's political fortunes is indeed discernible between 1865 and 1920. As wages converged after 1870, trade unionists suffered substantial losses in union membership and numbers of unions. Concurrently, radical labor organizations such as the Knights of Labor experienced heady expansion. But the fortunes of labor changed profoundly after 1890, when the wage ratio entered its second cycle. During the next fifteen years, wages and interests diverged sharply and conditions were ripe for the trade unions' strategy of expansion. Indeed, trade unions experienced a phase of vigorous growth in the large industrial cities. Radi-

38. Ober, "Occupational Wage Differentials"; Lydall, *The Structure of Earnings*, pp. 163–80, 182–85; David, "Industrial Labor Market Adjustments," p. 88.

cal labor politics, meanwhile, was in full retreat back into the preindustrial world following the complete collapse of the Knights in the
1890s. The revival of socialist principles in DeLeon's Socialist Labor
party and Debs's Socialist Party of America notwithstanding, socialism was not in a particularly healthy state at the turn of the century.

Prospects changed swiftly, however, after 1907. The resumption
of wage convergence promised to improve the Socialist position,
much as an earlier convergence in the turbulent 1870s and 1880s
had empowered workers and energized the Knights of Labor. For
a moment, at any rate, all things seemed possible. The steady narrowing in the wage differential after 1907 and the impressive performance of Socialist candidates in national, state, and local elections during the succeeding five years seemed harbingers of a powerful, class-based, socialist politics. Debs's presidential campaign, which
won only .6 percent of the popular vote in 1908, garnered 6 percent
four years later—more impressively, the campaign received some
37 percent of the nation's union vote, up from 12 percent in 1900.
And in the off-year elections in 1910 and 1911, Socialists won over
1,000 offices representing 324 municipalities and 36 separate states.

But euphoric talk of a Socialist millennium was premature. Convergent wages notwithstanding, the flood tide of socialism drained
away rapidly after 1912. The proportion of unionists voting for
Debs, which had reached 37 percent in the election of 1912, fell to
21 percent in 1916 and 18 percent in 1920. Local electoral victories
became the exception rather than the rule for the Party. And socialism's losses were trade unionism's gains. Trade union ranks—which
had thinned between 1907 and 1913—grew rapidly between 1915
and 1920. These facts cast doubt on a strictly materialist interpretation of labor power and politics. Socialism failed at the very moment
when radical politics seemed poised to achieve its greatest success and
when material conditions apparently insured that result.

Reversing history's powerful structural currents is usually difficult and almost always rare. Doing so requires nothing less than the
exercise of raw power by concerted agency and intervention. In the
case of socialism's unanticipated failure after 1912, a suite of countervailing forces was brought to bear upon radical labor politics and
its structural determinants. These included the Wilson administration's informal alliance with conservative trade unions, the passage of
the Clayton Act in 1914, and the establishment of the Department of
Labor—all of which favored trade unionists over socialists, intensi-

TABLE 11.2

Wage Ratios and Labor, 1865–1920

Year	Wage Ratio	Knights of Labor membership	Union membership	Socialist party vote	Socialist party vote as a percentage of trade union membership	Number of new AFL national unions
1865	152	—	—	—	—	—
1866	171	—	—	—	—	—
1867	169	—	—	—	—	—
1868	167	—	—	—	—	—
1869	166	—	—	—	—	—
1870	171	—	300,000	—	—	—
1871	167	—	—	—	—	—
1872	164	—	—	—	—	—
1873	168	—	—	—	—	—
1874	167	—	—	—	—	—
1875	165	—	—	—	—	—
1876	167	—	—	—	—	—
1877	163	—	—	—	—	—
1878	161	—	—	—	—	—
1879	161	13,400	—	—	—	—
1880	161	40,900	200,000	—	—	—
1881	—	31,800	—	—	—	—
1882	—	52,800	—	—	—	—
1883	—	85,800	—	—	—	—
1884	—	104,200	—	—	—	—
1885	—	158,600	—	—	—	—
1886	—	638,400	—	—	—	—
1887	—	1,708,000	—	—	—	17
1888	—	1,204,000	—	—	—	7
1889	—	616,000	372,000	—	—	8
1890	176	288,400	—	—	—	8
1891	177	352,800	—	—	—	6
1892	181	341,600	—	—	—	4
1893	185	215,600	—	—	—	7
1894	174	172,200	—	—	—	6
1895	181	140,000	—	—	—	7
1896	173	142,800	—	—	—	8

Year	Union Membership	Knights of Labor Membership	Wage Ratio Series	Socialist Party Vote		AFL National Unions
1897	440,000	—	179	—	—	5
1898	467,000	—	182	—	—	9
1899	550,000	—	186	—	—	8
1900	791,000	—	199	94,768	12.0%	11
1901	1,058,000	—	212	—	—	8
1902	1,335,000	—	225	—	—	13
1903	1,824,000	—	219	—	—	16
1904	2,067,000	—	—	402,460	19.5	8
1905	—	—	—	—	—	3
1906		—		—	—	3
1907	2,077,000	—	226	—	—	2
1908	2,092,000	—	204	420,820	20.1	3
1909	1,965,000	—	202	—	—	4
1910	2,116,000	—	188	—	—	2
1911	2,318,000	—	192	—	—	12
1912	2,405,000	—	194	897,011	37.3	3
1913	2,661,000	—	226	—	—	1
1914	2,647,000	—	187	—	—	1
1915	2,560,000	—	195	—	—	1
1916	2,722,000	—	189	585,113	21.5	5
1917	2,976,000	—	172	—	—	4
1918	3,368,000	—	140	—	—	4
1919	4,046,000	—	149	—	—	2
1920	5,034,000	—	146	919,799	18.3	1

NOTES AND SOURCES FOR TABLE 11.2:

Wage Ratio Series: This series contains the ratio of carpenters' wages (skilled labor) to the wages of common laborers (unskilled labor). Before 1881, the ratio is calculated on the basis of daily wages; after 1881, we use hourly rates. The pre-1881 wage ratio series is based on the Weeks Report. The post-1881 series is compiled from various publications: *Nineteenth Annual Report of the Commissioner of Labor 1904: Wages and the Hours of Labor* (Washington, D.C., 1905), pp. 444–71; U.S. Department of Labor, *Union Scale of Wages and Hours of Labor,* Bulletins 131, 143, 171, 194, 214, 245, 259, 274, 286 (Washington, D.C., 1913–21). The weakest link in the series covers the years 1907–13 when data are limited to four or five city wage observations. After 1913, the annual sample ranges from 12 to 26 observations. Between 1890 and 1903, the sample contains 19 urban observations. The strongest link in the series is the period before 1881. Sample size then ranged from 22 in 1865, to 41 in 1870, 57 in 1875, and 60 in 1880.

Knights of Labor Membership: Membership estimates are those made in Jonathan Garlock, "A Structural Analysis of the Knights of Labor: A Prolegomenon to the History of the Producing Classes" (Ph.D. diss., University of Rochester, 1974), p. 231. Garlock's projected membership offers an upper bound for the Knights. His procedure adds together the total reported membership for a particular year and the total of new members added during the succeeding year.

Union Membership: We use the estimates of the Bureau of Labor Statistics; for slightly higher estimates, see those of the National Bureau of Economic Research. Both series may be compared in Albert Blum, "Why Unions Grow," *Labor History,* 9 (1968), pp. 41–43.

Socialist Party Vote: Richard B. Morris, ed., *Encyclopedia of American History: Enlarged and Updated* (New York: Columbia University Press, 1970).

AFL National Unions: This series lists the number of national unions that affiliated with the American Federation of Labor for the specified year. See Gary M. Fink, ed., *Labor Unions* (Westport, Conn.: Greenwood, 1977), pp. 423–47.

fied intolerance for social and political heterodoxy (especially during the war years), and promoted state repression aimed at labor radicals such as the Industrial Workers of the World and the Socialist party.[39]

In one sense, the unleashing of these countervailing forces delivered the fatal blow to American socialism. This lethal punch, thrown ironically in socialism's finest American hour, dramatically reconfigured American politics. In the short term, it eliminated radical competition for "pure and simple" trade unionists and the proponents of a multi-class political system. Intermediately, it brought gains in trade union membership, at least to 1920. And in the long term, it favored wage-setting practices that greatly privileged the wages of the skilled over those of the unskilled.[40]

In another sense, however, socialism's failure was not so much the result of a single fatal blow delivered after 1912 as of structural causes deeply rooted in the dual geographies of American modernization and the historical divisions in the wages and interests of labor. Even in 1912, when socialism was experiencing a flood tide, its successes were confined largely to communities in transition from a pre-industrial to an industrial world. Socialism, like these cities in transition, was merely an ephemeral institution within the American geopolitical landscape. And in any event, socialist advance into indus-

---

39.   Weinstein, *The Decline of Socialism*; Marc Karson, *American Labor Unions and Politics, 1900–1918* (Carbondale: Southern Illinois Univ. Press, 1958), pp. 42–89; Graham Adams, Jr., *Age of Industrial Violence, 1910–15: The Activities and Findings of the United States Commission on Industrial Relations* (New York: Columbia Univ. Press, 1966), pp. 168–75, 219–26; David Montgomery, *Workers' Control in America: Studies in the History of Work, Technology, and Labor Struggles* (Cambridge: Cambridge Univ. Press, 1979).

40.   In 1926 Sam A. Lewisohn, chairman of the Board of the American Management Association, wrote that industrial leaders should not always try to drive a hard bargain with labor. He urged industrialists to enter into a consultative wage relationship with *organized* labor (read skilled trade unionists), a course that would ease tensions and where higher wages would be outpaced by the increased productivity of happier workers. Such a strategy left little room for consultation with the unorganized and the unskilled, who in any case fared poorly during the "roaring twenties." The demise of socialism perhaps accounts for Lewisohn's laconic tone on something as controversial as wage determination: "The problem of distribution, which has so often been regarded as a drama, with labor and capital as the conflicting characters, turns out to be largely the prosaic task of using wage policies to increase rational productivity." And, we might add, to further divide the ranks of labor. Insofar as Lewisohn is representative of American industry, wage determination in the 1920s seems to have been rooted more deeply in the relations of production than in marginalist economic theory. Sam A. Lewisohn, *The New Leadership in Industry* (New York: E. P. Dutton, 1926), p. 199. In an identical vein, but for different ends, Henry Ford increased unskilled and semi-skilled wages in order to ward off plant unionization. See Daniel M. G. Raff, "Wage Determination and the Five-Dollar Day at Ford," *Journal of Economic History* 48 (1988), pp. 387–99.

trial America had been effectively blocked by trade unionists ever since 1886, when the Knights of Labor and labor radicals conceded that realm in favor of constituencies in the small towns and communities of preindustrial America. Socialist politics had little space within which it could maneuver for power.

American wage differentials also mitigated against the success of class-based politics. Although the cycle of these differentials helps account for the oscillations in trade unionism and socialism (or labor radicalism), the main point is that no industrial nation in the nineteenth century had a differential as wide (on average) as that of the United States.[41] Wages might converge for short phases, as they did between 1865 and 1890 and again between 1907 and 1918, but they invariably reverted to their initial state. Indeed, wage divergence in the 1890s seems to have been especially critical in securing trade unionist hegemony in large industrial cities—a hegemony that the trade unions have never relinquished. Consequently, the divergences in the wages and the material and political interests of American labor have proven to be its most enduring truth. A proclivity toward schism in the house of labor was inherent, I believe, in modernizing America.

What, then, of the forces that brought socialism to its American denouement? It is clear to me that American society acted rashly and hyperbolically in repressing and eradicating socialism after 1912. In what amounts to a classic case of overreaction to a recurrent phase of American civil dissent, an alliance of industry, state, and trade unions succeeded in destroying a weak and hardly threatening foe and, perhaps worse, in draining the blood of interesting political conversation from the American body politic. Must it be ever this way in the disjunctive, adversarial American mind?

41. Phelps-Brown, *A Century of Pay*, pp. 47–48; Lydall, *The Structure of Earnings*, pp. 163–80, 182–85.

CHAPTER 12

The Periodic Structure
of the American Past

Rhythms, Phases, and
Geographic Conditions

A merican history offers an almost inexhaustible supply of problems for geographical inquiry, but the biggest of all concerns
what has been termed "the crisis in history." For several decades now, American historians have worried about the fate of their
discipline: its balkanization into special-interest histories; its elevation
of method and technique over substance; its inconclusive churning
in historiographic debate; and its loss of coherence and integrity in
the interpretation of the American past. History seems to have lost
its bearings, its capacity to tell an interesting story, its sense of structure and theme.[1] Some of us believe that the crisis encompasses historical geography as well.

I am neither the first to perceive this problem nor the first to
suggest a remedy for it. Indeed, historians have been responding
vigorously and creatively for some time. Their experiments span the
range of historical inquiry, from humanist to social science histories,
from the renaissance of historical fiction to the voraciously eclectic
approach of the *Annales* school, and from the revival of historical
narrative to concern for "big structures, large processes, and huge
comparisons" advocated by Charles Tilly and Immanuel Wallerstein.
Each in its own fashion attempts to make sense out of history, to give
it meaning, to make it comprehensible.[2] Such too are the aims of my
experiment in macrohistorical geography.

1. Theodore S. Hamerow, *Reflections on History and Historians* (Madison: University
of Wisconsin Press, 1987); Gertrude Himmelfarb, *The New History and the Old* (Cambridge,
Mass.: Belknap Press of Harvard University Press, 1987).
2. On historical fiction, see Larry Rohter, "Mexican Letter: Fighting Words, Poi-
soned Pens," *The New York Times Book Review*, 2 Oct. 1988, pp. 1, 31–32; and the ongoing

The American experience, though giving the illusion of youth, is really quite old: dated from the ill-fated Roanoke expedition, our past encompasses over four centuries. The achievement of longevity alone is worthy of more attention than it has previously received from historians and historical geographers. Our timidity is all the more surprising when compared to the bold forays of our European counterparts. French scholars associated with the *Annales* school, for example, range across centuries of the past, devising as they go a shimmering jargon of *longues durées*, conjunctures, and multilayered cyclical rhythms and a sparkling array of historical reinterpretations—Ladurie's motionless history, Aries's centuries of childhood, and Braudel's opus on the evolution of early capitalism.[3] Across the channel, English historians and geographers are effecting a similar transformation, prompted by the substantive problems of the origins of English individualism and the rise of capitalism over the course of nearly a millennium of history.[4] This revitalization of European history, due in part to macrohistory, is worthy of American emulation.

Geography, as I have tried to demonstrate, has much to contribute to the particularistic interpretation of American historical problems, but its most enduring contribution may lie beyond his-

debates over the historical fiction of Gore Vidal, William Styron, E. L. Doctorow, and Alex Haley in *The New York Review of Books*. Also see Richard N. Current, "Fiction as History: A Review Essay," *Journal of Southern History* 52 (1986), pp. 77–90. For other experiments in history, see Lawrence Stone, "The Revival of Narrative: Reflections on a New Old History," *Past and Present* 85 (1979), pp. 3–24. Charles Tilly, *Big Structures, Large Processes, and Huge Comparisons* (New York: Russell Sage Foundation, 1984). Immanuel Wallerstein, *The Capitalist World-Economy* (Cambridge: Cambridge University Press, 1979). T. Zeldin, "Social History and Total History," *Journal of Social History* 10 (1976), pp. 237–45. Alan R. H. Baker, "Reflections on the Relations of Historical Geography and the *Annales* School of History," in *Explorations in Historical Geography: Interpretative Essays*, ed. Alan R. H. Baker and Derek Gregory (Cambridge: Cambridge University Press, 1984), pp. 1–27.

3. Emmanuel LeRoy Ladurie, "Motionless History," *Social Science History* 1 (1977), pp. 115–36; *idem*, *The Peasants of Languedoc*, trans. John Day (Urbana: University of Illinois Press, 1974). Philippe Ariès, *Centuries of Childhood*, trans. Robert Baldick (London: Jonathan Cape, 1962). Fernand Braudel, *The Structures of Everyday Life: Civilization and Capitalism 15th-18th Century*, trans. Siân Reynolds (3 vols.; New York: Harper and Row, 1979–84), Vol. 1, *The Structures of Everyday Life*; Vol. 2, *The Wheels of Commerce*; Vol. 3, *The Perspective of the World*.

4. See especially Alan Macfarlane, *The Origins of English Individualism* (Oxford: Oxford University Press, 1978). The contours of this debate are nicely summarized in Richard Smith, "'Modernization' and the Corporate Medieval Village Community in England: Some Sceptical Reflections," *Explorations in Historical Geography*, ed. Baker and Gregory, pp. 140–79.

toricism in the realm of long-run or macrohistory. An American macrohistory affords unusual opportunities for a productive union of locational, ecological, and historical inquiries. I will sketch these opportunities at the outset in three spare propositions, which are, of course, provisional; their aim is to provoke further meditations on a more ambitious American historical geography—a story of macrohistorical rhythms, of periodic structures, and of the recurrent geographic processes of agrarian innovation and spatial diffusion that governed them.

PROPOSITION 1. *American history over its four centuries has a periodic structure.*

Traditional historical interpretations implicitly acknowledge a periodic structure in the American past—a series of historical periods spaced at intervals of about 50 years. Quite independently, a concurrent rhythmic structure has emerged from topical historical inquiries dealing with religious revitalization, policy cycles, and economic long waves. These remarkable symmetries in periods, cycles, and waves are unlikely to have arisen by chance. For heuristic purposes, we may provisionally regard them as historical realities that, when combined, constitute the macrohistorical periodic structure of the American past. That structure is old (dating back at least to the seventeenth century), periodic in rhythm, logistic in form, and dialectical in process.

PROPOSITION 2. *The periods of American history, in turn, consist of six shorter and typically overlapping phases: crisis, creativity, conflict, diffusion, dissent, and decline. These phases are recurrent and determinant, but historical responses within them are remarkably variable.*

Each period of American history has, if you will, a natural history—six more or less sequential phases establishing particular sets of conditions and constraints upon human action. In every half-century historical period, these phases unfold as follows: at the outset, society is mired in economic and social turmoil (crisis); it responds with experimentation and innovation at all societal levels and in most of its spheres (creativity); it contends soon after with international war (conflict); it experiences an acceleration in innovation diffusion (diffusion); it confronts in the midst of prosperity internal civil unrest (dissent); it then undergoes economic decline and a deepening social malaise as the period comes to an end (decline).

Phases are determinant: they define a general set of issues, conditions, and constraints that reappear at precise intervals in every period of American history. In this restricted sense, then, we may say that American history does indeed repeat itself. But rarely does this historical repetition produce the same behavioral reactions. Historical responses are wildly variable; that is to say, they are problematic. Take the dissent phase. In a few cases, dissent has boiled over into violent civil war (the American Revolution and the Civil War), but in other cases, protest has been nonviolent, albeit intense (the Civil Rights Movement of the 1950s and 1960s). Thus while phases do a pretty good job of predicting at any given moment the agenda for and the constraints upon historical behavior, they tell us very little about the specific nature of the response. Indeed, the most appealing aspect of the phase model is its delicate blending of contextual determinacy and historical freedom.

PROPOSITION 3. *The half-century periodic structure of American history is governed principally by the spatial and ecological processes underlying agrarian innovation and diffusion.*

The driving force behind the periodic structure of American history is recurrent and multiregional agrarian innovation and spatial diffusion. A list of the great innovations in American agriculture would show that most were installed during long-wave depressions—our crisis and creativity phases—and then diffused over the next 40 to 50 years. A few examples include the cotton gin, 1790s–1830s; the reaper, 1830s–80s; commercial fertilizers, 1880s–1930s; tractors, hybrid corn, soybeans, and the mechanical cotton harvester, 1930s–80s. The pattern is also evident in the colonial period: tobacco topping and housing, 1630s–70s; the tandem of slaves, tobacco, and diversified crops, 1680s–1730s. Recurrent agrarian innovations of this sort have initiated the revitalization of societies and economies in the American past.

While agrarian innovation initiates historical periods, it is spatial diffusion that accounts for the periodic rhythm of our history. The diffusion process typically follows an S-shaped or logistic curve that, in the case of fundamental agrarian innovations, consumes 40 or

50 years before adoption is saturated and the process comes to a halt. The logic of half-century logistic diffusion is as follows: at first, following a time of experimentation and contentious deliberation, a handful of innovations are selected and spread slowly among risk-taking adopters; then, as risk probabilities become known (owing to increased adoption and sample size), diffusion accelerates; finally, as the returns on a widely adopted innovation diminish, diffusion decelerates and then comes to a stop. Not much has changed in the diffusion process over the past several centuries. Despite more rapid communications and intervention by numerous agents of change, diffusion of a fundamental innovation to an agrarian majority takes as much time today as it did in the colonial period.

The process of agrarian diffusion translates directly into the cycle of economic growth. In the early stages of diffusion (the so-called upswing of the long wave) productivity gains are large and the economy grows rapidly; in the latter stages (the long downswing) productivity gains decline as a consequence of supply expansion, falling prices, diminishing returns, and adverse environmental impacts of innovation. The economy's growth slows to a crawl, then becomes negative as it enters the time of long-wave crisis. A new round of experimentation and innovation is thus required to initiate the next period in American history.

Let us take up these several propositions in turn, beginning with the evidence in favor of a macrohistorical periodic structure in the American past.

Proposition 1: Discerning the Periodic Structure of American Macrohistory

How do we uncover the structure of American history, if indeed one exists? That structure, I believe, has been right beneath our noses all along, lodged in an older and all-but-forgotten historiographic tradition. Implicit in these venerable, dust-covered works is a scheme of periodization, a periodic structure if you will, which informs almost every current text and course on the American past. Consider for a moment the organization of the typical introductory survey in American history, conventionally partitioned in the year 1877. Superficially this date signals the end of radical reconstruction, but 1877 also represents the end point of a historical period that began with Jacksonian democracy—the so-called "middle period," which lasted 50 years more or less. It was preceded, as we all know, by the early national period, extending from the Founding Fathers in the 1780s to Jackson in 1830—again about 50 years. This was preceded by what Gipson called the Age of Empire, that period of British neomercantilism stretching from King George's War in the mid 1740s to 1783—a duration of over 40 years. Before that came the era of "salutary neglect," a period of relatively free trade enduring from the Glorious Revolution until its rejection by neomercantilists in the 1740s—a span of about 55 years. And prior to that was the period of the emergence of mercantilism out of the English Civil War and the Cromwellian Protectorate and expiration in the Glorious Revolution—again, about 40 to 50 years in length. In sum, the typical first semester survey of American history consists of five historical periods of roughly a half-century each. That is to say that American history prior to 1877 has a periodic macrohistorical structure.[5]

The periodic structure persists after 1877 as well. The past century in fact divides nicely into two half-century historical periods. The first lasts from the Gilded Age and the Age of Reform in the 1880s and 1890s until the Great Depression in the 1930s; the second from Roosevelt's New Deal until Reagan's conservative revolution in the 1980s. Taken as a whole, the past three and a half centuries of American history consist of seven historical periods each lasting a half-century, more or less. These constitute the fundamental units in

5. No single citation suffices; my periodization reflects a wide range of sources and personal experience that began when I was a student in the introductory survey of American history and continues in my current inquiries into the American past. Further evidence of these periods appears in their remarkable correspondence with terminal datings employed in monographic studies of various topics in American history; see for example the dates listed in titles of books reviewed in any recent issue of the *Journal of American History*. The correspondence is too frequent for chance alone. Similarly, the half-century periodic structure of American history subsumes cyclical conceptions of American political and economic history such as the public-private political cycle identified by Arthur Schlesinger, Jr., *The Cycles of American History* (Boston: Houghton Mifflin, 1986), esp. pp. 23–48; and the 22-year economic cycles of Simon Kuznets, *Secular Movements in Production and Prices: Their Nature and Their Bearing upon Cyclical Fluctuations* (Boston: Houghton Mifflin, 1930). For quantitative attempts at periodization, see Jerald Hage, Edward T. Gargan, and Robert Hanneman, "Procedures for Periodizing History: Determining Distinct Eras in the Histories of Britain, France, Germany, and Italy," *Historical Social Research: The Uses of Historical and Process-produced Data* (Stuttgart, Germany: Klett-Cotta, 1980), pp. 267–83.

the periodic structuring of the American past.[6] In addition, I count an eighth period beginning in the 1980s.

Although skeptics might demur, citing the rough-and-ready dating or ill-defined taxonomic criteria, this periodic structure is readily discernable in traditional historiographic thought as well as in the periodizations that are taken for granted in contemporary historical instruction and text writing. When historians juxtapose their implicit outline of American history with the periodic structure proposed here, I am confident that the difference will not be glaring.

Assume for a moment that American history has a rhythmic half-century structure, or at least that the existence of such a structure is problematic. If it does exist, it should receive confirmation from independent sources. In fact, a good deal of supporting evidence is available in topical histories on American religion, policy, and economy. I will cite two provocative essays, one by William McLoughlin on religious revitalization, the other by Richard L. McCormick on national policy cycles, as well as the substantial body of work on long waves in the American economy. These works on the surface have little in common, but in their separate spheres, each examines periodic reformations in American social, political, and economic life— reformations that dovetail with virtually all of the major turning points in our periodic structure of the American past.[7]

6. Walter Nugent labels the period 1870–1920 as "the Great Conjuncture"; see his *Structures of American Social History* (Bloomington: Indiana University Press, 1981). To my knowledge, no historian has explicitly claimed a period running between the presidencies of Franklin Roosevelt and Jimmy Carter, though the justification for doing so is compelling. Certainly journalists and astute political observers do so regularly in commenting upon Reaganite conservatism's rather sharp break with a New Deal legacy. See, however, McCraw's argument on regulatory shifts in the 1930s and again in the 1970s; Thomas K. McCraw, *Prophets of Regulation: Charles Francis Adams, Louis D. Brandeis, James M. Landis, and Alfred E. Kahn* (Cambridge, Mass.: Harvard University Press, 1984). Also see Jay Winik, "The Neoconservative Revolution," *Foreign Policy* 73 (1988–89), pp. 135–52. Perhaps Reagan's most decisive legacy will be his conservative packing of the federal judiciary. The conservatism of their rulings will endure long after Reagan has left the political scene. For an analogous argument about earlier times, see Morton J. Horwitz, *The Transformation of American Law, 1780–1860* (Cambridge, Mass.: Harvard University Press, 1977); and James MacGregor Burns, *Roosevelt: The Lion and the Fox* (New York: Harcourt, Brace, 1956), pp. 291–315.

7. William G. McLoughlin, *Revivals, Awakenings, and Reform: An Essay on Religion and Social Change, 1607–1977* (Chicago: University of Chicago Press, 1978); on policy cycles, the brilliant essay by Richard L. McCormick, "The Party Period and Public Policy: An Explanatory Hypothesis," *Journal of American History* 66 (1979), pp. 279–98; see also Theodore J. Lowi, "Four Systems of Policy, Politics and Choice," *Public Administration Review* (July/Aug. 1972), pp. 298–310. On long waves, see Joseph Schumpeter, *Business Cycles* (2 vols.; New York: McGraw-Hill, 1939); and Joshua S. Goldstein, *Long Cycles: Prosperity*

Cycles of Religious Revitalization

William McLoughlin has identified five major religious revitalizations in the American past: those during the 1630s, 1740s, 1790s, 1890s, and 1970s and 1980s. In their timing, each of these revitalizations corresponds with turning points in the periods of American history. Indeed, of the eight periods we have identified, religious revitalizations inaugurate five. And of the three others, I suspect that two of them—those starting in the 1680s and 1830s—just missed satisfying McLoughlin's criteria. Certainly the late seventeenth century had more than its share of religious activity and ferment: the Salem witch trials, the establishment of the episcopacy in many colonies, and the migration of Quakers, Huguenots, and other dissenting groups to the Jerseys, Pennsylvania, and the Carolinas. Similarly the 1830s and 1840s were filled with religious dispute, revitalization, and awakening: the stormy birth of Mormonism, Quaker schism, Millerite millennialism, and Protestant revivalism.[8]

From the standpoint of religious ferment, only the 1930s is the odd period out. In this seemingly secular decade, one would be hard-pressed to make a case for religious revitalization, Father Coughlin and tent evangelism notwithstanding. Conversely, one might plausibly argue for the sacralization of American politics during these years by portraying Franklin Roosevelt as a charismatic divine preaching on the kingdom of this earth. Given the "evil" economic forces at work this interpretation has a certain appeal, but it is not necessary to our overall argument. The main point is that in seven out of eight cases between 1630 and 1980, the periodic revitalization of American religious life coincided with the turning points in the periods of American history. The deviant case remains an inviting hypothesis for inquiry.[9]

---

and War in the Modern Age (New Haven, Conn.: Yale University Press, 1988). For related cycling in the temperance movement, see Jack S. Blocker, Jr., *American Temperance Movements: Cycles of Reform* (Boston: Twayne, 1989).

8. I differentiate revitalizations as being of "high" and "low" intensity, the latter representing McLoughlin's "missing" cases in the 1680s–90s, 1830s–40s, and 1930s. Low intensity revitalizations are associated with policy cycles of free trade and democratic resource distribution; high intensity revitalizations with cycles of protectionism and elite distribution. See also George M. Thomas's thoughtful volume, *Revivalism and Cultural Change: Christianity, Nation Building, and the Market in the Nineteenth-Century United States* (Chicago: University of Chicago Press, 1989).

9. That the 1930s were a time of secular revitalization is a line of argument nibbled at by Burns, *Roosevelt: The Lion and the Fox*, esp. pp. 202–5.

Policy Cycles

Further confirmation for a periodic rhythm in American history comes from scholarship on policy cycles. Richard McCormick, in his sweeping critique of the new political history and its preoccupation with voting statistics, has asserted that the analysis of policy should take precedence over the study of electoral politics. The effectiveness of policy, according to McCormick, has at least as much influence on the way people vote as do voter ethnicity, religious affiliation, location, and the like. In his view, effective policies are the root cause of national electoral stability; ineffective policies, of rarer electoral realignments. Policies thus run in cycles.

They also run concurrently with the periodic structure of American history. McCormick's cycles of domestic resource distribution during the nineteenth century match up precisely with our half-century periodizations. His three cycles, each lasting four to five decades, are as follows: (1) 1790s to 1830s, an elite distributive resource policy; (2) 1830s to 1880s, a democratic or mass distributive resource policy; and (3) 1880s to the New Deal, a redistributive resource policy—which I take to be elite, based as it was on progressive notions of large-scale corporate efficiencies.[10] McCormick broadly hints at a fourth policy cycle commencing with FDR and the New Deal, what we might in retrospect call a "democratic redistributive resource policy." The latter of course has seen its day, having been displaced by Reagan's counterrevolutionary policy of elite distribution with its strong resemblances to the policies of the Founding Fathers some four cycles ago.[11]

10. The dating of the cyclical turning in late nineteenth-century policies varies slightly from one scholar to another. McCormick places the turning in the 1890s (perhaps because of his attempts to redress political history's overemphasis upon critical elections such as that of 1896); Lowi meanwhile dates the period from Cleveland's presidency to FDR's (1885–1930); and McCraw nicely joins the two by seeing two episodes of regulatory innovation—one in the 1870s and 1880s and another around 1900. It is worth noting that if McCormick's thesis is correct, namely that effective policy is a precondition for critical elections, then the turning of the policy cycle necessarily occurred prior to the election of 1896, perhaps beginning in the 1870s or 1880s. McCormick, "The Party Period and Public Policy"; *idem*, "The Realignment Synthesis in American History," *Journal of Interdisciplinary History* 13 (1982), pp. 85–105. Theodore J. Lowi, "American Business, Public Policy, Case Studies, and Political Theory," *World Politics* 16 (1964), pp. 677–715; *idem*, "Four Systems of Policy." McCraw, *Prophets of Regulation*. I do not wish to be misread as believing that a period is monolithic; antithetical views are continuously present, sometimes revising the period's policy paradigm in what amounts to a mid-period correction and at all times waiting in the wings for the dialectical moment of social and economic crisis when the prevailing paradigm is periodically discredited and replaced.

11. I follow McCormick's domestic policy schema for the first two cycles; also see

McCormick's policy cycles are highly suggestive. First, their timing and half-century duration independently confirm the accuracy and reliability of our periodic structure. Second, the cycles reveal a deeper structural pattern of periodic alternation, a dialectic, between elitist and democratic resource distribution policies.

McCormick's cyclical thesis applies also in the sphere of American foreign policy. Here, in the case of American trade policy, we may discern a rhythmic alternation that dates back to the 1790s and perhaps as far back as late Elizabethan times. During the national epoch of American history (post-1790 to the present), trade policy has alternated between protectionism and free trade in four long cycles. In the first cycle, Hamiltonian protectionist policies prevailed—albeit as matters of thorny sectional controversy—from the 1790s until the 1830s. In the second cycle, free trade displaced protectionism during the "middle period." In the third cycle, American protectionism resurfaced during the 1880s and 1890s as the capitalist world economy contemporaneously played out the drama of imperialism—protectionism writ at the global scale. And in the fourth cycle, free trade policies were resumed with FDR and the Great Depression. Thus, just as American domestic policies have cycled back and forth between the elitist and the democratic, our foreign policies have alternated between protectionism and free trade. Indeed these two cycles are so closely coupled that in large measure they define the nature of American political economy as alternating from elitism and protectionism in one cycle to mass democratic allocation and free trade in the next, and so on through the half-century rhythms of American macrohistory.[12]

Ralph Lerner, "Commerce and Character: The Anglo-American as New-Model Man," *William and Mary Quarterly*, 3rd ser., 36 (1979), pp. 3–26. I follow McCormick and Lowi for the third (1880s–1930)—a cycle of elite resource distribution, which was a cornerstone of progressive policies according to Samuel P. Hays, *Conservation and the Gospel of Efficiency: The Progressive Conservation Movement, 1890–1920* (Cambridge, Mass.: Harvard University Press, 1959); also Robert Weibe, *The Search for Order, 1877–1920* (New York: Hill and Wang, 1967). In understanding policy trends during the past century I have found useful the pungent essays by Lewis Galambos, *America at Middle Age: A New History of the United States in the Twentieth Century* (New York: New Press, 1983); and Forrest McDonald, *The Phaeton Ride: The Crisis of American Success* (Garden City, N.Y.: Doubleday, 1974). Also see Terry L. Anderson and P. J. Hill, "Institutional Change Through the Supreme Court and the Rise of Transfer Activity," in *Explorations in the New Economic History: Essays in Honor of Douglass C. North*, ed. Roger Ransom, Richard Sutch, and Gary M. Walton (New York: Academic Press, 1982), pp. 193–212.

12. The alternation of free trade and protectionist policies is evident in the level of effective tariff rates in the respective periods (cycles). See *Historical Statistics of the United*

McCormick's policy cycle thesis also seems applicable to the colonial period of American history. Although we know very little about colonial policies on domestic resource allocation—at least in the way that McCormick conceptualizes them—we do know a great deal about British trade and commercial policies. Though always premised on mercantilist principles, these policies ranged in fact from a formal mercantilism that was rigorously implemented to a loose mercantilism that was limply enforced and tantamount to free trade. From standard interpretations of the colonial period, we can extract three policy cycles: (1) mercantilism between the 1640s and 1680s, (2) free trade during the era of "salutary neglect," and (3) the neomercantilist revival of the mid-eighteenth century.[13]

The first cycle of mercantilism is officially dated from the English Navigation Act of 1651, though its origins probably lie earlier, in the depression of the 1630s and the English Civil War of the 1640s. Mercantilist policies aimed at driving American commerce exclusively through English channels. In addition to imposing stringent regulations on colonial trade and shipping, these policies strove for the military elimination of foreign competition, most notably the Dutch merchant interlopers in the American trade. By the 1670s, mercantilist policies had succeeded in binding the American colonies into an English colonial system.[14]

States, Colonial Times to 1970 (2 parts; Washington, D.C.: GPO, 1975), Part 2, p. 888. Import duties peaked in 1830, fell during the next 40 years, peaked again about 1870, remained relatively high until 1932 (another peak), then fell steadily until 1970. Tariff rate trends within any given period tend to reverse toward the end of each period—in what I will later describe as the phase of Decline. On foreign policy since 1800, see Samuel P. Huntington, "Coping with the Lippmann Gap," *Foreign Affairs* 66 (1988), pp. 453–77.

13. These policy cycles are rather well known, though colonial historians rarely put them in such bold relief. See Charles M. Andrews, *The Colonial Period of American History* (4 vols.; New Haven, Conn.: Yale University Press, 1934–38); Lawrence H. Gipson, *The British Empire Before the American Revolution* (15 vols.; Caldwell, Idaho, and New York: Caxton Printers and Knopf, 1936–70); and John J. McCusker and Russell R. Menard, *The Economy of British North America, 1607–1789* (Chapel Hill: University of North Carolina Press, 1985). Also see Jonathan R. T. Hughes, *Social Control in the Colonial Economy* (Charlottesville: University Press of Virginia, 1976).

14. A good deal of evidence suggests that the preceding period from the 1570s and 1580s to the 1620s was one of more liberal trade policy. Indeed liberalism (in the nineteenth-century sense of that term) was initiated by Elizabeth and extended by the early Stuarts, who, despite their reputed tyrannies, expanded trade and commerce by achieving an Anglo-Spanish peace in 1604 and passage of the Statute of Monopolies in 1624. The economic liberalism of the period provides the institutional foundation for the North-Thomas thesis on the commercial ascendancy of England. Douglass C. North and Robert

Mercantilism, however, did not weather events at the end of the century. A long depression that devastated the sugar islands in the Caribbean, the Glorious Revolution, and the establishment of parliamentary supremacy all contributed to the rise of a second policy cycle. But in a very real sense, the new trade policy was in effect no policy at all, characterizing what Edmund Burke later called the era of "salutary neglect." Prevailing from the 1690s to the 1740s, that liberal policy arising from the age of Locke damned mercantilist sanctions with faint praise. By ignoring mercantilism rather than rejecting it outright, the English in conjunction with the Scots (after the Act of Union in 1707) effected a remarkable liberalization of British and American commerce.[15]

But after a half century of free trade, "salutary neglect" succumbed to the next policy cycle. During the bad times in the 1730s and 1740s, Burke and other neomercantilists regained the upper hand in policy-making and instituted a third and final cycle of American colonial policy. They revitalized mercantilist principles and harnessed them to an imperial system. They insisted upon compliance with trade laws still on the books, extended the law to new commodities and trades, and established the administrative machinery of effective commercial surveillance—all of which provoked colonial anger, retaliation, and eventually rebellion.[16]

It would appear then that the British were no more immune to policy cycles before 1783 than were Americans afterward. In both cases, policy was cyclical in structure and alternating in pattern. Pasting together all of these policy cycles, domestic and foreign, we may sketch a pattern of seven periodic alternations stretching

---

Paul Thomas, *The Rise of the Western World: A New Economic History* (Cambridge: Cambridge University Press, 1973), esp. pp. 146–56. On the mercantilist resurgency in the middle third of the seventeenth century, see Charles Wilson, *England's Apprenticeship, 1603–1763* (New York: St. Martin's Press, 1965).

15. Bushman distinguishes what I take to be policy cycles of "limited monarchy" after 1688 and "administrative monarchy" after 1763 or, in more familiar language, salutary neglect and neomercantilism. Richard Bushman, *King and People in Provincial Massachusetts* (Chapel Hill: University of North Carolina Press, 1985), pp. 80–81. Also see Michael G. Kammen, *A Rope of Sand: The Colonial Agents, British Politics, and the American Revolution* (New York: Vintage Books, 1974); and James A. Henretta, *"Salutary Neglect": Colonial Administration Under the Duke of Newcastle* (Princeton, N.J.: Princeton University Press, 1972).

16. Kammen, *A Rope of Sand*; Thomas C. Barrow, *Trade and Empire: The British Customs Service in Colonial America, 1660–1775* (Cambridge, Mass.: Harvard University Press, 1967).

back to the 1630s. In tabular form, the progression looks something like this:

Mercantilism	1630s–1680s
Free trade ("salutary neglect")	1690s–1740s
Neomercantilism (the "Age of Empire")	1740s–1783
Protectionism and elite distribution	1790s–1830s
Free trade and democratic distribution	1830s–1880s
Protectionism and elite redistribution	1880s–1930s
Free trade and democratic redistribution	1930s–1970s

Note that policy cycles alternate in a pattern so firmly fixed that only once—1790s–1830s—was it broken. And that rupture required a very special set of historical circumstances. In this cycle, the Founding Fathers broke ranks with macrohistory. Instead of rejecting the protectionism of the previous cycle (the despised policies of the neomercantilists), they perversely reinstated high protectionist tariffs. But these were extraordinary times in history—"the best of times, the worst of times" according to Dickens, an Age of Revolution according to historians. In this cycle, nearly four decades of revolution and warfare cascaded over the Atlantic economy, first in America, then in France, and finally in Latin America. All of this thoroughly disrupted foreign markets, oceanic commerce, and international trade and rendered free trade a highly impractical policy. Resisting the dialectical policy imperative, the Founding Fathers chose protectionism as their only reasonable alternative.[17]

Macrohistory was momentarily thrown off course by the exceptional turbulence of the times. In effect, the policy cycle skipped a beat, jumping a full half-century ahead to a protectionist paradigm that was not scheduled to arrive until the 1830s. For many this was bad news, but the news could not have been better for the handful of infant industries scattered around the Atlantic arena.

17. Americans of course tried to have it both ways. Antifederalists attempted to maintain neutrality so as to trade with all belligerents; but free trade was blunted by the Napoleonic Wars, the War of 1812, and later the Latin American revolutions—all of which strengthened the case for Hamiltonian protectionist tariffs and bounties for infant industries. John C. Miller, *The Federalist Era: 1789–1801* (New York: Harper and Row, 1960); various essays in J. Rogers Hollingsworth, ed., *Nation and State Building in America: Comparative Historical Perspectives* (Boston: Little, Brown, 1971); and, on the War of 1812, Ronald L. Hatzenbuehler and Robert L. Ivie, *Congress Declares War: Rhetoric, Leadership, and Partisanship in the Early Republic* (Kent, Ohio: Kent State University Press, 1983).

Under protectionism's benign shelter, they effected somewhat ahead of schedule an industrial revolution.[18]

Economic Long Waves

To the triad of historical period, policy cycle, and religious revitalization cycle, we may add a fourth and final rhythm: the long wave in capitalist economies. Its correlation with our triad is so close that it cannot be dismissed as merely casual or coincidental; conversely, the association is far too intricate to be explained away by a simple-minded materialism. I will explore these matters after reconstructing the rhythmic structure of the long wave.

Long-wave rhythms were discovered earlier in this century by the Russian economist Nicolai Kondratieff—hence their occasional labeling as Kondratieff cycles. After examining countless price series, Kondratieff concluded that capitalist economies experienced recurrent waves, each lasting 45 to 60 years. He divided each wave into two principal parts: a long upswing of rising prices and prosperity and a long downswing of falling prices that culminated in a severe and protracted depression.[19]

In the years since Kondratieff's empirical discovery, economists have not known quite what to do with his long waves. Usually they have ignored them—as they have other business cycles—until the economy is knee-deep in the kind of depression the wave so presciently predicts. In these bad times, Kondratieff's cycles are dusted off (though never quite achieving the luster required for textbooks in economics) and a few serious scholars, along with a host of millenarian pop economists, explore the logic behind their relentless rhythm.

Indeed it was during the Great Depression of the 1930s that Joseph Schumpeter greatly advanced our understanding of these half-

18. Protectionist policies were elitist in that they favored a small but dynamic industrial sector in the northeast. On the elite cast of this policy cycle, see McCormick, "The Party Period and Public Policy" (cited in note 7); and Horwitz, *The Transformation of American Law* (cited in note 6). By shifting rates of return in favor of infant industries and domestic consumption of their products, protectionism sponsored biased regional economic growth based upon import replacement. This growth is nicely described, albeit divorced from its policy parameters, by Diane Lindstrom, *Economic Development in the Philadelphia Region, 1810–1850* (New York: Columbia University Press, 1978).

19. Nicolai Kondratieff, "The Long Wave in Economic Life," *Review of Economic Statistics* 17 (1935), pp. 105–15.

century rhythms. Among the many insights in his two-volume study of business cycles, one of the most useful is a description of long-wave rhythms between the 1780s and the 1930s. Thanks to Schumpeter and his intellectual heirs, scholars can agree that American society has experienced since the 1780s four long waves with perhaps a fifth just now commencing. The four waves correspond almost perfectly with the periodic structure of traditional history: (1) 1780s–1830s; (2) 1830s–80s; (3) 1890s–1930s; and (4) 1930s–80s. If the present wave persists, as some believe it will, we will have (5) 1980s–2030s.[20]

But what of the long wave prior to the 1780s? Opinion is divided. Following Walt Rostow, most economists believe that the wave originated with the Industrial Revolution in the latter half of the eighteenth century. Others, most notably Immanuel Wallerstein and Fernand Braudel, suspect that its origins are intertwined with the rise of capitalism in the sixteenth and seventeenth centuries. Schumpeter was noncommittal. He recognized that the wave might have begun before the 1780s, but felt that inferior data precluded a robust test of that proposition. Accordingly, he opted for the expedient solution of beginning his wave count in 1789.[21]

But much has changed since the 1930s. Our understanding of the colonial American economy has vastly improved. A massive literature has supplied us with price series, reasonably reliable esti-

20. These scholars disagree, however, on the precise dating of long-wave rhythms. Schumpeter, *Business Cycles* (cited in note 7). See also W. W. Rostow and Michael Kennedy, with the assistance of Faisal Nasr, "A Simple Model of the Kondratieff Cycle," *Research in Economic History* 4 (1979), pp. 1–36. Rostow's dating is as follows: (1) 1790–1848; (2) 1848–96; (3) 1896–1933; and (4) 1933–72. For slightly different turning points, see the comprehensive survey by Goldstein, *Long Cycles* (cited in note 7). My independently derived periods tend to fit best with Berry's long waves, which are based upon an impressive analysis of the growth in American prices over the past two centuries. See Brian J. L. Berry, *Long-Wave Rhythms in Economic Development and Political Behavior* (Baltimore, Md.: Johns Hopkins University Press, 1991), which I consulted as an unpublished manuscript entitled "The Clocks that Time Development" (1988). Scholars heatedly debate our current positioning on the long wave; some maintain that the worst came in the 1970s, others that it is yet to come. Berry's analysis suggests that the worst free fall of prices occurred in the 1970s but that following a short recovery, they will fall again before making their long rise in the first third of the twenty-first century. This interpretation is consistent with my labeling of these times as sequential phases of Crisis and Creativity.

21. Schumpeter, *Business Cycles*. Braudel, *The Perspective of the World* (cited in note 3). Wallerstein, *The Capitalist World-Economy* (cited in note 2); *idem*, "The Future of the World Economy," in *Processes of the World System*, ed. T. Hopkins and I. Wallerstein (Beverly Hills: Sage, 1980), pp. 167–80.

mates of economic growth, and a good sense of agrarian and mercantile innovation—all of which have been conveniently compiled by John McCusker and Russell Menard in their masterful survey of the economy of British North America. That evidence, as I have suggested elsewhere, makes a good case for a long-wave logistic rhythm that stretches back to the origins of the American colonies.[22]

Perhaps the best evidence of colonial long waves is the periodicity of bad times in that era. The absolutely worst depressions in the colonial period recur at intervals of a half century, plus or minus five to ten years. These bad times of plummeting commodity prices and falling real incomes came in the 1780s, the 1740s, the 1680s and 1690s, and the 1630s. (I would push the origins of the waves back at least to the crisis of the 1580s, when, of course, the Hakluyts wrote of England's extremity and the need to vent surplus Englishmen in overseas colonies.) Following each of these crises, prosperity resumed. The economy improved slowly at first and then at an accelerating pace during the wave's long upswing. Commodity prices went up; innovations in mercantile organization and agricultural practice spread rapidly; consumption increased; standards of living improved; and incomes and wealth, on average, rose. Growth continued impressively for two to three decades, whereupon the pace slackened and the economy entered a long downswing. In the ensuing two decades, the economy ran downhill into the abyss of long-wave depression and social crisis.[23]

To test this controversial proposition of long-wave rhythms in the colonial economy, I reexamined the evidence on frontier expansion. If long waves existed before 1790, then settlement processes should have been sensitive to their rhythms, slowing down during long-wave depressions and steadily expanding during the ensuing decades of prosperity (in the long upswings and early phases of the downswings). The test of this hypothesis unfolded in three steps. First, I delimited settled areas on Herman Friis's remarkable collection

22. Carville Earle, "Interpreting *The Economy of British North America:* Malthus, the Market, or the Logistic Curve?" in *The Economy of British America, 1607–1789*, Working Papers in Early Modern History (Minneapolis: Department of History, University of Minnesota, 1986), pp. 5–17. McCusker and Menard, *The Economy of British North America.*

23. My single disappointment with the McCusker-Menard account in *The Economy of British North America* is their description of the years between 1680 and 1720 as a long period of economic stagnation. Local and regional data reveal an earlier and a more rapid upturn than their argument allows.

of population maps (for 1650, 1675, 1700, 1720, 1740, 1760, 1770, 1780, and 1790). Second, I calculated for each sequential pair of maps the compounded annual growth in settled areas by region and for the colonies as a whole. Third, I compared expansion rates in the three long-wave depressions with the rates in the ensuing periods of prosperity. Depressions occurred within the map pairs of 1675/1700, 1740/1760, and 1780/1790; prosperity, generally speaking, within the balance of the map pairs.[24]

Insofar as settlement expansion is a proxy for the long wave, the test confirms the presence of this rhythm in the colonial economy. At the aggregate level, colonial settlement is highly responsive to long-run economic conditions. Settlement expansion rates fall to their lowest levels during half-century depressions. The rate is at its lowest (1.1 percent per annum) in the late-seventeenth-century depression—a widely acknowledged time of economic duress—and only slightly higher (1.6 percent) in the depressions of the 1740s and 1780s. At no other times in the colonial period did the rate fall to comparably low levels.

Conversely, in good times settlement expanded with increasing rapidity. Expansion rates grew modestly at first before accelerating to peaks of over 3 percent per annum—double or treble depression rates—toward the end of the long wave. The rate of settlement expansion then fell precipitously (to less than 1.7 percent per annum) when the colonial economy reentered the phase of long-wave depression.

Disaggregated regional rates of settlement expansion offer further confirmation of colonial long waves. Regional expansion rates slowed down significantly in virtually every colonial region during the three long-wave depressions. Of the sixteen separate cases, fourteen regions experienced a downtrend in frontier expansion. More precisely, in the late-seventeenth-century depression, three of four regional rates went down (New England's went up); in the depression of the 1740s, six of six went down; and in the 1780s, five of six did so (New York's went up). Moreover, the fall in regional expansion rates was often abrupt—in one case dropping from 20 percent per annum to 2 percent and in another from 9 to 4 percent. Long-wave depressions, therefore, seem to have had a ubiquitous and adverse

24. Herman R. Friis, "A Series of Population Maps of the Colonies and the United States, 1625–1790," *Geographical Review* 30 (1940), pp. 463–70. Expansion rates are compounded annually between sequential map pairs.

impact upon the rate of frontier expansion in the several regions of colonial America as well as in the colonies taken as a whole.

Long-wave prosperity, however, had mixed effects on regional settlement expansion. Generally speaking, expansion rates increased in half the regions and decreased or held steady in the other half. The variability in rates has no clear-cut pattern. Some regions bucked the colonial trend of rising rates in good times just once (Pennsylvania and the backcountry), some twice (New England, the Chesapeake, and the Carolinas), and one thrice (New York). This variability, however, should be set within a context of aggregate settlement expansion in the colonies as a whole.[25]

From this test of colonial settlement expansion, I draw three conclusions. First, the long-wave rhythm indeed operated during the colonial period from the mid-seventeenth century to 1790. Second, the waves' most ubiquitous and potent effects on the economy and society, both regionally and in the aggregate, occurred during the periodic depressions every half-century or so. Third, colonial long waves corresponded in their timing with the historical periods, policy cycles, and religious revitalizations of colonial history.

The Quadratic Conjuncture of American Macrohistory

The American past reveals a curiously persistent alignment of historical periods, policy cycles, religious revitalizations, and long-wave economic rhythms. This quadrad forms what the French would call a historical conjuncture of unusual proportion. Its several rhythms begin at almost precisely the same time and endure for the same half-century interval. Their synchronization is hardly coincidental. In fact, this indisoluble quadrad gets at the very essence of what we mean when we speak of historical periods. The period is, in

25. My regional units are those defined in D. W. Meinig, *The Shaping of America: A Geographical Perspective on 500 Years of History; Vol. 1, Atlantic America 1492–1800* (New Haven, Conn.: Yale University Press, 1986), pp. 79–256. The cyclical rhythm of frontier expansion endured until 1840, at which point the frontier was effectively closed (rates of increase in settled areas fell consistently below two percent per annum). The half-century cycling of American settlement persisted after 1840, however, as processes of spatial concentration replaced those of spatial extension. The concentrations of population density were highest during the difficult decades of the 1840s and 1880s and lowest during the more prosperous years in between. See Carville Earle and Changyong Cao, "The Rate of Frontier Expansion in American History, 1650–1890," in *GIS and the Social Sciences: A Handbook*, eds. Leonard Hochberg, Carville Earle, and David Miller (Basil Blackwell, forthcoming).

an important sense, nothing more than the sum of its political, social, and economic paradigms—the cyclically variable "rules of the game," which are established at the outset of every historical period. These paradigms—new policies, new religious ideas, new economic innovations—constitute a historical reformation: they set out the period's agenda; establish norms and constraints for thought, discourse, and actions; and exercise hegemony over daily life in the period's half-century duration.

Historicists understand this well; indeed, the equivalence of period and paradigm is the basic premise of their inquiry. For the historicist, historical paradigms give coherence to a period; they provide, as it were, its operating principles. It is because of them that past behavior is comprehensible, that it makes sense. And it is because of them that historicists anoint the period with methodological preeminence. The period—unique, distinctive, irreplaceable—is the supreme unit of historicist interpretation.[26]

The period is equally supreme for macrohistory, but in this case it is the relevant historical unit for comparative rather than particularistic interpretation. In place of the historicist strategy of studying periods one at a time ("on their own terms," as the historicist would say), macrohistory examines them all at once. Each period is positioned within a historical outline that we have called a periodic structure. Comparisons are made across that structure—comparisons of the variability in the internal structure of periods (phases), in conditions and constraints, in behavior. These comparisons introduce novel problems seldom conceived within the insular historicist paradigm. For example, why the periodic reformation in periods and their paradigms? Why the indissoluble links among their quadratic elements? Why their half-century viability? And, most baffling of all, why their disconcerting regularity—what manner of process has the

26. Historicist perspectives vary from that of the ultraists, who regard all past events as unique and contingent on free will, to that of the moderatists, who maintain that behavioral regularities are period- or epoch-specific. Along with Marxists and increasing numbers of social science historians, I take the latter position. Social science and historicism are not incompatible, provided that generalizations about behavior are acknowledged to be historically specific, that is, their scope conditions in time are middle range. Precisely how long these scope conditions endure and how they are transformed are central issues for contemporary students of history. Social science arguments that assume uniformitarian behavioral postulates cannot be taken seriously. See for example Robert E. Berkhofer, Jr., *A Behavioral Approach to Historical Analysis* (New York: Free Press, 1969), pp. 211–69. Tilly, *Big Structures, Large Processes, and Huge Comparisons* (cited in note 2).

capacity to shape so thoroughly the past three and a half centuries of American history? It is to these comparisons across periods that we now turn.

Proposition 2: The Several Phases in the Periods of American History

Strictly speaking, the historicists are right: every historical period, indeed every historical event, is unique. There will never be, for example, another Jacksonian democracy, another Great Awakening, or another depression quite like that of the 1930s. Yet at the same time, history teases us with a variety of irresistible analogies and parallels through time—what I will refer to as phases in the periods of American history. Certain historical situations, though widely separated in time, seem to incorporate the same kinds of conditions, constraints, and choices. We have a sense of déjà vu, that somehow we have been here before. No one has pursued these historical parallels as effectively as historians of American civil dissent of the most dramatic kind—the kind laden with a surplus of revolutionary rhetoric, polemical discourse, political polarization, and an ascribed "paranoid style." By touching briefly on a few of these distinguished comparisons, we edge closer to a comparative macrohistorical methodology—one that is more general and more systematic than prevailing methodologies and that is couched within the several phases in the periodic structure of the American past. .

The Dissent Phase in American History: An Illustration

For students of American civil dissent, the American Civil War has been the richest source of historical analogy. William Freehling, for example, has drawn parallels between the coming of the Civil War in the 1850s and the sectional strife of the 1810s and 1820s. The secessionist impulse of the Hartford Convention, the strident debate over slavery and the tariff, the emergent theory of nullification, and the spillover of violence into the halls of Congress during the 1810s and 1820s constituted a rehearsal for what was to come a half-century hence. Lee Benson has discerned parallels between the Civil War and the American Revolution—the most obvious being the eruption of civil dissent into internal civil war. Lastly, James McPherson has suggested provocative parallels between the antislavery dissent of the 1850s and the Black Civil Rights Movement in the 1950s and 1960s.[27]

In each of these cases, historical comparison proceeds by twos; by stringing these dyads together—a procedure not wholly illogical given their common analogical reference to the Civil War—we discover a revealing arithmetic progression in the history of American civil dissent. The Revolution and the sectional dissent of the 1810s and 1820s are separated by 40 to 50 years; the dissent of the 1810s and 1820s and the Civil War by another 30 to 50 years; and the Civil War and the Civil Rights Movement of the 1950s and 1960s by 90 to 100 years.

While mere arithmetic cannot explain history, it does in this case highlight a missing element in the half-century progression of civil dissent since the 1770s, namely a fifth moment of dissent at the turning of this century. Are we justified in proposing that such a moment exists, though its similarity to the other four episodes of civil dissent has not been noted? Perhaps, provided that we accept the candidacy of the intense conflict between labor and capital during the 1900s and 1910s. Some evidence suggests that the comparison is apt. Certainly the air was filled with the heady rhetoric of revolution and the occasional smell of dynamite and gunpowder. The arena of conflict, moreover, sprawled across the length and breadth of American society, encompassing the countryside (recall Richard Hofstadter's paranoiac populists) as well as the city, locus of much working-class radicalism. The venerable description of these times as an "age of reform" is testimony to the contentious civil claims of Americans aggrieved by capital's power over income and wealth, wages, working conditions, and freight rates. Four Constitutional amendments redressing these grievances were proposed and ratified between 1909

27. William W. Freehling, *Prelude to Civil War: The Nullification Controversy in South Carolina, 1816–1836* (New York: Harper and Row, 1966). Lee Benson, *Toward the Scientific Study of History* (Philadelphia: J. B. Lippincott, 1972), pp. 81–97, 225–340. James M. McPherson, *The Struggle for Equality: Abolitionists and the Negro in the Civil War and Reconstruction* (Princeton, N.J.: Princeton University Press, 1964); *idem, The Abolitionist Legacy: From Reconstruction to the NAACP* (Princeton, N.J.: Princeton University Press, 1975). Also see the provocative linkage of the Revolution and Civil War with the ferment of the 1960s—a comparison I find entirely apt—in Staughton Lynd, *The Intellectual Origins of American Radicalism* (New York: Vintage Books, 1969). Recall too Charles Beard's characterization of the Civil War as the nation's second American Revolution.

and 1920—a record rivaled only by the dissent interludes of 1865– 70 (three amendments) and 1960–67 (three amendments). Whatever reserve one may have about arithmetic progression as a historical method, it usefully pinpoints five of the most dramatic moments in American civil dissent.[28]

Although the issues and outcomes in these five cases of civil dissent vary considerably, their common features are sufficiently numerous for us to speak of "Dissent" as a recurrent phase in the periods of American history. In each case, dissent erupts midway through a half-century historical period. In each case, dissent is packed tightly into a span of one to two decades. In each case, enormous emotional energy and commitment are mobilized and channeled into collective protest. In each case, the nub of contention is in the civic relations between the individual and the state, that is, civil rights. And in each case, the end result is revision, reform, or revolution in these civic relations. To be sure, American civil dissent is not limited to this one phase, but at no other times does its expression have such potent effects.

It should not be surprising, therefore, that interpretations of civil dissent are as stylized as the phase itself. Certain historiographical themes are constantly reiterated in the parochial interpretations of these several cases of civil dissent: the general prosperity of the times, the inflated rhetoric, the paranoid style, the shadow of an earlier war, the juxtaposition of seemingly rational policy makers and irrational, even hysterical, dissidents, and so on.[29] Out of these stylized interpretations has emerged a richer interpretive context and a more precise definition of the situation from which dissent springs. Viewed in

28. Richard Hofstadter, *The Age of Reform: From Bryan to FDR* (New York: Knopf, 1955); Samuel P. Hays, *The Response to Industrialism, 1885–1914* (Chicago: University of Chicago Press, 1957); Weibe, *The Search for Order* (cited in note 11); Arthur S. Link and Richard L. McCormick, *Progressivism* (Arlington Heights, Ill.: Harlan Davidson, 1983). For Constitutional amendments, see Richard B. Morris, ed., *Encyclopedia of American History*, enlarged and updated (New York: Harper and Row, 1970), pp. 483–87.

29. Note the parallels in the stylized interpretations of, for example, Bernard Bailyn, *The Ideological Origins of the American Revolution* (Cambridge, Mass.: Harvard University Press, 1971); David Brion Davis, *The Slave Power Conspiracy and the Paranoid Style* (Baton Rouge: Louisiana State University Press, 1969); and Richard Hofstadter, *The Paranoid Style in American Politics and Other Essays* (New York: Knopf, 1965). A review of Hofstadter's essay on the paranoid style in American politics reveals that virtually all of his examples are drawn from Dissent phases in the American past. Is it coincidence that the Bailyn, Davis, and Hofstadter volumes all were written during the most recent phase of American dissent—1954–70? Should we expect that an interpretation of the 1960s paranoid style will prevail during the next phase of Dissent in roughly the 2010s?

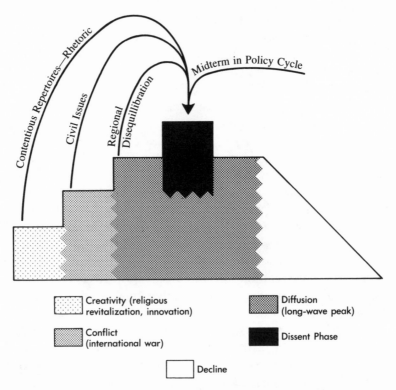

FIGURE 12.1. The Macrohistorical Context of the Dissent Phase. This schematic diagram illustrates the effects of earlier phases upon a later phase (in this case, the Dissent phase) in one period of a half century more or less. The nature of internal disagreements over civil issues during the Dissent phase is influenced by the residual effects of: 1) contentious repertoires and rhetoric deployed in the phases of Crisis and Creativity; 2) unresolved civil issues arising out of territorial acquisitions and the egalitarian consequences of the phase of Conflict (international war); 3) the differential growth of regional economies during the Diffusion phase; and 4) the political complacency that arises midway into a half-century policy cycle and affords an unusually wide berth for the exercise of civil dissent.

more general terms, the origins of the "Dissent phase" may be traced to the regular convergence of four key elements: (1) the disequilibration caused by economic prosperity; (2) the awareness of civil issues in a postwar society; (3) repertoires for contention; and (4) political policy constraints. All of these are embedded in the periodic rhythms of American society, economy, and polity (see Figure 12.1). Let us look more closely at this convergent configuration, starting with the economy.

Economic prosperity and its anxieties

The phase of civil Dissent occurs about midway in a historical period, and near the peak of long-wave economic growth. In these times, economic prosperity fuels rising expectations and regional economic disequilibrations. Anxieties ensue when expectations remain unfulfilled or when changes in one region prove profoundly unsettling in certain other regions (note for example Boston's relative spatial deprivation in the 1760s and 1770s or the fears engendered in the upper Midwest by the corn belt's acclaim for slave labor in the 1840s and 1850s). These regions become vanguards of revolution.

International war and the issues of dissent

Oddly enough, the controversial civil issues of the Dissent phase are triggered by international war. When the invariable phase of international war comes to an end (usually no later than 15 to 25 years into a half-century period), Americans suddenly confront a host of deferred, difficult, and politically controversial domestic issues: the need for postwar budget balancing, the disposition of acquired territory, the glaring contrasts between wartime military equality and postwar civilian inequalities, and so on. War has other effects as well, not least being the decisive style and the immediatist solution that are added to the repertoire of contention; but in these matters, religion plays a larger role.

Religious awakenings and contentious repertoires

The American language of dissent is suffused with the evangelical rhetoric handed down from the religious awakenings and revivals initiated at the outset of the historical period. Dissidents indulge *inter alia* the biblical penchant for disjunction: good versus evil, of right versus wrong, of moral versus immoral, of "all one thing or all the other." The language of civil dissent therefore is typically unreasoning, somewhat excessive, and stereotypically polarizing.

Policy cycles and the modesty of constraint

A generally prosperous, civilly aggrieved, and morally righteous population is a necessary condition for Dissent, but its sufficient condition lies in the sphere of politics, and more specifically in the domain of the policy cycle. Indeed, the phase of Dissent succeeds precisely because it attacks the soft underbelly in that cycle. Paradigmatic policies are most vulnerable to contentious civil dissent midway into the policy cycle, when governments are perhaps too secure in their triumph and too generous in their accommodation of critique (too willing to reason, one might say). By reacting reasonably and rationally to civil dissent, policymakers earn the admiration of a rationalist history and the contempt of their irrationalist historic constituencies. But the dissidents win out (however momentarily), compelling policymakers into what is described, too antiseptically, as a "mid-course correction" in policy paradigms.[30]

In the case of civil dissent, American history repeats itself, indeed with such regularity that we are justified in speaking of dissent as a recurrent phase in American history. But the recurrence of dissent, or any other phase for that matter, would not have been possible without the similarly regular recurrence of its causal context: of conditions, issues, repertoires, and constraints carried forward from earlier or concurrent phases. Understanding any one phase, therefore, requires understanding them all. But where do we start? As good a place as any is with historical analogy, and more particularly with the phases that are implicit in the rhythms of American religion, policy, and economy. Of these, we know the most about the rhythm of the economy's long wave. Its structure serves as a scaffolding upon which we may frame the several phases in the periods of American history.

A Scaffolding for the Phases of American History: The Logistic Curve

The continuous curve of the long wave can assume several forms—notably the tepee-like plot of commodity prices or the low dome of the rate of economic growth—but the most useful for discerning its phases is the S-shaped logistic curve of incomes per capita. Using this curve, economists have probed into the internal structure of the long wave. They have discovered in the logistic a recurrent

30. Critics of Whiggish interpretations usually see them as apologia for those in power—men and women presumably possessed of rationality, dispassion, and well-meaning policies. The Whig view of course presumes that policymakers accurately perceived the geographical realities that drove dissent. Chapter 4 in this volume should have disabused us of this peculiar notion; in these times, policymakers blunder because they ignore regional disequilibria associated with rapid economic growth, the social strains that ensue, and the spatial biases inherent in their policy measures. A classic example of Whig apologia occasioned by the omission of spatial biases in policy occurs in Lawrence Henry Gipson's otherwise brilliant essay "The American Revolution as the Aftermath of the Great War for the Empire, 1754–1763," *Political Science Quarterly* 65 (1950), pp. 86–104.

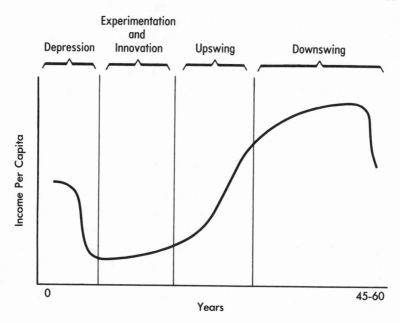

FIGURE 12.2. Generalized Phases in the Long-Wave Logistic.

pattern of phases, a natural history so to speak. Although the logistic is a continuous curve, its serifs and inflections partition the curve into four distinct phases: (1) severe and protracted depression; (2) creative experimentation and innovation (Schumpeter's phase of "creative destruction," when old technologies and infrastructures are displaced by new ones); (3) the long upswing, typified by rising incomes and prices; and (4) the long downswing, when income growth levels off and prices fall, eventuating in the next long-wave crisis when incomes drop abruptly. Figure 12.2 positions these several phases on a typical long-wave logistic.[31]

As a model of the economic past, the long-wave logistic is primitive in the sense that its predictions are modest. About the best the model can do is forecast a regular recurrence of 45- to 60-year long waves and their four internal phases (lasting on average 10 to 15 years each). It offers only educated estimates on the length or amplitude of a particular wave or phase, for example, whether a depression will be short or protracted, whether an innovation will be evolutionary or radically new, or whether an upswing or downswing

31. Schumpeter, *Business Cycles*. Rostow, Kennedy, and Nasr, "A Simple Model of the Kondratieff Cycle" (cited in note 20).

will be vigorous or timid. Nonetheless the long-wave model has considerable heuristic value. It provides us with temporal units—waves and phases—essential for macrohistorical comparison. Moreover, by drawing attention to their macrohistorical variability, the model generates comparative hypotheses on determinacy and contingency in historical behavior.[32]

The Six Phases of an American Historical Period

On the one hand, as currently constituted, the long-wave model is too parochial, too narrowly economic for a holistic American macrohistory. On the other hand, the long wave is an inextricable part of that history. We simply cannot appreciate historical behavior without including a large dose of economics. The question is how to join these two observations in a productive macrohistorical inquiry. Given the symmetry between long waves and the periodic structure of American history, the trick is to recast the long wave so that it is compatible with the multivariate perspectives of American history. The recasting involves two propositions.

The first proposition is that the long wave is merely a special case of the historical period—the former is narrowly economic, the latter is behaviorally inclusivist. The second proposition follows from the first: historical periods, because they are by definition inclusivist, have a richer texture than long waves—a texture that requires expanding the economists' four long-wave phases to at least six, and perhaps more, overlapping phases. This more textured structure transcends special-interest history; it invites synthesis of otherwise disparate findings.

Take just one provocative example. In the second macrohistorical phase—what economists speak of as a phase of experiment and innovation and what I call more generally the "phase of Creativity"—we may join under one roof Schumpeter's creative destruction, McCormick's policy-cycle paradigm, McLoughlin's religious awakenings, and a spate of fundamental innovation in agrarian

32. The model of the Kondratieff wave by Rostow and his associates illustrates the coarseness of the wave's predictions. Their attempts to model variations in the logistic requires assumptions about what needs to be explained. Several submodels, for example, regard such matters as war, rates of technical progress, and the "lumpiness" of capital investments as exogenous when in fact these are endogenous to the periodic structuring of the American past. Rostow, Kennedy, and Nasr, "A Simple Model of the Kondratieff Cycle."

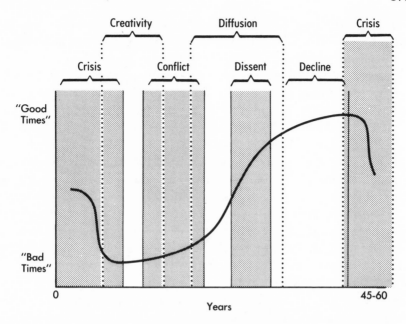

FIGURE 12.3 The Six Phases of an American Historical Period. The diagram illustrates a typical sequence of phases in a typical period of 45 to 60 years. In practice, phases vary considerably in their length, their overlap, and their clarity of definition from one historical period to another.

technology and organization. Creativity therefore extends far beyond microeconomics and embraces the multiple spheres and levels of organization within American society. Discerning these connections is what makes macrohistory interesting and what sets it apart from historicist inquiry.

There are six phases in our heuristic model of a historical period in American history. For ease of exposition, these are labeled Crisis, Creativity, Conflict, Diffusion, Dissent, and Decline. Figure 12.3 positions these phases on a typical long-wave logistic curve. These phases are invariant in two important respects. First, their sequence is the same in every historical period. Second, the general mode of behavior in specific phases, as described below, is identical across all historical periods. But all of the rest—the matters of phase length, overlap, magnitude—is enormously variable. Crisis, for example, may be very long and hard (as in the 1680s-90s and the 1930s) or more moderate in length and severity (as in the 1740s); Conflict, in which declared international war is an invariable feature, may be large (World War II) or small (the Spanish-American War). It is this sort of marvelous variability that constitutes the central problematic for macrohistorical inquiry.

Before delving into the issue of variability, however, it is necessary to summarize these several phases and their general modes of behavior. The phase summaries are desperately compressed, and historical examples are generally reserved for an ensuing discussion of phase variability. Each summary is accompanied by a table (Tables 12.1–12.6) listing the generalized dating of the given phase through the seven completed periods of American history and also the eighth period, which is now unfolding.[33]

The three phases of Crisis, Creativity, and Conflict are packed into the beginning of every historical period, typically the first fifteen years or so. Crisis initiates the period. These are bad times—for the society and polity as well as the economy. Things go wrong across the board. The economy sinks into a severe and usually protracted depression. Unemployment rises, pushing toward a fifth to a quarter of the labor force; prices fall to half-century lows. The economy's rate of growth sags below 1 percent per annum and generally dips into negative ranges. The glut of population relative to jobs becomes a matter of deep concern. Fears of overpopulation and population pressure are voiced; Malthusian concepts and notions of a constrained environment and resource base gain popularity. The frontier offers the only immediate remedy. It attracts migrants of two types: families fleeing economically depressed regions and families of dissenting religious groups fleeing the intensified persecution that accompanies hard times, for example, Massachusetts Puritans in the 1630s, Pennsylvania Quakers in the 1680s, and the Mormons in the 1840s. In these times, when the economy breaks down, when our vaunted tradition of pluralist toleration becomes a myth, the frontier assumes the dual role of safety valve and sectarian refuge.

Most Americans, however, remain in long-settled areas and suffer the privations of depression. As conditions worsen, the prevailing system of political economy is roundly criticized. Sporadic violence and organized opposition ensue: witness the recurrent rebellions and, more recently, the violence between labor and capital in the

33. It is impossible to cite all of the relevant authorities for each of the six phases over seven periods of American history. The illustrations listed in the tabulations must suffice. Selective footnotes point up particularly good comparative sources or amplify examples that might otherwise be misinterpreted.

TABLE 12.1

The Crisis Phase in American History

Period	Dating of phase	Illustrations
1	Late 1620s to 1630s	English depression; Puritan migration
2	Late 1670s to early 1690s	Bacon's Rebellion; Salem witch trials
3	Mid-1730s to mid-1740s	Backcountry migration (pluralist)
4	Late 1780s to early 1790s	Shays's Rebellion; Whiskey Rebellion
5	Mid-1830s to mid-1840s	Urban riots; Dorr's Rebellion (R.I.); Antirent War (N.Y.)
6	Mid-1870s to early 1890s	Strikes, episodically violent; Coxey's Army
7	Late 1920s to 1930s	Strikes, episodically violent
8	Late 1970s to 1980s	Farm protest

TABLE 12.2

The Creativity Phase in American History

Period	Dating of phase	Illustrations
1	Late 1630s to 1640s	Tobacco housing and topping; English Civil War; sugar in Barbados
2	1690s to 1710	Chesapeake slavery and plantation diversification; Carolina rice; Glorious Revolution
3	1740s to 1750s	European grain trade; Neomercantilist revival
4	Ca. 1790 to 1810	Cotton gin; steamboat; Constitution
5	Late 1830s to 1840s	Reaper; railroad; Jacksonian democracy
6	Mid-1880s to 1900	Tractor; American Federation of Labor; Socialist Party; Progressives (corporatism)
7	1930s to early 1940s	Hybrid corn; tractor; cotton harvesters; Congress of Industrial Organizations; New Deal
8	1980s	Corporate farming; microcomputers; superconductors; Reagan "Revolution"

TABLE 12.3

The Conflict Phase in American History

Period	Dating of phase	Illustrations
1	Late 1630s and early 1640s	Indian warfare in Virginia and New England
2	1689–97; 1702–13	War of the League of Augsburg; War of the Spanish Succession
3	1740–48; 1754–63	War of the Austrian Succession; French and Indian War
4	1801–5; 1812–15	Tripolitan War; War of 1812
5	1846–48	The war with Mexico
6	1898	Spanish-American War
7	1941–45	World War II
8	1990s	?

1870s and 1880s and again in the 1930s. Crisis is indeed a "dismal phase." Fortunately it lasts only for about a decade and rarely more than a decade and a half.[34]

Creativity arises out of Crisis. But in contrast to the dismal times of Crisis, this phase presents Americans at their best. Portraits of our national character, from Crèvecoeur's to Tocqueville's, capture our most flattering side. In this thin slice of time—rarely more than a decade—the cynicism and negativism of Crisis subtly fade into optimism, energy, and innovation. Worn-out ideas are set aside and the operative paradigms of a new historical period are installed. In this phase, Schumpeter's moment of "creative destruction," the nation's stock of fundamental technologies, institutions, and ideologies makes a quantum leap forward.

Creativity begins with a precocious search for solutions to the social, economic, and political malaise of Crisis. Experimentation takes place in all spheres of life and at all societal levels. Simultaneously, innovative ideas burst forth from households, farms, firms, religious groups, labor, communities, regions, states, and the nation at large. Of the multitude of experiments, a few prove exceptionally useful. Farmers and planters revise existing production practices or introduce new tools, machines, or crops; firms innovate new products and processes; religious groups experience revitalization and reformation; new institutions (corporations, religions or sects, and labor organizations) are born; politicians and parties (and before them, factions) construct a new political economy that replaces old, discredited, and ineffectual policies (this is the initiation of McCormick's policy cycle and the ensuing electoral realignment).

The clustering of technical innovations in this phase is well known. Less familiar are the recurrent innovations in the political economy (the Constitution, Jacksonian democracy, corporatist progressivism, and the New Deal), in religion (the revitalizations and reformations spelled out by McLoughlin), and in the economy (corporations and labor organizations). The historical significance of the

---

34. Note that in the 1620s, the contention over and the dissolution of the Virginia Company occurred on the eve of Crisis. Crisis is closely associated with "rebellions," which in addition to having their origins in conditions of regional socioeconomic deprivation, tend to be unsuccessful. History associates the term with a losing cause. Rebellions are put down; revolutions succeed. The geography of rebellion during Decline and Crisis has broadened its spatial range over time, from the frontier before 1790 to older settled agrarian regions and urban places in the 1830s to industrializing cities in the 1880s and 1930s.

innovations in all these spheres lies in their widespread and triumphant diffusion, which we take up momentarily.[35]

Ten to fifteen years into every historical period, Americans become entangled in international war—what we call a phase of Conflict. Unlike many other wars, the wars of the Conflict phase are officially declared and they elicit fairly widespread popular support. This is as true of the colonial period, when our entanglement arose from British imperial politics, as of the national period, when the United States consistently has been one of the principals in international war. The Conflict phase poses two sorts of issues: what causes war to recur and what are the ramifications of war for domestic society?

With respect to causality, the recurrence of war has led some scholars to regard war as the inevitable consequence of capitalist depression. War, in their view, rescues the economy from the desperate times of Crisis. However plausible this thesis may be in some cases, it is invalid as a general proposition. History offers too many counterexamples. Take for example the case of the War of 1812—a war that Americans did not want and did everything they could to avert. Instead of courting war as an escape from depression, American diplomats effectively deferred our involvement in international conflict for over a decade—an impressive achievement at any time, and all the more so in the Napoleonic era. In other cases, even though Americans may have been itching for war, we are hard-pressed to make a case for the depression thesis. In the "splendid little war" against Spain in 1898, it is difficult to imagine how a war so short could have made much of a dent in the troubled economy of the late nineteenth century. The causes of war are considerably more complex. At the moment, about all our period model allows us to say is that international war is a recurrent phase (Conflict); that it follows

---

35. The phase of Creativity may be regarded in Kuhnian terms as the moment of paradigmatic shift—the creative response to accumulating socioeconomic anomalies that eventuate in Crisis and discredit the preceding paradigm. I depart from Kuhn's model by regarding the process of paradigmatic social change as a contentious dialectic between elite and democratic innovations. Thomas S. Kuhn, *The Structure of Scientific Revolutions*, 2nd ed., enlarged (Chicago: University of Chicago Press, 1970). See also various essays in Peter B. Evans, Dietrich Rueschemeyer, and Theda Skocpol, eds., *Bringing the State Back In* (Cambridge: University of Cambridge Press, 1985). Americans thus far have been spared creative monstrosities the likes of Hitler and Mussolini, but these are no less the products of hard times. How the United States has managed to avert such personalities is of course a matter of the utmost significance. Hannah Arendt, *The Origins of Totalitarianism* (Cleveland: World, 1958).

the phase of Crisis; and that it overlaps with the phase of Creativity. Everything else about it—its causes, timing, duration, and magnitude—is so enormously variable from one conflict to another that interpretive caution is essential.[36]

In the rush to link war with economic depression, scholars have overlooked the fact that Conflict also arises out of Creativity, a phase that bears upon the recurrence of international war in two important ways. First, Creativity affects war through the emergence of a new elite with a new psychological profile. The emergent elites, flushed with the success of their innovations, are full of moxie and hubris; they are hard-working and forceful; and they are accustomed to taking risks and to solving difficult problems quickly and decisively. Such a profile of course is indispensable for overcoming bad times and social malaise at home; it is ill-suited, however, to the convoluted arena of diplomacy abroad.[37] Second, Creativity affects war through the mobilization of rhetoric and ideology. Innovations are useless unless diffused, and to encourage their adoption innovators employ the instruments of persuasive argument: reason, rhetoric, ideology, and, on occasion, bribery and brute force. And given a populace perplexed by the profusion of novelty in so many spheres, persuasion occurs more often through rhetoric and ideology than pure reason (this tendency is confirmed by the vast scholarship on innovation diffusion). Thus Creativity produces a new elite replete with a "quick-trigger" mentality and a demagogic capacity for rhetoric and ide-

36. While post-Crisis international war has been invariable throughout American history, the magnitude and duration of these conflicts are highly variable. On the deferral of post-Crisis Conflict, see Hatzenbuehler and Ivie, *Congress Declares War* (cited in note 17). Also see Goldstein, *Long Cycles*, pp. 99–147, 234–57 (cited in note 7); and Geoffrey Blainey, *The Causes of War* (New York: Free Press, 1973). Generalizations on warfare have been impeded by the indiscriminate grouping of all wars into the dependent variable; too little attention has been given to a careful specification of socioeconomic conditions (that is, the relevant phase) from which wars emerge. For example, given the Crisis phase in American history, international war invariably follows; by contrast, in the Dissent phase war is not invariable. War is rather one of several manifestations of internal conflict over civil issues. Consequently, analyses that group invariable international wars with more episodic internal wars confound interpretation by mixing radically different causal conditions and contexts (phases).

37. The daunting task of political economic reconstruction (that is, of shifting paradigms in domestic and foreign policy) usually exacerbates tensions across national boundaries. Yet we discount at our peril the critical role of the indomitable leaders (the new elite) in these times. The "great man" (and woman) conception of history is especially apt in phases of Crisis, Creativity, and Conflict; witness for example such principals as Elizabeth, Cromwell, Locke, Pitt, the Founding Fathers, Jackson, and FDR, as well as Hitler, Stalin, and Churchill.

ology—a combination perhaps too volatile and dangerous in matters of state. To understand our recurrent wars, therefore, we must come to grips with the militant predispositions of an American elite born, paradoxically, out of Creativity.[38]

Just as important as the causes of Conflict are its ramifications for domestic society. Let us hint at a few of these. First, war mobilization effects dramatic revisions in traditional roles and status: civilians of varying social rank, race, and creed dissolve into a soldiery of rough equality; jobs once reserved for "able-bodied" men are filled by women and marginal men; families formerly led by husbands are now run by wives; and so on. When war ends, American society is never quite the same again. Something like a law of compensation comes into play: veterans insist upon their entitlement to "catch-up" economic benefits and to the greater equality they enjoyed in wartime; women and marginal men, cast out of the postwar labor force, resent their loss of preferment. All of this strains social relations and the budget-balancing exercises of postwar governments.[39]

War also effects fundamental changes in national territory and, more recently, international hegemony. Peace treaties at the end of the Conflict phase have played key roles in American territorial expansion (note especially the 1763 Treaty of Paris and the 1848 Treaty of Guadalupe Hidalgo) as well as in the spread of American hegemony abroad—over the Caribbean after the Spanish-American War and over Europe and Japan following World War II. Territorial and

38. The irrationalist component of creativity has been underappreciated in the literature on innovation diffusion. Perhaps it is best treated in the study of political economy and ideology; for example, see Clifford Geertz, "Ideology as a Cultural System," in his *The Interpretation of Cultures* (New York: Basic Books, 1973), pp. 193–233; Kuhn, *The Structure of Scientific Revolutions*; and various essays in Evans, Rueschemeyer, and Skocpol, *Bringing the State Back In*, esp. pp. 107–63. Lawrence Brown, *Innovation Diffusion: A New Perspective* (London: Methuen, 1981), pp. 101–3, 110; and E. M. Rogers and F. F. Shoemaker, *Communication of Innovations: A Cross-cultural Approach* (New York: Free Press, 1971).

39. World War II, for example, dramatically altered attitudes toward racial segregation, and these new attitudes spilled over into the postwar Civil Rights Movement. Similarly, veterans benefits ranging from the post-Revolutionary land bounties to the GI Bill after World War II stimulated geographical expansion first to frontiers and later to cities and suburbs. These postwar effects have become more pronounced in the era of nationalist wars, which began with the American Revolution. Henceforth, a small cadre of professional soldiers was supplemented by masses of conscripts who returned to civilian life at war's end. See Russell F. Weigley, *The American Way of War: A History of United States Military Strategy and Policy* (Bloomington: Indiana University Press, 1965); various essays in Michael Howard, ed., *The Theory and Practice of War* (Bloomington: Indiana University Press, 1965); and Keith L. Nelson and Spencer C. Ohlin, Jr., *Why War?: Ideology, Theory, and History* (Berkeley: University of California Press, 1979).

hegemonic aggrandizement has its price, however, as we shall see when we examine how American society deals with the domestic ramifications of Conflict in the ensuing phases of American historical periods.[40]

Diffusion is the cool interlude between the emotionally charged Crisis, Creativity, and Conflict phases and the ensuing phase of civil Dissent. Overlapping the phase of Creativity, Diffusion usually begins about a decade into the period. The fundamental technical and social innovations of the Creativity phase start to spread over space when they are adopted by a small minority of risk takers—perhaps no more than 5 percent of the population. Their more cautious neighbors observe the successes and failures and assess the probabilities. As these people in turn adopt the successful innovations (those with small risk), the curve of diffusion inflects upward. Further success begets further adoption and the innovation spreads among the agrarian population. Although the rate of diffusion eventually decelerates, it is the early stages of adoption that make or break an innovation—the critical phase beginning about a decade into the historical period and ending near its midpoint, about two and a half decades into the period. In this span, fundamental innovations diffuse from a decided minority to a majority of the population; the diffusion of lesser innovations is truncated in its early stages.[41]

The Diffusion phase is one of unusual economic growth and prosperity. Confidently, the nation embarks upon a spectacular ex-

40. The extent of territorial or hegemonic acquisition is a key determinant of the magnitude of civil unrest in the ensuing phase of Dissent. An international war that begins during or soon after Crisis and produces large territorial acquisitions has invariably resulted in internal war during the Dissent phase. The three cases in point are the American Revolution, the American Civil War, and, if we consider the nation's vast hegemonic acquisitions after World War II, the Vietnam War.

41. The massive literatures on innovation diffusion and long waves rarely intersect; hence we lack both a time-specific theory of innovation diffusion and an integrated theory of long economic cycles. The problem, I believe, is that the diffusionists are inattentive to the half-century logistic of fundamental innovations and its synchronization with historic long waves. How far geographers have to go in achieving this integration is vividly illustrated in a recent statement by Pakes and Thrift: "Mandel associates each of these [Kondratieff] waves with a technological innovation of consequence. Such innovations must, however, be diffused spatially . . . in order for their impact to be of consequence. Linking cycle studies with spatial diffusion remains as a challenge to human geographers and economists alike. Cycles appear to be an endemic aspect of economic process as does diffusion"—which is to admit that we are just now at the primitive stage of pattern recognition. Don Pakes and Nigel Thrift, *Time, Spaces, and Places: A Chronogeographic Perspective* (Chichester, Eng.: John Wiley & Sons, 1980), p. 415. A substantial advance, however, has been made by Berry, *The Clock that Times Development* (cited in note 20).

TABLE 12.4

The Diffusion Phase in American History

Period	Dating of phase	Illustrations
1	1650s to 1660s	The rise of Boston's foreland; the Virginia land rush and servant mobility
2	1710s to 1720s	Boom in the American trade with the West Indies and associated urban growth; the spread of Scottish merchants in the southern colonies and the rise of the planter elite
3	1750s to 1760s	Direct grain trade with Europe; the "golden age of colonial culture"
4	1800s to early 1820s	Early industrialization; flush times in the rapidly expanding cotton belt; canals
5	Late 1840s to mid-1860s	Railroad and steamboat diffusion; regional economic specialization west of the Appalachians; origins of Megalopolis
6	1900s to 1918	Urban concentration of population and corporations; trucks, autos, "good roads," and urban subways
7	Late 1940s to 1965	Suburbanization and metropolitanization; interstate highway system
8	Mid-1990s to 2010?	?

pansion in settlement, transportation, and regional economic development—an expansion only hinted at by the illustrations in Table 12.4. Historians, however, have not been so confident about the meaning of these times of economic boom and material largesse. Indeed, their interpretations are remarkably ambivalent. On the one hand, traditional historians speak favorably of these decades as "the golden age of colonial culture" (1750s and 1760s) and the halcyon days (1820s cotton belt), and economists write admiringly of sustained growth and the eradication of cyclical depression (1950s and 1960s). On the other hand, social historians and commentators disparage these times as bland and excessively acquisitive (bourgeois one might say). They speak unflatteringly of a "nation of sheep," of "status seekers" and "lonely crowds," of semicyclical "private interest," of undistinguished leaders (the unknown presidents, for example, from Fillmore to Taft to Eisenhower). Yet neither side in this interpretive standoff fairly captures the ferment of civil dissent lying just beneath the cool exterior of the Diffusion phase.[42]

42. Vance Packard, *The Status Seekers: An Exploration of Class Behavior in America and the Hidden Barriers that Affect You, Your Community, and Your Future* (New York: D. McKay, 1959); Schlesinger, Jr., *The Cycles of American History*, pp. 23–48 (cited in note 5); Arthur M. Schlesinger, *Paths to the Present*, rev. ed. (Boston: Houghton Mifflin, 1964), pp. 89–114.

Politics enters into every phase in American history, but its influence is unusually important in two phases: first, the Creativity phase, when the paradigms of a new policy cycle are installed; and second, the phase of Dissent, a time of domestic political conflict that ranges from intense disagreement to internal war. In these times republican civic virtue and public purpose come to the fore and displace momentarily the narrower pursuit of private interests. This is to say that in matters of politics there is a cycle within a cycle—a Schlesingerian public-private cycle within McCormick's more encompassing policy cycle.[43]

The recurrence of Dissent may be specified quite precisely within the historical period. It recurs roughly 25 to 30 years into every historical period, about 20 to 25 years into the policy cycle (which begins in the Creativity phase), within 10 to 15 years of the conclusion of Conflict, and smack in the middle of long-wave economic prosperity. In these times, latent political issues are joined and their festering tensions erupt in the public arena. The issues invariably center on domestic politics, and more specifically on the civil rights of particular groups within the society and polity. The Dissent phase encompasses the great civil debates and struggles in the American past: the rights of colonial lower houses of assembly in the 1720s; the rights of the colonists in the 1770s; the morality of slavery in the 1810s and 1820s and again in the 1850s and 1860s; the rights of working

43. Arthur Schlesinger, Jr., argues that the cycle of public-private interests is about 30 years in length—a generation—but he acknowledges also a variability in cycle length from 24 to 30 years. Doubling his cycle produces a span of 48 to 60 years, which is the customary range in the duration of American historical periods. By focusing on the shorter cycle, Schlesinger mixes divergent socioeconomic contexts and confounds comparative interpretation. While it is true, for example, that Lincoln and FDR represent apogees of public interest, the former emerged from a context of legendary prosperity in which civil rights constituted the supreme political issue; the latter from the depths of depression in which political, economic, and social reconstruction surpassed all other concerns. Comparison detached from historical context produces limpid conclusions on causality; I cite Schlesinger speaking of this century: "Each period of public purpose has its detonating issue. In the early decades of the century, [it was] the concentration of economic power in the trusts [Dissent over the civil right of equality of opportunity or condition]. In the 1930s, the detonating issue was depression [Crisis and Creativity focused on political economic issues]. In the 1960s it was racial justice [Dissent over the civil rights of Black Americans]." What seems obvious is that the detonating conditions (context) and issues varied so dramatically between the public phases of Crisis and Dissent as to warrant treating them as analytically distinct phases within the half-century rhythm of American history. Schlesinger, Jr., *The Cycles of American History*, p. 33. On the importance of socioeconomic context, see Harold Kerbo, "Movements of Crisis and Movements of Affluence," *Journal of Conflict Resolution* 26 (1982), pp. 645–63.

TABLE 12.5
The Dissent Phase in American History

Period	Dating of phase	Illustrations
1	1650s–60s	Puritan and royalist contention in Virginia
2	1720s	Disputes between lower houses of assembly and royal or proprietary administrations
3	1770s	American Revolution
4	1810s–20s	Intensification of Sectionalism; slavery and tariff issues; Nullification
5	1850s–65	Slavery debate; Civil War
6	1900s–20	Progressive Reform (e.g., laws on child labor and income taxation); labor unrest; four Constitutional amendments
7	1950s–60s	Civil Rights Movement; Constitutional amendments
8	2000–2020?	?

people, women, and children in the first two decades of this century (one may speculate that World War I represents a European variant of our Dissent phase); and the rights of Black Americans in the 1950s and 1960s. Befitting these times of civil dissent, Americans customarily revise their system of governance. Of the thirteen Constitutional amendments since 1804, ten were proposed and ratified in Dissent phases: Articles 13–15 between 1865 and 1870, Articles 16–19 between 1909 and 1920, and Articles 23–25 between 1960 and 1967.[44]

In these times, moral and religious rhetorics infuse the debate over political and civil rights. Discourse becomes hyperbolic in form and militant in tone. Adversaries are polarized; enemies are named, and names are called. In sum, what Richard Hofstadter and David Brion Davis have called the "paranoid style" comes to prevail. Sporadic violence and intemperate rhetoric push the nation toward the brink of domestic warfare, and on two occasions—the American Revolution and the American Civil War—internal war in fact ensued.[45]

Like every other phase, Dissent has many causes and assumes

44. Dissent turns on civil issues of rights and power between the state and, variously, the individual, the section, and groups or classes. Most of these episodes are well known and thoroughly studied. Indeed they constitute a large share of what I have called "grand history." Among the less-known episodes is the conflict over the political rights of the lower houses of assembly in the 1720s; see the insightful analysis by Jack P. Greene, *The Quest for Power: The Lower Houses of Assembly in the Southern Royal Colonies, 1689–1776* (Chapel Hill: University of North Carolina Press, 1963). On Constitutional amendments, see Richard Morris, ed., *Encyclopedia of American History*, pp. 484–87 (cited in note 28).

45. Davis, *The Slave Power Conspiracy and the Paranoid Style* (cited in note 29); for arguments in a similar vein, see the other citations in note 29.

varied forms, but the fact remains that it is an invariant phase in the periods of American history. Certain generic conditions—the products of prior phases—seem to underlie it: unbounded prosperity, but with rising socioeconomic and spatial inequalities; a polarizing moral rhetoric carried over perhaps from earlier revitalization movements and wars; a new elite predisposed to decisive action; and a residuum of political and civil issues precipitated out of international conflict, for example, the disposition of newly won territory, paying off war debts, and equitable treatment of war veterans. In these times, when expectations rise faster than they are satisfied, American society enters into the explosive and dangerous phase of Dissent.[46]

About 25 to 30 years into the historical period, the pendulum of growth and prosperity swings the other way. Prices begin their long fall; recessions outnumber booms; pockets of unemployment emerge; firms retrench and workers complain about speedups, longer hours, lower wages, and competition from other supplies of cheap labor (immigrants, for example). Farmers, no longer reaping the preemptive benefits of innovation adoption, complain of cost-price squeezes and unfair transport rate structures. Economic stagnation creates many problems by itself, and these are compounded on several occasions by runaway inflation—a condition arising, it seems, out of resource scarcities exacerbated by warfare during the Dissent phase (for example, the Revolution and Civil War, but also note that the Vietnam War fits into the overall pattern). Calls for economic reforms in banking and currency become commonplace.[47]

Decline begins so subtly (recall the gradual slopes of the S-shaped long wave) that it goes unperceived for a decade or so; only in retrospect is the turning point evident in the economists' curves. Americans disregard the economy's early warnings. Accustomed to pros-

46. The geography of dissent is, in large measure, a consequence of regional disequilibrations resulting from spectacular but spatially uneven economic growth, for example, the cases of Boston in the American Revolution, the Midwest in the 1850s, and the Civil Rights Movement in the Deep South in the 1950s. Chapters 4 and 6 in this volume offer geographical interpretations of the Revolution and the Civil War, respectively; and while a satisfactory geographical interpretation of the Civil Rights Movement has yet to be written, historians have made a good start. See Aldon T. Morris, *The Origins of the Civil Rights Movement: Black Communities Organizing for Change* (New York: Free Press, 1984); and various essays in Charles W. Eagles, ed., *The Civil Rights Movement in America* (Jackson: University Press of Mississippi, 1986).

47. The classic case is late-nineteenth-century populism. Lawrence Goodwyn, *The Populist Moment: A Short History of the Agrarian Revolt in America* (Oxford, Eng.: Oxford University Press, 1978).

TABLE 12.6

The Decline Phase in American History

Period	Dating of phase	Illustrations
1	1660s to mid-1670s	Falling commodity prices (tobacco); rural unrest (eventuating, in the next period, in out-migration, charges of corruption)
2	Late 1720s to 1730s	Falling commodity prices; currency crises (e.g., in Massachusetts, 1739–41); slave rebellion
3	Late 1770s to early 1780s	Multiple currencies and currency inflation; frontier unrest over land, currency, and taxation
4	Late 1820s to early 1830s	Urban discontent; rural unrest in Rhode Island and New York; calls for banking reform
5	Late 1860s to early 1870s	Political corruption (Grant administration); critique of concentrated industrial wealth; initiation of extensive strikes; rural protest (the Grange)
6	1918 to late 1920s	Political corruption (Teapot Dome scandal); labor's critique of growing disparities in income and wealth; conflict and violence among racial and ethnic groups competing for increasingly scarce unskilled jobs; neo-Malthusian immigration quotas
7	1965 to mid-1970s	Declining productivity; farm unrest; inflation; resource scarcity; Watergate
8	2020s–30s?	?

perity and confident of its return, they dismiss indicators of Decline as anomalies, mere perturbations in economic progress. But as anomalies accumulate, the illusion of progress is unmasked. Within two decades, Decline is transformed into a full-fledged crisis requiring nothing less than a paradigmatic shift for its solution.[48]

But the creative solution lies in the future; in the interim, accusation and destructive polemic are the preferred style in the phase of Decline. This is not a high point in American political thought. While

48. On the assorted miseries of Decline, see Schumpeter, *Business Cycles* (cited in note 7). Recent economic history nicely illustrates the imperceptibility of Decline: it was not until the 1980s that economists generally acknowledged that the economy's turning point occurred in the mid-1960s. See Samuel Bowles, David M. Gordon, and Thomas E. Weisskopf, *Beyond the Waste Land: A Democratic Alternative to Economic Decline* (Garden City, N.Y.: Doubleday, 1984). Daniel Bell and Irving Kristol, eds., *The Crisis in Economic Theory* (New York: Basic Books, 1982). As a consequence of economic problems, families seeking relief from poverty and religious persecution migrate to the frontier or, in the case of the European exodus in the 1880s and 1890s, to the American city. See Chapter 2 in this volume; also David Ward, *Cities and Immigrants: A Geography of Change in Nineteenth-Century America* (New York: Oxford University Press, 1971).

social critics and ambitious politicians eagerly point out the shortcomings of the political economy, they offer little in the way of insightful analysis or constructive alternatives. Instead, they level ac-
cusations (often appropriately) of venality and corruption at politicians and parties in power, as if "kicking out the rascals" were the
cure for society's malaise. Decline offers numerous examples of the
accusatory mode, from the charges of corruption directed at the Virginia Company in the early 1620s and at Virginia's Governor Berkeley in the 1670s to the scandals of the Grant administration, Teapot
Dome, and Watergate in more recent times. Politics, politicians, and
political thought all fare badly in Decline. These are the times of
"the unknown presidents," the names every schoolchild forgets (save
those tarnished by corruption). As the senior Arthur Schlesinger's
famous essay confirms, Decline produces no great or near-great presidents and a disproportionate number of the impeachable and the
subpar; republican principles of civic virtue are in short supply.[49]

One of the few bright spots in these otherwise barren times is a
peculiar inventiveness (not, I underline, innovativeness). Just as the
diffusion of fundamental innovations slows to a crawl, a variety of
new inventions crowds in—the railroad, the telephone, hybrid corn,
and the reaper are good examples. But Americans regarded them
more as the curiosities they were than as vital new products. They
were, if you will, "ahead of their time" and "out of their place" (the
reaper was first tried in Maryland of all places; hybrid corn, in Massachusetts—both far from their eventual niches). Their time and
place would come, however, in the Creative phase of ensuing periods
in American history.[50]

49. Political scandal is not limited to the Decline phase, but it is more susceptible to
discovery by critics seeking explanation for the deepening social and economic malaise.
An image of corrupt politicians serves to personify (and to simplify) the exceedingly abstract and complex causes of Decline. On political corruption in America, see Jacob B.
Manheim, *Déjà Vu: American Political Problems in Historical Perspective* (New York: St. Mar-
tin's Press, 1976), especially the chapters on executive malfeasance, pp. 95–125; Abraham
S. Eisenstadt, Ari Hoogenboom, and Hans L. Trefousse, eds., *Before Watergate: Problems of
Corruption in American Society* (Brooklyn, N.Y.: Brooklyn College Press, 1978); Julian Roe-
buck and Stanley C. Weeber, *Political Crime in the United States: Analyzing Crime By and
Against Government* (New York: Praeger, 1978); and Francis A. Allan, *The Crimes of Politics:
Political Dimensions of Criminal Justice* (Cambridge, Mass.: Harvard University Press, 1974).
On presidential ratings, see Schlesinger, *Paths to the Present*, pp. 104–14; and Patrick J.
Kenney and Tom W. Rice, "The Contextual Determinants of Presidential Greatness,"
Presidential Studies Quarterly 18 (1988), pp. 161–69.

50. The clustering of inventions during economic decline is described in Christopher Freeman, John Clark, and Luc Soete, *Unemployment and Technical Innovation: A Study
of Long Waves and Economic Development* (Westport, Conn.: Greenwood Press, 1982),

Macrohistorical Variability: Patterns and Interpretations of American War

The rhythmic structure of American history is less an end than a beginning; less a rigid theory of macrohistory than an introduction to its potentialities. The virtue of macrohistory, and indeed the virtue of all good theory, is that it raises more problems than it resolves. Embedded in its superficially relentless rhythms and phases is the problematic of variability—variability in the structure itself and in the underlying historical action that shapes the structure. What at a distance appear to be fixed periods and phases are on closer examination characterized by sizable variations in duration and dramatic intensity. In some times and places, historical action is bled of its drama to such an extent that behaviors are predictable with a high degree of accuracy; in others, they are so random and refractory as to defy even the most rigorous models of social science. Indeed, such an enormous range of behavioral variability cannot but influence variability in the structure itself. Some historical periods, for example, are short, lasting only about 40 years, while others are half again as long. Similarly for phases: Dissent sometimes ends in internal war, other times in political accommodation and reform; Conflict (international war) may come quickly or it may be deferred for a couple of decades. Making sense of this variability is macrohistory's puzzle—or to use the parlance of social science, its dependent variable. Let us look briefly at this variability of historical action with an eye to discerning and interpreting its regularities. Of the many illustrations that come to mind, I have settled upon what is to me the most interesting and certainly the most dramatic of historical actions: the eruption of war abroad (in the Conflict phase) and at home (in the Dissent phase).

We begin our inquiry into American war by indirection, looking first at certain cliometric patterns (and nonpatterns) in American macrohistory, that is, the varying lengths of its periods and phases. In Table 12.7 we may discern a variety of patterns: the lengths of periods exhibit a sawtooth alternation between short periods and long dating back to the 1630s. The depressions that are the earmark

---

pp. 46–63; and Raymond S. Hartman and David R. Wheeler, "Schumpeterian Waves of Innovation and Infrastructure Development: The Kondratieff Cycle Revisited," *Research in Economic History* 4 (1979), pp. 37–85. For the invention and innovation of hybrid corn, see Allan G. Bogue, "Changes in Mechanical and Plant Technology: Corn Belt, 1910–1940," *Journal of Economic History* 43 (1983), pp. 1–26.

TABLE 12.7

Cliometric Measures of the Periods and Phases of American History: Chronologies

	Period	Depression	International war	Dissent
1	1630s to 1680s (1630)	Late 1620s to mid-1640s	[1618 to 1648]	1641 to 1660
2	1680s to 1740s (1684)	1670s to 1690s	1689 to 1713	1720s to mid-1730s
3	1740s to 1780s (1745)	Mid-1730s to mid-1740s	1754 to 1763	1763 to 1783
4	1780s to 1830s (1785)	Mid-1780s to mid-1790s	1812 to 1815	1812 to 1828
5	1830s to 1880s (1835)	Mid-1830s to mid-1840s	1846 to 1848	1848 to 1865
6	Late 1870s to 1930s (1877)	Mid-1870s to early 1890s	1898	1900 to 1919
7	1930s to 1980s (1929)	Late 1920s to 1941	1941 to 1945	1953 to 1970
8	1980s to 2030s? (1978)			

NOTE: Dates in parentheses in column one indicate my best estimate of when contemporaries perceived the existence of Crisis and the severity of economic depression.

TABLE 12.8

Cliometric Measures of the Periods and Phases of American History: Lengths

	Period	Depression	International war	Dissent	Crisis-Conflict interval
1	54 years	15	(30)	10–19	(?)
2	61 years	18	24	10–15	3
3	40 years	10	9	14–20	9
4	50 years	10	3	14–16	27
5	42 years	10	2	14–17	11
6	52 years	18	1	15–19	21
7	49 years	12	4	17	12

NOTE: Period and phase durations are calculated using the data in Table 12.7. The lengths of periods and phases shown here are approximations. Given the modest state of macrohistorical understanding, my intent is only to suggest a rough ordering of period and phase durations. The pertinent issue is whether the durations of periods and phases are long or short, increasing or decreasing, alternating or trending. For these purposes, the approximations are more than adequate. In period 1, international war is difficult to date; I use the Thirty Years War, which began in 1618 and thus precedes Crisis in that period. The Crisis-Conflict interval is measured as the length of time between the generally accepted beginning of a period (the dates in parentheses in Table 12.7, column 1) and the outbreak of international war.

of Crisis divide into a series of short phases between 1740 and 1875—that American boom time of seven-score years—flanked on either side by long Crises before 1740 and after 1875. Concurrently, the duration of international war (Conflict) exhibits a downslope descent, falling from over a quarter century in the 1600s to one year in 1898, albeit with an ominous reversal in duration and magnitude during World War II. Lastly, in contrast to all of the preceding, the duration of Dissent across all seven periods describes a flat line. Nothing is simple here; four cliometric measures of period and phase length describe four very different curves: periods varying cyclically, Crises in steplike fashion, international wars inversely, and Dissent not at all.

To precipitate some insight out of this fog, let us look at one other cliometric variable that bears upon American wars—the interval between the beginning points of Crisis and Conflict (see Table 12.8). In other words, do international wars come early or late in the historical period? In the four periods completed since 1780, the Crisis-Conflict interval alternates regularly between long intervals of a quarter century and shorter ones of a dozen or so years. This is to say that while war (Conflict) may be inevitable, one period defers or delays international hostilities, the next period delves into war on the heels of Crisis. More precisely, long intervals of peace occur in the periods 1790–1830s and 1875–1929; short intervals occur in the periods 1830s-1875 and 1929-late 1970s.

The cyclic nature of the Crisis-Conflict interval raises several interpretive questions. The first concerns the reasons for the origins of the interval in the 1780s rather than earlier or later. The most plausible explanation has to do with what military historians have characterized as a dramatic change in the strategy and conduct of war. Before the 1780s, wars were stylized, chesslike tests of endurance. International war entailed a 15- to 30-year commitment, thus precluding any interlude of peace and negotiation between the phases of Crisis and Conflict. The nature of war, however, was radically redefined in the latter half of the eighteenth century as a consequence of the Age of Revolution, the Industrial Revolution, and the Transportation Revolution. All contributed to a dramatic shortening of the duration of war. New technologies and the advent of nationalist warfare meant that troops and matériel could be mobilized literally at a moment's notice, that the resolution of war required but a few years rather than a few decades. Thus the 15 to 30 years once reserved for a protracted international war provided after 1780 ample room for negotiation and compromise, that is, for the emergence of modern diplomacy and a professionalized diplomatic corps.[51]

51. On the changing nature of warfare in the Age of Revolution, see Blainey, *The Causes of War* (cited in note 36); and John U. Nef, *War and Human Progress: An Essay on the Rise of Industrial Civilization* (New York: W. W. Norton, 1968).

But why, we may ask, has the Crisis-Conflict interval of modern times varied cyclically? Why do some wars occur soon after Crisis, while others are deferred? The answer lies in the perfect (and paradoxical) correlation of the intervals with American policy cycles. Long intervals between Crisis and Conflict coincide with the protectionist-elitist policy cycles of the 1790s-1830s and 1880s-1929; short intervals, with the free trade–democratic policy cycles of the 1830s-1877 and 1930s-1980. Conservatives defer war for about a quarter century, liberals only half as long (a dozen years or so on average). We have then the paradoxical situation of conservatives cast in the role of reluctant warriors. Their jingoistic rhetoric notwithstanding, conservatives historically engage in wars that are deferred, short, and low in magnitude.

Several factors contribute to an explanation of the paradoxical peacefulness of American conservatism (at least, when it has policy hegemony). The first factor, and perhaps the most important, was touched upon over a century ago in Tocqueville's prescient observation on the advantage of large states in an industrial world; a second factor is the introversive bonds between conservative policy cycles and high-intensity religious revitalization. In tandem, geography and religion predisposed American conservatism toward an introversive style and, perhaps unintentionally, relative peace in the international arena. Let us take up these factors in turn.

When Tocqueville forecast the future power of the United States and Russia, he based his prediction upon geography: sheer scale, territorial space, and variety of resources. American protectionists concurred, realizing that within the nation lay resources sufficient for economic growth and prosperity. Implied in the conservative strategy of economic introversion is a lessening of the potential for conflict in international affairs. Preoccupied with the development of America's vast space and resources, conservatives had neither motive nor opportunity for war. Conservatives, though invariably confronting international war, deferred it for as long as they could; and when war did come, they kept the hostilities short.[52]

52. Protectionist and mercantilist policies thus are pacific or warlike depending upon the luxuries of national space and resources. On the relevance of the geography of nation states, see Alexis de Tocqueville, *Democracy in America*, ed. J. P. Mayer (2 vols.; Garden City, N.Y.: Anchor Books, Doubleday, 1966), Vol. 1, pp. 411–13. Also see Max Weber's confirmation in his remarkable letter to the magazine *Die Frau* in the midst of World War I (February 1916) in which, after deprecating small states such as Switzerland, Denmark, and Norway, he asserts of Germany: "Because we are a power state and because we there-

By contrast, the American state was not big enough for liberal policies of American economic development. The world was the only suitable arena for liberal free traders; maximizing America's global interaction, however, maximized as well the risks of international war. Convinced that the basis of American prosperity lay in the international economic system, free traders insisted upon unrestricted access to markets and trade lanes—all predicated, of course, on freedom and democratic principles. When foreign nations balked at American policy, their opposition was regarded as petulant and obstructionist, requiring at times remedial intervention so as to insure the unfettered conduct of free trade based ironically on democratic principles. Thus in the interval between Crisis and Conflict, free trade provided both motive and ample opportunity for international war (though rarely the weapons, owing to liberal commitments to democratic resource allocation at home). In retrospect, liberal policy cycles have been the more aggressive, with international Conflict erupting usually within a decade of the origins of the free-trade paradigm.

The luxury of space has accorded American protectionists the role of reluctant warrior, but not all protectionists have been so reluctant. The aggressive history of European protectionism is a case in counterpoint. It offers a cautionary tale of the behavioral reversal that takes place when geography no longer suffices. European protectionist policy cycles are a horror story of violence and devastating warfare. Twice European society has been gutted and twice it has been remade under the diplomatic illusion that the likes of this horror would never come again. Think for example of the two wars to end all wars: the Napoleonic Campaigns and World War I. These occurred almost precisely a century apart, and both erupted almost

---

fore, in contrast to those 'little' peoples, can in this issue of history swing our weight into the scales—precisely on that account the accursed duty and obligation to history, which means to prosperity, lies on our shoulders and not on theirs—to swing ourselves in the way of the inundation of the whole world by those powers [Russia, France, and Britain]. If we reject this duty then the German Reich would be an expensive, vain luxury of a kind inimical to culture, which should not be able to support and which we should as quickly have to eliminate in favor of a 'Swissification' of our statehood, a dissolution into little, politically powerless cantons, perhaps with courts friendly to the arts—waiting to see how long neighbors would permit us the contemplative cultivation of the cultural values of small peoples ... which would remain the meaning of our existence for all time." Weber's imperial plea is quoted in Gordon A. Craig, "The Kaiser and the Kritik," *The New York Review of Books*, 18 Feb. 1988, pp. 17–20, esp. p. 19.

precisely in the midst of a protectionist policy cycle. American protectionists are timidity itself when compared to their aggressive European counterparts.

The crux of the difference, returning once again to Tocqueville, is in the geography of states. In America, introverted protectionist policies were economically viable given the vastness of space and resources; international conflicts were minimized (though American Indians would not agree). But in Europe, protectionist introversion was precluded by the small size of states relative to the resource base required of an industrial power. A single European state had neither the resources nor the scale economies (the space) sufficient for a viable protectionist political economy. Under such circumstances, protectionism could succeed only through territorial expansion—a process first exemplified by Napoleon's drive for continental dominance in the protectionist cycle 1790s–1830s, and later by overseas imperialism and German expansionism in the ensuing protectionist cycle 1880s–1920s. Thus in an industrializing world, protectionism in small states entailed an expansionist (and perforce militant) dynamic—a dynamic that Friedrich Ratzel faithfully captured in his concept of *lebensraum*.[53]

Europe's militant protectionism is puzzling to Americans in one other respect: the timing of conflict seems all wrong. In both Napoleon's nationalist war and World War I, war reached its highest fury not in the usual phase sequence of Crisis-Conflict but somewhat later, in the American equivalent of the internal civil Dissent phase (near the peaking of long-wave economic growth). Following a line of reasoning initially developed by Frederick Jackson Turner, we may hypothesize that both European wars were more nearly manifestations

53. The concept of *lebensraum*, for which Ratzel has been unjustly pilloried, insightfully captures the nearly inescapable geographical strategy for small and medium-sized states in protectionist macrocycles. See also the quote from Max Weber in the preceding note. Conversely, during the free-trade period from the 1830s to the 1880s, the arena of European conflict was diverted abroad, for example, to Crimea in the 1850s. The notable exception to this pattern occurred with the rise of fascism in western Europe during the 1930s—a time when macrohistory predicts a period of free trade. Hitler, in particular, sought the reversal of the historical dialectic by imposing statist protectionism upon an emergent paradigm of free trade—thus locking European states once again in mortal combat. That Hitler came so close to reversing history is testament to his terrible greatness and to the disproportionate influence of individuals in times of Crisis. Harriet G. Wanklyn, *Friedrich Ratzel: A Biographical Memoir and Bibliography* (Cambridge, Eng.: Cambridge University Press, 1961); see also Peter J. Hugill, "Structural Changes in the Core Regions of the World Economy, 1830–1945," *Journal of Historical Geography* 14 (1988), pp. 111–27.

of intra-European sectionalism and civil war (Dissent) than of inter-national conflict in the usual sense. An explanatory model might posit something like the following: the Industrial Revolution effectively increased the viable scale for national states; to achieve territorial thresholds in protectionist cycles, "small" states were compelled to expand; expansionism (usually undertaken most vigorously by the newest arrivals in the European system, for example the post-revolution French or the Germans after unification in 1871) encroached upon neighboring states; coalitions and alliances formed and, near the midpoint of the protectionist cycle, called expansionists to account; violent, high-magnitude war ensued.[54]

This European model of militant protectionist expansion applies not to the American past so much as to its future. Although American geography has provided protectionists with the luxury of ample room for internal expansion and development without the risk of devastating international conflict, at some point our resources may become insufficient for us to remain competitive in an expanding capitalist economy. What happened to Europe in the Industrial Revolution may be happening to the United States as we experience a scalar shift upward to a global economic system. If that is indeed the case, then the American frontier may at last be on the verge of closure; the nation may be too "small" for viable protectionism.

The alternative, of course, is a European-style protectionism modeled after the expansionist dynamics of Napoleon and imperialism. As the scale shifts toward the world system, American conservatives may be unable to resist the imperative toward external expansion and its nasty consequences. In that event, an expansive protectionism will provide both motive and opportunity for international war; worse, it will also provide the weapons that are such an important component in conservative policies of elitist resource distribution. When that fateful juncture arrives, the security and safety long afforded by American space and protectionist introver-

54. Turner offers the interesting hint that World War I represented Europe's equivalent of American sectional strife and civil war. See Frederick Jackson Turner, "The Significance of the Section in American History," *The Wisconsin Magazine of History*, 8 (1925), pp. 255–80, esp. pp. 263–64. See also Charles S. Maier, "August 1914: The Whys of War," *The New York Times Book Review*, 29 July 1984, pp. 22–23. Taking the longer view espoused by Modelski and Thompson, one might argue that global wars have been sponsored by mercantilist-protectionist-imperialist political economies since 1790 and by free-trading ones before that date (hence, perhaps, the justification for viewing the 1790s as the "true beginning" of the modern age); see George Modelski and William R. Thompson, *Seapower in Global Politics, 1494–1993* (Seattle: University of Washington Press, 1988).

sion will fade into the pages of a nostalgic history of American political economy.

It would be wrong, however, to conclude that the ample geography of the United States has been heretofore the exclusive cause of American conservatism's pacificity. Matters are more complex. We should not overlook, for example, the 350-year correlation between American protectionism and our high-intensity religious revitalizations. Each of these revitalizations—identified by McLoughlin as having occurred in the 1630s, 1740s, 1790s, 1890s, and 1970s and 1980s—coincides with the beginnings of a protectionist cycle. Indeed, the correlation is so strong that it holds even through the disruption of the regular alternation in policy cycles during the Age of Revolution (1790s–1830s).

Evangelism and protectionism are natural allies in several respects, but from the standpoint of war and peace, it is their domestic introversion that matters most. Each paradigm diverts attention from the world of nations abroad (so countenanced by liberal free traders) to the society and economy at home. While protectionists attend to internal economic development, divines attend to internal spiritual development. The vast social energy of sectaries, denominationalists, and evangelicals alike channels into spiritual disputations and "enemies" at home, rather than abroad. The alliance of evangelism and protectionism is thus the cyclical antithesis to free trade and republican ideologies. Protectionists reject categorically the principles of free trade and internationalism; evangelicals, it would seem, reject the cosmopolitan and quasi-sacred notions (free trade's spiritual handmaidens, as it were) of liberalism, republicanism, and civic virtue. Together they shape a larger introversive conservative paradigm that is relatively peaceful, albeit decidedly parochial.

But wherein are the causal mainsprings of conservative introversion? Are the antitheses of evangelism and protectionism coequals or is one cause and the other effect? The baffling case of the 1790s suggests that, in this case at any rate, religion played an especially decisive role. Recall that these were exceptional times. Given the "natural course" of policy cycles, the free-trade paradigm should have prevailed during the 1790s–1830s cycle. But the natural alternation was disrupted by the Age of Revolution; protectionism was the only viable policy alternative. In this context, it would appear that the Founding Fathers rejected free trade more out of expediency than principle (though one might argue that they were neomercantilist conservatives all along). In sharp contrast, the evangelical antithesis was hardly based on expediency. It involved a principled rejection of the deistic and atheistic excesses of the Enlightenment. In this case, religious revitalization was perhaps the driving force in the period's paradigmatic conservatism.

More generally, however, the likelihood is of a recursive and mutually reinforcing causality, such that a rising tide of evangelical popularity encourages conservative protectionists, whose positive reception in turn reinforces the evangelical appeal, and so on in a sequence of cumulative causation. The subtle interplay in our own day of political conservatism and evangelical fundamentalism commends seeing paradigmatic evolution as a cumulative and recursive process.

The last four policy cycles of American macrohistory are thus paradoxical: liberals speak of peace but effect war, quickly; conservatives speak of war, but effect a longer peace and very modest wars. But there is more involved here than paradox. International war has a direct bearing upon the probability of internal war in the ensuing phase of civil Dissent. Indeed, the timing and outcome of war abroad provide the necessary and sufficient conditions for war at home. Of the seven Dissent phases in American history, two have exploded into civil war: the American Revolution and the American Civil War. And a case can be made that on a third occasion, the Vietnam War, war was internal to an enlarged sphere of American hegemony. These three cases, aside from their uniform spacing a century apart, are bound together by two prior conditions. Their necessary condition is a short Crisis-Conflict interval preceding the Dissent phase. When the interval is short—that is, when international war comes early in the period—the effect is an elongation of the time span in which civil grievances accumulate, diffuse, and compound. These short intervals have occurred just four times in American history: the periods beginning in the 1680s, the 1740s, the 1830s, and the 1930s—the last three of which experienced internal wars.

But why did internal war fail to occur in the Dissent phase of the 1680s–1740s cycle? It failed precisely because that period lacked the sufficient condition for internal war: namely a vast territorial or hegemonic acquisition during the preceding Conflict phase. Conversely, in every case of internal war, large acquisitions were made at the conclusion of the Conflict phase: with the Treaty of Paris in 1763, the Treaty of Guadalupe Hidalgo in 1848, and—our largest hegemonic addition—at the conclusion of World War II (namely in East and Southeast Asia). Acquisition of such vast territories (effectively or hegemonically) created a panoply of problems—territorial status within the American polity, land disposition, defense, postwar finance—any one of which might trigger dissension among regions experiencing the disequilibrations caused by territorial gain or long-wave economic growth. Thus, given more time for the accumulation of grievance and more space for its expression, Dissent culminated in difficult, painful, and costly internal war.

American warfare thus exhibits certain macrohistorical regularities. International war (Conflict) since the 1790s has varied with American policy cycles: conservative introversion, reinforced by high-intensity religious revitalization, has deferred and truncated international conflict; liberalism, with its commitment to the global economy, has hastened and intensified foreign war. International war, in turn, has provided the determinants for less frequent internal warfare in the Dissent phase. The probability of internal war is high when international war occurs early in the period and when that war results in the acquisition of a vast national or hegemonic territory. When neither condition is present, Dissent rumbles but does not erupt.

This brief inquiry into American wars, abroad and at home, merely hints at the marvelous variability of American macrohistory and the profit from comparison across its periods and phases. To these we shall return, but at this juncture let me conclude this discussion of American macrohistory in anticipation of turning to our third proposition on its generative sources in recurrent agrarian innovation and spatial diffusion.

Any interpretation that espouses historical cycles and phases is bound to be overly mechanistic, sweeping away in its relentless rhythms the human spirit and will that so often make history. That is scarcely my intention—though it may be the result. The point that I am trying to make is more subtle—that history in the long run is a unique blend of structural forces and human agency. It is at once patterned and random, determined and indeterminate, routine and dramatic. Attempts to squeeze it into a preferred philosophy of history are, I believe, foredoomed to disappointment. History is too complicated and nuanced to be reduced to disjunctive choices. History's most satisfactory philosophy is one that reconciles and resolves historiographical conflicts by properly specifying them in time and ·

space. History is not the product of great men or of abstract structural processes; rather it is the product of both, operating at specific and I believe specifiable times and places in the past—at least in the capitalist past. And if the mechanistic rhythms and phases of capitalist history lend themselves to a certain predictability, the way we respond to them rarely does—at least not yet.[55]

Macrohistory thus leaves a wide berth for the maneuverings of the human spirit at certain times—or more accurately, in certain of its phases. My admiration for the younger Schlesinger's cycles of American history is predicated on these liberal sensibilities. What is most appealing in his generational cycling of public and private interests is its juxtaposition of historical philosophies, of "great men" exercising remarkable creativity and "small men" absorbed by the abstract forces that routinely drive them. Whatever our disagreements over historical cycles—and these turn on his conviction that the cycle of public and private interests is self-contained, and mine that it is subsumed by the macrohistorical period—we share a liberal philosophy of history that accommodates structure and agency as well as an abiding interest in the grand historical moment, those times of remarkable human ingenuity and unpredictable innovation in political economy (his phases of public interests and mine of Creativity) and civil rights (again his phases of public interests but mine of Dissent). Essentially we are describing the same things, and what distinguishes our approaches is that his describes historical behaviors

55. As one might expect, Hannah Arendt condenses the enormous philosophical problem of contingency and history with special eloquence: "The main characteristic of any event is that it has not been foreseen. We don't know the future but everybody acts into the future. . . . What actually happens is entirely contingent, and contingency is indeed one of the biggest factors in all history. Nobody knows what is going to happen because so much depends on an enormous number of variables, on simple hazard. On the other hand if you look at history retrospectively, then, even though it was contingent, you can tell a story that makes sense. . . . This is the real problem of every philosophy of history: how is it possible that in retrospect it always looks as though it couldn't have happened otherwise." "Hannah Arendt: From an Interview," *The New York Review of Books*, 26 Oct. 1986, p. 18. No methodology or philosophy of history has yet resolved Arendt's paradox, though the effort is made here as well as in a series of experimental structurationist interpretations that commendably attempt to integrate the contingency of human agency and history's structural forces. See Allan Pred, *Place, Practice and Structure: Social and Spatial Transformation in Southern Sweden: 1750–1850* (Totowa, N.J.: Barnes and Noble, 1986); Derek Gregory, *Regional Transformation and Industrial Revolution: A Geography of the Yorkshire Woollen Industry* (Minneapolis: University of Minnesota Press, 1982). The variability of national response to Crisis is concisely illustrated in Peter Temin, "Socialism and Wages in the Recovery from the Great Depression in the United States and Germany," *Journal of Economic History* 50 (1990), pp. 297–308.

only, whereas mine joins these behaviors with the issues and constraints appropriate to a specific historical context. Dissent over civil rights, though it shares a behavioral kinship with Creativity in political economy (what Schlesinger calls public interests), is conducted in radically different socioeconomic contexts and over fundamentally different issues.[56]

Nonetheless, it is in these two phases more than any others that macrohistory taps the springs of human agency. Both are characterized by an animation of the human spirit and its ancillaries: commitment, conviction, will, determination, organizational creativity, and rhetorical flourish. In these times, once begun, structural forces are impotent in predicting the course of human affairs. The rhetoric of historiography reflects (and, I believe, revels in) the milling about, the cacophony of confusion, and the indeterminancy of the times. Historians speak fondly of times out of control, of "riding the tiger," of "reaping the whirlwind." Less fondly, and with less elegance, social scientists mutter euphemisms of "random walks," "uncertainties," "catastrophe," and, most recent and the best of all, "chaos." All of this is further reflected in the methodology of historical inquiry. Science and logical positivism are in the descendant; narrative, thick description, and phenomenological history reign supreme. And rightly so, for without them, these times of Creativity and Dissent would be impenetrable to interpretation.

Matters are quite different in the lesser moments of American macrohistory. History tames the human spirit, disciplines it into patterns and routines that, if uninspiring to the historian, are melodic to the social scientist seeking refrains of regularity and predictability in human behavior. Schlesinger's phases of private interest and mine of Diffusion and Decline in particular lend themselves to economistic rational-actor interpretations. Thus specified and circumscribed in time, these models indeed do a good job of predicting the ways in which people have behaved in these thin slices of the past. Naturally, the interpretive rhetoric changes; all references to tigers or whirlwinds, random walks or chaos are dropped, and instead we speak grandiloquently of status seekers and lonely crowds, of narcissistic cultures and nations of sheep. All of this is as it should be—at least from a macrohistorical perspective and for these moments.[57] But

56. Schlesinger, Jr., *The Cycles of American History*, pp. 23–48 (cited in note 5).

57. Packard, *The Status Seekers* (cited in note 42); David Riesman, *The Lonely Crowd: A Study of the Changing American Character* (New Haven, Conn.: Yale University Press, 1950).

change ensues, blindsiding the probabilistic models of social science. Ironically, one suspects that the seeds of historical change lie fallow in the error terms of these models. What social science too often dismisses as errors, residuals, and deviant cases are in fact the agents of a new phase.

But structural forces should not be discounted too much, not even in phases of Creativity and Dissent. While great men and women may effect remarkably creative changes in these times, they do so within a context established by the periodic structure of American history. At this general level of analysis, human agency has always been constrained by macrohistory—which is perhaps what Marx meant in saying that men make their history, but it is not always of their own choosing. Take for instance the case of American policy cycles. Since the 1630s, these cycles have been relentlessly dialectical in their rhythm. And however creative and imaginative American policymakers may have been, it remains a fact that only one generation has managed to break the cycle's dialectical rhythm. For that achievement, we justly privilege the Founding Fathers above lesser mortals who have bent with macrohistory's rhythms. A contemporary case in point is Ronald Reagan's much-vaunted and creative policy of free trade—a policy that if effected would reverse the dialectic of American macrohistory for only the second time. The hubris of the "Reagan Revolution" would be more than justified. Conservative rhetoric notwithstanding, it would seem that the dialectic of macrohistory is winning out. Reagan's massive budget deficits and the falling dollar have resulted in a policy of protectionism by any other name. That protectionism in late summer of 1990 is almost a *fait accompli* reveals the considerable power of structural forces in the long run of American history.[58]

How remarkably different are these representations of American character from the buoyant Americans portrayed in the phases of Crisis and Creativity by among others Crèvecoeur in the 1780s, Tocqueville in the 1830s, and the senior Schlesinger in the 1930s and 1940s. See especially the latter's essays "What Then Is the American, This New Man?" and "Biography of a Nation of Joiners," written during World War II and reprinted in *Paths to the Present*, pp. 3–50.

58. On the Reagan economy, see Felix Rohatyn, "The New Chance for the Economy," *The New York Review of Books*, 24 Apr. 1986, pp. 20–23; *idem*, "On the Brink," *The New York Review of Books*, 11 June 1987, pp. 3–6. The ominous prospect of protectionism at a global scale is curiously juxtaposed in adjoining editorial commentaries in the Baltimore *Sun* by Mark Mahaney, editor of *SAIS Review: The Journal of the Johns Hopkins University Paul H. Nitze School of Advanced International Studies*, "Time for a New Isolation-

Breaking the cycle, indeed breaking the rhythm of American macrohistory, will be difficult, but it is not inconceivable. The rupture, however, will require more than sheer will, determination, creativity, and brilliant strategic and tactical organization. If and when the break occurs, it will take place when (a) society is "out of control," that is, in the phases of Creativity or Dissent, and (b) the conditions that prompt these phases are in their extreme ranges, for example, an Age of Revolution or the Great Depression. In these tempestuous times, macrohistory is lurched from its moorings and ordinary men and women are called upon to do truly "great things." But as Hitler's looming presence over this century attests, when human agency is unleashed, when history is out of control, what they do is not always for the best.

Until the forces that produce these macrohistorical tempests are understood, one branch of humanity will not rest easily at night, while another holds out hope for revolutionary exegesis, societal catharsis, and the dawning of a new epoch in history. Were the latter to occur, the half-century rhythms of American macrohistory as we have come to know them would cease to exist. A new epoch in history will have dawned and the conjunctural realignments in period, policy, religion, and economy that we now regard as revolutionary will be by comparison mere ripples in an expanded macrohistory. American society, for better or for worse, will have stepped outside the agenda of capitalist history.

Proposition 3: Agrarian Innovation, Spatial Diffusion, and American Macrohistory

Thomas Jefferson is reputed to have said that revolution is the prerogative of every generation. Macrohistory has proven him right, though not quite with the generational spacing he envisioned nor in ways he might have imagined. Were generational forces the cause of these revolutions, we would expect to see a 30-year rhythm in the periods of American history. But as we have at length suggested, a better case can be made for fixing our revolutions at half-century intervals, in the conjunctural realignments in the historical paradigms of period, policy, religion, and economy.

---

ism," *The Sun*, 10 July 1990, p. 9A; and Robert J. Hanks, retired Rear Admiral and former director of strategic plans and policy for the U.S. Navy, "Our Stake in East Asia," *The Sun*, 10 July 1990, p. 9A.

But if generational cycling falls short in explaining the half-century rhythms of American history, what is left? What manner of process explains a macrohistorical structuring that is *old*, dating back perhaps to our colonial origins; *periodic*, recurring regularly at half-century intervals; *logistic*, conforming with the S-shaped curvature of the long wave; and *dialectic*, alternating periodically between the conjunctural paradigms of liberalism and conservatism? These questions bring us to our third macrohistorical proposition: the explanation lies, I believe, in rural America's extraordinary capacity for agrarian innovation and spatial diffusion—ecological and locational processes that are as *ancient*, as sympathetically *periodic*, as symmetrically *logistic*, and as *dialectical* as the rhythmic structure of American history.

In the seven periodic crises in American history, ordinary rural Americans—farmers, planters, laborers, and sometimes even slaves—enlisted in a prosaic revolution. They revitalized their respective regional economies by introducing a variety of fundamental agrarian innovations and diffusing them during the ensuing half century. Their revolutions effected profound changes in American life: dramatic improvements in agrarian productivity, reconfigurations of agrarian practice, the restructuring of class relations in country and city; the revitalization of a society mired in long-wave depression. Indeed rural Americans, I would argue, have underwitten in large measure the several conjunctural realignments that periodically revolutionized the American past.

Innovation diffusion is by now a stock response to the periodic crises of American capitalism. That is to say that these revitalizing (and self-destructive) processes have been institutionalized, and the result has forever altered the habits of Western society. Crises that once brought the West to its knees and retarded progress for centuries have become staging areas for creativity and revitalization. Periodic adversities have been welded into a "succession of opportunities."[59] Viewed another way, Western society has willingly traded off the volatility of periodic crisis in return for impressive long-run advances in society and economy. Consequently in the West, and perhaps only there, the necessity arising out of institutionalized crisis has served as the mother of innovation and revitalization.

But the odd thing about this revolutionary new attitude, this institutionalization of innovation out of crisis, is its origins among pro-

59. The phrase comes from William N. Parker's essay "What Historians Must Explain," in his *Europe, America, and the Wider World: Essays on the Economic History of Western Capitalism* (Cambridge: Cambridge University Press, 1984), pp. 3–11, esp. 7–8.

saic and usually conservative agrarians. In coming to grips with these paradoxical agents of novelty, I will begin by sketching the pattern of recurrent crisis, innovation, and logistic diffusion in one time and place. Following innovation through two successive periods in the life of the Chesapeake tobacco economy, 1630–80 and 1680–1740, we gain entrance to the regenerative dynamics of agrarian innovation and diffusion. Next I will show that what occurred in the Chesapeake tobacco coast was repeated in virtually every other American (and, in some cases, British) region during the past three and a half centuries. These repetitions explain how otherwise parochial regional processes had the capacity to shape the rhythms of our nation's macrohistory. Finally I will sketch the outlines of a theory of American macrohistory. Analysis of the phases of agrarian innovation and diffusion— its natural history—affords the basis for certain provisional interpretations of, *inter alia*, the remarkable durability of these processes; their half-century periodicity; their logistic configuration; their dialectical alternation; and, most important, their modulation of American macrohistorical rhythms.

The Pattern of Innovation and Spatial Diffusion: Chesapeake Examples

The Chesapeake, 1630–80

Agrarian experimentation began with the first American Crisis. When the bottom fell out of the tobacco market in the late 1620s and early 1630s, Virginians despaired of their future. Prices that had made men rich in 1620—36 pence for a pound of leaf—promised little more than abject poverty in 1630, when a pound of the leaf sold at 1 to 2 pence. The end seemed at hand for a short-lived tobacco economy. But while most Virginians lamented their bad fortune or sought new lines of economic activity, a minority of planters struck out upon a more creative course, experimenting with new and more efficient methods for producing crops of tobacco. Their improbable and little-known achievements were to ensure the economic viability of the "stinking weed" for another 50 years.[60]

Indeed, two of their innovations were of such fundamental significance that even today tobacco planters continue to employ them: tobacco topping and tobacco-house air curing. Prior to the introduc-

60. Russell R. Menard, "The Tobacco Industry in the Chesapeake Colonies, 1617–1730: An Interpretation," *Research in Economic History* 5 (1980), pp. 109–77.

tion of topping in the 1630s and 1640s, Virginians let their tobacco plants "run to seed." Vital plant nutrients were allowed to flow up the stalk and into seed production rather than into the merchantable leaves of the plant. Leaf yield thus was modest, rarely amounting to more than 500 pounds of tobacco per worker. Innovative planters short-circuited the seeding process by cutting off the top or seeding portion of the tobacco plant, thereby diverting nutrients into the leaves. Tobacco leaves became fatter, heavier, and more valuable, and output per worker rose dramatically, from 500 pounds or so in the 1620s to 1,500 to 2,000 pounds by the 1650s and 1660s.[61]

As topping tripled or quadrupled yields, planters introduced a new method of curing that substantially improved tobacco's quality and price. In place of the crude practice of curing leaves in open-air piles, planters substituted the method of air curing in specially designed tobacco houses. By the 1650s, the leaves and stalks of harvested tobacco were hung on latticed rafters jamming the interior of these simple frame structures, there to be cured to a waxy brown by the damp, foggy air of Chesapeake Octobers and Novembers. The reputation of air-cured tobacco soon spread, and by mid-century its aroma and fine texture commanded a respectable price in the tobacco marts of Europe.[62]

These innovations in agrarian production salvaged, for the moment at any rate, the tobacco economy of the colonial Chesapeake. Although tobacco planting no longer offered an easy path to fortune, it held out the fair prospect of land ownership, independence, and a rude sufficiency that equaled or exceeded the annual earnings accrued by unskilled laborers in England.[63]

The Chesapeake, 1680–1740

Crisis revisited the Chesapeake economy nearly a half century later. The modest recovery in tobacco prices that had taken place during the 1650s and 1660s was all but wiped out in the depression of the 1680s. Prices fell from several pence per pound in the 1660s to less than a penny a pound by the 1680s. As in the 1630s, the via-

61. Lewis C. Gray, *History of Agriculture in the Southern United States to 1860* (2 vols., 1933; reprint, Gloucester, Mass.: Peter Smith, 1958), Vol. 1, pp. 213–76.

62. *Ibid.*

63. Gloria L. Main, *Tobacco Colony: Life in Early Maryland, 1650–1720* (Princeton, N.J.: Princeton University Press, 1982). Russell R. Menard, "From Servant to Freeholder: Status Mobility and Property Accumulation in Seventeenth-Century Maryland," *William and Mary Quarterly*, 3rd ser., 30 (1973), pp. 37–64.

bility of the tobacco economy was called into question. The response to the crisis was swift, particularly in the legislatures of Virginia and Maryland. Diagnosing the crisis as one of overproduction and marketing inefficiencies, they swiftly enacted laws stinting the per-worker output of tobacco (by restricting the number of plants) and establishing statutory towns for the collection of tobacco in advance of the arrival of the annual tobacco fleet (thereby shortening turnaround times and layover costs). Neither solution worked very well. Towns languished and the stint was often ignored.[64]

Planters, meanwhile, paid little attention to legislative panaceas; they preferred instead a more ambitious set of solutions. In just a few decades (between 1680 and 1710), they introduced innovations that at once preserved the region's tobacco economy and effected a fundamental restructuring of the region's agroecological system.

Faced with declining tobacco prices and soil exhaustion, Chesapeake tobacco planters introduced a series of innovations—shifting cultivation, massive numbers of slaves, and crop diversification—that reconfigured the region's agrarian system. During the ensuing half century, the diffusion logistic spread these innovations throughout the Chesapeake. In the parish of All Hallows in the upper Chesapeake, for example, inventories of decedents show that increasing numbers of people owned various agricultural products and implements; the proportion of inventories listing stocks of corn increased from 23 percent in the 1690s to over 50 percent in the 1720s and 70 percent in the 1730s; those listing peas and beans in the same years went from 8 to 19 to 40 percent; those listing cattle from 67 to 83 to 90 percent; and those listing plows from 8 to 40 to 60 percent (see Figure 12.4). Concurrently, the proportion of slaves in the Chesapeake population rose from nil to over 30 percent, virtually replacing white indentured servants along the way. Listed in this fashion, the innovations may appear to have been discrete additions to Chesapeake agriculture, but in fact all were tied in to a thorough revision of the entire agrarian system.[65]

64. Carville V. Earle, *The Evolution of a Tidewater Settlement System: All Hallow's Parish, Maryland, 1650–1783*, University of Chicago Department of Geography Research Paper No. 170 (Chicago, 1975); Arthur Pierce Middleton, *Tobacco Coast: A Maritime History of Chesapeake Bay in the Colonial Era* (Baltimore: Johns Hopkins University Press, 1984), pp. 105–232; Menard, "The Tobacco Industry"; and John C. Rainbolt, *From Prescription to Persuasion: Manipulation of Seventeenth-Century Virginia's Economy* (Port Washington, N.Y.: Kennikat Press, 1974).

65. Earle, *The Evolution of a Tidewater Settlement System*, pp. 101–41.

Since the full story of this revision is recounted elsewhere in this volume, let me attempt here merely a spare summary of its key components and functions. By the 1680s, the traditional agrarian system in the Chesapeake had reached its breaking point. As a consequence of long periods of continuous cultivation, yields were declining; efforts to reverse the trend through the application of animal manures met with little success. Falling tobacco prices exacerbated the situation and threw the Chesapeake economy into crisis. Once again, the ingenuity of Chesapeake planters was tested. They responded by assembling a variety of elements—land rotation, slavery, and crop diversification—into a remarkably novel agrarian system.

The crux of the new system was cyclical shifting cultivation, a form of land rotation aimed at ameliorating tobacco's exhaustion of the soil.[66] The cycle required considerable amounts of time and space, typically about twenty years or so and 50 to 60 acres per worker. The cycle ran as follows: a parcel of land (usually 3 acres per worker) was cleared and planted in tobacco for three years; the tobacco was then moved to a newly cleared second parcel and the first field planted in corn, wheat, peas, or beans for three to four years; after six or seven years, the first parcel was abandoned to a long fallow of twenty years or so, the second parcel put into diversified crops, and a new third parcel cleared and planted in tobacco. By the end of the fallow, nature had restored fertility (usually marked by the appearance of second-growth forest) to the first parcel, which was then recycled into tobacco production.

Though the Chesapeake farmers had previously neglected the strategy of maintaining soil fertility through cyclical land rotation, it was an old idea; indeed, it was common practice among many tribal populations, including the American Indians of the eastern forests. But the traditional practice required adaptation to a staple economy. One such adaptation was the integration of commercially valuable "following" crops. Although corn, wheat, peas, and beans were all useful for subsistence at home, the surplus was eagerly collected after 1700 by merchants trading to the burgeoning markets in the sugar islands of the West Indies. These "by-products" of shifting cultivation thus played an important role in increasing plantation profits.[67]

66. For full citations on the Chesapeake's novel agroecological system, see Chapter 7 in this volume.

67. On the emerging West Indian trade in diversified Chesapeake crops after 1700, see Chapter 3 and the sources cited therein.

The benefit of the Chesapeake planters' substitution of slave labor for short-term white indentured servants is less obvious. To be sure, during the depressed 1680s and 1690s, as the comparative costs of slaves and servants converged, slaves became more attractive investments; but slavery—a permanent labor force—had a particular advantage in a system of shifting cultivation. Unlike the old system of continuous cultivation, in which land clearing by servants effected a permanent capital improvement in land, the new system continuously created and destroyed capital in land. Servant improvements in land during their four- to seven-year terms were soon undone by the long fallow. An agrarian system of perpetual land clearance lent itself to a perpetual—and self-perpetuating—slave labor force. The truth of this assertion was affirmed several decades later, in the 1720s, when the comparative costs of slaves and servants returned to pre-1680 levels. If costs had been the principal determinant of labor systems, then Chesapeake planters would have abandoned slavery and reinstituted white servitude. That they did not do so testifies to the economic superiority of a perpetual slave labor force in an agrarian system that perpetually created and destroyed capital in land.[68]

The genius of agrarian innovation in the late seventeenth-century Chesapeake is that its various elements—mass slavery, crop diversification, and shifting cultivation—were of a piece, integral parts in a cleverly devised agronomic ecosystem. As one might expect of such a complex system, its diffusion had far-reaching regional ramifications. By 1740, when the diffusion logistic had run its course, slavery was commonplace; an elite class was aborning; and tenancy achieved often frightful proportions. Under the new agrarian system, a planter elite stood on the threshold of hegemony over a rural society that was increasingly poor or enslaved. Such inequalities, as we shall see, are too frequently the price of revitalization through elite agrarian innovation and spatial diffusion.[69]

68. The Menard and Galenson thesis explains the transformation of the Chesapeake labor system from servants to slaves as a consequence of the changing relative prices of these two forms of labor. Their economic argument, however, collapses in the case of the 1720s, when slavery persisted despite a swing of prices in favor of servants. Russell R. Menard, "From Servants to Slaves: The Transformation of the Chesapeake Labor System," *Southern Studies* 16 (1977), pp. 355–90; David W. Galenson, *White Servitude in Colonial America: An Economic Analysis* (Cambridge: Cambridge University Press, 1981); and my review of Galenson's book in *American Historical Review* 88 (1983), pp. 171–72.

69. The accumulating wealth of the planter elite between 1680 and the 1720s is fully documented in Main, *Tobacco Colony*; in the ensuing period of American history (1740s–1780s), tidewater elites added the refinements of power and ideology, thus transforming themselves into a class. Rhys Isaac, *The Transformation of Virginia, 1740–1790* (Chapel Hill:

Beyond the Chesapeake: The Case for Multiregional Simultaneity in Agrarian Revitalization

The agrarian revitalization of the colonial Chesapeake is hardly an isolated case in American history. That process, with minor variations, has been repeated over and over again in the regions of North America—and Britain—during the past three and a half centuries. When these cases are summed across regions, what at first appear to have been merely discrete instances of agrarian innovation and diffusion are marshaled into a powerful macrostructural force—a force capable of driving the half-century rhythms in American macrohistory.

My argument, to put it another way, is that American agrarian revitalization is not only periodic in macrohistorical time but simultaneous in multiregional space. The evidence in favor of multiregional simultaneity is surprisingly abundant, albeit of mixed quality and provenience. Some of the evidence is systematic, much is discursive (though often as persuasive); much of it is supplied by social science diffusionists, the rest by students of history. From this formidable literature, I have selectively culled a sample of about twenty-five cases, with a minimum of two for each of the seven periods of American history (see Table 12.9). Although representing only a small fraction of the theoretically possible cases—some 15 to 20 percent is my best guess—the sample is sufficient for testing the provisional hypothesis of multiregional simultaneity. Sketching out this evidence—and it is no more than a sketch—serves the dual purpose of suggesting the plausibility of the hypothesis while laying the groundwork for a general inquiry into the processes of recurrent agrarian innovation and logistic diffusion, their patterns, their variabilities, and their socioeconomic ramifications. Let us once again begin at the beginning, making our way from the first through the seventh period of American macrohistory.

Although English colonization had barely begun in the 1630s and 1640s, the pattern of multiregional simultaneity was already falling into place. In two regions, and nearly in a third, agrarian revitalization proceeded despite the disruptive effects of the English Civil War and the Interregnum. The Chesapeake story is by now familiar. Through innovations in tobacco topping and curing, Chesapeake

University of North Carolina Press, 1982); and Allan Kulikoff, *Tobacco and Slaves: The Development of Southern Cultures in the Chesapeake, 1680–1800* (Chapel Hill: University of North Carolina Press, 1986).

TABLE 12.9

The Case for Multiregional Simultaneity of Innovation Diffusion: Illustrations

1630–40s to 1670s	
Chesapeake	Tobacco topping and tobacco houses
Barbados	Tobacco replaced by sugar
1680s–90s to 1740s	
Chesapeake	New agroecological system—tobacco, shifting cultivation, diversified crops, and slavery on a large scale
Pennsylvania	Small grains and West Indian trade
Carolinas	Introduction of wet rice production and irrigation systems based on fluvio-estuarine hydraulics
England	Turnips, clover
1740s–50s to 1780s	
Chesapeake	Tobacco inspection systems (restructuring of tobacco coast by the elimination of marginal producers)
Bread Colonies	Wheat fans, cradles, Conestoga wagons, pioneering of South European direct grain trade
New England	First stirrings of commercial agriculture
1780s–90s to 1830s	
Northeast	High-farming reforms
Deep South	Upland cotton, cotton gin, slavery
U.S.	Cast-iron plow, steamboats, turnpikes, canals
1830s–40s to 1870s	
Midwest	Steel plow, reaper in wheat belt, cultivators in corn belt of lower Midwest
North	Mowing, haying, and threshing machines; first grain elevator, disc harrow
Deep South	Novel agroecological system—cotton-corn-cowpeas crop rotation for soil maintenance
U.S.	Railroad, telegraph
1880s–90s to 1930s	
North	Twine binder, spring-tooth harrows, corn-shucking and fodder-shredding machines, steam and gasoline tractors, corn binder
Deep South	Commercial fertilizer, introduction of rice farming and midwestern reapers (adapted)
Plains and the West	Giant combine harvesters on bonanza wheat farms
U.S.	Good-roads movement, trucks
1930 to 1980s	
Midwest	Hybrid corn, soybeans, no-till farming
Deep South	Cotton harvesters
U.S.	Tractors (diesel engine tractors, 1931) in multiple regions
England and Wales	Combine harvesters

planters were able to salvage the region's staple economy from the depression of the 1630s. Concurrently, tobacco planters in English Barbados took a radically different tack from their fellow colonists in Maryland and Virginia. Instead of trying to improve tobacco output and quality, they abandoned the crop altogether and replaced it with more profitable sugar cane. That conversion process, which has been lucidly described by Richard S. Dunn among others, was launched during the late 1630s and early 1640s and spread rapidly over Barbados in the ensuing decades. Export figures tell a tale of logistic diffusion on the island; from nothing in the early 1640s, exports rose to over 3,000 tons in 1651, over 7,000 by 1655, and nearly 10,000 by the 1670s, at which point, owing to overcrowding, overproduction, and falling prices, exports stagnated for a couple of decades. Periodic crisis had come again to Barbados as it had to the Chesapeake.[70]

That leaves only New England from among the principal areas of English settlement in North America. While agrarian revitalization clearly skipped over this region during this period, it was not for want of trying on the part of Boston's merchant community. Troubled by the dwindling flow of Puritan immigrants through the city, Boston merchants considered a variety of alternative economic bases for the city's commerce, one of which was a productive agrarian hinterland. But that alternative was choked off by the interior's inhospitable environs and a Puritan populace disinclined toward profit and commercial agriculture. Consequently, Boston merchants turned back on their own resources, fashioning in the 1650s and 1660s a unique and remarkably vigorous foreland trade with the Chesapeake and the West Indies. Yet it does not diminish Boston's accomplishments in the provisioning and wholesaling trades to say that these were ultimately contingent upon the fortunes of its principal trading partners in the Chesapeake and the West Indies and the simultaneous agrarian revitalizations that salvaged or transformed their respective regional economies. Boston's history, indeed America's history, would have been quite different in the absence of periodic and multiregional agrarian innovations elsewhere in English North America.[71]

The logistics of agrarian diffusion had run their course by the 1680s, and a new round of Crisis and innovation was set to begin. In the Chesapeake, planters installed an agroecological system consisting of tobacco, diversified crops, shifting cultivation, and slaves, as described above. To the north and south of the Chesapeake, the new

70. Richard S. Dunn, *Sugar and Slaves: The Rise of the Planter Class in the English West Indies, 1624–1713* (New York: W. W. Norton, 1972), pp. 46–116.

71. For Boston's strategies of economic development in the 1650s, see Bernard Bailyn, *The New England Merchants in the Seventeenth Century* (New York: Harper and Row, 1955), pp. 45–111.

colonies of Pennsylvania and Carolina simultaneously introduced specialized staple agrarian systems. Between 1680 and 1740, Pennsylvania emerged as the principal granary for the Caribbean trade in flour, corn, and meat provisions. And Carolinians—aided perhaps by slaves imported from Madagascar—introduced wet rice culture. This innovation, which was predicated on massive slaveholdings, extensive plantations, and a sophisticated understanding of fluvio-estuarine hydraulics, constituted the foundation for South Carolina's agrarian export economy by the 1710s.[72]

There are several ways of interpreting these dramatic transformations in the Atlantic economy in the period 1680–1740. One way is to see the commercial expansion in the Carolinas and the middle colonies as a response to the burgeoning demands of an urbanizing English population. But that interpretation merely begs the question of initial causes; nor does it offer a rationale for the half-century periodicity of American history. Another way is to trace the source of English consumer demand back to the recurrent processes of agrarian innovation and diffusion.

In a series of detailed studies of agrarian change in England between 1550 and 1740, Mark Overton has been doing precisely that. His studies have pointed out the revolutionary nature of these changes. In the case of wheat, the big advance in yields seems to have come between 1570 and 1640—a period with many of the earmarks of a long wave. Concerning the next period, roughly 1630s–70s, Overton makes little mention of agrarian innovation. Doubtless it was blunted somewhat by the disruption of the English Civil War and the Interregnum. But later in the century, from the 1670s until 1740, farmers in East Anglia introduced and diffused clover and turnips—a process that was logistic in form, a half century in duration, and simultaneous with American agrarian revitalizations (see Figure 12.4 which compares the English case with the diffusion of corn and wheat in the Chesapeake). American macrohistorical rhythms thus seem to have reinforced and been reinforced by simultaneous rhythms in English agrarian regions from the seventeenth century forward.[73]

72. See Chapter 3 in this volume and sources cited therein. Also see James T. Lemon, *The Best Poor Man's Country: A Geographical Study of Early Southeastern Pennsylvania* (Baltimore: Johns Hopkins University Press, 1972); Peter H. Wood, *Black Majority: Negroes in Colonial Carolina from 1670 Through the Stono Rebellion* (New York: Knopf, 1974).

73. Mark Overton, "Agricultural Revolution? Development of the Agrarian Economy in Early Modern England," in *Explorations in Historical Geography*, ed. Baker and Gregory, pp. 119–39 (cited in note 2); *idem*, "English Probate Inventories and the Mea-

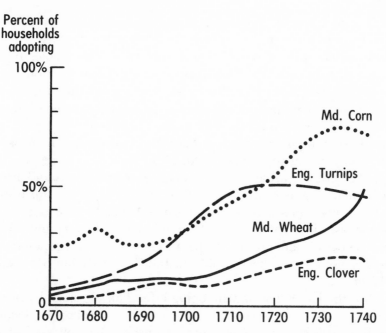

Percent of households adopting

FIGURE 12.4. The Diffusion of Agrarian Innovations in England and Maryland, 1670s–1740s. Sources: Overton, "The Diffusion of Agricultural Innovations in Early Modern England," pp. 205–21. Earle, *The Evolution of a Tidewater Settlement System*, pp. 122–23.

Overton's evidence, as I read it, implies that agrarian innovation (and the resulting expansion of the English food supply) rather than consumer demand provided the propulsion for Anglo-American economic history. The causal logic is as follows: periodic agrarian innovation and diffusion increased the English food supply, which permitted a sectoral shift toward urban centers, which stimulated a burgeoning demand for American goods. Thus, by increasing food output per worker, periodic agrarian innovation released (or evicted) rural labor to the pursuit of an urban life, with all its appetites for American exotics such as tobacco, sugar, indigo, and rice—appetites that ebbed and flowed in long waves generated by the deeper and more powerful currents of recurrent agrarian innovation and logistic diffusion in both England and America.

The next round of agrarian revitalization (1740s–80s) achieved equally spectacular results, albeit with much less fanfare. Indeed, this so-called "golden age of colonial culture" is attributable, in large measure, to the subtlety of multiregional agrarian innovation during the depressed decades of the 1730s and 1740s. Take the case of the colonial Chesapeake, where tobacco's quality, reputation, and price had fallen into a miserable state. To remedy these problems, legislators in both Virginia and Maryland crafted laws that insisted upon quality control. Henceforth, all tobacco was to be inspected and the "trash" (usually stems, stalks, and dirtied ground leaves) eliminated. The net effect of the legislative initiative seems to have been positive, losses from trash disposal being more than offset by increases in tobacco price. Although small planters and tenants forecast the ruination of their operations should the legislation pass, they do not seem to have fared much differently from the average planter.[74]

But the legislation had sweeping effects on the spatial structure of the tobacco coast. Recognizing that quality control paid a dividend in rising prices, mercantile interests pushed the policy of quality regulation to its logical conclusion. In place of the traditional practice of distinguishing just two varieties of tobacco, sweet-scented and oronoco, merchants differentiated the crop into a labyrinth of grades, varieties, and subregional production areas. While product differentiation benefited most subregions in the Chesapeake, the innovation devastated areas that produced low-quality tobacco. By the 1750s, marginal areas in the upper Chesapeake and North Carolina's Albemarle Sound were visited less frequently by tobacco merchants and the annual tobacco fleet. Planters in these regions, knowing that the end was near, cut their losses and switched from tobacco to diversified agrarian systems. Thus statutes and mercantile interests coincided in differentiating tobacco quality, eliminating inefficient and marginal production areas, and intensifying tobacco production in the most productive subregions of the Chesapeake. The net effect of quality-control innovations, therefore, was a reduction in tobacco supply from marginal areas, an expansion of supply in core regions, an overall improvement in tobacco quality, and a sharp increase in its

74. Mary McKinney Schweitzer, "Economic Regulation and the Colonial Economy: The Maryland Tobacco Inspection Act of 1747," *Journal of Economic History* 40 (1980), pp. 551–69; Earle, *The Evolution of a Tidewater Settlement System*, pp. 95–100; and Kulikoff, *Tobacco and Slaves*, pp. 109–16.

FIGURE 12.5. A mid-nineteenth-century representation of the mechanical reaper—one of many fundamental agrarian innovations introduced during a long-wave depression and diffused in the ensuing half century. Reproduced from Eminent Literary Men, *One Hundred Years' Progress of the United States* (Hartford, Conn.: L. Stebbins, 1872), p. 34.

price—processes we may collectively combine under the rubric of regional specialization.[75]

Elsewhere along the Atlantic Seaboard, agrarian revitalization introduced similarly subtle innovations. In the upper Chesapeake, marginal tobacco producers abandoned slavery and the "stinking weed" and adopted in their place an agrarian system of diversified grain production and free labor. Simultaneously in the "bread colonies" just to the north, wheat farmers adopted a variety of innovations ranging from mundane tools such as wheat fans and cradles, to massive Conestoga wagons for grain conveyance, to novel rural labor systems of by-employment that capitalized on the seasonal complementarities of grain production (wheat in spring and summer) and collieries (woodcutting and charcoal-making in winter).[76] Northward still, in the interior of New England, the 1750s produced the first stirrings of commercialized agriculture among subsistence farmers and farm villages. Specialists debate the causes of this mysterious re-

75. Paul G. E. Clemens, *The Atlantic Economy and Maryland's Eastern Shore: From Tobacco to Grain* (Ithaca, N.Y.: Cornell University Press, 1980).

76. Jerome Wood, *Conestoga Crossroads: Lancaster, Pennsylvania, 1730–1790* (Harrisburg: Pennsylvania Historical and Museum Commission, 1979); Lemon, *The Best Poor Man's Country*; Joan Jensen, *Loosening the Bonds: Mid-Atlantic Farm Women, 1750–1850* (New Haven, Conn.: Yale University Press, 1986); and Chapter 5 of this volume.

vitalization, but it surely had something to do with the synchronous innovations taking place among neighboring regions southward along the Atlantic Seaboard.[77]

Following the American Revolution, agrarian innovation became a point of national pride—and of fortune, owing, it would seem, to a new system of patents and the appurtenant profits. The fourth period of American history (1780s–1830s) contributed a spate of fundamental agrarian innovations: the complex of upland cotton, cotton gin, and slavery diffused across the Deep South; high-farming agrarian reforms and cast-iron plows spread from New England to the Chesapeake; and steamboats, turnpikes, and, in lesser degree, canals extended market access to inland farmers and planters throughout the young nation.[78]

No less spectacular was the burst of innovations that inititated the fifth period of American history (1830s–77): the reaper in the emerging wheat belt of the upper Midwest (northern Illinois and southern Wisconsin especially); corn cultivators and steel plows in the corn belt of the lower Midwest; haying, mowing, and threshing machinery along with grain elevators in other northern states; the ecological rotation of cotton, corn, and cowpeas (plus swine) in the cotton belt of the lower South; and all these overlain by the innovation and diffusion of railroads and telegraph lines. These innovations, and others too numerous to mention here, made the the nation's agricultural productivity the marvel, and envy, of the world.[79]

The revitalizing processes of agrarian innovation and logistic diffusion persisted in the century after the Civil War and Reconstruction, but with a difference. Prior to the 1870s, innovations were regionally specific; they were designed for and applied to particular crops in particular American agricultural regions. That is to say, innovative tools, techniques, and production methods were customized for staple regions rather than generalized for multiregional transfer and appli-

77.   Winifred B. Rothenberg, "The Market and Massachusetts Farmers, 1750–1855," *Journal of Economic History* 41 (1981), pp. 283–314.

78.   Curtis P. Nettels, *The Emergence of a National Economy, 1775–1815* (New York: Harper and Row, 1962), pp. 183–204, 243–62. Paul W. Gates, *The Farmer's Age: Agriculture, 1815–1860* (New York: Harper and Row, 1960); John R. Borchert, "American Metropolitan Evolution," *Geographical Review* 57 (1967), pp. 301–32.

79.   Allan G. Bogue, *From Prairie to Corn Belt: Farming on the Illinois and Iowa Prairies in the Nineteenth Century* (Chicago: Quadrangle Books, 1963), pp. 148–68, 193–215; Paul A. David, *Technical Choice Innovation and Economic Growth: Essays on American and British Experience in the Nineteenth Century* (London: Cambridge University Press, 1975), pp. 195–223; and Chapter 7 in this volume.

cation. Matters have changed somewhat since the 1870s. Innovations have become more generic, and multiregional technical transfers are, if not the rule, commonplace—a change attributable in large measure to the institutionalization of scientific agriculture in state and federal departments of agriculture as well as land grant colleges.

This tendency toward generic agrarian innovation and diffusion may be illustrated by four cases, two from the Deep South in the period 1880s–1930 and two from the period 1930s–80s. Shortly after the Civil War, commercial fertilizers—or more precisely manufactured manures—were first introduced in the eastern cotton belt of South Carolina and Georgia, not far from the phosphate deposits that provided the principal ingredient in the fertilizer. But the use of commercial fertilizer expanded rapidly beyond that region, achieving almost national scope by the end of the logistic cycle 1880s–1930. The rice farmers of Arkansas and Louisiana offer a second illustration. In the 1880s and 1890s, they successfully adapted the wheat combines employed in the northern plains to southern rice harvesting operations. The tractor offers a third case, but with a slightly different twist. Tractors diffused according to a double logistic—the first a small and principally Midwestern one between the 1890s and 1930; the second a much larger and regionally generic one between the 1930s and the 1970s. In the latter, tractors diffused simultaneously among multiple American regions. Of course in some regions tractors were diffused more widely than in others, but in each case the diffusion curves are logistic in form and half century in duration (see Figure 12.6). A fourth and final example of multiregional diffusion is the case of the combine harvester (1930–1980s), which spread in England and Wales much as it did in the United States (see Figure 12.7).[80]

Not all recent agrarian innovation is generic across multiple regions, however. In the most recent logistic cycle, environmental constraints have pretty much limited the diffusion of no-till farming to

80. Richard Wines, *Fertilizer in America: From Waste Recycling to Resource Exploitation* (Philadelphia: Temple University Press, 1985). Henry C. Dethloff, "Rice Revolution in the Southwest, 1880–1910," *Arkansas Historical Quarterly* 29 (1970), pp. 66–75; Pete Daniel, *Breaking the Land: The Transformation of Cotton, Tobacco, and Rice Cultures Since 1880* (Urbana: University of Illinois Press, 1985), pp. 39–61; Bogue, "Changes in Mechanical and Plant Technology" (cited in note 50); Richard Morrill, "The Diffusion of the Use of Tractors Again," *Geographical Analysis* 17 (1985), pp. 88–94; Sally Clarke, "New Deal Regulation and the Revolution in American Farm Productivity: A Case Study of the Diffusion of the Tractor in the Corn Belt, 1920–1940," *Journal of Economic History* 51 (1991), pp. 101–23; and David Grigg, *The Dynamics of Agrarian Change* (New York: St. Martin's Press, 1982), pp. 161–63.

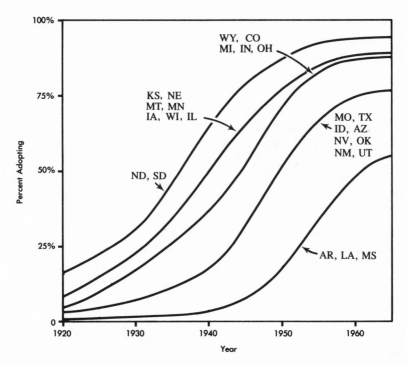

FIGURE 12.6. Percent of Farmers Adopting Tractors in the United States, 1920–64. Sources: Richard Morrill, "The Diffusion of the Use of Tractors Again," *Geographical Analysis* 17 (1985), pp. 88–94. In order to correct for an error in the temporal axis of Morrill's graph, I have recalibrated and replotted the original data supplied by E. Casetti and R. K. Semple, "Concerning the Testing of Spatial Hypotheses," *Geographical Analysis* 1 (1969), pp. 254–59.

the greater Midwest. Similarly in the Deep South, the innovation of the cotton harvester in the 1930s and 1940s produced a machine that in function was uniquely adapted to the picking requirements imposed by that crop. In modern agrarian history, accordingly, regionally specific and regionally generic innovations exist side by side; but perhaps the more important point is that both classes of innovation have arisen out of periodic crises and diffused simultaneously and logistically across multiple American regions. In that respect they differ hardly at all from innovations introduced and diffused some three and a half centuries ago.[81]

81.   Philip J. Gersmehl, "No-Till Farming: The Regional Applicability of a Revolutionary Agricultural Technology," *Geographical Review* 68 (1978), pp. 66–79; Gilbert C.

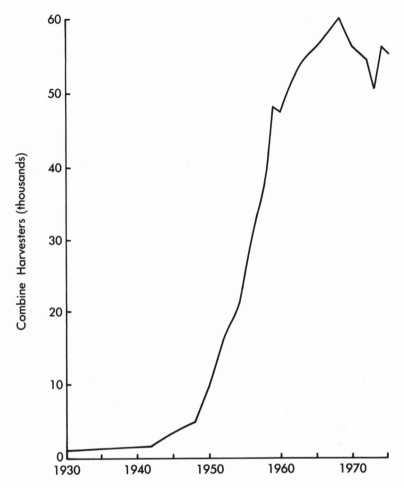

FIGURE 12.7. Growth of the Number of Combine Harvesters in England and Wales, 1930–75. Source: David Grigg, *The Dynamics of Agrarian Change* (New York: St. Martin's Press, 1982), pp. 161–63.

There is, this brief survey suggests, a persistent patterning in the processes of agrarian innovation and diffusion in the American past. That pattern is old, periodic, logistic, and, above all, synchronic. It is the multiregional simultaneity of these processes, I believe, that has enabled them to revive an economy and society in crisis, to revitalize economic growth, and to propagate the half-century rhythms of

Fite, "Recent Progress in the Mechanization of Cotton Production in the United States," *Agricultural History* 24 (1950), pp. 19–27.

American macrohistory. One parochial region innovating and diffusing alone could never have accomplished so much; but in tandem, many parochial regions behaving alike could, and indeed did, shape history—and at the grandest of scales.[82]

But what of the future? Is it conceivable that these agrarian processes will continue to shape American history, or will the drastic shrinkage in the nation's farm population—caused, ironically, by these successive innovations—render them impotent? My guess (and it is only that) is that so long as we live in a Malthusian world, these agrarian processes will retain their historical power.

My reasoning can be clarified by drawing a parallel between the United States, a nation poised at the portals of the eighth period in its history, and England some two centuries ago. Hanoverian England, though feeding itself, could not satisfy the food needs of the colonies and nations that had been drawn into its trading orbit. England's prosperity at home, therefore, was tied to the provisioning capacity of food producers abroad and most especially to the recurrent agrarian innovations first of North America and later, in Victorian times, of grain belts in Australia, South Africa, and Argentina. Like England in the eighteenth and nineteenth centuries, the United States in the late twentieth century finds its fate inextricably connected with agrarian innovation and diffusion in the third world. For us to enjoy the products of industry from Taiwan, Hong Kong, and Korea requires that somewhere in the system food supply is increasing at rates in excess of population (and, of course, that the food can be delivered where it is needed).

Just as Hanoverian England depended upon Pennsylvania's corn and New England's fish to feed the slaves producing sugar in the West Indies for English coffees, teas, cocoas, and cakes, Reagan's America depends upon a rice bowl somewhere in Southeast Asia that will feed the workers in enclaves of Asian commerce producing cameras and cars for American consumers. In such an interdependent world, not even Americans will escape the imperatives of agrarian innovation and the ongoing rhythms of capitalist macrohistory.

Thus an epitaph for agrarian innovation and diffusion processes

82. Multiregional simultaneity is itself a variable concept. Innovation and diffusion may be more extensive in some regions than in others; indeed, in a few regions these processes may be extremely weak or absent altogether. On these variations and their implications, see G. William Skinner, "The Structure of Chinese History," *Journal of Asian Studies* 44 (1985), pp. 271–92.

in American history is premature. While the loci of these processes may lie elsewhere in the future, there is no reason to believe that we have escaped from their hegemony over American history.[83]

A Theoretical Overview of Agrarian Innovation and Diffusion

Seven times American history has experienced periodic crises and seven times it has surmounted them by massive conjunctural realignments in national policy, economy, and religious life. These are extraordinary, even revolutionary, times—the stuff of which grand history is made. It is right and just, of course, to pay homage to the historical personalities who captained these realignments—leaders such as the Founding Fathers, Jackson, and FDR—provided that in doing so we do not overlook those prosaic agrarian processes that were vital to these revolutionary political and economic achievements. This theoretical overview tells that story of revolutionary change and structural continuity: how agrarian innovation and diffusion revitalized a society in crisis, sent it crashing back to earth a half century later (albeit with more wealth and power than it possessed in the preceding crisis), and revitalized it again, seven times in all.

The revolutionary dimensions of agrarian revitalization are striking, but from a theoretical point of view what is equally remarkable is the structural continuity of these processes in time and in space. Whether dealing with the innovation and diffusion of midwestern tractors and southern cotton harvesters between the 1930s and 1970s or Chesapeake slavery and English clover precisely two and a half centuries earlier, we see that these processes unfold in very much the same way in time and space. It is this structural continuity that suggests these processes are recurrent, self-generating, and replete with a distinctive natural history—one that begins amidst periodic crisis and ends with its reappearance a half century hence. A brief description of that natural history and its driving forces now seems in order.

The natural history of agrarian innovation and diffusion has, I believe, a relatively simple structure: it consists of a half-century logistic that divides into four distinct and rather short phases. The

83. We will, however, have surrendered effective control over these processes, which—as England learned—is one of the costs of living in a world system. Restoration of control, of course, was what late nineteenth-century European imperialism was all about.

achievement of continuity in this structure, however, is more complex; macrohistorical continuity is contingent upon the orderly completion of the several phases and upon the special contributions made by each one. *Phase one* is a time of creative experimentation amidst periodic crisis; *phase two*, of dialectical contention and early innovation diffusion; *phase three*, of prosperity and accelerating diffusion; and *phase four*, of decelerating diffusion (and the return of periodic crisis).

Phase one

Our natural history begins in the darkest hours of American history. In these times of periodic crisis, agrarian regions experience a remarkable burst of creative experimentation, from which emerge a few fundamental ecological innovations. These vary widely in form—from subtle improvements in prevailing methods (e.g., tobacco topping) to radically new machinery and hybrids—and in their class provenience—from folk innovations based on the epistemology of "practice" to elite innovations predicated on deductive agrarian science. In less than a decade, the process of agrarian revitalization has been set in motion.[84]

Experiments-cum-innovations are not created *ex nihilo*. History matters. Indeed, in times of crisis the entire stock of technical ideas and inventions is regarded as a vast resource to be unashamedly and mercilessly exploited. And we should not expect otherwise since innovators are, after all, an odd cast of technological tinkerers, plagiarizers, and cannibalizers. Their task is not to invent new products, machines, or methods so much as to reconfigure them in novel, practical, profitable, and expedient (owing to crisis) ways. Innovators are decidedly not inventors; indeed it is hard to imagine two groups any farther apart in style, substance, and macrohistorical context. Innovators are the products of hard times, men and women driven by the necessity imposed by periodic crisis. Inventors, in contrast, flourish in the halcyon phases of macrohistory, when material largesse permits them the luxury of purely intellectual solutions to technology's problems.

84. Here I follow Schumpeter's notions on entrepreneurial activity, with the proviso that innovations are class-biased and therefore the process of initial adoption is a contentious one. On innovation bias, see the insightful essays by Lakshman Yapa, "Green Revolution: A Diffusion Model," *Annals of the Association of American Geographers* 67 (1977), pp. 350–59; and *idem*, "Innovation Bias, Appropriate Technology, and Basic Goods," *Journal of Asian and African Studies* 17 (1982), pp. 32–44. Once innovations are selected and begin to diffuse, their unfolding class biases are discernable through staple theory.

Yet macrohistory has intertwined their separate lives. Without inventors, innovators would have but a modest stock of knowledge to exploit; and without innovators, inventors would have but a modest market for what most dismiss as impractical and laughable curiosities, conceptions "ahead of their time" and, as often, "out of their place." Three historical examples illustrate this interdependence. First, hybrid corn, though "invented" in the 1910s and 1920s in, of all places, Massachusetts, was not diffused until the periodic crisis of the 1930s and transplantation to Illinois and the Midwest. Second, the reaper, though initially developed in the 1820s and 1830s and tried first near Cincinnati and in Maryland, achieved its greatest successes in the upper Midwest following the crisis of the late 1830s and 1840s. Third, slavery, though introduced to the Chesapeake in the boom times of 1619, did not discover its niche until the innovation of cyclical shifting cultivation a full period and a half later in the depression of the 1680s and 1690s. By taking otherwise useless inventions and revising and repositioning them in time and space, agrarian innovators set in motion the rhythms of American macrohistory.[85]

Phase two

The profusion of experiment and innovation sets the stage for the second and most critical phase in the revitalization of agricultural systems. In this phase of early innovation diffusion, the multitude of agrarian experiments is whittled down to a few that are superior to all the rest. Whittling down to a few "fundamental innovations," however, is a tendentious process. An undercurrent of contentious class struggle flows beneath the seemingly placid dynamic of agrarian innovation. Though the struggle rarely is as brutal and covert as Marxists might imagine, the consequence of this contention for the hearts and minds of rural agrarians is, I believe, quietly revolutionary. For out of this struggle of elite and folk innovations, of scientific and practical epistemologies, is forged the ruling paradigm for the next half century of American history. And although the victor has been in most cases determined by an inexorable dialectic, the struggle for legitimation at crucial moments (that is, phase two) remains problematic and susceptible to the relative power and wit of the contending classes. In these respects, agrarian revitalization is not very different

85. Bogue, "Changes in Mechanical and Plant Technology"; Gates, *The Farmer's Age*, pp. 285–87; Percy W. Bidwell and John I. Falconer, *History of Agriculture in the Northern United States, 1620–1860* (New York: Peter Smith, 1941), pp. 286–90; Menard, "From Servants to Slaves" (cited in note 68).

from revitalization movements in other spheres of society, for example, religion and policy. All are in the business of introducing novelty, of running against the grain of established tradition. Tendentiousness is practically unavoidable: revitalization only succeeds if novelty is legitimated through means that are usually irrational and almost always contentious.[86]

Irrationalism is perhaps the only logic appropriate for justifying agrarian novelty under conditions of immense economic uncertainty. Lacking sizable and representative samples of an innovation's success and failure rates (upon which probabilistic risk assessments depend), agrarians cannot make rational choices. Legitimation of novelty therefore pursues other well-known avenues of irrationalist persuasion, including rhetoric, power, charisma, and the epistemologies of "science or practice." Irrationalist legitimation, whatever its lamentable qualities, is vital to the dynamic of recurrent agrarian innovation. Without it, society is frozen in uncertainty; novelty and progress as we know them simply cease to exist. And in this there is both great irony and the even greater dilemma of distinguishing in irrationalism's appeal the benign from the malignant. In agriculture as in politics, an unfortunate choice among alternative innovations at this juncture may have devastating social consequences.[87]

86. I accept Marx's main point that capitalist innovation, from enclosures in the sixteenth century to the present, has always been a contentious, class-based process; where I part company with Marxist interpretations is on the outcomes of these recurrent struggles. Contrary to Marx and his followers, elites do not always win. Periodically—and I would argue dialectically—folk (some might prefer the adjectives "mass" or "democratic") innovations proved victorious, and their diffusion spread benefits among a much larger proportion of the agrarian population than did elite innovations in their respective cycles. Dialectical alternations in the class-provenience of innovation thus may be regarded as an equilibrating mechanism—one that in the long run softened differences among and conflicts between American classes. That social scientists and historians have not pursued this line of argument probably has to do with the fact that we equate agrarian innovation with dramatic agrarian change—obvious things like the introduction of farm machines or the imposition of socially wrenching enclosures. Folk (or mass) innovations meanwhile usually go unnoticed in the scholarly record; such of course has been the fate of the cleverest and the wisest innovations made by southern agrarians between 1630 and 1870. On the Marxist dialectic, see John McLeish, *The Theory of Social Change: Four Views Considered* (London: Routledge & Kegan Paul, 1969), pp. 1–14; and on Marxism's contemporary responses to the failure of the Western proletariat "to arise on schedule," see Frederick Crews, "In the Big House of Theory," *The New York Review of Books*, 27 May 1986, pp. 36–42.

87. Geertz, "Ideology as a Cultural System." Also see Rogers and Shoemaker, *Communication of Innovations*; Brown, *Innovation Diffusion*, pp. 101–3, 110. (All cited in note 38.) Elite ideology sometimes has ensnared students of diffusion, notably in their distinc-

Contentiousness, meanwhile, is a product of the high stakes involved in choosing one innovation over another. Some innovations favor one or another group or class within the regional economy. This is especially true of elite innovations since they are almost always costly to implement. Hence, many members of the agrarian community are precluded by poverty from adopting an elite innovation and reaping its economic benefits—the classic case being the innovation of slavery in the Chesapeake and, a century later, in the cotton South. By benefiting only a fraction of the populace, elite innovations reinforce class divisions, solidify elite hegemony in the regional economy, and facilitate the triumph of paradigmatic conservatism in policy and religion. Folk innovations, in contrast, have low entry-thresholds and thus facilitate social mobility, egalitarian social structures, and liberal policy paradigms.[88] Given the revolutionary nature of these changes, contention over innovation is to be expected in this early phase of spatial diffusion.

In sum, innovation choices in the early stages of agrarian revitalization are made on grounds other than rational choice; class contention and irrationalist argument play important parts. But in practice, the choice is usually decided by a macrohistorical dialectic alternating between the elite scientific innovation of one period and the folk innovation of the next as each is discredited in turn by periodic crisis. But whatever the basis of an innovation's selection, the ramifications for regional society, economy, and landscape are enormous.[89]

The odd thing about this dialectic is that it should have existed at all. Given what was at stake—nothing less than the hegemony over economy and society—and given elite advantages of wealth, literacy, and science, the real question is how elites ever managed to lose. The fact of the matter is that neither elite nor folk epistemologies were privileged by the truth. Each could and did fail—often miserably, as

tion of two types of early innovators: the one solidly middle class and respectable (the elite's representation of themselves), and the other eccentric, "wild-eyed," and risk-taking (the elite's representation of their class adversary, the folk innovator). While hardly very useful as analytical descriptions, these ideological characterizations do get at the heart of the contentious class struggle over agrarian innovations.

88. The consequences of elite innovation in the early Chesapeake are deftly traced in Main, *Tobacco Colony* (cited in note 63); and Isaac, *The Transformation of Virginia* (cited in note 69).

89. See Chapter 7 in this volume for illustrations of periodic and dialectic alternation in the class provenience of innovation in the American South from the colonial period to the 1930s.

the history of elite innovations amply illustrates. It is these periodic failures that trigger the dialectic that revitalizes agrarian society.

When the elite innovations of one period fail, when they are discredited by declining profits, ecological destruction, and periodic crisis, the odds swing dialectically in favor of the folk in the next cycle of agrarian innovation and diffusion. Take the case of elite agrarian reform in the period between the 1780s and 1830. Intoxicated by Enlightenment thought, elite agrarians set about reforming American agriculture, making it more orderly, more intensive, and more productive. In short order, they imposed the innovations of crop rotations, plowing and clean tillage, neat rows, and organic manures and plaster. Several of these by the 1820s proved terribly destructive to environments and societies in the upper South. Plowing and clean tillage in particular vastly accelerated rates of soil exhaustion, erosion, drainage sedimentation, and economic deterioration—problems that, generally speaking, had been held in check by cyclical shifting cultivation.[90]

Ecological history repeated itself a half century later (1880s–1930) in the Deep South. In this case, the innovational culprit was the so-called "guano craze," which had been enthusiastically promoted after the war by scientific boosters and elite agrarian reformers. Few of them survived, however, to see what they had wrought by the early twentieth century: a landscape of gullied, eroded, and exhausted fields, worn out by commercial fertilizers (of inferior quality, unbeknownst to their promoters), and years of unrelieved cotton monoculture. Thus did elites fail. The crushing economic, social, and ecological costs of their bookish and scientifically inspired innovations vastly improved the odds for a macrohistorical dialectic, for the triumph of folk innovations in the ensuing period.[91]

Folk innovations triumphed in the South in the period sandwiched between the elite's Enlightenment reforms and the guano craze. Agrarian revitalization in the period 1830s-70s sprang from

90. On the destructiveness of elite agrarian reform in the Chesapeake, circa 1780–1830, see the convincing evidence of accelerating erosion and sedimentation supplied by Grace S. Brush, "Geology and Paleoecology of Chesapeake Bay: A Long-term Monitoring Tool for Management," *Journal of the Washington Academy of Science* 76 (1986), pp. 146–60; also Henry M. Miller, "Transforming a 'Splendid and Delightsome Land,'" *Journal of the Washington Academy of Science* 76 (1986), pp. 173–87.

91. On the guano craze and its destructive environmental effects, see Carville Earle, "Tillage Capacity and Soil Maintenance in the 19th-Century Cotton South: A New Theory of Crop Choice," *Working Papers of the Social Science History Workshop*, Paper No. 86–7 (Minneapolis: Department of History, University of Minnesota, 1986).

the practical empiricism of ordinary farmers and planters. Their introduction of a crop rotational system of cotton, corn, and cowpeas in the 1840s maintained soil fertility, moderated erosion, and sponsored astounding economic growth until interrupted by the Civil War and Reconstruction. These events in turn paved the way for the dialectical triumph of elite innovations in the 1870s.[92]

These examples reveal the functioning of the class dialectic over the course of a century, 1780s-1880s; but the process began much earlier, and it persists to the present day—with one difference. The role of the legitimating epistemologies of science and practice have been complicated by secular changes in their relative roles. Prior to the Enlightenment, science existed in what may only be described as a raw and primitive institutional form; although elites occasionally sought legitimacy through science (witness the rise of agrarian periodicals in England), most agrarian innovation was rooted in practice. Since the 1870s, however, agrarian innovation has emanated increasingly from an institutionalized scientific establishment. Thus the epistemological dialectic appears in its most unvarnished form in the century between the American Revolution and the end of Reconstruction. But if the roles of science and practice have changed over three and a half centuries, the class dialectic has endured.[93]

Recall for example the case of the Chesapeake in which folk-based innovations of the 1630s (tobacco topping and house curing) gave way in the 1680s to the elite-based innovation of shifting culti-

92. *Ibid.* and Chapter 7 in this volume. The cotton-corn-cowpeas rotation of the 1840s along with the guano craze after 1870 suggest that southern agriculture was more innovative and dynamic than prevailing interpretations allow. For the conventional view of technical backwardness in the region, see Gavin Wright, *The Political Economy of the Cotton South: Households, Markets, and Wealth in the Nineteenth Century* (New York: W. W. Norton, 1978), pp. 89–127.

93. Scientific epistemology was chiefly expressed before 1800 in English agricultural periodicals, books, and manuals—sources that were accessible to the English and American agrarian elite. See Richard J. Sullivan, "Measurement of English Farming Technological Change, 1523–1900," *Explorations in Economic History* 21 (1984), pp. 270–89. Sullivan's data show that for the span 1680–1800, the publication of English agrarian periodicals peaked in the phases of Crisis, Creativity, and Decline, that is, 1691–1700, 1721–40, and 1791–1800. Though literacy was widespread among yeomen by the seventeenth century, the majority of husbandmen were functionally illiterate until after 1750. Hence folk innovations based upon practice were unlikely to have appeared in the periodical literature. Since 1870, science has been increasingly institutionalized in the U.S. and state departments of agriculture. See Galambos, *America at Middle Age* (cited in note 11); Daniel, *Breaking the Land* (cited in note 80); Asa Gray, "Practice and Science Agree," *American Agriculturalist* 34 (1875), p. 140; Margaret W. Rossiter, *The Emergence of Agricultural Science: Justus Leibig and the Americans, 1840–1880* (New Haven, Conn.: Yale University Press, 1979).

vation with its capital-intensive emphasis on slave labor. Or consider the scene two centuries later when innovation was increasingly institutionalized in the agricultural establishment of state and federal government. The class dialectic of innovation did not disappear, but rather was refracted through prevailing policy paradigms. The triumph of large-scale plantations in the turn-of-the-century cotton belt, as Pete Daniel has emphatically shown, was a consequence of elite redistributive policies at state and national levels. In contrast, the mass democratic policies of the ensuing period, beginning with the New Deal in the 1930s, favored smaller and middling farmers by encouraging the diffusion of relatively low-cost innovations such as hybrid corn.[94]

Events in the cotton belt after 1930 might seem to contradict this conclusion since critics of the U.S. Department of Agriculture have accused it of devising policies that fostered the diffusion of cotton harvesters and thus hastened the dislocation of tenants and croppers. I would argue, however, that the most devastating blow may have been delivered in the preceding cycle of elite innovation. The initial round of tractor diffusion between the 1890s and 1930 had created a sharp imbalance in the seasonal demand for labor. Tillage—one of two highly labor-intensive tasks (the other being picking)—was increasingly performed by tractors. Tractors thus eliminated one of the principal labor bottlenecks, but plantation owners and managers still required large numbers of workers to handpick the crop in the fall. Under these dramatically new terms of employment, rational planters breached annual cropper and tenant contracts in favor of hiring labor for the unmechanized picking season. Thus by the 1930s, the traditional labor system in the cotton belt had experienced a radical change as a consequence of tractor mechanization. The cotton cropper and tenant were well on their way to becoming seasonal hired hands. The victim was already dead; consequently, interpretations that place the blame on USDA policies after 1930 seem ironic indeed.

94. Daniel, *Breaking the Land*. My tentative hypothesis is that the class dialectic of American agrarian innovation was out of synch with British policy cycles during the colonial period and in synch with American policy cycles after 1790. This hypothesis suggests a new basis for the persistent structural tensions between American colonists and British policymakers: as the British introduced conservative and elitist paradigms of political economy (for example, 1630s–40s and 1740s–50s), Americans were introducing folk innovations with egalitarian ramifications; and vice versa in the period 1680–1740. Hence the sustained political-economic strains that existed between the rulers and their colonial subjects seem to reflect divergent trends in welfare economics.

To be sure, USDA policies encouraged mechanization of the entire cotton production system, especially through the diffusion of the cotton harvester, but that policy may have been more humane in the long run—certainly it was less exploitive than a policy that would have preserved a system of underemployed and impoverished hired hands.[95]

These examples argue for a dialectical interpretation of agrarian revitalization, for a macrohistorical alternation in the class provenience of innovation (elite and folk) and their legitimating epistemologies (science and practice). The hegemonic class and epistemology of one period is thus the antithesis of the discredited epistemology of the period immediately preceding. When the class-based innovation of one period no longer works, when profits fall and destructive environmental effects are manifest, that is, when crisis comes, the way is cleared for its opposite epistemological number.

Was Marx right? Is the class dialectic indeed the locomotive of history? Perhaps, but in a manner in which he would hardly approve. Marx's dialectic departs radically from the macrohistorical dialectic proposed here. In Marx's world, the dialectic involves an unceasing and heroic struggle pitting the workers (antithesis) against the awesome power of capitalism and the state (thesis)—a struggle resolved only by violent conflict and the triumph of the working class in the fiery destruction of capitalism. In Marx's apocalyptic world, the dialectical locomotive is designed for self-destruction. In the macrohistorical world, the dialectics of class are reciprocating rather than linearly direct, revitalizing rather than destructive. The dialectic is more supple; it revitalizes agrarian regional systems through a periodic alternation of thesis (elite) and antithesis (folk). Whereas elites

95. Daniel presents some of the evidence supporting a thesis of a two-stage declension of the cotton cropper-tenant system—the first stage coming with the modest introduction of tractors for tillage (1890–1930), the second with cotton harvesters (1930–80). The tractor's advantages for the back-breaking and time-consuming task of tillage and its dislocative effects upon labor were evident prior to the New Deal. Daniel, *Breaking the Land; idem,* "The Transformation of the Rural South 1930 to the Present," *Agricultural History* 55 (1981), pp. 231–48; Jack Temple Kirby, "The Transformation of Southern Plantations, 1920–1960," *Agricultural History* 57 (1983), pp. 257–76; Gilbert C. Fite, "Mechanization of Cotton Production Since World War II," *Agricultural History* 54 (1980), pp. 190–207; Merle C. Prunty, Jr., "Renaissance of the Southern Plantation," *Geographical Review* 45 (1955), pp. 459–91. The spatial relocation of cotton production westward, presumably capitalizing on machine technologies, was equally dislocative for croppers and tenants in the eastern cotton belt; see John Fraser Hart, "The Demise of King Cotton," *Annals of the Association of American Geographers* 67 (1977), pp. 307–22.

exercise power and hegemony in one period, they surrender impressive gains to ordinary folk in the next. As a consequence of this reciprocating class dialectic, American macrohistory has managed to achieve long-run progress, relative social equilibrium, and the institutionalization of periodic revitalizations. All of which, parenthetically, has proven bewildering to Marxists whose dialectic prevents them from seeing that, on occasion, the antithesis has won.[96]

We are now fifteen to twenty years into the half-century logistic. The triumph of "fundamental" innovations is sealed: their privileged status has been clarified, their economic rationality demonstrated (by an increasing sample of adopters), and their contentious opposition put to bed.

Phase three

With these impediments to diffusion cleared away, only the superable constraints of space, time, and cost remain to fetter innovation's progress. The logistic at last takes off, makes a sharp turn upward, and then holds to that pace for two decades more or less. In that span, the progress of innovation diffusion transforms the economy and society of multiple regional systems: agrarian novelty spreads from the few to the many; economic prosperity (at least at the aggregate level) is restored; and regional welfare is refashioned in accordance with the class provenience of the innovation. Great changes these, and accomplished so swiftly and so unpretentiously that even contemporaries often failed to appreciate their grandeur.

About the inexorable rural progress of diffusion we know a large amount. From an initial handful of hearths, innovations diffuse lo-

---

96. The macrohistorical interpretation of a reciprocating class dialectic offers a more supple interpretation of the seemingly infinite capacity of capitalism to endure and to outwit the gloomy forecasts of Marx and his disciples (and, I might add, of Malthus and his students). So long as folk innovations (or their low-threshold equivalents from corporations or the USDA) emerge, diffuse, and work their egalitarian effects, capitalism seems likely to remain viable until the entire world is embraced by its hegemony. Marx notwithstanding, the threat to capitalism is not so much impending class violence as it is the danger of warfare arising out of protectionist and imperialist contention played out at the global scale. Ratzel, Tocqueville, and Weber more nearly than Marx are our best guides to political economy in a global system. The rapid emergence of regional trading "blocs" constitutes, in my view, an ominous warning for the twenty-first century's first cycle. Conversely, for the fearlessly optimistic view of the future, see W. Michael Blumenthal, "The World Economy and Technological Change," *Foreign Affairs* 66 (1988), pp. 529–50. See notes 52–54.

gistically in time and contagiously in space, that is, relying upon the persuasiveness of face-to-face adopter interaction and, most fundamentally, rational choice. Rational choice is a radically new method for decision making. Unlike the uncertainty and irrationalism that plagued earlier decisions, rational choice uses spartanly statistical criteria. Indeed, it entails an assessment of innovation risk based upon empirically derived probabilities of prior successes and failures. But risk probabilities in turn are only as good as the samples from which they are drawn; samples must be sufficiently large and representative if they are to be trusted. In this respect it is not merely coincidence that rational choice emerges as the decision criterion when the sample size of early adopters approaches a level of 5 to 10 percent—the so-called early majority. We can think of this group as constituting a first approximation to a representative sample upon which the accuracy of risk assessment and rational choice vitally depend. At this juncture, when statistical error is minimized by a sufficiently large sample and when empirically measured risk is demonstrably modest, agrarian adopters swarm (the so-called "bandwagon effect") to the innovation in order to earn the preemptive profits that attend early adoption.[97]

Given rational choice and certain other key factors—the location of initial adopters, the customary range of local travel, the costs of innovation, and the economic status of farmers—geographers and sociologists can model spatial contagion with a remarkably high degree of accuracy. They have observed that diffusion waves are propagated outward from initial hearth locations in increments proportional to the typical range of local information fields. They have predicted these patterns with probabilistic Monte Carlo models. What they have not done, however, is to tie the spatial process (contagion) to the half-century logistic characteristic of fundamental agrarian innovations. Any process in which adoption is predicated on face-to-face interaction takes time, even in the third phase of accelerated adoption. Time is consumed by the collection and evaluation of data on the risks of innovation, by the inefficiencies of oral information flows in space, by the conservative agrarian tendency to double-check information, and by the varying levels of certitude required by potential adopters (that is, what sample size sufficiently

97. Among many sources, see Brown, *Innovation Diffusion*; and Richard Morrill, Gary L. Gaile, and Grant Ian Thrall, *Spatial Diffusion* (Newbury Park, Calif.: Sage, 1988).

minimizes prediction errors in the calculation of profit probabilities). Indeed diffusion from a minority of adopters to a majority, which is what happens in phase three, takes as much time today—two decades—as it did some three centuries ago.[98]

What happens in the several decades of the first three phases profoundly transforms American geography. Regional geographies are recreated; a new tissue of space, society, and landscape is laid down. Scarcely any aspect of regional life is left untouched by the new agrotechnical system and its ecological ramifications. Tracing these ramifications into the recesses of regional life is the province of a staple approach to regional development, an approach deployed repeatedly in this volume. Various essays have explored the effects of agrarian innovation upon rural life (settlement, social structure, and labor systems), city life (urban wage determination and city-size differentials), and industrial life (the rise of machine production, wage differentials among skilled and unskilled, and the implications for the schism in the American working class).[99]

Of the scores of examples, I offer here just two concrete illustrations of the ecological ramifications of innovation. The first is from the Chesapeake in the late seventeenth century. The introduction of shifting cultivation in that region transformed rural labor systems and rural settlement. Servants were virtually eliminated, replaced by massive numbers of slaves. Concomitantly, rural settlement was restructured by the expansion of large slave plantations flanked by an array of small and middling plantations and an increasing proportion of tenant proprietors—in some cases, amounting to 30 percent or more of the rural households. A century later (1780s–1830), simi-

98. See, for example, the following works of Torsten Hägerstrand: "Aspects of the Spatial Structure of Social Communication and the Diffusion of Information," *Papers, Regional Science Association* 16 (1965), pp. 27–42; "On Monte Carlo Simulation of Diffusion," in *Quantitative Geography*, ed. W. Garrison and D. Marble, Northwestern University Studies in Geography, No. 13 (Evanston, Ill., 1967); *Innovation Diffusion as a Spatial Process*, trans. Allan Pred (Chicago: University of Chicago Press, 1967).

99. James Lemon notes that historical geographers have dwelt disproportionately on regional development during the long upswing of the Kondratieff wave while pretty much ignoring its downswing. That is ironic since the pattern disengages historical geography from the key debates in social science history that typically focus upon the phases of Decline, Crisis, and Creativity, where much of "grand history" lies. Historical geography has also abjured dealing with the internal civil protest and strife occurring principally in the Dissent phase. Lemon's observation appears in Carville Earle et al., "Historical Geography," in *Geography in America*, ed. Gary Gaile and Cort Willmott (Columbus, Ohio: Merrill, 1989), pp. 156–91.

larly dramatic transformations took place in the upper Chesapeake and the Middle States. Specialization in grain production and agrarian intensification created a distinctive regional landscape of modestly sized farms, an increasing proportion of landless rural laborers (15 to 30 percent of rural males by 1780), and an extensive network of urban places for the conveyance of grain to coastal entrepôts in Baltimore, Philadelphia, and New York. These ecological changes initiated by agrarian innovation redefined the character of regions and established new sets of conditions and constraints for ensuing developments within the regions; for example, the reservoir of grain-belt rural labor would after 1780 become the principal source of cheap labor that was instrumental for Mid-Atlantic industrialization. Staple theory thus has a particular relevance in times of accelerating diffusion. It is a theory subsidiary to the more encompassing theory of recurrent agrarian innovations and their spatial diffusion.[100]

To sum up, innovation diffusion during its first three phases still requires a half decade or so to deal with periodic crisis (phase one), a decade or two for determination of the fundamental innovation (phase two), and two decades to spread it from a tiny minority of agrarians to a majority (phase three). All of which consumes 35 to 45 years of the 45- to 60-year logistic. The decelerating phase of diffusion (phase 4) consumes the rest.

Phase four

Three to four decades into the logistic, the vigorous pace of diffusion is checked by a series of countervailing forces: the sheer mathematics of logistic spatial diffusion, diminished economic returns, and the appearance of destructive environmental conse-

100.   On elite transformations in the Chesapeake, ca. 1680–1740, see Main, *Tobacco Colony* (cited in note 63); Isaac, *The Transformation of Virginia* (cited in note 69); and Earle, *The Evolution of a Tidewater Settlement System* (cited in note 64). On elite transformations in Pennsylvania ca. 1780–1830, see Lemon, *The Best Poor Man's Country* (cited in note 72); Carville Earle and Ronald Hoffman, "The Foundation of the Modern Economy: Agriculture and the Costs of Labor in the United States and England, 1800–1860," *American Historical Review* 85 (1980), pp. 1055–94; Lucy Simler, "Tenancy in Colonial Pennsylvania: The Case of Chester County," *William and Mary Quarterly*, 3rd ser. 43 (1986), pp. 542–69; idem, "Those Who Live by Wages: Agricultural and Industrial Workers in Rural Pennsylvania, 1750–1820," paper presented at the Social Science History Association Meetings, Chicago, 5 Nov. 1988; and Lindstrom, *Economic Development in the Philadelphia Region* (cited in note 18).

quences. Diffusion stalls, the logistic curve arches downward, and a long-wave downswing in the regional economy quicky follows. At first, the occasional economic sputterings are dismissed as mere ephemera, but multiplication congeals them into an undeniable pattern of devolution.[101] Faced with impending economic crisis and a deepening social malaise, society behaves badly, venting its spleen in ethnocultural persecution and bigotry, rural rebellion, social discontent, otherworldly fatalism, pessimism, and Malthusian prescriptions of death, disease, war, and pestilence. And when Malthus's prophecy is fulfilled, that is, when population exceeds the economy's output of food production, the periodic crisis of regions and nations is at hand.[102]

The resurrection of bleak times has its origins in the earlier orgy of expansion. Diffusion falls victim to its own spectacular success. It sets in motion an array of countervailing forces (what systems thinkers refer to as "negative feedback"), several of which conspire in bringing heady expansion to a sobering denouement. In retrospect, three of these forces are most critical in slowing the pace of the logistic: (1) the rigid mathematical logic of logistic diffusion, (2) the perils of market "overshooting," and (3) the cumulating burden of "lagged" environmental costs. Each deserves brief comment.

101. The argument here parallels Kuhn's notion of accumulating anomaly and its challenges to the prevailing paradigm of science. Initially, as normal science uncovers anomalies, scientific theory is amended (much as economic theory is amended in the phase of Decline), but eventually they become so numerous as to undermine the paradigm, thus paving the way for a scientific revolution to install a new theoretical paradigm. Kuhn, *The Structure of Scientific Revolutions* (cited in note 35). The periodic structure of American macrohistory unfolds in much the same way.

102. The road from Decline to Crisis and then to Creativity is not a smooth one. Decline is triggered by an excess of commodity supply occasioned by the widespread diffusion of agrarian innovation. At the point at which most agrarians have adopted a fundamental innovation, aggregate supply overshoots aggregate demand (perhaps exaggerated by shorter Kuznets cycles and population cycles); prices begin their free fall into Crisis. Falling prices and diminishing returns to innovation pare down output by eliminating marginal producers and forcing others to reduce staple production. As Crisis settles in, what had been a glut of agrarian commodities turns into a food deficit. Urban dwellers in particular complain of food shortages, population pressure, and "overpopulation," that is, of Malthusian limits. The search for alternatives begins; but agrarian experimentation is foreshortened by a momentary recovery of prices, which is met by increased output followed by a secondary, albeit less dramatic, crash in prices. Twice chastened, agrarians resume their experimentation in earnest, seeking out new crops, novel methods, creative technologies, and innovative organizational arrangements, all designed to lead them out of Crisis. My characterization of these events is based on the remarkably identical behavior of prices in the four most recent long waves as documented by Berry in his manuscript *The Clock that Times Development* (cited in note 20).

The first countervailing force arises from a perverse property of logistic mathematics in time and space. Over time, diffusion steadily shrinks the pool of potential adopters; consequently, for the process to maintain a constant rate of adoption, it must operate at geometrically increasing efficiencies. A hypothetical illustration points up the mathematical bind. Imagine an initial adoption pool of 1,000 farmers and a diffusion rate of 20 percent per decade, that is, 200 new adopters. At the end of one decade, 20 percent have adopted; at the end of five decades, 100 percent. So far so good, but this is where the mathematical trouble begins. During the first decade, when the potential adoption pool stands at 1,000, adoption efficiencies are modest—20 percent—but by the third decade, when the adoption pool has shrunk to 600, efficiency rates must rise to 33.3 percent just to stay on pace. By the fourth decade, with just 400 in the pool, the rate must rise to 50 percent, and finally, in the fifth decade to 100 percent.

This example clearly shows why the sheer mathematics of logistic curves serve as a countervailing force to the rate of diffusion. A constant rate of expansion requires that the efficiency of diffusion must increase in inverse geometric proportion to the size of the shrinking pool of adopters. Operating at such high levels of efficiency becomes difficult when successful diffusion has trimmed the pool to 40 or 50 percent of its original size; and virtually impossible when it is a quarter or less of its original size. In this fashion, logistic mathematics alone can slow the pace of diffusion and force a downward inflection in the S-shaped curve.[103]

The mathematics of space further conspires against the rate of diffusion. Because agrarian innovation diffusion proceeds via spatial

103. Geographers and sociologists regrettably have mystified the issue of spatial and temporal efficiencies of diffusion by introducing complex logistic mathematics in place of a straightforward exposition of causality. It is a case of modeling without understanding. See for example Morrill, Gaile, and Thrall, *Spatial Diffusion*, pp. 57–73; and Robert L. Hamblin, R. Brooke Jacobsen, and Jerry L. L. Miller, *A Mathematical Theory of Social Change* (New York: John Wiley, 1973). For similar critiques, see J. Nicholas Entrikin, "Diffusion Research in the Context of the Naturalism Debate in Twentieth-Century Geographic Thought," in *The Transfer and Transformation of Ideas and Material Culture*, ed. Peter J. Hugill and D. Bruce Dickson (College Station: Texas A&M University Press, 1988), pp. 165–78; and Tilly, *Big Structures, Large Processes, and Huge Comparisons*, pp. 33–35 (cited in note 2). Tilly explains why these models have stirred so little interest among students of social change: "Specifications of the time-shapes of diffusion were not what students of social change needed. . . . The explicandum needs more than precision to make it interesting. It must also connect to Big Questions. . . . Even in a day of scientism, the social sciences have not—hallelujah—lost their ultimate concern with the fate of mankind." *Ibid.*, p. 35.

contagion, we find that the spatial arena of adoption increases exponentially as diffusion progresses. Since innovations typically spread gradually outward from an initial core or hearth, later adopters reside at greater distances from the initiating points of innovation. Although hearth-adopter distance increases arithmetically, the circular spatial arena of potential adoption increases by the square of distance. Diffusion thus faces a double whammy in its later stages: to maintain a constant rate, diffusion must not only achieve impractically high levels of efficiency over time, but must do so over an exponentially augmented rural space. These diffusion mathematics are usually sufficient in themselves for slowing the pace of innovation adoption and forcing downward inflection of the logistic curve.

A second countervailing force is an excess of supply—what Walt Rostow has called market "overshooting"—resulting from the extraordinary productivity of agrarian innovations. Rostow points out that long-wave dynamics are driven by persistent mismatches in aggregate supply and demand. In the upswing, as innovations are getting under way, supply undershoots aggregate demand. A combination of high prices and preemptive profits accrue to innovation adoption and thus speed the pace of diffusion. The reverse occurs in the downswing. Innovations are widely diffused, and their productivity causes supply to "overshoot" aggregate demand. Falling prices and profits retard the rate of innovation diffusion and the logistic begins its descent toward the hard landing of periodic crisis.[104]

Environmental costs constitute the third and perhaps most decisive force checking the further spread of agrarian innovation. Rarely are these long-run costs anticipated; and, to compound matters, the terribly slow rate of environmental feedback obscures their effects until late in the diffusion logistic, by which time the worst environmental damage to soils, water, and slopes is already done. To further complicate matters, the best environmental intentions often go awry. Innovations explicitly devised for improving the environment (for example, soil-maintaining practices) often prove to be the most destructive. Some of the classic environmental blunders have come from the scientifically legitimated innovations of an agrarian elite. Folk innovations also have adverse environmental effects, but per-

104.   Rostow, Kennedy, and Nasr, "A Simple Model of the Kondratieff Cycle" (cited in note 20).

haps because of their modesty in concept and design, folk innovations impose a smaller toll—one sufficient to dampen the rate of diffusion without (as elite innovations tend to do) plunging regions and nation into the depths of high-magnitude crises.[105]

These countervailing forces explain, in general terms, the downturn in the diffusion logistic; what they do not explain, however, is the timing of this deflection. Why do countervailing forces (logistic mathematics, market overshooting, and environmental costs) appear early in some periods—35 to 40 years into the cycle—and late in others—45 to 50 years into the cycle? The question is of more than passing interest since it has obvious theoretical implications for the varying length of historical periods themselves.

The turning of the logistic, I believe, has its determinants in the preceding phase of domestic dissent and the variable manifestations of political conflict. If the politics of dissent erupts in civil war, innovation diffusion speeds up. Rising prices for food and fiber on the demand side and rural labor scarcity on the supply side cause innovation diffusion to run well ahead of its regular schedule. After the war, when adoptions are widespread, diffusion decelerates rapidly and brings the historical period to a premature end. That was precisely the case in American history's three shortest periods: 1740s–80s, 1830s–1877, and 1929–70s. Each period was punctuated by internal wars (I include Vietnam), which accentuated the diffusion of agrarian innovation.

Take for example the case of machine mowing during the American Civil War. From a modest annual manufacture of 8,000 or so mowers in the 1850s, production exploded to 35,000 in 1862 and 70,000 in 1864. A doubling of mower output in just two years quite literally revised the logistic's gently sloping S-shape to an almost linear J-shape during the course of the war. The war-induced acceleration of diffusion further hastened the onset of countervailing forces. At war's end, supply and demand schedules shifted abruptly; simultaneously, the supply schedule shifted upward as returning veterans boosted regional agrarian outputs and the demand schedule shifted downward with the remission in the needs for military provisions. In sum, regional output increased, aggregate national demand decreased, and, on balance, regional supply overshot national demand.

105. On the lagged effects of an innovation's impact on the environment, see Chapter 7 in this volume and the sources cited therein.

In such cases, prices fell and regional innovation diffusion and economic growth crashed to a seemingly "premature" halt.[106]

The American Revolution gave a similar fillip to the diffusion of cradles, scythes, and seasonally complementary employment linkages in the grain belt of the Middle States; as perhaps did the Vietnam War to mechanical cotton and peanut harvesters, hybridization, soybeans, and no-till farming.[107] Let me be clear on these points. Internal war creates favorable conditions for the rapid diffusion of agrarian innovation. With its extraordinary demands for food, fiber, and manpower, a wartime economy foreshortens the diffusion logistic by a decade or more. Internal war speeds the phase of accelerating diffusion, hastens the onset of decelerating diffusion, and advances in time the Crisis that marks the endpoint of a historical period. Conversely, when civil war in the Dissent phase is averted, the logistic of agrarian innovation diffusion progresses at a more leisurely pace, its gentle swales spreading over five to six decades. The drawback is that this enlarged window provides ample time for the destructive play of countervailing environmental forces, which tend to intensify the ensuing periodic crisis, for example, in the 1830s and 1930s.[108]

The return of periodic Crisis rather unceremoniously marks the end of the first half-century cycle of agrarian innovation and diffusion. The cycle arises anew from an awkward mixture of optimism and pessimism, creativity and tradition, hope and despair—an ambivalence eloquently captured in Dickens's immortal opening line in

---

106. For mower diffusion during the Civil War, see Emerson David Fite, *Social and Industrial Conditions in the North During the Civil War* (New York: Frederick Unger, 1963), pp. 1–23.

107. On accelerated diffusion of agrarian innovation during the American Revolution, see Robert D. Mitchell, "Agricultural Change and the American Revolution: A Virginia Case Study," *Agricultural History* 47 (1973), pp. 119–32. Also see Lemon, *The Best Poor Man's Country*.

108. Historiographic ambiguity about the effects of war on the economy is largely a matter of context, timing, and macrohistorical phasing. In the Conflict phase, war typically serves as a stimulant to economic recovery from Crisis; conversely, in the Dissent phase, war accelerates diffusion and thus hastens the onset of economic and social Decline. Thus the effects of war on the economy are mixed, being more nearly positive in the early phases of a historical period and more nearly adverse in its later phases; hence the historiographic ambiguity arising from the literature. For history's divergent positions on the effects of war, see Nef, *War and Human Progress* (cited in note 51); and A. H. John, "War and the English Economy, 1700–1763," *The Economic History Review*, 2nd series, 7 (1955), pp. 329–44.

A Tale of Two Cities: "It was the best of times, it was the worst of times." His historical referent, the French Revolution, was a drama that could only have taken place in the crucible of capitalist macrohistory, in the bittersweet times of periodic crisis and conjunctural revolution.

The Genius of Capitalism: Institutionalizing Recurrent Agrarian Innovation and Diffusion

Any serious and sustained study of modern society invariably curves back upon what Max Weber called "the great problem": the institutions created by the rise of capitalism in the sixteenth and seventeenth centuries. Perhaps what most distinguishes capitalist society from traditional societies has been its institutionalization of recurrent innovation and diffusion—what William Parker described as a "succession of opportunities."[109] When did this institutionalization begin? What were its causes? Why has it persisted? Our inquiry into American macrohistory suggests that the half-century rhythm of innovation and logistic diffusion was in place by the 1630s. My best guess is that its origins lie in the golden twilight of Elizabeth's reign, and more precisely with the unmistakable injection of novelty during the 1570s and 1580s. In these depressed and difficult decades, when the Hakluyts lamented the nation's imbalanced trade, overpopulation, and unemployment, the range of English experimentation and innovation was breathtaking. To wit: the establishment of the royal exchange and the transfer of the capital market from Antwerp to London; new forms of company organization; a spate of company charters granted for trade in continental Europe and the Levant; the beginnings of North American colonization; the spectacular rise of privateering enterprise; and, as Mark Overton has documented, a tremendous upsurge in English grain production. Although one cannot rule out Henrican England of the 1530s as the ultimate source of recurrent innovation and diffusion, the tracings there lead more toward innovations in "high politics" rather than toward those in classically capitalist enterprises.[110]

109.   Parker, *Europe, America, and the Wider World*, pp. 7–8 (cited in note 59).
110.   Lawrence Stone, *The Causes of the English Revolution 1529–1642* (London: Routledge & Kegan Paul, 1972), pp. 26–117; Kenneth R. Andrews, *Elizabethan Privateering: English Privateering During the Spanish War 1585–1603* (Cambridge: Cambridge University Press, 1964); Theodore K. Rabb, *Enterprise and Empire: Merchant and Gentry Investment in*

The precise genesis of recurrent innovation, however, I leave to English historians who are better equipped than I am to elucidate its institutional origins. Nor do I have much to say about the causes and preconditions surrounding the sixteenth-century origins of recurrent agrarian innovation, save to rehearse the sophisticated interpretations already offered by students of those times. I do not doubt that the crucial causes are nestled among such well-known factors as the nation-state's provision of secure markets for commerce; the impulsive stimulation of European interregional trade by American bullion; institutional economic innovations (one of which was enclosure) that maximized private returns on investment; Puritanism's millennial quest for perfection in all spheres, including novelty and science; and the boost given to farm prices by an exploding population. I do have something to say, however, about what others have overlooked, namely the institutionalization of agrarian innovation and diffusion in response to systemic crises in capitalist society.

Although many societies have confronted crises and overcome them, only western European capitalism and its derivatives have succeeded in institutionalizing their response through the processes of recurrent innovation and diffusion. Some four centuries ago, western Europeans established a template, a set of routines, for overcoming the periodic half-century crises of capitalist society. We have described this template and its routines in some detail: wide-ranging experimentation; dialectical alternations in policy, in religion, and in economy, especially agrarian innovation; logistic spatial diffusion; and, as a consequence of countervailing forces, recurrent Crisis. But—and this is critical—the template of routines works only if the learning becomes an integral part of living collective memory. For that to have happened, learning must be transmitted efficiently via witnesses who have experienced one Crisis and have survived into the next—who can testify to the effectiveness of recurrent innovation and diffusion. And precisely that occurred, perhaps for the first time in human history, in the second half of the sixteenth century.

Two uniquely convergent forces permitted this to happen; one was rooted in capitalism, the other in demography. Capitalism short-

the Expansion of England, 1575–1630 (Cambridge, Mass.: Harvard University Press, 1967); Overton, "Agricultural Revolution?" pp. 119–39 (cited in note 73); North and Thomas, *The Rise of the Western World* (cited in note 14).

ened the cycle of macrohistory while demography lengthened the cycle of human life. In abrupt contrast with the "motionless" history experienced by premodern agrarian societies, capitalist innovation and diffusion dramatically stepped up the pace of change and of recurrent Crisis. Instead of recurring every two to two and a half centuries as in "motionless societies," capitalist Crisis returned every half century. Capitalism's condensed rhythm thus brought it within the experience of a small but ever-increasing proportion of the population.[111]

Which brings us to demography. The proportion of the population directly experiencing sequential crises was on the rise after 1550. As historical demographers tell us, the English lived longer on average, and increasing numbers lived into old age. This convergence in the durations of the life cycle and the capitalist cycle of Crisis-Creativity-Conflict-Diffusion-Dissent-Decline guaranteed to the elderly a new and vital role in capitalist learning and education. In contradistinction to the council of elders in motionless societies who discouraged innovation and venerated traditional, unchanging ways, the elderly of western Europe offered living testimony on past crises and how—with hard work, perseverance, intelligence, and novelty—crisis had been and could be overcome. Although contemporary youth are often contemptuous of their elders, dismissing their tales of hard times as just so many "war stories," they are in fact capitalism's chief source of nurturance and hope in its darkest hours.

It has been said, perhaps too glibly, that New Englanders invented the term "grandparents." Certainly their demographic role has been important, but the veneration and respect connoted by the term itself reflects as much our dependency upon them as the sages of "hard times." In their experience of Crisis is stored the wisdom of its resolution through hard work, austerity, experimentation, innovation, and diffusion. In the learning and recountings of the elderly

111. The convergence of the capitalist cycle and the life cycle was uniquely a phenomenon of western Europe and its mid-latitude colonies abroad until the turn of this century. On English longevity, see E. A. Wrigley and R. S. Schofield, with contributions by Ronald Lee and Jim Oeppen, *The Population History of England, 1541–1871* (Cambridge, Mass.: Harvard University Press, 1981). Printing and literacy also assisted in the transmission and institutionalization of recurrent agrarian innovation (though at first only among the elite and better-off agrarians). Sullivan, "Measurement of English Farming Technological Change" (cited in note 93); Roger Schofield, "The Measurement of Literacy in Pre-Industrial England," in *Literacy in Traditional Societies*, ed. J. Goody (Cambridge: Cambridge University Press, 1968).

lie the keys to capitalism's greatest achievement—the institutionalization of an optimistic faith in the revitalizing capacities of recurrent
innovation and diffusion. Or as one scholar has phrased it, "grandchildren think and act in ways similar to those of their grandparents"—but, I would add, not always and not everywhere, for social
interaction, like grand history, is contingent on particular times and
particular places.[112]

112.   The quote on grandparents and their grandchildren is from Gerhard Mensch,
Stalemate in Technology: Innovations Overcome the Depression (Cambridge, Mass.: Ballinger,
1979), p. 5.

Index

Index

In this index an "f" after a number indicates a separate reference on the next page, and an "ff" indicates separate references on the next two pages. A continuous discussion over two or more pages is indicated by a span of page numbers, e.g., "pp. 57–58." *Passim* is used for a cluster of references in close but not consecutive sequence.

Library of Congress Cataloging-in-Publication Data
Earle, Carville.
  Geographical inquiry and American historical problems / Carville Earle.
    p.   cm.
  Includes index.
  ISBN 0-8047-1575-0 (alk. paper) :
    1. United States—Historical geography.   2. Human geography—
United States.   3. Agriculture—United States—History.
4. United States—Population—History.   I. Title.
E179.5.E37 1991   91-19750
911'.73—dc20   CIP

∞ This book is printed on acid-free paper.